D1426868

Database
Development
and Management

THE AUERBACH
FOUNDATIONS OF DATABASE DESIGN SERIES

Database Design Using Entity-Relationship Diagrams
Sikha Bagui and Richard Earp
ISBN: 0-8493-1548-4

Physical Database Design Using Oracle
Donald K. Burleson
ISBN: 0-8493-1817-3

Logical Database Design Principles
John Garmany, Jeff Walker, and Terry Clark
ISBN: 0-8493-1853-X

Database Development and Management
Lee Chao
ISBN: 0-8493-3318-0

AUERBACH PUBLICATIONS

www.auerbach-publications.com
TO ORDER: Call: 1-800-272-7737 • Fax: 1-800-374-3401
E-mail: orders@crcpress.com

Database Development and Management

LEE CHAO

Auerbach Publications
Taylor & Francis Group
Boca Raton London New York Singapore

Published in 2006 by
Auerbach Publications
Taylor & Francis Group
6000 Broken Sound Parkway NW, Suite 300
Boca Raton, FL 33487-2742

International Standard Book Number-10: 0-8493-3318-0 (Hardcover)
International Standard Book Number-13: 978-0-8493-3318-7 (Hardcover)
Library of Congress Card Number 2005041241

Library of Congress Cataloging-in-Publication Data

Chao, Lee, 1951-
   Database development and design / Lee Chao.
     p. cm. -- (Foundations of database design)
   Includes bibliographical references and index.
   ISBN 0-8493-3318-0 (alk. paper)
   1. Database management. 2. Database design. I. Title. II. Foundations of database design series

QA76.9.D3C424 2005
005.74--dc22
                                                       2005041241

Taylor & Francis Group
is the Academic Division of Informa plc.

Visit the Taylor & Francis Web site at
http://www.taylorandfrancis.com

and the Auerbach Publications Web site at
http://www.auerbach-publications.com

Contents

APPENDICES

Preface

In this information age, database technology plays a key role in information management. As the center of information systems, database theory and technology are important components in today's computer science and information systems curriculum. Often, a database system and management course is taught after students have fulfilled the programming and introduction to computing requirements.

Today's E-commerce environment requires our students to understand how databases are used to manage information in various business processes. They should be able to develop database systems for database applications at the enterprise level such as client/server-based applications and Web-based applications.

To meet the curriculum requirements and to help students get a quick start in developing database systems, this book is designed to show what a database is, how to design a database system to meet business requirements, and how a database can be used to process information for an organization or a company.

Nowadays, many universities consist of branch campuses. It is a challenging task to cover the major steps in database development at the enterprise level on a small campus and in a distance education environment, where support from technology personnel is sometimes lacking. There, instructors maintain database servers and provide technical support to students. With a heavy teaching load per semester, research, and other responsibilities, there is little time left for faculty members to manage the database servers and clients. Often, those students who are not living in campus dormitories have to travel to campus to take classes and go home to complete their assignments. When something happens, caused either by misunderstanding of the content in the textbook, lack of instruction on how to get started on new projects, or incorrectly configured computing equipment at home, there is no teaching assistant around to help them figure out how to solve the problems. At home, students need help, most conveniently from the textbook, to enable them to complete their homework mostly by themselves.

I think we can do two things to help these faculty members and students. First, we can develop teaching materials based on a step-by-step approach to guide students in completing their projects. Second, we can create teaching materials based on low-cost and user-friendly database system development tools. Therefore, this book is written for the convenience of faculty members and students. It is self-contained. It provides detailed instruction that is suitable for classroom instruction and self-study while covering all the important topics to meet the requirements of today's business processes. It will help instructors develop their own labs for database classes. The book includes necessary tools for students to complete their homework and projects at home or through the Internet. I have tried to make this book an easy-to-follow guide for both instructors and students to get a particular database project done. Based on these intentions, the book is designed to have the following features.

Step-by-Step Instruction

For students who do not have experience in developing database systems, missing steps in the instruction can confuse them. Due to lack of experience, the trial-and-error method used in their problem-solving process often makes things worse. The step-by-step instruction in this book will help students master the techniques involved in database system development. In this way, the students will gain skills and confidence by implementing the components in the database systems developed in this book.

Example Approach

Learning through examples has been proven successful in learning new things. The examples can be used to clarify ambiguous concepts and understand complicated methodologies. The development of the integrated database systems in this book is illustrated by using case studies. Many examples are generated from these case studies and are used to illustrate how databases are designed, implemented, and applied in information management.

Emphasizing Both Theory and Hands-On Practice

In today's job market, our students are expected to know database theories and have hands-on skills. Emphasizing both theory and hands-on experience will help our students to meet these expectations. In each chapter of this book, we cover the basic theories, concepts, and methodologies needed to achieve the chapter objectives. A database system is an integrated project that consists of various technologies. This book aims at helping students understand how the technologies work together and at the same time gain problem-solving skills by using these technologies. Many hands-on examples are provided to enhance the understanding of the theories and concepts. The hands-on exercises are also used to improve students' problem-solving skills so that they are prepared to be professionals in the field.

Supplementary Materials

The instructor's manual contains PowerPoint presentations and all the data files for the examples used in this book. The PowerPoint presentations help instructors develop their lessons. The instructor's manual also provides a test bank, computer lab manual, and solution manual for the review questions and case study projects.

Software

The server and client software used in this book is supported by the MSDN Academic Alliance (MSDNAA) program at http://www.msdnaa.net/. The MSD-NAA package provides rich resources in developing database systems; it includes SQL Server for database servers and data analysis services, Visual Studio .NET for database applications and XML services, Microsoft Visio for database design, and Windows XP Professional and Windows Server 2003 for setting up the operating system. Under the agreement with MSDNAA, these software products can be used by the entire department. That is, they can be installed in the computer lab. Each faculty member or student in the same department can also install the software on a desktop computer or notebook computer at home or in the office. The MSDNAA program makes teaching and learning database systems easier and more affordable.

It is relatively easy to install and configure the software provided by MSDNAA for the class. It does not require a powerful computer to install the database server such as SQL Server in the lab, office, or at home. Once SQL Server is set up on the instructor's office PC, students can access it through the Internet to do their homework. SQL Server is also powerful enough to let us carry out the work for enterprise-level topics such as multi-tier architecture, database security, database management, Web database, data mart, data analysis, and XML-based Web services.

For the software on the client side, we use Microsoft Office, which is also widely available. Microsoft Office–based database applications are popular in today's IT industry. Developing skills of using this software will make students ready for the job market.

Objectives of the Book

The goal of the book is to help students achieve the following objectives:

- Understand the functionalities of database systems.
- Understand the database design process.
- Create a data model based on the requirements of a business process.
- Implement the physical database based on a data model.
- Use Structured Query Language in creating and managing databases.
- Develop database applications.
- Construct network-based database systems.
- Apply the techniques such as XML, ASP, and ADO in Web-based databases.
- Manage multi-user databases.
- Perform database administration tasks.
- Provide data analysis services.
- Gain hands-on experience in developing and managing databases.

The Intended Audience

This book is intended for a one-semester introductory database system course, assuming that the students taking this course have little previous database experience though some knowledge about personal databases such as Access is very helpful. Some of the chapters need some programming skills. One or two semesters' training in programming, such as programming in Visual Basic, will certainly be beneficial for understanding and implementing the hands-on projects.

Organization of the Book

Introduction

The book starts with an introduction to the database components. This chapter gives a brief discussion of the functions of these database components. It also presents an overview of the database system development process. The discussion in this chapter shows what has motivated people to develop database systems, what components are in a database system, what tools can be used to create and manage the database system components, and what steps are taken in the database system development process.

Data Modeling and Database Design

When building a car, the first step is for engineers to draw the blueprint of the car. Like the engineers, when we develop an enterprise-level database system, the first step is to develop the blueprint of the database, that is, the data model of the database. Data modeling is the foundation of the entire database system development. A case study is used to illustrate the data modeling process in Chapter 2. Because IDEF1X has been adopted as a national standard, E-R models are represented by using IDEF1X notations and symbols. Chapter 2 gives detailed instruction on how to develop the IDEF1X-version data model by using Microsoft Office Visio. Chapter 3 covers table structures and normalization. The discussion of transforming a data model to a relational database is covered in Chapter 4.

Structured Query Language (SQL)

After the database is designed, the next step is to physically implement the database with some database development and management tools. Since the 1970s, SQL has been a primary tool in database development. It is a portable tool that can be used in every Database Management System (DBMS) with some minor changes. Extensive knowledge about SQL will make it easier for us to manage different types of DBMS systems. To help students acquire in-depth knowledge about the usage of SQL, I cover views, cursors, triggers, functions, and stored procedures in detail and provide examples to illustrate the use of these database objects. In Chapter 5, I explain how to use SQL to implement and manage database objects. In Chapter 6, SQL is used to query databases. We discuss the development of functions, procedures, and triggers with Transact-SQL in Chapter 7. In order to build database applications in later chapters, views, indexes, and cursors are developed in Chapter 8.

Accessing Data

Once the database has been created, we want people to use it. There are several database-accessing tools available. Chapter 9 shows how to use the database-accessing tools to access data stored in a database server, even through a network environment. In this chapter, three major data-accessing techniques are discussed in detail.

Database Applications

From our survey, many entry-level database jobs are related to database application development. Practice in application development on existing databases will make our students more competitive in the job market. Some students feel that during the database design stage, they have created a well-designed database with a certain complexity. However, when they develop database applications in a programming class such as Java or VB, examples used to illustrate the development of forms are often based on a single database table. To fully utilize the functionalities provided by SQL Server, in Chapter 10 we develop some sophisticated database applications based on the database implemented in previous chapters. The views and cursors will serve as a bridge between databases and database applications. Through the development of database applications, students will strengthen their understanding of the concepts of database systems. Many students are not very clear on how and where the database objects such as views, stored procedures, and cursors are used in developing database applications for solving business problems. Through developing database applications, students will gain solid experience in applying these database objects.

Network-Based Database Systems

In a network database environment, we have a database server to support many database applications created for front-end users. To handle the database applications at a multi-user level, the network-based database system is the key. The discussion of how databases are used in a network environment for multiple users is covered in Chapter 11, where we develop client/server-based database systems, Web-based database systems, and XML Web services. Applications based on the technologies such as InfoPath and XML Web services are developed in this chapter. The database systems developed in Chapter 11 can be used to support daily business information processes on a local area network, wide area network, and the Internet.

Database Administration

A network database allows a large number of users to use the same database. Any database failure will have a great impact on many users and the entire organization or enterprise. This brings up some other tasks, such as how to maintain user accounts, database security, and reliability. In Chapter 12, we address issues such as managing user accounts and security, database backup and restoration, and database performance tuning. These tasks are normally handled by database administrators (DBAs). Some hands-on practices are given to make students familiar with the tasks performed by DBAs.

Data Analysis Services

As more and more data are collected and stored in an organization's databases, the organization can efficiently use these data to provide information for decision making. The On Line Analytical Processing (OLAP) system is one of the data analysis applications that support decision making. In Chapter 13, OLAP development tools provided by SQL Server are used to implement the OLAP projects. To effectively use data to support decision making, the data warehouse is a key component. Several tools used in data warehouse construction are introduced in Chapter 13. Another key component of data analysis is data mining, which helps identify trends and patterns of a business process for decision making. Data mining is discussed in Chapter 14.

Appendices

Appendix A provides detailed information on the databases used in this book. Appendix B offers some instruction and advice on how to set up a database server. It also gives directions on how to configure the database server in a computer lab. By following the instruction in Appendix B, the instructor and students will be able to set up a client/server computing environment for the class. Appendix C provides some resources for further reading; it includes Web sites, books, and articles.

The Approach

As you can see, a database system involves various technologies. This makes the process of database system development quite complicated. To make things easier, the following approach is adopted in explaining the content covered in this book. Each chapter starts with a discussion of related topics. First, the objectives for the chapter are given. Then I state the reasons why the topics should be introduced and describe the importance of the topics in a database system development process. In the discussion, I introduce the basic concepts and explain the methodologies used to achieve the chapter objectives. To demonstrate how to master the methodologies discussed in the chapter, hands-on examples are provided. Through these hands-on practices, students can not only enhance their understanding of the concepts and methodologies but also gain experience in problem-solving. A summary of the major topics covered in the chapter is given at the end of each chapter. To reinforce the learning, review questions are also given for each chapter. These review questions are closely related to the topics covered in the chapter. To further strengthen students' problem-solving skills, the instructor may assign some of the case study projects provided for each chapter. These projects are business-related comprehensive case studies. Therefore, the knowledge and skills needed to complete the projects may not be limited to the current chapter. The projects give students an opportunity to integrate what they have learned in different chapters.

Acknowledgments

My thanks go to my students, who first inspired me to write this book and then gave constructive suggestions and corrections on my writing. I am especially grateful to Dr. Jenny Huang, who helped me revise the writing and programming of this book.

My special appreciation extends to the wonderful editorial staff and other personnel at Auerbach Publications of Taylor & Francis for their cooperation and reviews: John Wyzalek, Senior Acquisitions Editor; Claire Miller, Managing Editor and Art Director; and all the people who have been involved in this project.

My loving gratitude goes to my family for their help, patience, and understanding of my seven-days-a-week work.

Chapter 1

Introduction to Database Systems

Objectives

- Learn the functions of a database management system.
- Understand some major database components.

1.1 Functions of a Database

To run a successful business, a company must have a good understanding of its customers, its employees, market competition, product performance, and the research of new products. A good understanding should be based on reliable information about these business processes. Without the information, a business is running in the dark. Think about it: If a real estate company has no records of the houses on the market, what can it sell? No business will be successful when nobody there knows what is going on. Reliable information is often based on data collected from a business process. The type of data from a business process may include text, charts, sound, image, and other multimedia data types. These data should be categorized, sorted, and analyzed to be useful. One of the efficient tools to manage business information is the database. The use of the database in a business process is to store business data, track business processes, and analyze business performance. In a business process, there is an immense amount of data to be stored. For example, a university uses databases to store student records, class schedules, enrollment information, and so on. A computer manufacturer uses databases to keep customer orders, employee data, sales data, revenue data, profit data, supply sources, product inventory, and so forth.

With the fast development of E-commerce, the amount of information needed has increased dramatically. In this information age, some companies need to store petabytes of data to support thousands of users simultaneously. One petabyte is equal to one million gigabytes. IBM has worked on petabyte databases for the U.S. Census Bureau and Seitel (a leading provider of seismic data for the oil industry), to name just two. The databases built for the U.S. Census Bureau can be used to maintain four petabytes of valuable national census storage. Thus, you can see that a tool such as a database used to store and manage a large amount of data is the key to a successful business.

The stored data on a database can be used to track business activities, customer information, and inventory. When a specific piece of information is needed, a utility provided by the database is available to query the data. A database can be used to categorize and sort raw data so that it is easier to retrieve them later. Data stored in the database can also be used to analyze customer behavior, predict future sales and business patterns, and then help make decisions. Business activities are designed based on information obtained from the database. For many companies, even a small gain in knowledge from data analysis could have a great impact on correct decision making. Today, the database is used as the information center of business. It is one of the most important parts of a business process.

As we show, virtually every type of business process requires databases. But, before you can successfully set up a database to handle your business, as an IT professional, you must have a thorough understanding of your business process and the technologies involved in database development and management. You need to have a lot of knowledge about database theories and technologies, whose development in processing business information has greatly enriched the computer science and computer information systems curriculum. In today's computer- and technology-related curricula, database theories and technologies have become a key component.

1.2 Database Management System

Even small amount of data is very hard to manipulate by hand. Since the late 1960s, computer scientists have developed and improved the data management tool *Database Management System* (DBMS). A DBMS is a software package used to store, manage, and analyze data. There are all sorts of DBMSs. Some of them can handle small amounts of data but are very user friendly, and even a nonprofessional can handle them. This kind of DBMS is called a personal DBMS. Some of them are built to handle data for a large enterprise. This type of DBMS is called an enterprise DBMS.

In this book, all our examples are developed on Microsoft SQL Server. We chose SQL Server for several reasons. First, it is easy to use so that beginners will not be overwhelmed by the complexity of an enterprise-level DBMS. On the other hand, SQL Server is complex enough to handle most of the enterprise-level database tasks. Another important reason to select SQL Server is its low cost. College students can obtain a copy of SQL Server through the MSDN

Figure 1.1   Database management tools in Microsoft SQL Server 2000

Academic Alliance (MSDNAA) program. For small- and medium-sized businesses, the ownership cost of SQL Server is lower than other major enterprise-level DBMSs. The installation of SQL Server is easier, too. It will help readers get a quick start on the hands-on practice included in this book.

With a DBMS, users can efficiently query the information needed for business processing. A DBMS also provides the users with a working environment for data management. An enterprise-level DBMS often includes the following database managing tools:

- Database configuration
- Database administration
- Executing query operations
- Creating database components
- Defining relationships among database components
- Data transformation
- Debugging
- Networking assistant utilities for a client/server environment

To get a quick overview of a DBMS, we use SQL Server as an example. After you have installed SQL Server 2000 by following the instruction in Appendix A, click the **Start** menu, then **All Programs**, and then **Microsoft SQL Server**. You will get a list of tools available in the DBMS package of Microsoft SQL Server 2000 (Figure 1.1).

With *Enterprise Manager*, you can create a new registration to an existing SQL Server. Enterprise Manager can be used to configure each database server registered in a server group. You can use Enterprise Manager to create and manage database components. Enterprise Manager includes wizards for database design, testing, and management. To open Enterprise Manager, click the menu item **Enterprise Manager** shown in Figure 1.1 and expand the tree of **Databases**. You will see a list of database objects, illustrated in Figure 1.2.

To effectively retrieve data, a DBMS uses a query language to select only those data requested by the user. In SQL Server 2000, *Query Analyzer* is the query management tool. In Query Analyzer, shown in Figure 1.3, you can

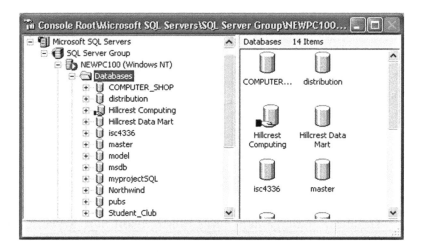

Figure 1.2   SQL Server 2000 Enterprise Manager window

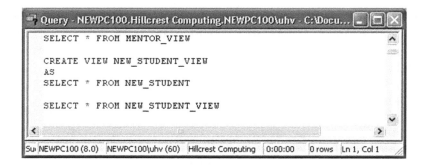

Figure 1.3   SQL Query Analyzer

create queries and other SQL scripts and execute them. Query Analyzer has a debugging tool that can be used to debug errors in query statements and solve problems that occur in performing a query. To explore Query Analyzer, click it on the menu in Figure 1.1. If you have installed SQL Server with the default Window's Authentication, click the **OK** button to start Query Analyzer. Otherwise, you need to enter your user name and password first. Click the down arrow sign of the combo box in the tool bar and select the **pubs** database. Type the SQL statement **SELECT * FROM AUTHORS**. You will learn more about SQL statements in later chapters. For now, we only use them to illustrate Query Analyzer. Press the **F5** key or click the **Execute Query** button on the tool bar, and you will get the result.

To extend the data management ability, programming languages can be integrated into the DBMS. Many DBMSs support the presentation of data on the Internet and support the creation of forms and reports. In SQL Server 2000, you can use the utility called *Configure SQL XML Support in IIS* for Internet-based database management. To open the utility, click **Configure SQL XML Support in IIS** on the menu, shown in Figure 1.4.

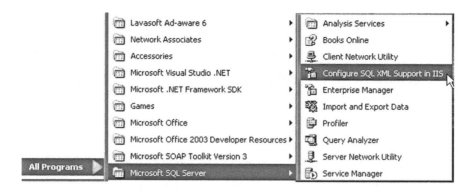

Figure 1.4   Configure SQL XML support in IIS

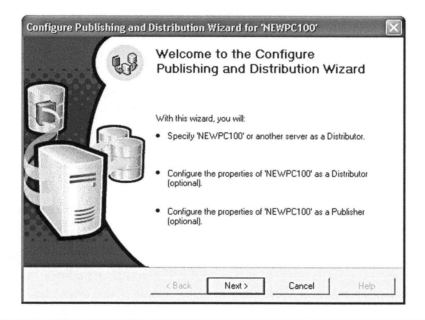

Figure 1.5   Configure Publishing and Distribution Wizard

To ease the management task, the *Graphical User Interface* (GUI) has become part of the DBMS. GUI administration utilities are used for designing databases, creating database applications, managing database users, performing database administration tasks such as database backup, restoring a damaged database, and performance tuning. *Wizards* are a type of interactive GUI tool used to simplify routine database maintenance. Many DBMSs create various wizards to help with data management. Figure 1.5 gives an example of the Configure Publishing and Distribution Wizard in SQL Server Enterprise Manager. To explore the database management wizards, click **Enterprise Manager**, as shown in Figure 1.1. Highlight one of the servers under the **SQL Server Group** node. Click the **Tools** menu. Then click **Wizards**, and a set of available wizards will appear. Expand the **Replication** node, and you will see

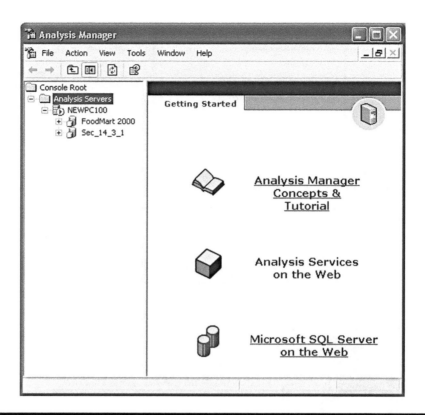

Figure 1.6   Analysis Manager window

all the wizards for replication maintenance. Double-click **Configure Publishing and Distribution Wizard**, and you will have the first screen of the wizard, as shown in Figure 1.5.

A DBMS may also provide tools for analyzing data. For example, SQL Server provides the *On-Line Analytical Processing* (OLAP) system, which has some advanced analytical tools that support business decision making. Some DBMS vendors also provide data-mining tools. The data-mining tools are used to analyze patterns of business data. The patterns can be used to model the behavior of business processes. For the purpose of decision support, some DBMSs provide tools for developing data warehouses used to store information for analysis. Figure 1.6 displays the Analysis Manager window in SQL Server, where you can perform OLAP analyses. If you have installed Analysis Manager as described in Appendix A, click **Analysis Services**, shown in Figure 1.1, and then **Analysis Manager** to conduct an OLAP analysis (Figure 1.6).

To manage the structure and the meaning of data, the DBMS provides metadata services. That is why *metadata* are also called the data about data. Metadata are normally stored in a specific table called a system table. You can use metadata to find all the tables that contain specific data types, such as `Date`, or all the columns that have specific names, such as `FirstName`. Metadata will help both database administrators and application developers to better understand the structure of data. To view the metadata in SQL Server,

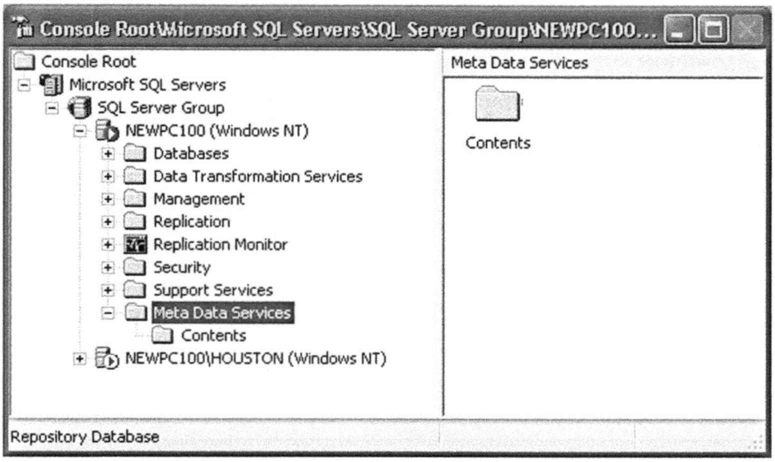

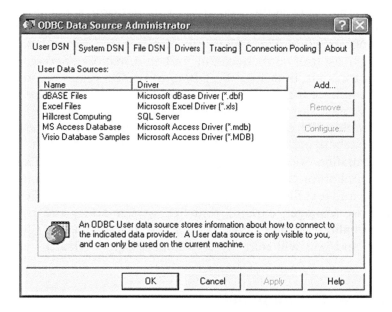

Figure 1.7   Metadata Service window

Figure 1.8   ODBC configuration dialog

open **Enterprise Manager**; you will see **Meta Data Services,** which is a metadata browser. There are also some metadata tools under *Data Transformation Services* (DTS), as shown in Figure 1.7.

The DBMS supports database-accessing interfaces such as *Open Database Connectivity* (ODBC) and *Active Data Objects* (ADO). Figure 1.8 shows the ODBC configuration dialog from the Control Panel. To explore the ODBC, click **Start**, then **Control Panel**. After opening the Control Panel, double-click the icon **Administrative Tools** and then the **Data Sources (ODBC)** icon. You will see the available ODBC data sources in Figure 1.8.

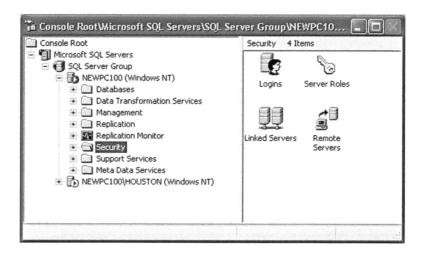

Figure 1.9   Security management tools

To ensure that only authorized users can perform specified activities, a database must have a dependable security system to control the accessing and modifying activities. The DBMS can also be used to implement security measures such as user authentication and information encryption. Security management tools are built into the DBMS to protect data from unauthorized users. An example of these tools is shown in Figure 1.9. To access the security tools in SQL Server, open **Enterprise Manager**. Expand your server's node, and then click the **Security** node. The security tools are displayed there.

Once a database table is created, it will be populated with data. In the **Data Transformation Services** in SQL Server, the **DTS Import/Export Wizard** provides the utility for copying data between data sources, such as databases, spreadsheets, and text files (see Figure 1.10). To start the **Import/Export Wizard**, open **Enterprise Manager**, expand your SQL Server node, and right-click the **Data Transformation Services** node to open the pop-up menu. Click **All Tasks**, then **Import**, and you will start the **DTS Import/Export Wizard**.

1.3   Database Components

In this section, we become familiar with the components created in a database management system. As an example, Figure 1.11 shows the commonly used database components in SQL Server 2000. To illustrate these components, open **Enterprise Manager** and expand your server node, and then open **Databases**. Click the **pubs** node; you will see database components such as tables, views, and stored procedures, as displayed in Figure 1.11.

In a relational database, data are stored in tables. Each *table* is used to store data related to the same object such as student. As you can see in Figure 1.12, a table is constructed with columns and rows. Each column represents an attribute that is used to describe the object. For example, the column emp_id in Figure 1.12 is the attribute used to describe the object employee.

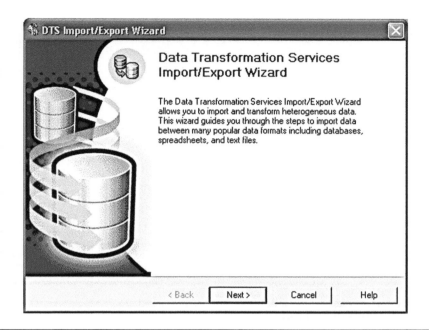

Figure 1.10   Data Transformation Services Import/Export Wizard

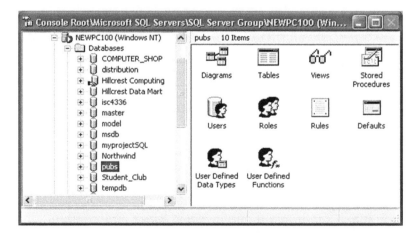

Figure 1.11   Commonly used database components in SQL Server 2000 DBMS

Here the employee object is a sample table in SQL Server, which contains eight columns. To view the contents of the table, click the **Tables** icon. Then right-click the **employee** table on the list, click **Open Table** on the pop-up menu, and then click **Return all rows**. The table window will appear and display the contents of the table, as shown in Figure 1.12.

Most relational databases have multiple tables. To make the tables work together, relationships must be correctly established among these tables. This is a task of database design. The diagram in Figure 1.13 presents a graphical display of relationships of the tables. A diagram is a convenient tool for

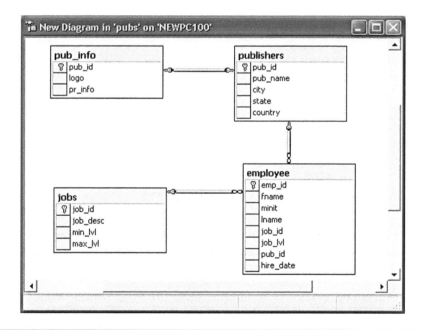

Data in Table 'employee' in 'pubs' on 'NEWPC100'

emp_id	fname	minit	lname	job_id	job_lvl	pub_id	hire_date
▶ PMA42628M	Paolo	M	Accorti	13	35	0877	8/27/1992
PSA89086M	Pedro	S	Afonso	14	89	1389	12/24/1990
VPA30890F	Victoria	P	Ashworth	6	140	0877	9/13/1990
H-B39728F	Helen		Bennett	12	35	0877	9/21/1989
L-B31947F	Lesley		Brown	7	120	0877	2/13/1991
F-C16315M	Francisco		Chang	4	227	9952	11/3/1990
PTC11962M	Philip	T	Cramer	2	215	9952	11/11/1989
A-C71970F	Aria		Cruz	10	87	1389	10/26/1991
AMD15433F	Ann	M	Devon	3	200	9952	7/16/1991
ARD36773F	Anabela	R	Domingues	8	100	0877	1/27/1993
PHF38899M	Peter	H	Franken	10	75	0877	5/17/1992
PXH22250M	Paul	X	Henriot	5	159	0877	8/19/1993
CFH28514M	Carlos	F	Hernadez	5	211	9999	4/21/1993
PDI47470M	Palle	D	Ibsen	7	195	0736	5/9/1993
KJJ92907F	Karla	J	Jablonski	9	170	9999	3/11/1994
KFJ64308F	Karin	F	Josephs	14	100	0736	10/17/1992
MGK44605M	Matti	G	Karttunen	6	220	0736	5/1/1994
POK93028M	Pirkko	O	Koskitalo	10	80	9999	11/29/1993
JYL26161F	Janine	Y	Labrune	5	172	9901	5/26/1991
M-L67958F	Maria		Larsson	7	135	1389	3/27/1992

Figure 1.12   Employee table

New Diagram in 'pubs' on 'NEWPC100'

pub_info
🔑 pub_id
logo
pr_info

publishers
🔑 pub_id
pub_name
city
state
country

employee
🔑 emp_id
fname
minit
lname
job_id
job_lvl
pub_id
hire_date

jobs
🔑 job_id
job_desc
min_lvl
max_lvl

Figure 1.13   Diagram

database design. You can find the diagram tool under the **Databases** node. Expand your database and right-click **Diagrams**. Then choose **New Database Diagram**; you will start the **Create Database Diagram Wizard**.

Sometimes an application (such as a form or a report) needs data from selected columns of multiple tables. A *view* is a database component that is

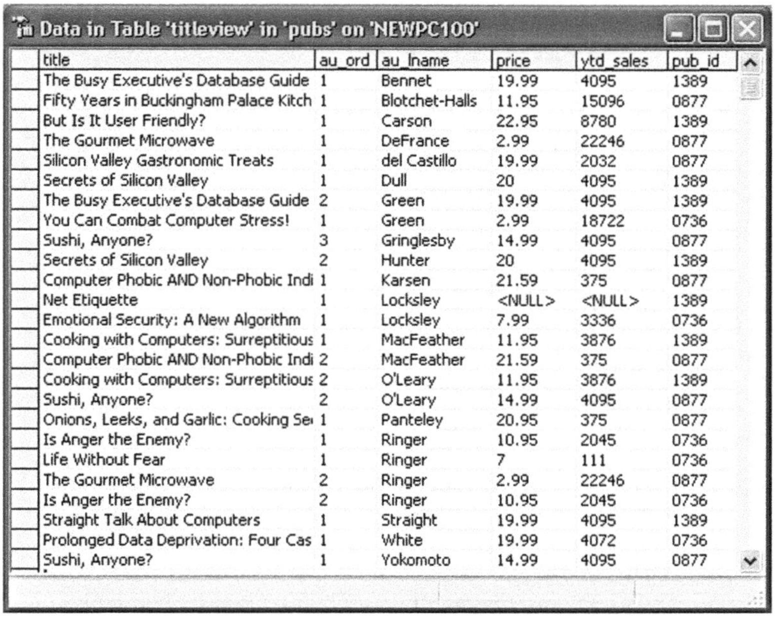

title	au_ord	au_lname	price	ytd_sales	pub_id
The Busy Executive's Database Guide	1	Bennet	19.99	4095	1389
Fifty Years in Buckingham Palace Kitch	1	Blotchet-Halls	11.95	15096	0877
But Is It User Friendly?	1	Carson	22.95	8780	1389
The Gourmet Microwave	1	DeFrance	2.99	22246	0877
Silicon Valley Gastronomic Treats	1	del Castillo	19.99	2032	0877
Secrets of Silicon Valley	1	Dull	20	4095	1389
The Busy Executive's Database Guide	2	Green	19.99	4095	1389
You Can Combat Computer Stress!	1	Green	2.99	18722	0736
Sushi, Anyone?	3	Gringlesby	14.99	4095	0877
Secrets of Silicon Valley	2	Hunter	20	4095	1389
Computer Phobic AND Non-Phobic Indi	1	Karsen	21.59	375	0877
Net Etiquette	1	Locksley	<NULL>	<NULL>	1389
Emotional Security: A New Algorithm	1	Locksley	7.99	3336	0736
Cooking with Computers: Surreptitious	1	MacFeather	11.95	3876	1389
Computer Phobic AND Non-Phobic Indi	2	MacFeather	21.59	375	0877
Cooking with Computers: Surreptitious	2	O'Leary	11.95	3876	1389
Sushi, Anyone?	2	O'Leary	14.99	4095	0877
Onions, Leeks, and Garlic: Cooking Se	1	Panteley	20.95	375	0877
Is Anger the Enemy?	1	Ringer	10.95	2045	0736
Life Without Fear	1	Ringer	7	111	0736
The Gourmet Microwave	2	Ringer	2.99	22246	0877
Is Anger the Enemy?	2	Ringer	10.95	2045	0736
Straight Talk About Computers	1	Straight	19.99	4095	1389
Prolonged Data Deprivation: Four Cas	1	White	19.99	4072	0736
Sushi, Anyone?	1	Yokomoto	14.99	4095	0877

Figure 1.14   View

constructed to contain the data from a set of selected columns from one table or multiple tables. A view can be used to support a database application that may use the data stored in multiple tables. For example, you may have a student grade report that is used to display data from multiple tables, such as STUDENT containing student personal data and ENROLLMENT containing grades of the student. In such a case, you may want to construct a view first to hold the data selected from multiple tables and then let the report use the data in the view. In the view of Figure 1.14, columns are selected from different tables. In this example, the column au_lname is from the table authors and the column pub_id is from the table publishers. To display the view, click the **Views** node under the **pubs** database node, right-click **titleview** to open the pop-up menu, choose **Open View,** and then choose **Return all rows**. You will have the result as illustrated in Figure 1.14. If you double-click **titleview**, you will see the SQL statement generating the view.

Sometimes you may want to let a DBMS run a set of SQL statements to accomplish a task. A *stored procedure* is a precompiled set of SQL statements stored in a database server (see Figure 1.15). You do not need to recompile the SQL statement in a stored procedure. The stored procedure is ready to run. The processing of a database can be faster if the often-used tasks are programmed as stored procedures. To view a stored procedure, click the **Stored Procedures** node under the **pubs** database node. Right-click the **byroyalty** icon on the right pane, and then click **Properties**. The **Stored Procedure Properties** window will open and the SQL statements for the stored procedure will be displayed.

A trigger is a specific kind of stored procedure. It will be executed automatically when a specific database action occurs, for example, when a table is modified by inserting a new record.

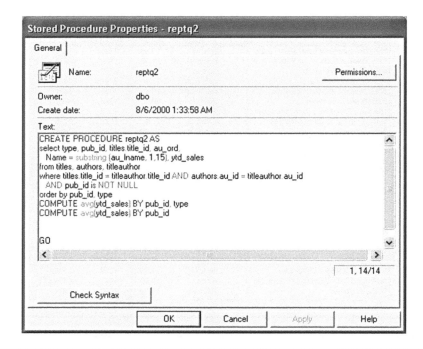

Figure 1.15   Stored procedure

To speed up the search for specified data, a DBMS provides a component called an *index*, which is created based on the key values in a table. By using an index, the search will look only at an appropriate column to match a given index key. This is just like searching the index at the end of a book to find specific information.

Constraints are used to specify characteristics of data in a column. There are integrity constraints and value constraints. *Integrity constraints* are used to define relationships among tables. *Value constraints* allow a user to specify, for example, if a column can take a NULL value, if the default value can be assigned to a column, if the values in a column should be unique, and what the range of values is in a column.

The *user* component defines users in a database (Figure 1.16). Many users may share the same database object, such as a table on a database server. To identify users who are sharing a database object, a user account is created for each individual user. Each user account can be configured to have ownerships and permissions on the objects in a database. An individual user can access his or her user account with the username and password. When you click the **Users** node under **pubs** in **SQL Server Enterprise Manager**, the database users are listed in the right pane.

When a group of users performs the same kind of job, you can create a role and grant appropriate permissions to that role. The *Role* component is a useful tool that allows you to group users with the same set of permissions. If a new user who performs the same job is created, instead of assigning a number of permissions to that user one permission at a time, you can assign

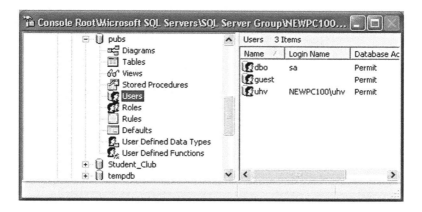

Figure 1.16   Users

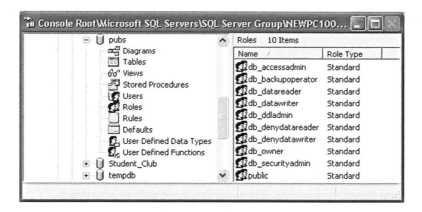

Figure 1.17   Roles

the role to that user. Then the user gets all the permissions assigned to that role at once. Also, when modifying permissions, instead of changing the permissions for each individual user, you can modify them for the role; then all the users with the same role will have the modified permissions automatically. The role component simplifies the process of permission assignment. To see the roles created in the database pubs, click the **Roles** node under **pubs** (Figure 1.17).

Rule components are used to restrict values entered in a column. Rules specify the range of valid values that can be entered into a column. You can implement rules when creating a table.

Defaults specify the default value in a column. For example, you can decide if a null value can be assigned to a column when inserting a row. If a column cannot accept a null value, the not null default should be used to prevent errors.

Most DBMSs allow users to create *user-defined database objects*, such as user-defined data types. To see a list of user-defined data types, click the **User**

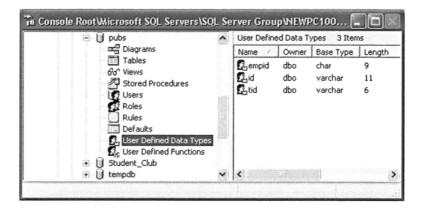

Figure 1.18   User-defined data types

Defined Data Types node under **pubs**; the list of user-defined data types will appear (Figure 1.18).

We have just completed a brief overview of some of the database components. There are more to come in later chapters. You will learn in more detail about these database components and how to use them to solve business problems.

1.4 Database Development Process

Before a database can be built, you must understand how the database will achieve its goals. You need to verify that the database will solve your specified business problems. Therefore, a careful design is necessary. A well-designed database is based on a good understanding of the business process. The first step in the development of a database is to identify business requirements and goals to be achieved by the new database. At this stage, one database designer or a team of database designers is involved in gathering information from users. They need to find out: What are the business requirements for the future database? What information needs to be stored in the database? How can the data be stored? How can the data be presented to the end users? They need to prepare the agreements and contracts and draft a timeline to fulfill those agreements.

Once you have figured out what information you want to keep track of, the next step is to understand the relationships among those things you want to keep track of through the data modeling process. At this stage, database designers translate the data model to database tables with integrity constraints. Based on the data model, the database designers can specify the tables and columns to organize the business data into a well-defined structure. After a data model is developed, the designers can use the data model to verify if the future database will meet the database requirements. Usually, several modifications are needed. It might take some time to make sure that the database design team and their business partners are all satisfied.

The next step is to implement the database with a DBMS package. It is the database designers' job to choose a proper DBMS package that will meet all the database management, data analysis, and data storage requirements. During the implementation process, the database designers or database administrators (DBAs) create the tables and populate them with business data. After the database is constructed, the database administrators and users need to test the newly created database before it can be used in the business process. The database design team may further modify the database to meet the users' requirements.

Once the database is ready to use, the database application developers need to create application objects to assist front-end users in accessing the database. A front-end user may access the database through the local network or through the Internet. This means that a well-built database must be able to provide networking functionalities. This kind of database is called a network database or Web database. For a large corporation, millions of users may access the database simultaneously. Such a database may not fit into a single computer. The database must be partitioned into multiple parts, and the partitioned database is distributed to multiple computers. The management of a distributed database system is a challenge. It is the database administrator's job to keep the organization's database running smoothly. Every database should enforce necessary security measures. Database security is an important issue that needs to be addressed by the DBA.

To support business decision making, a database should also provide data analysis tools, such as OLAP, data mart or data warehouse, and data mining. It is the information analyzer's job to provide the decision team with necessary analytical information. By using these data analysis tools, the information analyzer can store the history data for fast information search and identify the trend and patterns hidden in the daily business operation data.

During the development of databases in this book, we introduce some popular techniques. These techniques are used for learning purposes and are not designed as the optimal solution for some specific business management tasks.

1.5 Summary

We now summarize what we have done in this chapter. We have looked at the big picture of a database. First, we talked about the functions of a database and discussed why databases are needed and how they are used in business. Then database management systems were introduced. As an example, we discussed the management tools built into the SQL Server DBMS. We have also covered the major database components. Here, we discussed the following components: tables, views, stored procedures, triggers, indexes, constraints, rules, defaults, user-defined objects, roles, and users. In the last section of this chapter, we briefly stated the steps in a database development process. The roles of technology personnel who are involved in database development are described in this section.

Review Questions

1. Why is business process information important?
2. Describe the functions of a database in a business process.
3. What can be done with the administration tools in a DBMS system?
4. What are the functions of the Enterprise Manager?
5. What tasks can you accomplish by using Query Analyzer?
6. Describe a GUI and its functionalities.
7. Describe data analysis tools available in a database management system.
8. What is metadata?
9. Explain the functions of ODBC and ADO.
10. What do you do with Data Transformation Services?
11. Name the commonly used database components.
12. Describe tables and their structures.
13. What is a diagram?
14. What is a view in a database?
15. Why do we need stored procedures in a database?
16. Describe the functions of an index.
17. What are integrity constraints and value constraints?
18. Why do we need user accounts in a database?
19. When can you use a role?
20. What is the first step in database development?
21. What is a network database?
22. What do you need to support decision making?

Chapter 2

Conceptual Design and Data Modeling

Objectives

- Get a general idea about the process of database design.
- Learn how to collect information about a business process.
- Understand the concepts and theory of data modeling.
- Be able to represent a business process with a data model.

2.1 Introduction to Database Design Process

One of the functions of a database is to store data collected from a business process. The question is how to store the data so that database users can easily and quickly find them. Remember, there could be petabytes of data stored in a database. If we simply populate the database with data, live with it, later find out it does not meet the business requirements, and then rebuild it all over again, we will cause a lot of chaos in the entire business process. We must carefully design the database before we can populate it with data. We need to investigate the database requirements, construct a database structure to meet these requirements, classify the data to be stored in the database, come up with a plan of how to help the database users to access the data, and so on. A well-built database should clearly categorize business data and provide useful information for daily business processing. To achieve this goal, we carefully go through three major steps in the database design process: conceptual design, database design, and physical design.

The definitions of conceptual design, database design, and physical design may vary from one author to another author. For example, some authors may consider the database design software-dependent and others may not. Some may break the above three stages into five or six stages. To us, how to name the stages in a database process is not that important. The crucial thing is not to miss the major steps in a database design process.

Conceptual Design

At this stage, you, as a database designer, investigate business requirements and data used in a business process. You need to find out how data are used in the business process and how to present the data to the end user. Based on your investigation, you create a data model to represent the data transaction in the business process. After the data model is created, you will verify the business requirements against the initial data model. At the conceptual design stage, you should focus on developing a logical view based on the business requirements. You do not need to specify the hardware and software. The resulting data model is hardware- and software-free. The development of a data model is covered in this chapter.

Database Design

At this stage, the data model you created previously is converted into tables in a relational database. During the conversion, you must make sure that the table structures are good for data processing. A normalizing process will detect defects in the table structures. Chapter 3 covers the normalization process. In a relational database, tables, columns, and rows are used to represent the objects created in the corresponding data model. Primary keys and foreign keys used to connect the tables will represent the relationships established in the data model. Constraints will be implemented for attribute values. Sometimes, this stage is also called *logical design*. The database design is covered in Chapter 4, where we also use a graphical tool included in SQL Server to present table structures.

Physical Design

At this stage, you will specify the hardware, software, and physical environment for implementing a relational database. To successfully implement the database, you need to carefully determine what type of computer system will be used to hold the storage devices, how to import and export data, where to store the data, and how to enforce security measures on the database server. Some authentication issues are also specified in the physical design. At this level, the design is both hardware- and software-dependent.

In the next few sections, we discuss the conceptual design. We talk about how to get information on business requirements. You will learn what data modeling is and why you should care about it. You will also go through some of the practical steps to actually build a data model.

2.2 Understanding Business Process

As we mentioned earlier, to build a database that meets business requirements, you need to thoroughly understand the business process. In this section, you are going to learn how to do it. Several commonly used methods and procedures are discussed in this section.

At the beginning of the database design process, as a database designer, you will collect the following information:

- What works and what does not in the current business process
- The goals the database will achieve
- The type and amount of data information to be stored
- All the business rules
- How the information will be used in the business process
- Implementation problems and limitations

How and where can you find the above information? Here are the methods commonly used to collect the information:

- Examining the company's documents about its business process is a good starting point. You need to examine the office paperwork such as forms and reports used in the business process, business-related e-mail and screenshots, existing spreadsheets, and database backups. The company may have also documented some configurations and updates for its current system. If these documents are related to your projects, make sure to examine them carefully.
- You also need to observe how data are transferred from one location to another. It is very helpful to use diagrams and flowcharts to document the business process.
- To further understand the business process, you need to identify and interview the key players in the business process. The goal of the interview is to identify the business requirements. You should ask the interviewees what they want to achieve from the project, how they will use the data, where existing data are kept, and how they would like the data to be presented. During the interviews, you should take notes about your conversations and get clarification from the interviewees. Good interpersonal and communication skills are greatly helpful for data collection.

Your goal is to find out what the business requirements are for your project, what data should be stored in the database, and how the data are used in a business process. As an example, we consider a case study of a company we call `Hillcrest Computing`.

2.2.1 Business Process

The following example is used to demonstrate the process of information collection. It is for illustration purposes only; many real-world problems can be much more complicated.

Case Study: Hillcrest Computing Business Process

Hillcrest Computing manufactures and sells computer products such as desktop and notebook computers. It customizes computer systems based on customers' requests. It buys computer parts from different vendors. The company has four sales centers in Texas. At each sales center, there are about ten employees. Customer purchase orders are processed at each sales center. Each purchase order may contain different shipping addresses. One shipping address may also place multiple orders.

When a customer places an order, a purchase order form will be filled out. The form includes items such as

- Type of computer system
- Order date
- Price
- Shipping information such as customer name, address, and time
- Sales center where the order is processed

When purchase orders come in, the assembly workers will assemble the computer systems. One purchase order may include one or more types of computer system. On the other hand, different purchase orders may contain the same type of computer system. To assemble a computer system, several workers will participate in an assembly process. Each assembly worker may assemble many computer systems; that is, he or she may participate in many assembly processes.

In an assembly process, computer parts such as hard drives, memory, and motherboards will be put together to make a computer system based on the customer's request. Different computer systems may use the same kind of parts. For example, two computer systems with different operating systems may have the same kind of hard drive. Detailed information for each part is kept for reference.

After a computer system is assembled, the workers need to fill out a form that is used to track the products. The form includes the following items:

- Workers' ID numbers and names
- Time used to complete the job
- Type of computer system assembled
- Parts used for the job

The accountants will record computer system prices on purchase orders, costs of computer parts purchased from various vendors, and so forth. They need to keep records of the following items:

- Operation costs of the sales centers
- Costs of computer parts
- Revenue produced at each sales center
- Prices of computer systems sold to customers
- Salaries paid to Hillcrest Computing employees

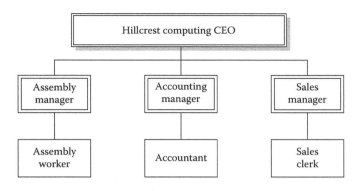

Figure 2.1   Key players in business process

The cost of a computer system will depend on the labor cost of the workers, the parts used for the computer system, and other miscellaneous costs. The company needs to keep track of the information about ordering, computer system assembling, computer parts, labor costs, and shipping. The company has decided to create a centralized database that can be used to assist the daily operation, such as producing reports to show job completion time, cost of each computer system, purchase orders, and shipping information.

2.2.2   *Investigating Business Requirements*

From the above description of the business process, the manager in the IT department, who will be the database designer for the proposed database, conducted an investigation by interviewing all the key players involved in the business process. He listed all the key players in the personnel diagram shown in Figure 2.1. The managers involved in production and sales report to the company's CEO. The assembly workers, who report to the assembly manager, assemble computer systems ordered by customers. The assembly workers are divided into several groups. There are four accountants, who work under the accounting manager. The accountants process purchase orders received from the sales centers. The sales clerks, who report to the sales manager, take customers' orders. After computer systems are assembled, the sales clerks will ship them to the customers.

From the interviews, the database designer recorded the following concerns:

- CEO: We are facing severe competition in the PC market. To attract and keep customers, Hillcrest Computing must meet the customers' demands better. We need to process customer orders as fast as possible. We also need to reduce production cost and pay competitive salaries to keep employees with good skills.
- Assembly manager: Sometimes the assembly workers forget to enter the costs of the parts. I have to track down the workers to get the costs. I need them in order to calculate the cost of each computer system. It takes too much time for me to do the calculation and the tracking as well.

- Assembly worker: Too much time has been used to fill the product tracking forms. Each day, we have to spend 20 percent of the time filling out those forms. The paperwork puts us behind. We would like to use that time to assemble more computer systems.
- Sales manager: Many times, the assembly workers cannot complete the orders on time. Our customers are not happy about the late shipments.
- Sales clerk: Filling out an order form manually takes too much time. To prevent the orders from getting lost during the process, we have to make a copy each time an order form is completed. Making copies wastes time and paper and costs money.
- Accounting manager: Currently, we don't have time to do productivity reports. This is because we are unable to efficiently relate the computer costs to the assembly workers' labor costs.
- Accountant: A sales clerk enters a computer system price on a purchase order. However, the actual cost for the computer system may vary due to the fluctuation of the market part prices. Manually entering customer order information into our computer is time consuming.

The database designer gathered ideas and suggestions for improvement as shown below.

- CEO: I would like to see how the computer system price is related to the labor cost and computer part cost. I would also like to improve our productivity and to better serve our customers. A monthly report should include all the costs, such as administrators' salaries, workers' salaries, costs of computer parts and computer systems, and expenses for advertising. The monthly report should also include the sales revenue and profit generated in the past month. From time to time, I would also like to read a detailed weekly report on sales and assembly processes to have a closer look at the business process.
- Assembly manager: I would like to have a requirement to fill out the cost, so nobody can submit a form without entering the cost. Also, I want the cost of a computer system to be calculated automatically after I enter separate costs such as parts and labor.
- Assembly worker: We should enter product information electronically about computer systems we assemble. This way, the sales manager will know the assembly progress and the accountants will know which parts have been used. There should be a system to calculate the total cost of parts for a computer system as soon as we enter the information about the parts. With a new electronic form that does most of the paperwork, we can complete customers' orders on time.
- Sales manager: I would like to know the progress of a computer assembly process, so we can better inform our customers. I need a report that shows sales in my location and detailed sales information about each type of computer system. A bar chart about the sales of each computer type would be helpful. Customers often ask us to recommend some popular computers. Through the bar chart, we would be able to provide some information and recommendations for our customers.

- Sales clerk: If we can electronically enter purchase information and keep it in a database, both the assembly workers and accountants can use the information without duplicating the data.
- Accounting manager: I would like to have the information of computer system costs, assembly workers' labor costs, and computer part costs, so we can report the productivity to the CEO. If the part cost information can be filled out by sales clerks and the usage of the parts by assembly workers, it would save us a lot of time and we could focus on employees' salaries and other costs and prepare detailed information on productivity.
- Accountant: We would like to be able to electronically enter detailed information about the parts when they arrive and track the cost of the parts for a computer system. To better compare prices of parts from different vendors, a graphic display would help us observe the trend and select the best vendors.

After having talked to the above key persons who are involved in the assembling, ordering, and shipping processes and in the administration and management, the database designer gave a careful review of the collected information and identified the goals of the database project.

- The first goal is to store necessary information in a database to reduce the time to complete forms.
- The second goal is to make sure that the sales manager is informed of the assembly progress.
- The third goal is to help the accounting manager collect productivity information.
- The fourth goal is to track market prices of computer parts and other details.

The database designer will create a database to fulfill these goals and meet all the business requirements. The designer has classified the information into the following categories:

- Order-Shipping System:
  - Sales center information management
  - Purchase order management
  - Shipping management
- Inventory System:
  - Computer parts inventory
  - Parts detail information
- Assembly System:
  - Assembly worker management
  - Assembly process information

From the above business processing systems, the database designer can determine what data to track and how to manipulate these data by queries and stored procedures to meet the business requirements.

Based on the understanding of the business process, the database designer will draft the structure of the database by analyzing the logical relationships among the data. By carefully interpreting the interview results, the database designer comes up with a logical representation of the database structure. The logical representation is also called a *data model*; it is the designer's view of the business data. At this point, the database designer will focus on the components of data modeling that include *entities, attributes, domains, relationships,* and *business rules*. In the development of a database, a data modeling process is used to discover the relationships among the data to be stored in the database. In later chapters, the relationships are used to integrate different types of information.

In Section 2.4, we discuss how to develop a data model for the business process shown in Figure 2.1. Before we develop the data model, we now become familiar with the components of the entity-relationship data model.

2.3 Entity-Relationship Data Model

Like most engineering projects, before physically building a project, a sketch or a scaled-down model should be built first. The model is used to make sure that the project to be built is feasible. Similarly, before you build a physical database, create a model first. As you will see after you have populated a database with data, it is very difficult to make changes to the structure of the database. Many data modeling tools have been developed since the 1970s. One of the most widely used modeling tools is the *entity-relationship model* (E-R model), introduced by Peter Chen in 1976. The entity-relationship data model is a graphical tool used to represent the logical structure of a database. E-R is not just a logical representation of the database structure. It is more than that. You can use the E-R model to verify if creating the database will satisfy the business requirements.

There are a number of modeling methodologies used to represent the data modeling components. One commonly used modeling methodology is the *Integration Definition for Information Modeling* (IDEF1X), which is based on the national standard called the Federal Information Standard, published in 1993. IDEF1X has the following abilities to meet data-modeling requirements:

- It is able to represent the modeling components such as entities, attributes, relationships, and domains.
- It has a relatively short learning curve in creating data models.
- It is powerful enough to cover most of the logical structures used in a relational database.
- It is suitable for converting a data model to a fully functioning database.

Due to the advantages of IDEF1X, some database modeling software packages, such as ERWin, Microsoft Visio, and Oracle Designer/2000, have adopted IDEF1X as one of their data modeling methodologies.

The elements used in an E-R model are entities, attributes, relationships, and so on. The meanings and the corresponding IDEF1X symbols are given below.

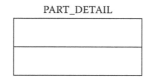

PART_DETAIL

Figure 2.2   IDEF1X graph for entity

2.3.1   Entities

An entity is a generic name for an object, such as a person, a computer, or a location that you want to keep in a database. Entities are things referred to as nouns from the grammar point of view. For example, if we are interested in keeping the information about employees, EMPLOYEE will be an entity.

By examining the objects whose information we will track in the business process in our case study, the database designer, who is the IT manager, identifies the following objects: shipping, purchase order, and sales center from the Order-Shipping System business process; assembly worker and assembly process from the Assembly System business process; and computer system, part, and part detail from the Inventory System business process. Therefore, SHIPPING, PURCHASE_ORDER, SALES_CENTER, ASSEMBLY_WORKER, ASSEMBLY_PROCESS, COMPUTER_SYSTEM, PART, and PART_DETAIL have become entities in the data model.

Graphically, an entity is represented by a rectangle with the entity name printed on it in capital letters. We now consider a group of assembly workers. Each worker in the assembly worker group is known as an *entity instance*. A collection of *entity instances* is called an *entity class*. The corresponding IDEF1X icon for the entity PART_DETAIL is shown in Figure 2.2.

2.3.2   Attributes, Identifiers, and Domains

Attributes are used to describe an entity, such as a person's name, Social Security number, and gender that describe a person. To illustrate the logical representation of an attribute, we can describe the PART_DETAIL entity by using the attributes ItemId, Price, Description, PartId, Maker, and Quantity. Figure 2.3a shows the PART_DETAIL entity with its attributes, and Figure 2.3b shows an instance of the entity. An attribute can be a *composite attribute* or a *multi-valued attribute*. A composite attribute is a set of related attributes, such as an Address attribute that consists of the Street, City, State, and Zip attributes. A multi-valued attribute has more than one value in it. For example, the attribute Car may contain two values if a person has two cars.

To identify the entity instances that are workers, an *identifier* such as worker ID is required. An identifier can consist of more than one attribute, for example, a combination of the first name and last name. When an identifier is used to identify each individual entity instance, it is unique. However, to

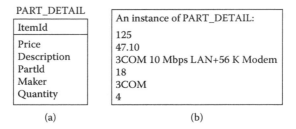

Figure 2.3   **(a)** `PART_DETAIL` **entity and (b) instance of** `PART_DETAIL` **entity**

PART_DETAIL

ItemId	smallint
Price	smallmoney
Description	char(50)
PartId	char(10)
Maker	char(30)
Quantity	smallint

Figure 2.4   **Attributes and their domains**

identify groups of instances, the identifier can be nonunique because all members in the same group are identified by the same id. A unique identifier is called a *key*. When there is no unique identifier from the attributes of an entity, a sequence of unique numbers can be used as a key. The numbers for this type of key can be generated automatically by a DBMS. Therefore, it is often called a *surrogate key*. In Figure 2.3a, the key attribute is in the top section and is separated from other attributes by a horizontal line.

The set of possible values that an attribute can use is called a *domain*. For example, the possible values for the attribute Gender are male or female. Then the set {male, female} is the domain for the attribute. Data types and constraints will be specified in the domain of an attribute. For example, we may specify the `ItemId` attribute as a *number* type. In the IDEF1X notation, the domain is placed on the right-hand side of the attribute name, as shown in Figure 2.4.

2.3.3   Relationships

Entities are often related to one another. For example, because apartments are built inside buildings, the `APARTMENT` entity is related to the `BUILDING` entity. As another example, an entity `PART` can be used to keep track of the computer part information such as part id and part name. In reality, we may purchase computer parts, such as monitors, from different vendors at different times. To keep track of detailed information for each part, in addition to the `PART` entity, we also need the entity `PART_DETAIL` to store the information about purchase time and vendors. Thus, the `PART_DETAIL` entity is related

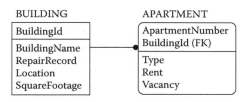

Figure 2.5   Identifying relationship

to the PART entity. Relationships are used to describe how entities are associated with each other. We first discuss four major types of IDEF1X relationships. There are more types of relationships, and we talk about them later.

1. *Identifying relationships:* Consider the relationship between APARTMENT and BUILDING. In reality, two apartments built in two buildings may have the same apartment number. To distinguish between these two apartments, you may need to attach the building number to the apartment number. In such a case, we can say that the apartment id depends on the existence of the building id. That is, the identifier for the APARTMENT entity should include the identifier for the BUILDING entity. Such a relationship is called the *identifying relationship*. In our example, the APARTMENT entity is the *child* entity, where the child record is based on the existence of the parent record from the *parent* entity BUILDING. To represent the identifying relationship in IDEF1X, use the symbols in Figure 2.5.

   The identifying relationship is represented by a solid line. The parent entity is represented by a square and the id dependent entity is represented by a round-cornered square. A filled-in black dot placed on the side of the child entity means that zero, one, or many apartments may be related to a single building. In a one-to-N relationship (or 1:N relationship), where N can be zero, one, or many, the entity with the filled-in black dot is on the N side of the relationship and the entity on the other side of the relationship is on the one side of the relationship. In an identifying relationship, the key for the child entity always includes the key from the parent entity. When the key from one entity is used by another entity, it is called the *foreign key* and is denoted by (FK).

2. *Nonidentifying relationships:* Consider the relationship between ADVISOR and STUDENT. A faculty member may advise zero, one, or many students. Therefore, the relationship between ADVISOR and STUDENT is a 1:N relationship. It is different from the example of the identifying relationship. Because each student has his or her own id, the faculty id is not part of the key for the STUDENT entity. Such a relationship is called a nonidentifying relationship. ADVISOR is the parent entity, which is on the one side of the relationship and STUDENT is the child entity, which is on the N side of the relationship. Although the entities are related by placing the advisor id to the STUDENT entity, this time the advisor id is not part of the key for the STUDENT entity. The IDEF1X symbol for the nonidentifying relationship is shown in Figure 2.6.

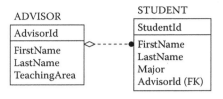

Figure 2.6   Nonidentifying relationship with optional parent

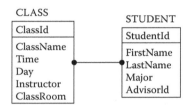

Figure 2.7   Nonspecific relationship

Again, because the filled-in black dot is on the STUDENT side, the STUDENT entity is on the N side of the relationship and the ADVISOR entity is on the one side of the relationship. The nonidentifying relationship is represented by a dashed line. The diamond sign on the side of the ADVISOR entity indicates that an advisor is optional. That is, some students may not have an advisor and the attribute AdvisorId in the entity STUDENT may contain null values. Here, some students may argue that every student at their university must have an advisor. Certainly, if the database is developed for that university, the diamond sign in the above relationship should be removed. The example is used for some universities where students do not have to have an advisor in their freshman year.

3. *Nonspecific relationships:* Consider the relationship between the STUDENT entity and the CLASS entity. A student may take many classes. On the other hand, many students may take the same class. Because such a relationship does not have a direction from the parent entity to the child entity, it is called a nonspecific relationship, which is also known as the many-to-many relationship (or M:N relationship). The IDEF1X representation of the nonspecific relationship is given in Figure 2.7.

As illustrated in the figure, the relationship is represented by a solid line with a filled-in black dot on each end. Physically, it is difficult to implement such a relationship. You cannot directly place the id of one entity to another entity as the foreign key as we did in a 1:N relationship. If you do so, it may generate a nonunique identifier. The nonspecific relationship is often represented by two specific 1:N relationships with an intersection entity, as shown in Figure 2.8.

The entity STUDENT_CLASS is the intersection entity. We discuss the M:N relationship further when we get to the physical implementation of a database.

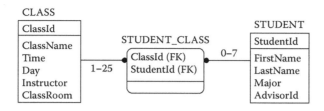

Figure 2.8   Nonspecific relationship with intersection entity

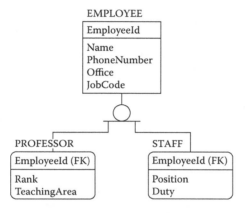

Figure 2.9   Incomplete categorization relationship

4. *Categorization relationships:* Categorization relationship is used to represent one entity that is a specific type of another entity. For example, consider the entity EMPLOYEE, which includes the faculty (professors) and staff. The faculty and staff have some unshared attributes. If we place all the unshared instances in the EMPLOYEE entity, the unshared attributes will contain a large number of null values. To avoid this problem, we can place the shared attributes into the *generic* entity EMPLOYEE and the unshared attributes into the *specific* entities PROFESSOR and STAFF. Such a relationship is called a categorization relationship (see Figures 2.9 and 2.10).

   In this categorization relationship, the generic entity EMPLOYEE is the parent entity, denoted by a square. The specific entities PROFESSOR and STAFF are the child entities, denoted by round-cornered squares. The *Category* icon ⚬ denotes a *discriminator* that is one of the attributes of the generic entity. Categorizing the generic entity instances into specific entities is based on this discriminator. If some possible categories are not included in the relationship, the categorization is called *incomplete* categorization, which is denoted by a single horizontal line, as shown in Figure 2.9. When every possible specific entity is included in the categorization relationship, such categorization is called *complete* categorization, which is denoted by two horizontal lines. As an example of complete categorization, suppose we have one more category of EMPLOYEE, student worker. By adding this category, we have generated a complete categorization, as shown in Figure 2.10.

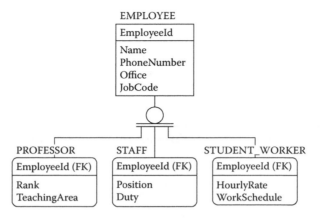

Figure 2.10   Complete categorization relationship

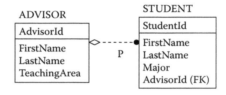

Figure 2.11   One-or-more cardinality

1:N relationships can also be categorized into two types commonly used by many database designers: HAS-A relationship and IS-A relationship. When a relationship associates entities of different logical types, the relationship is called a HAS-A relationship. In a HAS-A relationship, one or more attributes in the parent entity are used by the child entities. The nonidentifying relationship between entities CLASS and STUDENT is a HAS-A relationship. If the associated entities have the same logical type, we say the relationship is an IS-A relationship. In an IS-A relationship, the child entities are the specific types of the parent entity. The categorization relationship among entities EMPLOYEE, PROFESSOR, and STAFF is an IS-A relationship. The parent entity contains attributes that are common to all the child entities and each child entity contains attributes specific to itself.

2.3.4   Cardinality

Cardinality is the number of entity instances that can be involved in a relationship. For example, by the university rule, each student must have an advisor and each advisor must advise at least one student. Then the corresponding IDEF1X diagram will look like Figure 2.11.

Notice that the diamond icon is gone. This means that an advisor id is required for each student. The letter **P** indicates that each advisor must advise at least one student. That is, for each advisor id, there must be at least one STUDENT instance using this value for its AdvisorId attribute.

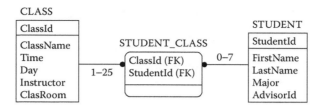

Figure 2.12   Cardinality of M:N relationship

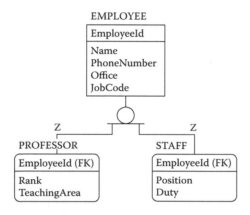

Figure 2.13   Zero-or-one cardinality

Consider another example. Due to the limitation of seats in the computer lab, a computer class can have a maximum of only 25 students. Therefore, the cardinality for the STUDENT entity enrolled in a class will be (1, 25). This means that a class can have 1 to 25 students. The 1 indicates that it is mandatory for a class to have at least one student. Assume that a student can take a maximum of 7 classes per semester. For the STUDENT entity, the cardinality for the CLASS entity may be given as (0, 7). The 0 indicates that it is optional for a student to take a class (see Figure 2.12).

In the following example, an employee is in one of the two categories. That is, the cardinality for each specific entity is either zero or one. The letter **Z** is used to represent this cardinality, as shown in Figure 2.13. The commonly used cardinality symbols are listed in Table 2.1.

2.3.5 Relationship Naming

To make a relationship more meaningful, you can name it as between parent and child. For example, to specify a relationship in which a building contains apartments, you can name the relationship with a verb phrase from parent to child, as shown in Figure 2.14.

You can also include the name from child to parent. For example, in the relationship between the entity ADVISOR and the entity STUDENT, advisors

Table 2.1   Symbols for Cardinalities and Relationships

Cardinality Symbol	Description
─●	Child entity with zero or more children
Z─●	Zero or one child
P─●	One or more children
n - m─●	Ranging from n to m children
1─●	Exactly one child
◇─	Optional parent
───	Identifying relationship
─ ─ ─	Nonidentifying relationship

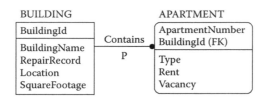

Figure 2.14   Relationship naming from parent to child

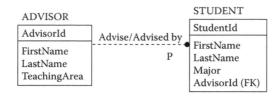

Figure 2.15   Relationship naming from parent to child and from child to parent

advise students and students are advised by advisors. The relationship is named with two verb phrases from parent to child and from child to parent, as shown in Figure 2.15.

2.3.6 Recursive Relationships

In the above examples, each relationship connects two entities. Such a relationship is called a *binary relationship*. Although the binary relationship

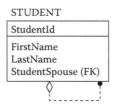

Figure 2.16   Recursive relationship with optional parent

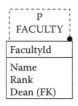

Figure 2.17   Recursive relationship with required parent

is the most commonly used relationship, there are other types of relationships, such as the *recursive relationship*. In a recursive relationship, an entity associates with itself. The recursive relationship represents a self-join relationship. In such a relationship, the parent entity and the child entity are the same entity. As an example of a recursive relationship, consider the entity STUDENT (see Figure 2.16). The attribute StudentSpouse is specified to be the spouse, who may also be a student. Thus, a student has a 1:N relationship with StudentSpouse where the value for N is either 0 or 1. On the other hand, a student is someone's spouse, and that someone may or may not be a student. Therefore, for StudentSpouse, the student is optional. The IDEF1X representation for the recursive relationship is shown in Figure 2.16.

The cardinality symbol **Z** indicates that a student may have zero or one spouse and the diamond icon indicates that the student is optional to StudentSpouse.

As another example, consider the entity FACULTY, as shown in Figure 2.17. Because a college dean is also a faculty member who is managing many other faculty members, there is 1:N relationship among faculty members. The cardinality symbol **P** indicates that a dean manages one or more faculty members. There is no diamond icon. That means that each faculty member must work for the dean.

2.3.7 Ternary Relationships

In a ternary relationship, three or more entities are involved. For example, consider the situation in which there are many classes and each may have multiple sections at the same time. A professor teaches four class sections each semester. On the other hand, each class section may be taught by more than one professor and each section may use more than one classroom, such

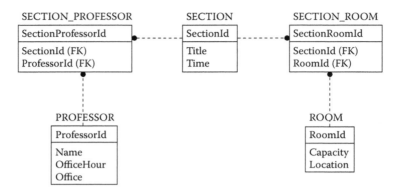

Figure 2.18   Ternary relationship

as a lab-based class that uses a regular classroom and a lab. As a result, there is an M:N relationship between SECTION and PROFESSOR and an M:N relationship between SECTION and ROOM. The ternary relationship can be used to associate the entities PROFESSOR, SECTION, and ROOM. In most cases, the ternary relationship is treated as two separate binary relationships, as shown in Figure 2.18.

To find a class taught by a given professor and the classroom assigned to this professor, you can search the SectionId with the given ProfessorId in the entity SECTION_PROFESSOR. After SectionId is found, the information about the section can be found in the SECTION entity. Through SectionId, you can find the corresponding RoomId in the SECTION_ROOM entity. By using RoomId, you can find the information about the classroom.

In general, the number of entities associated in a relationship is called the *degree* of the relationship. In a recursive relationship, the degree of the relationship is one. In a ternary relationship, the degree of the relationship is three or more.

2.3.8   Business Rules

Business rules are set up by companies to control business behaviors. A database designer can identify business rules from a company's documents about its regulations and by interviewing key players in a business process. The database designer should carefully document these rules for future reference. For example, who is qualified as the manager of the sales department? It will depend on the company's policy. After the database designer has identified the business rules, he or she will follow the steps below to include those rules in the database.

1. Identify the entities to which the business rules can be applied.
2. If the business rules can be implemented in a data model, add these rules to the data model.
3. In fact, except for the rules that can be implemented through cardinalities, other business rules may not be added to the E-R model. Although some

business rules cannot be added to the E-R model at this stage, the database designer can write a note about these rules, so that they can be used later.

4. During the database implementation phase, you may be able to implement some of the business rules in a DBMS with proper constraint checking.
5. If the DBMS package does not provide the desired functionality for the business rules, you may implement them in the application programs.

A well-defined database should implement these rules. Missing business rules can cause serious problems.

2.4 Representing Business Process with Entity-Relationship Model

A business process can be described by an entity-relationship model. Representing the business process correctly is an important step in database design. Usually, we cannot do it perfectly during the first try. Repeated modifications are needed as we go through the design process. In the following, we continue to use our case study to illustrate the development of an E-R data model.

2.4.1 Determining Entities from Business Information

The first step in developing an E-R data model is to identify the entities. We can identify them by examining the nouns in the business requirements. As an example, let us consider the case study of `Hillcrest Computing`.

■ Based on the business requirements, the first goal is to help assembly workers and others to fill out forms electronically. On the forms, one needs the information about assembly workers, assembly process, computer systems, and parts. Thus, we should create four entities — `ASSEMBLY_WORKER`, `ASSEMBLY_PROCESS`, `COMPUTER_SYSTEM`, and `PART` — to keep track of the information for completing the forms.

■ The second goal is to allow the sales manager and sales clerks to check the production progress. The assembly progress data will get them informed. The data on purchase orders and shipping will help them inform customers. The entities `PURCHASE_ORDER`, `SALES_CENTER`, and `SHIPPING` should be created to help the sales manager and sales clerks.

■ The third goal requires information about costs of computer parts and assembly workers. From examining the business requirements, we can see that the cost of a computer system depends mainly on the skill level of a worker and the type of computer system to be assembled. To meet the third goal, the accounting manager and accountants should be able to access the computer system information. Entities such as `SYSTEM_PART` and `SYSTEM_WORKER` should be created to store information about labor cost and system cost.

■ The cost of a part depends on detailed market information. Therefore, we create the entity `PART_DETAIL` for this purpose. The accountants should be able to read the updated prices of computer parts.

```
                    Assembly Process Report Card

Assembly Process:                    Assembly Worker:

Process ID: 1015                     Worker ID: 10
Starting Time: 7/1/2002              Labor Cost: 64000
Ending Time: 7/2/2002               Name: Mary Smith

Progress: Completed on time          Worker ID: 12
Reason for Delay:                    Labor Cost: 36000
                                     Name: Sam Carter
Computer System Information:

System ID: N0003
System Type: Notebook computer
System Description:
          1.0 GHz intel P3, 512 MB RAM, 60 GB hd, 12X DVD, 56K, 10/100
          Ethernet, Windows XP Pro, 15" XGA
```

Figure 2.19   Assembly process report card

```
            ASSEMBLY_WORKER
            ┌─────────────────┐
            │ WorkerId        │
            ├─────────────────┤
            │ FName           │
            │ LName           │
            │ Wages           │
            └─────────────────┘
```

Figure 2.20   `ASSEMBLY_WORKER` entity and its attributes

After the entities are created, we add attributes to the entities. Next, we demonstrate how to describe each entity with a set of attributes.

2.4.2   *Identifying Attributes from Business Information*

Each entity contains several attributes used to describe the entity. You can specify the attributes by examining the description of the business and business requirements. For example, by examining the Assembly Process Report Card (Figure 2.19) that will be completed after assembling a computer system, you will be able to identify which attributes are to be included in the entities ASSEMBLY_WORKER, ASSEMBLY_PROCESS, and COMPUTER_SYSTEM.

From the Assembly Worker section, the entity ASSEMBLY_WORKER should include the attributes WorkerId, Wages, and Name. The attribute WorkerId is used as the unique identifier for an assembly worker. The attribute Name is a so-called multi-valued attribute; that is, it can be split into first name and last name (FName and LName). The labor cost partially depends on the assembly worker's skill level, which is shown as wages. Therefore, the attribute Wages should be added to the ASSEMBLY_WORKER entity. The ASSEMBLY_WORKER entity can then be described as in Figure 2.20.

Similar specifications apply to the descriptions of other entities. For instance, with the business requirements, information related to the assembly process is the time used to complete a job and the type of system assembled. The

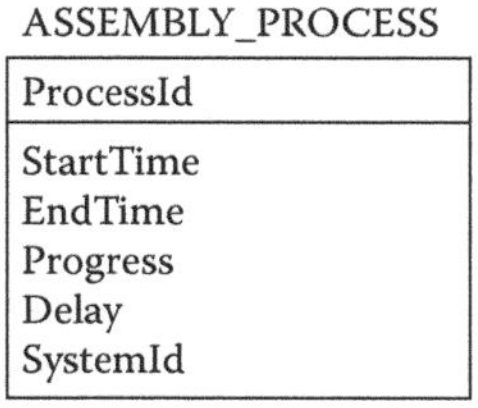

ASSEMBLY_PROCESS

ProcessId
StartTime
EndTime
Progress
Delay
SystemId

Figure 2.21 `ASSEMBLY_PROCESS` **entity and its attributes**

COMPUTER_SYSTEM

SystemId
Type
Description

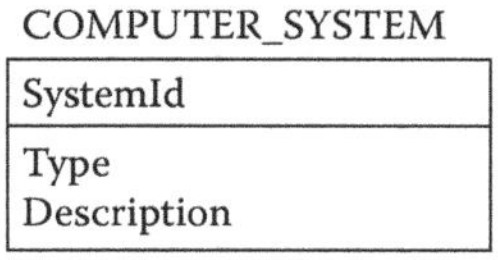

Figure 2.22 `COMPUTER_SYSTEM` **entity and its attributes**

SALES_CENTER

CenterId
Name
Phone

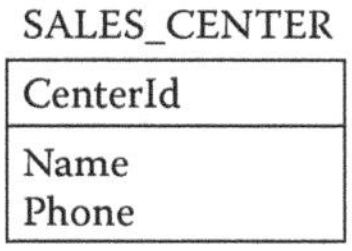

Figure 2.23 `SALES_CENTER` **entity and its attributes**

`Time` attribute can be broken into two values: one is the starting time, and the other is the finishing time. The `ASSEMBLY_PROCESS` needs its own identifier `ProcessId`. The assembly workers who are working in the assembly process need to report the progress. If the completion is delayed, they need to report the reason for the delay. Therefore, the entity `ASSEMBLY_PROCESS` should include the attributes `ProcessId`, `StartTime`, `EndTime`, `Progress`, and `Delay`. We also need to include the id number of the computer system that is assembled in this assembly process. The description of `ASSEMBLY_PROCESS` is as in Figure 2.21.

For the `COMPUTER_SYSTEM` entity, we need the attributes such as `SystemId`, `Type`, and `Description` (see Figure 2.22). For each sales center, the center identifier should be included in this entity. Add the sales center's name and phone number, as shown in Figure 2.23.

For the `PURCHASE_ORDER` entity, the `OrderId` attribute should be included. Also, we must indicate at which sales center a purchase order is processed. Thus, we should include the sales center's identifier to indicate where the purchase order is processed. For each purchase order, we should also include the order date (see Figure 2.24).

Information included in the `SHIPPING` entity is shipping identification, customer name, address, and shipping date. The attribute `Address` is a *composite attribute*, which consists of a set of attributes: `Street`, `City`,

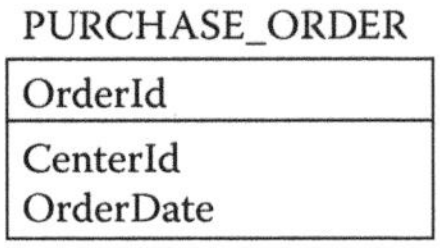

PURCHASE_ORDER

OrderId
CenterId
OrderDate

Figure 2.24   PURCHASE_ORDER **entity and its attributes**

SHIPPING

ShippingId
FName
LName
Street
City
State
Zip
ShippingDate

Figure 2.25   SHIPPING **entity and its attributes**

PART

PartId
PartName

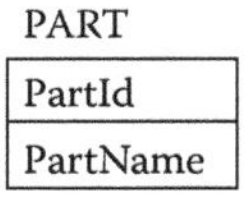

Figure 2.26   PART **entity and its attributes**

PART_DETAIL

ItemId
PartId
Price
Description
Maker
Quantity

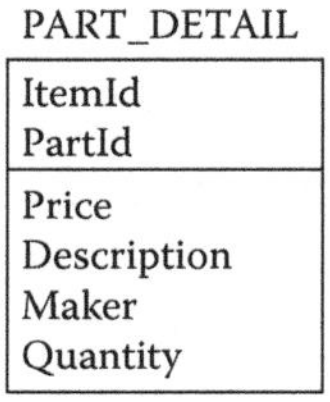

Figure 2.27   PART_DETAIL **entity and its attributes**

State, and Zip. The customer name has two values: first name and last name. There are two ways to deal with the composite attribute. We can create a new entity ADDRESS or we can create the new attributes Street, City, State, and Zip in the SHIPPING entity. Similarly, we can use two new attributes, FName and LName, to represent the multi-valued attribute Name (see Figure 2.25).

In the PART entity, we include the part identifier and the part name (see Figure 2.26). In the PART_DETAIL entity, more detailed information is included. The attributes are identifier, price, description, maker, and quantity. Because PART_DETAIL is an id-dependent entity, its existence depends on the existence of the entity PART. We must include the identifier from the parent entity, which is the PartId (see Figure 2.27).

Table 2.2 Business Requirements and Relationships between Entities

Description of Business Process	Indicated Relationship
Several workers participate in one assembly process. Each assembly worker may assemble many computer systems; that is, he or she may participate in many assembly processes.	The verb "participate" indicates that there is a relationship between the entities ASSEMBLY_WORKER and ASSEMBLY_PROCESS. From the description, it is an M:N nonspecific relationship.
One purchase order may include one or more types of computer systems. On the other hand, different purchase orders may purchase the same type of computer system.	There is an M:N nonspecific relationship between the entity PURCHASE_ORDER and the entity COMPUTER_SYSTEM.
Purchase orders are processed at each sales center.	There is an N:1 nonidentifying relationship between the PURCHASE_ORDER entity and the SALES_CENTER entity.
The costs of computer systems include the costs of labor and computer parts.	There is an M:N nonspecific relationship between the COMPUTER_SYSTEM entity and the entity ASSEMBLY_WORKER.
Each purchase order may contain different shipping addresses. One shipping address may also place multiple orders.	There is an M:N nonspecific relationship between the PURCHASE_ORDER entity and the entity SHIPPING.
Computer parts will be assembled together to make a computer system, and the same type of part may be installed on different systems.	There is an M:N nonspecific relationship between the COMPUTER_SYSTEM entity and the entity PART.
Detailed information for each type of part is kept.	There is a 1:N nonidentifying relationship between the PART entity and the entity PART_DETAIL.
In an assembly process, a computer system is assembled.	There is a 1:1 nonidentifying relationship between the ASSEMBLY_PROCESS entity and the COMPUTER_SYSTEM entity.

At this point, we have created all the entities identified in the previous section. To develop the data model based on these entities, we need to identify the relationships among these entities.

2.4.3 *Identifying Relationships among Entities*

The next step is to identify the relationships among entities. A relationship can be identified by finding verbs between related entities. For example, the descriptions in Table 2.2 indicate the relationship between each pair of entities. In Table 2.2, several relationships have been identified through the description

Figure 2.28   Relationship between ASSEMBLY_WORKER **and**
ASSEMBLY_PROCESS

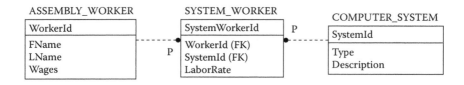

Figure 2.29   Relationship between ASSEMBLY_WORKER **and**
COMPUTER_SYSTEM

of the interviews. Similarly, other relationships can be identified by examining the information collected by the database designer.

2.4.4   Identifying Cardinalities

Based on the relationships described in Table 2.2, we analyze the cardinalities of the entities. As you can see, there are several M:N relationships. In practice, an M:N relationship can be broken into two 1:N relationships. Such a representation makes the database design in the next step easier. In the relationship that involves the entities ASSEMBLY_WORKER and ASSEMBLY_PROCESS, an assembly process must have at least one worker and there is an unspecified upper bound. Thus, the minimum–maximum cardinality is (1, N) for the entity ASSEMBLY_WORKER. On the other hand, an assembly worker participates in at least one assembly process. For the ASSEMBLY_PROCESS entity, the minimum–maximum cardinality is (1, M). An intersection entity WORKER_PROCESS is used to connect the entities ASSEMBLY_WORKER and ASSEMBLY_PROCESS. The intersection entity contains identifiers from ASSEMBLY_WORKER and ASSEMBLY_PROCESS. It can have some other attributes, too. Usually, the intersection entity does not have its own identifier. You can combine the two identifiers from both sides of the relationship as a combination key to enforce the uniqueness (see Figure 2.28).

In Figure 2.28, the letter **P** represents that each parent has one or more children. That is, each assembly worker can participate in one or more assembly processes and each assembly process can have one or more workers involved.

Another M:N relationship is between the COMPUTER_SYSTEM entity and the ASSEMBLY_WORKER entity. Its representation is shown in Figure 2.29.

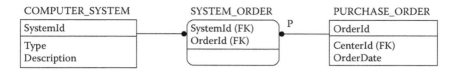

Figure 2.30   Relationship between `COMPUTER_SYSTEM` **and** `PURCHASE_ORDER`

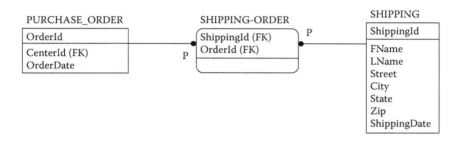

Figure 2.31   Relationship between `SHIPPING` **and** `PURCHASE_ORDER`

The intersection entity `SYSTEM_WORKER` relates multiple instances of the `COMPUTER_SYSTEM` entity to the multiple instances of the `ASSEMBLY_WORKER` entity. In this intersection entity, we include the identifiers from both `COMPUTER_SYSTEM` and `ASSEMBLY_WORKER`. The third attribute, `Labor-Rate`, is the labor cost rate to complete a job. The labor cost to complete a job depends on both the skill level of a worker and the system to be assembled. That is why we add `LaborRate` to the intersection entity. The higher the skill level, the less time is used to complete the job. Although skilled workers are paid higher salaries at Hillcrest Computing, they create much more revenue. Overall, the skilled workers' labor rate may be lower.

In the relationship that involves the entities `PURCHASE_ORDER` and `COMPUTER_SYSTEM`, a purchase order must include a computer system and there is an unspecified upper bound. Consequently, the minimum–maximum cardinality is (1, N) for the entity `PURCHASE_ORDER`. On the other hand, a specific kind of computer system does not have to be on a purchase order; the minimum–maximum cardinality is (0, M). The corresponding relationship diagram is shown in Figure 2.30.

In the relationship that involves the entities `PURCHASE_ORDER` and `SHIPPING`, each purchase order may contain different shipping addresses. Thus, the minimum–maximum cardinality is (1, N) for the entity `PURCHASE_ORDER`. On the other hand, each shipment may take care of one or more purchase orders. Therefore, the minimum–maximum cardinality is (1, M) for the entity `SHIPPING`. The corresponding relationship diagram is shown in Figure 2.31.

In the relationship that involves the entities `PART` and `COMPUTER_SYSTEM`, a computer system consists of many different computer parts and there is an unspecified upper bound. Therefore, the minimum–maximum cardinality is

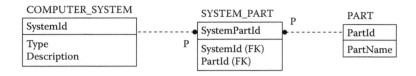

Figure 2.32   Relationship between PART **and** COMPUTER_SYSTEM

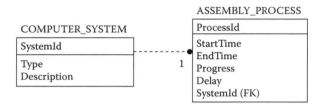

Figure 2.33   Relationship between COMPUTER_SYSTEM **and**
ASSEMBLY_PROCESS

(1, N) for the entity COMPUTER_SYSTEM. On the other hand, a type of
computer part can be put on one or more computer systems. The minimum–maximum cardinality is (1, M) for the entity PART. It is possible that
the same system uses the same part more than once. Therefore, an identifier
SystemPartId is added to the intersection entity SYSTEM_PART for the
uniqueness. The corresponding relationship diagram is shown in Figure 2.32.

In the relationship that involves the entities ASSEMBLY_PROCESS and
COMPUTER_SYSTEM, each assembly process assembles one computer system.
Thus, the minimum–maximum cardinality is (1, 1) for the entity ASSEMBLY_
PROCESS. Also, a computer system must be assembled in one and only one
assembly process. Therefore, the minimum–maximum cardinality is (1,1) for
the entity COMPUTER_SYSTEM. The corresponding relationship diagram for
this 1:N relationship is shown in Figure 2.33. Note that the value for N here
is 1 in a nonidentifying relationship.

In the relationship that involves the entities PURCHASE_ORDER and
SALES_CENTER, a purchase order must come from one, and only one, of
the sales centers. Thus, the minimum–maximum cardinality is (1, 1) for the
entity SALES_CENTER. On the other hand, a sales center must have at least
one purchase order and there is an unspecified upper bound. Therefore, the
minimum–maximum cardinality is (1, N) for PURCHASE_ORDER (see Figure
2.34).

In the relationship that involves the entities PART and PART_DETAIL, a
type of part contains many items and there is an unspecified upper bound.
Thus, the minimum–maximum cardinality is (1, N) for the entity
PART_DETAIL. On the other hand, an item of a computer part must belong
to one, and only one, part type. The minimum–maximum cardinality is (1,1)
for the entity PART. The existence of the PART_DETAIL entity instance
depends on the existence of the PART. Therefore, the part id is required. The

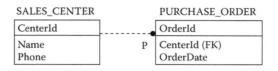

Figure 2.34 Relationship between SALES_CENTER **and** PURCHASE_ORDER

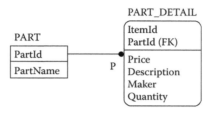

Figure 2.35 Relationship between PART **and** PART_DETAIL

corresponding relationship diagram for this identifying relationship is shown in Figure 2.35.

During the development of a data model, it is likely that additional entities and relationships will be discovered. In many practical problems, additional entities and relationships come from additional interviews and re-examination of the documents. The data model development process may need several modifications based on the feedback from reviewing the newly built data model. The process of a data model development is not a sequential process. The modification continues until the data model satisfies the business requirements.

2.4.5 Creating Entity-Relationship Diagrams

Now that we have identified the entities and relationships, we take some time to create these objects with Microsoft Visio. To create an entity diagram using IDEF1X in Microsoft Visio, follow the instructions below.

Creating Entities

In the following instructions, a bold-lettered word or phrase means that it is an important item, or you need to click or type it. Here is how to get started.

1. Start Visio by clicking **Start**, **All Programs**, **Microsoft Office**, and **Microsoft Office Visio 2003**. Click **File**, **New**, **Database**, and **Database Model Diagram (Metric)**. You may also select the (US Units) option.
2. To set the options for our data model, click **Database** on the menu bar and select **Options** and then **Document**.
3. Under the **General** tab, check the **IDEF1X** option for **Symbol set** (see Figure 2.36). Click the **Table** tab and uncheck the **Show** option for **IDEF1X**

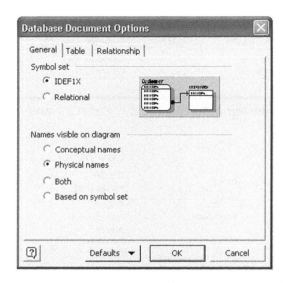

Figure 2.36   Database model diagram options

> **optionality '(O)'**. Under the tab **Relationship**, check the option **Cardinality**, and then click **OK**.
4. To add an entity to the drawing page, click the **Entity** icon in the Entity Relationship pane and drag it to the drawing page.
5. To specify the entity just added to the drawing page, right-click the entity and select **Database Properties**. Specify the entity name as, for example, **PART**.
6. To specify the attributes, click **Columns** in the **Categories** list box. Enter two new attribute names **PartId** and **PartName**. To view the result, drag the **Database Properties** window to the bottom of the screen and zoom the diagram to 100 percent.

Similarly, you can create other entities listed in Table 2.3.

Table 2.3   Entity and Attribute Summary

Entity	Attributes
ASSEMBLY_WORKER	WorkerId LName FName Wages
ASSEMBLY_PROCESS	ProcessId StartTime EndTime SystemId Progress Delay

Table 2.3   Entity and Attribute Summary (continued)

Entity	*Attributes*
COMPUTER_SYSTEM	SystemId Type Description
SALES_CENTER	CenterId Name Phone
PURCHASE_ORDER	OrderId CenterId OrderDate
SHIPPING	ShippingId LName FName Street City State Zip ShippingDate OrderId
PART	PartId PartName
PART_DETAIL	ItemId Price Description Maker PartId Quantity
SYSTEM_WORKER	SystemWorkerId SystemId WorkerId LaborRate
SYSTEM_PART	SystemPartId SystemId PartId
SYSTEM_ORDER	SystemId OrderId
WORKER_PROCESS	WorkerId ProcessId

Note: The above steps are performed on Windows XP Professional with Microsoft Visio 2003 installed. If you have Microsoft Visio 2002 installed, you may find Microsoft Visio directly from the **All Programs** list.

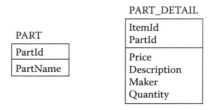

Figure 2.37   PART **Entity and** PART_DETAIL **entity**

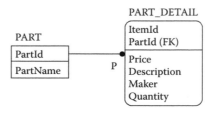

Figure 2.38   **Relationship between** PART **and** PART_DETAIL

Creating Relationships

By using Microsoft Visio, you can create relationships such as identifying relationship, nonidentifying relationship, nonspecific relationship, categorization relationship, and recursive relationship, as mentioned earlier. The following steps show you how to create various relationships among entities.

1. *Creating identifying relationship:* In the following steps, we create an identifying relationship between the entities **PART** and **PART_DETAIL**.
   a. First, you need to create two entities, as shown in Figure 2.37.
   b. Click the **Connector Tool** icon on the tool bar. Move the mouse cursor over the parent entity **PART**. When a red rectangle appears, click the parent entity. Then hold the mouse and move the cursor over to the child entity **PART_DETAIL**. Click the child entity when a red rectangle appears. A nonidentifying relationship connector is automatically drawn from the parent entity to the child entity.
   c. Click **Pointer Tool** on the tool bar. Right-click the **PART_DETAIL** entity and select **Database Properties**. Select **Columns** in the **Categories** pane. Make sure the column **PartId** has the **PK** option checked. The connector should be automatically changed to represent the **identifying relationship**.
   d. To specify the cardinality, double-click on the new relationship connector line and select **Miscellaneous** in the **Categories** pane. Check the option **One or More**. The letter P should appear near the relationship connector line, as shown in Figure 2.38.
2. *Creating nonidentifying relationship:* To create a nonidentifying relationship, we use the entities SALES_CENTER and PURCHASE_ORDER.
   a. Create SALES_CENTER and PURCHASE_ORDER, as shown in Figure 2.39.

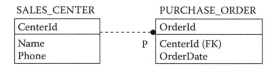

Figure 2.39   Relationship between SALES_CENTER **and** PURCHASE_ORDER

Figure 2.40   Nonspecific relationship between ASSEMBLY_WORKER **and**
ASSEMBLY_PROCESS

b. Because each sales center processes many purchase orders, we consider
SALES_CENTER as the parent entity and PURCHASE_ORDER as the
child entity. Click **Connector Tool** on the tool bar. Move the mouse
cursor over the parent entity **SALES_CENTER**. When a red rectangle
appears, click the parent entity. Then hold the mouse and move the
cursor over to the child entity **PURCHASE_ORDER**. Click the child
entity when a red rectangle appears. A nonidentifying relationship
connector is automatically drawn from the parent entity to the child
entity.

c. Because purchase orders must be processed at a sales center, the parent
is required. To enforce the presence of the parent, click the child entity.
In the **Database Properties** window, select **Columns** in the **Categories**
pane. Make the column **CenterId** required by checking the **Req'd** option.
You should see the diamond icon disappear on the connector line.

d. To specify the cardinality, click the newly created relationship connector
line. In the **Database Properties** window, select **Miscellaneous** in the
Categories pane. Check the **One or More** option. You should have the
result in Figure 2.39.

Similarly, you can create a nonidentifying relationship for the entity pair
ASSEMBLY_PROCESS and COMPUTER_SYSTEM.

3. *Creating nonspecific relationship:* For a nonspecific relationship, use two
nonidentifying 1:N relationships with an intersection entity. For example,
the M:N nonspecific relationship between ASSEMBLY_WORKER and
ASSEMBLY_PROCESS can be represented as in Figure 2.40.

Similarly, you can create nonspecific relationships for the entity pairs
PURCHASE_ORDER and COMPUTER_SYSTEM, PART and COMPUTER_
SYSTEM, and ASSEMBLY_WORKER and COMPUTER_SYSTEM.

4. *Creating categorization relationship:* To illustrate the creation of a categorization relationship, consider the relationship among the entities EMPLOYEE,

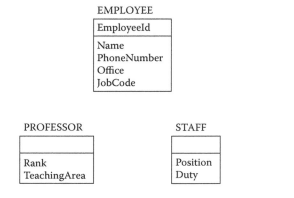

Figure 2.41   Generic and specific entities

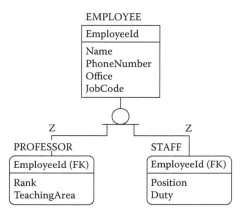

Figure 2.42   Relationship among EMPLOYEE, PROFESSOR, **and** STAFF

PROFESSOR, and STAFF. To create the categorization relationship, follow the steps below.

a. Create the entities shown in Figure 2.41. The entities PROFESSOR and STAFF are specific entities and the entity EMPLOYEE is a generic entity.

b. After the generic and specific entities are created, drag the **Category** icon from the **Entity Relationship** pane to the drawing page.

c. Choose **Connector Tool** from the tool bar. Drag the **Parent to category** icon from the **Entity Relationship** pane over the generic entity **EMPLOYEE**. When a red rectangle appears, release the mouse. Click the connector line, hold the mouse, and move the cursor to the **Category** icon in the diagram. When a red rectangle appears, release the mouse. Also, connect the **Category** icon to the two specific entities with two **Category to child** connectors. Make sure to drag the connector line to the top blank row of each specific entity so that EmployeeId (FK) will automatically appear (see Figure 2.42).

d. To specify the discriminator for **Category**, right-click the **Category** icon in the diagram and select **Database Properties**. In the **Database Properties**

Figure 2.43 FACULTY **entity**

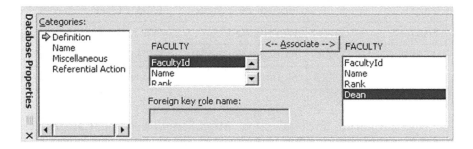

Figure 2.44 Configuring database properties

Figure 2.45 Recursive relationship

window, select **This attribute**, and then select the **Jobcode** in the list box. Because we assume that this categorization relationship is incomplete, make sure that the check box of **Category is complete** is unchecked. The specification result is shown in Figure 2.42.

5. *Creating recursive relationship:* For the recursive relationship, we consider the example that faculty members are recursively related to their deans.
   a. Create the entity **FACULTY**, as shown in Figure 2.43.
   b. Click on the newly created entity **FACULTY**. In the **Database Properties** window, select **Columns** in the **Categories** pane. Highlight **Dean** and check the option **Req'd**.
   c. Click **Connector Tool** on the tool bar. Start from the entity **FACULTY**, move the connector around the **FACULTY** entity, and drag the connector back to **FACULTY**. When a red rectangle appears, release the mouse.
   d. Click on the newly created connector line. In the **Database Properties** window, select **Definition** in the **Categories** pane. In the left **FACULTY** pane, select **FacultyId**. In the right **FACULTY** pane, select **Dean**. Click the **Associate** button to relate the attribute **FacultyId** to the attribute **Dean** (see Figure 2.44).

Table 2.4   Relationship Summary

Entity	Relationship	Entity
ASSEMBLY_WORKER	Nonspecific (M:N)	ASSEMBLY_PROCESS
PURCHASE_ORDER	Nonspecific (M:N)	COMPUTER_SYSTEM
SHIPPING	Nonspecific (M:N)	PURCHASE_ORDER
SALES_CENTER	Nonidentifying (1:N)	PURCHASE_ORDER
PART	Nonspecific (M:N)	COMPUTER_SYSTEM
PART	Identifying (1:N)	PART_DETAIL
ASSEMBLY_WORKER	Nonspecific (M:N)	COMPUTER_SYSTEM
ASSEMBLY_PROCESS	Nonidentifying (1:1)	COMPUTER_SYSTEM

e. To specify that a dean manages one or more faculty members, click the connector line and select **Miscellaneous** in the **Categories** pane. Check the option **One or more**. As a result, we have Figure 2.45.

Now that you have learned how to create entities and relationships in Microsoft Visio, you can create the data model for our case study.

2.4.6   Entity-Relationship Modeling

To summarize, the entities and the attributes for our case study Hillcrest Computing are listed in Table 2.3.

In the above discussion, we have examined five types of relationships, and three of them are for our case study: the nonspecific relationship, nonidentifying relationship, and identifying relationship, and we have examined the cardinalities associated with them. Through these relationships, we have illustrated the 1:N and M:N types of connectivity. Table 2.4 summarizes the data model.

After the entities and the relationships are created, the corresponding IDEF1X data model diagram for the case study Hillcrest Computing is given in Figure 2.46. Figure 2.46 shows the E-R model for the Hillcrest Computing business process. The data model includes entities, attributes, and relationships. Consider the entity COMPUTER_SYSTEM, which is associated with the entities SYSTEM_ORDER, SYSTEM_WORKER, and SYSTEM_PART through three relationships. In theory, an entity may involve multiple relationships. In this case, there are three relationships connecting the COMPUTER_SYSTEM entity to the other entities. These relationships form a relationship class. Because the entity COMPUTER_SYSTEM involves the most relationships, it is called a *central entity*.

Suppose you are the database designer. After the initial E-R model is created, you need to explain it to the key business players you have interviewed to find out if your data model meets their expectations. You may need to use the following verifications against the newly created E-R model:

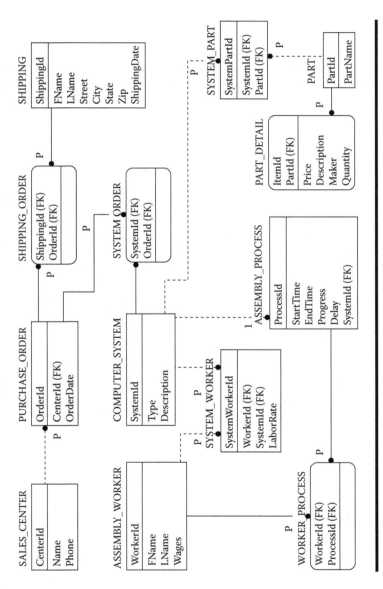

Figure 2.46 E-R model of Hillcrest Computing business process

- Verification of all the users' requirements
- Verification of all the data constraints
- Verification of all the business rules
- Verification of all possible data transactions

You may have to modify the initial E-R model several times before you can get approval from your customer. Do not overlook this step. If you create a database without the approval of your customer, you will be very sorry when something goes wrong. It is difficult to make changes in the database structure if the database is populated with data.

So far, we have developed a data model for a database. It is a hardware- and software-free model. A well-built data model should be able to be implemented on any DBMS software package. In the next two chapters, we demonstrate how to represent the data model with tables.

2.5 Summary

This chapter has discussed the concepts and the development of data models. First, we talked about the interview process through the case study of Hillcrest Computing. Through the interviews with the key players in a business process, the database designer was able to identify the users' requirements for the database project and set up the design goals accordingly. To represent the data by a conceptual structure, the concepts of the Entity-Relationship data model were introduced. The major components, such as entities, attributes, and relationships, in an E-R data model were explained with examples. By examining the business process, the database designer was able to create the entities and the relationships among these entities.

In this chapter, you have learned about IDEF1X, which is a national standard representing data models in database development. The IDEF1X symbols were used to illustrate entities and relationships in the data models. As hands-on experience, we used Microsoft Visio to create the entities and relationships using IDEF1X. In the last section of this chapter, we developed the IDEF1X data model to represent the Hillcrest Computing business process for our case study.

Review Questions

1. What are the major steps in a database design?
2. Describe the conceptual design.
3. What information do you need to collect for the database design process?
4. How do you collect information needed for the conceptual design?
5. Why is data modeling important in a database development process?
6. What are the abilities IDEF1X has to meet data modeling requirements?
7. What is an entity? Give an example of an entity.

8. Explain the difference between an entity class and an entity instance.
9. What is an attribute? Give an example of an entity with some attributes.
10. What is an identifier? Give an example of an identifier.
11. Explain what a surrogate key is.
12. What is a domain? Give an example of a domain.
13. Describe the identifying relationship and give an example of it.
14. Describe the nonidentifying relationship and give an example of it.
15. Describe the many-to-many relationship and give an example of it.
16. What is a categorization relationship? Give an example of a categorization relationship.
17. Describe the HAS-A relationship.
18. Describe the IS-A relationship.
19. What is cardinality? Give an example of cardinality.
20. What does the letter Z stand for as a cardinality symbol?
21. Describe the recursive relationship. Give an example of the recursive relationship.
22. How do you represent a nonspecific relationship?

Case Study Projects

Three case study projects are given in the following. In later chapters, you will create database systems based on these case studies.

1. Computer Service

Awesome Computer Service (ACS) is a computer repair company located in Houston, Texas. The competition in the computer repair business is intense in the local area. To compete successfully, the company must provide great services for its customers. To better serve the customers, ACS has decided to develop a database system to store customer information and provide online forms to allow customers to place service orders through the Internet.

Currently, ACS has five service centers in Houston and its suburbs. The largest service center is located in downtown Houston, which is also the headquarters of the company. Mr. Smith is the head of the company. Each repair center has a service manager, five to ten repair technicians, and one to two cashiers. The service centers are open from 9:00 AM to 6:00 PM. Customers bring defective computers to the service centers. The service manager at a center talks to the customer to find out his or her computer problems and estimates the cost for the repair. If the customer agrees with the cost, the manager will make a schedule for the customer to pick up the computer. At the time the customer picks up the repaired computer, the cashier at the service center will work with the customer to get the payment.

Suppose that the company has hired you to develop a database system to help it to better serve its customers. You may start your database project with the following steps:

- Conduct interviews with the key players to find out what the problems are in the current business process, what requirements from these key players are, and how to meet these requirements by developing a database project.
- Based on your interviews, draw a flowchart that represents the business process.
- Identify the entities for the database. With Microsoft Visio, develop an E-R model with at least five entities, with each entity having at least three attributes. The possible entities are CUSTOMERS, SYSTEMS, SERVICES, EMPLOYEES, and PARTS.

2. University Registration

Victoria University is a small four-year university. The campus has about 2500 students studying in three departments: education, business, and arts and sciences. The Admissions Office handles student registration and keeps track of students' records. To better serve the students, the director of the Admissions Office has decided to develop a database so the students can register classes through the Internet.

Currently, to register for next semester's classes, students need to pick up the course schedule in the Admissions Office, find the courses to enroll in, and then fill out the registration form. The Admissions Office keeps student information in a database developed on Microsoft Access. The registrars need to manually type the student information into the database. When a student requests information such as graduation status, a registrar can print a report on the printer located in the Admissions Office for the student.

Suppose that you are taking an Information Systems Internship class and are assigned to the Admissions Office to develop the student registration database. You may start your database project with the following steps.

- Interview the key players in the student registration process to find out what it takes to upgrade the registration process for the Internet and what goals should be achieved by the database project.
- Based on your interviews, draw a flowchart that represents the student registration process.
- Identify the entities for the database. With Microsoft Visio, develop an E-R model with at least five entities, with each entity having at least three attributes. The possible entities are STUDENTS, COURSES, CLASSES, ENROLLMENT, and CLASSROOMS.

3. Mail Order

Wellbeing is a mail-order health product company that specializes in vitamins, herbs, and antioxidant products. To increase the sales and reach out to more customers, the company wants to take customer orders through the Internet.

Currently, Wellbeing takes customer orders through telephone, mail, and fax. It distributes its catalogues to five states: Texas, Okalahoma, New Mexico, Louisiana, and Arkansas. When a customer order arrives, a sales representative checks if the items ordered by the customer are in stock. If they are in stock, he will place the order by typing the order information and customer information. Then the sales representative will manually reduce the quantity of the items in stock. Based on the order form, the shipping department will mail the items to the customer. The staff in the shipping department also needs to record the shipping time and shipping method.

Suppose that Wellbeing has hired a local consulting company to develop a Web-based database system and you are assigned by the consulting company to develop the database. You may start your project by using the following steps:

- Interview the key players in the mail-order process to find out the goals for the database project and what it takes to upgrade the current mail-order system to a Web-based database system.
- Based on your interviews, draw a flow chart that represents the mail-order process.
- Identify the entities for the database. With Microsoft Visio, develop an E-R model with at least five entities, with each entity having at least three attributes. The possible entities are CUSTOMERS, ORDERS, PRODUCTS, INVENTORY, and SHIPMENT.

Chapter 3

Table Structure and Normalization

Objectives

- Learn in detail about database tables.
- Link tables.
- Identify problems in table structures.
- Normalize the tables.

3.1 Introduction to Tables

In this chapter, we discuss how to convert a data model to a relational database. Because a database is constructed with tables, you must get to know the tables first. Then you will learn how to modify the table structure so that it will be suitable for data processing in a database.

3.1.1 Tables

In the previous chapter, we introduced data models to represent business processes. We investigated the main data model components such as entities, attributes, and relationships. Now it is time to think about how to convert a data model to a relational database where tables are used to store data. Thus, how do we relate tables to data model components? Here are the definitions from database theory. A logical structure containing a set of related entity instances is called a *table*. Each table consists of rows and columns. Each *row* in a table represents an entity instance and each *column* in the table represents an attribute. As an example, consider the **JOBS** table in the pubs database in

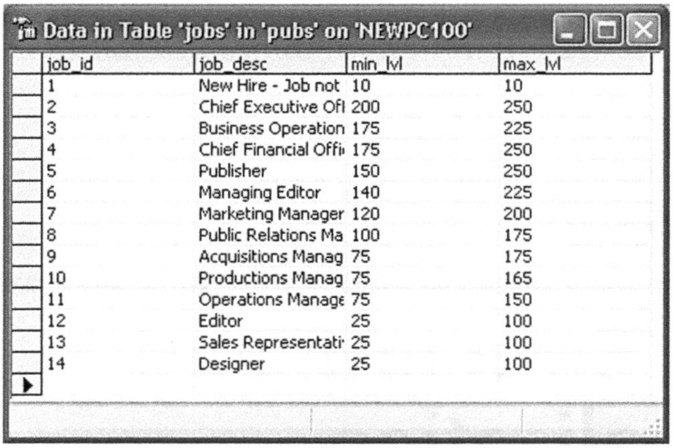

job_id	job_desc	min_lvl	max_lvl
1	New Hire - Job not	10	10
2	Chief Executive Offi	200	250
3	Business Operation	175	225
4	Chief Financial Offi	175	250
5	Publisher	150	250
6	Managing Editor	140	225
7	Marketing Manager	120	200
8	Public Relations Ma	100	175
9	Acquisitions Manag	75	175
10	Productions Manag	75	165
11	Operations Manage	75	150
12	Editor	25	100
13	Sales Representati	25	100
14	Designer	25	100

Figure 3.1 Example of table

the SQL Server DBMS (Figure 3.1). (Note: We capitalize the table names of the pubs database in this chapter.)

The `job_id` column is a unique identifier of the entity instances. As you may already know, the unique identifier is also called a *key*. Each cell in the table contains a data value. For each column, the data values have the same data type. The data type of the column `job_desc` is character string. The data type in each of the other three columns, `job_id`, `min_lvl`, and `max_lvl`, is fixed length integer. From the programmer point of view, the corresponding technical terms for table, column, and row can also be called *file*, *field*, and *record*. These words are often used in file systems and programming languages such as Visual BASIC, C++, and Java.

The more rigorous names for table, column, and row are *relation*, *attribute*, and *tuple*. The words relation, attribute, and tuple are from a mathematical set theory from which E.F. Codd created the relational model in 1970. The word *relation* is often confused with the word *relationship* in an E-R model. In fact, the word relation is closely related to table. For a table to be a relation, each cell in a table must contain a single value, there should be no duplicated rows, and all the cells in a column must contain the same type of data. There is no requirement for the order of columns and rows. Therefore, the table in Figure 3.1 is a relation. As an example, the `jobs` relation displayed in Figure 3.1 can be expressed as `JOBS(job_id, job_desc, min_lvl, max_lvl)`.

3.1.2 Keys

When we convert a data model to a relational database, the concept of key plays an important role. In this subsection, we do a quick review about keys. As you have learned in Chapter 2, a key is an attribute or a group of attributes that can uniquely identify rows in a table. Unlike a determinant, a key is always unique. That is, each key value in a table can occur only once. For a table to be a relation, we must include a key in the table inasmuch as no

Data in Table 'publishers' in 'pubs' on 'NEWPC100'

pub_id	pub_name	city	state	country
0736	New Moon Books	Boston	MA	USA
0877	Binnet & Hardley	Washington	DC	USA
1389	Algodata Infosyste	Berkeley	CA	USA
1622	Five Lakes Publishir	Chicago	IL	USA
1756	Ramona Publishers	Dallas	TX	USA
9901	GGG&G	München	<NULL>	Germany
9952	Scootney Books	New York	NY	USA
9999	Lucerne Publishing	Paris	<NULL>	France

Data in Table 'employee' in 'pubs' on 'NEWPC100'

emp_id	fname	minit	lname	job_id
PMA42628M	Paolo	M	Accorti	13
PSA89086M	Pedro	S	Afonso	14
VPA30890F	Victoria	P	Ashworth	6
H-B39728F	Helen		Bennett	12
L-B31947F	Lesley		Brown	7
F-C16315M	Francisco		Chang	4
PTC11962M	Philip	T	Cramer	2
A-C71970F	Aria		Cruz	10
AMD15433F	Ann	M	Devon	3
ARD36773F	Anabela	R	Domingues	8
PHF38899M	Peter	H	Franken	10

Figure 3.2 Linked tables: (a) `PUBLISHERS` table and (b) `EMPLOYEE` table

relation allows duplicated rows. A key attribute can be used to define an entity relationship. We can summarize the concepts of keys as the following:

- *Combination key:* Corresponding to the combination determinant, a combination key consists of more than one attribute. These attributes are called key attributes.
- *Candidate key:* A candidate key is a nonredundant attribute or a set of attributes that can uniquely identify each entity instance. In the `EMPLOYEE` table displayed in Figure 3.2, both `emp_id` and `lname` can serve as a key to determine the values of `job_lvl`. Consequently, we have three sets of key attributes:

  ```
  emp_id → job_lvl
  lname → job_lvl
  (emp_id, lname) → job_lvl
  ```

  In this case, the candidate keys are `emp_id` and `lname`. However, the combination (`emp_id, lname`) is not a candidate key because `emp_id` and `lname` have already been used as candidate keys.
- *Primary key:* In a relation, a primary key is a candidate key selected by the user to uniquely identify entity instances.
- *Foreign key:* A foreign key is an attribute or set of attributes whose values match the values of the primary key in another relation.

3.1.3   Linking Tables

As discussed in the previous chapter, entities are associated by relationships. To relate the tables in a relational database, we can link tables based on a relationship connecting the entities. This can be done by creating a common column in each table, as illustrated in Figure 3.2. Consider the tables PUB-LISHERS and EMPLOYEE in the built-in database pubs in SQL Server.

There is a 1:N relationship between PUBLISHERS and EMPLOYEE. That is, many employees are working for a publisher. To link these two tables, the attribute pub_id is placed in both the table PUBLISHERS and the table EMPLOYEE. In PUBLISHERS, the attribute pub_id is used as an entity identifier. As an identifier, the values in the pub_id column are unique and not null. A *null* value represents an unknown value or a missing value. Therefore, pub_id is the primary key. However, pub_id in the table EMPLOYEE is not an identifier. Thus, it can have a repeated value; for example, the value 0877 occurs four times. The pub_id column in the table EMPLOYEE is a foreign key used to link to the primary key pub_id in the table PUBLISHERS. The primary key and foreign key pair implement an entity relationship.

3.1.4   Functional Dependency

In a table, through a given value in an attribute, we can find related values in other attributes. For example, through the pub_id value 0877 in the PUBLISHERS table, we can find Binnet & Hardley for the attribute pub_name, Washington for the attribute City, DC for the attribute State, and USA for the attribute Country. The value of the attribute pub_id determines the values of the other attributes in the same entity. The attribute pub_id is called a *determinant,* and the other attributes that are determined by pub_id are called *dependents*. The notation below means that the attribute pub_id determines the attributes pub_name, City, State, and Country.

```
pub_id → pub_name, City, State, Country
```

From the above notation, we can say that the attributes pub_name, City, State, and Country are *functionally dependent* on the attribute pub_id.

Also, notice that pub_id is a key, which is used to uniquely identify other attributes. Therefore, a key is a determinant; however, in general, a determinant may not necessarily be a key. Any attribute that determines the values of other attributes is a determinant. For example, the attribute lname in table EMPLOYEE may also be used to determine the job_lvl. The above discussion can be summarized as the following.

▼

In general, if a value of the attribute *X* determines the value in the attribute *Y*, we say that the attribute *Y* is functionally dependent on the attribute *X*.

▲

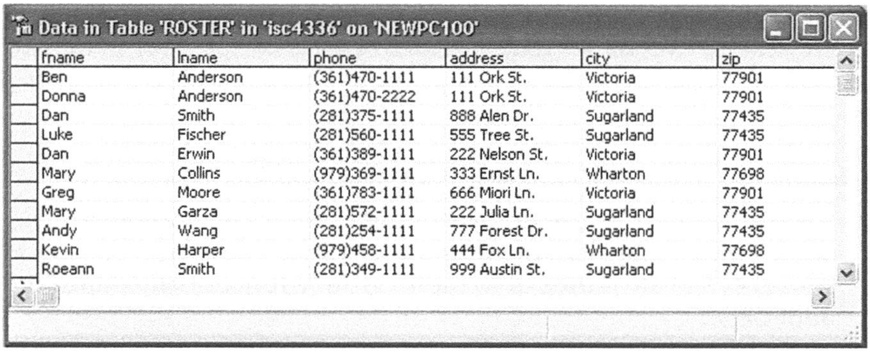

Data in Table 'ROSTER' in 'isc4336' on 'NEWPC100'

fname	lname	phone	address	city	zip
Ben	Anderson	(361)470-1111	111 Ork St.	Victoria	77901
Donna	Anderson	(361)470-2222	111 Ork St.	Victoria	77901
Dan	Smith	(281)375-1111	888 Alen Dr.	Sugarland	77435
Luke	Fischer	(281)560-1111	555 Tree St.	Sugarland	77435
Dan	Erwin	(361)389-1111	222 Nelson St.	Victoria	77901
Mary	Collins	(979)369-1111	333 Ernst Ln.	Wharton	77698
Greg	Moore	(361)783-1111	666 Miori Ln.	Victoria	77901
Mary	Garza	(281)572-1111	222 Julia Ln.	Sugarland	77435
Andy	Wang	(281)254-1111	777 Forest Dr.	Sugarland	77435
Kevin	Harper	(979)458-1111	444 Fox Ln.	Wharton	77698
Roeann	Smith	(281)349-1111	999 Austin St.	Sugarland	77435

Figure 3.3 Combination determinant

From the above statement, we can say that functional dependency is a relationship among attributes where one attribute or a combination of attributes determines another attribute. To illustrate the concept of functional dependency, consider the `EMPLOYEE` table, where the attribute `emp_id` is not functionally dependent on the attribute `job_lvl`. The value 35 is related to two `emp_id` values, PMA42628M and H-B39728F. On the other hand, the attribute `job_lvl` is functionally dependent on the attribute `emp_id`; each value of `emp_id` is only related to any single value of `job_lvl`. For example, the value PMA42628M is related to 35 and H-B39728F is related to 35. Notice that the value 35 is a single value even though it has been related twice. This situation leads to another conclusion.

> In general, if a value of the attribute *X* determines some values in the attribute *Y*, and each value of *X* has a 1:N relationship to the values of *Y*.

Sometimes, a combination of attributes is needed to form a determinant. For example, if the attribute `lname` or `fname` in Figure 3.3 is used as the key by itself, there may be a repeated last name or first name related to the values in the attribute phone. Therefore, `lname` or `fname` alone is not the determinant. The attributes have a better chance to be a determinant if we combine them. Figure 3.3 shows that the combination determinant (`fname, lname`) can determine the attribute phone. (Note: Although the combination determinant (`fname, lname`) works for the table in Figure 3.3, there are some situations where even the combination (`fname, lname`) is not enough to be a determinant.)

Notice that, in the table `PUBLISHERS`, if `pub_id` → `pub_name, city, state, country`, then `pub_id` → `pub_name`, `pub_id` → `city`, `pub_id` → `state`, and `pub_id` → `country`. On the other hand, for the table in Figure 3.3, (`fname, lname`) → `phone` does not mean `fname` → `phone`, nor does it mean `lname` → `phone`. The value Mary will not determine the values in the attribute phone, because there are two persons named Mary who are related to two values (281)572-2828 and (979)369-2451 in the attribute phone. The above discussion leads to a new concept called *fully functional dependency*.

▼

If the attribute *Y* is functionally dependent on the combination key *X* which consists of multiple attributes but not on any subset of the attributes of *X*, then *Y* is fully functionally dependent on *X*.

▲

Consider the attribute phone in Figure 3.3. This attribute determines the attribute city. Consequently, the phone attribute is a determinant. However, the phone attribute is not a unique determinant. The value (361)470-6618 appears twice. For this kind of determinant, we have the following rule.

▼

If the attribute *X* determines the attribute *Y*, the duplicated value in *X* must match the corresponding duplicate value in *Y*.

▲

That is, if (361)470-6618 in the phone attribute determines the value Victoria in the city attribute, then the duplicated value (361)470-6618 in the second row should also determine the same value Victoria in the city attribute.

3.2 Table Normalization

Tables are the building blocks of a database. Database performance and functionalities largely depend on the structure of tables. A good table structure will improve database performance, reduce the size of data storage, and ensure correct database operations. Unfortunately, a table that satisfies the requirements of a relation is not good enough to handle all the data-changing operations. This kind of table may cause database malfunction and may contain a large amount of redundant data.

3.2.1 Why Table Normalization

To answer the question of why we need table normalization, let us consider the STUDENT_CLUB_INFO table, which includes club names, membership fees, the duty of each member, students' mentors, skill training offered by the mentors, and so on (see Table 3.1). (Note that this is just an example for illustration purposes; in reality, the data will be more complete.) In addition to the data in STUDENT_CLUB_INFO, we need to use business requirements to guide the normalization process. The business requirements for the student clubs are listed below.

Table 3.1 STUDENT_CLUB_INFO **Table**

SID	Student Name	Mentor Name	Skill	Duty	Club Name	Membership Fee	Enroll Date
10258	Liz	Jones	Leadership	President	Book	60	10/02/01
11690	Joe	Lee	Typing	Secretary	Book	60	11/12/01
12105	Linda	Smith	Web-develop	Recruiter	Book	60	02/11/02
12153	Don	Long	Leadership	President	Poetry	50	02/11/02
13654	Jan	Garza	Typing	Secretary	Poetry	50	11/16/01
12784	Liz	Smith	Web-develop	Recruiter	Poetry	50	04/14/02
11505	Bruce	Moore	Leadership	President	Soccer	150	09/12/01
11690	Joe	Lee	Typing	Secretary	Soccer	150	03/30/02
12153	Don	Wang	Web-develop	WebMaster	Soccer	150	07/31/02

- Each club charges a membership fee.
- Each student can enroll in more than one club.
- Each club can have many students.
- Each student can have more than one mentor.
- A student can have more than one duty in different clubs, but not in the same club.
- Each mentor can offer training in one type of skill.
- Each mentor can train many students.
- More than one mentor can offer training in the same type of skill.
- One skill may serve different duties.
- Each club member must serve one of the duties.
- No student should have the same training by more than one mentor.
- No student can enroll in the same club twice.
- Each duty can be served by many students.
- The minimum value for the membership fee is $40.

These business requirements indicate how the student clubs work. The clubs' daily operations, standards, qualifications, and activities are described by these business requirements.

The table satisfies all the requirements of a relation. The combination (SID, Duty, ClubName) is the primary key of the relation. Students can join any clubs listed in Table 3.1. The membership fees of the clubs are charged differently.

By examining Table 3.1, you will see that it has a data redundancy problem. Every time a student joins a new club, both the student information and the club information need to be entered again. This has caused data redundancy. Suppose that a student mentored by Smith wants to join the Soccer Club; we enter a row with the values

```
12125 Eric Smith Web-develop Recruiter Soccer 150 10/12/02
```

to match the attributes SID (for student id), StudentName, MentorName, Skill, Duty, ClubName, MembershipFee, and EnrollDate. Notice that the information about the mentor and the Soccer Club already exists in the table. All the information we have entered is redundant data. In practice, many student clubs may have hundreds of students enrolled and one student may be enrolled in several clubs. This will generate a large amount of redundant data. The redundant data will waste a lot of data storage space and the labor to enter these data.

Changing data in such a table may also cause undesired results, which are called *modification anomalies*. There are three types of *modification anomalies*:

- *Update anomalies:* Suppose that the Soccer Club wants to raise its membership fee due to the increasing cost of club uniforms. All the rows with the ClubName as Soccer must be modified accordingly. For a large table, you may need to perform thousands of modifications.
- *Insertion anomalies:* Suppose we want to add a computer club and the membership fee. We cannot add Computer to the ClubName attribute in the table until a student enrolls in the club. Without a student id, the row with the ClubName as Computer cannot be identified. The information about the club cannot be inserted until we have the information about a student. This situation is called insertion anomaly.
- *Deletion anomalies:* Suppose the students with the ids 11505, 11690, and 12153 have graduated. We are going to delete these three students from the table in Table 3.1. The problem is that, after we delete these students, the information about the Soccer Club is lost, too. The situation in which deleting information about a student causes the deletion of information about a club is called deletion anomaly.

To find out what causes a modification anomaly in Table 3.1, consider the key attributes (SID, Duty, ClubName) that determine all other attributes:

```
(SID, Duty, ClubName) → StudentName, MentorName, Skill,
    MembershipFee, EnrollDate
```

There are two partial dependencies in the table. That is, the attribute MentorName depends on the key attributes (SID, Duty) that are part of the determinant (SID, Duty, ClubName). It is also true for MembershipFee, which depends on the key attribute ClubName:

```
(SID, Duty) → MentorName
ClubName → MembershipFee
```

The problem we have is caused by the fact that two partial dependencies are placed in the same table. When we modify the information of one partial dependency, we must modify the information of the other partial dependency. To solve the problem, we must split the relation into two relations, as follows:

Table 3.2 STUDENT **Table**

SID	Student Name	Mentor Name	Skill	Duty	Enroll Date
10258	Liz	Jones	Leadership	President	10/02/01
11690	Joe	Lee	Typing	Secretary	11/12/01
12105	Linda	Smith	Web-develop	Recruiter	02/11/02
12153	Don	Long	Leadership	President	02/11/02
13654	Jan	Garza	Typing	Secretary	11/16/01
12784	Liz	Smith	Web-develop	Recruiter	04/14/02
11505	Bruce	Moore	Leadership	President	09/12/01
11690	Joe	Lee	Typing	Secretary	03/30/02
12153	Don	Wang	Web-develop	WebMaster	07/31/02

Table 3.3 CLUB **Table**

Club Name	Membership Fee
Book	60
Poetry	50
Soccer	150

```
STUDENT(SID, StudentName, MentorName, Skill, Duty, EnrollDate)
CLUB(ClubName, MembershipFee)
```

The corresponding relations are displayed in Tables 3.2 and 3.3.

After the split, the tables appear to have better structures. If we want to add a new club, we can simply add the new club in the CLUB table without waiting for student information. On the other hand, if we want to delete the students 11505, 11690, and 12153, we can delete them in the STUDENT table without deleting the Soccer Club. The process of breaking up a table to get better table structures is table *normalization*. Normalization helps eliminate modification anomalies and reduce data redundancies.

The ultimate goal of table normalization is to make each table contain only a single dependency. There is a disadvantage of splitting a table into two smaller tables because we have to establish a relationship between these two tables by creating a foreign key. Consider the tables corresponding to the entities STUDENT and CLUB. From the business requirements, we know that each student is allowed to join multiple clubs and each club has many students. Therefore, the entity STUDENT has an M:N relationship with the entity CLUB. To represent the M:N relationship, you have learned in Chapter 2 that we need an intersection entity. To implement the M:N relationship, we place the foreign keys in the intersection table STUDENT_CLUB, which is displayed in Table 3.4.

Table 3.4   STUDENT_CLUB **Table**

SID	Club Name
10258	Book
11690	Book
12105	Book
12153	Poetry
13654	Poetry
12784	Poetry
11505	Soccer
11690	Soccer
12153	Soccer

In the intersection table, SID is the foreign key corresponding to the primary key in the STUDENT table and ClubName is the foreign key corresponding to the primary key in the CLUB table. If a student wants to join a club, we must check if the club name exists in the CLUB table before we can add the student id and club name to the STUDENT_CLUB table. A constraint like this is called a *referential integrity constraint*. Checking constraints uses extra time and slows down performance. Also, retrieving data from a database, we may need to go through many small tables. As we show later, a query retrieving data from multiple tables uses many joins. Too many complex joins can reduce data-querying performance and make the programming of the query more challenging. Although normalization is necessary, for some tasks, the highest level of normalization is not always desirable. For example, if a database is used mainly for decision support, its tables should be more efficient for queries and more understandable for users. In such a case, it is better to use tables that are not fully normalized. On the other hand, for update-intensive databases, fully normalized tables will do a better job.

3.2.2 *Normal Forms*

Depending on the table structure, a table may be classified as being in the

- First normal form (1NF)
- Second normal form (2NF)
- Third normal form (3NF)
- Boyce–Codd normal form (BCNF)
- Fourth normal form (4NF)
- Domain-key normal form (DKNF)

Higher-level normal forms are nested; that is, if a table is in the 2NF, it is also in the 1NF. If a table is in the 3NF, then it is in the 1NF and 2NF. If a table is in the DKNF, then it is in all the other normal forms. The higher the normal form is, the fewer modification anomalies exist. The DKNF will eliminate all the modification anomalies. For many business applications, the 3NF is sufficient. Even though higher-level normal forms can further reduce or eliminate modification anomalies, these normal forms are less likely to be used in a business environment.

First Normal Form (1NF)

All relations satisfy the first normal form requirements. That is, a table meeting the following requirements is in the 1NF.

- Each cell in the table contains a single value, not a set of values.
- All the entries in a column have the same data type.
- Each column has a unique column name.
- The key attribute or a set of key attributes must be defined in the table. This means there are no identical multiple rows in the table.

The STUDENT_CLUB_INFO table in Table 3.1 meets all the above requirements. Therefore, it is in the 1NF.

Second Normal Form (2NF)

As mentioned earlier, the STUDENT_CLUB_INFO is not a desirable table. It contains all kinds of modification anomalies. The problem is caused by the fact that there are partial dependencies in the table. As discussed earlier, in the combination key (SID, Skill, ClubName), (SID, Duty) determines MentorName and ClubName determines MembershipFee. That is, each value in ClubName can uniquely determine the value in MembershipFee. However, there is no unique correspondence between the values in MembershipFee and the values in (SID, Duty). Consequently, MembershipFee is partially dependent on the combination key (SID, Duty, ClubName). This indicates that MembershipFee does not have to be determined by the combination key. It can be determined by ClubName separately. Similarly, MentorName does not have to be determined by (SID, Duty, ClubName) because it can be determined by (SID, Duty). Converting the 1NF to the 2NF by dividing the STUDENT_CLUB_INFO table can eliminate the partial dependencies.

For a table to be in the second normal form, it must meet the following requirements:

- The table is a relation; that is, it meets all the requirements for the 1NF.
- There is no partial dependency in the table.

The requirements for the 2NF indicate that all relations with a single key attribute are in the 2NF. The discussion of the 2NF is relevant only when a table has a combination key. To convert the table STUDENT_CLUB_INFO to the 2NF, let each component of the combination key be the primary key in the divided tables. Table 3.3 shows that the component ClubName in the original combination key (SID, Duty, ClubName) becomes the primary key in the table CLUB and ClubName → MembershipFee. In Table 3.2, the STUDENT table has the combination key (SID, Duty). We can further split it into two tables. However, it can be used to illustrate the next level normalization. Thus, we leave it as it is for instructional purposes.

Third Normal Form (3NF)

When we try to modify data, the second normal form still has modification anomalies. Consider the table STUDENT in Table 3.2.

- *Update anomalies:* The Duty information is redundant. Any change to a duty type will cause a full table search to locate the rows that need the same modification. For example, if we want to change the duty type Recruiter to WebMaster, we have to search the entire table to find all rows with the value Recruiter so that we can replace it with WebMaster. Full table search is time consuming. We need to avoid it as much as possible.
- *Insertion anomalies:* Suppose we want to add a new duty, Treasurer, into the table STUDENT. We cannot add it to the Duty attribute until a student who will serve as a treasurer is added to the table.
- *Deletion anomalies:* Suppose the students with student ids 11690 and 13654 are deleted. The deletion removes the Duty value Secretary. This deletion anomaly causes the loss of the Secretary duty.

The problem of the modification anomalies here is caused by *transitive dependency* that exists in the STUDENT table (see Table 3.2). From the business requirements listed above, each mentor can offer training in one type of skill, which means that the Skill attribute depends on the attribute MentorName. However, the MentorName attribute is not a primary key. That is, in the relation STUDENT(SID, StudentName, MentorName, Skill, Duty, EnrollDate), we have

```
(SID, Duty) → MentorName, Skill
MentorName → Skill
```

Here, a non-key attribute determines another non-key attribute. The problem with transitive dependency is that it still generates modification anomalies. Converting the 2NF to the 3NF will eliminate some of the modification anomalies.

For a table to be in the 3NF, we must eliminate the transitive dependency in the table. A table is in the 3NF if

- It is in the 2NF.
- It contains no transitive dependency; that is, the values in a non-key attribute except for the foreign key attribute cannot determine another non-key attribute.

Table 3.5 STUDENT **Table**

SID	Student Name	Duty	Enroll Date
10258	Liz	President	10/02/01
11690	Joe	Secretary	11/12/01
12105	Linda	Recruiter	02/11/02
12153	Don	President	02/11/02
13654	Jan	Secretary	11/16/01
12784	Liz	Recruiter	04/14/02
11505	Bruce	President	09/12/01
11690	Joe	Secretary	03/30/02
12153	Don	WebMaster	07/31/02

Table 3.6 MENTOR **Table in 3NF**

Mentor Name	Skill
Jones	Leadership
Lee	Typing
Smith	Web-develop
Long	Leadership
Garza	Typing
Moore	Leadership
Wang	Web-develop

Table 3.7 CLUB **Table in 3NF**

Club Name	Membership Fee
Book	60
Poetry	50
Soccer	150

By eliminating the transitive dependency, we mean that the table with the transitive dependency should be split into two tables. After we split the table STUDENT into the tables STUDENT and MENTOR, the original table STUDENT_CLUB_INFO in Table 3.1 becomes three smaller tables, Tables 3.5 through 3.7.

From the new STUDENT table, each student can serve more than one duty and has multiple enrollment dates in different clubs. You may be wondering

Table 3.8 FACULTY **Table**

FID	Dept	Specialty
10022	Computer	Networking
10023	Statistics	Applied statistics
10023	Biology	Biometrics
10024	Math	Matrix theory
10025	Computer	Database
10026	Statistics	Applied statistics

if StudentName determines EnrollDate. In Table 3.5, there are two students named Liz and, therefore, StudentName cannot determine Enroll-Date. The same is true about the attribute Duty, which cannot determine the attribute EnrollDate. According to the business requirements, one student may enroll in more than one club to perform different duties. This means that a student may have different enrollment dates and, therefore, SID alone cannot be the key for the STUDENT table. You still need the combination key (SID, Duty) for the table STUDENT. In Table 3.6, each mentor can offer only one type of skill and more than one mentor can offer the same type of skill. For example, Lee and Garza offer the Typing training and Wang and Smith offer the training in Web development. Because each of the tables MENTOR and CLUB has a single non-key column, it cannot have transitive dependency. Thus, both MENTOR and CLUB are in the third normal form.

By observing the tables in the 3NF, we conclude that each of the tables has a single key attribute to avoid partial dependency. By examining each pair of the non-key attributes in turn, we see that the non-key attributes except the foreign key attribute in each table directly depend on the primary key to avoid transitive dependency. However, because SID determines Student-Name in the table STUDENT, we have a partial dependency here. Therefore, STUDENT is not in the third normal form yet, but we keep it for instructional purposes.

Boyce–Codd Normal Form (BCNF)

Although the 3NF is sufficient for some business applications, it still cannot eliminate all the anomalies. Consider the table FACULTY (see Table 3.8). The dependencies are listed below.

```
Primary Key: FID, Dept
Dependency: Specialty → Dept
```

The combination (FID, Dept) will determine the attribute Specialty. Accordingly, the primary key can be the combination (FID, Dept). Some faculty members may have positions in two different departments and have research interest in two related fields. For example, the FID value 10023 is related to two Dept values, Biology and Statistics. Therefore, FID cannot determine the attribute Specialty. Similarly, the attribute Dept cannot determine Specialty because one department often covers several fields. That is, even though a professor is in the Computer department, you may still not know if his or her specialty is Database or Networking. Based on the above observation, we know that there is no partial dependency and the table FACULTY is in the second normal form.

The FACULTY table has no transitive dependency because there is only one non-key attribute Specialty. Thus, FACULTY is in the third normal form. Although the FACULTY table is in the 3NF, it can still generate some anomalies. There is another dependency, Specialty → Dept, in the table FACULTY. This dependency is not partial dependency because the determinant Specialty is not a key attribute. For example, if we want to insert a new specialty, Data Mining, into the FACULTY table, we cannot insert it until a faculty member who has this specialty is entered into the table first. This has generated an *insertion anomaly*. On the other hand, if the faculty members with FIDs 10022 and 10025 are deleted from the table, we will lose the Computer department. This is *deletion anomaly*. The modification anomalies are caused by the dependency where Specialty → Dept. The attribute Specialty is a determinant but it is not a candidate key because it cannot uniquely identify the values in FID. To solve the problem, we need to further split the table FACULTY to get to the next level of normalization. The next level normal form is called the *Boyce–Codd normal form*. A table is in the BCNF if it meets the following requirements:

- It is in the 3NF.
- Every determinant must be a candidate key.

The requirements listed above indicate that a table in the 3NF with only a single key attribute and a single non-key attribute is already in the BCNF because the only determinant is the primary key. In our example, we need to split the FACULTY table into multiple tables (see Tables 3.9a,b). First, place the dependency (Specialty → Dept) into a table by itself. Then place the dependency (FID → FacultyName) into the FACULTY table. Note that we have added the FacultyName column to FACULTY to make it look better; otherwise, we would have a single column in that table.

Consider Tables 3.9a,b. These tables are broken down to the level where there are only two columns in each table. We have eliminated all the anomalies caused by the dependency.

We are not at the end of the normalization process yet. There are other types of dependencies that can cause modification anomalies. Next, we work on the fourth normal form.

Fourth Normal Form (4NF)

To see a table with other types of dependencies, consider the STUDENT table in Table 3.10. The table consists of four columns — SID, StudentName,

Table 3.9(a)   SPECIALTY **Table**

Specialty	Dept
Networking	Computer
Applied Statistics	Statistics
Biometrics	Biology
Matrix Theory	Math
Database	Computer

Table 3.9(b)   FACULTY **Table in BCNF**

FID	Faculty Name
10022	Smith
10023	Jones
10024	Fox
10025	Long
10026	Fry

Table 3.10   STUDENT **Table**

SID	Student Name	Duty	Enroll Date
10258	Liz	President	10/02/01
11690	Joe	Secretary	11/12/01
12105	Linda	Recruiter	02/11/02
12153	Don	President	02/11/02
13654	Jan	Secretary	11/16/01
12784	Liz	Recruiter	04/14/02
11505	Bruce	President	09/12/01
11690	Joe	Secretary	03/30/02
12153	Don	WebMaster	07/31/02

Duty, and EnrollDate. A student can serve multiple duties and enroll in different clubs.

In this STUDENT table, the student with StudentId 11690 participates in two clubs. The enrollment dates for the two clubs are different with the same type of duty. The attributes SID, StudentName, and Duty are related to multiple values of enrollment dates. Therefore, the table contains duplicated values in SID, StudentName, and Duty. As another example, there are three students, Liz, Don, and Bruce, who serve as presidents. That is, the duty `President` is related to three values in `StudentName`, so the `President` value is duplicated. This is called *multi-value dependency* and is denoted below:

```
SID  →→  EnrollDate
Duty  →→  StudentName
```

Multi-value dependency is different from functional dependency, where one attribute or a combination of attributes determines another attribute (e.g., the transitive dependency discussed earlier). Notice that the `SID` cannot determine the attribute `EnrollDate`. Thus, there is no functional dependency between the attribute `SID` and the attribute `EnrollDate`. The same is true between the attribute `Duty` and the attribute `StudentName`. Multi-value dependency can generate update anomalies. For example, if the student with `SID` 11690 wants to update the duty from `Secretary` to `Recruiter` for both of his clubs, we must update two rows in order to make the update complete. From Table 3.10, we can see that multi-value dependency may happen if there is more than one non-key attribute. If a table has only a single key attribute and a single non-key attribute, we will have no multi-value dependency. To eliminate the update anomaly caused by multi-value dependency, we should split the table STUDENT in Table 3.10.

Now we demonstrate that normalization is not a forward-only process. It requires revisions based on new needs from feedback. For example, instead of splitting STUDENT in Table 3.10, we actually can do a better job by using a ternary relationship. Now we revisit the original STUDENT_CLUB_ INFO table in Table 3.1. We can see that the table actually contains four entities, STUDENT, CLUB, MENTOR, and SERVICE. For the ease of demonstration, we first separate MENTOR from the original table. Then we use a ternary relationship to represent the relationship among STUDENT, CLUB, and SER-VICE. Because one club can have many students and one student can enroll in several clubs, there is an M:N relationship between STUDENT and CLUB. Similarly, there is an M:N relationship between STUDENT and SERVICE. As shown in Figure 3.4, except for the foreign keys in the intersection tables, each of these three tables contains only one non-key attribute so that there will be no multi-value dependency.

The contents of the three tables are shown in Tables 3.11a,b,c, where each table has a single non-key attribute. This means we no longer have multi-value dependency in these tables. This leads to a new type of normalized form, *fourth normal form* (4NF).

A table is in the 4NF if it meets the following requirements:

- It is in BCNF.
- It has no multi-value dependency.

As you have seen, the normalization process improves the structure of the tables. It gradually removes some of the modification anomalies. Now the question is whether there is a normalization form that can guarantee the

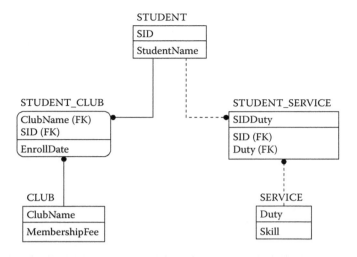

Figure 3.4   Structure with no multi-value dependency

Table 3.11(a)   STUDENT Table

SID	Student Name
10258	Liz
11690	Joe
12105	Linda
12153	Don
13654	Jan
12784	Liz
11505	Bruce

Table 3.11(b)   CLUB Table

Club Name	Membership Fee
Book	60
Poetry	50
Soccer	150

Table 3.11(c)   SERVICE Table in 4NF

Duty	Skill
President	Leadership
Recruiter	Web-develop
Secretary	Typing
WebMaster	Web-develop

elimination of all types of anomalies. Theoretically, the answer is yes. The Domain-Key normal form will eliminate all types of anomalies.

Domain-Key Normal Form (DKNF)

The ultimate goal of table normalization is to eliminate all kinds of anomalies. This goal can be achieved by normalizing a table so that it is in the *domain-key normal form* (DKNF). Theoretically, the DKNF is great. If a table is in the DKNF, it does not have any type of anomaly. In other words, if a table has no anomaly, it is in the DKNF. However, there is no general procedure to convert a table to be in the DKNF. The converting process is mostly based on the designer's knowledge about business requirements and his or her design experience. Once entities, attributes, relationships, and business rules are identified for a database project, the designer can start the converting process. Based on the business requirements, the designer creates tables that consist of attributes logically involved in a specific business requirement. For those business requirements that cannot be converted, the designer implements them later in a DBMS or in an application program.

The difficulty is that there are no general rules that will tell us which business requirements can be implemented during the database design stage and which ones should be implemented in the application programs. However, for some design problems, the converting process is not that uncertain. Once the conversion is completed, we will eliminate all the anomalies in the DKNF.

We first look at the definition of the DKNF. Then we go through the process to make the relations in the DKNF by fulfilling the business requirements. The definition of the domain-key normal form defined by Fagin in 1981 is stated below.

▼

A relation is in the DKNF if and only if every constraint on the relation is a logical consequence of key constraints and domain constraints.

▲

The words such as constraint, key, and domain used by Fagin have very general meanings. The word constraint includes all types of rules enforced on functional dependency, multi-value dependency, interrelation dependency, and intravalue dependency, except the time-dependent rules. As we have defined earlier, key is the unique identifier of the entity instances in a table and domain is the description of the format, restriction, type, and range of the allowed values for an attribute. The definition says that by checking the key values to make sure that they are unique and by enforcing the values in each attribute to meet the definition of the attribute domain, we can make the resulting relation in the DKNF.

If the above explanation still sounds too abstract, consider the table STUDENT_CLUB_INFO in Table 3.1. The STUDENT_CLUB_INFO table contains information about the clubs in which the students are participating. The table

Table 3.12   List of Constraints

Business Requirements	Constraints
Each club charges a membership fee.	ClubName → MembershipFee
Each student can enroll in more than one club.	SID →→ Club
Each club can have many students.	Club →→ SID
Each student can have more than one mentor.	SID →→ Mentor
Each mentor can train many students.	Mentor →→ SID
A student can have more than one duty in different clubs.	SID →→ Duty (SID, Duty, Club) is unique
Each duty can be served by many students.	Duty →→ SID
Each mentor can offer training in one type of skill.	Mentor → Skill
More than one mentor can offer training in the same type of skill.	Skill →→ Mentor
One skill may serve different duties.	Skill →→ Duty
No student can have the same mentor twice.	(SID, Mentor) is unique
No student can enroll in the same club twice.	(SID, Club) is unique
Each club member must serve one of the duties.	Duty cannot be null
Minimum value for MembershipFee is $40	MembershipFee >= $40

includes club names, membership fees, and enrollment dates for each club; duty of each participating student; students' mentors; skills trained by the mentors; and so on.

The first step of the process that converts a relation to be in the DKNF is to examine the business requirements, so that we can define the keys and domains to fulfill these requirements. We have listed the business requirements for the student clubs at the beginning of the Table Normalization section. Based on these business requirements, we define the constraints in terms of the functional dependencies, multi-value dependencies, and the ranges of data values in Table 3.12.

The goal of the DKNF conversion here is to define the keys and domains to meet all the constraints listed in Table 3.12. If we can meet these constraints by enforcing the keys and domains, we will be able to create relations in the DKNF.

In the next step, we examine the themes of the information contained in the table STUDENT_CLUB_INFO in Table 3.1 so that we can categorize the constraints for each theme. The STUDENT_CLUB_INFO table contains the following themes:

- Information about clubs
- Skill training offered by mentors
- Information about students

Table 3.13 CLUB **Relation**

Club Name	Membership Fee
Book	60
Poetry	50
Soccer	150

- Skill requirement by each duty
- Mentor, duty, and club information for each student
- Information about data value restrictions

In the following, we examine each theme and enforce the constraints involved in it.

1. *Information about clubs:* By examining the constraints of the clubs, we get the following constraints:

   ```
   ClubName → MembershipFee
   MembershipFee >= $40
   ```

   If we enforce `ClubName` as the key attribute, the constraint will be satisfied. To make `ClubName` the key attribute, we can create a relation CLUB containing the primary key attribute `ClubName` and the non-key attribute `MembershipFee`. The CLUB relation is illustrated in Table 3.13. The constraint `MembershipFee >= $40` is a domain constraint. It can be enforced on the attribute `MembershipFee` when we create the corresponding table in a DBMS.

2. *Skill training offered by mentors:* For information about the training offered by the mentors, we have the following constraints:

   ```
   MentorName → Skill
   Skill →→ MentorName
   ```

   Because the attribute `MentorName` determines the attribute Skill, we can create a table MENTOR that contains the attributes `MentorName` and `Skill`. Make the attribute `MentorName` the primary key and the `Skill` the non-key attribute. The MENTOR relation is illustrated in Table 3.14.

3. *Information about students:* Similarly, the information about students has the following constraint:

   ```
   SID → StudentName
   ```

   Consequently, we have the relation about students (Table 3.15) by enforcing the SID primary key.

4. *Skill requirement by each duty:* For the information about skill requirements, we have the following constraint:

   ```
   Skill →→ Duty
   ```

Table 3.14   MENTOR **Relation**

Mentor Name	Skill
Jones	Leadership
Lee	Typing
Smith	Web-develop
Long	Leadership
Garza	Typing
Moore	Leadership
Wang	Web-develop

Table 3.15   STUDENT **Relation**

SID	Student Name
10258	Liz
11690	Joe
12105	Linda
12153	Don
13654	Jan
12784	Liz
11505	Bruce

Table 3.16   SERVICE **Relation**

Duty	Skill
President	Leadership
Secretary	Typing
Recruiter	Web-develop
WebMaster	Web-develop

That is,

```
Duty → Skill
```

To meet the constraint Duty → Skill, create the relation SERVICE (Table 3.16) with the attribute Duty as the primary key and Skill as the non-key attribute. Because the Skill attribute is in both MENTOR and SERVICE, it is better to use a ternary relationship by adding a SKILL relation. Here, we add the SKILL relation with two attributes, SkillId and SkillName, and modify the SERVICE and MENTOR relations accordingly (see Figure 3.5). The modified relations are shown in Tables 3.17a,b,c.

Figure 3.5 **Relationship among** SERVICE, SKILL, **and** MENTOR

Table 3.17(a) SKILL **Relations**

Skill Id	Skill Name
1	Leadership
2	Typing
3	Web-develop

Table 3.17(b) MENTOR **Relations**

Mentor Name	Skill Id
Jones	1
Lee	2
Smith	3
Long	1
Garza	2
Moore	1
Wang	3

Table 3.17(c) SERVICE **Relations**

Duty	Skill Id
President	1
Secretary	2
Recruiter	3
WebMaster	3

5. *Mentor, duty, and club information for each student:* For information about the students' mentors and duties, and the clubs the students participate in, we have the following constraints:

```
SID  →→ MentorName | Duty | ClubName
Mentor →→ SID
Duty  →→ SID
Club  →→ SID
(SID, Duty, Club) is unique
```

Table 3.18   STUDENT_MENTOR **Relation**

SID	Mentor Name
10258	Jones
11690	Lee
12105	Smith
12153	Long
13654	Garza
12784	Smith
11505	Moore
12153	Wang

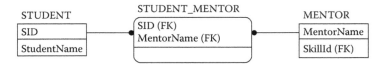

Figure 3.6   Relationship between STUDENT **and** MENTOR

```
(SID, Mentor) is unique
(SID, Club) is unique
Duty cannot be null
```

According to the business rules, a student can serve more than one duty, have one or more mentors, and join one or more clubs. For the constraint SID →→ MentorName, SID is the key in the STUDENT table and MentorName is the key in the MENTOR table. Because a mentor can advise many students and one student can choose several mentors, we can place the attributes MentorName and SID in the intersection table STUDENT_MENTOR. To satisfy the constraint (SID, Mentor) as unique, let us make the pair (SID, Mentor) be the key for the table. The resulting relation STUDENT_MENTOR is given in Table 3.18. The corresponding relationship diagram is shown in Figure 3.6.

For the constraints SID →→ Duty and Duty →→ SID, we can create an intersection table to relate the attributes SID and Duty. Because SID is the key in the STUDENT table and Duty is the key in the SERVICE table, the intersection table STUDENT_SERVICE is used to implement the constraints. Because a student can serve the same type of duty more than once in different clubs, the constraint that (SID, Duty, ClubName) is unique should be enforced by a key. The ClubName column is a foreign key from CLUB. To enforce this key constraint, we make a combination key for the table STUDENT_SERVICE (see Figure 3.7). The corresponding relation is illustrated in Table 3.19. We implement the constraint, Duty cannot be null, in a DBMS later.

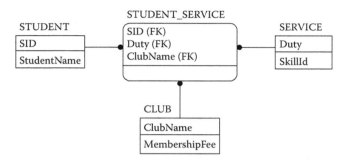

Figure 3.7   Relationship between STUDENT **and** SERVICE

Table 3.19   STUDENT_SERVICE Relation

SID	Duty	Club Name
110258	President	Book
111690	Secretary	Book
112105	Recruiter	Book
112153	President	Poetry
113654	Secretary	Poetry
112784	Recruiter	Poetry
111505	President	Soccer
111690	Secretary	Soccer
112153	WebMaster	Soccer

For the constraints SID →→ ClubName and ClubName →→ SID, we can create a table STUDENT_CLUB to relate SID and ClubName. Because a student cannot enroll in the same club twice, the pair (SID, ClubName) can be enforced as the key for the table. As the combination key, the pair can also determine EnrollDate. Adding EnrollDate to the relation STUDENT_CLUB, we have the result in Table 3.20.

In Table 3.20, SID is the key from the relation STUDENT and ClubName is the key from the table CLUB. Accordingly, STUDENT_CLUB can be used as an intersection table. The corresponding relationship is shown in Figure 3.8.

At this point we have defined all the keys and domains to meet the constraints. To implement the keys, we have to create tables to hold these keys and make sure that these tables satisfy the requirements for relations when we create them. The relations created to implement the keys are in the DKNF. For the theme, information about data value restrictions, we use the domain definitions to implement the value restrictions, and we do not discuss the theme separately. We summarize the keys, domains, and relations in Figure 3.9.

Table 3.20 STUDENT_CLUB **Relation**

SID	Club Name	Enroll Date
10258	Book	10/02/01
11690	Book	11/12/01
12105	Book	02/11/02
12153	Poetry	02/11/02
13654	Poetry	11/16/01
12784	Poetry	04/14/02
11505	Soccer	09/12/01
11690	Soccer	03/30/02
12153	Soccer	07/31/02

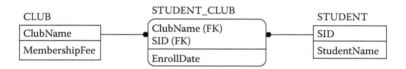

Figure 3.8   Relationship between CLUB **and** STUDENT

Domain Definitions

Duty:	not null
MembershipFee:	minimum value = 40

Key Definitions and Resulting Relations

CLUB (<u>ClubName</u>, MembershipFee)
Key: ClubName

MENTOR (<u>MentorName</u>, *SkillId*)
Key: MentorName

STUDENT (<u>SID</u>, StudentName)
Key: SID

SERVICE (<u>Duty</u>, *SkillId*)
Key: Duty

SKILL (<u>SkillId</u>, SkillName)
Key: SkillId

STUDENT_CLUB (<u>*SID*</u>, <u>*ClubName*</u>, *EnrollDate*)
Key: (SID, ClubName)

STUDENT_MENTOR (<u>*SID*</u>, <u>*MentorName*</u>)
Key: (SID, MentorName)

STUDENT_SERVICE (<u>*SID*</u>, <u>*Duty*</u>, <u>*ClubName*</u>)
Key: (SID, Duty, ClubName)

Figure 3.9   Domain-key normal form

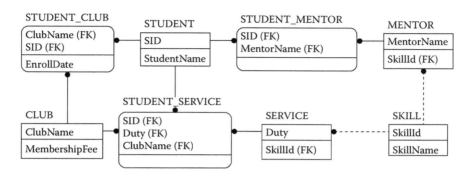

Figure 3.10   Relationship diagram for `Student_Club` **database**

By adding the relationships to these relations, the E-R data model diagram for the above relations is given in Figure 3.10.

For some small projects, the DKNF converting process is easier than the table splitting process mentioned earlier. Database designers are more familiar with the *key* and *domain* concepts. In most DBMSs, keys and domains are used for table creation. Therefore, proper use of the DKNF converting process will help us in theory and practice.

Denormalization

For some decision-support systems, high-level normalization is not always desirable. Tables used in a decision-support system have few modifications and search performance is more important. In such a case, it is better to use tables that are not fully normalized.

For example, consider the CUSTOMER table, CUSTOMER(CID, Cname, Phone, Street, City, State, Zip). There are two themes here:

```
CID  →  CustomerName, Phone
(Street, Zip)  →  City, State
```

Normally, we should break CUSTOMER into two smaller tables. However, for the purpose of information presentation, it is more convenient to keep the original CUSTOMER table so that a specific customer's information can be retrieved at once without searching another table. Using tables in low-level normalization can get information faster for a decision-support system.

As you have seen in this chapter, during the normalization process, you may need to modify the initial E-R model. Sometimes, you may need to add new entities or attributes or delete some entities or attributes until the initial E-R meets the business requirements.

3.3 Summary

This chapter has discussed tables and table normalization. We discussed how to use primary keys and foreign keys to link tables. To prepare the conversion from a data model to a relational database, we need to properly normalize the table structures. First, the chapter introduced the concepts of tables and functional dependencies that will be used in a normalization process. To eliminate modification anomalies in tables, you learned how to convert tables to be in normalized forms. We went over the normal forms 1NF, 2NF, 3NF, BCNF, 4NF, and DKNF in detail. Through examples, you learned how to use these normal forms to eliminate various modification anomalies. A case study of the student clubs was used to illustrate the method of the DKNF. The last topic covered in this chapter was denormalization. Once the table structures are normalized, you are ready to convert the data model to a relational database and implement the database with one of the DBMS packages. In the next chapter, you will learn how to implement the database in SQL Server.

Review Questions

1. What is a table?
2. What are the conditions for a table to be a relation?
3. How do you link a table to other tables?
4. What is functional dependency? Give an example of functional dependency.
5. What is fully functional dependency?
6. What is a combination key?
7. Explain the meaning of a candidate key.
8. What is a primary key?
9. What is a foreign key?
10. Describe update anomalies using an example.
11. Describe insertion anomalies using an example.
12. Describe deletion anomalies using an example.
13. Why do tables need to be normalized?
14. Why is the highest-level normalization not always desirable?
15. For what type of task will fully normalized tables do a better job?
16. What are the requirements for the first normal form?
17. What are the requirements for the second normal form?
18. What is a third normal form?
19. What is a Boyce–Codd normal form?
20. What is a fourth normal form?
21. What is a domain-key normal form?

Case Study Projects

In the previous chapter, you created a data model for each case study project. Now, to make the entities in the data model have a consistent structure, you need to perform a normalization process. We examine the characteristics of the attributes in the entities.

1. Computer Service

Based on the data model for Awesome Computer Service created in the previous chapter, perform the following tasks to normalize the tables in the data model:

- Identify the key attributes for the entities in your data model.
- Check if there are any partial dependencies and transitive dependencies among the attributes.
- Normalize each table in your project up to the third normal form.

2. University Registration

Examine the University Registration data model created in the previous chapter and normalize the tables according to the following steps:

- For the entities in your data model, identify the key attributes.
- List partial dependencies and transitive dependencies among the attributes, if there are any.
- For each table in your project, normalize it up to the third normal form.

3. Mail Order

Perform the following activities for the Mail Order data model created in the previous chapter:

- Specify the attribute(s) that can be used as the key for each entity.
- Are there any partial dependencies or transitive dependencies among the attributes? If so, list your findings.
- If any table in your project is not in the third normal form, normalize it up to the third normal form.

Chapter 4

Transforming Data Models to Relational Databases

Objectives

- Select a Database Management System (DBMS).
- Transform an E-R data model to a relational database.
- Describe and create constraints.
- Create a database diagram in SQL Server.

4.1 Introduction

Before a database can be created on a specified Database Management System (DBMS), you need to map all the objects in a data model to table representations and specify the relationships by primary and foreign keys. The process of transforming data models to table representations is part of the logical design. After a data model is represented in normalized table structures, it is ready to be implemented in a specified database management system.

In the previous chapter, we briefly discussed how to represent relationships with primary/foreign keys. The concepts of primary and foreign keys were used to illustrate the normalization process. We did not really implement the relationships created in a data model with the primary and foreign keys. In this chapter, you will convert the entities to tables and implement the relationships between a pair of entities with the primary or foreign keys. You will create database objects such as database, tables, and diagrams with SQL Server 2000. Seeing is believing. For readers who are new to the database processing system, this is a good time to implement the database objects with a graphical tool right after the table structure is normalized.

4.2 DBMS Selection

To convert a data model to tables with a specified DBMS, we need to select a DBMS first. Some popular DBMS systems are Microsoft Access, Microsoft SQL Server, IBM DB2, Oracle, and Informix Cloudscape.

Microsoft Access is a personal DBMS; it is good for single users or small businesses. In a client/server environment, Microsoft Access can be used as an application development tool. It is not for an environment where many people are accessing the same database simultaneously. Microsoft Access has fewer security capabilities.

Microsoft SQL Server is designed to handle a relatively large database. It can manage a database with terabyte storage. It can work in a truly client/server environment to allow many people to access the database simultaneously. Many enterprise database functionalities can be implemented on a SQL Server DBMS. Not only is it relatively powerful, but it is also user friendly. For those relatively less complex database projects, it takes less time to get the job done on SQL Server. It also includes security management utilities and data analysis tools. To meet the demands of E-commerce, SQL Server 2000 provides tools for transforming a database in a DBMS to one in XML for portability and Web presentation. A more important advantage is that it costs less when compared with other business database DBMSs. For small- and medium-sized companies, SQL Server is a good choice.

Oracle and IBM DB2 are designed for even larger databases. They are a good choice for medium to large companies. Many large E-commerce companies use these types of DBMSs for 24-hours-a-day and 7-days-a-week continuous business operations. These DBMSs require much more powerful hardware to support the data storage devices. Their costs are also higher.

When you select a DBMS, consider the following factors:

- The maximum number of users who need to access the database simultaneously. Oracle, IBM DB2, and Microsoft SQL Server can handle thousands of users at the same time.
- The cost of the DBMS, hardware, and daily operations.
- The volume of data. If the business grows continuously, you need to reserve enough storage space. It also influences the choice of hardware.
- Web-development capability. It is a consideration for those who will implement the database for E-commerce.
- Application-development tools for creating forms and reports. Some DBMSs do not include these tools. For quick development of applications, you need to use a DBMS with these tools, for example, Microsoft Access.

Our choice of DBMS is SQL Server, due to the fact that it comes with a variety of graphical database development tools to assist us in building databases and applications. For someone who is new to the database processing system, graphical tools make the development of database projects easier. On the other hand, it is powerful enough to cover all the topics in database management, database security, and database analysis in this book.

It also provides the tools for developing Web-based databases and the support for XML technologies. The cost of SQL Server is relatively low and it requires less storage for hosting the database server.

4.3 Transforming Data Models to Relational Databases

A database design and creation process includes the following tasks:

- Convert a data model to tables in a relational database.
- Relate the tables with foreign keys and primary keys.
- Implement data constraints when creating the tables in a DBMS.
- Create a database diagram to represent the data model.

In Chapter 2, we created some data models for business processes. A data model consists of objects such as entities, attributes, and relationships. Now we are going to transform them into table-related objects in a relational database. To represent an entity in a relational database, we first convert the entity to a relation, which is a table that contains single-value entries and no duplicated rows, and then normalize the table so that the table is in a proper normal form, as discussed in Chapter 3.

As mentioned in Chapter 3, a table contains a set of entity instances. Each row in a table represents an entity instance. Each column of a table represents an attribute of the entity.

4.3.1 Representing Entities

When we represent entities with tables in SQL Server, table names should follow the rules for identifiers used in SQL Server. The following are the rules for naming tables, columns, or other database objects.

- The length of names can be from 1 to 128 characters, numbers, or symbols.
- The first character in an object name must be [a–z], [A–Z], _, @, or #.
- The symbols @, $, #, or _ can be used in subsequent characters.
- A Transact-SQL reserved keyword such as System cannot be used as an object name.
- Embedded spaces cannot be used to name tables, columns, views, and so on, except for naming a database.

For names that do not follow these rules, you must delimit them with either double quotation marks " " or brackets [ ] when they are referenced. For example, if you have a table name such as SYSTEM-PART or a table name with a space such as COMPUTER SYSTEM, you must delimit the names when you use them in a Transact-SQL statement as [SYSTEM-PART] and [COMPUTER SYSTEM]. Also, notice that the symbols # and @ at the beginning of an identifier have special meanings. For example,

Table 4.1   Naming Convention

Database Object	Naming Example
Database	MyDatabase or My Database
Table	MYTABLE or MY_TABLE
Intersection table	TABLE1_TABLE2
Column	MyColumn

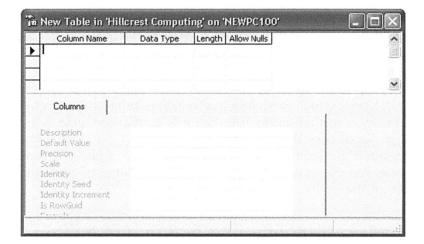

Figure 4.1   Table structure in SQL Server

- A name beginning with the sign @ represents a local variable or parameter.
- A name beginning with the sign # represents a temporary table or procedure.
- A name beginning with ## or @@ denotes a global temporary object.

Before a database is implemented, a general rule should be established about its object naming. For example, we are going to use the naming convention in Table 4.1 for our database objects.

Each company may have its own naming convention. It is important to keep the naming convention consistent. In general, it is not a good idea to use a space or a reserved keyword to name a database object. It may cause confusion during programming. We try to follow the convention to avoid confusion.

After you have learned the naming convention, it is time to create tables and columns with SQL Server's graphical tools. Before you do that, you should get to know the table structure better. A table in SQL Server has a structure as shown in Figure 4.1.

Table 4.2 Commonly Used Data Types

Data Type	Default Length	Description
char	10	Fixed-length non-Unicode character data type with a maximum length of 8000 characters
datetime	8	Date and time data from January 1, 1753, to December 31, 9999
decimal	9	Fixed precision and scale numeric data type ranging from $-10^{38} - 1$ to $10^{38} - 1$
float	8	Floating-precision number data type ranging from $-1.79E + 308$ through $1.79E + 308$
image	16	Variable-length binary data representing an image. The maximum length is $2^{31} - 1$ bytes
int	4	Integer data type ranging from -2^{31} through $2^{31} - 1$
money	8	Monetary data values from -2^{63} to $2^{63} - 1$ with accuracy to a ten-thousandth of a monetary unit
nchar	10	Fixed-length Unicode data type with a maximum length of 4000 characters
ntext	16	Variable-length Unicode data type with a maximum length of $2^{30} - 1$ characters
numeric	9	Same as decimal
nvarchar	50	Variable-length Unicode data type with a maximum length of 4000 characters
text	16	Variable-length non-Unicode data type with a maximum length of $2^{31} - 1$ characters
varchar	50	Variable-length non-Unicode data type with a maximum of 8000 characters

In SQL Server, you can create a maximum of 1024 columns in a table. Each column can be described by its name, data type, and other properties, as listed below:

- *Allow Nulls:* A column is allowed to have null values.
- *Column Name:* The name of a column.
- *Data Type:* The data type of a column. The commonly used data types are listed in Table 4.2.
- *Default Value:* A value automatically assigned to a column when a new row is inserted.
- *Identity:* A system-generated number that is used as a row identifier. It will be automatically incremented when each new row is inserted.
- *Is RowGuid:* A column that is used as a globally unique identifier (GUID).
- *Length:* The length of data values. You may change the default length listed in Table 4.2.
- *Precision:* The maximum number of digits used in decimal data.
- *Scale:* The maximum number of digits used to the right of the decimal point.

PART_DETAIL

ItemId	smallint
Price	smallmoney
Description	char(50)
PartId	char(10)
Maker	char30)
Quantity	smallint

Figure 4.2 `PART_DETAIL` **entity**

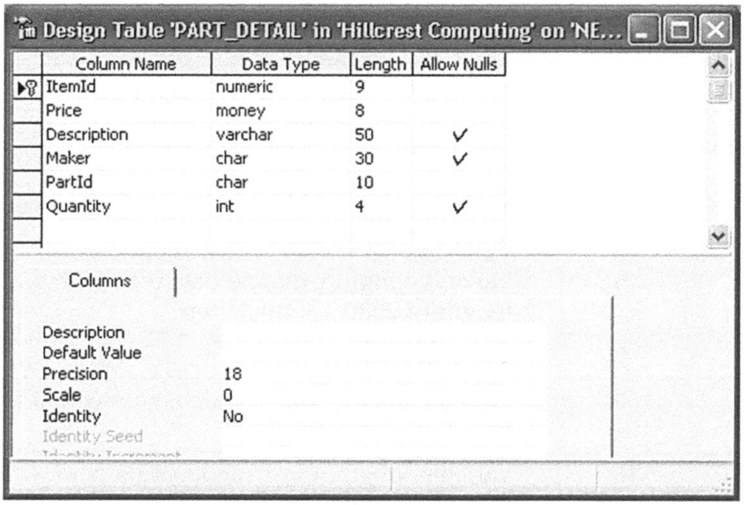

Figure 4.3 `PART_DETAIL` **table design in SQL Server**

Next, we implement entities in terms of tables in SQL Server. Consider the `PART_DETAIL` entity (Figure 4.2) created in Chapter 2. The entity in Figure 4.2 can be represented by the table notation used in database design as shown below:

`PART_DETAIL(`<u>`ItemId`</u>`, Price, Description, `*`PartId`*`, Maker, Quantity)`

The underlined column name shows that the column is a primary key and the column name in italics indicates that the column is a foreign key. The corresponding table design in SQL Server is shown in Figure 4.3.

In this table design, `ItemId` is the primary key for the table. The data types and their lengths are also displayed. The check marks in the Allow Nulls column indicate that null values can be used in the columns `Description`, `Maker`, and `Quantity`. The column properties `Precision`, `Scale`, and `Identity` are also specified in the design.

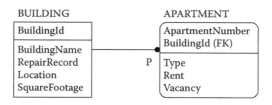

Figure 4.4   Identifying relationship

4.3.2   *Representing Relationships*

For two tables to be linked, they need to share a common column. That is, the primary key column of one table is placed in the other table. To learn how to implement relationships in a DBMS, consider the following cases.

1. *Identifying relationship:* In Chapter 2, we discussed the relationship between APARTMENT and BUILDING. The relationship between them is an identifying relationship (see Figure 4.4). To represent this kind of relationship in table notation, place the primary key in the parent table BUILDING to the child table APARTMENT as the foreign key. The primary key and foreign key pair is used to implement the relationship. The table APARTMENT has a primary key that partially depends on `BuildingId` defined in the BUILDING table. Thus, the primary key for APARTMENT includes both `BuildingId` and `ApartmentNumber`. This combination key is necessary because the APARTMENT table may contain duplicated rows without both `BuildingId` and `ApartmentNumber` as the primary key. The designs of these two tables in SQL Server are shown in Figure 4.5. In SQL Server, you can represent the relationship by the relationship diagram shown in Figure 4.6. From Figure 4.6, we can see that the key end in the relationship is the parent side and the ⊐⊐ end is the child side.

2. *Nonidentifying relationship:* In Chapter 2, the nonidentifying relationship was established between the entities ADVISOR and STUDENT, shown in Figure 4.7. The ADVISOR entity is the parent entity on the optional side (with a diamond) of the relationship and the STUDENT entity is the child entity on the N side (with a solid dot) of the relationship. Notice that `AdvisorId` is not part of the primary key in the child entity.

   To find a student's advisor's name, we first go to the STUDENT table and find the student's ID and then obtain the advisor's ID, which is in the `AdvisorId` column of that row. Then we go to the ADVISOR table and find the advisor's ID in the `AdvisorId` column. After finding the advisor's ID, we can obtain the advisor's name from that row. On the other hand, given an advisor's name, we can get the advisor's ID and find all the students advised by the adviser through searching the `AdvisorId` column in the STUDENT table.

   As mentioned before, N can be 0, 1, or any positive integer. When N is equal to 1 in a 1:1 relationship, we can put the primary key in any of the two tables. However, in a one-to-many relationship, we must place

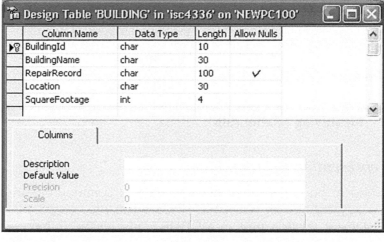

[a]

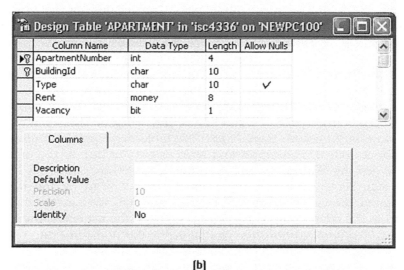

[b]

Figure 4.5   Table designs of (a) BUILDING **and (b)** APARTMENT

the primary key in the one-side table and put it in the many-side table as a foreign key, not the other way around. The reason is that if we place the key of the many-side table to the one-side table, we will have many duplicated rows in the key column(s) of the one-side table because each row in the one-side table corresponds to many rows in the many-side table. We now look at the table designs for ADVISOR and STUDENT, shown in Figure 4.8. For AdvisorId in Figure 4.8b, the check mark under the column Allow Nulls indicates that the advisor id is optional. The corresponding relationship diagram in SQL Server is shown in Figure 4.9.

3. *Nonspecific relationship:* Consider the entities STUDENT and CLASS. They are connected by a nonspecific relationship, which is used for many-to-many (M:N) relationships. As mentioned in Chapter 2, an intersection table

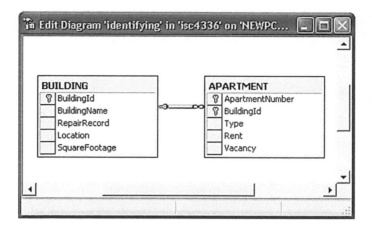

Figure 4.6 **Identifying relationship between** BUILDING **and** APARTMENT

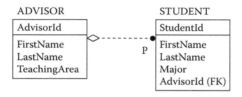

Figure 4.7 **Nonidentifying relationship between** ADVISOR **and** STUDENT

should be added to represent an M:N relationship. Here, STUDENT_CLASS will be the intersection table. Each row in the intersection table contains the key values from the tables on both sides of the M:N relationship. Here, STUDENT_CLASS has a primary key that consists of the attributes StudentId and ClassId. Now, the M:N relationship can be represented by the 1:M relationship between STUDENT and STUDENT_CLASS and the 1:N relationship between CLASS and STUDENT_CLASS, as illustrated in Figure 4.10. The CLASS and STUDENT_CLASS tables are designed as shown in Figure 4.11. The STUDENT table design is displayed in Figure 4.8.

Notice in Figure 4.11 that the column names Time and Day are enclosed by the delimiter [ ] because both are reserved words. Make sure that the data format for StudentId and ClassId in the STUDENT_CLASS table is consistent with the corresponding columns in the tables STUDENT and CLASS. Figure 4.12 shows the M:N relationship diagram.

4. *Categorization relationship:* In Chapter 2, we investigated the categorization relationship among the entities EMPLOYEE, PROFESSOR, and STAFF shown in Figure 4.13. The shared attributes are placed in the generic entity EMPLOYEE and the unshared attributes are placed in the specific entities PROFESSOR and STAFF. Each row in the specific tables PROFESSOR and STAFF corresponds to a single row in the generic table EMPLOYEE. The identifier of each specific table is the identifier used in the generic table. The corresponding table designs in SQL Server are given in Figure 4.14.

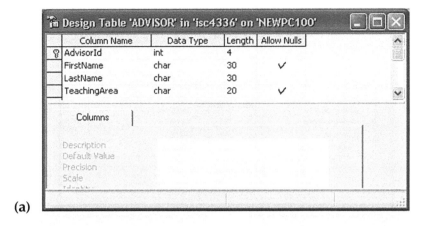

(a)

(b)

Figure 4.8   Table designs of (a) ADVISOR **and (b)** STUDENT

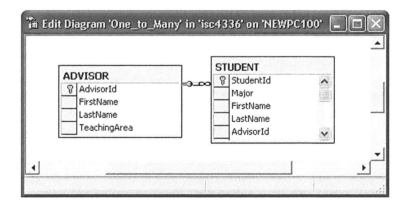

Figure 4.9   Nonidentifying relationship between ADVISOR **and** STUDENT

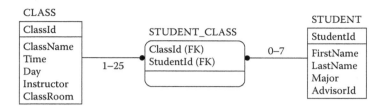

Figure 4.10 Nonspecific relationship with intersection table

Design Table 'CLASS' in 'isc4336' on 'NEWPC100'

Column Name	Data Type	Length	Allow Nulls
ClassId	numeric	9	
ClassName	char	50	
[Time]	char	20	
[Day]	char	20	✓
Instructor	char	30	
ClassRoom	char	10	✓

Columns

Description
Default Value
Precision
Scale

(a)

Design Table 'STUDENT_CLASS' in 'isc4336' on 'NEWPC...

Column Name	Data Type	Length	Allow Nulls
StudentId	numeric	9	
ClassId	numeric	9	

Columns

Description
Default Value
Precision
Scale

(b)

Figure 4.11 Table designs of (a) CLASS and (b) STUDENT_CLASS

Because the word Name is a reserved word in SQL Server, we change it to EmployeeName here.

Make sure that the data format for EmployeeId in the specific tables PROFESSOR and STAFF matches EmployeeId in the table EMPLOYEE. Figure 4.15 shows the categorization relationship diagram.

Notice that the connection between two tables has key icons on both ends. This means that it is a one-to-one connection.

In this table implementation, to create a record for a new employee who is a professor, you have to add the information in both EMPLOYEE

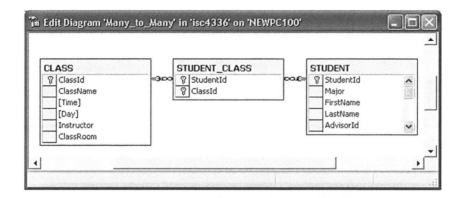

Figure 4.12   Nonspecific relationship between CLASS **and** STUDENT

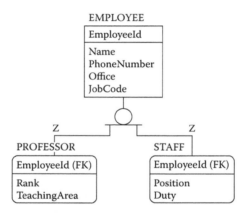

Figure 4.13   Incomplete categorization relationship

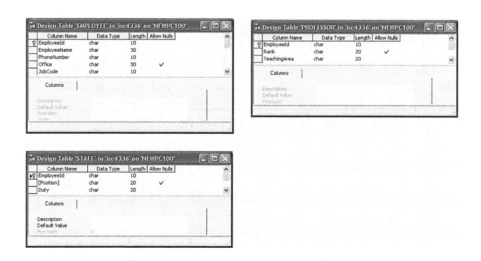

Figure 4.14   Table designs of (a) EMPLOYEE, **(b)** PROFESSOR, **and (c)** STAFF

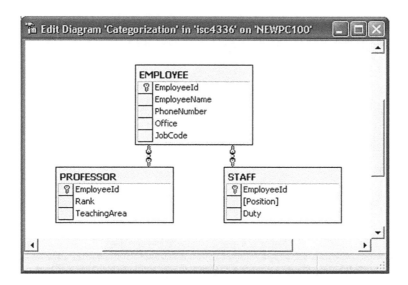

Figure 4.15   Categorization relationship among EMPLOYEE, PROFESSOR, **and** STAFF

and PROFESSOR. Also, to display a list of employees that includes both professors and staff members, you need to first select the data for professors from the tables EMPLOYEE and PROFESSOR, then select the data for staff members from the tables EMPLOYEE and STAFF, and finally put the selected data together. Although this is doable, it is awkward and slows down database performance. For some categorization relationships that contain similar attributes in their specific entities, we may consider limiting the use of the categorization relationship. For example, for the categorization relationship in Figure 4.13, the attributes in PROFESSOR and STAFF have similar meanings. The attribute Rank is similar to the attribute Position, and the attribute TeachingArea is similar to Duty. In such a case, we may implement the relationship with a single table, as in Figure 4.16. If the attributes in the specific tables do not have much in common, putting these attributes in a generic table can cause a lot of data redundancy. In that case, it is better to implement the categorization relationship.

5. *Recursive relationship:* As we have seen in Chapter 2, only one entity is involved in a recursive relationship. The recursive relationship we have developed is shown in Figure 4.17. In this relationship, a student is related to a student spouse who is also a student. In the column StudentSpouse, you can place the student spouse's student id. The corresponding recursive relationship diagram in SQL Server is shown in Figure 4.18.

In a university course catalogue, you may find that some courses have many prerequisite courses and many courses may require the same course as a prerequisite. In this situation, the entity COURSE has an M:N recursive relationship. For the M:N recursive relationship, to avoid duplicated rows in the table COURSE, two tables are used to implement the relationship:

```
COURSE (CourseId, Title, Credit)
PREREQUISITE (CourseId, Prerequisite)
```

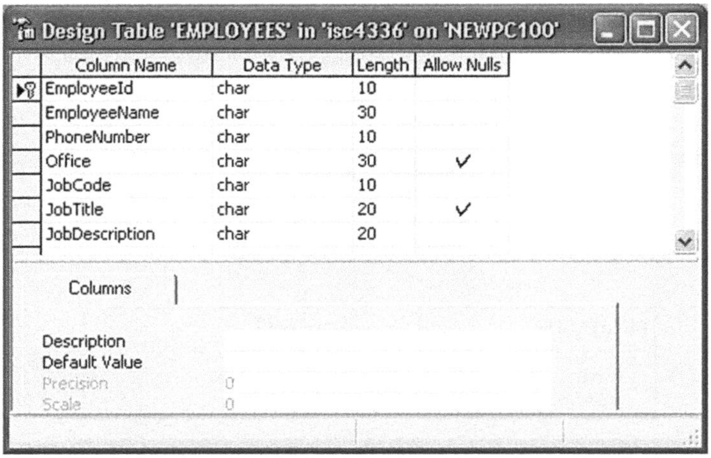

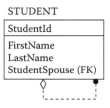

Figure 4.16   Table design of EMPLOYEES

STUDENT

StudentId
FirstName
LastName
StudentSpouse (FK)

Figure 4.17   Recursive relationship with optional parent

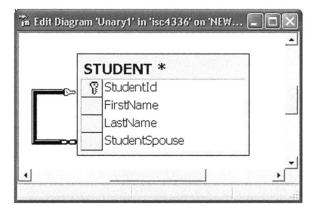

Figure 4.18   Recursive relationship diagram

In the table PREREQUISITE, the CourseId column contains course ids that require other courses. The Prerequisite column contains course ids that are required by the courses in the CourseId column as prerequisites. If a course has no prerequisite, the value in the Prerequisite

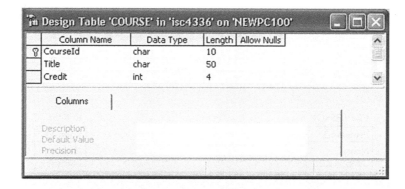

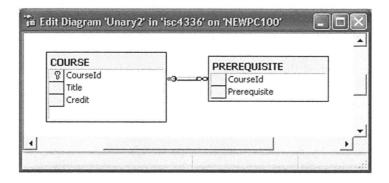

Figure 4.19 **Table designs of (a)** COURSE **and (b)** PREREQUISITE

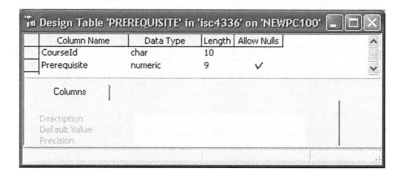

Figure 4.20 **M:N recursive relationship diagram**

column can be set to null. The table designs for COURSE and PREREQ-UISITE are given in Figure 4.19. The diagram for the table representation is shown in Figure 4.20.

6. *Ternary relationship:* Because database designers are more familiar with binary relationships, the binary relationships are often used to represent a ternary relationship. If possible, converting a ternary relationship to binary relationships is a better design. Let us consider the ternary relationship in Figure 4.21.

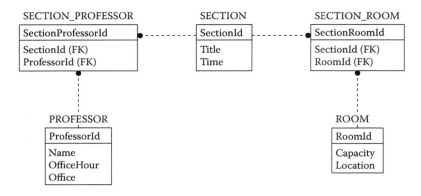

Figure 4.21   Ternary relationship

In this example, assume that there is an M:N relationship between the SECTION entity and the ROOM entity and an M:N relationship between the entities PROFESSOR and SECTION. To implement the M:N relationship between SECTION and PROFESSOR, an intersection table SECTION_PROFESSOR is added. The non-key columns in the SECTION_PROFESSOR table are the foreign keys from the tables SECTION and PROFESSOR. Similarly, an intersection table is added to implement the M:N relationship between SECTION and ROOM.

Given a professor id, we will be able to find the classes (sections) he or she is teaching and the classrooms assigned to her classes. Through the table SECTION_PROFESSOR, we can find the section ids corresponding to the given professor id. From section ids, we can find information about the sections in the SECTION table. In the table SECTION_ROOM, we will be able to find the corresponding classroom ids through the section ids. By using the classroom ids, we can find information about these classrooms in the ROOM table. On the other hand, if we know the classroom id, we can find the corresponding section ids and also find information about the professors who are teaching in that classroom. The designs for these tables are given in Figure 4.22. The diagram representing the ternary relationship is given in Figure 4.23. This ternary relationship is represented by two M:N binary relationships. Not all ternary relationships can be represented by two M:N relationships or 1:N relationships. In those cases, application programs can be used to enforce constraints.

4.4 Enforcing Constraints

Before we can create those tables shown in the previous section, we need to consider adding constraints to them. Suppose we have a database. How can we be sure that the related tables are properly connected? That is, when inserting, updating, and deleting data in one of the tables, the consequence of these activities should not cause malfunction in the other tables. We may need to take some measures to make sure there are no duplicated values in a column that requires unique values. When inserting data into a table, not

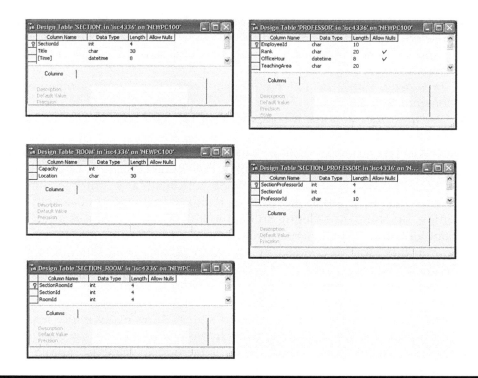

Figure 4.22 Table designs (a), (b), (c), (d), and (e) in ternary relationship

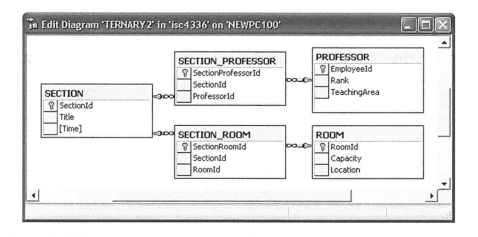

Figure 4.23 Ternary relationship diagram in SQL Server

all of the values are desirable. We need to find a way to restrict the undesirable values from entering the tables. We may also need to implement business policies and regulations in the database. Constraints are used to accomplish these tasks. We can use constraints to protect the integrity of our database, control data values entered in a column, ensure the uniqueness of key columns, and implement business rules. There are four types of commonly used constraints:

- *Relationship constraints:* Enforce referential integrity and cardinality among related tables.
- *Uniqueness constraints:* Ensure that no duplicated values are entered in a column.
- *Domain constraints:* Enforce domain restriction by controlling values entered in a column.
- *Business rules:* Enforce a company's policies and regulations.

There two types of relationship constraints, *integrity constraint* and *cardinality constraint*. Foreign key and primary key constraints are used to implement integrity constraints. Most DBMSs automatically enforce integrity constraints. That is, a DBMS prevents a database management activity such as inserting, updating, or deleting an item in a database if it causes an integrity constraint violation. In SQL Server, when you create a relationship by dragging a column in one table to connect to a corresponding column in another table in a database diagram, a foreign key constraint is automatically placed on the foreign key column corresponding to the column with a primary key or uniqueness constraint in the other table.

A cardinality constraint can be used to specify how many entity instances from one entity are associated with each entity instance in another entity. Most of the cardinality constraints are implemented in database applications. We discuss this type of constraint in later chapters.

Business rules are often implemented in database application programs inasmuch as they are application dependent. In later chapters, we study triggers and stored procedures that can be used to implement business rules.

4.5 Creating Database for Business Process

In this section, we create a database that consists of tables, relationships, and constraints with the graphical tool Enterprise Manager provided by SQL Server. Through step-by-step hands-on practice, you will learn to actually build the database based on a data model developed in Chapter 2. We created the E-R data model of `Hillcrest Computing` in Chapter 2. We revisit the data model, shown in Figure 4.24.

Now we use tables to represent the data model in Figure 4.24. Because the `PART` entity has an identifying relationship with `PART_DETAIL`, we should place `PartId` in the `PART_DETAIL` table. The detailed descriptions of the columns for the tables `PART` and `PART_DETAIL` are given in Tables 4.3 and 4.4, respectively.

When parts are bought from a wholesaler, the part ids are assigned by accountants using a predefined format, for example, NICPCI230 to represent the PCI Network Interface Card with the subtype identification number 230. For more detailed information about the part, we can go to the `PART_DETAIL` table. `ItemId` is simply a sequence number for a specific part. `ItemId` must be used with `PartId` to uniquely identify a part. `PartId` is a foreign key used to connect `PART_DETAIL` to `PART`. The reason to place the attributes

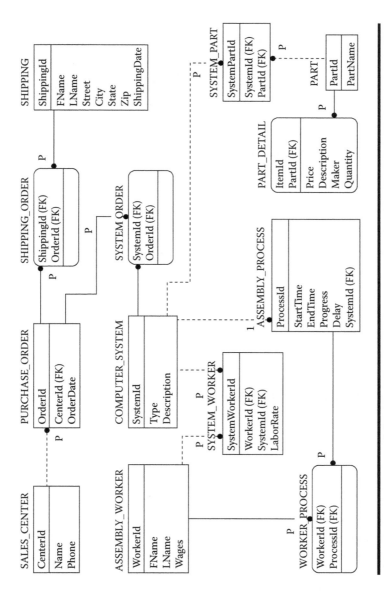

Figure 4.24 E-R model of Hillcrest Computing **business process**

Table 4.3   Column Descriptions for the `PART` **Table**

Column Name	Data Value	PK or FK	Reference Table
PartId	String of characters	PK	
PartName	String of characters		

Table 4.4   Column Descriptions for `PART_DETAIL` **Table**

Column Name	Data Value	PK or FK	Reference Table
PartId	String of characters	PK, FK	PART
ItemId	Numerical identifier	PK	
Quantity	Integer		
Price	Decimal number		
Description	String of characters		
Maker	String of characters		

Table 4.5   Column Descriptions for `SALES_CENTER` **Table**

Column Name	Data Value	PK or FK	Reference Table
CenterId	Numerical identifier	PK	
Name	String of characters		
Phone	String of characters		

Table 4.6   Column Descriptions for `PURCHASE_ORDER` **Table**

Column Name	Data Value	PK or FK	Reference Table
OrderId	String of characters	PK	
CenterId	Numerical identifier	FK	SALES_CENTER
Order_Date	DateTime		

`Price`, `Description`, and `Maker` in the table `PART_DETAIL` is that the same type of part may come from different manufacturers with different prices and descriptions. For the `Quantity` column, a constraint that a value should be greater than or equal to zero can be added, so there will be no negative number in the column.

Similarly, we have the following detailed descriptions for the 1:N relationship between the `SALES_CENTER` table (see Table 4.5) and the `PURCHASE_ORDER` table (see Table 4.6).

Note: In `SALES_CENTER`, the keyword `Name` is used as a column name. Later, if you want to use this column name for queries, you should use brackets

[ ] to enclose it. Although Query Analyzer under SQL Server may allow you to use this column name without brackets, conventionally you should use them to avoid conflicts.

When a purchase order is created, it should include information about the sales center, shipping, computer system ordered, and the order date, so we will know which computer system is ordered from which sales center, where to ship the product, and so on. We place the sales center id in the PURCHASE_ORDER table as a foreign key. For detailed information about the sales center, we need to trace back to the SALES_CENTER table. To get the information about the computer system and shipping, we look at the M:N relationship between PURCHASE_ORDER and COMPUTER_SYSTEM and the M:N relationship between PURCHASE_ORDER and SHIPPING, covered in the following paragraphs.

The PART table has an M:N relationship with COMPUTER_SYSTEM. An intersection table is needed for this M:N relationship. Sometimes, a computer system may use two identical parts, for example, two 20-GB hard drives. Also, the same type of computer system will use the same parts repeatedly. For example, if we are going to assemble 50 notebook systems, then the same type of motherboard will be used 50 times. This means we are going to have 50 identical SystemId and PartId pairs. In this case, the combination (SystemId, PartId) cannot be used as the primary key. We need to add a column SystemPartId and use it as the primary key in the intersection table SYSTEM_PART, where SystemPartId is a surrogate key that contains a sequence of numerical values automatically generated by SQL Server. Thus, every time a part is installed on a system, an identifier is automatically attached to the system and part pair. The detailed column descriptions for the tables SYSTEM_PART and COMPUTER_SYSTEM are given in Tables 4.7 and 4.8, respectively.

Table 4.7 Column Descriptions for SYSTEM_PART **Table**

Column Name	Data Value	PK or FK	Reference Table
SystemPartId	Integer	PK	
SystemId	String of characters	FK	COMPUTER_SYSTEM
PartId	String of characters	FK	PART

Table 4.8 Column Descriptions for COMPUTER_SYSTEM **Table**

Column Name	Data Value	PK or FK	Reference Table
SystemId	String of characters	PK	
Type	String of characters		
Description	String of characters		

Table 4.9   Column Descriptions for SHIPPING

Column Name	Data Value	PK or FK	Reference Table
ShippingId	Numerical identifier	PK	
Lname	String of characters		
Fname	String of characters		
Street	String of characters		
City	String of characters		
State	String of characters		
Zip	String of characters		
ShippingDate	DateTime		

For an M:N relationship, an intersection table stores the ids from both sides of the relationship. For example, to get the information about the parts in a computer system, search the column SystemId in the COMPUTER_SYSTEM table to get the specific system id and find all the PartId values corresponding to that system id in the intersection table SYSTEM_PART. If you want to find which computer systems have a certain part, you need to search the PartId column to obtain the id of that particular part and find the SystemId values that correspond to the same PartId value in the SYSTEM_PART table. To further find the descriptions of these computer systems, you can search the COMPUTER_SYSTEM table to find the descriptions of the computer systems based on the SystemId values obtained from the SYSTEM_PART table.

Similarly, we can develop table representations for the M:N relationships between the COMPUTER_SYSTEM entity and the PURCHASE_ORDER entity, between PURCHASE_ORDER and SHIPPING, between COMPUTER_SYSTEM and ASSEMBLY_WORKER, and between ASSEMBLY_WORKER and ASSEMBLY_PROCESS. The column descriptions for the tables SHIPPING, SHIPPING_ORDER, SYSTEM_ORDER, SYSTEM_WORKER, ASSEMBLY_WORKER, WORKER_PROCESS, and ASSEMBLY_PROCESS are illustrated in Tables 4.9 through 4.15.

There are some redundant address data in the SHIPPING table (see Table 4.9), which could be split into two tables, SHIPPING and ADDRESS. However, it is more convenient to read the information if we keep the shipping address in the SHIPPING table. Therefore, we do not normalize the SHIPPING table, even though there are some redundant data.

In the intersection table SHIPPING_ORDER (see Table 4.10), you can obtain shipping information from a given purchase order. On the other hand, from a given ShippingId value, you can get all the OrderId values for that shipment. These OrderId values can be used to get information about purchase orders.

SYSTEM_ORDER is an intersection table (see Table 4.11) used to connect the COMPUTER_SYSTEM table and the PURCHASE_ORDER table. It can be used to search for information about computer systems on an order list.

Table 4.10   Column Descriptions for SHIPPING_ORDER

Column Name	Data Value	PK or FK	Reference Table
ShippingId	Numerical identifier	PK, FK	SHIPPING
OrderId	String of characters	PK, FK	PURCHASE_ORDER

Table 4.11   Column Descriptions for SYSTEM_ORDER

Column Name	Data Value	PK or FK	Reference Table
SystemId	String of characters	PK, FK	COMPUTER_SYSTEM
OrderId	String of characters	PK, FK	PURCHASE_ORDER

Table 4.12   Column Descriptions for SYSTEM_WORKER

Column Name	Data Value	PK or FK	Reference Table
SystemWorkerId	Integer	PK	
SystemId	String of characters	FK	COMPUTER_SYSTEM
WorkerId	Numerical identifier	FK	ASSEMBLY_WORKER
LaborRate	Money		

The intersection table SYSTEM_WORKER (see Table 4.12) is used to find which workers are involved in assembling which computer systems. The more systems that are assembled per day, the lower the labor cost. This table can be used to calculate the productivity of the assembly workers. You may also be interested in how to calculate the productivity of the sales representatives or accountants. To simplify our case study, let us assume these have been done by the sales department and the accounting department, so that we do not have to include them in this newly created database.

For the SYSTEM_WORKER table, we need to add the primary key column SystemWorkerId due to the fact that the same worker may assemble the same type of computer system many times.

The LaborRate column contains productivity information. It has the ratio of each worker's daily wages divided by the average number of computer systems he or she assembles each day.

The assembly workers' information is stored in the table ASSEMBLY_WORKER (see Table 4.13). Because workers work as a group to complete an assembly process, the workers with higher salaries may take more responsibility assembling the portions that need more skills.

Through the table WORKER_PROCESS (see Table 4.14), you can find information about workers involved in an assembly process. You can also find the progress of an assembly process by looking at the ASSEMBLY_PROCESS table (see Table 4.15). Each day, a group of workers may complete several assembly processes.

Table 4.13   Column Descriptions for ASSEMBLY_WORKER

Column Name	Data Value	PK or FK	Reference Table
WorkerId	Numerical identifier	PK	
Lname	String of characters		
Fname	String of characters		
Wages	Money		

Table 4.14   Column Descriptions for WORKER_PROCESS

Column Name	Data Value	PK or FK	Reference Table
ProcessId	Numerical identifier	PK, FK	ASSEMBLY_PROCESS
WorkerId	Numerical Identifier	PK, FK	ASSEMBLY_WORKER

Table 4.15   Column Descriptions for ASSEMBLY_PROCESS

Column Name	Data Value	PK or FK	Reference Table
ProcessId	Numerical identifier	PK	
StartTime	DateTime		
EndTime	DateTime		
SystemId	String of characters	FK	COMPUTER_SYSTEM
Delay	String of characters		
Progress	String of characters		

There is a 1:1 relationship between the entity ASSEMBLY_PROCESS and the entity COMPUTER_SYSTEM. For the 1:1 relationship, we can either place ProcessId in the COMPUTER_SYSTEM table or place SystemId in the ASSEMBLY_PROCESS table.

Now that the tables are defined, we can implement them in SQL Server and use a diagram to demonstrate the data model.

4.5.1   *Creating the* Hillcrest Computing *Database*

Before creating tables, we need to create a database that is part of the physical implementation process. In the next chapter, you will learn how to create a database with a more general method. Here, to get a quick start, we use a graphical tool that is specific to SQL Server. For the Hillcrest Computing case study, we create a database first. Then we design tables for this database. To create a database, follow the steps below:

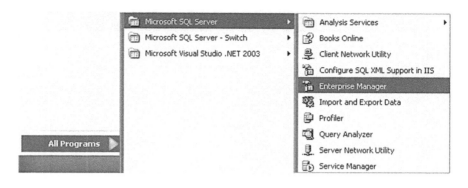

Figure 4.25   Open enterprise manager

1. Click **Enterprise Manager** in the **Microsoft SQL Server** menu, as shown in Figure 4.25.
2. Expand **SQL Server Group** by clicking the **+** sign on the left, and then expand your server node. If SQL Server is installed on your local computer, the name for your server is your local computer's name.
3. Right-click on **Databases**. Choose **New Database** on the pop-up menu to open the **Database Properties** page. Enter the database name, **Hillcrest Computing**, in the **Name** textbox. Click **OK** to close the properties page (see Figure 4.26). Expand the **Databases** node to check if the newly created Hillcrest Computing database is present. If the Hillcrest Computing database is successfully created, you will see its name under the **Databases** node (see Figure 4.27).

4.5.2   Designing Tables

The following steps show you how to design tables in SQL Server. To get started, we first design the table ASSEMBLY_WORKER.

1. Expand the **Hillcrest Computing** node. Right-click the **Table** node. Choose **New Table** on the pop-up menu to start the New Table page.
2. Enter the attributes' names under **Column Name**. For example, type **WorkerId** in the first cell.
3. Press the **Tab** key or click the cell under **Data Type**. Select the **numeric** type for the identifier **WorkerId**. For some columns, you may also need to specify **Length** for the selected data type.
4. To make the column WorkerId the primary key column, highlight the **WorkerId** row and then click the **Set primary key** button on the tool bar to make WorkerId the primary key.
5. Define the other columns based on Table 4.13; the result is shown in Figure 4.28. Click the **Save** button on the tool bar, and you will be prompted to enter the table name. Enter the name **ASSEMBLY_WORKER**, and then click **OK**.

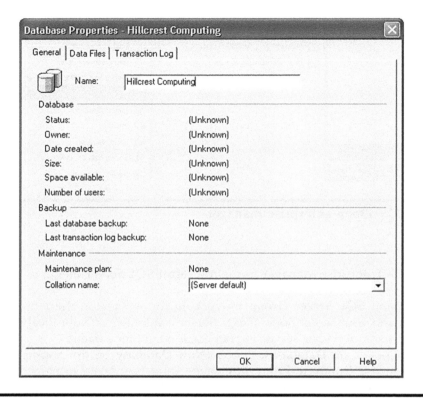

Figure 4.26   Database properties page

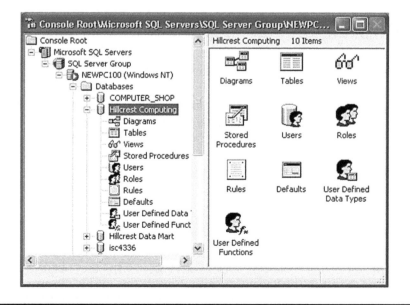

Figure 4.27 `Hillcrest Computing` **database**

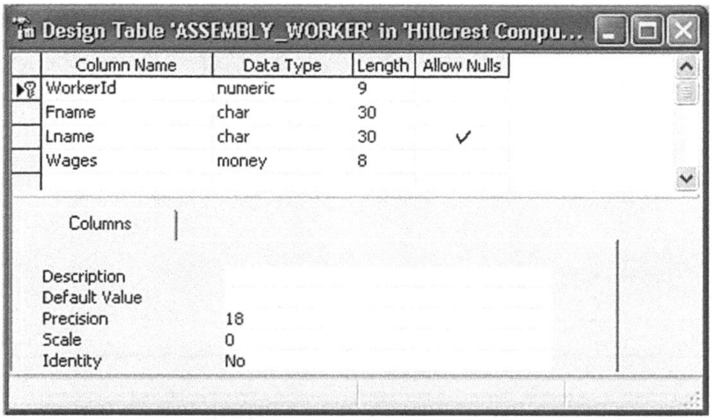

Figure 4.28   Design of ASSEMBLY_WORKER **table**

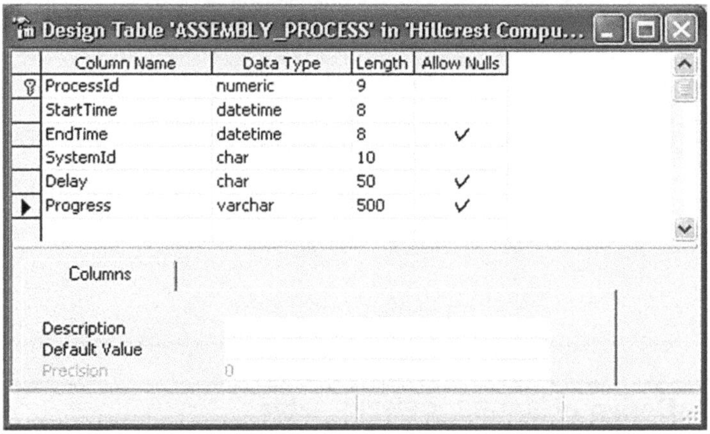

Figure 4.29   Design of ASSEMBLY_PROCESS **table**

Similarly, you can design the tables for the other entities, as shown from Figure 4.29 to Figure 4.38 in this subsection and Figures 4.39 and 4.40 in the next subsection, *Creating Surrogate Keys*.

4.5.3   *Creating Surrogate Keys*

In the SYSTEM_PART table (see Figure 4.39), the data type for the column SystemPartId is *bigint*. The bigint data type allows the column System-PartId to be configured as an identity column to which an id value will be automatically inserted when a new row is added to the table. Set the **Identity** property to **Yes**, **Identity Seed** to **1**, and **Identity Increment** to **1**. Similarly, the table SYSTEM_WORKER, which also needs a surrogate key, is defined in Figure 4.40.

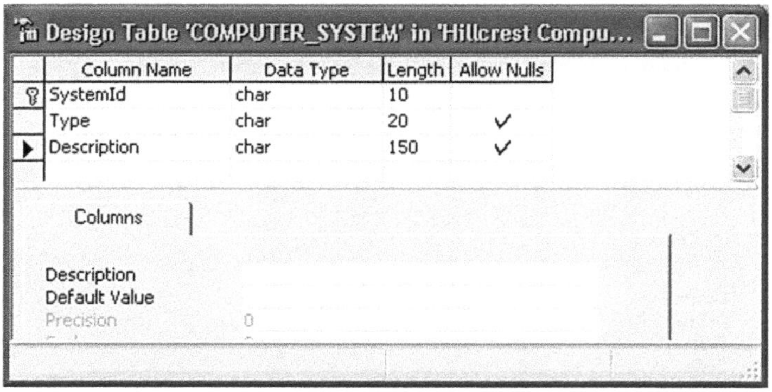

Figure 4.30   Design of COMPUTER_SYSTEM **table**

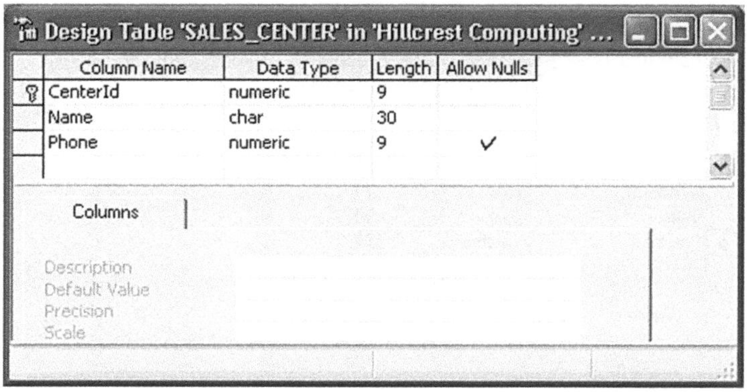

Figure 4.31   Design of SALES_CENTER **table**

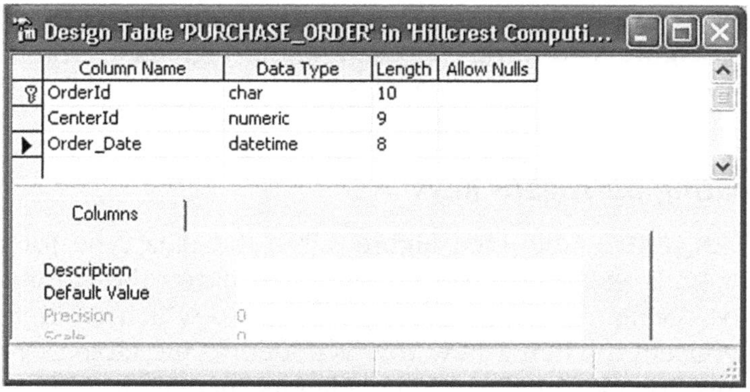

Figure 4.32   Design of PURCHASE_ORDER **table**

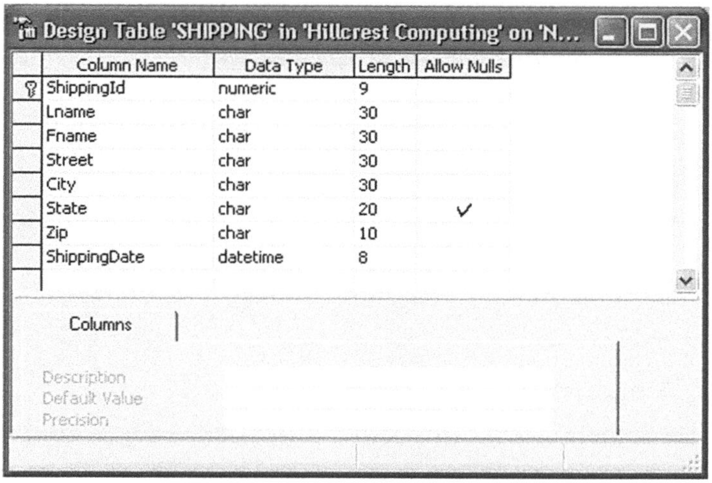

Figure 4.33   Design of `SHIPPING` **table**

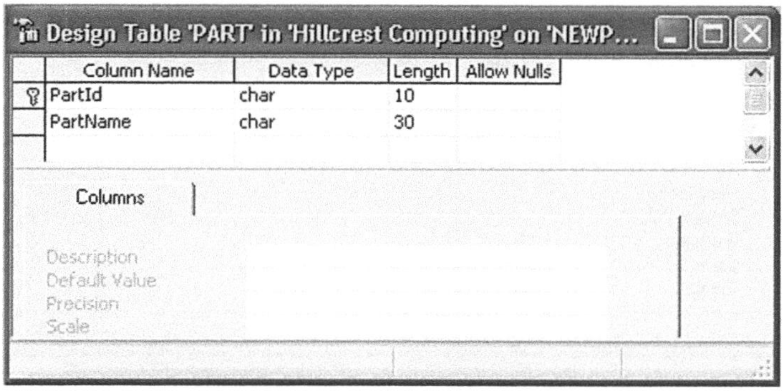

Figure 4.34   Design of `PART` **table**

4.5.4   Enforcing Constraints

To learn how to enforce a domain constraint, you may create a **CHECK** constraint by following the steps below. As an example, we are going to add a constraint to a column. Let us modify the column Quantity in the table `PART_DETAIL` by adding a constraint that will make the column accept only zero or positive values (see Figure 4.41).

    1. Right-click on the table **PART_DETAIL**, and select **Design Table**.
    2. In the Design Table window, right-click on the column **Quantity**, and then select **Check Constraints** on the pop-up menu. Click the **New** button. Type the constraint **Quantity >= 0** in the textbox under the label **Constraint expression**, and close the **Properties** dialog.

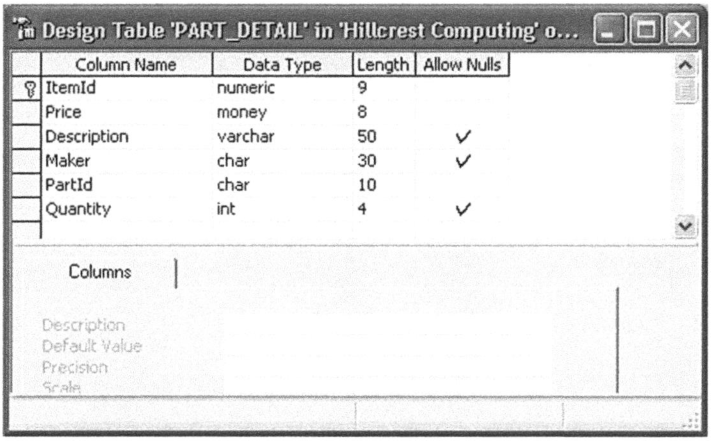

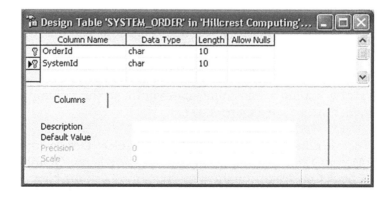

Figure 4.35   Design of `PART_DETAIL` **table**

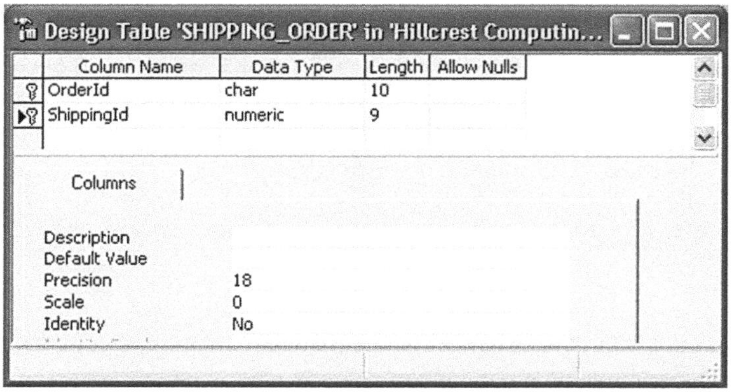

Figure 4.36   Design of `SHIPPING_ORDER` **table**

Figure 4.37   Design of `SYSTEM_ORDER` **table**

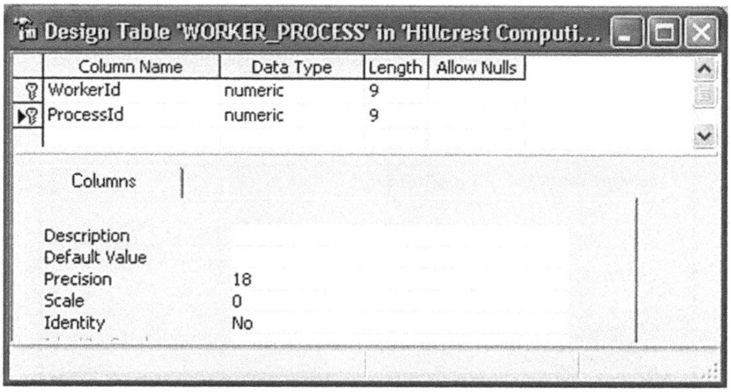

Figure 4.38 Design of `WORKER_PROCESS` **table**

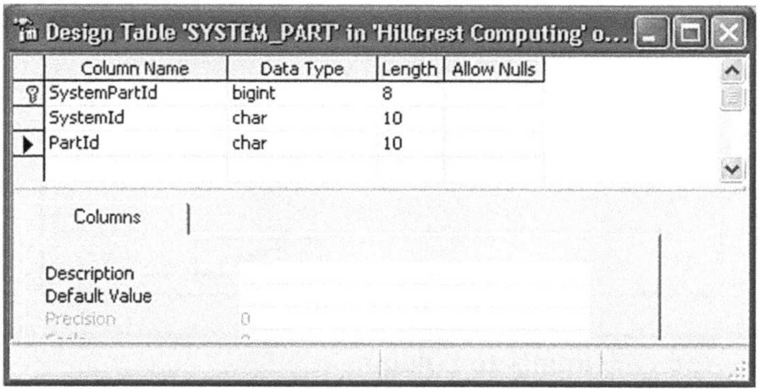

Figure 4.39 Design of `SYSTEM_PART` **table**

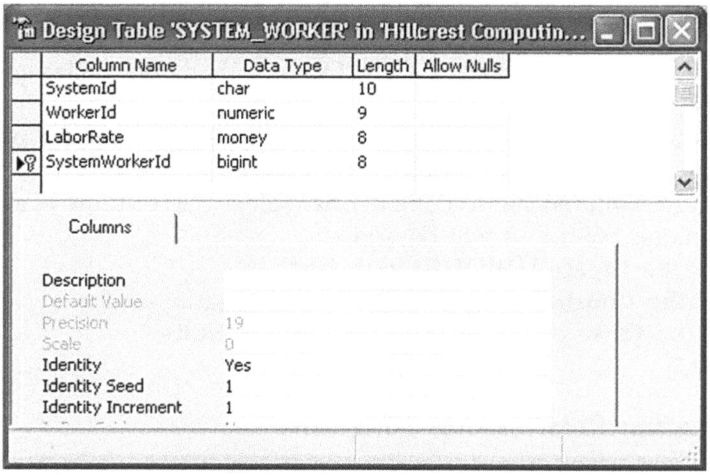

Figure 4.40 Design of `SYSTEM_WORKER` **table**

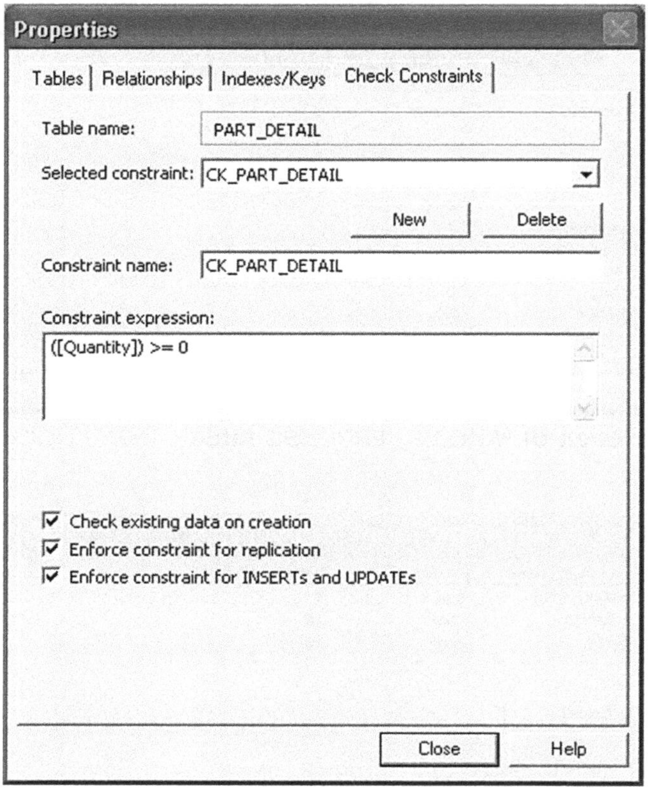

Figure 4.41   Add constraints to column

You can also create a unique constraint on a column that is not a primary key. For example, you can enforce the unique constraint for the column Name in the table SALES_CENTER (see Figure 4.42). Follow the steps below to add a unique constraint in SQL Server Enterprise Manager:

1. Right-click the table **SALES_CENTER**, and then select **Design Table** from the pop-up menu.
2. Right-click on the column **Name**. Select **Indexes/Keys** from the pop-up menu.
3. Click the **New** button and enter the new index name.
4. From the **Column name** combo box, select the column **Name** to which the unique constraint will be added.
5. Check the **Create UNIQUE** check box.
6. Select the **Constraint** option, as shown in Figure 4.42.
7. Click the **Close** button and uncheck **Allow Nulls**.

4.5.5   Creating Relationship Diagrams

Now we create a diagram that will display all the relationships for the database Hillcrest Computing in SQL Server. The diagram created here will match the E-R data model displayed in Figure 4.24.

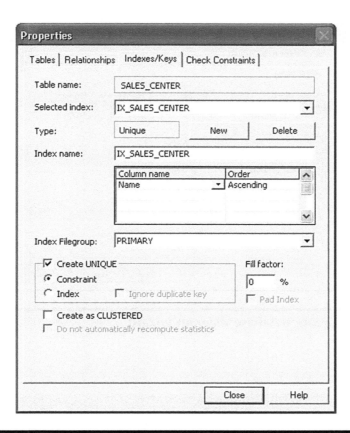

Figure 4.42   Create unique constraint

1. Under the `Hillcrest Computing` database node, right-click **Diagrams**; then select **New Database Diagram** to start the **Create Database Diagram Wizard**.
2. Click **Next** to move to the **Select Tables to be Added** screen, where we will add the tables to the diagram, as shown in Figure 4.43.
3. Add all the tables defined for the database `Hillcrest Computing` to the **Tables to add to diagram** pane on the right-hand side. Go to the next page and click **Finish**.
4. After we rearrange the tables to the proper positions, we will click on the identifier from the one-side of the 1:N relationship and then hold the mouse and drag it to the corresponding column in the many-side of the relationship. For example, for the 1:N relationship between SALES_CENTER and PURCHASE_ORDER, click the column **CenterId** in the **SALES_CENTER** table, and then hold the mouse and drag the mouse pointer to the column **CenterId** in the **PURCHASE_ORDER** table. On the diagram, the one-side of the relationship is represented by the key pointer, and the many-side of the 1:N relationship is represented by the ∞ sign. For a 1:1 relationship, the key is on both sides of the relationship. The SQL Server diagram for the E-R data model of the database `Hillcrest Computing` is displayed in Figure 4.44.

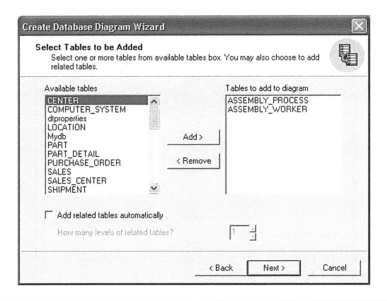

Figure 4.43   Create database diagram wizard

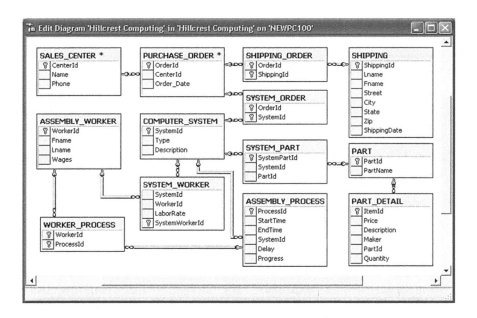

Figure 4.44   Diagram of `Hillcrest Computing` **database**

By comparing this diagram with that in Figure 4.24, you can see that we have converted the E-R data model to a collection of related tables. In the next chapter, you will learn how to populate the tables with data. After that, our first basic database will have been physically implemented.

4.6 Summary

In this chapter, we have discussed and implemented database design. First, we discussed the selection of a DBMS system. The DBMS we selected is SQL Server. To materialize the data model created in Chapter 2, we first designed the tables in SQL Server to represent the entities. We examined the naming convention and data types for defining tables. Surrogate keys were created to allow SQL Server to automatically create a sequence of numerical values as the primary key. Diagrams have been created in SQL Server to represent the relationships in the E-R models. These diagrams were used to represent identifying relationships, nonidentifying relationships, nonspecific relationships, categorization relationships, recursive relationships, and ternary relationships. We also discussed constraint types and practiced how to enforce constraints in SQL Server. As an example, we developed the table representations and the database diagram for the `Hillcrest Computing` business process.

Review Questions

1. What type of DBMS is good for single users?
2. What are the advantages of SQL Server?
3. How does Oracle meet the needs of large companies?
4. What factors should be considered when selecting a DBMS?
5. What are the tasks in the database design and creation process?
6. List the naming rules in SQL Server.
7. Why do you need to use the delimiter " " or [ ]?
8. When a name starts with the symbol #, what does the symbol represent?
9. What is the range for values in the decimal data type?
10. What type of data represents image?
11. Describe the data type of money.
12. What is the default length for the varchar data type?
13. What is identity?
14. State the meaning of precision.
15. What is scale?
16. Use an example to explain how to represent an identifying relationship in table notation.
17. Use an example to explain how to represent a nonidentifying relationship in table notation.
18. When N is equal to one, how can you represent a nonidentifying relationship between the tables?
19. Use an example to represent a nonspecific relationship with table notation.
20. Use an example to explain how to represent a categorization relationship in table notation.
21. Describe the difficulties when representing a categorization relationship in tables.
22. When should a categorization relationship be implemented with tables?
23. How do you represent a recursive relationship with tables?

24. How do you represent an M:N recursive relationship with tables?
25. Use an example to explain how to represent a ternary relationship in table notation.
26. What are the four types of constraints?
27. What are the functions of an integrity constraint? How do you implement an integrity constraint?

Case Study Projects

After you have created the data models and performed the normalization process, it is time to represent the data models with tables in a selected DBMS. For the following projects, you need SQL Server Enterprise Manager.

1. Computer Service

For the data model of Awesome Computer Service created in the previous chapters, complete the following tasks:

- Convert the entities in your data model to tables in a database called `Computer_Service` in SQL Server. Also, create constraints, if any, for the columns in each table.
- Create a surrogate key for the SERVICES table.
- Create a database diagram with SQL Server Enterprise Manager for the tables in your database.

2. University Registration

Represent the University Registration data model with the following steps:

- Convert the entities in your data model to tables in a database called `Registration` with SQL Server. Add constraints, if any, to the columns in the tables.
- Create a surrogate key for the table ENROLLMENT.
- Use SQL Server Enterprise Manager to create a database diagram for the tables in your database.

3. Mail Order

To represent the Mail Order data model, perform the following tasks:

- By using SQL Server, convert the entities in your data model to tables in a database called `Mail_Order`. Add constraints, if any, to the columns in the tables.
- For the table ORDERS, create a surrogate key as its primary key column.
- Represent the tables with a database diagram in SQL Server Enterprise Manager.

Chapter 5

Physical Design and Database Implementation with SQL

Objectives

- Learn about issues that need to be addressed in physical design.
- Familiarize yourself with Structured Query Language (SQL).
- Use SQL to implement relational databases.
- Manage and manipulate database objects.
- Import and export database data.

5.1 Introduction

In the previous chapter, we discussed how to transform a data model developed in logical design to a relational database. For most database projects, it is not wise to just physically install the selected DBMS on a PC and hope everything will come out exactly as you expected. As business grows, sooner or later you will find that there is not enough space in your server computer to add another hard drive, your server is not powerful enough to handle data transactions, or the database users are not able to access the data stored on your database. Sometimes, it is too costly or too late for you to start all over again. To successfully implement your database to meet the business requirements, some additional design issues need to be addressed. In this chapter, we perform the following database implementation tasks:

- Investigating issues in physical design
- Creating and modifying database structure in a DBMS

- Specifying data and integrity constraints
- Allocating storage space (often required for mainframe DBMS products)
- Importing data into and exporting data from a database

We first consider some physical design issues, such as specifying I/O and storage devices and why, as a database designer, you should care about these issues. We investigate what type of server to be used to hold the storage devices, how to import and export data, where to store the data, and how to enforce security measures on the database server. Some authentication issues are also introduced in this chapter. To successfully carry out these tasks, we introduce a powerful tool, *Structured Query Language* (SQL), which is used to create, control, and modify database objects. We use SQL to create and manage database objects, implement some security measures on those database objects, and import data into or export data from those database objects. The last part of this chapter is about copying and pasting databases.

5.2 Physical Design

At the stage of physical design, the goal is to make the database meet the business requirements physically. Therefore, we need to consider the following issues:

- Database system architecture
- Data type and size
- Database accessing
- Data usage

5.2.1 Database System Architecture

Before the database can be implemented, it is important to get the whole picture into which the future database will fit. As a database designer, you need to know if the system architecture is a Web-based system, a three-tier client/server system, or another type of system. If the database is network-based, you need to find out what the network limitation is. You also need to be aware of the budgetary limitation for the current database project.

5.2.2 Data Type and Size

The selected hardware should have a large-enough capacity to hold the existing data and to handle future data growth. The best way to decide on the hardware is to interview the key players in the business process. As a database designer, you need to find information related to data size, such as how large the existing data sets are, what the annual growth rate is, if there is an upper bound for the data growth, and how long the data have to be stored in the database. You also need to know the types of data to be stored in the database. Some types of data such as BLOB may require more storage space than other types. Based on the obtained information, you can figure out what the necessary hard drive capacity, CPU speed, and RAM size should be.

5.2.3 Database Accessing

From business requirements, you can learn how database users access the database. The users may access the database through the Internet or a local area network. Find out what interfaces are used for data accessing from the client side. If the data are accessed through a Graphic User Interface (GUI), more powerful front-end personal computers are needed. Find out if the data will be shared by different types of database applications or computer systems. If so, what data-accessing requirements and what types of data conversion software should be installed? Are there any types of data other than relational database data that need to communicate with the database? If so, what software and hardware should be used to fulfill the communication need?

5.2.4 Data Usage

The decision on the selection of hardware depends on how many users will be using the database, how many users will simultaneously log on to the database, and time requirements for operations. It is also helpful if you can find out how data are used in the business process, for example, whether data are used for decision support or for data transaction. From data transaction records, you may find data usage information such as the frequency of transactions per day and the data usage trend. You should find out from the business requirements how valuable the data are. For valuable data, extra equipment should be added for data protection. Data security is another important issue to be addressed. You need to find out which groups of users are allowed to access what kinds of data and what hardware and software should be added to protect the data. Also, to protect the data from operation failure, additional equipment should be added for database replication and backup.

Before you physically implement your database, make a checklist of the above questions. Make some effort to get the answers. Remember the famous saying, "Failure to plan is a plan to fail."

5.3 Creating, Controlling, and Modifying Database Objects with SQL

To implement, query, and manage the databases designed earlier, we need tools to handle these tasks. It is nice to know that some of the DBMS products, such as SQL Server, provide graphical tools to help us create databases and design tables. However, each DBMS product has its own graphical tools and other DBMS products cannot share them. A more portable solution is to use Structured Query Language. This query language can be used to implement and manipulate database information. You can use SQL statements to create databases, tables, and views; you can insert, update, and delete records in a table; and you can also define constraints to maintain database integrity. Since the early 1970s, SQL has been a primary tool in database development. In this chapter, the databases are implemented by SQL.

As SQL became more and more popular as a database development tool, the American National Standards Institute (ANSI) published the standard for SQL. The latest version is SQL-92. The ANSI-based SQL is a very basic SQL language that contains about 30 commands. Various vendors have made different extensions on top of the basic ANSI-based SQL. In SQL Server, the extended SQL language is called Transact-SQL, which supports three types of commands:

- *Data Definition Language (DDL):* Used to manage databases, tables, attributes, and properties of a database. The most-often used DDL commands are:
  - **CREATE:** Used to create database objects such as tables, users, or views.
  - **ALTER:** Used to modify database objects.
  - **DROP:** Used to delete database objects.
- *Data Control Language (DCL):* Used to control permissions on database objects. The most common DCL commands are:
  - **GRANT:** Used to permit a user to use a database or execute some SQL commands.
  - **REVOKE:** Used to remove previously granted permissions.
- *Data Manipulation Language (DML):* Used to select, insert, update, and delete data in a database object. The most often used DML commands are:
  - **SELECT:** Used to select information from a database. Columns are selected from database tables or views.
  - **INSERT:** Used to insert rows into database tables.
  - **UPDATE:** Used to modify rows in database tables.
  - **DELETE:** Used to delete rows in database tables.

Although different vendors have extended SQL-92, the difference is minor. It will not take too much effort for users to change from one version of SQL to another version. There are many different DBMS packages on the market. Learning SQL is particularly important for those who will work with multiple DBMS products.

More specifically, in this section, SQL Query Analyzer, a built-in utility in SQL Server, is used to enter, debug, and execute the SQL statements. We use SQL statements to create database objects such as users, tables, and views. After they are created, we grant permissions for some of the objects. We also modify the structures of tables with SQL statements.

5.3.1 *Creating Database Objects*

Creating Databases

Before we can create database objects such as tables, we must first create a database to contain the tables. In SQL Server, you can use **Create Database Wizard** to create a database. Most DBMS vendors also use the SQL statement

CREATE DATABASE to create it. As we have mentioned before, for better portability, we use Data Definition Language (DDL) to create databases, tables, and the other database objects. For example, if you want to create the Student_Club database with the initial size of 2 MB and the maximum size of 10 MB, and want the database file to be saved to student_club.mdf, you can use the following statement in SQL Server:

```
CREATE DATABASE Student_Club
ON
(
   NAME = Student_Club,
   FILENAME = 'c:\program files\Microsoft SQL
      Server\mssql\data\Student_Club.mdf ',
   SIZE = 2,
   MAXSIZE = 10,
   FILEGROWTH = 1
)
```

SQL statements are not case sensitive. We use capital letters to indicate keywords or table names for clarity. After executing the command, we will be able to add tables to the database.

Defining Data Types

For each attribute in a table, we must specify its data type when creating a table. The example below shows how to define commonly used data types in SQL Server.

1. *Character data types:* Character data consist of any combination of letters, symbols, and numeric characters.
   a. CHAR: fixed-length character data. Example: To define the column Club_Name of CHAR data type with length 30, use

   ```
   Club_Name CHAR(30)
   ```

   b. VARCHAR: variable-length character data. Example: To define the attribute Description of VARCHAR data type with maximum length of 300, use

   ```
   Description VARCHAR(300)
   ```

   A column with VARCHAR data type has a variable length. This means that there is no wasted storage space. On the other hand, a column with CHAR data type may have many blank spaces if the fixed-length column has many values that will not fill up the column width. However, with the fixed-length, a column of CHAR can be processed faster.
2. *Number data types:* Number data types include integers and decimals.
   a. INT: The integer data type consists of positive, zero, and negative whole numbers. The range of INT is from –2,147,483,648 to 2,147,483,647. Usually, INT is used for id numbers. Example: To define the integer type column SID, use

```
SID INT
```

   b. DECIMAL (or NUMERIC): DECIMAL is used for the positive and negative decimal numbers. Example: To define the decimal type column Rate, use

```
Rate DECIMAL
```

3. *Date and time data type:* This type is used for date and time combinations.
   a. DATETIME: It represents date and time from 1–1–1753 to 12–31–9999. Example: To define the date and time data type column Start_Time, use

```
Start_Time DATETIME
```

4. *Monetary data type:* This type is used to show amounts of money.
   a. MONEY: MONEY represents money values. Example: To define the money data type column Cost, use

```
Cost MONEY
```

For the definitions of other data types, please refer to SQL Server Help.

Creating Tables

Now it is time to create some tables in the database Student_Club. In Chapter 3, we developed several entities for the database Student_Club. To create tables representing these entities, we take a closer look at the table representations for these entities. The following are the tables developed from the conceptual design (see Tables 5.1 to 5.8), with corresponding table notations:

```
CLUB(ClubName, MembershipFee)
Key: ClubName
MENTOR(MentorName, SkillId)
Key: MentorName
STUDENT(SID, StudentName)
Key: SID
SERVICE(Duty, SkillId)
Key: Duty
SKILL(SkillId, SkillName)
Key: SkillId
```

There are several intersection tables used to represent the M:N relationships (see Tables 5.6 through 5.8).

```
STUDENT_CLUB(SID, ClubName, EnrollDate)
Key: SID, ClubName
```

In the intersection table STUDENT_CLUB, the combination primary key is (SID, ClubName). The columns SID and Club_Name are also foreign keys.

To connect the STUDENT and SERVICE tables and enforce the constraint that (SID, Duty, Club) is unique, use the intersection table STUDENT_SERVICE as defined below and shown in Table 5.7:

Table 5.1   Column Descriptions for CLUB **Table**

Column Name	Data Type	PK or FK	Reference Table
ClubName	CHAR(30)	PK	
MembershipFee	MONEY		

Table 5.2   Column Descriptions for MENTOR **Table**

Column Name	Data Type	PK or FK	Reference Table
MentorName	CHAR(30)	PK	
SkillId	INT	FK	SKILL

Table 5.3   Column Descriptions for STUDENT **Table**

Column Name	Data Type	PK or FK	Reference Table
SID	INT(4)	PK	
StudentName	CHAR(20)		

Table 5.4   Column Descriptions for SERVICE **Table**

Column Name	Data Type	PK or FK	Reference Table
Duty	CHAR(30)	PK	
SkillId	INT	FK	SKILL

Table 5.5   Column Descriptions for SKILL **Table**

Column Name	Data Type	PK or FK	Reference Table
SkillId	INT	PK	
SkillName	CHAR(30)		

Table 5.6   Column Descriptions for STUDENT_CLUB **Table**

Column Name	Data Type	PK or FK	Reference Table
SID	INT(4)	PK, FK	STUDENT
ClubName	CHAR(20)	PK, FK	CLUB
EnrollDate	DATETIME		

Table 5.7   Column Descriptions for STUDENT_SERVICE **Table**

Column Name	Data Type	PK or FK	Reference Table
ClubName	CHAR(30)	PK, FK	CLUB
SID	INT(4)	PK, FK	STUDENT
Duty	CHAR(30)	PK, FK	SERVICE

Table 5.8   Column Descriptions for STUDENT_MENTOR **Table**

Column Name	Data Type	PK or FK	Reference Table
SID	INT	PK, FK	STUDENT
MentorName	CHAR(30)	PK, FK	MENTOR

```
STUDENT_SERVICE(ClubName, SID, Duty)
Key: (SID, Duty, ClubName)
```

All three columns in STUDENT_SERVICE are combined as the combination key. In the intersection table STUDENT_MENTOR, SID and MentorName are foreign keys (see the following notations and Table 5.8).

```
STUDENT_MENTOR(SID, MentorName)
Key: SID, MentorName
```

When creating database objects, try not to use the DBMS reserved keywords as an object's name, such as the keywords ORDER, NAME, TRANSACTION. If you have to use a keyword as your database object name, enclose the name with the square brackets [ ] or with " ". After the tables have been specified, we can use the CREATE TABLE statement to create them. The following SQL statements show you how to define tables with primary constraints:

```
CREATE TABLE CLUB
(
   ClubName CHAR(30) PRIMARY KEY,
   MembershipFee MONEY
)
CREATE TABLE SKILL
(
   SkillId INT PRIMARY KEY,
   SkillName CHAR(30)
)
CREATE TABLE STUDENT
(
   SID INT PRIMARY KEY,
   StudentName CHAR(20)
)
```

The keyword PRIMARY KEY indicates that a column is defined as the primary key. The keyword CONSTRAINT can also be used to define the constraints such as *primary key constraint, foreign key constraint, table constraint*, and *value constraint* for columns. Using the keyword CONSTRAINT is particularly useful in defining an *integrity constraint* that consists of a pair of primary key and foreign key constraints.

To define a foreign key constraint with the keyword CONSTRAINT, you can use the following syntax:

```
CONSTRAINT constraint_name FOREIGN KEY (column_name)
   REFERENCES Table_where_the_primary_key_comes_from
   (primary_key_column)
```

Usually, the word xxx_fk is used for the name of the foreign key constraint. The keyword FOREIGN KEY indicates that the constraint is a type of foreign key. The keyword REFERENCES specifies the name of the host table where its primary key column is used as the foreign key column in the current table. To learn how to use the keyword CONSTRAINT to define a foreign key column, see the creation of the tables with foreign key constraints listed below:

```
CREATE TABLE MENTOR
(
   MentorName CHAR(30) PRIMARY KEY,
   SkillId INT,
   CONSTRAINT Mentor_SkillId_fk FOREIGN KEY (SkillId)
      REFERENCES SKILL (SkillId)
)
CREATE TABLE SERVICE
(
   Duty CHAR(30) PRIMARY KEY,
   SkillId INT,
   CONSTRAINT Service_SkillId_fk FOREIGN KEY (SkillId)
      REFERENCES SKILL (SkillId)
)
```

If the primary key column is referenced by a FOREIGN KEY constraint in another table, its content cannot be deleted. If you really need to delete the content in a column referenced by other tables, you must delete the FOREIGN KEY constraint first.

Another way to specify a column as the primary key is to use the keyword CONSTRAINT. The syntax for defining a primary key by using the keyword CONSTRAINT is given below:

```
CONSTRAINT constraint_name PRIMARY KEY
   (column_name, ..., column_name)
```

If a table has a primary key that consists of multiple columns, using the keyword CONSTRAINT will allow us to define a combination primary key. To illustrate the use of the keyword CONSTRAINT, consider the creation of the STUDENT_CLUB table:

```
CREATE TABLE STUDENT_CLUB
(
   SID INT,
   ClubName CHAR(30),
   EnrollDate DATETIME,
   CONSTRAINT Club_ClubName_fk FOREIGN KEY (ClubName)
      REFERENCES CLUB (ClubName),
   CONSTRAINT Student_SID_fk FOREIGN KEY (SID)
      REFERENCES STUDENT (SID),
   CONSTRAINT SID_ClubName_pk PRIMARY KEY (SID, ClubName)
)
```

Also, for the table STUDENT_SERVICE, you can define a combination primary key as shown below:

```
CREATE TABLE STUDENT_SERVICE
(
   ClubName CHAR(30),
   SID INT,
   Duty CHAR(30),
   CONSTRAINT Club_ClubName_fk1 FOREIGN KEY (ClubName)
      REFERENCES CLUB (ClubName),
   CONSTRAINT Student_SID_fk FOREIGN KEY (SID)
      REFERENCES STUDENT (SID),
   CONSTRAINT Service_Duty_fk FOREIGN KEY (Duty)
      REFERENCES SERVICE (Duty),
   CONSTRAINT ClubName_SID_Duty_pk PRIMARY KEY (ClubName,
      SID, Duty)
)
```

The combination primary key can also be used for the table STUDENT_MENTOR:

```
CREATE TABLE STUDENT_MENTOR
(
   SID INT,
   MentorName CHAR(30),
   CONSTRAINT Mentor_MentorName_fk FOREIGN KEY (MentorName)
      REFERENCES MENTOR (MentorName),
   CONSTRAINT Student_SID_fk FOREIGN KEY (SID)
      REFERENCES STUDENT (SID),
   CONSTRAINT SID_MentorName_pk PRIMARY KEY (SID, MentorName)
)
GO
```

In the above SQL statement, GO is used to signal the end of a group of SQL commands, but it is not a SQL command itself. Here, it is used to separate a CREATE TABLE statement from other SQL statements. The use of GO is optional.

In addition to the primary key and foreign key constraints, there are other types of constraints. To define value constraints that check the range of values, use

```
CONSTRAINT constraint_name CHECK( ( value > lower_bound )
   AND ( value < upper_bound ))
```

The AND keyword is used to check if both of the two constraints are true before returning a "True" value.

Creating Views

Similar to creating tables, the keyword CREATE can also be used to create other database objects such as views, indexes, and users. A view is a database object composed of columns that may come from different tables. Often, views are used to implement database applications for end users. An *index* is used to improve performance in sorting and data accessing. It can also be used to set a unique constraint for some columns. A *user* object can define database user profiles. The following statement can be used to create a view from two tables:

```
CREATE VIEW view_name
AS
SELECT T1.column_name, …, T2.column_name
FROM table_name1 T1 JOIN table_name2 T2
ON T1.column_from_first_table = T2.column_from_second_table
```

At this point, you have seen SQL statements used to create databases, tables, and views. Next, you will learn how to enter and execute the SQL statements in SQL Server.

Creating Database Objects in Query Analyzer

SQL Server provides a utility tool, Query Analyzer, that is convenient for executing SQL statements. We use SQL statements to create the Student_Club database tables in Query Analyzer. To do so, click **Query Analyzer** in the **Microsoft SQL Server** menu, as shown in Figure 5.1.

After clicking Query Analyzer, you will be prompted to enter the SQL Server name; by default, this is your computer host name. (You can find the host name by going to **Control Panel**, **System**, and clicking the **Computer Name**

Figure 5.1   Open Query Analyzer

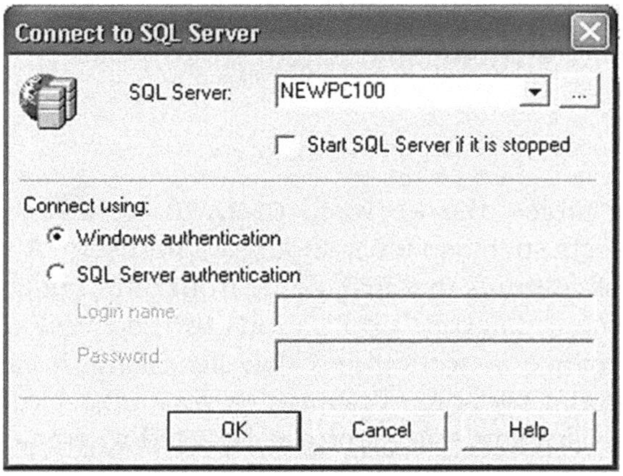

Figure 5.2 Connect to SQL Server

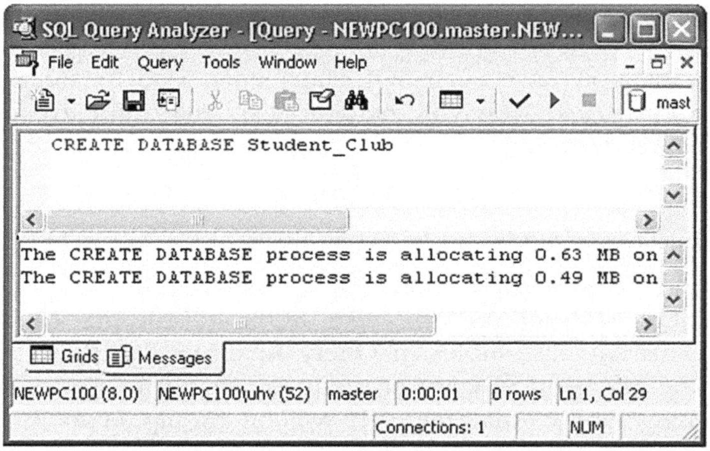

Figure 5.3 Create `Student_Club` database

tab.) Enter the computer name and make sure that **Windows authentication** is selected if you are working on the same computer where the database server is currently installed. If you are working in a client/server environment and you need to log on to the database server from different computers, select **SQL Server authentication**. In Figure 5.2, we have selected **Windows authentication**. Click **OK** to open **Query Analyzer**.

Note: If you try to log on to a remote server, enter the server name in the **SQL Sever** combo box, check the **SQL Server authentication** option, and then enter the log-in name and password.

The next step is to enter the statement to create the **Student_Club** database. After the statement is entered, click the **Execute Query** button ▶ on the tool bar, or press the **F5** key. The execution result is given in the lower pane, as shown in Figure 5.3.

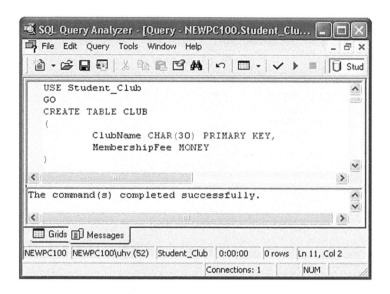

Figure 5.4   Create CLUB **table**

After you have successfully created the database Student_Club, you can add tables in it. Type **USE Student_Club** to indicate that tables will be created in the Student_Club database, and then enter the **CREATE TABLE** statement, as shown in Figure 5.4.

To execute the SQL statement, you can either press the **F5** key or click the **Execute Query** button ▶ on the tool bar. Similarly, you can create the tables SKILL and STUDENT. Then create tables MENTOR and SERVICE. Last, create tables STUDENT_CLUB, STUDENT_SERVICE, and STUDENT_MENTOR. Make sure that you create the tables in the above order so that the foreign key columns in the tables created later can reference the primary key columns in the tables previously created. Figure 5.5 shows how to implement a primary key that consists of multiple columns.

To verify that the database and all the tables have been successfully created, click **Enterprise Manager** in Microsoft SQL Server and expand the **Databases** tree. You should see the database Student_Club. Expand the **Student_Club** node, and you should see all the tables created by the SQL commands. In Figure 5.6, the owner of these tables is **dbo**, the database owner. The user who created the database is a dbo. As a dbo, the user has the permission to perform all activities in the database. A dbo user is present in every database and cannot be deleted.

If errors occur, check the spelling and the definition of the statement where the errors occur. After the correction, highlight the modified CREATE command, and then click the **Execute Query** button on the tool bar to run the CREATE command again.

SQL Server provides you with graphical tools to create database objects such as tables and automatically allocates storage space for these objects. However, the graphical tools may not be available for some of the DBMS products. In such a case, you need to create database objects and allocate

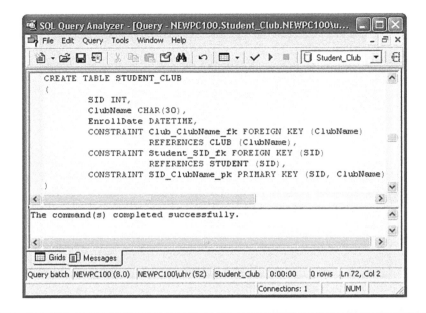

Figure 5.5   Create `STUDENT_CLUB` **table with combination primary key**

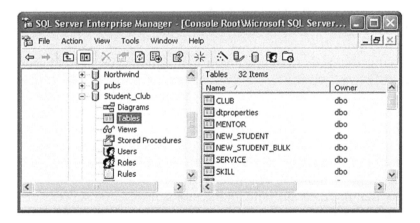

Figure 5.6   Tables created by SQL commands

storage space through SQL statements. When allocating storage for a database structure manually, an allocation plan must be carefully carried out. The allocation will be based on information such as whether a data file is a system file or nonsystem file, the life span of data files, and the degree of the data files' fragmentation. You need to place the data files on different disks if they have different life spans or different fragmentation propensities. Do the same for the system files and nonsystem files.

5.3.2 Modifying Database Objects

After the tables have been created, the tables can be viewed and modified by SQL commands and stored procedures. You will see some examples for

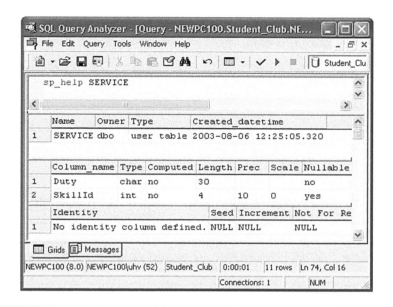

Figure 5.7   Use stored procedure to obtain table definition

these operations. For more detailed descriptions, please refer to SQL Server Help. To view the table properties, you can use SQL Server Enterprise Manager or the following stored procedures or command in SQL Server:

- `sp_help`: A built-in stored procedure used to view table definitions
- `sp_depends`: A built-in stored procedure used to view table dependencies
- `COLUMNPROPERTY`: a command used to return information about columns in a database

After you enter the `sp_help` statement in the Query Analyzer, you will have the results shown in Figure 5.7.

The syntax of COLUMNPROPERTY is given as

`COLUMNPROPERTY (id, column, property)`

where the arguments are defined as below:

- *Id:* The identifier of a table or procedure
- *Column:* The name of the column or parameter
- *Property:* The column property information to be returned

An example of using `COLUMNPROPERTY` is given in Figure 5.8. To return the column property, you need the `SELECT` statement, which can be used to specify the column to be obtained.

Often you need to modify the original table structure, such as changing the length of a column, renaming a column or a table, modifying constraints, adding new columns, or changing the data type of a column. The `ALTER`

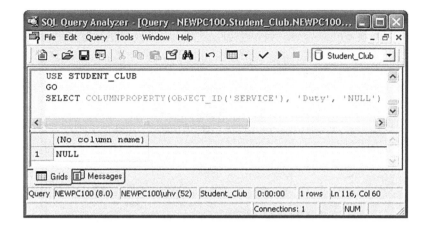

Figure 5.8   Use COLUMNPROPERTY **to obtain column information**

TABLE statement is used to change the table structure. For example, if you did not set the primary key in the SERVICE table, you can add a primary key constraint to the column Duty by using the following SQL statement:

```
ALTER TABLE SERVICE ADD
  CONSTRAINT Duty_pk PRIMARY KEY (Duty)
```

If you do not have a foreign key in the STUDENT_MENTOR table, you can add one with an ALTER TABLE statement. For example, you can add a foreign key to the column MentorName in the table STUDENT_MENTOR:

```
ALTER TABLE STUDENT_MENTOR ADD
  CONSTRAINT Mentor_MentorName_fk FOREIGN KEY (MentorName)
    REFERENCES MENTOR (MentorName)
```

To add a check constraint to the column MembershipFee in the CLUB table, use

```
ALTER TABLE CLUB ADD
  CONSTRAINT MembershipFee_ck CHECK
  MembershipFee BETWEEN 0 AND 300)
```

To add a column to a table, use the following statement:

```
ALTER TABLE Table_name ADD Column_name Data_type
```

For example, if you want to change StudentName in the STUDENT table to LastName and FirstName, the statement in Figure 5.9 will do so. Note that you may not be able to add new columns if the existing table contains data.

You can also modify a column definition by using the following statement:

```
ALTER TABLE Table_name ALTER COLUMN Column_name Data_type
```

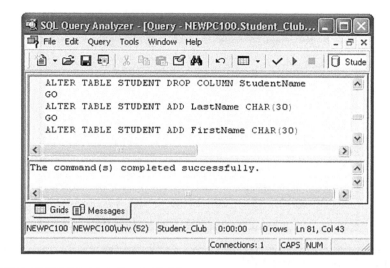

Figure 5.9   Drop and add columns

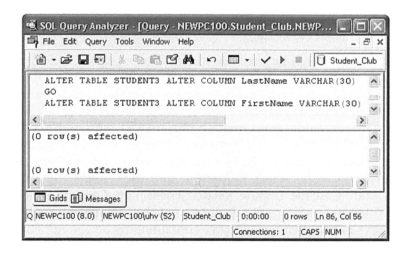

Figure 5.10   Modify column definition

For example, if you want to change the data type for the columns Last-Name and FirstName from CHAR(30) to VARCHAR(30), use the statement in Figure 5.10.

SQL Server allows you to change the length of columns, even if they contain data. When the length of a column is reduced to less than the length of data in that column, the data will be truncated to fit in that column. This is also true for changing data types. However, you may lose some data values by changing the data types.

To drop the table STUDENT in the database Student_Club, use the following statement or use the statement in Figure 5.11 if the database Student_Club is selected in the combo box on the tool bar.

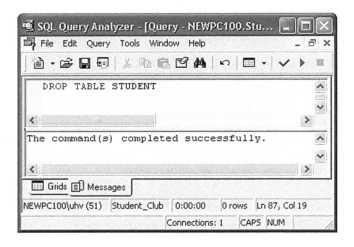

Figure 5.11 Drop existing table

```
USE Student_Club
GO
DROP TABLE STUDENT
```

If a table has a foreign key connection with other tables, deleting the rows in the table or dropping the table could cause problems to the tables that are referencing it. SQL Server prevents you from dropping a table referenced by another table. You must drop the referencing table before you can drop the referenced table. Deleting and updating the rows in the referenced table can also cause problems. To solve the problem on modifying the referenced table, you need to open the relationship diagram in **Enterprise Manager**. Right-click on the referenced table, select **Properties**, and then select the **Relationships** tab. Check both **Cascade Update Related Fields** and **Cascade Delete Related Records**. In this way, if an attempt is made to update or delete a row referenced by foreign keys in other tables, all rows containing those foreign keys in other tables are also updated or deleted.

5.3.3 Manipulating Data in Tables

For an existing table, you may insert a row of data by using the INSERT command, modify data by using the UPDATE command, and delete data by using the DELETE command. The example in Figure 5.12 shows you how to insert a row into the table STUDENT.

Make sure that the order and data types of the data values listed in the VALUES(…) statement are consistent with the definitions of the columns listed in the INSERT INTO statement. For example, if the data type of the LastName column is defined as CHAR(30), then the corresponding data value Smith must be quoted by a pair of single quotes to specify that Smith is a character string.

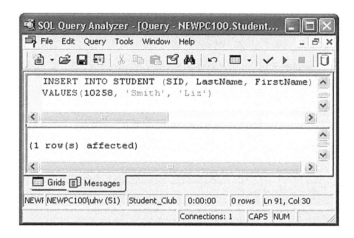

Figure 5.12   Insert data into table

To modify existing data, consider the following example that will change a student's last name from Smith to Taylor:

```
UPDATE STUDENT
SET LastName = 'Taylor'
WHERE LastName = 'Smith'
```

WHERE is used to specify the condition in which a value will be modified. If the condition statement WHERE is missing, all the values in the same column will be changed. The SET keyword is used to modify a column value. To delete a row from the STUDENT table, use the following statement:

```
DELETE FROM STUDENT
WHERE LastName = 'Taylor'
```

After executing the statement, the row(s) containing Taylor will be deleted.

5.3.4 Controlling Database Object Privileges

If you have created some database objects, other users of SQL Server cannot automatically access these objects. To allow them to modify or execute your database objects, you can grant them permissions. For example, to let the public update the table STUDENT, you can use the statement in Figure 5.13. (In reality, you will not let the public update the STUDENT table, which has private information.)

The statement REVOKE can be used to remove previously granted privileges on a database object. The following statement will remove the UPDATE privilege granted to the public on the table STUDENT:

```
REVOKE UPDATE
ON STUDENT
TO PUBLIC
```

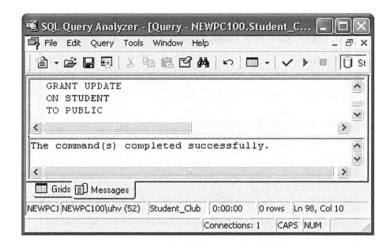

Figure 5.13　Grant update privilege on STUDENT **table**

A database manager has the privilege to create, delete, and grant database-accessing privileges to other users.

5.4　Transporting Database Data

In this section, we cover topics such as how to import and export database data, access external data, and move or copy database files. After a table is created, the next step is to enter data or import data to the table. You can enter the data manually in SQL Server Enterprise Manager. However, it is not a practical way if the data file has a large amount of data. The easiest way to generate database data is to move data from a data file that contains the data with a proper format. Transporting data is an important part of database implementation. Without data, no matter how good the structure is, the database will not serve its purpose.

5.4.1　Entering Data Manually

To enter data into a table manually, you can use the INSERT SQL statement, as shown earlier. The data entry job can also be done through Enterprise Manager. The following steps show you how to enter data into the STUDENT table in Enterprise Manager:

1. Start **Enterprise Manager** in SQL Server. Expand the **Databases** node, and then expand the **Student_Club** node.
2. Click **Tables** in the **Tree** pane. Right-click the table **STUDENT** in the **Tables** pane and then select **Open Table**. In the submenu, select **Return all rows**.
3. Enter the data as shown in Figure 5.14.

Similarly, you can enter data for the other tables built for the database Student_Club. When you enter data, make sure to enter the data into the

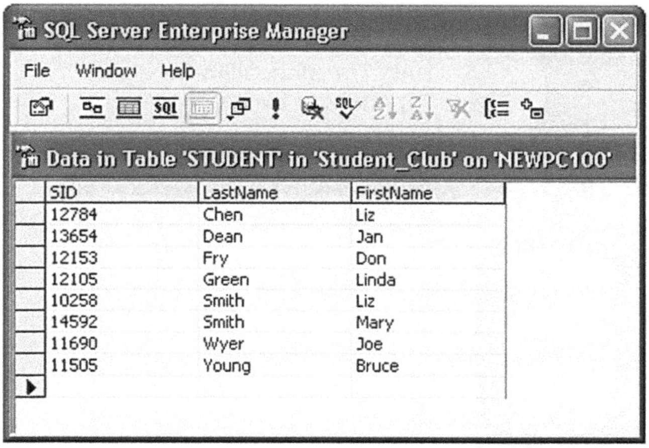

Figure 5.14　Enter records in STUDENT **table**

tables without foreign key columns first. Then enter the data into the tables
with the foreign key columns. In this way, the data values entered into foreign
key columns can be verified by the integrity constraint. If the values entered
into a foreign column do not match the data values in the primary key column,
you will get an error message.

5.4.2 Importing and Exporting Data

If the data you need are available in a text file or in an existing database,
instead of entering the data manually, you can import them by using the *bulk
copy program* (**bcp**), bulk INSERT, or **Import/Export Wizard** in Data Transformation Services (DTS).

Import/Export Wizard

The **Import/Export Wizard** built into SQL Server is a convenient tool for
transporting data into and out of a database. In the case in which you want
to export data from an existing database to a text file and then import the
data from the text file to a table in a new database, use the following steps:

1.　To export data in a database to a text file, click **Enterprise Manager**, and
expand the database tree. Right-click on the database where data will be
exported, for example, the database **Hillcrest Computing**.
2.　Click the menu item **All Tasks**, and then click **Export Data** to start the
Import/Export Wizard (see Figure 5.15).
3.　Click **Next** to go to the **Choose a Data Source** page. This page asks you
to enter the information about your SQL Server, the database authentication
method, and the database to be exported. Because we opened the wizard
by clicking the database to be exported, all the necessary information has
been entered by default.

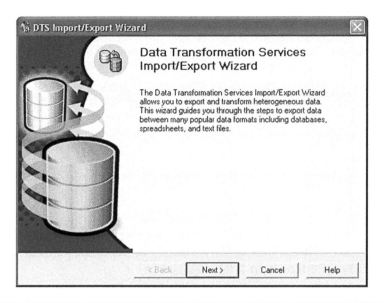

Figure 5.15   Import/Export Wizard

4. Click **Next** to go to the page that prompts you to enter the destination and file name. Because we have decided to export the database as a text file, choose **Text File** as the destination and **Mydb** as the file name.
5. Click the button on the right side of the file name and save **Mydb**.
6. Click **Next** until you get to the **Select destination file format** page. On this page, you need to tell the Wizard which table will be exported and the format of the text file. In this example, you can specify any table in the **Source** combo box. For our purpose, it does not matter if the columns in the text file are separated by a character or each column has a fixed column width. Thus, we take the default option **Delimited**.
7. Click **Next.** The Wizard page asks you to decide if you want to run the export process immediately or export the table later at a prescheduled time. Because we really want to see the result now, take the default option **Run immediately**. Click **Next** and then click **Finish**.

To import the text file into your database, you need to design the table first and then import the data, so that the column names and types will match those in the table from which you import data.

1. To import data, right-click on the database you want to use to hold the table. Click **All Tasks**, and then click **Import Data** to start the **Import/Export Wizard**.
2. Click **Next** to go to the page that prompts you to enter the data source and file name. The Wizard needs to know what type of file you want to import. Enter **Text File** as the data source and **Mydb** as the file name by using the browse button. If you cannot see **Mydb** in **Text Files**, select **All Files** in the **Files of type** combo box.

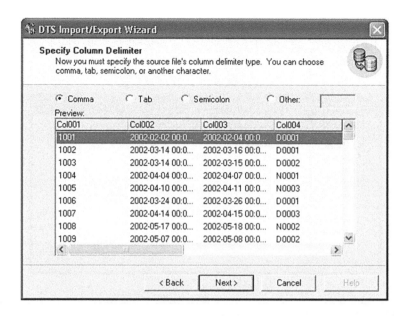

Figure 5.16   Specify column delimiter

3. Click **Next** and choose **Delimited** on the **Select file format** page.
4. Click **Next** again and select **Comma** in the **Specify Column Delimiter** page, as shown in Figure 5.16.
5. Then click **Next** several times. In the **Preview**, you can see the result. After you click **Finish**, you may need to log on again or use **Refresh** under the **Action** drop-down list to see the change.

Bulk Copy Program (bcp)

Another frequently used tool to copy data to or from database files is the bcp utility. The bcp utility is a flexible tool. It allows you to export and import SQL Server data to and from tables in other DBMSs or even data files in other software packages such as Microsoft Excel. When importing or exporting data, the bcp utility has the following requirements:

- The rows and columns should be separated by terminators such as Tab and Newline.
- Data in a data file should be in character format, Unicode format, or bcp native format (SQL Server–specific).
- The order and the number of columns in a data file do not have to be the same as in the SQL Server table.
- The destination table should be built before you can import data into it.
- You should have the INSERT and SELECT permissions to use the bcp utility.

The following is the format of the bcp command:

```
bcp [[db_name.]owner.]table_name | "query" {in | out | format |
    queryout} datafile_name [ -parameter 1] …[ -parameter n]
```

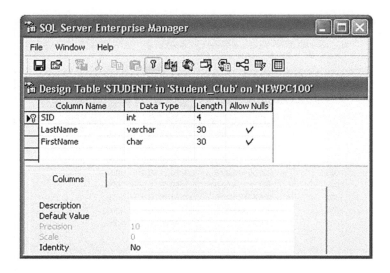

Figure 5.17   Design of STUDENT **table**

The square bracket means optional. Here, "query" is a SQL statement that generates the export result set. The {in | out | format | queryout} expression gives the data transfer direction. The vertical bar represents the OR operator. The word format is used to create a format file. When exporting results from a SQL statement or stored procedure, you need to use the keyword queryout. To specify the data format or other options, use the SQL Server switch -parameter. The commonly used switches are

```
[-m max_errors] [-f format_file] [-e err_file]
  [-F first_row] [-L last_row] [-b batch_size]
  [-n native data type] [-c char data type] [-w unicode data type]
[-N native export for nonchar data or unicode export for char
  data]
[-6 use 6.x data types] [-q use quoted identifier]
[-C code_page] [-t field_terminator] [-r row_terminator]
  [-i input_file] [-o output_file] [-a packet_size]
  [-S server_name[\instance_name]] [-U login_id] [-P password]
  [-T use trusted connection to SQL Server] [-v bcp version]
[-k preserve null values] [-E preserve id values] [-h "hint
  [,...n]"]
```

To see how the bcp utility works, we export data from a SQL Server table to a text file and then import the data from the text file to a SQL Server table. Before you start the exporting process, you need to check the structure of the source table, for example, STUDENT (see Figure 5.17). From Figure 5.17, we can see that the STUDENT table has three columns: SID, LastName, and FirstName. Next, we export the data in the table STUDENT to a data file STUDENT.txt, with Tab as the column terminator and Newline as the row terminator. The commonly used terminators are

Terminator	Indicated by
Tab	\t
Newline character	\n
Carriage return	\r
Backslash	\\
Null terminator	\0
User-defined terminator	character(^, %, *, ...)

Figure 5.18   Use bcp command to export data

The switches −t and −r are used to specify the terminators for the column and row, respectively. If there is no specification, the export file from a SQL Server table uses **Tab** as the column terminator and **Newline** as the row terminator. Go to **Start**, **Run**, and type **cmd** in the combo box. Then click **OK**. Enter the following command in the command prompt window:

```
bcp Student_Club..STUDENT out STUDENT.txt −c −T
```

In the **Command Prompt** window, we have the result shown in Figure 5.18.

Note: You need to run the above command in the folder for the current user. For example, if you log on as Student, change to the folder **C:\ Documents and Settings\Student** to run the command.

The out keyword specifies that the data in table STUDENT will be exported to the STUDENT.txt file. Student_Club is the database containing the table STUDENT. The switch **–c** specifies that the character format is used and **–T** indicates that the trusted connection is used to connect to SQL Server. The exported text file will be saved under the user's folder of **C:\Documents and Settings**. Open the exported file STUDENT.txt in the notepad, and we have the data shown in Figure 5.19.

Now we can import the text file STUDENT.txt into a new table NEW_STUDENT. Figure 5.20 shows the structure of the table NEW_STUDENT. Run the following command in the command prompt window to import the text file into the table NEW_STUDENT:

```
bcp Student_Club..NEW_STUDENT in STUDENT.txt −c −T
```

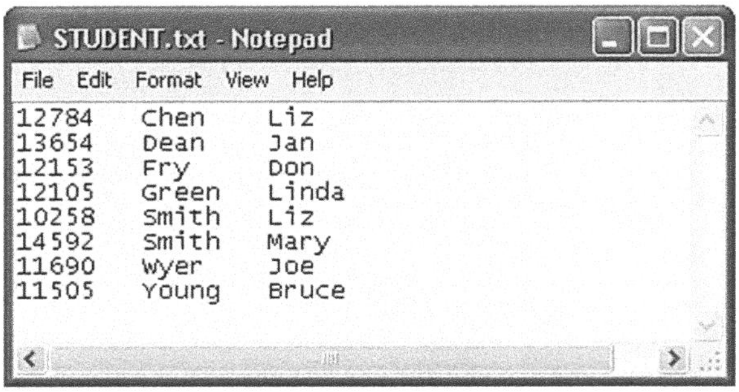

Figure 5.19   Data exported to text file by bcp command

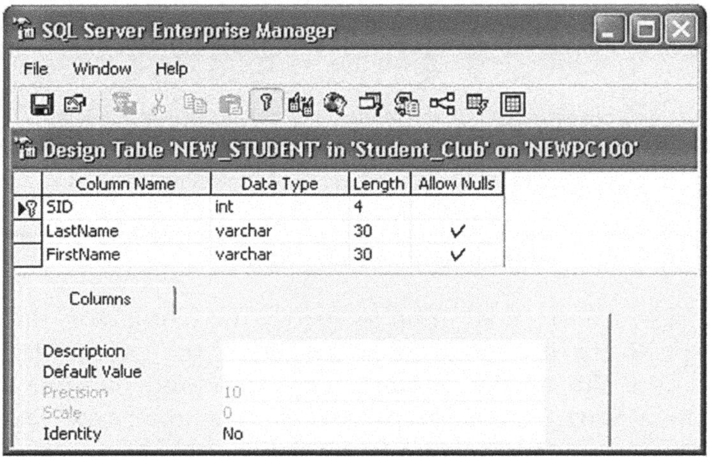

Figure 5.20   Design of NEW_STUDENT **Table**

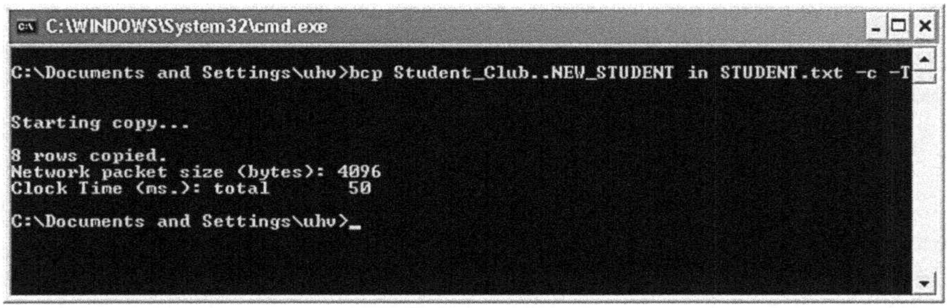

Figure 5.21   Use bcp command to import data

You should see the result shown in Figure 5.21.

To verify that the data have been imported into the table NEW_STUDENT, open the **Enterprise Manager**, expand the **Student_Club** database node, and right-click on the table **NEW_STUDENT**. Select **Open Table** and then select **Return all rows**. You should see the imported data as shown in Figure 5.22.

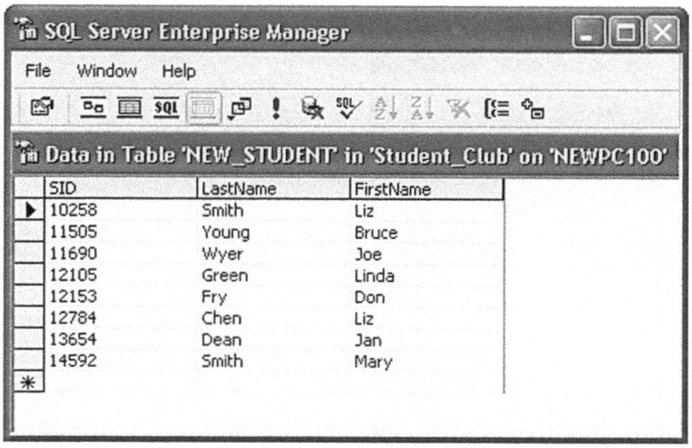

Figure 5.22   Data imported to table by bcp command

Bulk Insert

BULK INSERT cannot export data from a SQL Server table to a data file. It can only import data from a data file to a table created in SQL Server. The advantage of BULK INSERT is that you can copy data to a table using Query Analyzer rather than the command prompt. To use BULK INSERT, open **Query Analyzer** and enter the following statement:

```
BULK INSERT NEW_STUDENT_BULK
FROM 'C:\STUDENT.txt'
WITH (DATAFILETYPE = 'char')
```

NEW_STUDENT_BULK is a table created with the same structure as the table NEW_STUDENT. Run the statement, and we have the result shown in Figure 5.23. To verify, open the table NEW_STUDENT_BULK and return all rows of the table, and you will have the data in Figure 5.24.

5.4.3 Accessing External Data

Sometimes you may need to access external data that are from various data sources such as Oracle, Excel, Access, or text files by using SQL statements. For example, from SQL Server, you may want to query data stored in Microsoft Access. To help you accomplish this task, SQL Server provides you with the tool, distributed query, to access external data if the data are provided by OLE DB, which is an interface to external data. To access external data with distributed query, follow the steps below:

1. Create a linked server that includes the information used to access OLE DB–based external data.
   a. Open **Enterprise Manager** and expand the **Security** node.
   b. Right-click **Linked Servers** and then select **New Linked Server** to open the **Linked Server Properties** page.

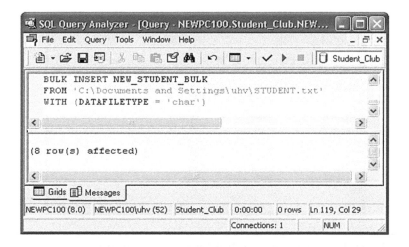

Figure 5.23   Import data to table by `BULK  INSERT`

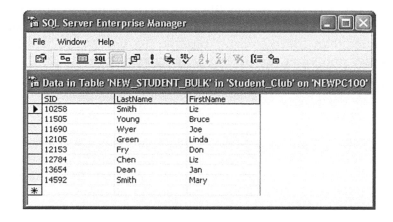

Figure 5.24   Data imported to `NEW_STUDENT_BULK` **table by** `BULK  INSERT`

   c. Under the **General** tab, enter the name of the linked server, such as **MY_SERVER**, in the **Linked server** text box. You can name it anything you like.

   d. You need to select the server type. For our example, we need to query the data in **Access**, so we select the option **Other data source**. In the **Provider name** combo box, choose **Microsoft Jet 4.0 OLE DB Provider**.

   e. Enter the path and the name of the Access database in the **Data Source** text box, for example, **C:\Program Files\Microsoft Analysis Services\Samples\foodmart 2000.mdb**. This is the Access database file created for the OLAP Analysis Manager. See Figure 5.25 for the configuration of the linked server `MY_SERVER`.

   f. Click **OK** to add the `MY_SERVER` to the **Linked Servers** list.

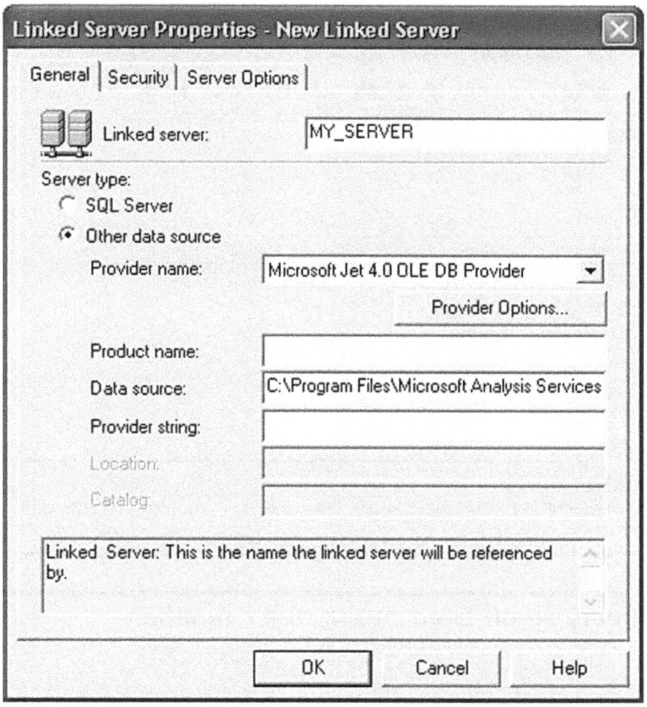

Figure 5.25   Configuration of linked server

2. After you have created the linked server, you can now use a built-in OPENQUERY function to query the external data source specified by MY_SERVER. To do so, open **Query Analyzer** and enter the following statement:

```
SELECT *
FROM OPENQUERY(MY_SERVER,
    'SELECT FName, LName FROM CUSTOMER')
```

Your query result is given in Figure 5.26. OPENQUERY is a convenient tool to query data in an external OLE DB–supported data source. Besides the Microsoft products, another major DBMS vendor that participates in the OLE DB technology is Oracle. This means that you can query data stored in an Oracle database from SQL Server.

3. Similar to the OPENQUERY function, you can also query external data by querying the linked server MY_SERVER with a SELECT statement as shown below:

```
SELECT FName, LName
FROM MY_SERVER...CUSTOMER
```

The SELECT statement is used to specify the columns to be obtained. The keyword FROM is used to specify the table(s) from where the columns in the SELECT statement come. The ellipsis is used as a placeholder for the four-part name defined as

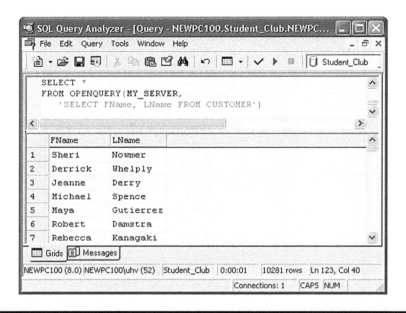

Figure 5.26   Query result from `OPENQUERY` **function**

```
linked_server.catalog.schema.object_name
```

The meaning of each part's name is listed below:

Linked_server: The name of the linked server
Catalog: The catalog in the OLE DB data source such as a database name
Schema: The schema in the catalog, such as an owner ID
Object_name: The data object in a schema, such as a table owned by
      the user

The query result by the four-part SQL statement is given in Figure 5.27.

As you can see, the data import/export tools provided by SQL Server are quite handy. These tools make the data transfer from a data source to your newly created database much easier. Try to use these tools whenever it is proper. Manually entering data into your database should be your last option.

5.4.4 Copying Database

Sometimes you may want to copy your database created on a SQL Server database from one computer to another computer. In the case in which these two computers are not connected with a network, you may copy the database from one computer to a portable storage device such as a CD or USB external hard drive and then copy the database from the portable storage device to the other computer. To copy a database on SQL Server, you need to detach it first from the SQL Server. Copy the data file to a portable storage device. To re-create the database on the other computer, you need to attach the data files to that SQL Server. The following example shows you how to copy the

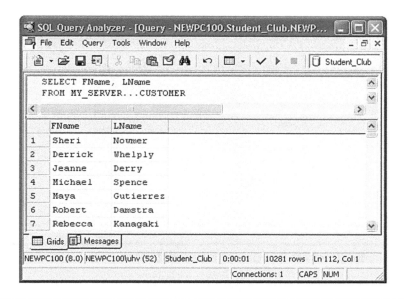

Figure 5.27   Query result from SQL statement

database `Student_Club` to a new location. For illustration purposes, this new location is still on your current computer but in a different folder.

1. Detach the database that you want to copy. For example, if you want to copy the database `Student_Club`, enter the following statement in **Query Analyzer** to detach the database:

    ```
    EXEC sp_detach_db @dbname = 'Student_Club'
    ```

    After you have entered the SQL statement, click the **Execute Query** button.
2. Open **Windows Explorer**. Go to the directory **C:\Program Files\ Microsoft SQL Server\MSSQL\Data**. There are two files related to the database Student_Club: `Student_Club.mdf` and `Student_Club_ Log.ldf`. You can copy the database-related files to another directory or to a CD. To simplify the task, we copy the files to the directory **C:\ Documents and Settings\Administrator\My Documents\dbcopy**.
3. From **Query Analyzer**, execute the following SQL statement to reattach the database from the new location:

    ```
    EXEC sp_attach_db @dbname = 'Student_Club',
    @filename1 = 'c:\Documents and Settings\Administrator\
       My Documents\dbcopy\Student_Club.mdf',
    @filename2 = 'c:\Documents and Settings\Administrator\
       My Documents\dbcopy\Student_Club_Log.ldf'
    ```

    (Note that, in Query Analyzer, when you execute the above statements, you may want to keep the file name and the path in a single line.) To verify that the database is reattached, open **Enterprise Manager**. You should see the reattached database `Student_Club` under the **Databases** node (Figure 5.28).

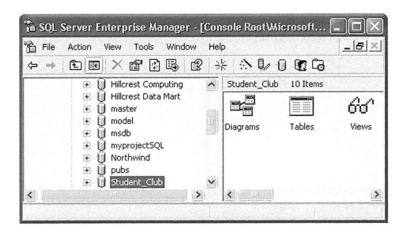

Figure 5.28   Reattached `Student_Club` **database**

In the above section, you have learned how to copy a database to a different location and then reattach the database. Although we accomplished the task through executing the SQL statement, you can also detach and attach a database by using the Detach and Attach wizards in Enterprise Manager. As you have read earlier, SQL is a more portable database management tool. Suppose you want to copy a database from SQL Server to another database managed by a DBMS product without graphical tools. In such a case, SQL is the tool to accomplish the database copying task.

5.5   Summary

This chapter started with the introduction of physical design issues. To physically create a database itself and other database objects, we have introduced the primary database management tool Structured Query Language (SQL). We then used SQL to implement relational databases. We discussed how to create, alter, and delete database objects such as databases, tables, and views. The tool Query Analyzer included in SQL Server was used to run SQL statements. After a database was created, the Data Control Language (DCL) and Data Manipulation Language (DML) statements were used to manage the database objects. Populating tables is an important task in database implementation. In this chapter, you first learned how to enter data to a table manually and then how to work with several utilities to export data from and import data to a database.

Review Questions

For the questions 13 to 19 and 21 to 25, write and run SQL statements in Query Analyzer.

1. What are the concerns at the physical design stage?
2. Explain why SQL is important to database development.
3. What is the SQL extension used in SQL Server?
4. What does DDL stand for?
5. What are the tasks that can be done by DDL?
6. What are the commonly used DDL commands?
7. What does DCL stand for?
8. What are the tasks that can be done by DCL?
9. What are the commonly used DCL commands?
10. What does DML stand for?
11. What are the tasks that can be done by DML?
12. What are the commonly used DML commands?
13. Create a database named `Computer_Shop` with an initial size of 1 MB and a maximum size of 8 MB. The database file should be saved as `Computer_Shop.mdf`.
14. Create the table ORDER(<u>OrderId</u>, OrderDate, ShippingCharge, Total).
15. Write a SQL statement to create a table COMPUTER with the definition COMPUTER(<u>ComputerId</u>, Maker, Model, Price).
16. Write a SQL statement to create a table with the following information:

    HARDDRIVE(<u>SerialNumber</u>, Maker, Model, Price)

17. Write a SQL statement to create a table with the following information:

    ORDER_HARDDRIVE(SerialNumber, OrderId)

18. Write a SQL statement to create a table with the following information:

    ORDER_COMPUTER(OrderId, ComputerId)

19. In Query Analyzer, alter the table HARDDRIVE by adding a new column Description with the CHAR(100) data type.
20. Explain the meaning of Cascade Delete Related Records.
21. Use the INSERT statement to insert the following information into the table HARDDRIVE:

11111	KEM	TI20GB	168
12293	QVT	SL40GB	243
23412	TTP	FK100GB	405

22. For the table HARDDRIVE, update the price for the hard drive with the serial number 12293 to $220.
23. Use the GRANT statement to grant the insert privilege to the public on table HARDDRIVE, and then use the REVOKE statement to remove the insert privilege to the public.
24. Insert the following data into the table ORDER created in Question 14:

10	7/9/04	90	1290
11	7/11/04	56	1456

12	7/15/04	78	2078
13	8/1/04	103	1903
14	8/3/04	50	1650
15	8/7/04	90	1896

Insert the following data into the table COMPUTER created in Question 15:

1	CQ	DT4135	1200
2	DP	NS2190	1400
3	CQ	DT6135	1800
4	GN	HK4900	1600
5	BN	CT1289	2000

Insert the following data into the table ORDER_HARDDRIVE created in Question 17:

```
12293 10
11111 12
23412 15
```

Insert the following data into the table ORDER_COMPUTER created in Question 18:

```
10  1
11  2
12  5
13  3
14  4
15  3
```

25. Create a table COMPUTER_NEW with the same structure as COMPUTER created in Question 15. Then export the data in COMPUTER to a text file. Import the text file to the table COMPUTER_NEW.

Case Study Projects

Continue from the previous chapter. Start Query Analyzer in SQL Server and write SQL statements to perform the following activities.

1. Computer Service

Based on the database diagram created in the previous chapter, populate the Awesome Computer Service's database Computer_Service with SQL statements.

- Insert at least five rows of data for each table in the diagram. Modify some of the rows in the tables, and delete one of the rows in one of the tables.
- Detach the Computer_Service database. Copy it to the folder dbcopy created in My Documents. Then restore the database with Query Analyzer.

2. University Registration

Based on the database diagram created in the previous chapter, perform the following activities:

- Insert at least five rows of data for each table in the diagram.
- Create a linked server Registration to link to the data source, the Registration database, with Microsoft OLE DB Provider for SQL Server.
- By querying the linked server Registration in Query Analyzer, select data from some of the tables in the Registration database.

3. Mail Order

Perform the following activities for the Mail_Order database:

- Insert at least five rows of data for each table in the Mail_Order database.
- In Query Analyzer, create a new database Catalog Shopping, with the database structure matching that of the database Mail_Order.
- Use the bcp command to export the data in the tables to text files and then import the text files to the tables in the new database with the bcp command.

Chapter 6

Querying Databases

Objectives

- Use basic query statements to select data from tables.
- Use subqueries to obtain data from multiple tables.
- Join multiple tables.
- Use built-in group functions.

6.1 Introduction

After a database is created and populated with data, it is ready for database users to retrieve information for its applications. For example, a user of the database `Student_Club` may want to know who is a member of the Book Club or which club charges the highest membership fee. To provide information that meets users' needs, queries are used to select specified records from a database. Based on their needs, users can specify their query search constraints that will limit the returns, so that the output of their queries can provide useful information.

In this chapter, you will learn how to execute SQL statements in Query Analyzer and how to use SQL statements to retrieve information from single or multiple tables.

6.2 Retrieving Data from Tables

To retrieve data from a database, the SQL statements are used for database querying. You can use a combination of three basic statements, `SELECT`, `FROM`, and `WHERE`, in the following format:

```
SELECT Column_name(s)
FROM Table_name
WHERE condition(s)
```

To illustrate the use of SQL statements for retrieving data, we need to populate the tables created in the `Student_Club` database as shown in Figure 6.1. Now that data have been entered in each table, we can practice data retrieving from these tables.

6.2.1 *Querying with SELECT, FROM and WHERE Statements*

We start with the `SELECT-FROM` statement that will return all the data from a table. Type the following statement into Query Analyzer:

```
SELECT *
FROM CLUB
```

The keyword `SELECT` is used to specify the columns to be selected in the query. The symbol * means that all columns in the table are selected. The keyword `FROM` specifies the table from which the columns are selected. SQL statements are not case sensitive. We capitalized the keywords and table name just for clarity purposes. Also, you do not have to break the `SELECT` statement into two lines. If you write the statement as `SELECT * FROM CLUB` in a single line, it is perfectly acceptable. However, breaking the statement into different lines makes it easier to read. By running the above SQL statement in Query Analyzer, we have the result shown in Figure 6.2.

For most retrieving tasks, data are selected based on some conditions or constraints. Adding the `WHERE` condition to the `SELECT` statement will accomplish this goal. For example, to select the information such as `SID`, `LastName`, and `FirstName` about the students who have the first name Liz, we can use the following `SELECT` statement:

```
SELECT *
FROM STUDENT
WHERE FirstName = 'Liz'
```

Although the SQL statement is case insensitive, the character string in the `WHERE` condition is case sensitive. The character string inside the single quotation marks is used to match the values in the column `FirstName`. The selection result is shown in Figure 6.3. Different types of conditions or constraints can be entered following the `WHERE` keyword. We work through some of the commonly used operators that will enrich the constraints used with `WHERE`.

Logical Operators

Logical operators are used to combine multiple search conditions and set limits for values to be selected (see Table 6.1). To illustrate the use of logical operators, consider the following examples. To select the rows with the duty as `Recruiter` or `WebMaster` in the `SERVICE` table accompanied by `SkillId`, use the SQL statement shown in Figure 6.4.

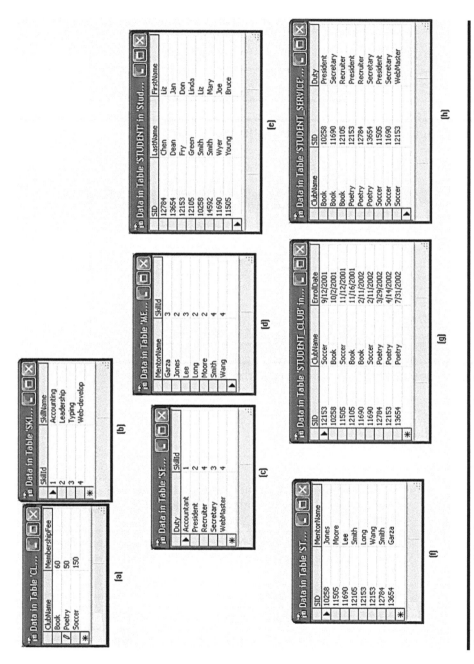

Figure 6.1 **Tables in** Student_Club **database: (a)** CLUB, **(b)** SKILL, **(c)** SERVICE, **(d)** MENTOR, **(e)** STUDENT, **(f)** STUDENT_MENTOR, **(g)** STUDENT_CLUB, **and (h)** STUDENT_SERVICE

[a] Data in Table 'CL...'

ClubName	MembershipFee
Book	60
Poetry	50
Soccer	150

[b] Data in Table 'SKI...'

SkillId	SkillName
1	Accounting
2	Leadership
3	Typing
4	Web-develop

[c] Data in Table 'SE...'

Duty	SkillId
Accountant	1
President	2
Recruiter	4
Secretary	3
WebMaster	4

[d] Data in Table 'ME...'

MentorName	SkillId
Garza	3
Jones	2
Lee	3
Long	2
Moore	2
Smith	4
Wang	4

[e] Data in Table 'STUDENT' in 'Stud...'

SID	LastName	FirstName
12784	Chen	Liz
13654	Dean	Jan
12153	Fry	Don
12105	Green	Linda
10258	Smith	Liz
14592	Smith	Mary
11690	Wyer	Joe
11505	Young	Bruce

[f] Data in Table 'ST...'

SID	MentorName
10258	Jones
11505	Moore
11690	Lee
12105	Smith
12153	Long
12153	Wang
12784	Smith
13654	Garza

[g] Data in Table 'STUDENT_CLUB' in...

SID	ClubName	EnrollDate
12153	Soccer	9/12/2001
10258	Book	10/2/2001
11505	Soccer	11/12/2001
12105	Book	11/16/2001
11690	Book	2/11/2002
11690	Soccer	2/11/2002
12784	Poetry	3/29/2002
12153	Poetry	4/14/2002
13654	Poetry	7/31/2002

[h] Data in Table 'STUDENT_SERVICE'...

ClubName	SID	Duty
Book	10258	President
Book	11690	Secretary
Book	12105	Recruiter
Poetry	12153	President
Poetry	12784	Recruiter
Poetry	13654	Secretary
Soccer	11505	President
Soccer	11690	Secretary
Soccer	12153	WebMaster

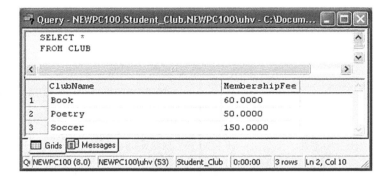

Figure 6.2 **Select all columns from** CLUB **table**

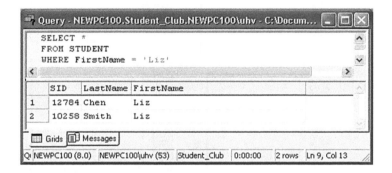

Figure 6.3 **Select students with first name Liz**

Table 6.1 **Logical Operators**

Logical Operator	Description
AND	If both conditions combined by the AND operator are true, the row or rows that meet both conditions will be displayed in the output.
OR	If one of the conditions combined by the OR operator is true, the row or rows that meet one of the conditions will be displayed in the output.
NOT	Exclude the rows that satisfy the NOT constraint from the output.
BETWEEN	Use to define the value range for a given operand.
EXISTS	Use to determine if a subquery returns any rows.
IN	Use to determine if a list of values contains a given value.
IS NULL	Use to determine if a column contains any null (unknown) value.
LIKE	Use to determine if a given value matches a specific pattern.

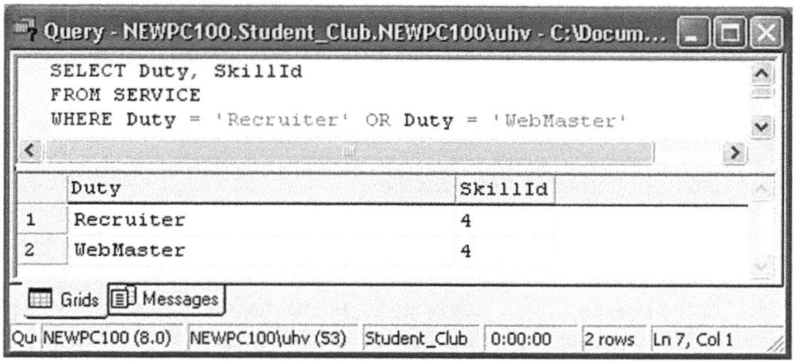

Figure 6.4   Use OR **logical operator**

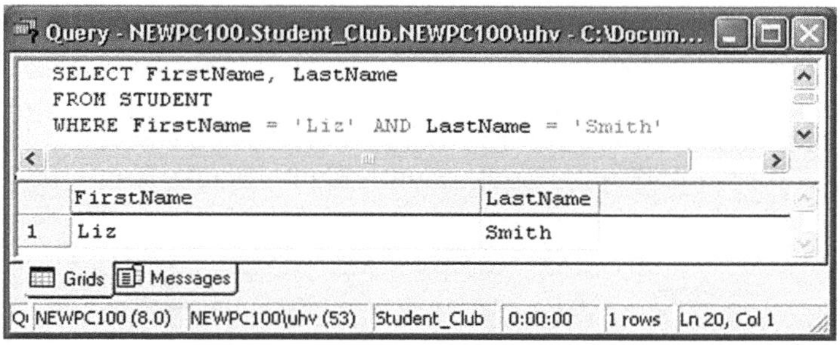

Figure 6.5   Use AND **logical operator**

Two rows are selected in the query output. One row matches the condition Duty = 'Recruiter' on the left-hand side of OR and the other row matches the condition Duty = 'WebMaster' on right-hand side of OR. To look for the student who has the first name Liz and last name Smith, consider the SELECT statement shown in Figure 6.5. The row selected in the output matches the conditions on the left and right sides of the AND operator. The example in Figure 6.6 uses datetime values to select information of students who enrolled between November 15, 2001, and April 15, 2002.

As you have learned, single quotes are used for the character string. In SQL Server, single quotes are also used for datetime values. However, for numerical values, no quotation mark is needed.

The keyword IN is used to determine if a column has any of the values specified in the parentheses. The IN operator is similar to the OR operator. A row will be displayed in the query output if any of the given values is matched by the search condition. Look at the example in Figure 6.7. Four rows are selected; two rows match the search condition that SID is 12153 and the other two rows match the search condition that SID is 11690.

To make the LIKE operator more flexible, wildcard characters are often used. The common wildcard characters are shown in Table 6.2. As an example of using a wildcard, we select students who have last names with a beginning letter between R and Z (see Figure 6.8).

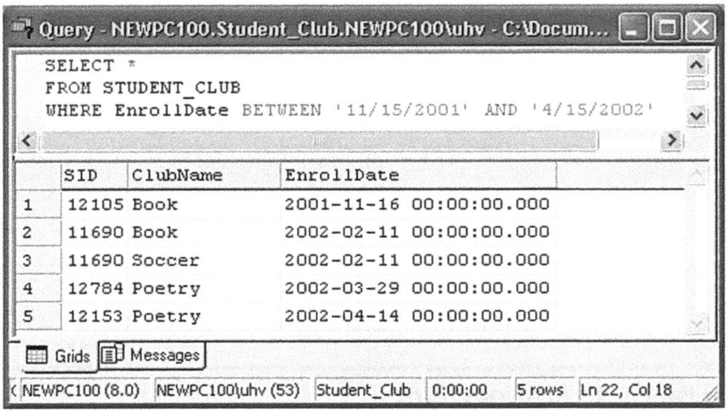

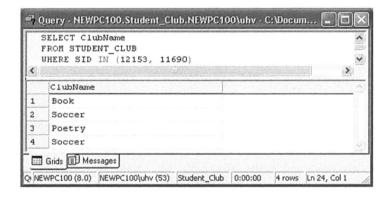

Figure 6.6   Use DateTime data and `BETWEEN` **operator**

Figure 6.7   Use `IN` **logical operator**

Table 6.2   Wildcard Characters

Wildcard Character	Description
%	Any string of characters, e.g., 'B%' means any string that starts with B
_ (Underscore)	Any single character, e.g., 'A_' means any two-letter string that starts with A
[ ]	Any range of characters, e.g., 'F[a-c]' means any two-letter string that starts with F and ends with a or b or c

The example shown in Figure 6.9 uses the `NOT` operator to select mentors who are not mentoring the student with `SID` 12153. Because the student with `SID` 12153 has Long and Wang as mentors, the output of the query does not include Long and Wang in the list.

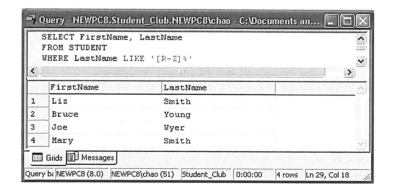

Figure 6.8 Use `LIKE` **operator with wildcard**

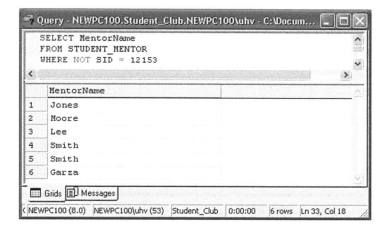

Figure 6.9 Use `NOT` **logical operator**

Any combination of the three Boolean operators (`AND`, `OR`, and `NOT`) can be used for more complicated queries. For example, if you want to select mentors who are not advising the student with `SID` 12153 or the student with `SID` 11505, enter the query in Figure 6.10. As expected, the mentors for the students with `SID` 12153 and `SID` 11505 are not on the printout list.

To find `NULL` values, use `IS NULL` in the `WHERE` clause. For example, to find if there is a club that has no membership fee listed, the statement in Figure 6.11 can be used. As expected, there is no club that does not list a membership fee. Be aware that `NULL` is not equal to 0 or empty space. `NULL` means unknown, so it does not have a value.

Comparison Operators

The operators in this category will select data within the range defined by a constraint. Comparison operators are normally used to set limitations (see Table 6.3).

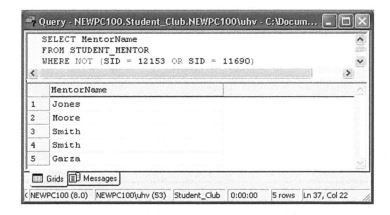

Figure 6.10   Combination of NOT **and** OR **logical operators**

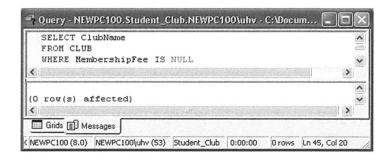

Figure 6.11   IS NULL **operator**

Table 6.3   Comparison Operators

Comparison Operator	Description
>	x > y, x is greater than y
<	x < y, x is less than y
>=	x >= y, x is greater than or equal to y
<=	x <= y, x is less than or equal to y
<>	x <> y, x is not equal to y
!=	x != y, x is not equal to y

The operators <> and != are equivalent. Some DBMS vendors may include only one of the not-equal-to operators. As an example, consider a query that selects mentors for the students with SIDs greater than or equal to 12153. The selection result is shown in Figure 6.12.

Comparison operators can also be used to compare two character strings. The comparison is based on the order of the ASCII character set. There are

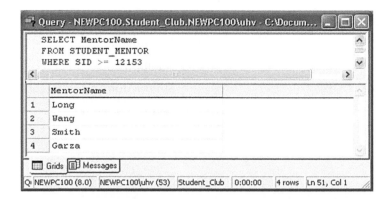

Figure 6.12   Use >= comparison operator

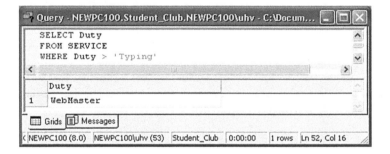

Figure 6.13   Use comparison operator on character string

256 characters in the set. In ascending order, the numerical characters and English letters are arranged as 0–9, A–Z, and a–z. The date order is different from the order for the ASCII characters. When comparing date values with the format dd/mm/yy or dd/mm/yyyy, the comparison starts from the year value, not the date value. The comparison of money values is the same as that of numbers. The example in Figure 6.13 shows a character string comparison.

Arithmetic Operators

These operators can perform mathematical operations on values of the numeric data type (see Table 6.4).

Consider the example in Figure 6.14, which will select the club whose membership fee costs more than twice the fee of the Book Club, which is $60. Some of the above operators can also be used with other keywords such as `UPDATE` and `DELETE`. For example, except for the Soccer Club, the other clubs decide to raise their membership fees by 10 percent. The SQL statement in Figure 6.15 will accomplish this goal.

To better present the result from a `SELECT-FROM-WHERE` statement, `DISTINCT`, `ORDER BY`, and `UNION` can be used. The keyword `DISTINCT`

Table 6.4   Arithmetic Operators

Arithmetic Operator	Description
+	Addition
-	Subtraction
*	Multiplication
/	Division

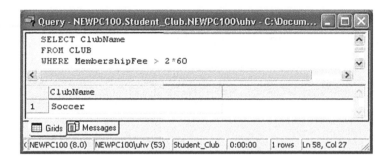

Figure 6.14   Use * arithmetic operator

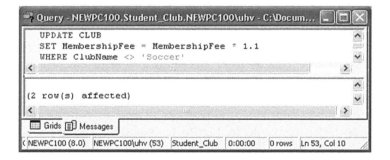

Figure 6.15   Use arithmetic operator in UPDATE **statement**

will eliminate duplicated rows. ORDER BY will sort the result in an ascending or descending order. As an example, we redo the query that selects the mentors who are not mentors for students with SIDs 12153 and 11505 and enter the following query. However, this time we want the result with no duplicated rows and in a descending order (see Figure 6.16). The ascending order is the default for ORDER BY. If you use the ORDER BY MentorName statement, the result will be in the ascending order.

The UNION operator is good for combining the output of two different queries. The query in Figure 6.17 will print the student name with SID 12105 and her mentor together.

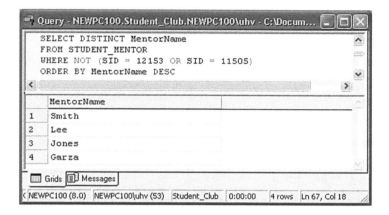

Figure 6.16 Use `DISTINCT` **and** `ORDER BY`

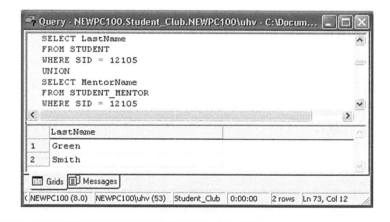

Figure 6.17 Use `UNION` **operator**

The `EXISTS` operator will return values such as True or False. `EXISTS` can be used in the `WHERE` clause to specify a subquery to test for the existence of rows. We discuss subqueries in the following section.

6.2.2 Subqueries

Sometimes a condition in a `WHERE` clause depends on the result from a `SELECT` subquery that returns an intermediate result that is used in the main query's search condition. The subquery may return one or more values. When a single value is returned, the `=` operator is used to match the comparison value in the `WHERE` clause. If the subquery returns more than one value, the `IN` operator is used to determine if a given value matches any value(s) in the list returned from the subquery. For example, one way to list the `SID`s and enrollment dates of the Soccer Club members is to use the statement shown in Figure 6.18 with a subquery.

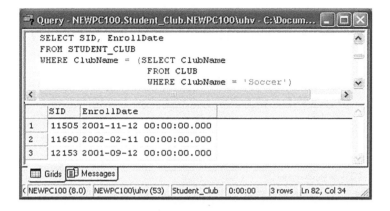

Figure 6.18   Use subquery that returns a single value

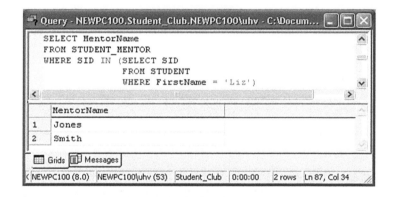

Figure 6.19   Use subquery that returns multiple values

A single `ClubName` value, Soccer, is returned by the subquery. Therefore, the = operator is used in the `WHERE` clause. A subquery must be enclosed in parentheses. The next example shows that there are two students with the same first name Liz. To find their mentors, we can use the following query. Because the subquery returns two student id numbers, the keyword `IN` is used in the `WHERE` clause (see Figure 6.19). Basically, a subquery is used to select information from another table. If you need to select information from more than two tables, you can use multiple subqueries. Next, we select the names of students who have Smith as their mentor and perform duties other than WebMaster (see Figure 6.20).

A subquery can contain another subquery in a nested query. The innermost subquery will be executed first. We consider an example that selects the student id(s) and club name(s) of student(s) who are club presidents and pay a membership fee of more than $100. This query can be represented by a nested query, which selects club(s) that charge more than $100 and has the additional condition that the student(s) serve as club president(s) (see Figure 6.21).

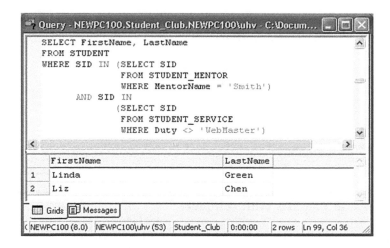

Figure 6.20   Use multiple subqueries

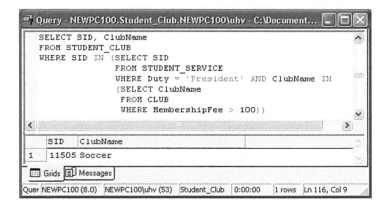

Figure 6.21   Use nested subqueries

The logical operator EXISTS can be used to determine if a subquery returns any row(s). If it does, the search condition in the WHERE clause becomes TRUE; otherwise, the search condition becomes FALSE. The logical operator NOT EXISTS is just the opposite of EXISTS. In the example (Figure 6.22), the main query returns student name(s) if they are mentored by Garza.

In the above query, the alias S stands for the table STUDENT and M stands for STUDENT_MENTOR. The alias used here is to distinguish between the two SIDs that appeared in the WHERE clause. The subquery will check if any student id from the STUDENT table in the main query matches the student id related to the mentor Garza from the STUDENT_MENTOR table. If the search condition is satisfied, the WHERE clause returns TRUE and the student name is selected in the main query. Notice that the table name is placed in front of the column name to identify from which table the column comes (e.g.,

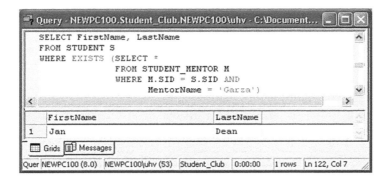

Figure 6.22   Use EXISTS with subquery

STUDENT.SID). When using the operator EXISTS or NOT EXISTS with a subquery, you should use a condition that will connect the table in the subquery and the table in the main query, for example, the condition M.SID = S.SID in Figure 6.22.

By using EXISTS and NOT EXISTS, you can apply subqueries to the following operations that deal with multiple tables:

- *Intersection:* The intersection of two tables contains all rows that exist in both of the original tables.
- *Difference:* The difference of two tables contains the rows that exist only in the first table of the two original tables (not including the rows in both tables).
- *Union:* The union of two tables contains all rows that exist in either of the original tables.
- *Product:* The product (or Cartesian product) of two tables contains all the matches that associate every row of the first table with every row of the second table.

For example, the intersection of SKILL and MENTOR over the SkillId column is the set of skills that mentors are providing (see Figure 6.23). Because no mentor is providing the Accounting skill, there is no accounting in the output in Figure 6.23. The next example shows the difference between SKILL and MENTOR over the SkillId column, where the skill(s) that the mentors are not providing will be returned (see Figure 6.24). Because Accounting is the only skill that mentors are not teaching, it is the only item in the output.

Another useful application of subqueries is to copy data from one table to another. The example in Figure 6.25 copies the data from the table STUDENT to NEW_STUDENT by using an INSERT statement and a subquery.

6.2.3   Joining Multiple Tables with SQL

When you want to select the contents of two or more tables, you can do it based on the primary–foreign key pair. The columns in a join condition must

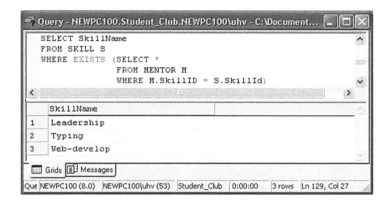

Figure 6.23 Apply `EXISTS` **to intersection with subquery**

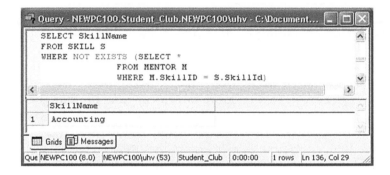

Figure 6.24 Apply `NOT EXISTS` **to difference with subquery**

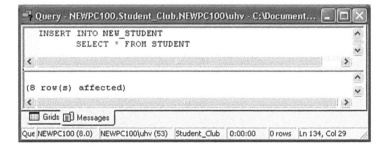

Figure 6.25 Copy data from one table to another

have the same domain. The statement to retrieve data from multiple tables is as follows:

```
SELECT column1, column2, ...
FROM table1, table2, ...
WHERE table1.column  = table2.column
```

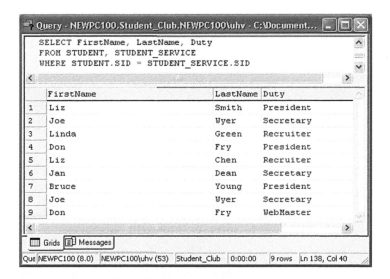

Figure 6.26   Use inner join to select data from two tables

In this statement, the WHERE clause contains the join condition. Joins are used to merge the rows from two or more tables if those rows satisfy the join condition. In SQL Server, two or more tables can also be joined by specifying table names in the FROM clause with the keyword JOIN. That is, a join condition can be placed in the FROM clause or in the WHERE clause. It is clearer if the join condition is placed in the FROM clause and the search condition is placed in the WHERE clause. When specifying the join condition in the FROM clause, use the following basic statement:

```
SELECT column1, column2, ...
FROM table1 JOIN table2 ON table1.column   =   table2.column
WHERE search_condition
```

Joins can be categorized as inner, outer, or self joins. DBMS vendors support the inner join and self join. Many DBMS vendors, including SQL Server, also support the outer join. Next, we illustrate these joins with examples.

Inner Join

An inner join returns rows that match both sides of the join condition. Suppose we want to retrieve information about the students along with their duties. To do this, we should use a query that selects the students' names and their duties from the tables STUDENT and STUDENT_SERVICE by an inner join on the SID column (see Figure 6.26).

Two tables, STUDENT and STUDENT_SERVICE, are involved in this join. To make the join work, the tables must have a common column to implement the join condition. In the output, if the student ids in the STUDENT table match the student ids in the STUDENT_SERVICE table, the rows that contain the first name and last name values from the STUDENT table and duty values

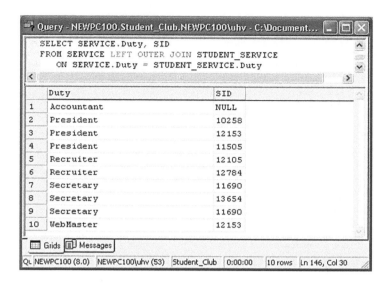

Figure 6.27   Use left outer join to select data from two tables

from the STUDENT_SERVICE table are merged and displayed. In the WHERE clause, to indicate which table the SID column is from, we need the table names in front of the column names. The inner join in the above example is specified in the WHERE clause. You can also specify the inner join in the FROM clause as shown below:

```
SELECT FirstName, LastName, Duty
FROM STUDENT JOIN STUDENT_SERVICE ON
    STUDENT.SID = STUDENT_SERV ICE.SID
```

Outer Join

SQL Server has three types of outer joins: left, right, and full. For a left outer join, all rows from the left table are included, even those with no corresponding rows from the right table. The rows from the right table that satisfy the join condition will be included. The example in Figure 6.27 selects the duties that may or may not be served by students. Because no student currently serves as accountant, the corresponding value from the right-hand side table STUDENT is NULL.

Similarly, you can use a right outer join which will include all rows from the right table and place a NULL value in the rows from the left table that do not match the corresponding rows from the right table. When using a right outer join, replace the LEFT keyword with the RIGHT keyword. For the full outer join, the selection result will include all rows from both tables, no matter if there is a match or not. When using a full outer join, you should use the keyword FULL. As an example of the right outer join, we select all the available duties from the table SERVICE on the right-hand side and the SIDs of students who are serving duties on the

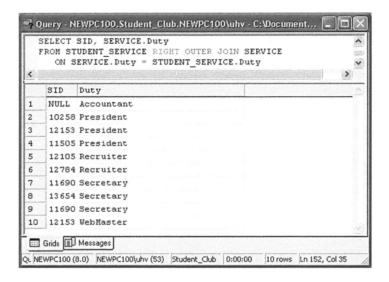

Figure 6.28   Use right outer join to select data from two tables

left-hand side (see Figure 6.28). We have selected the students who serve the duties and all the duties that are available.

As we can see from Figure 6.28, there is a NULL value in the SID column because no student serves as an accountant.

Multiple Joins

You can also join more than two tables using the FROM clause. We consider a selection that will retrieve information of a student's first name, the club he or she has enrolled in, and his or her mentor's name. In this example, for SID 11505, the student's first name is from the table STUDENT, the club name is from the table STUDENT_CLUB, and the mentor's name is from the table STUDENT_MENTOR. To select the information from the three tables, we need to join them in a select statement (see Figure 6.29).

In the above example, the join condition is specified in the FROM clause. You can also specify the join condition in the WHERE clause by using the following statement:

```
SELECT FirstName, ClubName, MentorName
FROM STUDENT S, STUDENT_CLUB C, STUDENT_MENTOR M
WHERE S.SID = C.SID AND
   C.SID = M.SID AND
   S.SID = 11505
```

Self Join

Sometimes you need to join a table to itself. For example, if you want to pair the students who are from the same club, consider a comparison that involves

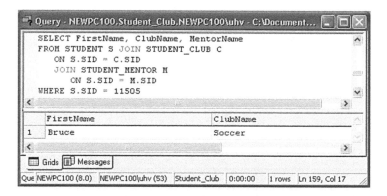

Figure 6.29 Use multiple inner joins to select data from three tables

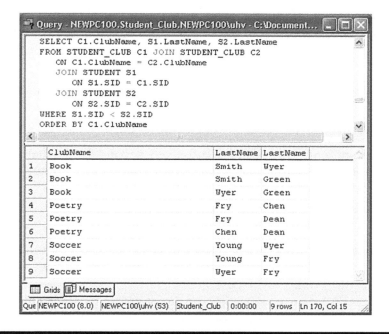

Figure 6.30 Use self join to select data

club names. After you select a club name in the table STUDENT_CLUB, you want to find the matching values of the club name. To do this, you need to compare the values in the ClubName column. Because, in the comparison, both club names come from the same table STUDENT_CLUB, you must distinguish their roles by giving the table two different aliases in the FROM clause. Here, you can name the aliases as C1 and C2. As shown in Figure 6.30, this is a self join that involves a join of the STUDENT_CLUB table with itself. The aliases are used to distinguish the column names in the rest of the query. To match the club names in the table STUDENT_CLUB, you need a join condition

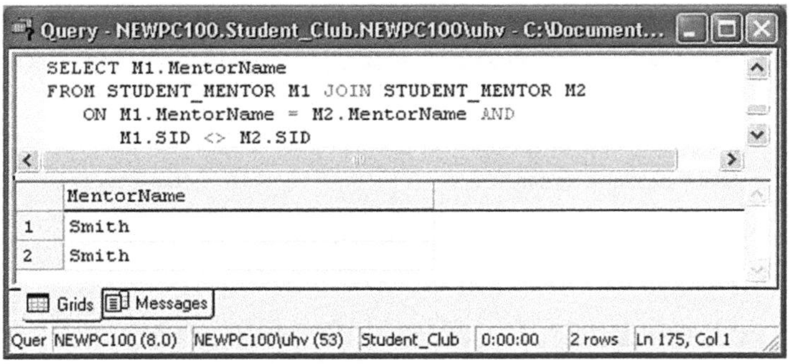

```
Query - NEWPC100.Student_Club.NEWPC100\uhv - C:\Document...  [_][□][X]

   SELECT M1.MentorName
   FROM STUDENT_MENTOR M1 JOIN STUDENT_MENTOR M2
      ON M1.MentorName = M2.MentorName AND
         M1.SID <> M2.SID
```

	MentorName
1	Smith
2	Smith

```
  Grids   Messages

Quer  NEWPC100 (8.0)  NEWPC100\uhv (53)  Student_Club  0:00:00  2 rows  Ln 175, Col 1
```

Figure 6.31   Find duplicated values by using self join

```
C1.ClubName = C2.ClubName
```

To display a pair of student names who are enrolled in the same club, you can use two aliases S1 and S2 for the table STUDENT. The join condition

```
S1.SID = C1.SID
```

matches the students who will be displayed first in the name pairs. Use

```
S2.SID = C2.SID
```

to match the students who will be displayed second in the name pairs. To eliminate duplicates such as the pairs (Smith Green) and (Green Smith), the WHERE condition below is used:

```
S1.SID < S2.SID
```

From the output of the query, for example, the pair Smith and Wyer are from the Book Club. Similarly, the pairs Smith and Green and Wyer and Green are also from the Book Club (see Figure 6.30).

The ORDER BY clause is used to group students by their club names so that it is easier to find the names of the club members. Self joins can also be used in other tasks such as locating duplicated values in a column. For example, to display the names of mentors who advise more than one student, use the self join shown in Figure 6.31. As you can see, Smith advises more than one student. In the above SQL statements, the condition

```
M1.MentorName = M2.MentorName
```

is used to match all the possible duplicates of a mentor name. The second condition

```
M1.SID <> M2.SID
```

is used to eliminate the duplicated values in SID.

Table 6.5   Built-In Functions

Function	Meaning	Example
COUNT	Counts how many non-null rows are in a given column	SELECT COUNT(MembershipFee) FROM CLUB
SUM	Sums the values in a given numerical column	SELECT SUM(MembershipFee) FROM CLUB
MAX	Finds the maximum value in a given numerical column	SELECT MAX(MembershipFee) FROM CLUB
MIN	Finds the minimum value in a given numerical column	SELECT MIN(MembershipFee) FROM CLUB
AVG	Calculates the average for the values in a given numerical column	SELECT AVG(MembershipFee) FROM CLUB
GETDATE	Returns current date and time	SELECT GETDATE( )
DATEDIFF	Returns the difference between two dates	SELECT DATEDIFF(Day, EnrollDate, GETDATE( )) FROM STUDENT_CLUB

Figure 6.32   Use built-in function in subquery

6.2.4   SQL Built-In Functions

SQL built-in functions perform calculations on a set of rows. Table 6.5 shows the commonly used built-in functions and their descriptions. Each of these built-in functions returns a single value. Some of these functions do not work with all types of columns. For example, the SUM function will not be suitable for columns with character data types. The built-in functions can be used with the SELECT clause. For example, if you want to find which club charges the highest membership fee, try the query in Figure 6.32. In this example, a subquery is used in the WHERE clause.

The mixed use of a column and a function after a SELECT keyword will cause an error. For example, the following SQL statement is not correct because the SELECT statement will return three rows from ClubName and only a

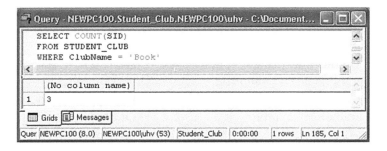

Figure 6.33 Use built-in function COUNT

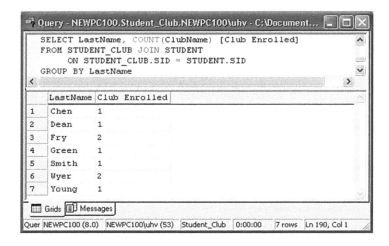

Figure 6.34 Use built-in function with GROUP BY

single value from MAX(MembershipFee). The numbers of rows returned do not match, so an error will occur.

```
SELECT ClubName, MAX(MembershipFee)
FROM CLUB
```

The next example, Figure 6.33, will count how many students are currently enrolled in the Book Club. As shown in the figure, there are three students enrolled in the Book Club.

The built-in functions can also be applied to a set of values grouped by the GROUP BY clause. GROUP BY is used to group rows with the same data value in a column. If we add GROUP BY to the above SQL statement and make sure that the column in the GROUP BY clause is in the SELECT clause, we will have the correct output for mixing a column and a built-in function in a SELECT clause (see Figure 6.34).

When using the built-in functions with the WHERE clause, you will get an error message. To apply conditions to the result returned from built-in functions, you should use the HAVING clause. HAVING is used to select only certain

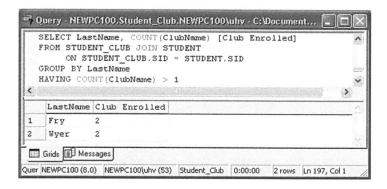

Figure 6.35 **Use** `HAVING` **clause with** `GROUP BY`

groups out of all the groups returned by the `GROUP BY` clause. As an example, we add a condition that returns the last names of students who participate in more than one club (see Figure 6.35).

By now, you have learned some commonly used built-in functions in query statements. There are more built-in functions to come. We cover them in the next chapter.

6.3 Summary

In this chapter, we first populated the database `Student_Club` with data. Through working with several hands-on examples, you have learned how to query information from database tables by using a combination of three basic statements: `SELECT`, `FROM`, and `WHERE`. You have worked with the logical operators `AND`, `OR`, `NOT`, `IN`, `EXISTS`, `NOT EXISTS`, `IS NULL`, `DISTINCT`, `BETWEEN`, and `LIKE`. Examples were also given to illustrate how to use these logical operators. The comparison operators and arithmetic operators have been used with condition statements in the `WHERE` clause. To better display information retrieved from a database, `ORDER BY`, `HAVING`, and `GROUP BY` statements were used to organize output data.

Subqueries were used to retrieve information from multiple tables. Several examples were given to demonstrate the applications of subqueries in operations such as intersection, difference, union, and product. As another subquery application example, a subquery was used in an `INSERT` statement to import data to a new table. You have also learned how to join tables to query information from multiple tables. A table join can be classified as an inner join, left outer join, right outer join, full outer join, or self join. By working on several join examples, you have learned how to retrieve data from multiple tables. Two self join examples were given to help you better understand the concept and application of the self join.

You have also learned how to use built-in functions to perform calculations on a set of rows. We have discussed seven commonly used built-in functions: `COUNT`, `SUM`, `MAX`, `MIN`, `AVG`, `GETDATE`, and `DATEDIFF`. As a query gets more and more complicated, it is important to write more efficient code and execute the code in a more efficient way.

In the next chapter, you will learn how to execute a list of SQL statements automatically. You will also learn how to call a precompiled list of SQL statements in the current SQL statement.

Review Questions

To answer the following questions, you need to enter the data in Figure 6.1 to the tables in the Student_Club database. For each question below, show the result by executing the query in Query Analyzer.

1. Execute a SQL statement to display all the columns in the table CLUB for the club named Poetry.
2. Execute a SQL statement to display the columns FirstName and Last-Name in the table STUDENT, where the student has the first name Liz and last name Chen.
3. Execute a SQL statement to display all the columns in the table CLUB for the membership fee between $60 and $200.
4. Execute a SQL statement to display the mentor name(s) with SkillId of either 2 or 4.
5. Execute a SQL statement to display the first name(s) and last name(s) of the student(s) with the last name starting with A or B or C.
6. Execute a SQL statement to display the student id(s) of the student(s) who is (are) neither a member of the Book Club nor a member of the Poetry Club.
7. Execute a SQL statement to display the last names of the students whose ids are between 11000 and 12000.
8. Execute a SQL statement to display the names of the clubs that charge less than half the membership fee of the Soccer Club.
9. Execute a SQL statement to display, in descending order, the names of the students who are enrolled in the Soccer Club.
10. Execute a SQL statement to display the student's last name and his or her mentor's name for the student whose id is 12153 with a UNION statement.
11. Execute a SQL statement to display the mentor name(s) of the student(s) who has (have) the last name Smith.
12. Execute a SQL statement to display the first name(s) and last name(s) of the student(s) whose mentor is Smith and who is (are) enrolled in the Book Club.
13. Execute a nested query statement to display the student ids and club names of the students who are recruiters and pay less than $100 for membership fees.
14. By using the EXISTS operator, execute a SQL statement to display the first and last names of the students who are enrolled in the Book Club.
15. By using the NOT EXISTS operator, execute a SQL statement to display the names of the skills not required by the duty President.

16. Create a table NEW_CLUB with the same structure as CLUB. Execute a SQL statement to copy the records from CLUB to NEW_CLUB.
17. By using an inner join, display the students' names along with their mentors' names.
18. By using the LEFT OUTER JOIN operator, execute a SQL statement to display the names of the skills from the table SKILL and the names of mentors who provide training for these skills from the table MENTOR.
19. By using the RIGHT OUTER JOIN operator, execute a SQL statement to display the names of the mentors who provide training for the skills from the table MENTOR and the names of the skills from the table SKILL.
20. By using a self join, execute a SQL statement to display the mentors' names and the pairs of the last names of the students who are mentored by the same mentors. Order your result by the mentors' names.
21. Display the name of the club that charges the lowest membership fee.
22. Find out how many students are mentored by Smith.
23. Find out how many students are mentored by each mentor.
24. By using the HAVING clause, display the names of the clubs and the last names of the students who have enrolled in more than one club.

Case Study Projects

Continue from the previous chapter. Start Query Analyzer in SQL Server and write queries for the following case studies.

1. Computer Service

For the Computer_Service database, write and execute SQL queries to display the following information:

- A list of services performed by each technician
- The names and addresses of the customers who have been served by at least two technicians
- A list of computer system ids and types for those computers that have been serviced at least twice
- A list of services and their costs, including the service charge and the cost of parts that are more than $50

2. University Registration

Display the following information from the Registration database:

- A list of students who have enrolled for more than three credits
- Information about a student, the courses he or she has taken, and the terms when the courses were taken
- Calculation of the accumulated GPA for a given student

3. Mail Order

Query the database `Mail_Order` to display the information specified in the following:

- A list of the customers who have used VISA cards for their purchases
- Information about a given customer and the shipping information related to the customer
- The information about a given order, the customer who made the order, the quantity of the product ordered by the customer, the product description and price, and the quantity in stock after the ordering

Chapter 7

SQL Procedures

Objectives

- Learn the procedural extension of ANSI SQL.
- Create, execute, and use stored procedures.
- Create, execute, and use triggers.
- Debug SQL procedures.

7.1 Introduction

In the previous chapter, we used SQL statements to query information from a database, and the SQL statements we created were executed one at a time. Sometimes you may need to execute a list of SQL statements automatically or you may want to call a precompiled list of SQL statements in the current SQL statement. The list of multiple SQL statements contained in a program is called a *SQL procedure*. The current ANSI standard SQL does not support procedural SQL programs. Many DBMS vendors provide their own versions of procedural SQL, such as PL/SQL supported by Oracle and Transact-SQL supported by SQL Server. Transact-SQL is an extension of the standard ANSI SQL. It has some procedural programming components such as variables, user-defined functions, and control-of-flow statements. To avoid writing the same SQL codes repeatedly, procedural SQL programs are often saved on a server so that other programs can call them.

A *stored procedure* is a prebuilt procedure or group of procedures. We can invoke a stored procedure dynamically by calling its name and passing a set of parameters into and out of it. Using stored procedures can improve performance because there is no need to compile a procedure before using it. Often, a built-in stored procedure is optimized for best performance. Stored procedures are also used to improve database programmers' productivity

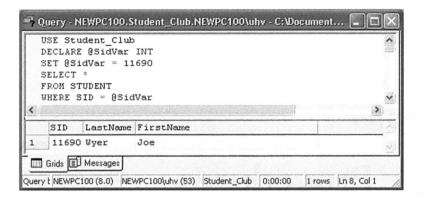

Figure 7.1   Declare and use variable

because the programmers do not have to re-create codes for some common tasks.

When a row in a table is inserted, updated, or deleted, often a prebuilt SQL procedure called a *trigger* is automatically invoked to perform some updating maintenance job. Triggers can be used to update referential integrity constraints, to provide warning messages, or to enforce complex constraints that may be too difficult to be enforced at the time of database design.

In the next few sections, you will learn about these new database objects. You will work through several examples in order to clearly understand these objects.

7.2 SQL Programming Extension

To meet the requirements of procedural programming, SQL Server has added extensions to the standard ANSI SQL, such as declaration of variables, flow-control structures, and error handling. We discuss some of the extensions in this section and then use them in stored procedures and triggers.

7.2.1   Variables

In Transact-SQL, you can define a *variable* to hold a data value. A value in a variable can be dynamically modified. In the following example, a variable is created and assigned a student id value. The variable is then used in a SELECT statement to query data from the table STUDENT (see Figure 7.1). The @ sign indicates that a name is used as a variable. Variables are often used in arithmetic calculations, as illustrated in Figure 7.2, which raises the membership fee for the Poetry Club to $100.

In Figure 7.2, a MONEY type variable **@Fee** is declared first. The variable **@Fee** is assigned a value of 50. Next, in the **UPDATE** statement, the value stored in **@Fee** is multiplied by 2 and the result is assigned to the row in the MembershipFee column that matches the club name Poetry.

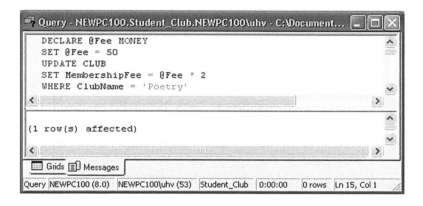

Figure 7.2   Use variable in arithmetic calculation

In a procedure, a variable can be used to hold a returned value from a function call or used as a counter in a loop. You will see the use of a variable in a function call or as a counter in a loop later in this chapter. In addition to defining variables with data types already built, SQL Server 2000 allows users to define their own data types. For example, we can define the data type EnrollTime as a character type with ten letters. To implement this user-defined data type:

- Open **Enterprise Manager** and expand the database **Student_Club** under the **Databases** node.
- Right-click **User Defined Data Types** and select **New User Defined Data Type**. When the dialog opens, enter the information in Figure 7.3.
- Click **OK** to save the new data type.
- Click on the **Tables** node. Right-click on the table **STUDENT_CLUB**, and select **Design Table**. When the table design window opens, we can select the user-defined data type **EnrollTime** from the data type drop-down list for the **EnrollDate** column, as shown in Figure 7.4.

7.2.2   Flow-Control Structures

By now, the examples we have used are sequential programs; that is, the order of execution is the same as the order in which the code appears in the program. Sometimes you may want to change the execution order based on certain conditions, or you may want to execute a block of code repeatedly. To accomplish these goals, flow-control structures are used to change the order of executing SQL statements. The commonly used flow-control structures are shown in Table 7.1.

To illustrate the use of these flow-control keywords, we consider a case in which we are going to increase the membership fee for each student club. A decision has been made to increase the membership fee if at least one club has a membership fee less than $100. However, we will stop increasing the membership fee if any of the clubs has a fee greater than $170. The rate of

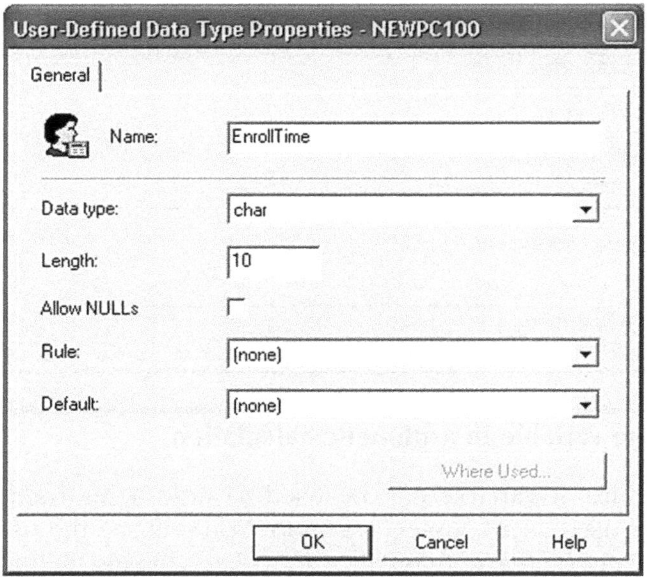

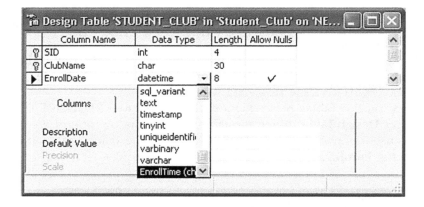

Figure 7.3   User-defined data type

Figure 7.4   User-defined data type

increase is $10 each time. We use a WHILE loop to test if there is a club that charges a fee less than $100. If so, a $10 fee increase will be applied to every club. An IF...THEN structure is used to test if any club charges a membership fee greater than $170. If so, break the WHILE loop to stop the increase of fees. If not, continue the increase until some club charges a fee greater than $170. For the IF...THEN structure, if the code block contains more than a one-line statement, BEGIN...END is needed to enclose all the statements. In this example, we have used WHILE, BEGIN...END, IF...ELSE, BREAK, and CONTINUE to illustrate the use of flow-control structures. At the end of the program, a SELECT statement is used to display the current membership fee after several increments (see Figure 7.5).

Table 7.1 Flow-Control Keywords and Descriptions

Keyword	Description
BEGIN...END	Defines a block that contains a list of SQL statements.
BREAK	Exits a WHILE loop when a specified condition is met. If the WHILE loop is embedded in another WHILE loop, exits the inner WHILE loop.
CONTINUE	Continues the currently running WHILE loop.
GOTO label	Jumps to the label defined by the keyword *label* and continues to process the statements starting from that label.
IF...ELSE	Determines if a condition is true. If true, the block of statements under IF is executed. Otherwise, the block of statements under ELSE is executed.
RETURN	Exits processing SQL statements unconditionally.
WAITFOR	Delays a statement execution by a specified time.
WHILE	Processes a block of SQL statements repeatedly while a specific condition continues to be TRUE.

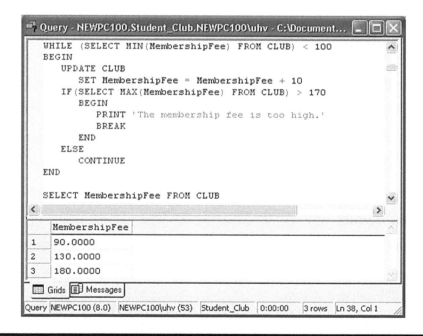

Figure 7.5 Use flow-control structures

Messages are printed in the Messages pane. Click on the **Messages** tab, and you will see the message we entered (see Figure 7.6).

To make Transact-SQL act like a procedural programming language, SQL Server also allows us to create functions and procedures. To trace errors in a

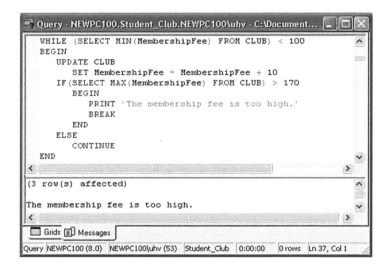

Figure 7.6   Information printed in Messages pane

code, SQL Server has added some debugging utilities and a debugger specific for procedures. These topics are covered in the next few sections.

7.3 Procedures and Functions

If a list of SQL statements has multiple input and output parameters, it is called a *procedure*. A *function* is a list of SQL statements that can take multiple input parameters but will return only a single value output. A variable is used to receive the returned value from a function. In other words, a function is commonly used for returning a single calculated value, whereas a procedure is commonly used for performing activities that involve a set of values for multiple variables. We look at functions and procedures here.

7.3.1   Functions

There are two types of functions, *built-in functions* and *user-defined functions*.

- Built-in functions are prebuilt in Transact-SQL. SQL Server users cannot modify these functions.
- User-defined functions are created by database users with the CREATE FUNCTION command. The CREATE FUNCTION command allows a maximum of 1024 input parameters. Unlike procedures, a user-defined function returns a single value or table and does not have an output parameter.

To see how to use the built-in functions and how to create user-defined functions, see the following subsections.

Built-In Functions

SQL Server provides a function library where built-in functions are categorized into three types: *rowset, scalar,* and *aggregate.* The group functions covered in Chapter 6 are built-in aggregate functions. We first look at these three types of built-in functions:

- *Rowset functions*: These functions can be used like table references in a SQL statement. In fact, we used the rowset function OPENQUERY in Chapter 5 to access an external data file. The commonly used rowset functions are the following:

      OPENQUERY(linked_server , 'query')

  - OPENQUERY is used in the FROM clause as a table name to access external data. It can also be used in INSERT, UPDATE, and DELETE statements as a target table. When the query parameter returns multiple result sets, OPENQUERY returns only the first one.

        OPENDATASOURCE(provider_name, init_string)

  - OPENDATASOURCE is also used to access external data. Its parameters pass in the external data file connection information used as part of a four-part object named

        linked_server.catalog.scheme.object_name

    Periods are used to separate the four parts. As an example, we use the function OPENDATASOURCE to access an external Access data file **c:\ dbbook\GPA.mdb**. The data are saved in the table STUDENT_GPA. The object_name in the last part is the table name (see Figure 7.7).

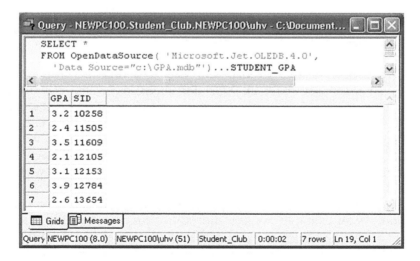

Figure 7.7 Use OPENDATASOURCE

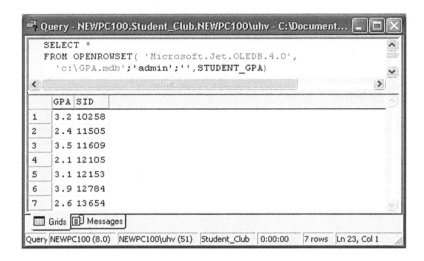

Figure 7.8   Use OPENROWSET

Note: For this example, you may need to create the table with two columns GPA and SID in Microsoft Access and save it as GPA.mdb in an easy-to-work-with folder. Your folder may not be like c:\. I just made that up.

```
OPENROWSET ( 'provider_name', { 'datasource' ; 'user_id' ;
    'password' | 'provider_string' }, { [ catalog. ] [ schema.
    ] object | 'query' })
```

— Like OPENDATASOURE, OPENROWSET can be used in the FROM clause of a query to access remote data from an OLE DB data source (see Figure 7.8). It can also be used in an INSERT, UPDATE, or DELETE statement as a target table.

```
OPENXML(idoc int [in],rowpattern nvarchar[in],[flags
    byte[in]]) [WITH (SchemaDeclaration | TableName)]
```

— OPENXML is used to map XML data to a relational rowset to provide a rowset view over an XML document. OPENXML can be used with rowset providers such as a table, a view, or an OPENROWSET function in a Transact-SQL statement. We talk more about XML later.

- *Aggregate functions*: This is a set of group functions used with SELECT, GROUP BY, or HAVING statements. The commonly used aggregate functions are COUNT, AVG, SUM, MAX, and MIN. These functions were discussed in Chapter 6.
- *Scalar functions*: A scalar function returns a single value in a valid expression. As an example, we use the ROUND function that has a format as

```
ROUND( numeric_expression , length [ , function ] )
```

to return a rounded number for updating MembershipFee (see Figure 7.9).

Figure 7.9   Use scalar function ROUND

The number to be rounded is 66. The second argument −1 is used to indicate that the precision to be rounded is one digit to the left of the decimal point. As you can see, MembershipFee is updated to 70.0000. If the second argument is a positive number, the number in the first argument is rounded to the right of the decimal point.

User-Defined Functions

User-defined functions can be classified into two categories: *scalar functions* that return a scalar value and *table functions* (or *table-valued functions*) that return a table. To create a user-defined function, use the statement CREATE FUNCTION with the following format:

```
CREATE FUNCTION [ owner_name. ] function_name
( [{@parameter_name [AS] scalar_parameter_data_type [ = default ]
   }[ ,...n ] ] )
RETURNS scalar_return_data_type
[WITH < function_option> [ [,] ...n] ]
[AS]
BEGIN
   function_body
   RETURN scalar_expression
END
```

- *Scalar functions:* A scalar function can return any scalar value, *bigint*, or *sql_variant* that allows a variable to store values of different data types. For example, a single sql_variant column can hold int, decimal, char, binary, and nchar values. The following example illustrates how to create and use a user-defined scalar function. The function is used to update the MembershipFee column in the CLUB table (see Figure 7.10).
    The function has two input parameters, Fee and Rate. The returned data type is money. The function code is placed in the BEGIN ... END block. In this function, Fee is updated according to a given Rate. The New_Fee will be returned. To illustrate the use of the user-defined function, we update the original MembershipFee by increasing it by 5 percent. The SELECT state-

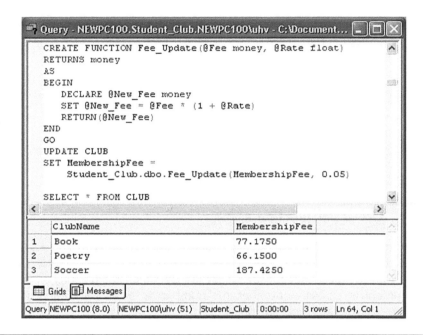

Figure 7.10   Create and use user-defined scalar function

ment is used to show the updated MembershipFee. To modify the code of the user-defined function, you need to replace the keyword CREATE with ALTER in the above example. To delete a function, use DROP followed by the function name.

■ *Table functions:* There are two types of table functions: *inline function* and *multi-statement function*. In an inline table function, the returned table is a rowset from a single SELECT statement. In a multi-statement table function, a TABLE variable is used to store and accumulate the rows returned from multiple SELECT statements.

  – To illustrate the use of inline table functions, we create a function called Registration that returns detailed registration information for a given student id (see Figure 7.11). The function Registration returns a table constructed from three tables, STUDENT, STUDENT_MENTOR, and STUDENT_CLUB. We can use this function as a table or view.

  – To illustrate the use of a multi-statement function, consider the case in which we can return a student's information such as id, name, mentor's name, and the club(s) in which the student is enrolled. After this student's information is available, we can add the information about the students who have the same mentor. Because we cannot run the second selection before the information becomes available in the first selection, it is difficult to express this logic in a single query. This is a good case for implementing a multi-statement table function that can accumulate information from multiple SQL statements and return the information to the calling program at once. Another difference between an inline function and a multi-statement function is that the multi-statement function returns a table variable with the @ sign as the first

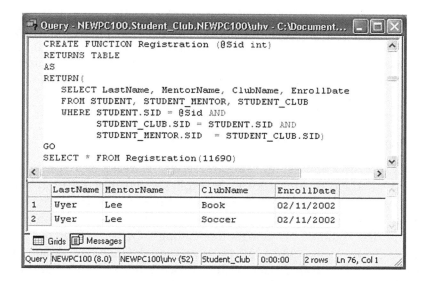

Figure 7.11   Create and use user-defined inline table function

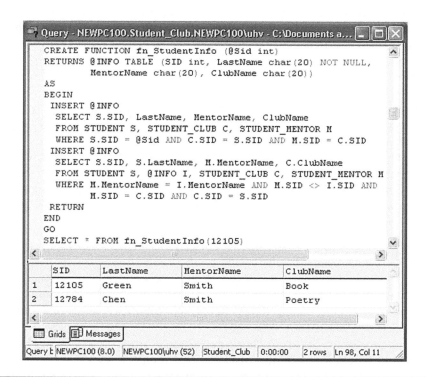

Figure 7.12   Create and use user-defined multi-statement table function

letter in its name (see Figure 7.12). In Figure 7.12, the returned variable is defined as the table @INFO. There are two INSERT statements. The first one inserts information about a student specified by the @Sid parameter. Because Green has the student id 12105, the first line of the output is the information about Green. The second `INSERT` statement inserts information about the students who have the same mentor as Green. Chen's mentor is also Smith, so Chen's information is placed in the second row of the output. In the last `SELECT` statement, the function `fn_StudentInfo` is called in the `FROM` clause and the table `@INFO` is returned.

7.3.2 Procedures

Like functions, procedures are predeveloped Transact-SQL programs. The difference is that a procedure does not explicitly return a value. A procedure does not use the `RETURN` keyword to return a value to the calling SQL program. It uses output parameters to return values; this means that a procedure can return multiple values to the calling SQL program. If parameters cause an error in a procedure, all the transactions that have been done by the procedure will be rolled back. Often, procedures are stored and executed on a database server. They are called stored procedures. Stored procedures have the following advantages:

- Once created, stored procedures are available to all database users with the proper privileges. Many database applications can share the same stored procedures.
- Using stored procedures can improve performance because they are already executable files and there is no need to parse them again when called by multiple users.
- Stored procedures can be written by experienced programmers and optimized by DBMS systems. When shared by many users, stored procedures have fewer programming errors and run faster.
- Because stored procedures are installed on servers, they are protected by better security measures.
- When clients call stored procedures on the server, only the final computation results are returned to the clients. In this way, network traffic can be reduced.

There are five types of stored procedures:

- *System-stored procedures:* These stored procedures are created by SQL Server and used for database administration, security management, and providing system data to database applications. The names of system-stored procedures often start with `sp_`.
- *Local stored procedures:* These procedures are stored on user-built databases and used to conduct user-defined database tasks.
- *Temporary stored procedures:* These are temporary local procedures. They will be deleted when the database server is shut down or when the database connection is terminated.
- *Extended stored procedures:* These stored procedures are written in other programming languages such as C and are compiled as *Dynamic Link Library* (DLL) files. SQL Server can dynamically load and execute these stored procedures.

■ *Remote stored procedures:* These procedures can be executed on a remote SQL Server database.

You can use stored procedures to do the following:

■ Calculate complicated application logic
■ Invoke other stored procedures or functions
■ Process multiple databases
■ Submit Transact-SQL programs to SQL Server

Viewing and Executing Stored Procedures

Many system-stored procedures have been built into SQL Server and are stored in the master database. To explore these system procedures, follow the steps below.

1. Log on to Windows as a system administrator and open **Query Analyzer** in **Microsoft SQL Server**.
2. By default, the **Object Browser** is on the left-hand side of the screen. If it is not there, click **Tools**, then **Object Browser**, and then **Show/hide**.
3. Expand the **master** database, and you will see the folders of **Stored Procedures**, **Extended Procedures**, and **Functions**. Expand the **Stored Procedures** folder.
4. There are many stored procedures, for example, **dbo.sp_spaceused,** where dbo is the owner of the stored procedure. This stored procedure is used to report storage space used by a table or the entire database if the table name is not specified. There are two folders, **Parameters** and **Dependencies**, under **dbo.sp_spaceused**.
5. To see the parameters used by the stored procedure, expand the **Parameters** folder; you will see three parameters, **@RETURN_VALUE(int, Return Value)**, **@objname(nvarchar(776), Input)**, and **@updateusage(varchar(5), Input)**, for this stored procedure. The first argument in parentheses defines the data type of the parameter and the second argument specifies the functionality of the parameter. All stored procedures should contain the **@RETURN_VALUE** parameter.
6. Expand the **Dependencies** folder; there are four system tables: **dbo.sysobjects**, **dbo.sysindexes**, **dbo.sysfiles**, and **dbo.spt_values**. To find how much storage space is used by a table or the entire database, the system-stored procedures will search these four system tables. The **Dependencies** folder lists all the tables depending on or depended by this stored procedure.
7. To view the content of the stored procedure **dbo.sp_spaceused**, use another system-stored procedure **sp_helptext**, as shown in Figure 7.13.
8. To execute the stored procedure dbo.sp_spaceused, expand the **master** database node in the **Object Browser** pane. If Object Browser is not open, click the **Tools** menu, click **Object Browser**, and then select **Show/hide**. Expand the **Stored Procedures** node. Right-click on the **dbo.sp_spaceused** stored procedure and elect **Open**. Highlight the parameter **@objname.** Type the system table name **sysobjects** in the **Value** textbox. Click the **Execute** button, and you will have the code and information about the system table **sysobjects** (see Figure 7.14).

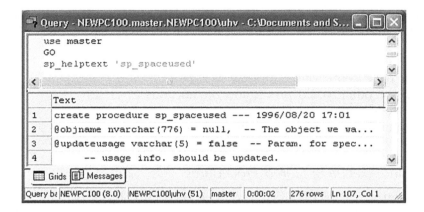

Figure 7.13 View content of stored procedure sp_spaceused

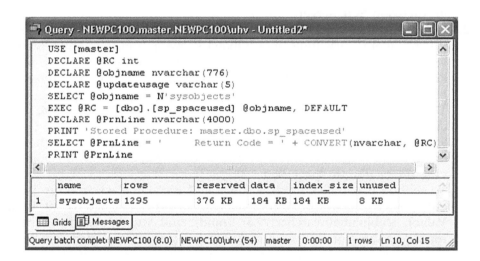

Figure 7.14 Execute stored procedure sp_spaceused

You can also execute the stored procedure by executing the following Transact-SQL statement in Query Analyzer:

```
USE master
EXEC sp_spaceused 'sysobjects'
```

The above statement will give you the same result as that shown in Figure 7.14.

Creating, Modifying, and Deleting Stored Procedures

You can create a stored procedure using Enterprise Manager or Create Stored Procedure Wizard in Enterprise Manager or by executing the CREATE PRO-CEDURE statement in Query Analyzer. Suppose that we need a stored procedure to update the membership fee for a given fee increment.

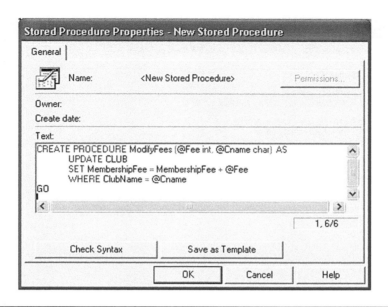

Figure 7.15   Create stored procedure with Enterprise Manager

To create a stored procedure with **Enterprise Manager**, use the following steps:

1. Open **Enterprise Manager** and expand the **Databases** folder under the **SQL Server Group** node.
2. Expand the database **Student_Club**, and right-click **Stored Procedures**.
3. Click **New Stored Procedure**. Enter the SQL statements of the stored procedure in the text area (see Figure 7.15). In the above example, there are two input parameters, **@Fee** and **@Cname**. The value in the column MembershipFee is increased by adding the value passed in from the input parameter **@Fee**.
4. To debug the SQL statement, click **Check Syntax**.
5. To save the new stored procedure, click **OK**.
6. Click the **Cancel** button to exit.
7. To verify that the newly created stored procedure is saved, right-click the **Stored Procedures** node; then select **Refresh**. You should be able to see the new stored procedure.

To create a stored procedure with **Create Stored Procedure Wizard**, use the following steps. In this example, a new value will be assigned to the MembershipFee column.

1. Open **Enterprise Manger** and expand the **Databases** folder under the **SQL Server Group** node.
2. Expand the database **Student_Club**, and then highlight **Stored Procedures**.
3. Click the **Tools** tab, and then select **Wizards**.
4. Expand the **Database** node, highlight **Create Stored Procedure Wizard**, and then click **OK**.

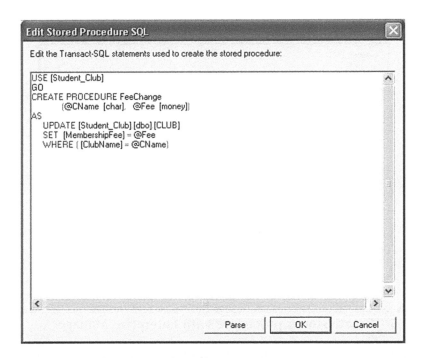

Figure 7.16   Create stored procedure with Create Stored Procedure Wizard

5. Click **Next** and select the database **Student_Club**. Then click **Next** again to move to the **Select Stored Procedures** window.
6. Check the cell crossed by **CLUB** and **Update**. Then click **Next**.
7. To edit SQL statements, click the **Edit** button. Then click the **Edit SQL** button.
8. Enter the SQL statements as shown in Figure 7.16.
9. Click the **Parse** button to debug the code. Click **OK** and then click **Finish**.

To create a stored procedure by Transact-SQL statements in Query Analyzer, use the following steps:

1. Enter the SQL statements shown in Figure 7.17 directly into Query Analyzer. The stored procedure name has been changed to avoid conflicts.
2. Highlight the code and click the **Execute Query** button ▶ on the tool bar.

To modify a stored procedure, you can use Enterprise Manager or the ALTER PROCEDURE statement in Query Analyzer. To modify a stored procedure with Enterprise Manager, use the following steps:

1. Open **Enterprise Manager** and expand the **Databases** folder under the **SQL Server Group** node.
2. Expand the database **Student_Club**, and then expand the **Stored Procedures** node.
3. Right-click on the stored procedure to be modified, for example, **Modify-Fees**, and then select **Properties**.

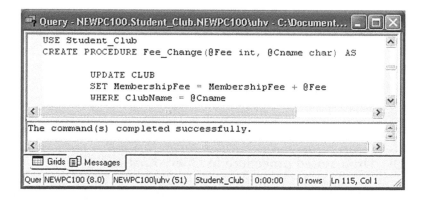

Figure 7.17   Create stored procedure using Transact-SQL statements

```
SET QUOTED_IDENTIFIER OFF
GO
SET ANSI_NULLS OFF
GO

ALTER   PROCEDURE ModifyFees (@Fee int, @Cname char)   AS
        UPDATE CLUB
        SET MembershipFee = MembershipFee + @Fee
        WHERE ClubName = @Cname
GO
SET QUOTED_IDENTIFIER OFF
GO
SET ANSI_NULLS ON
GO
```

Query - NEWPC100.Student_Club.NEWPC100\uhv - Untitled3*

Read NEWPC100 (8.0)   NEWPC100\uhv (55)   Student_Club   0:00:00   0 rows   Ln 16, Col 1

Figure 7.18   Modify stored procedure in Query Analyzer

4. In the **Stored Procedure Properties** dialog box, you can modify the SQL statement accordingly.
5. Click **OK** to save the change and exit.

To modify a stored procedure with **Transact-SQL** statements, use the following steps:

1. Open **Query Analyzer**. Expand the database **Student_Club** in **Object Browser**, and then expand the **Stored Procedures** folder.
2. Right-click on the stored procedure **ModifyFees** and select **Edit**, and the dialog box shown in Figure 7.18 will appear.
3. Modify the SQL statements accordingly, and then execute the SQL statements.

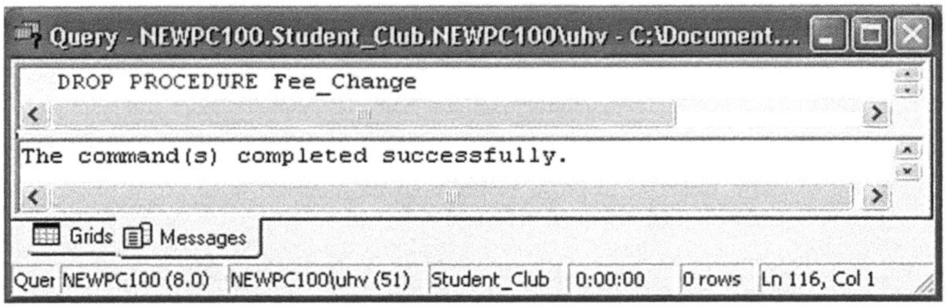

Figure 7.19   Drop stored procedure in Query Analyzer

There are two ways to delete a stored procedure. First, in **Enterprise Manager**, expand the **Stored Procedures** node in a database, right-click the stored procedure to be deleted, and then select **Delete** on the pop-up menu. Click the **Drop All** button to delete the stored procedure. The second way to delete a stored procedure is to execute the Transact-SQL statement in Query Analyzer as shown below:

```
USE database_name
DROP PROCEDURE stored_procedure_name
```

Execute the statement; the stored procedure will be deleted. As an example, let us drop the stored procedure Fee_Change (see Figure 7.19).

7.4 Triggers

Triggers are a kind of stored procedure that is executed automatically for updating, inserting, and deleting database objects. For example, if a student has graduated, you want to remove the student's id and name from the STUDENT table in the Student_Club database. In such a case, you may want to create a trigger to automatically delete the records from the STUDENT_MENTOR, STUDENT_SERVICE, and STUDENT_CLUB tables that are associated with that student. As mentioned in the introduction section, triggers are a key component in implementing database application logic and database maintenance. Triggers are useful in the following cases:

- Modifying data values in associated tables when a record in a table is changed
- Updating the content of a view that is constructed on multiple tables
- Invoking external programs such as stored procedures
- Displaying warning messages when data in a database have been modified
- Enforcing complex data constraints that may be difficult to enforce at the database design stage
- Computing data values for columns containing calculated values
- Validating data values in associated tables before a record can be modified
- Implementing dynamic application logic
- Rolling back transactions

When using triggers, keep the following in mind:

- A trigger can be defined in only one table or one view. If you need the same trigger to be used in another table, define it again with the same SQL code body but a different name.
- Triggers cannot be created for system tables or temporary tables.
- A trigger can be fired by multiple INSERT, UPDATE, or DELETE statements.
- Triggers do not accept input parameters.
- Too many triggers may slow down database performance.

7.4.1 About Triggers

SQL Server categorizes triggers by the types of SQL statements that cause them to fire or by what time they fire. Because SQL statements that cause triggers to fire are INSERT, UPDATE, and DELETE, a trigger can be categorized as one of these types or any combination of them.

A trigger can be fired either before or after a SQL statement. An *INSTEAD OF* trigger defined on a table or view is fired before a change is made to the underlying table or view by a SQL statement. Instead of executing the SQL statement, the INSTEAD OF trigger will run the other SQL statements preprogrammed in the trigger. The INSTEAD OF trigger is used for situations in which more complicated database processing is needed to overwrite the relatively simple activities such as insert, update, or delete. For example, instead of simply deleting a student from the STUDENT table, we can use an INSTEAD OF trigger to delete all of this student's information, such as his or her mentor(s), duty (duties), and enrollment date(s), from other tables. Depending on the SQL statements, there are INSTEAD OF INSERT, INSTEAD OF UPDATE, and INSTEAD OF DELETE triggers. Notice that INSTEAD OF DELETE and INSTEAD OF UPDATE cannot be created on the tables that have corresponding ON DELETE and ON UPDATE cascading referential integrity constraints. Also, you cannot create multiple INSTEAD OF triggers on one table.

An AFTER trigger is fired after an INSERT, UPDATE, or DELETE statement is executed. The AFTER trigger is used to enhance the modification done by a simple INSERT, UPDATE, or DELETE trigger. For example, after a student is added to the table STUDENT, an AFTER trigger should be used to update the student's information in related tables. Another use of the AFTER trigger is for view modification. You can create more than one AFTER trigger for a table and specify the order of firing these triggers. The AFTER trigger cannot be defined on a view. The default trigger type is AFTER.

Trigger Execution

The way of executing a trigger is different from that of executing other stored procedures. A trigger can be fired (executed) only when valid data modification events such as INSERT, UPDATE, or DELETE occur. Triggers cannot be fired manually.

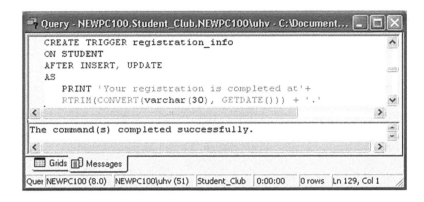

Figure 7.20 Create trigger in Query Analyzer

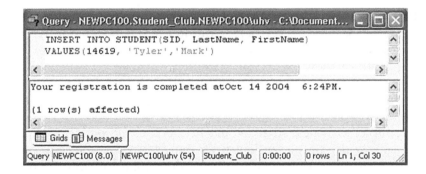

Figure 7.21 Test trigger in Query Analyzer

Creating, Modifying, and Deleting Triggers

You can create a trigger by using either Query Analyzer or Enterprise Manager. To create a trigger using Query Analyzer, you need to specify the following:

```
CREATE TRIGGER trigger_name
ON associated_table_names or associated_view_names
FOR trigger_types; may include AFTER, or INSTEAD OF, plus any
   combination of INSERT, UPDATE, DELETE
AS Transact-SQL statement as the trigger body
```

You may use AFTER or INSTEAD OF to replace FOR. For example, after a student is added to or updated in the STUDENT table, we can print out a message to display the time the enrollment is completed by creating a trigger using the SQL statement in Figure 7.20. Notice that the built-in function RTRIM is used to trim the empty spaces on the right-hand side.

To test the trigger we have just created, we can add a new student to the STUDENT table with the student id 14619, first name Mark, and last name Tyler (see Figure 7.21).

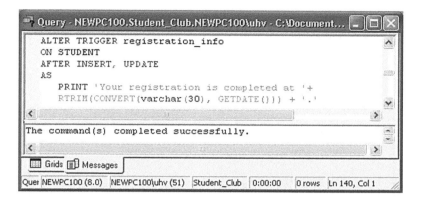

Figure 7.22   Modify trigger using ALTER TRIGGER

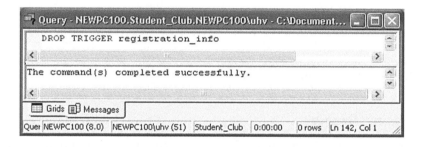

Figure 7.23   Delete trigger using DROP TRIGGER

You can use the ALTER TRIGGER command to modify an existing trigger. For example, to add a space between "at" and the month in the above output, you can use the statement in Figure 7.22.

To delete a trigger from a database, you can use the DROP TRIGGER command. For example, to delete the registration_info trigger, enter the statement in Figure 7.23 in Query Analyzer.

You can also create, modify, and delete triggers using Enterprise Manager in SQL Server. The following steps will show you how to create a trigger in Enterprise Manager:

1. Open **Enterprise Manager** and expand the **Databases** folder under the **SQL Server Group** node. Click **Tables** under the database **Student_Club**.
2. Right-click on the table **STUDENT**. Select **All Tasks**, and then select **Manage Triggers**.
3. Enter the **CREATE TRIGGER** statement in the **Text** pane, as shown in Figure 7.24.
4. Click the **Check Syntax** button. If there is no syntax error, click **OK** to save and exit.

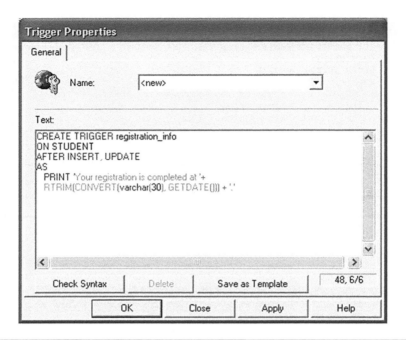

Figure 7.24   Create trigger in Enterprise Manager

7.4.2   Using Triggers

As mentioned at the beginning of this section, triggers have many uses in database management and business logic implementation. In the following, we use several examples to demonstrate how to use triggers.

Validating Business Constraints

The following is one of the business rules for the Student_Club database given in Chapter 3:

■ No student should have the same training by more than one mentor.

If a student serves as a recruiter and a Web master, both positions require the Web-development skill; the student should get training from one mentor who offers Web-development training. You can implement the rule in the following way. Use an INSTEAD OF trigger for the table STUDENT_MENTOR to check the constraint whenever a new row is added or an existing role is updated.

When a trigger fires, transactions are logged in the logical tables such as INSERTED or DELETED. These are pseudo tables that can be used for database maintenance and dynamic modification of data values. An insert event will generate the INSERTED logic table that contains the record set that has been inserted. The delete event will generate the DELETED logic table that contains the deleted record set. The update event will generate both the INSERTED

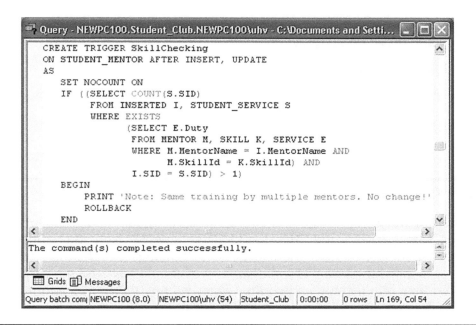

Figure 7.25 Trigger for verifying constraints

and DELETED logic tables that contain the original record set in the DELETED table and the modified record set in the INSERTED table.

To illustrate the use of these logic tables in a constraint-checking trigger, consider the following example. In this example, a student will switch his or her mentor to learn a different skill. This will lead to the modification of the STUDENT_MENTOR table. After the table STUDENT_MENTOR is updated, we need to check if the student has the same type of training by more than one mentor. If so, the change will be rolled back.

In the above code, an IF structure is used to verify if a student has the same training by more than one mentor (see Figure 7.25). The WHERE condition

```
EXISTS (SELECT E.Duty
   FROM MENTOR M, SKILL K, SERVICE E
   WHERE M.MentorName = I.MentorName AND
      M.SkillId = K.SkillId)
```

is used to find all duties that match the skill provided by the mentor whose name is listed in the table INSERTED. The next WHERE condition

```
I.SID = S.SID
```

is used to match the student who made the change in the table STUDENT_MENTOR. If the count for the same training is greater than 1, the message is printed and the update operation is terminated. In the code of Figure 7.25, the statement **SET NOCOUNT ON** is used to conceal the output of the SELECT statements. To test the trigger, enter the statement in Figure 7.26 in the Query Analyzer.

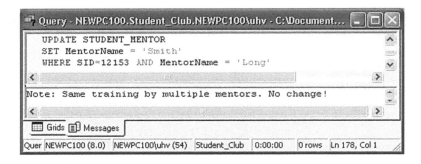

Figure 7.26   Test constraint trigger

The student with id 12153 has two mentors, Long and Wang. Wang is the mentor who provides the Web-development training. Now the student is adding the mentor Smith who also provides training in Web development. This has violated the business rule "No student should have the same training by more than one mentor." When the trigger is fired, the user is informed of the problem and the transaction is rolled back.

Implementing Dynamic Application Logic

In this application of triggers, we are going to calculate membership fees. Suppose that membership fees depend on the following rules:

- If a student is enrolled in two clubs concurrently, he or she will get a $10 discount on the membership fee for the second club.
- If a student is enrolled in three clubs concurrently, he or she will get a $10 discount on the membership fee for the second club and a $20 discount for the third club.

Suppose we want the membership fee calculation to be done automatically whenever a change is made to the enrollment. To do so, we create a trigger that will count how many clubs a student is currently enrolled in and calculate the membership fees accordingly. Enter the following code in Query Analyzer:

```
CREATE TRIGGER FeeCalculation
ON STUDENT_CLUB AFTER INSERT, UPDATE
AS
-- Declaring variables.
DECLARE @ClubCount As int,
   @MembershipFee As Money,
   @UpdatedFee As Money
BEGIN

-- Assign the regular membership fee to variable @membershipFee.
SET @MembershipFee = (SELECT MembershipFee
   FROM CLUB C, INSERTED I
   WHERE C.ClubName = I. ClubName)
```

```
/*If a student is enrolled in a new club,
  count how many clubs the student is enrolled in.*/
SET @ClubCount = (SELECT COUNT(S.ClubName)
  FROM STUDENT_CLUB S, INSERTED I
  WHERE S.SID = I.SID)

/*Update the membership fee based on the number of clubs enrolled.*/

IF (@ClubCount = 2)
BEGIN
  SET @UpdatedFee = @MembershipFee - 10
  PRINT 'Your membership fee is $' + CONVERT(varchar(10),
      @UpdatedFee)
END
ELSE IF (@ClubCount = 3)
BEGIN
  SET @UpdatedFee = @MembershipFee - 20
  PRINT 'Your membership fee is $' + CONVERT(varchar(10),
      @UpdatedFee)
END
ELSE IF (@ClubCount = 1)
    PRINT 'Your membership fee is $' + CONVERT(varchar(10),
      @MembershipFee)

END
```

In the above code, three variables have been declared. **@ClubCount** is used to hold the number of clubs in which a student is currently enrolled. **@MembershipFee** is used to hold the original membership fee. **@UpdatedFee** is used to hold the updated membership fee based on the number of clubs in which a student is currently enrolled. We set the values for variables **@MembershipFee** and **@ClubCount** by querying the corresponding information in the database. The SID in the table **INSERTED** is used to match the SID values in the table STUDENT_CLUB. Based on the value in **@ClubCount**, the updated value is assigned to the variable **@UpdatedFee**. Then the updated fee is displayed on the screen. The built-in function is used to convert the Money data type to the char data type for printing to the screen. To test the trigger, run the INSERT statement in Figure 7.27 in Query Analyzer.

Keeping Referential Integrities

Triggers are used to ensure referential integrities after data have been inserted, deleted, or updated. In the next example, a trigger is used to prevent the delete operation from deleting the last duty in each duty category. After the deletion, the trigger checks if this type of duty still exists in the table STUDENT_SERVICE. If not, it will display a message and roll back the transaction. A trigger called KeepIntegrity is created to accomplish this task. Enter the code in Figure 7.28 in Query Analyzer.

To test the trigger, we delete the duty WebMaster from the table STUDENT_SERVICE. Because there is only one WebMaster in the table, the

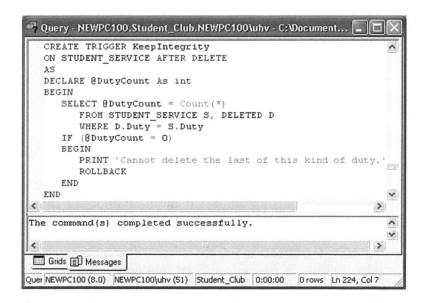

Figure 7.27   Test dynamic logic implementation trigger

```
CREATE TRIGGER KeepIntegrity
ON STUDENT_SERVICE AFTER DELETE
AS
DECLARE @DutyCount As int
BEGIN
    SELECT @DutyCount = Count(*)
        FROM STUDENT_SERVICE S, DELETED D
        WHERE D.Duty = S.Duty
    IF (@DutyCount = 0)
    BEGIN
        PRINT 'Cannot delete the last of this kind of duty.'
        ROLLBACK
    END
END
```

The command(s) completed successfully.

Figure 7.28   Keeping referential integrity trigger

trigger will roll back the transaction and inform the user (see Figure 7.29). The message indicates the deletion operation is prevented.

7.5 Debugging SQL Procedures

For more complex stored procedures and triggers, finding and fixing errors in the code is a difficult task. SQL Server displays compiling errors in a message pane. The error code, the associated error message, and the error location are displayed to assist the debugging process. Sometimes, the error location does not indicate the exact line where an error occurs; instead, it indicates the starting line of a code block. In such a case, you may want to comment out some lines to narrow down the location of the error.

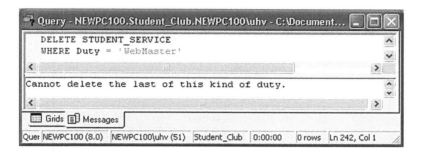

Figure 7.29   Test referential integrity trigger

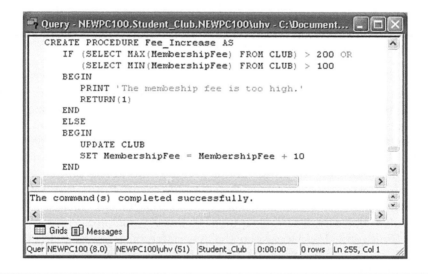

Figure 7.30   Stored procedure `Fee_Increase` **for debugging**

A logic error often leads to undesired output. The logic error may be caused by incorrect input, syntax, or calculation. The debugger that runs in Query Analyzer is the tool to let a database developer view the values in the variables during the execution of procedures. The debugger can be used to do the following:

- Validate input and output parameters for a procedure
- Set a breakpoint to check variable values
- Trace statements step by step in a procedure

7.5.1   Procedure Debugger

Before you start a debugger, make sure that the target procedure exists. To illustrate the use of a debugger, we first create the stored procedure `Fee_Increase`, as shown in Figure 7.30. To debug the stored procedure `Fee_Increase` by the debugger in Query Analyzer, follow the steps below:

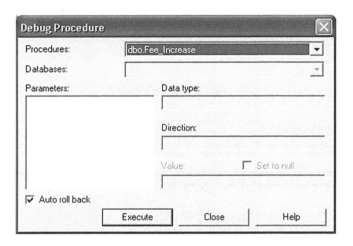

Figure 7.31 Debugger dialog box

1. Open **Query Analyzer**. Expand the **Stored Procedures** node in **Object Browser,** which is on the left-hand side of the Query Analyzer window. Right-click the stored procedure **Fee_Increase**. In the pop-up menu, select **Debug**. A dialog box appears when the **Transact-SQL Debugger** starts. In the dialog box, you can set values for input parameter variables. In our example, there is no input variable, so the **Parameters** pane is empty (see Figure 7.31).

2. Click **Execute** to continue. After the Execute button is clicked, a five-pane window appears. The descriptions of these panes are:
   a. Code pane: Used to display the SQL statements that are being debugged.
   b. Local variable pane: Used to display the names and values of local variables.
   c. Global variable pane: Used to display the names and values of global variables.
   d. Callstack pane: Used to list the procedure calls that are still not completed. This pane tracks the procedure calling history.
   e. Result text pane: Used to display the output of the stored procedure that is being tested.
   Figure 7.32 shows the debugger window. In this window, the debugger is running against the stored procedure Fee_Increase. As shown, the cursor in the code pane is on the second line. At this point, two global variables identified by the @@ sign are listed in the Global variable pane. In the **Callstack** pane, the uncompleted procedure call is from the stored procedure Fee_Increase. The status bar indicates that the current stored procedure is running.

3. On the menu, there are several buttons related to debugger activities. The descriptions of these buttons are listed below:
   a. Go: Runs the stored procedure in the code pane.
   b. Toggle Breakpoints: Sets or removes a breakpoint at the line where the cursor is placed.

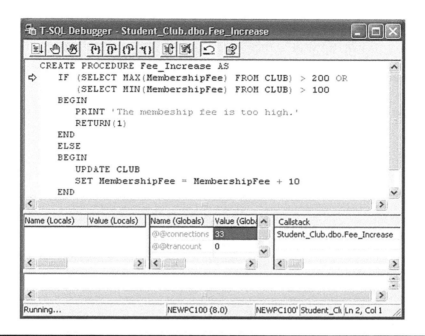

Figure 7.32 Debugger panes

    c. Remove All Breakpoints: Removes all the breakpoints created in the code pane.

    d. Step Into: Executes the SQL statements in the code pane one at a time.

    e. Step Over: When step-by-step execution comes to a statement that is used to call another procedure, Step Over returns the message that contains only the final result from the procedure call.

    f. Step Out: Executes the remaining statements of the current procedure.

    g. Run to Cursor: Executes the statements up to the current cursor.

    h. Restart: Restarts the existing debugging process.

    i. Stop Debugging: Stops the current debugging process.

    j. Auto Rollback: Automatically rolls back all the work that has been done during the debugging process.

As an example, Figure 7.33 shows that two breakpoints have been set, and the execution of the SQL statement stops at the first breakpoint.

7.5.2 *RETURN Statement*

To verify that a certain value has been achieved during calculation, the RETURN statement can be used to unconditionally return the code of either 1 or 0 to identify the consequence. The following code will illustrate the use of RETURN in the procedure Fee_Increase. As shown in Figure 7.30, if the membership fee is too high, the code 1 is returned by the RETURN statement and the message "The membership fee is too high" is printed.

    To test the stored procedure with the RETURN statement, enter the codes from Figures 7.34 and 7.35 in Query Analyzer. If the membership fees are

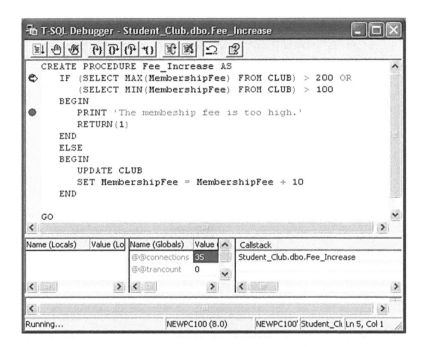

Figure 7.33   Breakpoints in debugger pane

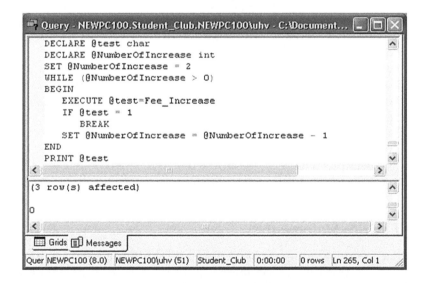

Figure 7.34   Test RETURN **statement for allowable membership fee**

between $100 and $200, the code 0 is returned; otherwise, the code 1 is returned and the message "The membership fee is too high" is printed. The RETURN statement is also used to test values in variables such as testing if a variable contains NULL values.

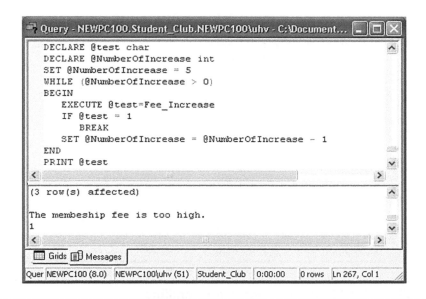

Figure 7.35 Test RETURN **statement for error handling**

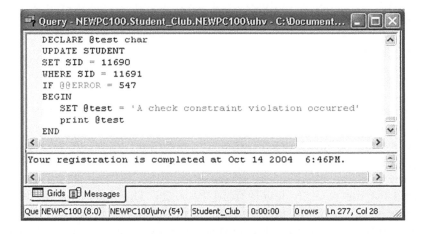

Figure 7.36 Use @@ERROR **for error handling**

7.5.3   @@ERROR

The @@ERROR function can return up to more than 3000 database-related errors for the last executed SQL statement. To illustrate the use of the @@ERROR function, run the example in Figure 7.36 that updates a student id. The result in the figure shows that the update is complete and there is no error.

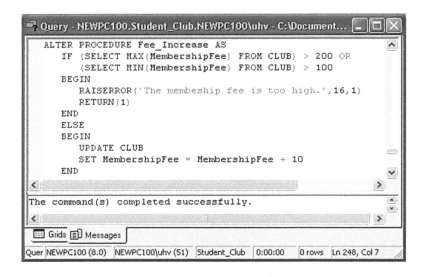

Figure 7.37   Use RAISERROR **for error handling**

7.5.4   *RAISERROR*

The RAISERROR statement can be used to return a user-defined error message. After an error message is defined by a user, it can be used as a server error message. The syntax of RAISERROR is given below:

```
RAISERROR ( { msg_id | msg_str } { , severity , state }
    [ , argument [ ,...n ] ] )
    [ WITH option [ ,...n ] ]
```

The example in Figure 7.37 shows how to use the RAISERROR statement to return the user-defined message "The membership fee is too high."

In the syntax of RAISERROR, the severity is set to 16. A user can define the range of severity levels from 0 to 18. Only members of the sysadmin fixed server role can use severity levels from 19 to 25. The WITH LOG option is required for the severity levels from 19 to 25. The state argument is set to 1. The state is an arbitrary integer from 1 through 127. The state integer can be used to represent information about the state of an error. To test the use of the RAISERROR statement, set the membership fee to $50 for the Book Club, $60 for the Poetry Club, and $210 for the Soccer Club and run the statement shown in Figure 7.38.

As expected, a user-defined message with message id 50000 is returned. The user-defined message "The membership fee is too high" is printed in the Messages pane.

To further extend ANSI SQL to procedural programs, you can create extended stored procedures in other programming languages such as C++ or Visual Basic. In such cases, the debugging process can be done by copying the stored procedure DLL to SQL Server. For more detailed information, please read the SQL Server manual.

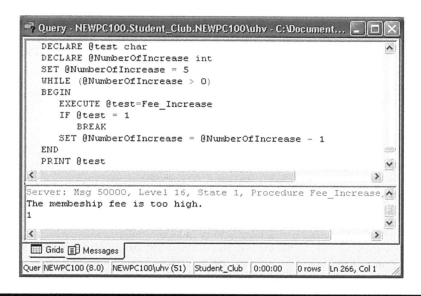

Figure 7.38 Use RAISERROR **to return user-defined error message**

7.6 Summary

In this chapter, you have learned the ANSI SQL programming extension, Transact-SQL. You have learned how to use Transact-SQL to create, execute, and test functions, stored procedures, and triggers. Examples were used to illustrate how to declare and use variables and use loop control structures. You have seen different types of functions. In this chapter, the advantages of the stored procedures and triggers have been discussed in detail. Through some hands-on practice, you have learned to create, execute, and test stored procedures and triggers with both Enterprise Manager and Query Analyzer. To further understand the importance of triggers, you have developed various trigger applications in database maintenance and implementation of business logic. To better assist procedure programming with Transact-SQL, you have been provided with some error-handling tools such as the Query Analyzer debugger and other error-handling methods such as the use of the RETURN statement, RAISERROR statement, and @@ERROR function. In this chapter, examples were given to illustrate the use of these methods in error handling. There is much more to Transact-SQL. In the next chapter, we discuss the concepts and applications of some other important database objects such as View, Index, and Cursor.

Review Questions

1. For students who join both the Book and Soccer clubs, use the variable Fee to set the Book Club membership fee at $50 and set the Soccer Club membership fee as 70 percent higher than the Book Club fee. Run your SQL statement in Query Analyzer.

2. Use a flow-control structure to reduce the membership fee to $120 if any of the clubs charge more than $120. Make sure to reduce $5 each time and reduce only the membership fees of the clubs that overcharge. Run your SQL statement in Query Analyzer.
3. State the difference between a function and a procedure.
4. How do you use the built-in function OPENQUERY?
5. Create a data file and then use the OPENDATASOURCE function to display the data in Query Analyzer.
6. What types of data can the sql_variant hold?
7. In Query Analyzer, create a user-defined function that updates the membership fee based on a given rate. Use an UPDATE clause to demonstrate the usage of your function by updating the membership fee of the Soccer Club by 10 percent.
8. Describe the table-valued user-defined functions.
9. For a given student id, create an inline table function to return a student's duty and the skill needed to perform the duty. Use a SELECT statement to show the result. Run your SQL statements in Query Analyzer.
10. What are the advantages of a stored procedure?
11. How is a stored procedure used?
12. Where can a trigger be used?
13. What do we need to be careful about when using a trigger?
14. How can an INSTEAD OF trigger be used? Give an example.
15. What are the tasks that an AFTER trigger can accomplish?
16. What is the default trigger type?
17. How can a trigger be executed?
18. Explain what the logical tables INSERTED and DELETED do.
19. What tasks can the Query Analyzer debugger accomplish?
20. Create a stored procedure that uses the RAISERROR statement to return a user-defined error message.

Case Study Projects

Continue from the previous chapter. Start Query Analyzer in SQL Server and create functions, procedures, and triggers to conduct the following tasks.

1. Computer Service

For the Computer_Service database, perform the activities below:

- Create a stored procedure, FeeProc, which is used to update the total costs including the service charge and the costs of parts. Use ServiceId as the input parameter. Run the stored procedure in Query Analyzer.
- Create a trigger on the table PARTS_SERVICES to reduce the cost by 10 percent if the customer has more than one service. Test the trigger by using an INSERT statement in Query Analyzer.

2. University Registration

Perform the following activities on the Registration database:

- Create a trigger to check if a student is enrolled in the same class twice. If so, and if the student passed the class before, roll back the insert operation. Test your trigger by using an INSERT clause in Query Analyzer.
- For a given student, create a multi-statement table function to return information about other students who are taking the same class as the given student and the class information. Use a SELECT statement to show the result. Run your SQL statements in Query Analyzer.

3. Mail Order

On the database Mail_Order, perform the following activities:

- For a given product id, create an inline table-valued function, Customer_Product, to return information about customers who have bought a product and the number of purchases. Use a SELECT statement to show the result. Run your SQL statements in Query Analyzer.
- Create a trigger that displays the message "Hello xxx. Thank you for ordering from Wellbeing" after a customer places an order; xxx is the customer's first name. Run the SQL statement in Query Analyzer.

Chapter 8

Database Views, Indexes, and Cursors

Objectives

- Create and manage views.
- Create and manage indexes.
- Create and manage cursors.
- Develop views and cursors for database applications.

8.1 Introduction

After a database is created, the next step is to prepare application programs to assist database application users in accessing and working with data stored in the database. Many application users have limited knowledge in computer information technology. Computer professionals need to help the users to access databases. Because these users often access databases through desktop personal computers, application programs for accessing databases are included as part of the desktop solutions. Database application users are also called front-end users.

We often display data from multiple data sources for many database applications, such as forms and reports. SQL statements for this type of application logic are complicated and may slow down performance. It is difficult for many front-end users to create complicated SQL statements to collect information. For many interaction-intensive applications, using tables directly will generate frequent table updating that also holds back performance.

Security is another concern if front-end users directly access database tables. They may corrupt data in a database table. Sometimes, you may want to allow front-end users to access certain rows or columns in a table but not the entire table.

For some database applications, you may need to provide calculated values. For example, the price of a product on sale is calculated by subtracting the deduction and adding the sales tax based on the reduced price.

In this chapter, views and indexes are introduced to overcome the above-mentioned problems. A *view* is a virtual table. It is created by selecting data from one or multiple data sources, such as tables from one or more databases, other views, calculated values, or even data from Excel, but looks like a single table and can be used as a single table. The use of views will simplify a front-end user's task in collecting data from multiple tables. A SQL statement that selects data from a view is just like a SQL statement that selects data from a table.

A user may have the privilege to read and update data in a view but may not be given the privilege to read or update the associated table(s). In this way, we can avoid accidentally erasing or updating data in database tables. By using a view, we can also restrict users from accessing certain rows or columns in a table. For example, if a table contains employee information such as name, address, and salary, a secretary may only be allowed to access information about an employee's name and address, but not salary. You can create a view with employees' names and addresses and let the secretary access the view only. Views are much safer to be used by front-end users. Also, views are dynamically created in memory. Updating data in memory instead of in database tables also speeds up performance.

For many database applications, you should create views first and then bind the views to applications. The applications will use these views as tables. The advantages of using views are summarized below.

- Views can be used to limit the actions such as inserting, deleting, and updating tables directly by front-end users. They are more secure. For example, instead of letting front-end users access an entire table, we can create a view to include only the columns and rows that the front-end users are permitted to access and to grant the view access permission to the front-end users.

- A view can contain data from multiple tables and can be used as a single table. For example, if front-end users need information about students, the clubs they are enrolled in, and their mentors, instead of letting the front-end users query three tables, you may create a view to integrate all the information so that the front-end users need to query only the single view for the information. This advantage of views is often used to improve performance of a decision-support system.

- Views reduce the complexity of data manipulation tasks for users. For example, if the name of a base table has been changed, we can redefine the view to use the new table name and keep the name of the view the same as before. In this way, the users do not need to change the database application code.

- Views can be used to display results calculated by using columns in tables. For example, instead of saving the discount membership fee in a table, we can create a view that contains all the columns needed for the calculation and a calculated column that stores the calculation results.

■ Views can have triggers different from the triggers originally defined on the tables. This provides database administrators with more flexibility in maintaining databases.

A view can be referenced by other views. SQL Server 2000 allows up to 32 nested view references. As mentioned earlier, a view can be referenced as a table, so you can apply stored procedures and the INSTEAD OF trigger to a view. Although a view is created by selecting data from one or multiple data sources, it cannot select data from a temporary table.

Searching specified data in a large table or view takes time. Like an index at the end of a book, *indexes* are created on tables or views to improve data searching performance. The following are situations in which indexes will improve query performance:

■ You may want to create indexes on columns that are often used in the WHERE clause as part of a searching condition. When the WHERE clause has an exact match, a clustered index created on a column with unique values will speed up the search for a matched pair. For example, a clustered index on ClubName will make the following query perform better:

```
SELECT ClubName
FROM CLUB
WHERE ClubName = 'Poetry'
```

■ If a wildcard search condition or a range search condition is used in a WHERE clause, the use of an index can also improve query performance. For example, the following query performance can be improved if an index is used:

```
SELECT MentorName
FROM STUDENT_MENTOR
WHERE MentorName BETWEEN 'F%' AND 'L%'
```

Because the index on the column MentorName arranges the mentors' names alphabetically, it takes less time to match all the qualified names with the condition.
■ When joining two tables with a foreign key column that is used to match the join condition, you can use an index to improve performance.

Besides improving search performance, indexes are also used for sorting rows in a table and enforcing uniqueness. You can create many indexes on a single table or view. In some situations, an index will not improve query performance. Every time the data in an indexed column are changed or the structure of the column is changed, the index is automatically updated. The updating of indexes slows down query performance. For those frequently updated tables, creating too many indexes is not a good idea.

Running the stored procedure sp_helpindex can retrieve information about an index. There are two types of indexes in SQL Server: *clustered index* and *nonclustered index*. These indexes are stored in a data structure called a balance tree or *B-tree*, which is a topic covered in a data structure course in the computer science curriculum. A clustered index places each row in a table to the leaf node of the B-tree. A nonclustered index places the reference to each row in a table to the leaf node of the B-tree. Because you can access rows directly in a cluster, query performance of a clustered index is better. In SQL Server, each table can have one clustered index. If a clustered index has been created on a table, it can be used by a nonclustered index to improve performance. Therefore, you should create nonclustered indexes after a clustered index is created.

When a table is created, SQL Server automatically creates a clustered index on the primary key and foreign key columns. An index can be created by including multiple columns. For example, an index is created on a primary key that consists of multiple columns. Such an index is called a *composite index*. The column on which a clustered index is created does not have to be unique. The clustered index enforces the uniqueness by creating an associated sorting column containing only unique values. However, if an index is created on multiple columns, each row in the combination must be unique.

In most database application developments, SQL statements are used to access data stored in a database. The result from a SQL statement is called a *result set*. In SQL Server, data stored in a result set does not have the row-by-column format. This has caused some difficulties when a database application needs to process certain rows or columns. A SELECT statement returns a complete set of rows that meet the search criteria, even though sometimes interactive applications need only a small portion of the entire returned result or only one row of the entire output. To efficiently use the results from SELECT statements, cursors have been introduced to manage result sets.

A *cursor* is a database object that can be used to pick up certain rows or columns for an application program. With a cursor, you can keep track of records used by a database application. By using a cursor, you can browse a result set. In a cursor, data are arranged in the row-by-column format so that a user can browse through the result set more easily. Once a specified row is located, you can perform database operations, such as modifying data in a result set and searching for and retrieving specified rows. As database objects, cursors have their own data and methods. There are four types of commonly used cursors: *forward only*, *static*, *keyset*, and *dynamic*.

- *Forward only:* With the forward only cursor, you can only browse forward through a result set from the first to the last record. If changes are made to the result set, the forward only cursor can let you see only the changes ahead of it. The forward only cursor is faster than the other types of cursors.
- *Static:* With the static cursor, you can make a snapshot of the records from a result set returned by a SQL statement or a database application. As the name indicates, the records returned by the static cursor will not show changes made by other transactions. That is, the static cursor cannot let you see other users' modifications. It allows back and forth movements when you search for a record.

- *Keyset:* For a keyset cursor, a set of keys that uniquely identify the records in a result set is created. The key values are used to improve performance in searching and sorting. However, because the keys are created when the cursor is opened, the newly inserted records will have no key values assigned to them. Consequently, these inserted records are not visible. If a row is deleted by other transactions and we try to fetch the deleted rows, we will get the record unavailable message from the variable @@FETCH_STATUS of −2. Updating data in a key column involves deleting the old value and inserting a new one. Because the cursor owner will not be able to see the inserted value, the updated data in a key column will not be visible until the result set is refreshed. However, if the update is done through the cursor by using the WHERE CURRENT OF clause, the updated value will be visible.
- *Dynamic:* With a dynamic cursor, you are able to move back and forth and see all data changes made to the records in a result set without refreshing it. This means that all the modifications from inserts, updates, and deletes are visible as you browse around the cursor. When data are selected in the cursor, you can change the data values and order of the rows.

By the end of this chapter, we develop views and cursors for the applications created for the Hillcrest Computing database that is designed and implemented in Chapter 4.

8.2 Creating and Managing Views

In this section, you will learn how to create and manage views. You will also learn how to use a view to access data stored in a database.

8.2.1 Creating Views

There are three ways to create a view. You can create a view by using Enterprise Manager, by using **Create View Wizard**, or by executing the CREATE VIEW statement in Query Analyzer. When creating a view, the following restrictions may apply:

- The name of a view must be unique within the database.
- The query used to create a view cannot contain the ORDER BY, COMPUTE, and INTO keywords.
- You must specify the column name in a view if the column is derived from an arithmetic expression, a built-in function, a constant, or columns from different tables that have the same column name.

Creating a View Using Enterprise Manager

Suppose that we want to create a view by Enterprise Manager in the database Student_Club to display student information such as student names, clubs

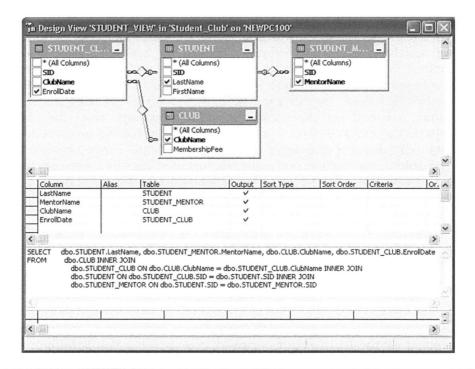

Figure 8.1 Create view by Enterprise Manager

that students are enrolled in, students' mentors, and so on. This view will be created by selecting data from the tables STUDENT, CLUB, STUDENT_MENTOR, and STUDENT_CLUB, as shown below.

1. Open **Enterprise Manager**. Expand the **Student_Club** node.
2. Right-click **Views**; then select **New View**.
3. Right-click on the top pane. Click the **Add table** button on the tool bar. Add the tables **CLUB**, **STUDENT**, **STUDENT_MENTOR**, and **STUDENT_CLUB**.
4. Check the columns **LastName**, **ClubName**, **MentorName**, and **EnrollDate**, and then click the **Run** button (with the **!** sign) on the tool bar.
5. Save the view as **STUDENT_VIEW**.

In Figure 8.1, there are four panes: Diagram, Grid, SQL, and Result. The Diagram pane shows the relationship among the tables that are associated with the view. The Grid pane displays the columns, tables, and other information used in creating the view. In the SQL pane, the SQL statement used to create the view is displayed. The Result pane displays the result set generated by the view. The result set is generated dynamically and is placed in memory.

Creating a View by CREATE VIEW Statement

The syntax to create a view is

```
CREATE VIEW [ db_name .] [owner.] view_name [ ( column [ ,...n ] ) ]
[WITH < view_attribute > [ ,...n ]]
AS
select_statement
[WITH CHECK OPTION]
< view_attribute > ::=
    { ENCRYPTION | SCHEMABINDING | VIEW_METADATA }
```

- *View_name* specifies the name of the view. The name must be unique in the database.
- *Column* is the name of a specified column. As mentioned earlier, some columns in the view should have specified names.
- WITH CHECK OPTION ensures that the modified data are visible in the modified view.
- *Select_statement* is a SQL statement that queries data for a view. To merge data from different sources, the JOIN and UNION statements are often used with SELECT statements. From time to time, subqueries are also used in SELECT statements.
- ENCRYPTION encrypts columns in a system table if the columns have the text of CREATE VIEW statements.
- SCHEMABINDING binds a view with a specific database schema.
- VIEW_METADATA returns metadata information about a view.

To illustrate the use of the CREATE VIEW statement, we consider an example that selects information about a mentor and his or her students from the tables STUDENT_MENTOR and STUDENT.

For this example, open **Query Analyzer**. Enter the SQL statement shown in Figure 8.2. Run the query (by clicking the ▶ button on the tool bar). Before you run the CREATE VIEW statement, make sure that the database Student_Club is selected from the pull-down list on the tool bar.

The query used in creating the view joins the tables STUDENT and STUDENT_MENTOR on the column SID. A SELECT statement is used to display the content of the view MENTOR_VIEW.

Creating a View by Create View Wizard

You can also create a view by using **Create View Wizard**. To do this,

1. Open **Enterprise Manager**. Click the **Databases** node. Click **Tools**, and then click **Wizards**. In the **Select Wizard** dialog, expand the **Database** node, highlight **Create View Wizard**, and then click **OK**.
2. Click **Next** to start the process of creating a view. In the **Select Database** dialog, choose **Student_Club** and click **Next**. Check the tables **STUDENT** and **STUDENT_MENTOR**.
3. Click **Next** to select columns for the view to display. Select the columns **LastName**, **FirstName**, and **MentorName**.
4. Click **Next** to define the condition in the **WHERE** clause. Enter the **WHERE** condition as shown in Figure 8.3.

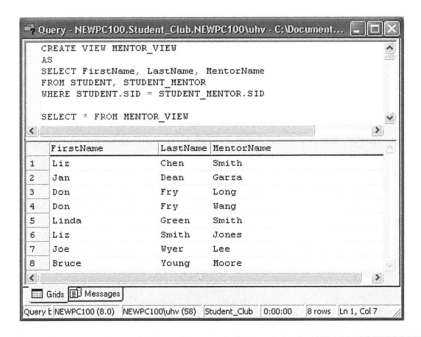

Figure 8.2　Create view by `CREATE VIEW` **statement**

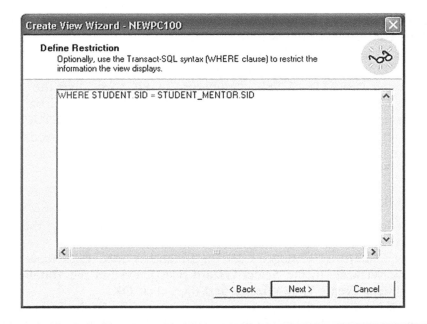

Figure 8.3　Create view by Create View Wizard

5. Click **Next** to specify the name for the view. Name the view **STUDENT_ MENTOR_VIEW**.
6. Click **Next**. Verify the SQL statement. If everything is right, click **Finish**.

Now you have created the view by **Create View Wizard**. To verify this, expand the **View** node under the database **Student_Club** in Enterprise Manager.

8.2.2 Modifying Views

If you want to modify views without dropping and re-creating an existing view, you can use the ALTER VIEW statement. ALTER VIEW keeps the original indexes, stored procedures, or triggers created for the view. The syntax for the ALTER VIEW statement is

```
ALTER VIEW [ db_name .] [owner.] view_name [ ( column [ ,...n ] ) ]
[WITH < view_attribute > [ ,...n ]]
AS
select_statement
[WITH CHECK OPTION]
< view_attribute > ::=
   { ENCRYPTION | SCHEMABINDING | VIEW_METADATA }
```

This statement is similar to the CREATE VIEW statement. There are two ways to modify a view. You can modify a view using Enterprise Manager or using the ALTER VIEW statement in Query Analyzer. For example, if you want to add the mentors' skills to MENTOR_VIEW, you need to add the SkillName column from the SKILL table to MENTOR_VIEW. Figure 8.4 shows the modification to MENTOR_VIEW.

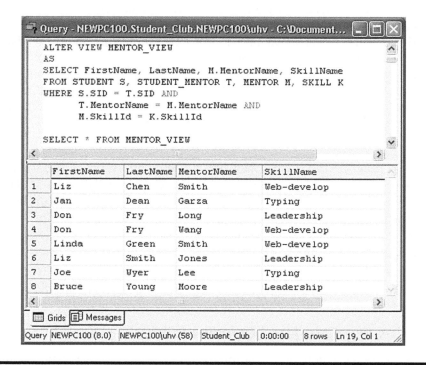

Figure 8.4   Modify view

Note that modifying a view may cause its dependent database objects such as triggers or stored procedures to become invalid. If this happens, you need to modify its stored procedures or triggers accordingly.

8.2.3 Modifying Data in Views

After a view is created, you can use the view to modify data in an underlying table as long as you have the permission to modify data in that table. However, you will not be able to use the DELETE statement to modify the data through the views created in the above section such as STUDENT_VIEW, because the view contains more than one table. You may, however, be able to insert, update, and delete data in a view according to the following rules:

- A view based on a single table may be updated (including insert, update, and delete) if the SQL statement creating the view satisfies conditions as stated below and all the NOT NULL columns in the table are present in the view.
- Views based on any number of tables with or without calculated columns may be updated if INSTEAD OF triggers are defined for the views.

For a single table based on which a view is created to be updateable, you need to meet the following restrictions on SQL statements while creating the view:

- If NOT NULL is specified for some columns in a table, you must specify the values in the INSERT statement.
- If the clause WITH CHECK OPTION is used in the CREATE VIEW statement, you cannot delete the row from the view.
- The modified data in an underlying table should maintain the data constraints and integrity constraints created for the table.
- The query used to create a view should have no aggregate functions such as AVG, SUM, COUNT, ... in the SELECT list. Also, the SELECT statement should not contain the keywords GROUP BY, UNION, DISTINCT, or TOP.
- No calculated columns, which are derived from other columns, should be allowed in the SELECT list if you want to modify the columns later.

Now we practice modifying data in an underlying table. First, we create a view based on a single table called NEW_STUDENT (see Figure 8.5). Then we perform several modifications. We first insert a row with the data (15438, Rice, John) into the underlying table through the view, then change Joe Wyer's id to 11606, and, last, delete the row (15438, Rice, John), as shown in Figure 8.6. The modification result will be illustrated by using a SELECT statement on the underlying table (see Figure 8.7). As we can see, the row with SID 15438 is removed and the SID for Joe Wyer is changed to 11606.

8.2.4 Creating Calculated Columns in Views

It is good to place calculated columns in a view. In such a way, the performance can be improved significantly. As an example, we create a view

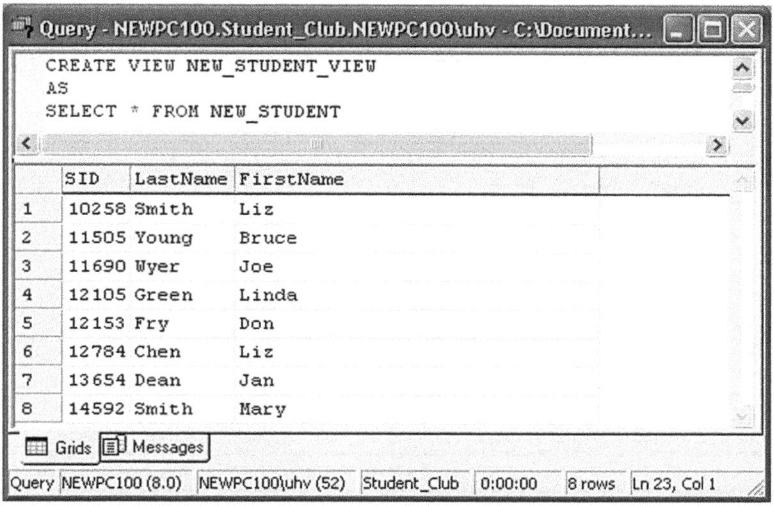

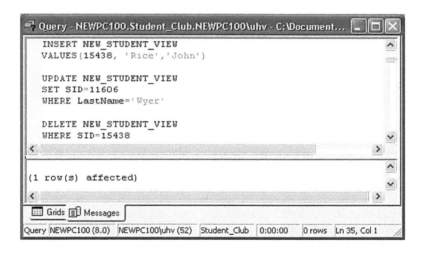

Figure 8.5   Create view based on single table

Figure 8.6   Modify data through view

FEE_CHARGE that contains the column StudentName consisting of both FirstName and LastName from the STUDENT table. The view also has the column Fee containing the membership fee charged to the students. Suppose that we give a 10 percent discount for both clubs if a student is enrolled in two clubs concurrently and a 20 percent discount for all three clubs if a student is enrolled in three clubs concurrently. First, we create a function fn_FeeCharge that calculates the membership fee based on the number of clubs in which a student is currently enrolled. Then we create a view that calls the function to get the updated membership fee. Enter the following code to create the function in Query Analyzer:

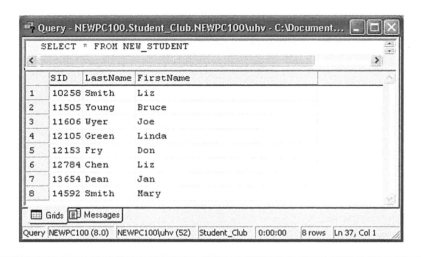

Figure 8.7 Data in table modified through view

```
CREATE FUNCTION fn_FeeCharge( )
RETURNS @UPDATEDFEE TABLE(SID int, CName char(30), Fee money) AS
BEGIN

    DECLARE @CLUBCOUNT TABLE(SID int, EnrollCount int)
-- Assign the initial value to UPDATEDFEE table
    INSERT @UPDATEDFEE
    SELECT SID, C.ClubName, MembershipFee
    FROM CLUB C, STUDENT_CLUB S
    WHERE C.ClubName = S.ClubName

-- Count how many clubs the student is enrolled in
    INSERT @CLUBCOUNT
    SELECT SID, COUNT(SID) AS EnrollCount
    FROM STUDENT_CLUB
    GROUP BY SID

-- Calculate UPDATEDFEE based on the number of clubs enrolled
    UPDATE @UPDATEDFEE
    SET Fee = Fee * 0.9
    WHERE SID IN (SELECT SID
                    FROM @CLUBCOUNT
                    WHERE EnrollCount = 2)
    UPDATE @UPDATEDFEE
    SET Fee = Fee * 0.8
    WHERE SID IN (SELECT SID
                    FROM @CLUBCOUNT
                    WHERE EnrollCount = 3)
    RETURN

END
```

To create a view that displays the students' names, club names, and updated membership fees, enter the code shown in Figure 8.8.

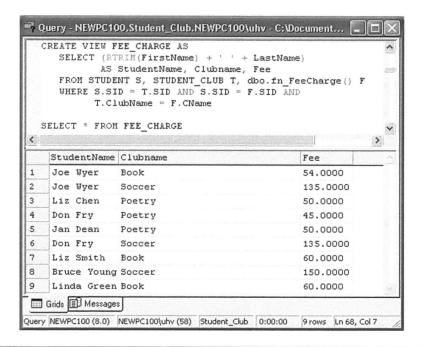

Figure 8.8   View with calculated columns

From the data selected from the view, we can see that the column StudentName includes both first and last names. Also, both Joe Wyer and Don Fry get a 10 percent discount because they join two clubs concurrently. With a view like this, front-end users can easily display information such as student names and membership fees on their desktop computers.

8.2.5   Deleting Views

You can delete a no-longer-used view from your database. When deleting a view, you are deleting the view's definitions. The data selected for the view are still kept in the database table(s). Again, there are two ways to delete a view. You can delete a view using Enterprise Manager or using the DROP VIEW statement in Query Analyzer. Figure 8.9 shows an example that deletes the view NEW_STUDENT_VIEW.

To verify that NEW_STUDENT_VIEW is deleted, you can expand the Views node under the Student_Club database in **Object Browser** on the left-hand side of the Query Analyzer window after refreshing Views (by right-clicking **Views** and clicking **Refresh**). You will see that NEW_STUDENT_VIEW is gone.

8.3 Creating and Managing Indexes

In this section, you will learn how to create and modify indexes. You will also learn how to view information about existing indexes created in a database.

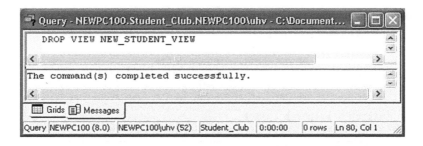

Figure 8.9   Delete view

8.3.1   Creating Indexes

There are different ways to create an index. You can use the CREATE INDEX statement in Query Analyzer, use Enterprise Manager, or use the **Create Index Wizard**.

Creating Indexes with Enterprise Manager

To create an index using Enterprise Manager, you need the **Manage Indexes** tool. For example, we create an index on the column EnrollDate in the table STUDENT_CLUB. To do this,

1. Open **Enterprise Manager**. Expand the database **Student_Club**. Right-click on the table **STUDENT_CLUB**, select **All Tasks**, and then select **Manage Indexes** on the pop-up menu.
2. Click the **New** button to open the **Create New Index** dialog where you are prompted to enter the index name; check the column on which you want to create the index. You are then prompted to choose the type of index and to configure the index properties such as uniqueness constraint, pad index, fill factor, computing statistics, and file group. You can specify the type of index as clustered or nonclustered. Usually, the clustered index is automatically created on the primary key column. You can have only one clustered index on a table. In this case, the check box for the clustered index is grayed out. The name of an index must be unique. If there is an existing index with the same name as the new index, you will be asked if you want to delete the existing index. You can check **Pad index** that is used to allocate additional space for each interior node of the index. The additional space can be used for index updating. You can also specify the fill factor that is used to reserve some spare storage space for the index page at the creation of an index to avoid page splitting caused by future index modification. Page splitting reduces database performance. The default fill factor value is 100, which means there is no spare space. The **Up** and **Down** buttons are used to change the order of columns in a composite index. For this example, enter the index name **Enroll_Index** and check the column **EnrollDate**. Check the fill factor and enter **80** as the fill factor. You should have the configured dialog as shown in Figure 8.10.

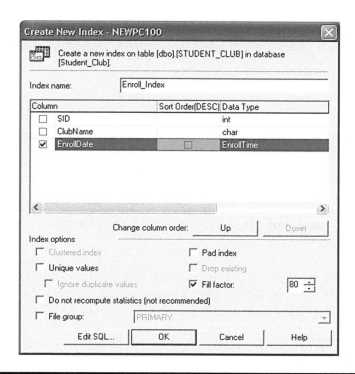

Figure 8.10   Create index by Enterprise Manager

3. Click the **OK** button to complete the configuration. In the **Manage Indexes** dialog, you should see the created index **Enroll_Index**. Click **Close** to exit **Manage Indexes**.

Creating Indexes with Wizard

The second graphical tool to create an index is the **Create Index Wizard**. To start the wizard, open **Enterprise Manager**. Highlight the **Databases** node, and click **Tools** on the menu bar. Select **Wizards**, and then expand the **Database** node. Select **Create Index Wizard** and click **OK** to start the wizard. Click **Next** to go to the next page. Choose the database and table, and then click **Next** twice. Select the column on which the index will be created. Specify the sorting order, fill factor, and other properties, and then click **Finish**.

Creating Indexes with CREATE INDEX Statement

In Query Analyzer, you can enter a CREATE INDEX statement to create an index. The CREATE INDEX syntax has many optional parameters similar to those used in the Create New Index dialog in Enterprise Manager discussed earlier. The syntax is given below:

```
CREATE [ UNIQUE ] [ CLUSTERED | NONCLUSTERED ] INDEX index_name
   ON [ table_name | view_name ] ( column_name [ ASC | DESC ] [
   ,...n ] )
[ WITH  [index_property]  [ ,...n] ]
[ ON filegroup ]
```

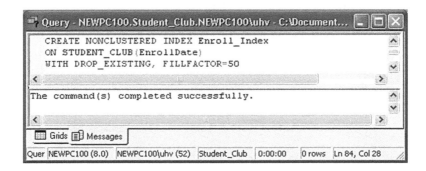

Figure 8.11   Create index by `CREATE INDEX` **statement**

In the above syntax, [,...*n*] is used to indicate that multiple columns or multiple options can be listed. The *index_property* in the WITH clause can be any of the following.

```
{ PAD_INDEX |
    FILLFACTOR = fillfactor |
    IGNORE_DUP_KEY |
    DROP_EXISTING |
    STATISTICS_NORECOMPUTE |
    SORT_IN_TEMPDB    }
```

The example in Figure 8.11 is used to illustrate the use of the CREATE INDEX statement. In this example, we create a nonclustered index with the fill factor equal to 50 on the column EnrollDate in the STUDENT_CLUB table. Because the index already exists, we use the DROP_EXISTING option.

8.3.2   Managing Indexes

After an index is created, you can view, modify, and delete it. SQL Server provides several ways to manage existing indexes. You can do it in Enterprise Manager, Query Analyzer, or by stored procedures.

Managing Indexes with Enterprise Manager

You can view and modify index properties using the **Manage Indexes** tool built into Enterprise Manager. In the next example, we view the properties of the index Enroll_Index.

1. Open **Enterprise Manager**, and expand the database **Student_Club**. Right-click on the table **STUDENT_CLUB** and select **All Tasks**, and then click **Manage Indexes**.

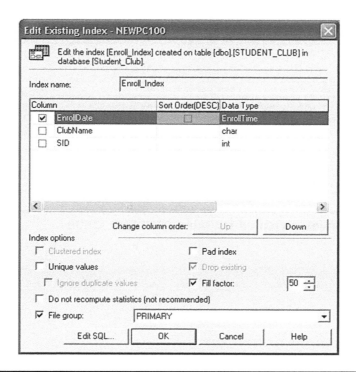

Figure 8.12   Edit index by Enterprise Manager

2. Highlight the index **Enroll_Index**, and then click the **Edit** button to change the properties. In the Edit dialog, you can change the properties such as Fill factor (see Figure 8.12).

Managing Indexes with Query Analyzer

In Query Analyzer, you can use **Object Browser** (on the left-hand side of the screen) to view the information about an existing index.

1. Open **Query Analyzer**. If **Object Browser** is not open, click the **Object Browser** button on the toolbar or press the **F8** key.
2. Expand **User Tables** under the Student_Club database. Expand the table **dbo.STUDENT_CLUB**, and then expand the **Indexes** folder. You should see the index **Enroll_Index**.
3. Right-click on **Enroll_Index**, and select **Edit** on the pop-up menu. The **Edit Existing Index** dialog will open as shown in Figure 8.12.

Managing Indexes with Stored Procedures

For a given table, you can use the stored procedures `sp_help` and `sp_helpindex` to obtain information about an index. For example, if you want to know the information on indexes created for the table `STUDENT_CLUB`, enter and run the statement shown in Figure 8.13 in Query Analyzer.

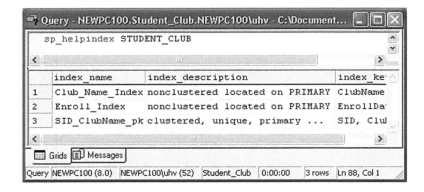

Figure 8.13   Indexes created for table STUDENT_CLUB

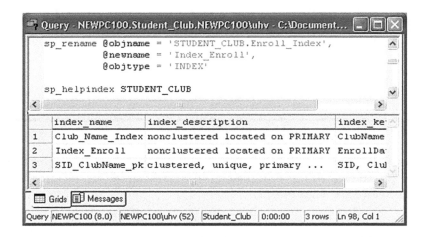

Figure 8.14   Rename index by sp_rename stored procedure

There are two indexes created for STUDENT_CLUB. Enroll_Index is a nonclustered index created manually by the user. SID_ClubName_pk is the clustered index created automatically on the primary key.

You can rename an index using the system stored procedure sp_rename. Its syntax is

```
sp_rename [ @objname = ] 'object_name' , [ @newname = ] 'new_name'
    [ , [ @objtype = ] 'object_type' ]
```

If the identifier *object_name* is specified as an index built on a table, use the combination table_name.index_name. The table name is required. Otherwise, the sp_rename stored procedure cannot find the specified index to give it a new name. If the object to be renamed is an index, you need to specify the *object_type* as INDEX. As an example, we rename Enroll_Index as Index_Enroll. In Figure 8.14, the system-stored procedure sp_ helpindex is used to show that the name of Enroll_Index has been changed to Index_Enroll.

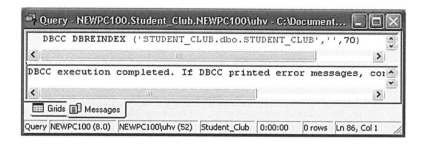

Figure 8.15   Modify index by DBCC   DBREINDEX **statement**

Updating Indexes

To update an index manually, you can use either the CREATE   INDEX statement with the DROP_EXISTING option or the statement DBCC   DBRE-INDEX. The syntax for DBCC   DBREINDEX is given as

```
DBCC DBREINDEX ( [ 'database.owner.table_name'
   [ , index_name  [ , fillfactor ] ] ]
) [ WITH NO_INFOMSGS ]
```

When executing the DBCC   DBREINDEX statement, one or more indexes can be rebuilt based on the indexes specified in the *index_name*. If the *fillfactor* is specified, you must specify all preceding parameters. You can use DBCC   DBREINDEX on user-created tables but not system tables. The example in Figure 8.15 shows the use of DBCC   DBREINDEX to change the fill factor to 70 percent. Because no index has been specified, all the indexes built into table STUDENT_CLUB are modified to have the fill factor equal to 70.

Deleting Indexes

If an index is no longer used, you can delete it by using the DROP   INDEX statement, which has the following syntax:

```
DROP INDEX 'table.index | view.index' [ ,...n ]
```

You need to specify the table name to make sure that the right index gets dropped. The notation [,...*n*] indicates that you can drop multiple indexes. In the example in Figure 8.16, we delete the index Index_Enroll. As shown by the stored procedure sp_helpindex, the STUDENT_CLUB table no longer has the *Index_Enroll* index.

8.4 Creating and Managing Cursors

When database applications such as forms and reports are developed based on result sets returned by SQL statements, they may need to access only certain rows or columns in the result sets. Cursors are used to search for the

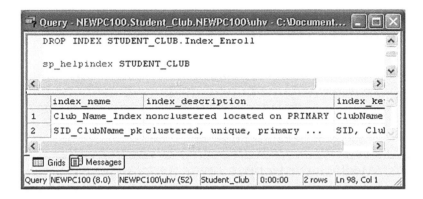

Figure 8.16   Delete index by `DROP INDEX` **statement**

specified records for the database applications. In a client/server structure, cursors can be implemented in three ways in SQL Server. On the server side, you can implement a cursor as a Transact-SQL cursor or API cursor. On the client side, cursors are implemented as client cursors.

8.4.1   Client Cursors

On the client side, client cursors include forward only and static types of cursors. The entire result set is saved on the client side and all the cursor operations are performed on the client side. Client cursors are implemented by SQL Server ODBC and DB-Library.

The SQL Server ODBC driver and DB-Library DLL implement client cursors internally and by DLL that implements ADO API. To implement client cursors, all the result set rows are cached on the client computer. Because a client cursor does not support full cursor operations, we should consider using server-side cursors if possible.

8.4.2   Application Programming Interface (API) Server Cursors

ODBC, ADO, OLE DB, and DB-Library make up a set of data-accessing tools called *Application Programming Interface* (API), which is covered in later chapters. API cursors are a type of server cursor. You can manage API cursors by calling API cursor methods or functions built into OLE DB, ODBC, ADO, and DB-Library. These database APIs have built-in stored procedures for cursor operations, such as the following:

- *sp_cursoropen:* For creating SQL statements to open and populate a cursor
- *sp_cursorfetch:* For fetching one or more rows from a cursor
- *sp_cursorclose:* For closing and deallocating a cursor
- *sp_cursor:* For requesting location updates in result sets
- *sp_cursorprepare:* For preparing a cursor by creating an execution plan but not the cursor
- *sp_cursorexecute:* For creating and populating a cursor from the execution plan

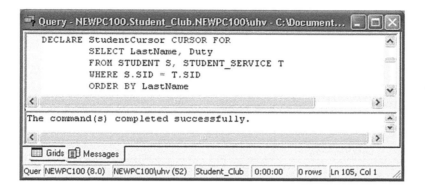

Figure 8.17   Create Transact-SQL cursor

You do not access an API cursor directly. Instead, you access it using the stored procedures built into the database APIs. Requests for API cursor functions are passed to an API server cursor by the OLE DB provider, ODBC driver, or DB-Library DLL. With stored procedures built into an API cursor, you can open a connection to tables in a database, execute one or more SQL statements, set cursor properties, and fetch rows from result sets.

8.4.3   Transact-SQL Cursors

Although a Transact-SQL cursor is implemented on a server, clients can manage Transact-SQL from client computers. You can also create a Transact-SQL cursor in a trigger or in a stored procedure. If you are not clear whether to create a client cursor or a server cursor, you should create the server cursor. To implement a Transact-SQL cursor, you can use the DECLARE CURSOR statement in Query Analyzer. For example, you can create a cursor called StudentCursor that contains student names and their club duties (see Figure 8.17).

The cursor's structure is created with no data in it. To use the cursor, you need to populate it with data by using the OPEN statement and then fetching the data in the cursor by the FETCH statement. When the OPEN statement is executed, the SQL statement defined in the DECLARE CURSOR statement is processed. The data returned by the SQL statement are used to populate the cursor. The FETCH statement retrieves data in the cursor one record at a time. The example in Figure 8.18 is used to get the data in the cursor Student-Cursor with a WHILE loop.

You can see in the output that you fetch one record at a time by using a cursor. For many interactive database applications, it is often desirable to work with one record at a time or a set of specified records at a time. Cursors play an important role in database application development. When a cursor is no longer needed, you can close and deallocate the cursor to free the memory storage used by the cursor (see Figure 8.19). The freed memory can be used by other tasks. The message indicates that the cursor StudentCursor is successfully deallocated.

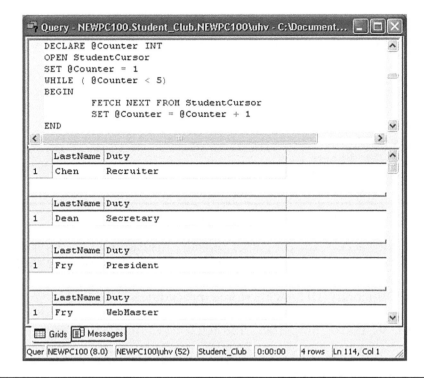

Figure 8.18   Use Transact-SQL cursor

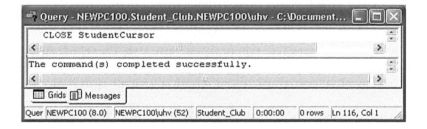

Figure 8.19   Close and deallocate Transact-SQL cursor

8.5 Case Study: Hillcrest Computing

The information about the company Hillcrest Computing is given in Chapter 2. The database Hillcrest Computing was created in Chapter 4. The definitions of the tables and the diagram of the tables were also created in Chapter 4. In this section, you will accomplish the following tasks for Hillcrest Computing:

- Create a view called LABOR_RATE_VIEW that includes computed values.
- Create a view called PART_COST_VIEW that calculates the cost of parts used for each computer system.

- Create a view called `RETAIL_PRICE_VIEW` that calculates the total cost of each computer system and the retail price based on the cost.

The tables we use in this section are `SYSTEM_WORKER`, `SYSTEM_PART`, `PART`, `PART_DETAIL`, and `COMPUTER_SYSTEM`. In Appendix A, we list the corresponding tables that contain the data used in the views and cursors developed in this section.

As mentioned earlier, views are used to improve database security, filter data, and present computation results. In the following example, we create a view that includes a column that calculates the average labor cost rate for each computer system. For each worker, the company assigns a cost rate based on the salary paid to the worker and the hours needed to complete a job. The rate is calculated by the following formula:

```
Labor Cost Rate = Worker's Hourly Cost * Hours Needed to Complete
    a Job
```

A job assignment is designed by the company to evaluate workers' levels of skill. The average time needed to complete a job (assembling a computer system) is about nine hours. It takes five hours for the most-skilled workers to complete the job, and it takes about fifteen hours for the least-skilled workers to complete the same job. Two workers assemble a given computer system together. The group arrangement is given in the table `SYSTEM_WORKER`, along with the labor cost rate. We would like to see, after two workers team up, what the average labor cost rate is for the group. We add the workers' labor costs for the group and divide the sum by the number of workers in that group. A view is going to be used to hold the calculated column. In the view `LABOR_RATE_VIEW` in Figure 8.20, the calculated values are placed in the column `Avg_LaborRate`. Later, a database application can retrieve the calculated data from `LABOR_RATE_VIEW` directly without recalculating these values. This will improve the performance of the database application. The SQL statement that creates the view is illustrated in Figure 8.20. A `SELECT` statement is used to show the calculation result. Although more-skilled workers are paid more, their labor costs can be less because they are more efficient and are usually assigned to assemble high-end (expensive) computer systems.

For the next example, we create a view `PART_COST_VIEW` to calculate the total part cost of each computer system. We add the costs for the parts used for a computer system. To create this view, we need to identify the parts used in the computer systems in the table `SYSTEM_PART`. Once the part ids are available, we add the prices of these parts by looking them up in the table `PART_DETAIL`. An inner join is used to join these two tables. A `GROUP BY` statement is used to group the parts for each type of computer with the aggregate function `SUM()` that calculates the total part cost for each computer system. When the view is used by a database application, there is no need to rejoin these two tables. Not only is the performance improved, but the security of the database is also enhanced. In Figure 8.21, the `CREATE VIEW` statement and the data in the created view are displayed.

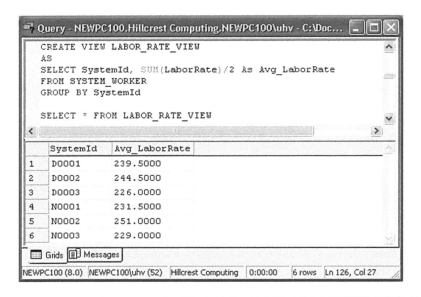

Figure 8.20   View with computed values

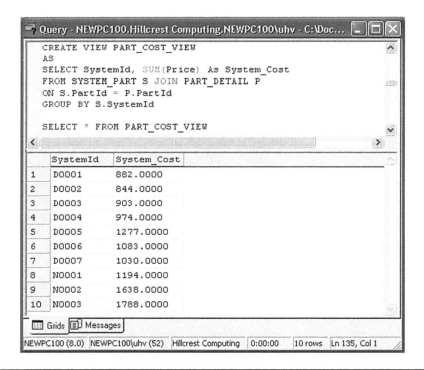

Figure 8.21   PART_COST_VIEW based on joined tables

The output gives the total cost of the parts for a given computer system. You may wonder why some of the high-end systems are less expensive. This is because they do not include certain peripheral parts, or the system is using the Linux operating system that costs less.

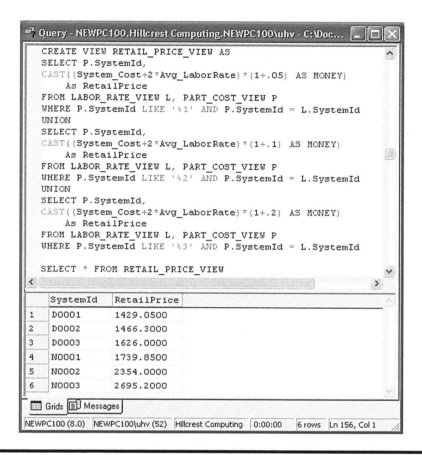

```
Query - NEWPC100.Hillcrest Computing.NEWPC100\uhv - C:\Doc...

CREATE VIEW RETAIL_PRICE_VIEW AS
SELECT P.SystemId,
CAST((System_Cost+2*Avg_LaborRate)*(1+.05) AS MONEY)
    As RetailPrice
FROM LABOR_RATE_VIEW L, PART_COST_VIEW P
WHERE P.SystemId LIKE '%1' AND P.SystemId = L.SystemId
UNION
SELECT P.SystemId,
CAST((System_Cost+2*Avg_LaborRate)*(1+.1) AS MONEY)
    As RetailPrice
FROM LABOR_RATE_VIEW L, PART_COST_VIEW P
WHERE P.SystemId LIKE '%2' AND P.SystemId = L.SystemId
UNION
SELECT P.SystemId,
CAST((System_Cost+2*Avg_LaborRate)*(1+.2) AS MONEY)
    As RetailPrice
FROM LABOR_RATE_VIEW L, PART_COST_VIEW P
WHERE P.SystemId LIKE '%3' AND P.SystemId = L.SystemId

SELECT * FROM RETAIL_PRICE_VIEW
```

	SystemId	RetailPrice
1	D0001	1429.0500
2	D0002	1466.3000
3	D0003	1626.0000
4	N0001	1739.8500
5	N0002	2354.0000
6	N0003	2695.2000

```
Grids  Messages
NEWPC100 (8.0)  NEWPC100\uhv (52)  Hillcrest Computing  0:00:00  6 rows  Ln 156, Col 1
```

Figure 8.22 Create and use RETAIL_PRICE_VIEW

For the retail prices of these computer systems, the company takes 5 percent, 10 percent, and 20 percent profit from the low-end (e.g., D0001), medium, and high-end (e.g., D0003) computer systems, respectively. (Notice that the profit here is not pure profit. The company has to pay other costs such as other personnel salaries, buildings and their maintenance, tools, and advertising. After paying all the costs, the actual profit is probably about five to six percent.) The company is using the following formula to calculate the retail prices:

```
Retail Price = (labor cost + part cost) * (1 + percentage of profit)
```

We place the retail prices in the view RETAIL_PRICE_VIEW. Labor and part costs are from the previously built view LABOR_RATE_VIEW and PART_COST_VIEW. Because labor and part costs are directly from the views with values that have already been calculated, the performance is much improved. RETAIL_PRICE_VIEW is created as shown in Figure 8.22.

The code pane of Figure 8.22 shows the SQL statement of creating the view RETAIL_PRICE_VIEW based on joined views. The keyword UNION is used to combine the rows of the outputs with identical formats but different profit percentages. The result pane shows the retail prices stored in RETAIL_PRICE_VIEW. (Here, we assume that computer systems with id numbers whose last digits are higher than 3 are customized systems and their retail prices should be calculated in the same way as high-end computer systems.) In later chapters, forms are created based on this view so that the sales manager can figure out the cost after a customer has decided on the configuration of his or her computer system.

The database Hillcrest Computing is designed to work in a client/server environment. When developing your database applications, you need to pay attention to the following tasks:

- Make sure that changes of records are shown simultaneously on both the client and server sides.
- Avoid transmitting the entire result set over the network that connects the client and server. Transmitting a large result set will significantly slow down performance. Most database applications need only a small portion of an entire result set.
- Multiple users must be allowed to access the same result set.

Using cursors can help you accomplish these tasks. In the following example, suppose that a customer is interested only in the high-end notebook systems. Instead of showing the entire view RETAIL_PRICE_VIEW to the customer, we can create a cursor that returns only the prices of the systems with dual CPU. This cursor can be used in a form that contains a list of computer systems. After the customer selects a computer system, the price of the system will be displayed in a textbox on the form for purchasing.

The cursor SystemPrice_Cursor is used to return the price of the high-end notebook computer system with the system id N0003 (see Figure 8.23). Transferring the single value back to the form on the client computer will reduce network traffic and improve performance.

Some of the database applications allow front-end users to update database values in a database. In the following example, the assembly manager wants to upgrade the D0002 system by adding a 19-in monitor to it. First, the cursor SystemChange_Cursor is declared (see Figure 8.24).

Next, we use the cursor to insert and update the database. In Figure 8.25, a WHILE loop is used to search for the computer system to make the change. Once the system is located, an INSERT statement is used to add the monitor to the current computer system in the table SYSTEM_PART, and an UPDATE statement is used to update the system description in the table COMPUTER_SYSTEM. Because the word Description is a reserved keyword, square brackets [ ] are used to include it. Keep in mind that the keyword TRANSACTION is special to SQL Server. You could not use it even if it were enclosed in the square brackets.

Four variables are declared in Figure 8.25. The variables **@Desc** and **@Monitor** are used to update the values in the Description column. They have the **VARCHAR** data type so that it is easier to concatenate two strings held by these two variables. Two **SET** statements are used to assign description strings

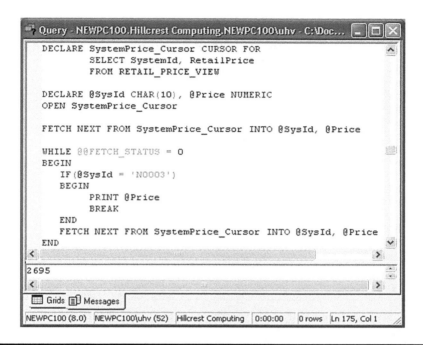

Figure 8.23 `SystemPrice_Cursor` **based on** `RETAIL_PRICE_VIEW`

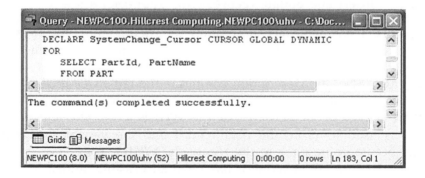

Figure 8.24 **Declare** `SystemChange_Cursor`

to the variables. The variable **@Desc** holds the original description, and the variable **@Monitor** holds the name of the part to be added to the Description column. After opening the cursor `SystemChange_Cursor`, we use the **FETCH** statement to place the data from the result set to the variables **@PartId** and **@PartName**. The **WHILE** loop is used to search for the part id of the given part name. The built-in variable **@@FETCH_STATUS** has the following values:

- 0: The FETCH statement has successfully returned a value.
- 1: The FETCH statement has failed to return a value.
- 2: The record fetched by the FETCH statement is missing.

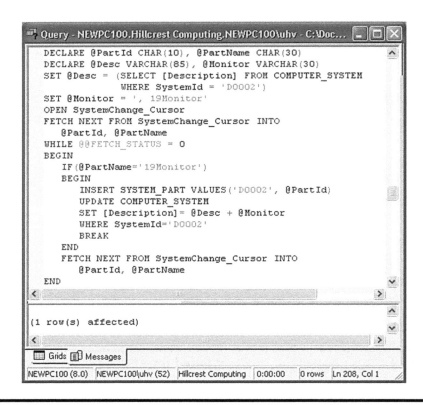

```
DECLARE @PartId CHAR(10), @PartName CHAR(30)
DECLARE @Desc VARCHAR(85), @Monitor VARCHAR(30)
SET @Desc = (SELECT [Description] FROM COMPUTER_SYSTEM
            WHERE SystemId = 'D0002')
SET @Monitor = ', 19Monitor'
OPEN SystemChange_Cursor
FETCH NEXT FROM SystemChange_Cursor INTO
    @PartId, @PartName
WHILE @@FETCH_STATUS = 0
BEGIN
    IF (@PartName='19Monitor')
    BEGIN
        INSERT SYSTEM_PART VALUES('D0002', @PartId)
        UPDATE COMPUTER_SYSTEM
        SET [Description]= @Desc + @Monitor
        WHERE SystemId='D0002'
        BREAK
    END
    FETCH NEXT FROM SystemChange_Cursor INTO
        @PartId, @PartName
END
```

```
(1 row(s) affected)
```

Grids Messages

NEWPC100 (8.0) NEWPC100\uhv (52) Hillcrest Computing 0:00:00 0 rows Ln 208, Col 1

Figure 8.25   Insert and update records with `SystemChange_Cursor`

If the **FETCH** statement has successfully returned a value, the **IF** statement is used to test whether the **PartName** matches the given part name. If there is a match, insert the corresponding system id and part id into the table **SYSTEM_PART**. Also, the Description column in the table **COMPUTER_SYSTEM** is updated by concatenating **@Desc** and **@Monitor**. After making the changes, the **BREAK** statement is used to exit the **WHILE** loop. The second **FETCH** statement is used to place the next record into the variables **@PartId** and **PartName** before going back to the top of the **WHILE** loop.

To show that the 19-in monitor has been successfully added to the table SYSTEM_PART, run the statement shown in Figure 8.26 to retrieve the names of the parts used for the computer system D0002. As shown in Figure 8.26, the 19-in monitor is indeed added to the computer system D0002. Next, we can show that the description corresponding to the system D0002 is also updated by adding the information about the 19-in monitor (see Figure 8.27).

In the above SQL statement, a variable **@Desc** is declared and is assigned the updated description. The **PRINT** command is used to print the content of the variable **@Desc**.

In this example, we have manually entered the information, such as the computer system id and the parts to be added to the table SYSTEM_PART in the script in Figure 8.25. In many practical applications, it is not a good idea to directly program the source code. It is much better if we can create a procedure and pass the information for updating as parameters to the SQL

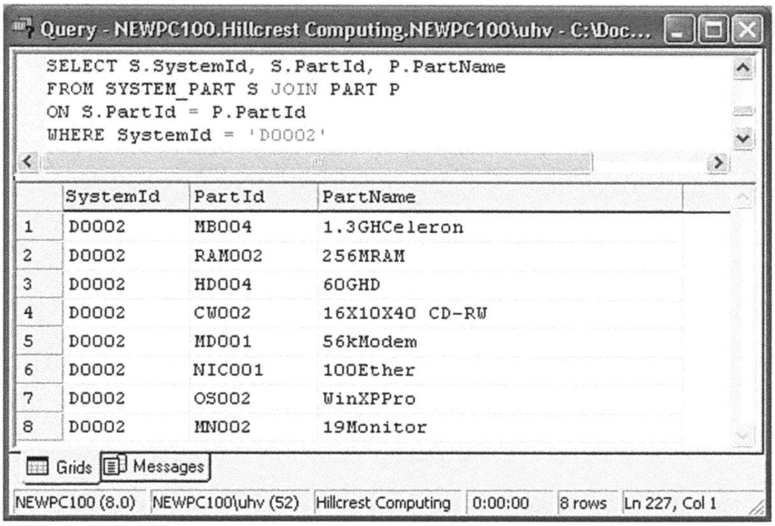

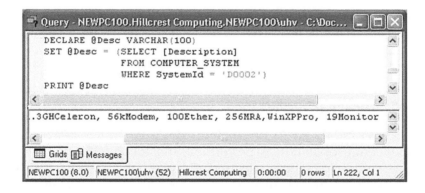

Figure 8.26   Add monitor to computer system D0002

Figure 8.27   Add monitor to description of computer system D0002

source code. Next, we create a procedure to accomplish this task. The first step is to create a procedure by using the statement

```
CREATE PROCEDURE UpdateProc   @SysId CHAR(10),
   @Action CHAR(10), @Item VACHAR(30)
AS
```

where **UpdateProc** is the name of the procedure. **@SysId** is the parameter used to pass the id of a computer system. **@Action** is the parameter used to define if a part is added to a computer system or is deleted from it. **@Item** is the parameter used to pass the part name to be added or deleted. Comparing the code in Figure 8.28 with that in Figure 8.25, the code in the procedure is an improvement in several ways. The parameter **@Action** is added to allow a user to add or delete parts. The **IF...ELSE IF...** structure is used to determine

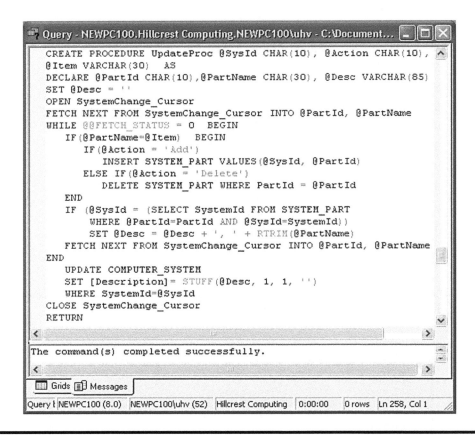

Figure 8.28   Update procedure

if a part should be added to or deleted from a computer system. After the adding or deleting operation is performed, the second **IF** statement is used to create a description about the updated computer system. The **UPDATE** statement is used to modify the Description column in the table **COMPUTER_SYSTEM**. The **STUFF** function is used to remove the ',' sign in front of the description.

Once the procedure UpdateProc is created, it can be executed by the command **EXEC**. Three variables are created to hold the given input values. Let us assign three values, D0002, Add, and 19Monitor, to the variables. (In real-life practice, an input variable is usually assigned a value entered in a textbox on a form.) Figure 8.29 shows the execution result.

After UpdateProc is executed, we have inserted one record to the SYSTEM_PART table and modified the Description column in the table COMPUTER_SYSTEM. To verify the changes, we list all the parts used for the system D0002 in Figure 8.30 and show the content in the corresponding Description column in Figure 8.31.

We can see that the 19-in monitor is added to the computer system D0002 and the description of the system is modified accordingly. When the variable **@Action** is assigned the value **Delete**, the corresponding item will be removed from the specified computer system and the description of the system should

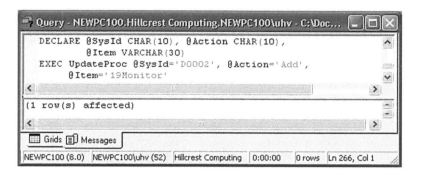

Figure 8.29 **Execute** `UpdateProc` **procedure**

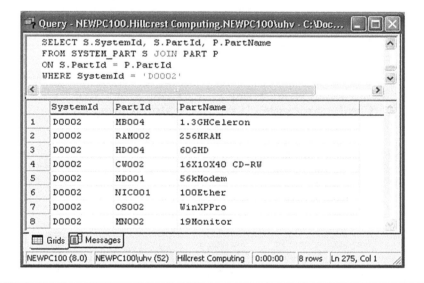

Figure 8.30 **Parts used for system D0002**

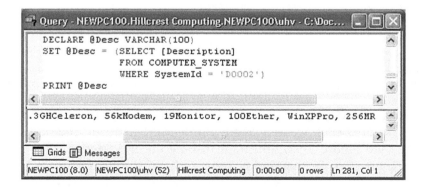

Figure 8.31 **Content in** `Description` **column**

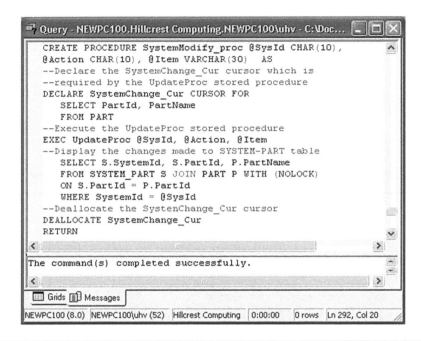

Figure 8.32   Create `SystemModify_proc` **stored procedure**

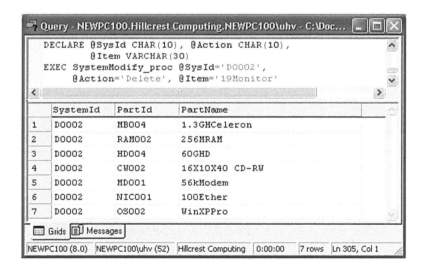

Figure 8.33   Execute `SystemModify_proc` **procedure and execution result**

be changed accordingly. In the next example, we delete the 19-in monitor from the system D0002. We first create a procedure that calls the `UpdateProc` procedure (see Figure 8.32) and then display the modified results.

The execution of **SystemModify_proc** and the results are given in Figures 8.33 and 8.34. As we can see, the 19-in monitor is deleted from the table `SYSTEM_PART` and the description in the `COMPUTER_SYSTEM` table is also modified to exclude the 19-in monitor.

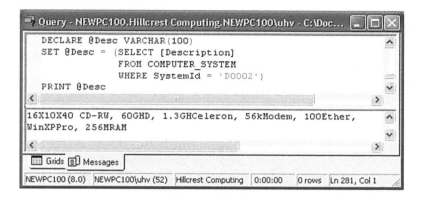

Figure 8.34   Item deleted from computer system D0002

In this section, you have learned how views and cursors are used to develop database applications. In later chapters, we develop some database applications such as forms and reports based on these views and cursors. You will see the importance of views and cursors to database applications.

8.6 Summary

In this chapter, you have learned the concepts of views, indexes, and cursors. The application of views in database applications was discussed in detail. We also discussed the forward only, static, keyset, and dynamic cursors. For indexes, we defined two types of indexes: the clustered index and nonclustered index. We have created, executed, and tested views, indexes, and cursors. You have also learned how to delete a no-longer-needed view, index, and cursor. Examples were used to illustrate how to declare and use these database objects. We used Enterprise Manager, wizards, or Query Analyzer to create, execute, and test these objects. To illustrate how to use views and cursors in a database application, we have created some views and cursors for the `Hillcrest Computing` case study. As mentioned earlier, these views and cursors are used to develop database applications such as forms and reports later.

Review Questions

1. What are the advantages of using views in database applications?
2. How can indexes be used to improve query performance?
3. In what situations will indexes not improve performance?
4. What is a clustered index? What is the advantage of a clustered index?
5. What is a nonclustered index?
6. What is a composite index?
7. What is a result set?
8. What is a cursor?

9. Why do we need a cursor?
10. Describe the forward only cursor.
11. Describe the static cursor.
12. Describe the keyset cursor.
13. Describe the dynamic cursor.
14. What are the restrictions when creating a view?
15. When can a view be updated?
16. In Query Analyzer, create a view NEW_CLUB_VIEW including all the rows from the single table NEW_CLUB, which is a copy of the table CLUB. Perform the insert, delete, and update operations to modify the table NEW_CLUB through the view.
17. In Query Analyzer, create the index, Fee_Index, for the column MembershipFee in the table NEW_CLUB with the fillfactor = 70.
18. In Query Analyzer, create a cursor, NameCursor, to include students' last names and their mentors' names.
19. In Query Analyzer, fetch the records in the cursor NameCursor created in the previous question by using a WHILE loop.
20. Close and deallocate the cursor NameCursor.

Case Study Projects

Continue from the previous chapter. Create views, indexes, and cursors in Query Analyzer for the following case study projects.

1. Computer Service

For the Computer_Service database, perform the following activities:

- In Query Analyzer, create a view, CUSTOMERS_VIEW, which includes information about the customers, their technicians, and the computer systems that have been repaired.
- Modify CUSTOMERS_VIEW created in the previous activity by adding the service cost information to the view.
- Create an index, Parts_Index, for the PartName column in the table PARTS with the fillfactor = 80. Then demonstrate how to delete the index.

2. University Registration

Perform the following activities on the university's Registration database:

- Create a view, STUDENTS_VIEW, to include information about the students and their enrollment. Include a name column that consists of both first names and last names from the STUDENTS table. Test the view in Query Analyzer.
- In Query Analyzer, create a cursor, EnrollmentCursor, to include students' last names and their enrollment information. Test the cursor by using a WHILE loop.

3. Mail Order

On the database `Mail_Order`, perform the following activities:

- In Query Analyzer, create a view, ORDERS_VIEW, which includes customer information and order information, and a calculated column to display the total price of each order.
- In Query Analyzer, create an index, Products_Index, for the product description column in the table PRODUCTS with the fillfactor = 70.
- In Query Analyzer, create a cursor, OrderCursor, to include both the order and shipment information. Also in Query Analyzer, use a WHILE loop to test the cursor. Then demonstrate how to close the cursor.

Chapter 9
Accessing Data

Objectives

- Access data from database applications.
- Use Open Database Connectivity (ODBC).
- Understand Object Linking and Embedding Database (OLE DB).
- Learn about Active Data Object (ADO).

9.1 Introduction

After a database is created and populated with data, it is time for database application developers to develop applications for accessing and retrieving the data stored in the database. The database applications may include forms, reports, and spreadsheets. These applications may be built with programming languages or with some software packages such as Microsoft Access, Microsoft Excel, or InfoPath. On the other hand, databases may be created by various DBMSs such as Oracle, SQL Server, or Access. The task to establish communication between a database and a database application is challenging because, between them, data formats and commands are not consistent. An application can communicate with a database by passing the data-retrieving information through a database's native interface. Although accessing databases can be done through native DBMS libraries provided by DBMS vendors, the native DBMS libraries are a DBMS-specific access method and tedious work is required to configure database-accessing functions. Even worse, there are a large number of DBMS vendors that are providing various data sources for a database application; it is cumbersome to write database-accessing code for each of these DBMS libraries.

To assist front-end users in accessing data, various database-accessing interfaces are created by application developers. The universal data-accessing interfaces such as *Open Database Connectivity* (ODBC) and *Object Linking and Embedding Database* (OLE DB) have been developed to process data maintained by various DBMSs. Basically, an interface is a package of objects that supports certain activities, such as database accessing, by letting users configure some built-in procedures and functions. These interfaces allow application programs to access various DBMS systems. ODBC, developed in the early 1990s, has been accepted by most database vendors such as Microsoft Access, Microsoft SQL Server, Oracle, and IBM DB2. With the ODBC technology, a database application developer can access the database from various programming languages such as Visual Basic, C++, C#, and Java, or from scripting languages such as VBScript and JScript. Many Windows-based products provide graphics-based tools to help front-end users access data. For example, Microsoft Access and Microsoft Excel can call a prespecified ODBC connection to access databases.

It is likely that the ODBC technology will not be updated further. Microsoft has developed the newer, more powerful database-accessing technology OLE DB, which is an object-oriented interface designed for accessing data over an enterprise's network. In the mid-1990s, OLE DB was developed to process not only relational database data but also other types of data such as Excel data. OLE DB is a database-accessing tool created to feature Microsoft products such as SQL Server and Microsoft Office. Microsoft has tried to make these products comply with the OLE DB standard so that front-end users can access these products through OLE DB. Other database vendors such as Oracle and IBM also participate in the OLE DB standard. From now on, all new products from Microsoft will be compatible with OLE DB.

OLE DB is a low-level database-accessing interface and is complex. A database application that uses OLE DB must use some complex COM interfaces. (COM stands for *Component Object Model* that is used to develop object-oriented components.) You can access OLE DB through C++ directly, but you cannot access OLE DB directly through languages such as JScript, VBScript, or Visual Basic because these languages do not have pointers to access COM interfaces. To allow application programs created by Visual Basic and a scripting language to access the OLE DB objects, a specific interface called *Active Data Object* (ADO) has been created. These database applications access OLE DB through ADO indirectly. ADO is much simpler to use than OLE DB.

9.2 Database Accessing

In an enterprise client/server environment, information is transferred back and forth between front-end users and data sources on the Web or local area network. To get data stored on a database server, the application on the client establishes a connection to the data source on the server. The data source can be a relational database, a text file, e-mail, or Web-based information. After the connection to the data source is established, SQL statements created by the application will be passed to the server. By executing the SQL statements on the server, data will be retrieved from the database and sent to the

Table 9.1 Compare Database-accessing Methods

	ODBC	OLE DB	ADO
Object-oriented computing	Weak	Strong	Strong
Nonrelational data sources	Weak	Strong	Strong
Performance	Fair	Strong	Fair
Ease of use	Strong	Fair	Strong

application on the client. If an error occurs, the error information will be sent from the server to the client application.

An application communicates with a database by passing the data-retrieving information through a database's native interface. A program communicating with a database through its native interface is very complex, inflexible, and limited to the current database only. It is very difficult and time consuming for a database to communicate with other databases this way. Various database connection utilities have been developed to make the job easier.

There are three possible ways to help us handle database-accessing tasks:

- Convert data stored in a data source to ASCII code, and then import the code to the database application.
- Use *Object Linking and Embedding* (OLE) to access stored data directly.
- Use database-accessing technologies such as ODBC and ADO to access stored data.

With several ways to choose, which is better for your project? The use of the technologies introduced above will depend on the database application, the data source, and the programming environment. ODBC will let you access relational data such as data from your relational database. If you have non-relational data types such as Extensible Markup Language (XML) files, Microsoft Office Word documents, or e-mail integrated in your data source, consider using OLE DB. ADO is a good choice if you want to create a new application project. ADO has several advantages. It is easier to access nonrelational data by using ADO than by OLE DB. ADO allows front-end users to access a data source through almost any programming language, such as C++ or Visual Basic, or scripting languages such as VBScript or JScript. Table 9.1 lists relative strengths and weaknesses of the database-accessing methods.

As seen in Table 9.1, ADO offers a good combination of flexibility and simplicity with decent performance. When creating a new data-accessing project with script programming languages, ADO should be considered as an ideal choice. Although the use of OLE DB for older front-end applications is not an easy task, OLE DB as a database-accessing tool is quite convenient for some newer front-end applications such as Microsoft Office XP or later, which have the built-in OLE DB-based GUI tools for database accessing. OLE DB is the new standard for Microsoft database-accessing functionalities.

If your front-end applications are Windows-based, understanding OLE DB and ADO is particularly important. Next, we take a minute to see how each of the three methods can be used to accomplish the database-accessing tasks.

9.3 Open Database Connectivity (ODBC)

By using ODBC, a database application can access data stored in various relational databases or spreadsheets. Proposed by the SQL Access Group committee and supported by Microsoft, IBM, Oracle, and many other DBMS vendors, ODBC is an industry standard in accessing tablelike data resources such as relational database data. The high points of ODBC are as follows:

- ODBC is a universal data-accessing interface, which means that it allows an application to use SQL statements to access many different DBMS systems without rewriting the database-accessing interface.
- ODBC is an interface that can be used to connect a Web server to various databases. ODBC plays an important role in today's E-business environment.
- By using ODBC, each DBMS product can support a variety of applications created in a multiple-tier client/server environment.

On the other hand, ODBC is an older technology. Nowadays, many database applications do not just access database data. They may also need to access the data stored on other data sources. When accessing nonrelational data such as text files by ODBC, front-end users need to specify a lot of detailed information such as the data type for each column, the column delimiter, the length of each column, and other format-related details. Thus, ODBC is not a convenient tool to use for creating the interface between an application and a nonrelational data source.

ODBC consists of two major components, the ODBC driver manager and ODBC driver. The architecture of ODBC is illustrated in Figure 9.1, which shows four components. We take a closer look at these components. The *database application* component includes forms and reports built with application software products such as a spreadsheet, personal database, word processor, Web browser, or programs written in C++.NET, Java, Visual Basic.NET, C#, and other programming languages. These applications pass SQL statements to the ODBC driver manager.

After receiving a request from the application component, the *ODBC driver manager* component, which is a Dynamic-Link Library file, will be used to determine the type of DBMS requested by the application component. Once the type of DBMS is determined, the driver manager loads the DBMS-specific ODBC driver into memory. The driver manager is also used to verify the number of arguments and the data type passed into the interface functions.

The *ODBC driver* component for each specified DBMS is also a DLL file that is used to process an application request passed by the driver manager. The driver will translate the SQL statements from the application request to

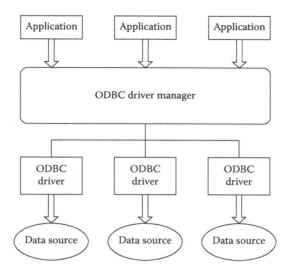

Figure 9.1   ODBC architecture

the native SQL syntax supported by the data source. If the data source does not process the SQL statements, the driver may process them to retrieve data from the data source. When errors are generated in the data source, the driver converts the error message in the data source to the format supported by ODBC.

The *data source* component consists of a database, the DBMS that manages the database, the operating system that runs the DBMS, and the network used to access the DBMS. For example, SQL Server is one of the data sources.

ODBC is a powerful database-accessing tool. It can handle all kinds of database-accessing tasks, from connecting to data sources to calling transaction libraries. It will take a great effort for a DBMS vendor to implement all these functionalities. The good news is that drivers supplied by DBMS vendors do not have to utilize the complete power of ODBC. This allows more DBMS vendors to participate in the ODBC standard, even though some of the vendors are able to comply with only a portion of the standard.

A driver's *application program interface* (API) can be made at different conformance levels. An API is a group of functions or procedures accessible by programmers to call ODBC built-in functions to connect data to, retrieve data from, manage data in, and disconnect data from a data source. There are three API conformance levels: *Core API level*, *Level 1 API*, and *Level 2 API*. The descriptions of the three conformance levels are listed in Table 9.2. The higher levels can use the features of ODBC and SQL more fully. However, they require software producers to put more effort into developing the driver. On the other hand, the lower-level API requires less effort in software development but will have less functionality. Most of the software vendors use Level 1 API.

Next, we use the case study `Hillcrest Computing` to illustrate the use of ODBC. For a database application, Microsoft supports the driver manager,

Table 9.2   Conformance Levels

Conformance Level	Description
Core API level	This is the basic level. It does basic jobs such as connecting to data sources, implementing SQL statements, converting error information, and managing transactions.
Level 1 API	This has all the functionalities of Core API plus more advanced functions such as managing partial results, passing driver-specified information to data sources, and retrieving driver information.
Level 2 API	This is the highest level. It has all the functionalities of Level 1 plus higher-level functionalities such as processing a scrollable cursor, calling transaction libraries, and managing detailed information about connection and data sources.

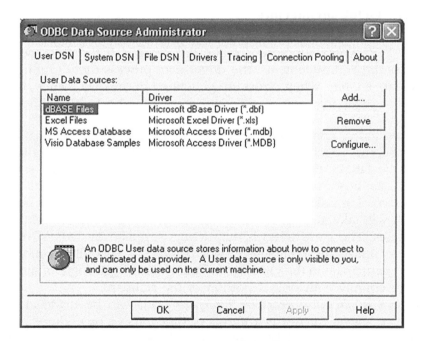

Figure 9.2   ODBC data source administrator dialog

which is built into Windows. A DBMS vendor who supports an application provides the driver. You need to specify the appropriate ODBC data sources and drivers for your applications.

If SQL Server is installed on your computer with the Windows XP Professional Edition operating system or above, open **Administrative Tools** in the **Control Panel**. In the Administrative Tools window, double-click the icon labeled **Data Sources (ODBC)**, and the **ODBC Data Source Administrator** dialog will be open for configuration (see Figure 9.2).

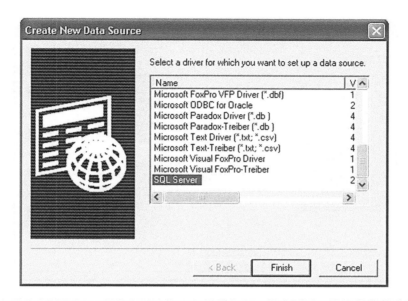

Figure 9.3   Create new data source dialog

The next step is to configure the *Data Source Name* (DSN). There are three DSNs: *User DSN*, *System DSN*, and *File DSN*. User DSN is available only to the current user. The other users of the computer are not able to use the DSN configured by the current user. System DSN is available to all the users who have an account on the current computer system. File DSN allows all the users who have the proper permission to access a DSN file. System DSN has a balance of security and convenience. It is a good choice for Web-based applications. Next, we configure a User DSN for the SQL Server data source that contains the database `Hillcrest Computing`.

Make sure that the **User DSN** tab is selected. Click on the **Add** button. When the **Create New Data Source** dialog is open, select **SQL Server**. Then click the **Finish** button (see Figure 9.3). The **Create a New Data Source to SQL Server** dialog is open for us to enter detailed data source information (see Figure 9.4). Enter **Hillcrest Computing** for the **Name** textbox and **SQL Server data source** for the **Description** textbox. Select or enter your SQL Server for the **Server** combo box and click **Next**.

In Figure 9.5, you have two authentication options: Windows NT authentication and SQL Server authentication. If you select the Windows NT authentication, you are automatically permitted to access SQL Server once you have logged on to the computer. If you select the SQL Server authentication, after you have logged on to the computer, you still need to provide the SQL Server user name and password before you can log on to SQL Server. We have chosen the **Windows NT authentication**.

Click **Next** to go to the database selection dialog (see Figure 9.6). It allows you to select the default database. Check the **Change the default database to** box and select the **Hillcrest Computing** database. Then click **Next**. Choose the default setting in the next page and click **Finish**.

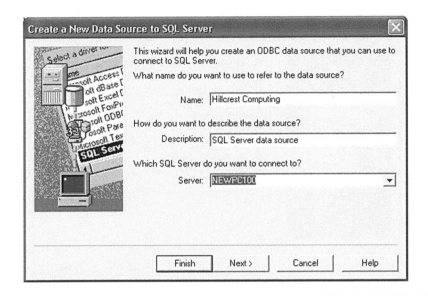

Figure 9.4   Create a new data source to SQL Server dialog

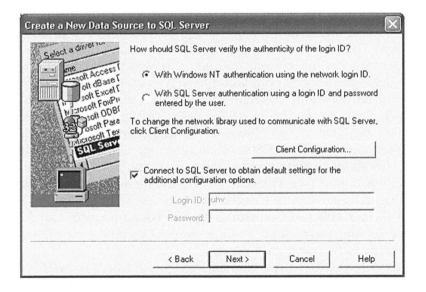

Figure 9.5   Authentication options

On the **ODBC Microsoft SQL Server Setup** message page, a summary of the configuration is listed for examination (see Figure 9.7). To test the data source configuration, click the **Test Data Source** button.

Click **OK** to go back to the **ODBC Data Source Administrator** dialog. Click **OK** again to complete the configuration. At this point, a data source named Hillcrest Computing is ready to be used by a database application. This data source can be called from application programs in Visual Basic, C++, or other

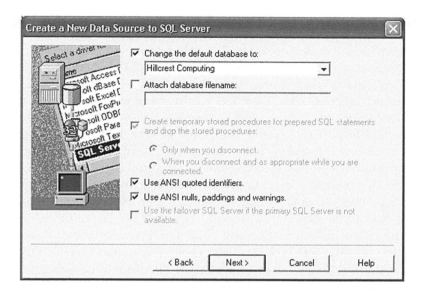

Figure 9.6   Change default database

Figure 9.7   ODBC SQL Server setup page

programming languages. For accessing a relational data source, ODBC is an adequate database-accessing technology. It is likely that ODBC will not be upgraded in the future. If you want to include nonrelational data sources such as XML files, Microsoft Office Word documents, or e-mail, consider the OLE DB database-accessing technology below.

9.4 Object Linking and Embedding Database (OLE DB)

OLE DB provides access to relational or nonrelational data, structured or flat data, and data accessible or inaccessible through ODBC. Like ODBC, OLE DB is a low-level database-accessing technology. Compared with ODBC, OLE DB has two improvements. First, OLE DB allows database applications to access both relational and nonrelational data sources. Second, OLE DB data sources provide well-defined COM-based components. The COM-based components are used to deliver features and functionalities of a data source to data consumers. Such COM-based components are called *data providers*, which are provided by vendors of data sources. Data providers are programs that enable native access to data. A data provider retrieves data from a data source, constructs RecordSet objects, and populates them with retrieved data. The data providers we use are Microsoft OLE DB Provider for SQL Server and Microsoft Jet 4.0 OLE DB Provider. The other advantage of OLE DB is that a database vendor does not have to provide the functionalities from a data source all at once. The database vendor may provide some basic functionalities first and then add more functionalities later.

The database application connected to a data provider is called a *data consumer*. Data consumers are used to access data. For example, Microsoft Access and a Microsoft Visual C++ program are data consumers. A data consumer receives a set of records provided by a data provider. RecordSet objects returned by OLE DB can be accessed by multiple data consumers and can be loaded on client computers for offline processing. They even provide several data management tools such as sorting and filtering for data consumers. As you can see in Figure 9.8, the data provider has components that can talk to the ODBC data source. This allows database applications to access those data sources that have the ODBC driver but do not yet have the OLE DB provider.

Using OLE DB often involves detailed programming. However, if Microsoft Access 2002 and Excel 2002 are available as data consumers, you can connect to the OLE DB data provider from Access 2002 and Excel 2002 or later by using graphical tools such as **Data Link**. Connection information is specified by a data link. Microsoft Access has powerful tools for creating front-end applications such as forms and reports. On other hand, SQL Server can be used to create databases to store information for an enterprise with much better security measures. If we use Microsoft Access as a data consumer and SQL Server as a data provider, we can take advantage of both products. The following steps show you how to configure **data link** properties to connect Access 2003 to SQL Server.

1. Open **Microsoft Access 2003** and click the **Create a new file** link in the Getting Started pane.
2. Click **Project using existing data** in the **New File** task pane and enter the project name such as **Mytest**, and then click the **Create** button to open the **Data Link Properties** dialog box.
3. Select the database server in the **Select or enter a server name** combo box.

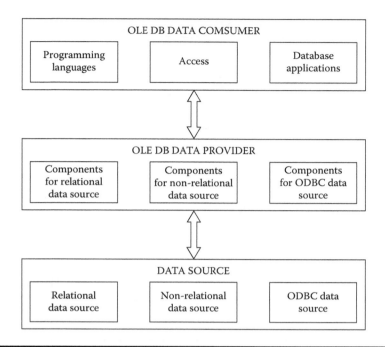

Figure 9.8   OLE DB structure

4. For authentication options, you have two choices, **Use Windows NT Integrated security** or **Use a specific user name and password**. If your SQL Server and Access are installed on the same computer, you may select the first one. Once you log on to your computer, you are automatically permitted to access SQL Server. If you are working in a client/server environment, you should select the second one. Through the client computer, you access SQL Server by providing your user name and password. In Figure 9.5, we have chosen the first one.
5. Select the database **Hillcrest Computing** from the combo box, as shown in Figure 9.9.
6. Click the **Test Connection** button to verify if the connection is successful. If it is successful, click **OK**. The tables created for the `Hillcrest Computing` database will be displayed in the Access Project window, as shown in Figure 9.10.

From Figure 9.10, we can see that the tables from SQL Server are ready to be used in Access. On the left-hand side of the window, **Forms** and **Reports** are listed in the **Objects** pane. In the next chapter, we use these objects to create some front-end applications.

Note: To run this example, you may need to attach the database `Hillcrest Computing` to your SQL Server (as shown in Chapter 5) if the database is not there. The view `PART_COST_VIEW` below is included in the `Hillcrest Computing` database.

If the front-end applications are built in Microsoft Excel or Word, similar methods can be used to access a data provider. For example, to import the

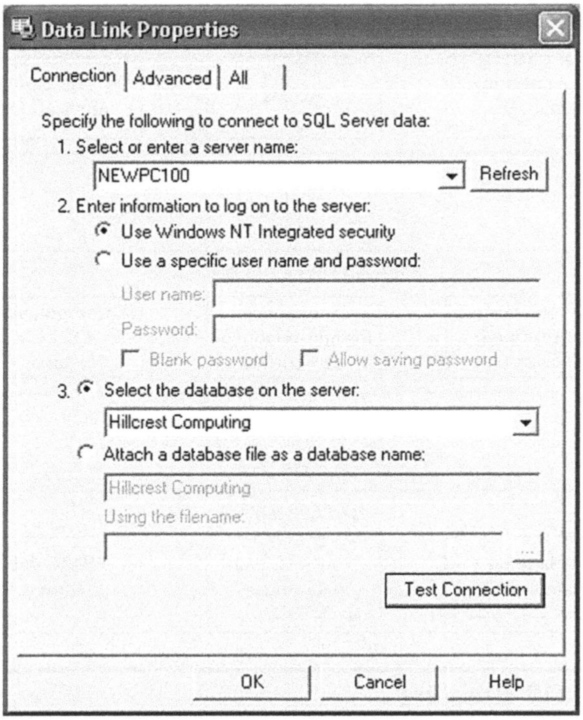

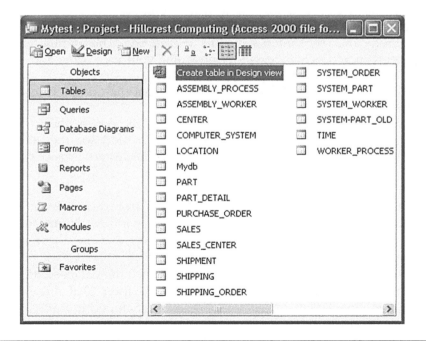

Figure 9.9   Configure data link properties

Figure 9.10   Connect Access to database created in SQL Server

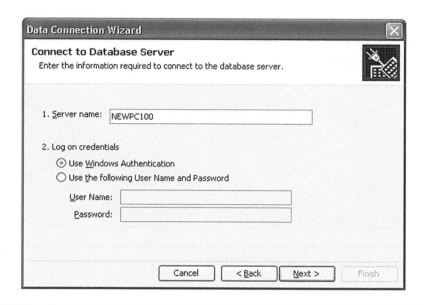

Figure 9.11   Configure Data Connection Wizard

data in the view PART_COST_VIEW stored in the database Hillcrest Computing, try the following steps.

1. Open **Microsoft Excel 2002** or **2003**. Click **Data** on the menu bar. Select **Import External Data**, and then select **Import Data**.
2. In the **Select Data Source** dialog box, double-click **+New SQL Server Connection** and you will have the dialog box in Figure 9.11.
3. Enter your server name and choose the **Log on credentials** option, and then click **Next**.
4. Select the **Hillcrest Computing** database and the view **PART_COST_VIEW**, and then click **Next**.
5. Enter the description of your data link and the search keywords.
6. Click **Finish** to complete the configuration. Figure 9.12 shows the result of the data connection.

As we have seen, OLE DB is a convenient tool that can be used to connect a front-end database application to a data provider.

Note: When you work on the above example, make sure that you are the **dbo**. If you copy the database from somewhere else, you may not be able to see the tables or stored procedures.

9.5 Active Data Object (ADO)

ADO is a relatively new database-accessing technology built on top of the OLE DB technology; that is, ADO is a high-level database-accessing technology. For database application developers, a high-level database-accessing technology requires less programming and is easier to use in developing

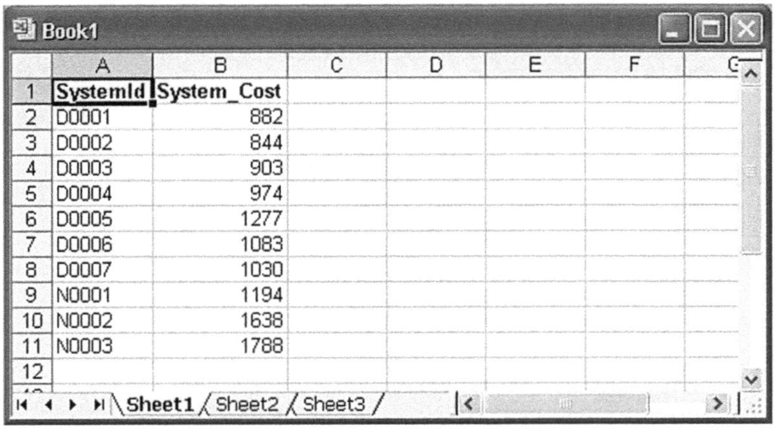

	A	B	C	D	E	F
1	SystemId	System_Cost				
2	D0001	882				
3	D0002	844				
4	D0003	903				
5	D0004	974				
6	D0005	1277				
7	D0006	1083				
8	D0007	1030				
9	N0001	1194				
10	N0002	1638				
11	N0003	1788				
12						

Figure 9.12 Result of data connection

database applications. Because ADO is built on top of OLE DB, an OLE DB data provider can be considered a data source for ADO. The ADO technology was first developed for *Active Server Pages* (ASP) to access databases through the Internet. Since the release of Version 2.5, ADO has been able to access a wide variety of data sources. It is used to access relational or nonrelational databases, structured or flat files, shared folders, and e-mail. When used with SQL Server 2000, ADO allows us to execute XML commands against SQL Server. It can now be called from Internet browsers, database products, and programming languages such as Visual Basic and scripting languages. The further developed ADO.NET is also XML-compatible. As the name indicates, ADO contains objects or collections of objects for database accessing. The object hierarchy is represented in Figure 9.13.

In Figure 9.13, the rectangle blocks represent objects and the round-cornered rectangle blocks represent collections of objects. Often, ADO objects are built and used with scripting languages such as VBScript or JScript, or with commonly used programming languages such as Visual Basic, Java, and C++. Some programming is involved in implementing ADO objects. However, programming for the implementation of ADO objects is fairly simple because ADO is a high-level database-accessing technique. Each object contains properties, methods, or other objects. Properties are used to describe the characteristics of an object such as the type and location of a data source. Methods are used to perform some activities such as opening a data source. Here we discuss some objects commonly used in database applications. For more detailed information about ADO objects, please refer to books specializing in ADO. The description and use of these objects are listed below.

- *Connection object:* Before you can get data from a data source, you must establish a connection between your database application and the data source. A `Connection` object can be used to help accomplish this task. It has some transaction control methods, such as `Open`, `BeginTrans`, `CommitTrans`, and `RollbackTrans`. When executing a command, you

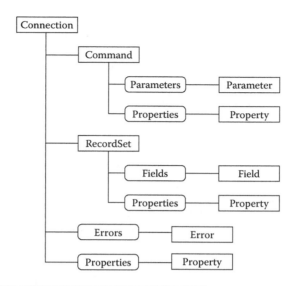

Figure 9.13   ADO object architecture

can use these methods to open a connection or create multiple nested transactions. Also, a `Connection` object can be used to make sure that changes made to a data source in a transaction occur either successfully together or not at all.

- *Command object:* After a connection is established, a `Command` object can be used to execute SQL statements, stored procedures, or user-defined functions stored in a data source to retrieve data.
- *RecordSet object:* The `RecordSet` object is used to process results returned by SQL statements, user-defined functions, or stored procedures in a `Command` object.
- *Error object:* The `Error` object is used to handle errors and messages. It contains error messages generated during an ADO process.
- *Parameter object:* When executing parameterized queries or stored procedures in a `Command` object, the `Parameter` object is used to pass input or output values.
- *Field object:* The `Field` object is used to represent a column in a `Record-Set` object.
- *Property object:* Each object supports some `Property` objects that contain a set of values defining the general characteristics of the object. An object may have two types of properties, built-in and dynamic. Built-in properties are prebuilt properties that are common to any new object. On the other hand, dynamic properties are specific to each data provider and are implemented when a data provider is connected.

To open a connection to a data source, you can use the `Open` method defined in a `Connection` object. The `Open` method has several parameters such as `ConnectionString`, `UserID`, `Password`, and `OpenOptions`. `ConnectionString` is a `Property` object; that is, it contains several values used to characterize the connection to a data source. The values in `Connection-String` are:

- *Provider:* The name of a data provider in a connection, such as the name of an OLE DB data provider for SQL Server. Examples of commonly used providers are:
  - Access: Provider=Microsoft.Jet.OLEDB.4
  - SQL Server: Provider=SQLOLEDB.1
  - Oracle: Provider=MSDAORA.1
- *Data source:* The name of a data source in a connection, such as the name of a database server or the path to the Microsoft Access mdb file. You may use the keyword `Server` for `Data Source`.
- *Initial catalog:* The name of a database that you want to connect to, such as the database `Hillcrest Computing`. You may use the keyword `Database` for `Initial Catalog`.
- *Integrated security:* The name of a security setting for the Windows authentication mode. For the SQL Server authentication mode, use the keywords `User Id` and `Password`.

One of the ADO's advantages is that all these objects, properties, and methods are already built into the ADO package. As an application developer, your task is to learn how to use these objects and their properties and methods in your application code. The following code shows a specified `ConnectionString` of `Property` object in VBScript:

```
MyConnStr = "Provider='SQLOLEDB.1';Server='NEWPC100';" & _
"Database='Hillcrest Computing';Integrated Security='SSPI';"
```

To help application developers set up ADO `Connection` objects, Microsoft developed the *Universal Data Link* (UDL) wizard to assist in the configuration of `ConnectionString`. The following are the steps for setting up a connection to an OLE DB data provider from a database application.

1. Make sure that **Microsoft Data Access Components (MDAC)** is installed on your computer. MDAC 2.5 should be installed if you have installed Microsoft Visual Basic 6.0, Microsoft Data Access SDK 2.*x*, or Windows 2000 or later. Otherwise, you can download the latest version from http://www.microsoft.com/data/download.htm.
2. Open **Windows Explorer**. Click the **Tools** menu, and then click **Folder Options**. Click the **View** tab, uncheck the **Hide extensions for known file types** checkbox, and then click **OK**.
3. Right-click on the desktop screen, select **New**, and then click click **Text Document**. A new text file **New Text Document.txt** is created.
4. Right-click on the file **New Text Document.txt** you just created and select **Rename**; rename the file as **MyLink.udl** and press **Enter**.
5. Double-click the **Mylink.udl** file to open the **Data Link Properties** dialog.
6. Click the **Provider** tab and select **Microsoft OLE DB Provider for SQL Server**, as shown in Figure 9.14.
7. Click **Next** to proceed to the **Connection** tab.
8. Enter your database server name in the **Select or enter a server name** combo box.

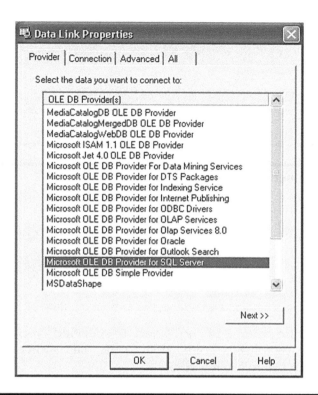

Figure 9.14   Select Microsoft OLE DB provider for SQL Server

9. Select **Use Windows NT Integrated security**. Then select the database **Hillcrest Computing** from the combo box.
10. Click the **Test Connection** button to verify if the connection is successful. If the connection is successful, click **OK**.

After the OLE DB data provider is set up, you can access the data provider from different types of data consumers. For example, you may access the data provider from ASP files or from programming languages such as Visual Basic. If you want to use the ConnectionString object created in the above procedure in your VBScript code, simply do the following:

- For the **MyLink.udl** file on the desktop, change the file name to **MyLink.txt**. Then click **Yes** to the warning message. Then double-click the **MyLink.txt** file. You should have the message shown in Figure 9.15. (At this point, the connection string is fully tested.)
- Later, you can copy the connection string to the ConnectionString object in your VBScript or VB programs.

Note: Here we assume that you are currently working with the computer where SQL Server is installed and that you are the administrator of that computer. For the remote log-on from a client computer, you should choose the option **Use a specific user name and password**. Then enter your username

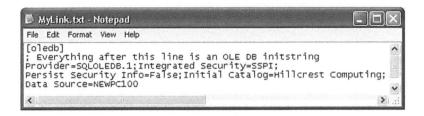

Figure 9.15   Connection message in `MyLink.txt`

and password for SQL Server. The connection string should look like the one below:

```
Provider=SQLOLEDB.1;Persist Security Info=False;
Initial Catalog=Hillcrest Computing;
User Id=Group1;Password=student;Data Source=NEWPC100
```

Once the `ConnectionString` object is specified, you pass it into the method `Open` to establish a connection to the data source. To accomplish this task, consider the following code:

```
Dim objConn As New ADODB.Connection
objConn.ConnectionString = "Provider=SQLOLEDB.1;" & _
"Integrated Security=SSPI;" & _
"Persist Security Info=False;" & _
"Initial Catalog=Hillcrest Computing;" & _
"Data Source=NEWPC100"
objConn.Open

    (You may later insert some code using the ObjConn object.)

objConn.Close
Set objConn = Nothing
```

The code above shows how to build a **Connection** object. The first line

```
Dim objConn As New ADODB.Connection
```

creates a **Connection** object. By convention, the first three letters in a variable name are the abbreviation of the variable type. Because we are creating an object variable, the first three letters in the name of the variable are **obj**. For those of you who are not familiar with Visual Basic, **Dim** is the keyword used to declare a local variable. The object ADODB is a built-in object. It is the root object in the ADO object hierarchy. The **Connection** object is inherited from the **ADODB** object. The statement **ADODB.Connection** means that the variable type for **objConn** is an ADO Connection object. You may find more ways to create an object in a VBScript book. The code

```
objConn.ConnectionString = "Provider=SQLOLEDB.1;_
   Integrated Security=SSPI;_
   Persist Security Info=False;_
   Initial Catalog=Hillcrest Computing;Data Source=NEWPC100"
```

is used to specify the **ConnectionString** object. As you can see, the specification of the **ConnectionString** object is copied from the **MyLink.txt** file. The line

```
objConn.Open
```

is used to open a connection to the database `Hillcrest Computing`. The syntax **objConn.Open** indicates that **Open** is the method that belongs to the object **objConn**. After the connection is established, you can run the **Command** object to retrieve data. We do this in a moment. The code

```
objConn.Close
Set objConn = Nothing
```

is used to close and delete the connection. Here, **Close** is the method included in the object **objConn**.

Now that a connection is established to a data source, you can create a `Command` object to retrieve data by executing SQL statements or stored procedures. You may also use a `Command` object for other operations such as managing a database by using INSERT, UPDATE, and DELETE SQL statements. Like `Connection` objects, a `Command` object can have collections of other objects, methods, or properties, depending on the functionality of the provider. For the `Command` object, the commonly used properties and methods are as follows:

- Properties:
  - *CommandText:* This property contains a string that has the command to be executed. The command can be a SQL statement, stored procedure, or other statement that can be recognized by the data provider.
  - *CommandType:* This property defines the type of command that the data provider will execute.
  - *CommandTimeout:* This property specifies the number of seconds that a `Command` object will wait before the execution of the command expires.
  - *ActiveConnection:* This property contains the reference to a `Connection` object. When using this property in a `Command` object, you can open a data source connection without using a connection string.
- Methods:
  - *Execute:* This method is used to execute a command specified by the `CommandText` and `CommandType` properties.
  - *Cancel:* This method is used to cancel a command execution.

In the following, we illustrate the use of a `Command` object to retrieve data from the Hillcrest Computing database.

```
Dim objCmd As New ADODB.Command

objCmd.CommandText = "SELECT SystemId, System_Cost " & _
   "FROM Part_Cost " & _
   "WHERE System_Cost > 1500 " & _
   "ORDER BY System_Cost"

objCmd.CommandType = adCmdText
```

In this code, the first line is used to create a **Command** object **objCmd**. Then the **CommandText** property is specified by a SQL statement to select the records with **System_Cost** higher than 1500 in ascending order based on **System_Cost**. The last line indicates that the command type is a text string.

Once the command is executed, the selected data are returned to the RecordSet object used to process the data. RecordSet is an abstract object. Being abstract, it loses some details but gains some abilities to work with more types of database components such as e-mail data. Properties and methods in a RecordSet object are used to locate and modify data. The descriptions of some commonly used methods and properties are shown below.

- Methods:
  - *Addnew:* It is used to create a new record in a RecordSet object. The new record will not be written to a database until the Update method is executed.
  - *Cancel:* It is used to cancel the execution of a command.
  - *Clone:* It is used to duplicate a RecordSet object.
  - *Delete:* It is used to delete records in a RecordSet object.
  - *MoveFirst, MoveNext, MovePrevious,* and *MoveLast:* These methods are used to locate the first, next, previous, and last records in a RecordSet object.
  - *Open:* It is used to open a RecordSet object for data manipulation.
  - *Update:* It is used to write changes made in the editing process back to the database.
- Properties:
  - *AbsolutePosition:* It is used to indicate the current record position in a RecordSet object. It contains three values, adPosUnknown, adPosBOF, and adPosEOF, which indicate that the current position is unknown, at the beginning of a RecordSet object, and at the end of a RecordSet object, respectively. Often it is used to track a looping process.
  - *BOF and EOF:* It is used to show the beginning and ending position of a RecordSet object.
  - *EditMode:* It is used to indicate that the current record is being edited. It contains four values: adEditAdd, adEditDelete, adEditIn-Progress, and adEditnone.
  - *Bookmark:* It is used to create variables to locate a record in a Record-Set object.
  - *CursorLocation:* It is used to indicate the location of a cursor.
  - *CursorType:* It is used to specify the kind of cursor being used in a RecordSet object.

  — *LockType:* In a multi-user environment, `LockType` is used to determine how records are locked when being edited.
  — *MaxRecords:* It is used to count the maximum number of records in a `RecordSet` object.
  — *RecordCount:* It is used to count the number of records in a `RecordSet` object.

The properties `CursorType` and `LockType` are especially important for a database in a client/server environment where multiple users log on to a remote database server. There are several difficulties when multiple users manipulate data stored in a remote database. The following questions may be raised:

■ When one of the clients makes a change to the data, how should other clients know about the change?
■ Client/server computing may cause a traffic jam on a network. How can we minimize network traffic?
■ Multiple users may attempt to change the same records. How do we resolve conflicts among the users?

A cursor object can be used to answer the first two questions. The last question can be answered by specifying a proper `LockType`. Previously, we introduced the cursor concepts and implemented cursors in Transact-SQL for manipulating data returned from a `SELECT` statement. To simplify database accessing, some cursor functionalities have already been built into ADO. A built-in cursor object provides tools to synchronize changes and minimize network traffic. A cursor object can be specified through the properties `CursorLocation` and `CursorType`. `CursorLocation` can be set to one of the two values

■ *adUseClient:* This value indicates that the cursor is on the client computer. If the `RecordSet` object is created on the client computer, using a local client cursor to manipulate the `RecordSet` object will minimize network traffic.
■ *adUseServer:* This value indicates that the cursor is on the data provider side. It is the default setting.

The property `CursorType` can be set as one of the four values in Table 9.3. When two users attempt to modify the same record, the data provider provides a locking tool to prevent the conflict. There are four different lock types available in SQL Server, as shown in Table 9.4.

To illustrate the use of a `RecordSet` object, consider the following example that combines the code for creating a `Connection` object and a `Command` object. An `Error` object is also used to handle errors. In the following example, we are going to create a `RecordSet` object by retrieving data from `PART_COST_VIEW` in the database `Hillcrest Computing`.

Table 9.3   Cursor Types and Their Descriptions

Cursor Type	Constant Name	Description
Forward only	adOpenForwordOnly	A forward only cursor can move in the forward direction only. It supports fetching, but not scrolling.
Static	adOpenStatic	A static cursor provides forward and backward scrolling. It is a snapshot of a `RecordSet` object, so it cannot detect changes made to the `RecordSet` object by other users. A static cursor can be set to either read only or read/write.
Dynamic	adOpenDynamic	A dynamic cursor supports forward and backward scrolling. It can detect any changes made to a `RecordSet` object by other users.
Keyset	adOpenKeySet	A keyset cursor supports scrolling manipulated by keys that are built on a set of columns that uniquely identify the rows in a `RecordSet` object. It can detect changes to the values of rows in the `RecordSet` object but cannot detect newly added records to the `RecordSet` object.

Table 9.4   Lock Types and Their Descriptions

Lock Type	Constant Name	Description
Read only	adLockReadOnly	It tells the data provider to create a read-only `RecordSet` object. The content in the read-only `RecordSet` object cannot be modified. It is the default setting.
Pessimistic	adLockPessimistic	When the lock on a data provider is specified as pessimistic, a record is locked as soon as the editing process begins. The lock remains effective until the editing process is complete. No other users can access the record before the record is unlocked. When a `RecordSet` object is set to a remote client side, the `adLockPessimistic` lock type is not supported.
Optimistic	adLockOptimistic	When the lock on a data provider is specified as optimistic, a record is locked only when the Update method is called.
Batch optimistic	adBatchOptimistic	This value is used to set optimistic locking for batch updates. When a `RecordSet` object is set to a remote client side, the lock type can only be set to `adLockBatchOptimistic`.

9.5.1 Example: Creating an ADO RecordSet Object

```
'Begin the example creating Connection, Command, and RecordSet
   objects.

   On Error GoTo ErrHandler: 'If error, go to the ErrHandler
       'section

   Dim objConn As New ADODB.Connection 'Create a Connection object
   Dim objCmd As New ADODB.Command 'Create a Command object
   Dim objRs As New ADODB.RecordSet 'Create a RecordSet object

'The SQL statement in the CommandText property is used to
'retrieve data from PART_COST_VIEW in the Hillcrest Computing
'database.

   objCmd.CommandText = "SELECT SystemId, System_Cost " & _
   "FROM PART_COST_VIEW " & _
   "WHERE System_Cost > 1500 " & _
   "ORDER BY System_Cost"

   objCmd.CommandType = adCmdText 'Specify the CommandType as
       'adCmdText

'Connect to the OLE DB data source.

   objConn.ConnectionString = "Provider=SQLOLEDB.1;" & _
       "Integrated Security=SSPI;" & _
       "Persist Security Info=False;" & _
       "Initial Catalog=Hillcrest Computing;Data Source=NEWPC100"
   objConn.Open

'Tell the Command object to use the Connection object objConn.

   objCmd.ActiveConnection = objConn

'Set the CursorLocation, CursorType and LockType properties and
'open the RecordSet object by passing the parameter objCmd.
objRs.LockType = adLockOptimistic
   objRs.CursorLocation = adUseClient
   objRs.CursorType = adOpenKeyset
   objRs.Open objCmd

'Display the records stored in the RecordSet object objRs.

   Debug.Print "    SystemId    System_Cost"
   Do While Not objRs.EOF
        Debug.Print vbTab & objRs(0) & vbTab & objRs(1)
        objRs.MoveNext
   Loop

   'Clean up

   objRs.Close
   objConn.Close
```

```
   Set objRs = Nothing
   Set objConn = Nothing
   Set objCmd = Nothing
   Exit Sub

'Error handling section.

ErrHandler:
'Clean up

  If objRs.State = adStateOpen Then
      objRs.Close
  End If

  If objConn.State = adStateOpen Then
      objConn.Close
  End If

  Set objRs = Nothing
  Set objConn = Nothing
  Set objCmd = Nothing

  If Err <> 0 Then
      MsgBox Err.Source & "-->" & Err.Description, , "Error"
  End If

'End of the example.
```

Note: The connection string assigned to **objConn.ConnectionString** is based on the fact that I have a server named NEWPC100 with the database named Hillcrest Computing and I use the **Windows NT Integrated security** to log on to the server. You need to modify your connection string. For example, if you want to log on to a database named **WindingRiver** on a server named **FC121** and use a specific username and password for log-on, you should use the connection as shown below:

```
objConn.ConnectionString = "Provider=SQLOLEDB.1;" & _
   "Persist Security Info=False;" & _
   "Initial Catalog= WindingRiver;" & _
   "User Id=sa;Password=student;Data Source= FC121"
```

In the code of the **Creating an ADO RecordSet Object** example, the lines starting with the sign ' are comments. The first line

```
On Error GoTo ErrHandler:
```

says that if an error occurs during the execution of the code, go to the error-handling section labeled as **ErrHandler**. In the first part of the error-handling section, the code is used to close and delete the RecordSet and Connection objects. In the last **If** statement, the error information is printed in the message box with the box title as **Error**. **Err** is a built-in object that contains error information. The code

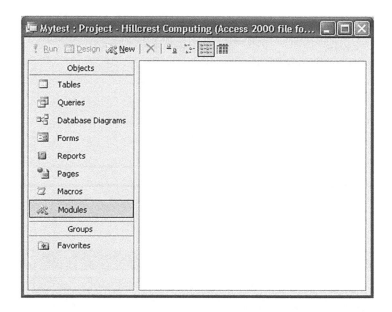

Figure 9.16   Open module window

```
objRs.LockType = adLockOptimistic
objRs.CursorLocation = adUseClient
objRs.CursorType = adOpenKeyset
```

is used to set the properties related to a cursor and lock. The code

```
objRs.Open objCmd
```

is used to open the `RecordSet` object **objRs** by using the `Command` object **objCmd**. The **objCmd** is used as an input parameter that is passed to the **Open** method in **objRs**. The command **Debug.Print** is used to print the message in the **Immediate** window, which we use later. The **Do ... Loop** is used to print one record at a time until the end of the `RecordSet` object. The following steps will show you how to run the code.

1. If you have created the project Mytest.adp, open **Microsoft Access 2003**, and then open **Mytest.adp**.
   Note: If you have not created the project Mytest yet, click **Create a new file** and **Project using existing data** in the **New File** task pane. Enter the project name such as **Mytest**. You may use another name; any name will do. Then click the **Create** button. You will also need to connect to the database `Hillcrest Computing` as shown in the earlier sections.
2. Click **Modules** in the **Objects** pane and then click the **New** button on the menu (see Figure 9.16). At this step, you have opened a **Module** window where you can enter the code.
3. Click ▶ (**Run Sub/User Form**) and enter a name (e.g., MyModule) under **Macro Name**. Then click **Create** (see Figure 9.17).

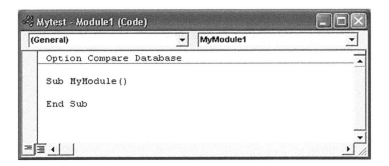

Figure 9.17   Open code window

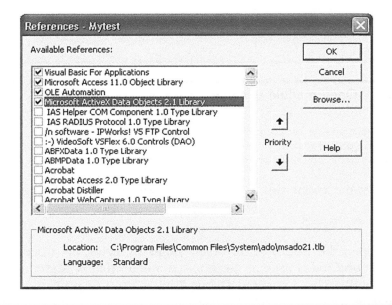

Figure 9.18   Add Microsoft ActiveX Data Objects library

4. Paste the code from the **Creating an ADO RecordSet Object** example. The code should be pasted between **Sub MyModule()** and **End Sub**. You also need to add the **Microsoft ActiveX Data Objects 2.1 Library** to your code by clicking **Tools** and then **References** (see Figure 9.18).
5. Click ▶ again to print out the content of the RecordSet object **objRs** in the **Immediate** window. If the **Immediate** window is not shown on the screen, click **View** and then **Immediate Window**. You will see the printout as shown in Figure 9.19.

At this point, you have seen a simple example of how to create and use ADO objects to access data. We have created ADO objects such as `Connection`, `Command`, and `RecordSet` and displayed the content stored in the `RecordSet`

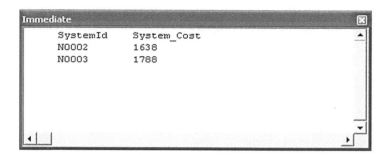

Figure 9.19   Data contained in `RecordSet` **object objRs**

object in Microsoft Access. You can also perform other data manipulation operations such as add, update, and delete in a `RecordSet` object. You are going to learn these data manipulation operations in later chapters when we use a `RecordSet` object to build our front-end applications.

9.6 Summary

In this chapter, you have learned different methods of accessing data. We discussed three database-accessing methods, ODBC, OLE DB, and ADO. Detailed descriptions of the three methods were given. Comparisons of these methods were also given in this chapter to help you make the right choice. You learned how to apply these database-accessing methods to retrieve data for database applications. Examples were used to illustrate how to use these methods to connect data providers to data consumers. You have learned how to access data through graphic user interface tools and through object-oriented programming. You have revisited the cursor from the object point of view. A cursor was used as an object to manipulate data in a `RecordSet` object. Cursors and locks have been emphasized as particularly useful in a client/ server environment. By working on an example, you created connections to database components with the three database-accessing methods for the database `Hillcrest Computing`. These connection methods are used to develop database applications such as forms and reports in the next chapter.

Review Questions

1. Why is accessing data through a database's native interface inappropriate for many database applications?
2. Compare the database-accessing methods ODBC, ADO, and OLE DB. State the advantages and disadvantages of each method.
3. Why is ADO a better database-accessing method?
4. Why is ODBC important to database?
5. Describe the application component in the ODBC architecture.
6. Describe the driver manager component in the ODBC architecture.

7. Describe the ODBC driver component in the ODBC architecture.
8. Describe the data source component in the ODBC architecture.
9. What tasks can Core API level, Level 1 API, and Level 2 API accomplish?
10. Which DSN is good for Web-based applications?
11. Create an ODBC connection to the database Student_Club with System DSN.
12. What is a data provider?
13. What are the improvements by OLE DB over ODBC?
14. What is a data consumer?
15. What can OLE DB do to help data consumers?
16. Why is it important for OLE DB to connect to ODBC data sources?
17. Describe the Connection object.
18. Describe the Command object.
19. Describe the RecordSet object.
20. Explain the purpose of the Open method.
21. Describe the four parameters used in the Open method.
22. What is the purpose of the Universal Data Link wizard?
23. What are the questions raised when multiple users use the same data source?
24. The property CursorLocation can be specified by adUseClient and adUseServer. Explain what we can do with these two values.
25. Describe the four lock types.

Case Study Projects

In the following case study projects, create the indicated database-accessing connections from the client applications to the database developed in the previous chapters.

1. Computer Service

For Awesome Computer Service's database, create the following database-accessing connections from the client applications:

- Create an ODBC connection with System DSN to the Computer_Service database.
- Use the data link to create a connection from Access to the SQL Server database Computer_Service.
- In Access, display the service information if the service charge is greater than $100. Get the service information from the database Computer_Service on SQL Server by using the ADO database-accessing technology.

2. University Registration

Create the following database-accessing connections to the Registration database:

- Create an ODBC connection with System DSN to the `Registration` database.
- Use the data link to create a connection from Access to the SQL Server database `Registration`.
- In Access, display the information of students who have enrolled for more than six credits. Get the student information from the database `Registration` on SQL Server by using the ADO database-accessing technology.

3. Mail Order

To allow the client to access the database `Mail_Order`, create the following database-accessing connections:

- Create an ODBC connection with System DSN to the `Mail_Order` database.
- Use the data link to create a connection from Access to the SQL Server database `Mail_Order`.
- In Excel, display the data in the `ORDERS` table of the `Mail_Order` database.

Chapter 10

Database Application Development

Objectives

- Learn user interface design.
- Create forms.
- Create reports.

10.1 Introduction

With the database-accessing tools available, it is time for database application developers to develop various applications to assist front-end users in using databases. Through these applications, the users can interact with a database to perform tasks such as importing and exporting data; enforcing constraints and securities; implementing business application logic; and developing, modifying, reading, and executing database objects such as views, functions, and stored procedures.

Front-end users may not be computer technology professionals. They may be business managers or secretaries who process business documents. To assist them in using databases, various database applications are created. Forms are used to enter, display, and update data stored in a database. Reports are used to present information. Data stored in a database can also be used for data analysis and for decision making. In a GUI, controls and menus are created for data manipulation. Applications can be created with programming languages such as Visual Basic, C++, and Java; scripting languages such as JavaScript, VBScript, and Jscript; or enhanced SQL languages such as Transact-SQL from Microsoft and PL/SQL from Oracle. Microsoft Access is a DBMS mainly for small businesses or personal database use. But that is not all you will like about Microsoft Access. It is also a good application development tool used to create forms and reports.

10.2 Understanding Business Process

To make a form easy to use and make sense to front-end users who are involved in a business process, you should understand how business is processed. A good understanding of the business process and related database operations often leads to good database application designs. When designing a database application, we need to make decisions on how to best represent paper forms and reports used in the business process with electronic forms and reports. To learn how to design a database application, you will be guided through some easy-to-follow examples in the case study Hillcrest Computing. The first step to achieve this goal is to identify data entry and data updating tasks in the business process. For example, the following data entry and updating tasks can be identified for our Hillcrest Computing case study:

- At each sales center, the sales manager and sales clerks need to enter and update the purchase order data stored in the PURCHASE_ORDER, SYSTEM_ORDER, SHIPPING, and SHIPPING_ORDER tables. When a customer places an order, the order information is entered into the PURCHASE_ORDER, SHIPPING_ORDER, and SYSTEM_ORDER tables. The shipping information is entered into the SHIPPING and SHIPPING_ORDER tables. If the order is cancelled, the order and shipping information should be removed from these tables. In addition, the sales manager needs to update the COMPUTER_SYSTEM table if a customer has some special requirements. The manager will also need to read sales reports.
- The accounting manager and accountants need to enter and update data for the tables SYSTEM_PART, COMPUTER_SYSTEM, PART, PART_DETAIL, and ASSEMBLY_PROCESS. In addition, the accounting manager needs to access ASSEMBLY_WORKER and WORKER_PROCESS tables to calculate productivity.
- Assembly workers need to enter assembly progress information in the table ASSEMBLY_PROCESS and update the tables PART and PART_DETAIL as to what parts have been used to assemble a computer system.
- Like the assembly workers, the assembly manager needs to update the tables ASSEMBLY_PROCESS, PART, and PART_DETAIL. In addition, the assembly manager needs to update the tables ASSEMBLY_WORKER, COMPUTER_SYSTEM, and SYSTEM_PART. He or she needs to assign jobs to assembly workers and update the configuration of computer systems. The assembly manager reads the assembly process report.
- The CEO of the company will read productivity reports, sales reports, and assembly process reports.

Based on the understanding of the business process, you should create the following forms and reports for the front-end users:

- For the sales clerks and managers, a **customer order form** needs to be created for entering and updating data on customers' orders and shipping information. This form should also include information about available computer systems. Customer-specified requirements should also be entered in this form. (An **assembly process report** will be created mainly for the assembly manager. However, both the sales clerks and sales managers should be able to read the **assembly process report**, which shows the scheduling of each assembly process, including starting and ending date, and day-by-day progress. If an assembly job is delayed, the reason for the delay should be given. When a customer asks about the progress of the assembly job, this report should help a salesperson answer the customer's questions.)

- For the sales managers, a **sales report** should be created. This report should list sales of different types of computer systems for a specified sales center. A bar chart used to display the sales of each type of computer system would be helpful. Through the bar chart, the sales managers will understand the customers' purchasing preferences at each sales center and provide some sales information for the company.

- For the accountants and accounting manager, a **receiving form** should be created to enter and update information about parts. When new parts arrive, an accountant will record their specifications and cost. A sales report and assembly process report will help the accountants to compare the sales prices and costs of computer parts. The comparison will help the accountants select a better computer-part vendor.

- For the accounting manager, a **productivity form** should be created so that he or she can enter data about the sales revenue, cost of labor and parts, and time used by an assembly process. The accounting manager will also need to read the sales report.

- For the assembly workers, an **assembly process form** should be created to enter the starting and ending time of an assembly process. Also, the form can be used to enter information about the parts used in a computer system. If, for some reason, an assembly job cannot be completed on time, the assembly workers can enter the reason for the delay.

- For the assembly manager, a **system form** is created and is used to enter information such as the configuration of custom-made computer systems and the assembly workers who are assembling these computer systems. Once all the parts are entered for a computer system, the cost of the computer system will be automatically calculated and displayed on the **system form**. The NOT NULL constraint should be enforced for the system cost so it will not be missing.

- For the CEO of Hillcrest Computing, all the reports should be available for him or her to see how the business is running. Some of the information on the reports, such as the office personnel's salaries and the expense on advertising, may come from other data sources. Here, we assume that it is available in a spreadsheet file generated from other databases.

A flowchart is a convenient tool that we can use to understand a business and its related practice needed to support the business process. As an example, consider the flowchart for the assembly process of our case study (see Figure 10.1).

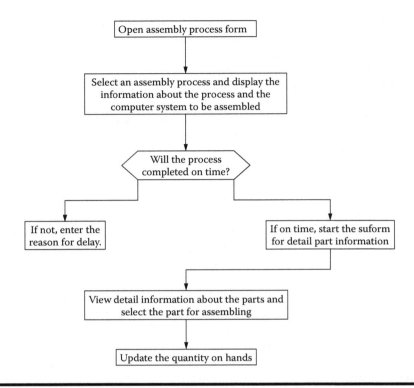

Figure 10.1   Example of business process and database applications

In this process, computer parts are used to assemble a computer system. The assembly manager needs to know the information about the computer system, such as when the assembly is started and when it is finished and the reason for delay, if that is the case. The assembly manager is also likely to keep track of the transaction activities of parts, such as automatically updating the quantity on hand, parts being used in an assembly process, and the availability of parts for an assembly process.

After you have identified the possible forms and reports to be used in your business process, the next step is to design a graphical user interface to make the front-end users' job easier.

10.3   User Interface Design and Format

10.3.1   *Graphical User Interface*

In this section we introduce the commonly used **Graphical User Interface** components and some guidelines for the appearance of GUI to make it easier to use. To assist front-end users in processing data, many GUI components are developed to allow the users to manipulate data without memorizing and typing commands. GUI components can also reduce errors caused by typing commands. Before developing a GUI, let us examine some GUI examples for database applications and get familiar with the functionality of GUI.

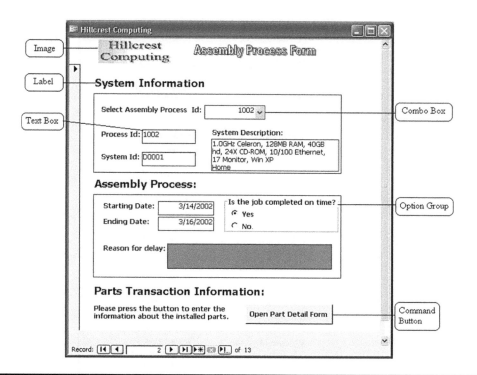

Figure 10.2 Example of form

The example shown in Figure 10.2 is an *electronic form* that we build in this chapter. This form can be used to help the assembly manager and assembly workers update information for a specified assembly process. Users can enter a reason or reasons for a delayed assembly process. They can also enter the item ids for the parts that have been installed on a computer system. Once an assembly process is selected, the information about the computer system being assembled in this process will be displayed. The information about the assembly process, such as the starting date and ending date, is also given. The assembly manager can modify the assembly process information through this form.

In Figure 10.2, several application controls have been displayed. These application controls are used to help front-end users manipulate data. At the top of the form, there are two **Image** controls that are used to present the company logo and the title of the form. On the top left-hand side of the form, we have a **Label** control, which can be used to display the name of another control or the section title. The **Text Box** on the left-hand side of the form is used to enter, update, or display information related to a column in a database table. On the top right-hand side, we have a **Combo Box** control, which can be used as a list box to select a value in a short list of values or can be used as a text box. In this example, a list of assembly processes is available. Users can choose one process on which to work. The **Option Group** control on the right-hand side is used to represent a set of candidates to be chosen. In our example, you can select either "Yes" or "No" for the question "Is the job

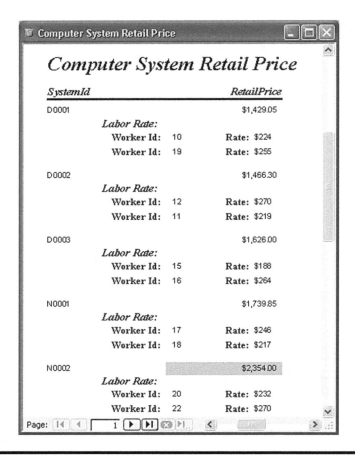

Figure 10.3   Example of report

completed on time?" If it is "No," you can enter a reason or reasons for the delay in the text box. On the bottom right-hand side, there is a **Command Button** control, which is used to start an action. In our example, it is used to open another form that contains detailed information about the parts used in an assembly process.

Report is another important database application, which is used to display data from a database in a certain format. Similar to a form, a report contains controls and graphics. Unlike a form, the main task of a report is to display data. A report may include some components such as **Report Header**, **Page Header**, **Detail**, **Page Footer**, and **Report Footer**. To make a report easier to read, a report is often divided into several sections. In such a case, a report may have multiple header components, multiple detail sections, and multiple footer components. Figure 10.3 shows an example of a report.

In this report, the report title **Computer System Retail Price** is placed in the **Report Header** section. The column titles, **SystemId** and **RetailPrice**, are placed in the **Page Header** section. The system ids and the retail prices are displayed in the **Detail** section. Also in the **Detail** section, we have included a subreport that shows the labor rate. As a special effect, when the retail price is greater then $2000, the background of the price darkens to attract the reader's attention.

There are some general guidelines about how a GUI should be properly designed so that it is easy to use and properly reflects the view structure. These guidelines are listed below:

- The locations of controls should be convenient for the application user. For example, place the controls related to an assembly process together and use a frame box to surround these controls.
- A GUI should be designed to help front-end users avoid mistakes. In our example, the **Delay** text box is grayed out if a job is completed on time.
- The design of a GUI should reflect the structure of an underlying table, view, or stored procedure. That is, the names of the columns from the same table should be placed close to each other in a form.
- In the case that an application needs to display detailed information related to an item displayed on the main form or main report, a subform or subreport should be created. The content displayed on the subform or subreport should be consistent with the item selected from the main form. The main or subform structure can also be used to represent the structure that needs multiple SQL statements to query data. For example, if we have a report to display retail prices of computer systems, the view RETAIL_PRICE_VIEW (created in Chapter 8) is used to retrieve the price information for each computer system. If, in addition, we also want to display the labor rate of the workers who assemble the computer systems, a subreport should be created to display the data returned by another SQL statement.

There are many different GUI designs that represent the same set of data. It is hard to say which one is better. It all depends on where and how the GUI is applied. The ultimate goal of a GUI design is to create a form or a report that reduces the anxiety of front-end users and helps them process data stored in a database. You may have to modify the original design many times based on users' response.

10.3.2   Enforcing Cardinality Constraints

When we develop a database application, it is possible that database management activities such as insert, update, and delete may generate some violations to cardinality constraints. In a parent–child relationship, cardinality constraints are used to specify each row from the parent table in relation to a certain number of rows in the child table. Depending on whether a row is required when making a modification to a table, a cardinality constraint can be either mandatory or optional. When a row must exist, we have a mandatory cardinality constraint. Otherwise, we have an optional cardinality constraint. For example, in the 1:N relationship between the PART and PART_DETAIL tables, before you insert an item in the PART_DETAIL table, you must have a corresponding part id in the parent table PART. This means the cardinality constraint for the part id is mandatory. On the other hand, for each part id, there may or may not be an item related to it. Here, you have an optional

Table 10.1   Conditions to Preserve Cardinality Constraints

Relationship	Table	Activities		
		Insert	*Key Update*	*Delete*
Mandatory to mandatory	Parent	Require at least one child row	Modify the key values for all matching child rows	Delete all matching child rows
	Child	Require at least one parent row	A parent row with a matching key value exists	Keep at least one matching child row
Mandatory to optional	Parent	No requirement	Modify the key values for all matching child rows	Delete all matching child rows
	Child	A parent row exists	A parent row with a matching key value exists	No requirement
Optional to mandatory	Parent	At least one child row with a matching key exists	At least one child row with matching key exists	No requirement
	Child	No requirement	At least one child row exists	At least one child row exists
Optional to optional	Parent	No requirement	No requirement	No requirement
	Child	No requirement	No requirement	No requirement

cardinality constraint. The above example shows that the 1:N relationship has a mandatory–optional constraint.

As another example, consider the relationship between PURCHASE_ORDER and SALES_CENTER. Suppose that we require that a purchase order must come from a sales center and a sales center must issue at least one purchase order. That is, when a row is inserted into PURCHASE_ORDER, a sales center id must exist. On the other hand, before a row is deleted from the SALES_CENTER table, we must make sure that the SALES_CENTER table has more than one row. If you must delete a sales center, make sure its purchase orders have been transferred to another sales center or other sales centers with a trigger. This relationship has a mandatory–mandatory cardinality constraint. A row that exists without a required parent or child is called a *fragment*. In our case, if a row exists in PURCHASE_ORDER without the required sales center, this row is a fragment. Table 10.1 shows the conditions that allow database-manipulating activities to preserve the cardinality constraints.

Triggers, stored procedures, and front-end application software such as Microsoft Access can be used to implement cardinality constraints. As an example, we create a trigger that will determine if a part id exists in the table PART when a new row is added to the PART_DETAIL table. If not, a new

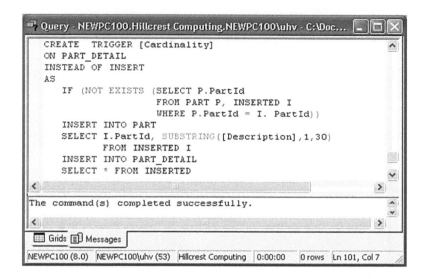

Figure 10.4 Create trigger to verify cardinality

row will be created with a new value in the PartId column of the PART table. The trigger is created as shown in Figure 10.4.

This trigger will be fired when a row is inserted into the PART_DETAIL table. Instead of inserting the row directly into the table, which may generate a fragment if the PART table does not have the PartId value, the trigger will verify if the PartId value exists in the PART table. If not, the trigger will insert a row in the PART table with the new PartId value and the part name and then insert the new row into the PART_DETAIL table. As mentioned in previous chapters, the two special tables, DELETED and INSERTED, are automatically created when creating a trigger. You will not be able to alter the data in these two tables directly. You can use them only to set conditions for trigger actions and verify data-updating effects.

Microsoft Access and SQL Server provide some graphic-based tools to verify cardinality constraints. Start Microsoft Access and open the **Mytest** project. You can go to **Database Diagrams** in the **Objects** pane and open the **Hillcrest Computing** diagram. If you right-click the relationship connection line between PART and PART_DETAIL and select **Properties**, you will open the Properties page as shown in Figure 10.5.

On this Properties page, the functions of the check boxes are listed below:

- *Check existing data on creation:* When a relationship is added to a child table, force the existing data to follow the constraint.
- *Enforce relationship for replication:* When tables are copied to a different database, keep the proper relationship.
- *Enforce relationship for INSERTs and UPDATEs:* When data are inserted or updated in a child table, make sure there is a matching row in the parent table. Prevent a row in the parent table from being deleted when there is a matching row in the child table.

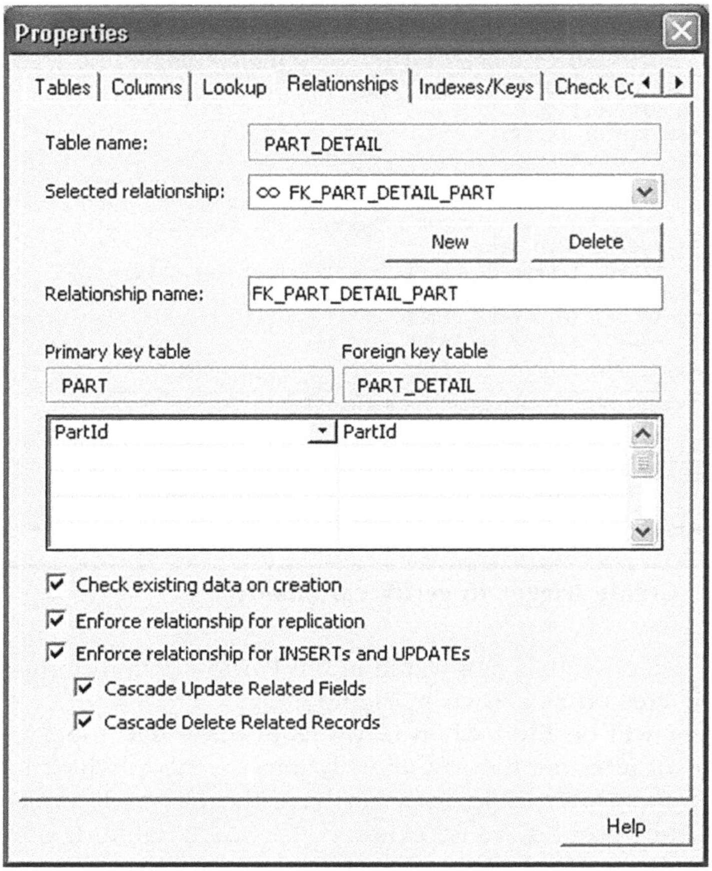

Figure 10.5 Relationship properties

- *Cascade Update Related Fields:* When a key value in the parent table is updated, automatically update the matching values in the child table.
- *Cascade Delete Related Records:* When a key value in the parent table is deleted, automatically delete the matching values in the child table.

These functions are used to check constraints. If a violation occurs, an error message will be displayed to inform the user. They do not fix problems as does the trigger we have just created.

10.4 Creating Forms

In a previous chapter, you learned how to use SQL statements such as INSERT, DELETE, and UPDATE to manipulate database data. For many front-end users without much computer background, using SQL statements to manipulate data is a tough job. These users are familiar with paper forms used for daily business. As a database application developer, if you can create an electronic form similar to the paper form and present data on the electronic form, you will greatly help these users improve their productivity.

When working with electronic forms, front-end users can enter data through a text box, make a selection by using a combo box, and perform certain functionalities by clicking corresponding buttons. In this way, they do not have to know SQL statements. Therefore, you as a database application developer need to program the form so data entered in the text box will be saved to the corresponding tables in the back-end database and the users can select the right data from the database to be displayed on the electronic form.

Microsoft Access offers many easy-to-use tools to quickly develop database applications. One of these tools is **Form Wizard**, used to create forms based on tables, views, and stored procedures constructed on SQL Server in a client/server environment. Microsoft Access not only provides **Form Wizard** for developing forms but also provides programming tools such as **Visual Basic for Applications** for us to create more sophisticated form applications for table updating, record searching, form synchronizing, and information filtering. Programming code is used to capture events generated by a database application and to perform certain activities according to the events.

10.4.1   Creating Forms with Form Wizard

By using **Form Wizard**, you can create a simple form against a table or a record set returned by a view and stored procedure. As an example, let us create a form that can be used to insert records into the table PART.

1. Creating Forms Based on Views with Form Wizard

Usually, for security and performance reasons, views are used to support forms and reports. When connecting to a view, you may not update columns in the base table through the form due to the restrictions of a view. Similar to forms that are connected to tables, you can create a form connected to a view by using **Form Wizard**. In the following example, we create a form for PART_COST_VIEW created in Chapter 8.

- Start Microsoft Access. If you have created the OLE DB data link as shown in Chapter 9, click **Mytest.adp** in the **New File** window. If you are using an older version of Access, you may create an ODBC connection, as also shown in Chapter 9. Click **Forms** in the **Objects** pane as shown in Figure 10.6.
- Double-click **Create form by using wizard** to open **Form Wizard**. At first, the wizard wants you to select the table or view on which the form will be created. From the **Tables/Queries** combo box, choose PART_COST_VIEW. You can specify the columns to be included in the form. Select all the columns by clicking the ⟦>>⟧ button. Click **Next** to choose a layout. You can select a layout style by clicking one of the radio buttons. Here, we select **Columnar** and click **Next**. You are prompted to select a form style. We select **Industrial** and then click **Next**. Change the form title to **Computer System Cost Form**, and then click **Finish**. Now we have the simple form shown in Figure 10.7.

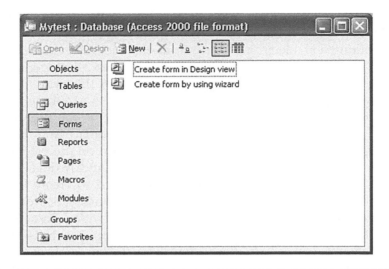

Figure 10.6   Create form using wizard

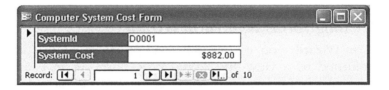

Figure 10.7   Simple form created by Form Wizard

This form contains several GUI components. The labels are used to display the column names of PART_COST_VIEW. The column values are displayed in the text box. At the bottom of the form, there is an ADO data control ⏮ ◀ ⬚ 1 ▶ ⏭ ▶✳ ⊗ ▶⌗ which is a specially designed GUI component. An ADO data control can be used to establish a connection to a database table at runtime. It functions as do the ADO objects introduced in Chapter 9 but with no programming. The ADO data control can also be used to locate a record in a table by clicking the **move next** ▶ , **move previous** ◀ , **move last** ⏭ , and **move first** ⏮ buttons. To insert a new record, click the ▶✳ button. The **Cancel Query** button ⊗ is used to stop retrieving data from a database table. The ▶⌗ button is used to set the maximum number of records. Front-end users can use this form to find computer system prices. Because the form is based on a view, the front-end user will not be able to modify the contents of the base tables.

2. Creating Forms Based on Tables with Form Wizard

In the next example, we create a data entry form, **Receiving Form**, for the accountants and accounting manager. This form can be used to enter and update information on the parts. When new parts arrive, an accountant records

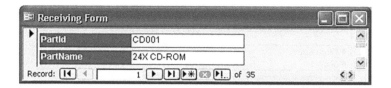

Figure 10.8   Receiving Form created by Form Wizard

ItemId	Price	Description	Maker	PartId	Quantity
1	$25.00	24X Max Internal CD-	QMC	CD001	17
2	$27.00	24X Max Internal CD-	Mega	CD001	21
3	$39.00	48X Max Internal CD-	HC	CD002	25
4	$77.00	48X Max External CD	Mega	CD002	21
5	$46.00	52X Max INternal CD	Chos	CD003	23
6	$29.00	24X Max Internal CD-	HD	CD001	34
7	$20.00	24X Max Internal CD-	QMC	CD001	31
8	$25.00	24X Max Internal CD-	Yam	CD001	32
9	$28.00	24X Max Internal CD-	HD	CD001	21
10	$29.00	24X Max Internal CD-	Mega	CD001	45
11	$41.00	48X Max Internal CD-	HD	CD002	32
12	$112.00	8X internal DVD	Mega	DD001	21

Figure 10.9   Receiving Detail Form created by Form Wizard

their specifications and costs. Forms connected to tables allow front-end users to update the content of the underlying tables. Because part information must be entered in both the PART and PART_DETAIL tables, we create a form with a **master/detail** structure. This structure contains two forms, the master form and the detail form. In general, the master/detail structure is used for one-to-many relationships. In our example, the form connected to the table PART is the master form and the form connected to PART_DETAIL is the detail form. **Form Wizard** will use the primary key and foreign key pair to link these two forms. The first step is to create two forms, one for the table PART and the other for the table PART_DETAIL. Similar to creating a form connected to a view, we have created the two forms **Receiving Form** (see Figure 10.8) and **Receiving Detail Form** (see Figure 10.9). When creating **Receiving Detail Form**, use the **Datasheet** layout shown in Figure 10.9.

The next step is to link these two forms. To do this, right-click on **Receiving Form**, and then select **Design View** on the pop-up menu. Figure 10.10 shows the design view of **Receiving Form**. Click **Receiving Detail Form** in the **Mytest:Project** window and drag it to the design view of **Receiving Form**. Rearrange **Receiving Detail Form** to place it under **Receiving Form**. In Figure 10.11, the complete design of **Receiving Form** is displayed.

The design view is usually not for front-end users. They should use the form view for their daily business operations. Right-click the title area of **Receiving Form**, select **Form View**, and you will have the form shown in Figure 10.12.

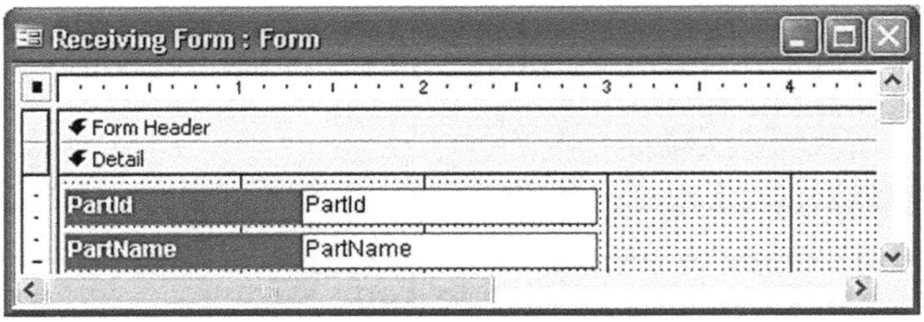

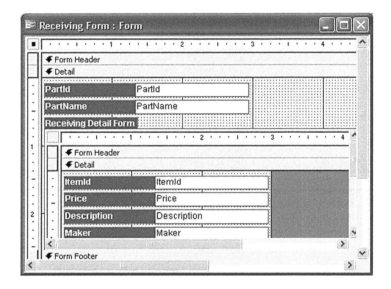

Figure 10.10   Design view of Receiving Form

Figure 10.11   Receiving Detail Form linked to Receiving Form

In this form view, selecting a record of a computer part will cause the detail form to list all the information about the part. In Figure 10.12, when the record CD001 is selected, the detail form will list several different brands of 24X Internal CD-ROM along with detailed information such as `ItemId`, `Price`, `Description`, `Maker`, `PartId`, and `Quantity`. Notice that all these 24X Internal CD-ROM drives have the same `PartId`. By clicking the **move next** button in the ADO data control, you will get the next part and its detailed information.

3. Creating Forms Based on Stored Procedures with Form Wizard

Execution of a stored procedure returns a record set. By connecting the record set, you can create a form that uses a stored procedure as the data source. A stored procedure–based form will ask users to enter values for input parameters. In the next example, we create a form, **System Form**, from a simple stored procedure that is used to return information about computer systems.

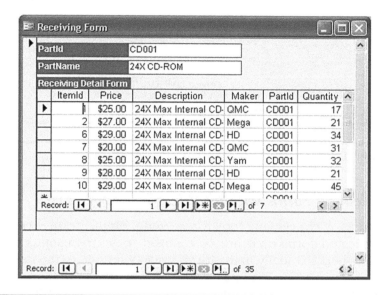

Figure 10.12   Receiving Form with Receiving Detail Form

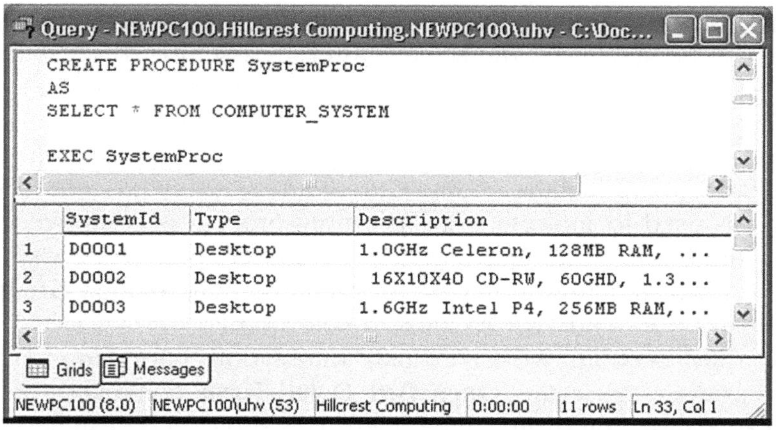

Figure 10.13   SystemProc stored procedure

The stored procedure–based form in the next example can be used to allow a user to update the computer system information interactively. It can also be used to enter the information of a new computer system customized according to a customer's request. The stored procedure that will be used in this form is created in Query Analyzer, as shown in Figure 10.13.

Make sure to execute the stored procedure **SystemProc** once to return a record set. To build the form, start Access and open the **Mytest** project file. Click **Forms** in the **Objects** pane. Double-click **Create form by using wizard** and select the **SystemProc** stored procedure. Click **Next** a few times, enter the form name as **System Form**, and then click **Finish**. You can see the form in Figure 10.14.

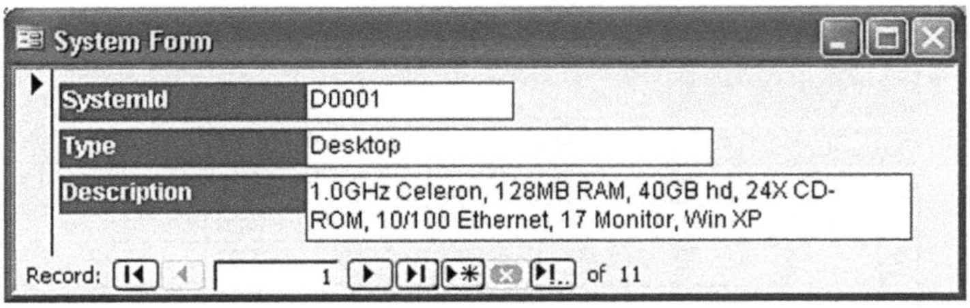

Figure 10.14   Create form based on stored procedure

10.4.2   Creating Forms without Wizard

Form Wizard is a convenient tool for creating simple forms. However, for more sophisticated forms that are customized to your business needs, you need to create them manually in the form design window. In the next example, we create a form for the assembly workers who need an assembly process form to enter assembly progress information in the table ASSEMBLY_PROCESS and update the tables PART and PART_DETAIL when parts have been used to assemble computer systems. The **Assembly Process Form** we are creating has three major sections. The first section gives computer system information. When the **Assembly Process Id** combo box is clicked, a list of assembly processes will be shown on the screen. After an assembly process is selected from the list, the corresponding values such as System Id and the underlying computer system information will be displayed on the form.

The second section of the form is the assembly process section. Here, we have the starting date and the ending date of an assembly process. The **Option Group** box is used to indicate if an assembly process is completed on time. If it is on time, the **Delay** text box will be grayed out. Otherwise, the text box will be used to enter the reason for the delay. The **Option Group** control is used for the front-end user to make a selection.

In the third section, we enter part transaction information. Once the assembly workers click the **Open Part Detail Form** command button, the subform **Part Transaction Form** will be open. This subform is designed to reduce tedious typing work for the assembly workers. They do not need to type the information into the **Progress** text box. Once a worker has decided which part to use in the assembly process, he or she can enter the part description in the **Progress** text box by clicking the item id for that part and clicking the **Update** command button. Then the corresponding **Quantity** value will be automatically reduced by one and the **Progress** column in the ASSEMBLY_PROCESS table will be automatically updated. The other information about this part, such as the part's price, id, description, maker, and quantity, is given in the embedded subform **Part Detail Information Subform** to help the assembly workers make a choice. The **Assembly Process Form** is displayed in Figure 10.15.

The subform **Part Transaction Form** and the embedded subform **Part Detail Information Subform** are displayed in Figure 10.16.

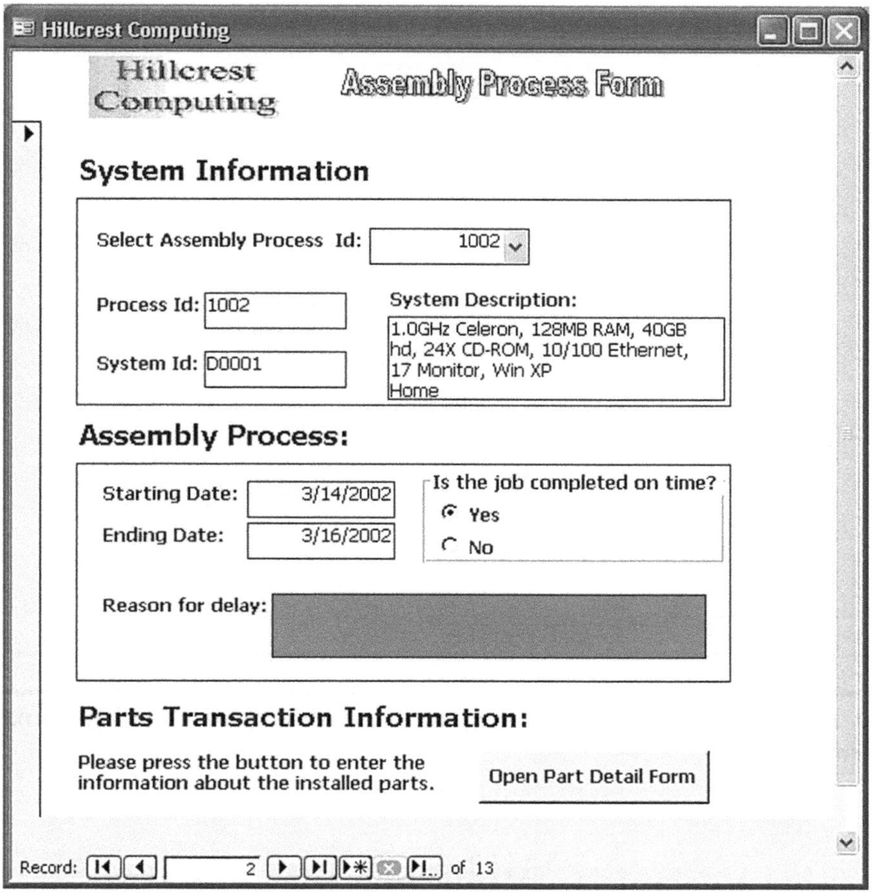

Figure 10.15   Assembly Process Form

These two forms are more sophisticated than the ones we created using the **Form Wizard**. We build these two forms manually. We use the **Query Designer** built into Microsoft Access to create a record set for the forms and create an event procedure for the calculation behind the forms.

10.4.3   Creating Company Logo

The first step in the form development is to add the company logo to the form. We use Microsoft Word to create a simple company logo and a form title with some art effect. Open Microsoft Word, click the **Insert** menu, select **Picture**, and then select **WordArt**. Choose a style you like, type the company's name, `Hillcrest Computing`, and then click the **Insert** button. You can also use **Clip Art** or **WordArt** to select a proper icon for your company. Here, we choose **Blends** from **Theme** in the **Format** menu to add the shade to the company name. Crop the icon into a suitable size like the one shown in Figure 10.17.

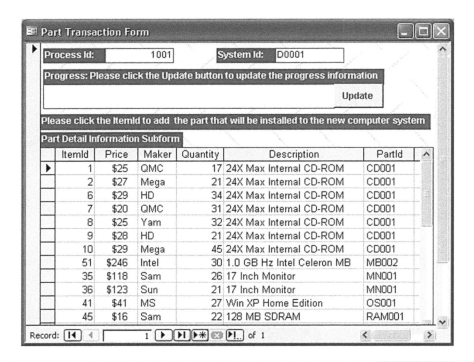

Figure 10.16   Part Transaction Form and embedded Part Detail Information Subform

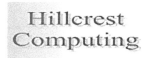

Figure 10.17   Hillcrest Computing logo

Select the icon you have just created and copy it by right-clicking on it, and select **Copy**. Start Access, and open the **Mytest** data link. Click on **Forms** in the **Objects** pane and click **New** to create a new form. Choose **Design View** from the list. Right-click in the middle of the empty form, and select **Form Header/Footer**. Paste the icon under **Form Header** to add the company's logo to the form header. Right-click on the icon and choose **Properties**. Set both the **Back Style** and **Border Style** properties as **Transparent**. Save the form as **Template Form**. You will reuse it later.

To create the **Assembly Process Form**, copy the **Template Form** and paste it as **Assembly Process Form** into the **Mytest** project window. Next, we add a form name in the form header. To create the form name, open Microsoft Word, click the **Insert** menu, select **Picture**, and then select **WordArt**. Choose a style you like, type the form name, and then click the **Insert** button to obtain the form name like the one shown in Figure 10.18.

Assembly Process Form

Figure 10.18   Assembly Process Form

Right-click the form **Assembly Process Form** and choose **Design View** from the list. Paste the form name under **Form Header**. Right-click on the form name and select **Properties** on the pop-up menu. Set both the **Back Style** and **Border Style** properties as **Transparent**.

10.4.4   Creating Views for Forms

Some controls such as **Text Box**, **Combo Box**, and **List Box** are used to display data retrieved from a database. *Views* can be used to retrieve necessary data from a database to support the controls on a form. To include a view in a form, you can specify the control source property by the name of the prebuilt view. Another way is to create a view using the **Query Designer** in Microsoft Access to support the form. Here, we use the **Query Designer** to build a view for our Assembly Process Form.

1. Open the **Design** window of the form **Assembly Process Form**. Right-click on the form and select **Properties**.
2. Select **Form** from the combo box and then click the **Data** tab.
3. Click the **Record Source** property and open the **Query Designer** pane by clicking the button [...] on the right-hand side of the **Record Source** property.
4. Because we need data to support the text boxes **txtProcessId**, **txtSystem**, **txtDesc**, **txtStartDate**, **txtEndDate**, and **txtReason** and the combo box **cboProcessId**, click the **Add Table** button 🏢 and then select the table **ASSEMBLY_PROCESS**. Do the same to add the table **COMPUTER_SYSTEM**.
5. Check the columns **SystemId** and **Description** from the table **COMPUTER_SYSTEM** and the columns **ProcessId**, **StartDate**, **EndDate**, **Delay**, and **Progress** from the table **ASSEMBLY_PROCESS**. The **Query Designer** will automatically generate the SQL statement for the view to support the form (see Figure 10.19).
6. Close the **Query Designer**. You should see that the SQL statement is placed in the **Record Source** property.

10.4.5   Placing Controls to Forms

Next, we create controls such as combo boxes, check boxes, and text boxes for a form. Open **Assembly Process Form** in **Design View**. Click 🛠 in the **Toolbox** menu. You will see that there are many controls available for constructing a form. The basic controls listed in Table 10.2 are available in Microsoft Access (see Figure 10.20).

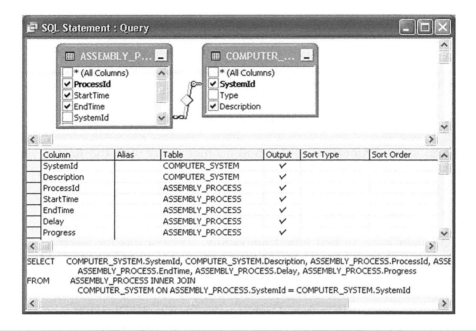

Figure 10.19   Create view for Assembly Process Form by Query Designer

We add some controls to the Assembly Process Form and rearrange the controls such as **Label**, **Combo Box**, **Command Button**, **Option Group,** and **Text Box** as shown in Figure 10.21. We also need to change the font size for the labels and program some application logic for the **Command Button** and **Option Group** controls. To change the appearance of these controls and to make them work together, we need to configure the properties for these controls.

10.4.6   *Configuring Properties for Controls*

In the following sections, we use more tools to configure the properties that handle dynamic data transactions. To specify the control properties, right-click on the control, and then select Properties from the pop-up menu. For example, to configure the label control representing the subtitle **System Information**, type the subtitle **System Information** for the **Caption** property, and then change the **Font Size** property to 16. Find the **Name** property under the **Other** tab and name the label as **lblSystem** (see Figure 10.22).

To name the controls, we usually place three letters representing the control type as the first three letters of the control name. For example, use **txt** as the first three letters for a text box name and use **lbl** as the first three letters for a label name, and so on. Similarly, you can add the controls in Table 10.3 to the form and configure their properties accordingly. We create the command button later because it requires the existence of the subform **Part Transaction Form**.

Table 10.2   Basic Controls in Microsoft Access

Aa	Label control	Used to display a label
abl	Text box control	Used to display text or accept data entry
[xyz]	Option group control	Used to select one item from a list of mutually exclusive items
⇄	Toggle button control	Used to toggle on and off
⦿	Option button control	Used to represent Boolean values
☑	Check box control	Used to represent a list of alternative values to be selected
📊	Combo box control	Used for a short list of values from which you can select a value
📋	List box control	Used to display a list of values from which you can select a value
⌐	Command button control	Used to start actions
🖼	Image control	Used to set the path and file name for an unbound image
🖼	Unbound object frame control	Used to set the path and file name for an unbound object
🖼	Bound object frame control	Used to display a bound object in a form
▤	Page break control	Used to add a page break
⌐	Tab control	Used to activate a page
▦	Subform/subreport control	Used to add a subform/subreport to a form
＼	Line control	Used to add a line in a form
▭	Rectangle control	Used to add a rectangle in a form

Figure 10.20   Commonly used controls in Access

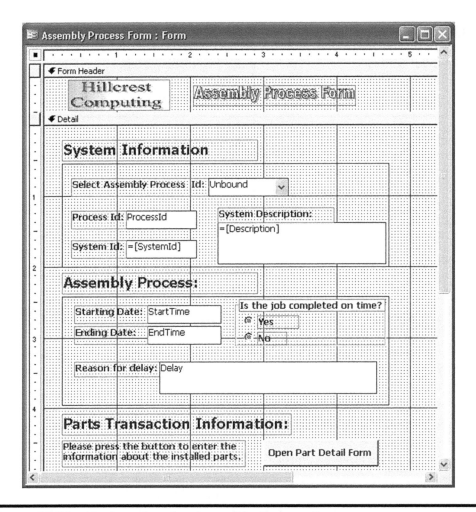

Figure 10.21   Design view for Assembly Process Form

When adding some of the controls, configuration wizards will automatically start to assist you to get the configuration job done. The following section shows you how to configure an option group with the configuration wizard.

10.4.7   Configuring Option Group with Control Wizard

The **Option Group** control allows the assembly workers to choose if the assembly process is completed on time or delayed due to some reason. If it is completed on time, the **Delay** text box is grayed out to prevent possible mistakes. If an assembly process is not completed on time, the assembly workers are allowed to enter the reason for the delay in the **Delay** text box. Later, we will use various techniques to implement these actions. You can use **Control Wizard** to ease configuration tasks. As an example, we configure the **Option Group** control.

Figure 10.22   Properties page for lblSystem

1. Click **Option Group** in **Toolbox**. Make sure that the **Control Wizard** icon in **Toolbox** is selected to enable the wizard.
2. Put the **Option Group** control in **Assembly Process Form**, and you will be automatically prompted to configure the **Option Group** control.
3. Type the labels for the choices **Yes** and **No** and then click **Next** (see Figure 10.23).
4. Make **Yes** the default, and then click **Next** four times.
5. Enter the title "**Is the job completed on time?**" for the **Option Group** label, and then click **Finish**.

10.4.8   Configuring Text Box with Conditional Formatting

You can use the **Conditional Formatting** tool to enable or disable a control based on a given condition. **Conditional Formatting** can dynamically change the setting for a property. In our example, the text box **txtDelay** is grayed out if **Yes** is selected from the **Option Group** control and allows a user to enter the reason for delay if **No** is selected. The following steps are used to show you how to implement this function.

1. Click the text box **txtDelay** with the control source displayed as **Delay** in the **Design** pane. Click **Format** on the menu bar. Then select **Conditional Formatting** to open the dialog box.
2. Select **Expression Is** from the combo box and enter the control expression **[FrameOptGrp] = 1** in the text box. As mentioned earlier, the value 1 represents the choice **Yes**. FrameOptGrp is the name for the **Option Group** control. If the name for the option group is different, rename it in the property page.

Table 10.3   Configuration of Properties for Assembly Process Form

Control Name	Configuration of Properties
frameSystem	Name: frameSystem
lblSystem	Name: lblSystem Font Size: 16 Caption: System Information
lblSelectProcess	Name: lblSelectProcess Caption: Select Assembly Process Id:
txtProcessId	Name: txtProcessId Control Source: ProcessId
cboProcessId	Name: cboProcessId Row Source Type: Table/View/StoredProc Row Source: SELECT ProcessId FROM ASSEMBLY_PROCESS Bound Column: 1 Column Count: 1 Column Width: 1 in
lblProcessId	Name: lblProcessId Caption: Process Id:
lblDesc	Name: lblDesc Caption: System Description:
txtDesc	Name: txtDesc Control Source: =[Description]
lblSysId	Name: lblSysId Caption: System Id:
txtSystemId	Name: txtSystemId Control Source: =[SystemId]
frameAssembly	Name: frameAssembly
lblAssembly	Name: lblAssembly Font Size: 16 Caption: Assembly Process
lblStartDate	Name: lblStartDate Caption: Starting Date:
lblEndDate	Name: lblEndDate Caption: Ending Date:
txtStartDate	Name: txtStartDate Control Source: StartTime
txtEndDate	Name: txtEndDate Control Source: EndTime
frameOptGrp	Name: frameOptGrp

Table 10.3   Configuration of Properties for Assembly Process Form (continued)

Control Name	Configuration of Properties
optYes	Name: optYes Option Value: 1
optNo	Name: optNo Option Value: 2
lblYes	Name: lblYes Caption: Yes
lblNo	Name: lblNo Caption: No
lblReason	Name: lblReason Caption: Reason for Delay
txtDelay	Name: txtDelay Control Source: Delay
lblParts	Name: lblParts Font Size: 16 Caption: Part Transaction Information
lblButton	Name: lblButton Caption: Please press the button to enter the information about the installed parts
cmdPartDetail	Name: cmdPartDetail On Click: (Will create a subprocedure to open the subform Part Transaction Form later)

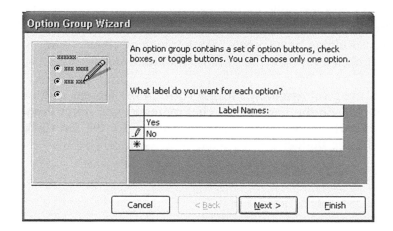

Figure 10.23   Configure option group with Option Group Wizard

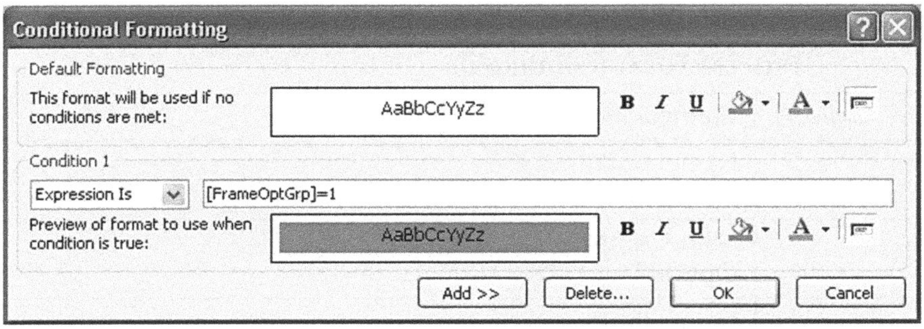

Figure 10.24   Conditional formatting dialog

3. Click the **Fill/Back Color** icon to gray out the text box, which means that the text box is grayed out if the condition **[FrameOptGrp] = 1** is met.
4. Click **OK** to accept the configuration and close the dialog (see Figure 10.24).

10.4.9   Programming Event Procedures

As mentioned in earlier chapters, triggers and stored procedures are attached to a table and used to perform some activities once a condition is satisfied. Very much like triggers, event procedures allow forms to perform certain desired activities. In our example, we program event procedures in the **Properties** dialog. The advantage of event procedures is that it includes the ADO object, which will make the programming task easier.

10.4.10   Configuring Click Event for Combo Box

The combo box **cboProcessId** gives a list of process ids for an assembly worker to choose. After one of the process ids is chosen, related information such as the id for the system built in the process, the process's starting date and ending date, and the description of the system will be automatically displayed in the corresponding text boxes. To implement this feature, we need to program the click event for the control **cboProcessId**.

1. Open the form **Assembly Process Form** in the **Design** window.
2. Right-click on the combo box **cboProgressId** and select **Properties**.
3. Click **Event** tab and open the code window for the **On Click** event.
4. Select **Code Builder** and type the code as shown below:

```
Private Sub cboProcessId_Click()

Me.txtProcessId.SetFocus
DoCmd.FindRecord cboProcessId

End Sub
```

Here, the first and the last lines are automatically given once you open the code window. The first line represents the beginning of the event procedure with the procedure's name. **Private Sub** indicates that this subprocedure cannot be accessed from other procedures. On the second line, **Me** represents the current form object, and **txtProcessId** is the control on **Me**. **SetFocus** is the method used to set the focus (mouse cursor) to **txtProcessId**. Once the focus is set to a process id, the **FindRecord** method will find the information related to the selected process id. You need to set the focus to a unique column for **FindRecord**. **DoCmd** is an object that allows you to run Access actions from Visual Basic. The method **FindRecord** will find the record identified by the process id and place related information into the text box.

5. After you have entered the code, go back to Access. Click the **Form View** icon ⊞ on the menu bar to change to the form view.

6. Click the combo box and select the **1003** assembly process; you have the output as shown in Figure 10.25. The system id, starting date, ending date, and system description have all changed to match to the **1003** assembly process. As you can see, the focus is set to the **ProcessId** text box.

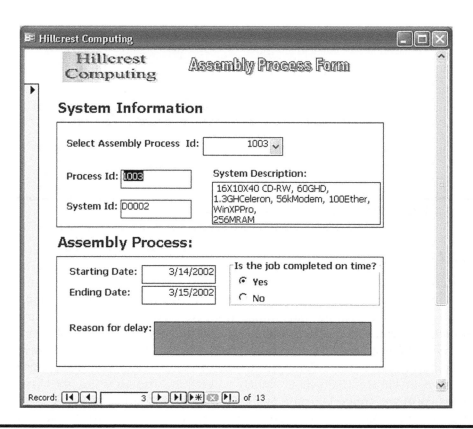

Figure 10.25   Result of combo box selection

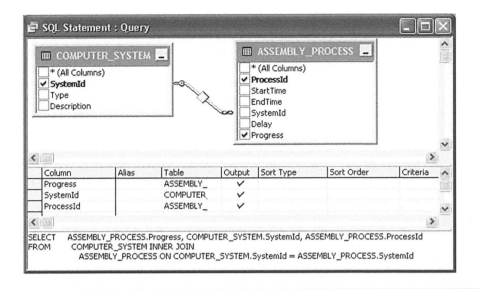

Figure 10.26   Create view for Part Transaction Form by Query Designer

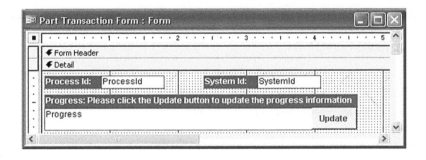

Figure 10.27   Initial Part Transaction Form

10.4.11   Creating Subforms

The third section of the **Assembly Process Form** gives part transaction information. On the form **Assembly Process Form**, the button **Open Part Detail Form** is used to open a form for part transaction. Next, we create the subform **Part Transaction Form**. Open a new form from the design view or simply copy the form **System Form** created earlier and paste it as the **Part Transaction Form**. We first create a view for the **Part Transaction Form** by using the **Query Designer**, as shown in Figure 10.26. It is similar to creating the view for the **Assembly Process Form** we created earlier. We then add labels and text boxes as shown in Figure 10.27. As shown in Figure 10.27, the data sources for the text boxes **txtProcessId**, **txtSystemId**, and **txtProgress** are ProcessId, SystemId, and Progress, respectively. For the controls on the **Part Transaction Form**, the configuration information is given in Table 10.4.

Table 10.4   Configuration of Properties for Part Transaction Form

Control Name	Configuration of Properties
lblProcessId	Name: lblProcessId Caption: Process Id:
txtProcessId	Name: txtProcessId Control Source: ProcessId
lblSystemId	Name: lblSystemId Caption: System Id:
txtSystemId	Name: txtSystemId Control Source: SystemId
lblProgress	Name: lblProgress Caption: Progress: Please click the Update button to update the progress information
txtProgress	Name: txtProgress Control Source: Progress
lblItemId	Name: lblItemId Caption: Please click ItemId to add the part that will be installed in the new computer system
cmdUpdate	Name: cmdUpdate Caption: Update
subform	Name: Part Detail Information Subform Source Object: Part Detail Information Subform

In the **Part Transaction Form**, there will be another embedded subform **Part Detail Information Subform**. This subform is developed for detailed part information such as ItemId, Price, Description, Maker, Quantity, ProcessId, SystemId, and PartId. We first create the subform using the **Form Wizard** to include the columns to match the information needed in the subform.

10.4.12   Creating Subform with Wizard

To use the Form Wizard to create the subform **Part Detail Information Subform**, follow the steps below.

1. First, copy the form **Receiving Detail Form** and paste it as the **Part Detail Information Subform**.
2. Open the form in **Design View** and right-click on it.
3. Then go to **Properties** and choose **Form** in the combo box.
4. Click the **Data** tab and the ⟦...⟧ button to open the **Query Designer**.
5. To create a view for the subform, add the tables **PART**, **PART_DETAIL**, **COMPUTER_SYSTEM**, **SYSTEM_PART**, and **ASSEMBLY_PROCESS**, and then select the columns **ItemId**, **Price**, **Description**, **Maker**, **Quantity**, **ProcessId**, **SystemId**, **Progress**, and **PartId**. Arrange the tables so that they look like the ones in Figure 10.28.

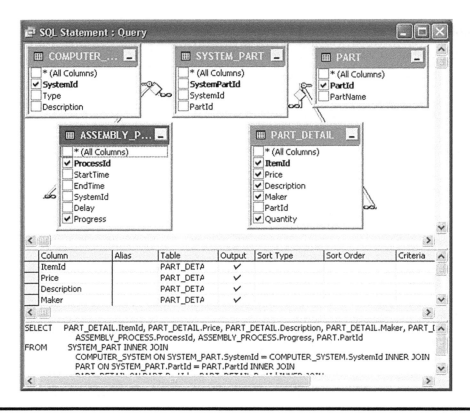

Figure 10.28   Create view for Part Detail Information Subform using Query Designer

6. Close the **Query Designer**. Add more controls as shown in the bottom half of Figure 10.31 with the property configuration listed in Table 10.5.
7. On the form's **Properties** page, change the **Default View** property to **Datasheet**.

Next, we embed the **Part Detail Information Subform** in the **Part Transaction Form** (see Figure 10.29). To do so, follow the steps below.

1. Open the **Design** window of **Part Transaction Form**.
2. Click the subform icon ▦ in **Toolbox**, and draw a subform control with a proper size. **SubForm Wizard** will automatically start.
3. Check the radio button of **Use an existing form** and select **Part Detail Information Subform** as shown in Figure 10.29. Then click **Next**.
4. Define the fields that will link the subform to the main form as shown in Figure 10.30 and click **Next**.
5. Click **Finish** to complete the configuration. The result is shown in Figure 10.31.

Next, we create the **Update** button for the **Part Transaction Form**. During an assembly process, assembly workers are required to enter information for

Table 10.5 Configuration of Properties for Part Detail Information Subform

Control Name	Configuration of Properties
lblItemId	Name: lblItemId Caption: ItemId:
txtItemId	Name: txtItemId Control Source: ItemId
lblPrice	Name: lblPrice Caption: Price:
txtPrice	Name: txtPrice Control Source: Price
lblDescription	Name: lblDescription Caption: Description:
txtDescription	Name: txtDescription Control Source: Description
lblMaker	Name: lblMaker Caption: Maker:
txtMaker	Name: txtMaker Control Source: Maker
lblQuantity	Name: lblQuantity Caption: Quantity:
txtQuantity	Name: txtQuantity Control Source: Quantity
lblProcessId	Name: lblProcessId Caption: ProcessId:
txtProcessId	Name: txtProcessId Control Source: ProcessId
lblSystemId	Name: txtSystemId Caption: SystemId:
txtSystemId	Name: txtSystemId Control Source: SystemId
lblPartId	Name: lblPartId Caption: PartId:
txtPartId	Name: txtPartId Control Source: PartId

the parts used in a new computer system. Typing the information into the database is time consuming. Thus, the database developer will try to do something to reduce the tedious work. The following section shows how to manually program event procedures that will allow the assembly workers to enter part information without typing.

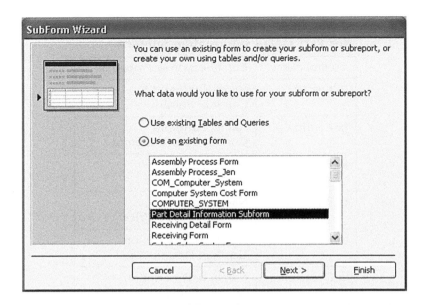

Figure 10.29   Configure subform with Subform Wizard

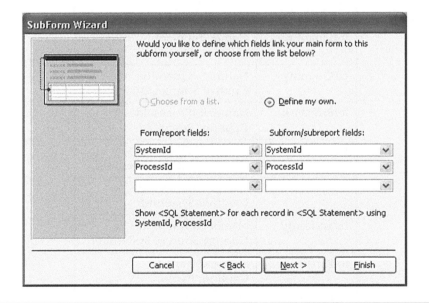

Figure 10.30   Define fields to link subform to main form

10.4.13   Configuring Click Event for Command Button

The **Command Button Wizard** generates the Visual Basic code for event procedures. This makes the application developer's job much easier. The other way to implement form activities is to manually program event procedures. This is a more powerful and more flexible way for developing database applications.

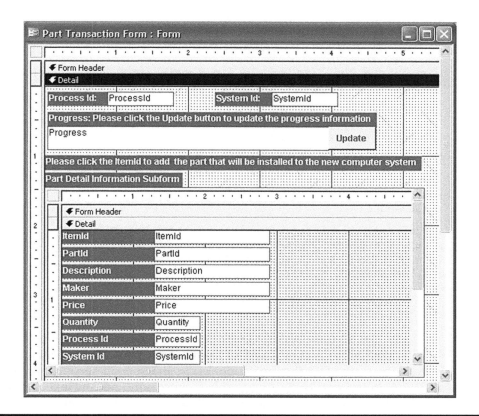

Figure 10.31   Design view of Part Transaction Form

For many database activities, you have to manually program event procedures to get the job done. Systematically covering programming languages is beyond the scope of this book. If needed, readers can refer to textbooks for Visual Basic, VBScript, or other programming languages.

The first example is to update the ASSEMBLY_PROCESS table when a user clicks on an ItemId value. When a command button is clicked, the **On Click** event is generated. We program an **On Click** event procedure to perform two functions. First, it updates the **Progress** column in the ASSEMBLY_PROCESS table. Second, it reduces the **Quantity** value by one. The following steps show you how to program this event procedure.

1. In the **Design** view of the the **Part Transaction Form**, click **Part Detail Information Subform**.
2. Right-click on the **ItemId** text box and select **Properties,** and rename **ItemId** as **txtItemId** under the tab **Other**.
3. Click the **Event** tab and open the code window for the **On Click** event.
4. Choose **Code Builder** and click **OK**. Enter the following code for this event procedure:

```
Private Sub txtItemId_Click()

'Declare local variables
```

```
Dim strSQL As String
Dim cmd As New ADODB.Command
Dim rst As New ADODB.Recordset

'Connect to the data source and specify the Command object
cmd.ActiveConnection = CurrentProject.Connection
cmd.CommandType = adCmdText

'Update the Progress column in the ASSEMBLY_PROCESS table
strSQL = "Update [ASSEMBLY_PROCESS] SET Progress = " & _
    " ' " & Me.[Description] & " ' " & "+ Progress WHERE ProcessId
    = " & _
    Me.ProcessId.Value
cmd.CommandText = strSQL
cmd.Execute

'Update the Quantity column in the PART_DETAIL table
strSQL = "Update [PART_DETAIL] SET Quantity = Quantity - 1" & _
    "WHERE ItemId = " & Me.txtItemId.Value
cmd.CommandText = strSQL
cmd.Execute

End Sub
```

In the first section of the code, three local variables are defined. The variable **cmd** is defined as an **ADO Command** object and the variable **rst** is defined as an **ADO RecordSet** object. In the second section, we have specified the current project as the data source and **adCmdText** as **CommandType** because a SQL statement will be used as the command. In the third section, the SQL statement that will be used to update the **Progress** column is assigned to the string **strSQL**. The string **strSQL** is then assigned to the **cmd.CommandText** constant. Execute the command by invoking the **Execute** method. The last section is similar to the third one. This time, a SQL statement used to decrease the **Quantity** value is assigned to **strSQL**.

5. Close the code window and return to **Design View**.

Once a value in the **ItemId** column is clicked, the item's description is added to the **Progress** text box.

The second example is a simple example that will update the assembly progress information after a computer part is installed on a system. Follow the steps below to accomplish this task.

1. Make sure that you are in the **Design** view of **Part Transaction Form**.
2. Place a **Command Button** control on the form and cancel **Command Button Wizard** if it pops up. Configure it according to the configuration for **cmdUpdate** in Table 10.4.
3. On the **Properties** page of the **Update** button, click the **Event** tab and open the **On Click** event procedure's code window.
4. Enter the following code:

```
Private Sub cmdUpdate_Click()
Me.Requery
End Sub
```

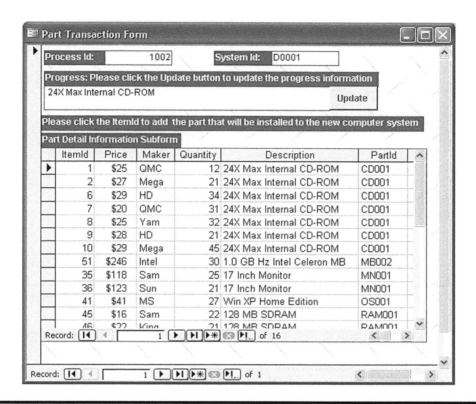

Figure 10.32   Update assembly progress information

> **Requery** is the method that updates a record set, so that changes can be displayed on the screen.

5. Switch to the form view. Click **1** in the **ItemId** column of **Part Detail Information Subform** and click the **Update** button, and you will have the result shown in Figure 10.32.

As you can see from Figure 10.32, the part description of the item number 1 is displayed in the **Progress** text box, which shows that the CD-ROM has been installed.

10.4.14   *Configuring Command Button Using Wizard*

On the Assembly Process Form, the command button **Open Part Detail Form** is used to open the subform **Part Transaction Form**. You can use the **Command Button Wizard** to specify the activities behind the command button. The following steps show you how to use the wizard to configure the command button.

1. Open the form **Assembly Process Form** in **Design View**. Click the **Command Button** control in **Toolbox** and place it on the form. **Command Button Wizard** will start automatically.

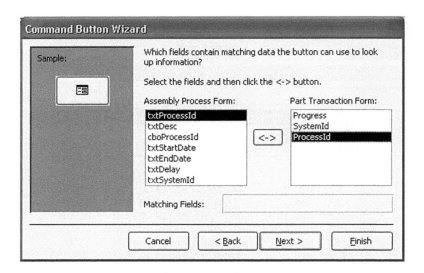

Figure 10.33   Configure command button with Command Button Wizard

2. From the **Categories** list, select **Form Operations**, and choose **Open Form** in the **Actions** list. Click **Next** to move to the next page.
3. Click **Part Transaction Form** from the selection list, and then click **Next**.
4. Check the radio button of **Open the form and find specific data to display**, and click **Next**.
5. Match **txtProcessId** in **Assembly Process Form** with **ProcessId** in **Part Transaction Form**, as shown in Figure 10.33. In this way, the values of **ProcessId** will be passed to **Part Transaction Form**. Click **Next** to move to the next page.
6. Check the radio button **Text** and enter **Open Part Detail Form** as the caption for the button, and click **Next**.
7. Enter **cmdPartDetail** as the command button name, and click **Finish** to complete the configuration.

After the configuration is completed, the control wizard automatically creates the Visual Basic code for the **On Click** event to handle error checking and data link activities. To view the code, change to the **Design** window, right-click on the button **Open Part Detail Form**, and select **Properties**. Click the **Event** tab, and then click the **On Click** property to open the **Microsoft Visual Basic** code window. Later, you will learn how to add to the code manually.

In this section, you have learned various ways to create a form. For quick development of a simple form, you can use the form wizard. For developing more sophisticated forms, you can manually design a form in the form design window and create a view by using the Query Designer. In a form design window, you can place the controls at desired locations and then configure the properties for these controls with Control Wizards or manually. *Control Wizards* is a convenient tool to configure controls that perform certain activities. Some examples have been given to illustrate how to configure event procedures by programming. Programming is a powerful tool to implement activities that are not covered by Control Wizards.

10.5 Creating Reports

Microsoft Access provides a report creation tool called **Report Designer**. In the **Report Designer** window, you can use the **Report Wizard**. **Report Designer** has some controls that can be used by application developers. It also provides programming tools for making more sophisticated reports. You can also create charts on a report by using a chart wizard.

10.5.1 Creating Reports Using Wizards

By using a report wizard, you can quickly create a simple report. Report and subreport wizards allow you to configure the style of a report, specify sorting and grouping options, and embed subreports in a main report.

1. Creating Report Based on Table or View

If you want to create a report based on a view or a single table, **Report Wizard** is the tool to use. Suppose that we would like to see a report about the price for each computer system. We can create this report based on the view RETAIL_PRICE_VIEW. To accomplish this task, consider the following steps.

1. Open the **Mytest** project in Access.
2. Highlight **Reports** in the **Objects** pane and double-click **Create report by using wizard**.
3. Select **RETAIL_PRICE_VIEW** and all its fields. Click **Next** twice.
4. To sort records in ascending order, select **SystemId** in the first combo box. Make sure that **Ascending** is on. Click **Next** to move to the next page.
5. Select **Tabular** for the layout and **Portrait** for the orientation, and then click **Next**.
6. Select **Corporate** for the style; then click **Next**.
7. Enter **Computer System Retail Price** for the report title and click **Finish**. You have the result in Figure 10.34.

As seen in Figure 10.34, we have created a simple report with a title and a couple of columns. The rows are sorted in ascending order according to SystemId.

2. Embedding Subreport in Main Report

A report can also be placed in another report or form. An embedded report can be used to display additional information or information obtained by using multiple SQL statements. In the previous example, we listed the retail price for each computer system. In some cases, an accountant may also want to

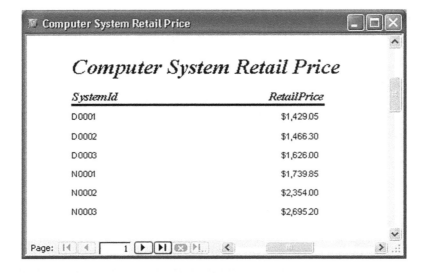

Figure 10.34   Create report with Report Wizard

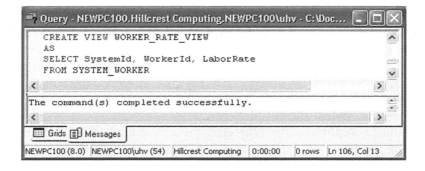

Figure 10.35   Create WORKER_RATE_VIEW

see the labor rate for a given system. In such a case, an additional view is used to select the labor rate information. We can add a subreport to the main report **Computer System Retail Price**. To do this, follow the steps below.

1. Create the view **WORKER_RATE_VIEW** using **Query Analyzer** in Microsoft SQL Server to select the assembly workers' labor rate with the SQL statement shown in Figure 10.35. Make sure to select the Hillcrest Computing database.

2. Open the report **Computer System Retail Price** in **Design View** in Microsoft Access.

3. Click the **Subform/Subreport** icon in **Toolbox**. Then place the subreport below the column names in the **Detail** section.

4. **SubReport Wizard** automatically starts and prompts you to enter the data source for the report. Click the radio button of **Use existing Tables and Queries**. Click **Next** to move to the next page.

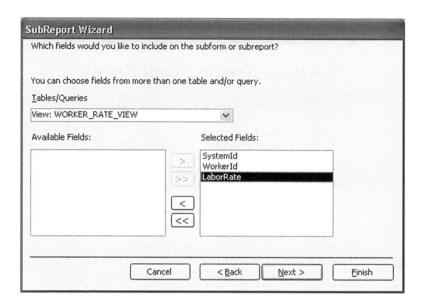

Figure 10.36   Configure subreport

5. Select the view **WORKER_RATE_VIEW**, and move all the columns to the right pane as shown in Figure 10.36. Click **Next**.
6. On this page, you can connect the main report to the subreport. Select **SystemId** for both the main report and subreport. Click **Next**.
7. Enter **Labor Rate:** as the name of the subreport, and then click **Finish**.
8. You may want to simplify the subreport by deleting the header and items related to **SystemId** in the subreport in the design view. After simplifying, add the labels **Worker Id:** and **Rate:** and rearrange the controls to have the report look like the one in Figure 10.37.

3. Creating Report Based on Stored Procedure

We can use **Report Wizard** to create a report based on a stored procedure in Access 2002 or later. Suppose that we are interested in the sales of computers from each sales center. We can build a report that will display the sales information at each sales center. First, we create a stored procedure that will return the record set containing sales at each sales center. When executing the stored procedure, the front-end user needs to specify a sales center by typing its name as the input parameter. To help the user specify the input parameter conveniently, we can develop the report to automatically prompt the user to enter the sales center's name. To create the stored procedure `SalesCenter_proc`, open **Query Analyzer** in **Microsoft SQL Server** and enter the code as shown in Figure 10.38.

In the stored procedure, we sum the retail price for each system id and use the value as the sales value. In the WHERE clause, we match the sales center name with the input parameter @Name. We also need to match the sales center ids between the tables SALES_CENTER and PURCHASE_ORDER,

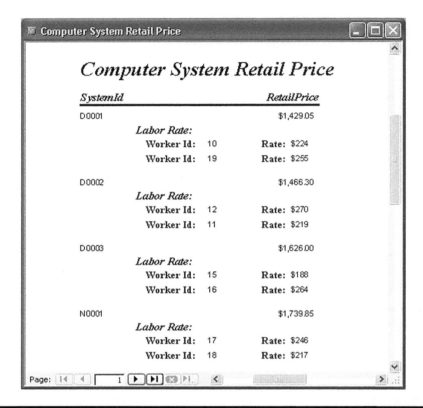

Figure 10.37   Computer system retail price report with labor rate subreport

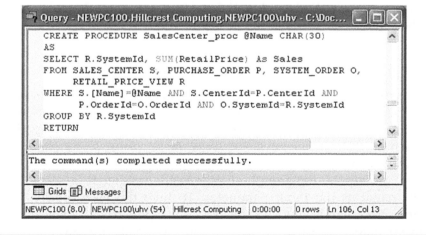

Figure 10.38   Create stored procedure to obtain sales information of sales center

then match the order ids between the tables PURCHASE_ORDER and SYSTEM_ORDER, and finally match the system ids in SYSTEM_ORDER and RETAIL_PRICE_VIEW. After the code is executed, the stored procedure is

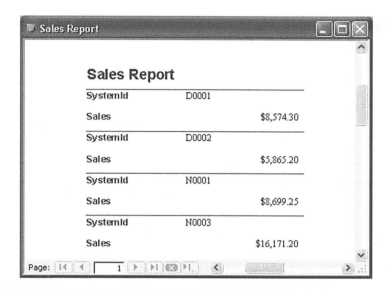

Figure 10.39   Report based on stored procedure

ready to be used in the report. The next step is to create a report based on this stored procedure. To do this, consider the following steps.

1. Open the **Mytest** project in Access and select **Reports** in the **Objects** pane.
2. Click the **New** button on the menu bar, select **Report Wizard**, and click **OK**.
3. From the **Tables/Queries** combo box, select the stored procedure **SalesCenter_proc** and move both the **SystemId** and **Sales** columns to the **Selected Fields** list box by clicking the double arrow button **>>**.
4. Click **Next** twice to move to the record sorting page. Sort the records in ascending order according to **SystemId** first and **Sales** second.
5. Click **Next**, and choose **Columnar** as the layout.
6. Click **Next**, and select **Bold** as the style.
7. Click **Next**, enter the report name as **Sales Report**, and then click **Finish**.
8. Enter the sales center name **Houston** as the input parameter and click **OK**.
9. Open the **Design** view of the newly created report. Change the **Border Style** property to **Transparent** for both the **SystemId** and **Sales** text boxes.
10. Click the preview icon, and you will be prompted to enter an input parameter value. If you enter the input parameter as **Houston** and press **Enter**, you will get the report in Figure 10.39.

4. Dynamically Formatting Report Using Conditional Formatting

As we have seen in creating forms, conditional formatting can be used to dynamically change the settings of properties. As an example, we use conditional formatting to identify the computer systems that cost more than $2000 by changing their background color. If the cost of a system is changed later, the background color will adjust accordingly.

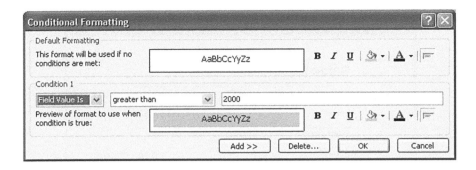

Figure 10.40   Conditional formatting for RetailPrice text box

1. Open the report **Computer System Retail Price** in the **Design** view.
2. Highlight the text box **RetailPrice**, click **Format** on the menu bar, and select **Conditional Formatting**.
3. After the **Conditional Formatting** dialog opens, select **Field Value Is** under **Condition 1**. Select **greater than** as the operator, enter **2000** as the condition, and change the background color to gray, as shown in Figure 10.40.
4. Click **OK** to complete the configuration. Switch to the preview window, and we have the report in which the price greater than $2000 has a gray background (see Figure 10.41).

10.5.2   Creating Comprehensive Reports Using Forms, Reports, and Graphics

Next, we develop a more sophisticated report for the sales managers. We review the required tasks for the sales report.

- Open the sales report for the sales center selected by the user.
- List the sales of each type of computer system.
- Display the sales of each type of computer system with a bar chart.

In this project, we first create a form called **Select Sales Center Form**, which allows the user to select a sales center. After the sales center is selected, the form will list the sales for each type of computer in the report **Sales Report**. A bar chart that shows the sales for each type of computer will be attached to the report. The flowchart of the sales report process is given in Figure 10.42.

1. Creating More Sophisticated Sales Report

We have previously created the stored procedure `SalesCenter_proc`, which returns the sales information at a sales center specified by the input parameter. The simple report **Sales Report** based on `SalesCenter_proc` was already created in the previous section with **Report Wizard**. We can reuse that report and build on it here.

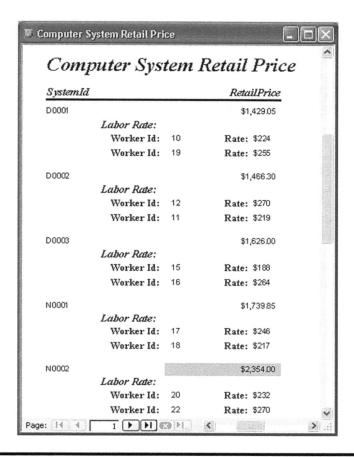

Figure 10.41   Conditional formatting effect on RetailPrice

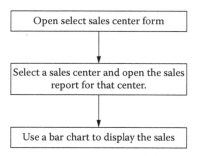

Figure 10.42   Business process of sales report

2. Creating Sales Chart

To add a chart to the simple report **Sales Report**, we work through the following steps. The first thing we need to do is to create a report that contains the sales bar chart only. The following steps show how to do this.

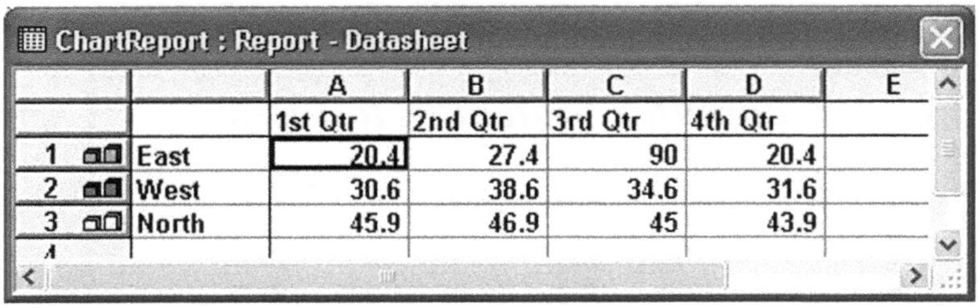

Figure 10.43   Default datasheet

1. Open a blank report in the **Design** view, name the report **ChartReport**, and place an **Unbound Object Frame** control with the icon 🖼 to the report.
2. The **Microsoft Office Access** dialog box is open for configuration. Make sure that the **Create New** option is checked. Select **Microsoft Graph Chart** in the **Object Type** list box. Click **OK**.
3. Change the control name to **oleSalesChart** under the **Other** tab in **Properties**.
4. Remove the **Header/Footer** sections for both **Report** and **Page** to reduce empty space. This will make the report embedded with the chart look better. You do this by right-clicking the **Page Header** or **Report Header** bar and then selecting **Page Header/Footer** or **Report Header/Footer**. After you are done, you should have only the **Detail** section in the report.
5. You may also want to delete the default datasheet. To do this, double-click the chart in the **Design** view to open the default datasheet, as shown in Figure 10.43. Mark the content of the datasheet, and then press the **Delete** key. Save the report as **ChartReport**.
6. In this step, you will insert the chart into the report **Sales Report**, which serves as the main report. Open **Sales Report** in the **Design** view. Place a **Subform/Subreport** control in the **Report Footer** section, as shown in Figure 10.44.
7. **SubReport Wizard** will open automatically. Check the **Use an existing report or form** option and select **ChartReport**.
8. Click **Next** and enter **Sales by Computer System Chart** as the subreport title. Click **Finish** to complete the configuration.
9. Delete the **Page Header** and **Page Footer** sections as shown earlier to reduce empty space.
10. Right-click on the subreport control and select **Properties**. Change the **Border Style** property to **Transparent**. Also, for the subreport title label control, change the **Font Size** property to **14**.

Now you have the report with a chart ready. As mentioned earlier, the chart will display the sales at a specified sales center. Next, we create a form that allows front-end users to select a sales center for which the sales data will be displayed.

3. Creating Select Sales Center Form

This is a form that includes a combo box and a command button. The combo box is used to select a sales center. After the sales center is chosen, click the

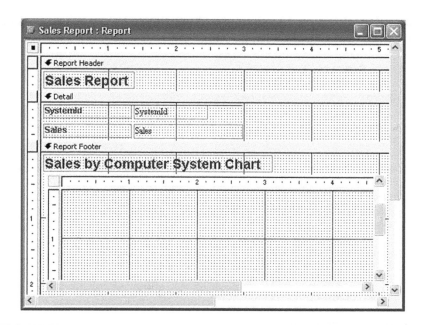

Figure 10.44   Place subform/subreport into report footer

command button to open the Sales Report for the selected sales center. The following steps show you how to create the form.

1. Create a new form with the company logo and the form name **Select Sales Center Form** by making a copy of **Template Form** created earlier in Section 10.4. To edit the form title, double-click on it in the **Design** view and click it again to obtain the **WordArt** window. Change the form title to **Select Sales Center Form**.

2. Add a combo box to the **Detail** part in the **Design** view. The **Combo Box Wizard** will start automatically. Check the radio button of **I want the combo box to look up the values in a table or query**. Click **Next** and select the table **SALES_CENTER**. Click **Next** and move the **Name** field from the **Available Fields** list box to the **Selected Fields** list box. Click **Next** a couple of times and enter **Select a Sales Center** as the combo box label. Click **Finish** to complete the configuration. Right-click on the combo box to open the **Properties** window. Click the **Other** tab and change the name of the combo box to **cboCenter**.

3. Add a command button to the form. The **Command Button Wizard** will start automatically. Select **Report Operations** in the **Categories** list box and **Preview Report** in the **Actions** list box. Click **Next** and select **Sales Report** to preview. Click **Next** again. This page asks you to enter the caption for the command button. Select the **Text** option and type **Open Sales Report** as the caption. Click **Next** and change the button name to **cmdOpenReport**; then click **Finish**.

4. The command button will open the report **Sales Report** with the content based on the selected value in the combo box **cboCenter**. To accomplish this, we need to program the **On Click** event. Right-click on the **Open**

Sales Report button and open the **Properties** window. Click the **Event** tab and open the **On Click** event. Enter the following code:

```
Option Compare Database
Private Sub cmdOpenReport_Click()
On Error GoTo Err_cmdOpenReport_Click

'Declare a string variable to hold the report name.
  Dim stDocName As String

'Open the report, update the input parameter, and then close
  'the report.
  stDocName = "Sales Report"
  DoCmd.OpenReport stDocName, acViewDesign
  Reports(stDocName).InputParameters = "@Name = '" & _
    Me.cboCenter.Value & "'"
  DoCmd.Close acReport, stDocName, acSaveYes

'View the report with the updated input parameter.
  DoCmd.OpenReport stDocName, acViewPreview

'Exit the event procedure.
Exit_cmdOpenReport_Click:
  Exit Sub

Err_cmdOpenReport_Click:
  MsgBox Err.Description
  Resume Exit_cmdOpenReport_Click

End Sub
```

5. The above code opens **Sales Report** twice. First, it opens the report in the **Design** view and specifies the input parameter as the value selected in the combo box **cboCenter** for later use of the stored procedure `SalesCenter_proc`. Then it closes the **Design** view. Next, it opens the report again in the **Preview** view to display the report **Sales Report** with the content specified by the input parameter. Several lines of error-handling code will be used to display an error message if an error occurs during the process.

6. The report **Sales Report** has a chart to visually display sales at a specified location. To dynamically reconfigure the record source property based on the value selected in the combo box, you need to add the code for the **On Mouse Up** event. Right-click on the **Open Sales Report** button and open the **Properties** window. Click the **Event** tab and open the **On Mouse Up** event. Enter the code shown below:

```
'Make sure to close the open report before running this program.
Private Sub cmdOpenReport_MouseUp(Button As Integer, Shift As
    Integer, X As Single, Y As Single)

'Declare the variables.
Dim rep As Report
```

```
Dim cmd As ADODB.Command
Dim par As ADODB.Parameter
Dim rst As ADODB.Recordset
Dim str As String

'Open the report ChartReport.
DoCmd.OpenReport "ChartReport", acViewDesign
Set rep = Reports(0)

'Connect to the stored procedure SalesCenter_proc
Set cmd = New ADODB.Command
cmd.ActiveConnection = CurrentProject.Connection
cmd.CommandType = adCmdStoredProc
cmd.CommandText = "SalesCenter_proc"

'Define the Parameter object.
Set par = cmd.CreateParameter("@Name", adChar, adParamInput, 30)
cmd.Parameters.Append par
par.Value = Me.cboCenter.Value

'Create the record set rst.
Set rst = New ADODB.Recordset
Set rst = cmd.Execute

'Add a blank row in the record source.
str = ";;"

'Append the data stored in the record set.
Do Until rst.EOF
   str = str & rst("SystemId") & ";" & rst("Sales") & ";"
   rst.MoveNext
Loop

'Update the properties for the unbound OLE container.
With rep.oleSalesChart
   .RowSourceType = "Value List"
   .RowSource = str
   .ColumnCount = 2
End With

'Save the configuration.
DoCmd.Close acReport, "ChartReport", acSaveYes

End Sub
```

In this code, we have created some ADO objects such as `Command`, `RecordSet`, and `Parameter`. The `Command` object is used to connect to the stored procedure `SalesCenter_proc`. The `Parameter` object is used to specify the input parameter for the stored procedure. The following code

```
DoCmd.OpenReport "ChartReport", acViewDesign
```

opens the chart **ChartReport** in the **Design** view for configuration. After the command is executed, the values returned by the stored procedure are

Figure 10.45   Select Sales Center Form

assigned to the `RecordSet` object `rst`. A blank line is added to the beginning of the record source property because **Microsoft Graph Chart OLE Class** does not read the first row of the record source. **Until rst.EOF** in the do loop is the test condition that allows the adding of values to the value list that iterates through the rows of a record set until the end. **DoCmd.Close** is used to close the record set to release the resources consumed by the client and server. To configure the `RowSource` and `RecordSourceType` properties, use the following code:

```
With rep.oleSalesChart
   .RowSourceType = "Value List"
   .RowSource = str
   .ColumnCount = 2
End With
```

`RowSourceType` is specified as **Value List** because `RowSource` is specified by a string **str**, which contains a list of sales values returned from the stored procedure. We set **ColumnCount = 2** to preserve the value in the **Name** column for creating the chart later. **oleSalesChart** is the name of the chart. When creating the chart **oleSalesChart**, make sure that the name is consistent. After you have programmed the events, you can start the form by clicking the form view icon ▣ on the menu bar. The form will look like the one in Figure 10.45.

Select **Houston** from the combo box and click the **Open Sales Report** button, and you will open the sales report with the bar chart to illustrate the sales at the Houston sales center. The report is illustrated in Figure 10.46.

In this section, several reports have been created. Report Wizard can be used to create a new report based on an existing table, view, and stored procedure. For more sophisticated reports such as those that can be dynamically updated based on the user's decision, you need to manually configure the properties and program the events. You can take advantage of programming to make several reports work together, dynamically reconfigure report properties, and dynamically modify the content displayed on a report.

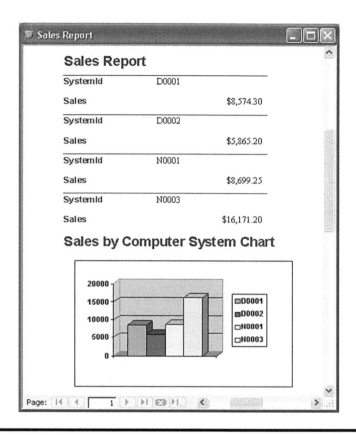

Figure 10.46   Open sales report by clicking Open Sales Report button

10.6 Summary

In this chapter, you have learned various ways of developing database applications such as forms and reports. We first discussed the application design issues. A good database application design should meet front-end users' requirements. Carefully analyzing users' needs and requirements is the key to successfully developing a database application. Some commonly used application design guidelines were listed to help application developers. Detailed descriptions of database application controls were given in the early sections of this chapter. These are controls used to construct the graphical user interface that will help front-end users interact with a database.

Form Wizard and Report Wizard were used for quick development of forms and reports. These wizards can generate forms and reports against existing tables, views, functions, or stored procedures. Wizards are a convenient tool in developing database applications; they usually need only a few clicks and require no programming skills. To make multiple forms and reports work together consistently or to make forms and reports respond to specific events, you need to manually program the properties and events of a form or report.

Programming is powerful and gives great flexibility. By working through the examples, we have built some forms and reports against the tables, views, and stored procedures created in the database `Hillcrest Computing`.

In a real-life business environment, a database can be accessed by multiple remote users through a network. Although our database applications are created on the same computer where the database is installed, they can be installed on multiple-client computers in a network environment. In the next chapter, you will learn how to develop network-based database applications.

Review Questions

1. What are forms and reports for?
2. Explain the role of an Image control.
3. Explain the role of a Label control.
4. Explain the role of a Text Box control.
5. Explain the role of a Combo Box control.
6. Explain the role of an Option Group control.
7. Explain the role of a Command Button control.
8. What are the components a report may include?
9. How can a form be designed to make it convenient for the user?
10. Give an example to show how to design a GUI to help users avoid making a mistake.
11. How can a GUI be designed to reflect the structure of a data source?
12. Give an example in which the main or subform or main or subreport structure is appropriate.
13. What is a mandatory–optional cardinality constraint?
14. Explain the meaning of fragment in a cardinality constraint.
15. Summarize the four cardinality constraints: mandatory–mandatory, mandatory–optional, optional–mandatory, and optional–optional.
16. In the graphical tools provided by Microsoft Access for checking cardinality constraints, summarize the functionalities for those check boxes in the Relationship Properties dialog.
17. Describe the form-developing tool provided by Microsoft Access.
18. By using Form Wizard, create a form that can be used to enter and display the data for the table `ASSEMBLY_WORKER`.
19. What is the role of an event procedure?
20. What is the role of an embedded report?

Case Study Projects

In the following case study projects, create some database applications with Microsoft Access.

1. Computer Service

For the Computer_Service database, create the following database applications for front-end users.

- For the service manager, create a data entry form for inserting new rows into the table SERVICES. On the form, the **StartDate** textbox automatically enters the current date. A combo box is used to select the customer id and a list box is used to select the job id. Create an Insert button to insert new rows to the table SERVICES.
- Create a view to show each customer's id, the number of services for each customer, and the cost of the services. Create a report to display the information in the view. In the report, dynamically change the background of the cost values that are greater than $200.

2. University Registration

Create the following database applications for the Registration database.

- Create a form to allow the user to enter information about a new student and enter the enrollment information based on a list of available classes.
- Create a report that includes a bar chart to display the enrollment of each class.

3. Mail Order

To allow the front-end user to use the database Mail_Order, create the following database applications.

- Use the master or detail structure to create a form that allows the user to enter information about a customer and his or her order.
- Create a form for the user to select a customer. After the customer is selected, display the order(s) placed by the customer in a report.

Chapter 11

Network Databases

Objectives

- Understand three-tier client/server architecture.
- Develop client/server database applications.
- Develop Internet database applications with ASP.NET.
- Develop Internet database applications with XML.

11.1 Introduction

In this chapter, we discuss how databases are used by multiple users in a network environment. Nowadays, more and more companies do not just live in one place. In fact, virtually every business requires its database to be accessed by multiple users through a local area network, a wide area network, or the Internet. In a network database environment, we have a database server to support many database applications created for front-end users. In Chapter 10, we created some database applications for front-end users. Although these applications are created on the same computer where the database is installed, we can consider it as a special case of a network database environment.

In this chapter, you will first learn the concepts of network-based databases such as client/server architecture, Web services, and ASP. Then, by walking through some examples, you will actually develop some network-based database applications. The examples covered in this chapter are used for learning purposes and are not particularly optimized for a specific networked database. They are relatively easy to follow. For some business applications at the enterprise level, a network-based database can be much more complicated and requires a group of well-trained IT professionals to develop and manage.

Now we see exactly what tasks are involved in a network database computing environment.

1. *Displaying Data:* A network database can be used to supply data and display information in a report at multiple remote locations. It returns static query results to a front-end user who has sent a query to the network database server at a central location. For these types of applications, the database performs a one-way operation; that is, it sends the requested data to the front-end user.

2. *Receiving data:* A network database is also used to store data received from a data entry form. Once the data are received, the network database server may send a response back to the front-end user.

3. *Sharing data:* The network database allows front-end users to download and share the data stored on a network server. These data can be used in various database applications on the client side.

4. *Managing databases at remote locations:* The network database server provides authentication tools and database management tools, so that a database administrator can log on remotely to perform database management tasks.

5. *Implementing business logic:* The network database server provides stored procedures and triggers that are used to perform business logic. Front-end users may be allowed to execute these procedures remotely from client computers.

6. *Supporting client GUI activities:* The network database server supports all the GUI activities and allows front-end users to interact with multiple network databases graphically.

7. *Publishing database on Internet:* With the rapid development of Internet technology, network databases have become the heart of many interactive Web sites. Data are published on Web pages to allow front-end users to interactively communicate with a database through the Internet.

Most of the above activities can be done through the client/server computing architecture. The client side requests services and the server side provides them.

11.2 Client/Server Computing

In a network database environment, a database server (referred to as a network database server in this chapter) can handle multiple users at remote locations. The database applications (front end) on the client side send requests across the network. When the requests arrive at the database server (back end), the database server processes them by retrieving data from the database, conducting the requested activities such as sorting or filtering, and then sending the final results back to the client through the network. The advantages of a client/server solution to business processes are that it

- Generates less network traffic by reducing the network load
- Improves database performance by reallocating some of the tasks to client computers
- Makes database processing more reliable by providing tools for handling failures, recovering from failures, and managing transactions

- Allows more flexibility for clients to present data the way they want
- Provides the database server with tools for handling a large amount of data for multiple users with better security measures

With these advantages, the client/server architecture should be considered if your business has many computers running simultaneously. It has a great impact on the design and use of databases at the enterprise level. To support the implementation of the client/server architecture, many client/server software packages have been developed by companies such as IBM, Microsoft, Oracle, SAP, PeopleSoft, and Sun. In this section, you will learn how to develop a client/server solution based on the forms and reports developed by using Microsoft Office and Microsoft Visual Studio .NET as the front end, and SQL Server as the back end. Internet Information Services and XML Web services are used to process front-end users' requests and retrieve data from database servers based on the users' requests.

To help you master database applications in a client/server environment, examples are provided for hands-on practice. In order to run the examples, you should have the Mytest.adp data link project created in Chapter 9, Microsoft Office 2003 or later, Visual Studio .NET, and SQL Server. The Access project files (.adp files) are used to connect to a SQL Server database at the back end and allow users to develop front-end applications through MS Access. Through OLE DB, an Access project file will be connected to data providers such as relational databases constructed on SQL Server, e-mail files, text files, or spreadsheets. InfoPath, a database application development tool provided by Office 2003, is used to connect the Web service developed with Visual Studio .NET.

For a client/server computing environment, a database computing task can be logically divided into several parts. Each part will take a certain processing load. The word *tier* means an individual part in the partition of the database computing task.

11.2.1   Two-Tier Architecture

If a database-processing task is divided into two parts (the database application on the client side and the database management on the server side), such a computing architecture is called a *two-tier client/server architecture* (see Figure 11.1).

In a *two-tier client/server* system, database applications can be installed on either the client or server side. In fact, if you install database applications on

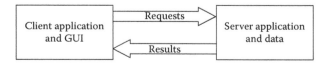

Figure 11.1   Two-tier client/server architecture

the server side, they will be available to all the client users all the time. The client users can run the applications from any client-side computer. On the other hand, if you install the database applications on the client side, they will reduce the database-processing load on the server side and reduce traffic over the network.

The advantages of the two-tier architecture are its ease of development and its suitability for an environment that has fewer than 100 users accessing the database simultaneously over a local area network. One of the disadvantages of the two-tier architecture is that it has difficulty handling large-scale database-processing tasks. The limitation is caused by the fact that the two-tier architecture maintains a keep-alive session for each user who is accessing the database. When more than 100 client users are accessing the database at the same time, the performance begins to slow down and soon the client users will find that they are no longer able to carry out database-processing tasks. Another difficulty with the two-tier system is that it is not flexible. For example, technologies from different vendors or different versions from the same vendor are often not compatible. In such a case, system upgrading could be a problem for the two-tier system. Not only do you have to stay with the same DBMS vendor, but you also have to make sure that the new version is backward-compatible with the old version.

The two-tier architecture allows the client to develop and use database applications such as data entry, a decision-support system, and an Internet-based database process through GUI. The applications such as the forms and reports developed in Chapter 10 are examples of two-tier systems. The computation tasks are shared by both the client and the database server. The server-side applications include triggers, stored procedures, and views. The client-side applications include forms and reports. Usually, a two-tier system is implemented on different computers. It can also be implemented on the same computer. For learning purposes, it is convenient to implement the two-tier system on the same computer.

11.2.2   Three-Tier Architecture

To overcome the difficulties of the two-tier structure and meet the requirements of today's fast-developing business environment, a *middle tier* is added to the two-tier structure (see Figure 11.2). The *middle tier* can be used to implement business computing tasks such as a transaction-processing service, message service, Internet application service, and business logic implementation service. When a client requests an activity, the request is passed to an appropriate middle-tier service; the middle-tier service will decide which database to contact and communicate with that database to retrieve data based on the request from the client. Then the data or message will be returned to the client. Each tier may have its own operating system and communicate with a standard network protocol. By comparing it with the two-tier architecture, the *three-tier architecture* has the following advantages:

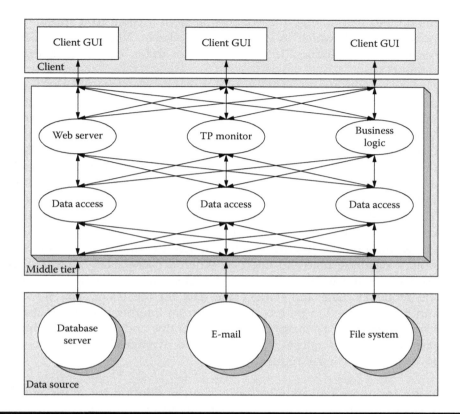

Figure 11.2   Three-tier client/server architecture

- Client-side computing is much less complex. Most of the business application computing is done at the middle tier.
- It is more secure because many security measures such as verification of user priorities for database accessing are implemented on the middle tier.
- It is much easier to scale up a three-tier system. The middle tier can be used to distribute the load across multiple server systems. The middle tier can also be used to transact data among heterogeneous databases.
- It is much more flexible. The middle tier can be implemented on multiple computers at different locations or implemented on the database server. With the middle-tier structure, it is easier to add clients and database servers to the existing system or remove them from the system. It is also easier to add more components to the middle tier to handle rapidly increasing requests from the client side and keep the current database operation unchanged. The middle tier can be used to process business computing tasks in multiple programming languages, so that you can use your favorite programming language for data processing.
- It can handle a large number of clients. To manage connections of a large number of clients, the middle tier implements a *transaction-processing* monitor to let the clients share a pool of resources. The resource-pooling technique keeps available components in the pool. When requested, the

middle tier will arrange the connection from a client to a specified component through which to contact the database. When the connection is released, the component is back in the pool and is ready to handle another request.

- Performance is improved because the middle tier does most of the computation for data transaction and implementation of business logic. The middle tier communicates with the database server only for necessary data. When the requests from the clients ask for different business-processing tasks to be done, multiple components can work simultaneously. Because the components in the resource pool are ready to be connected, initiating a connection from a client to a component on the middle tier is much faster than creating a direct connection between the client and the database.

- The three-tier architecture is an excellent structure to support Internet computing. The middle tier can be built as a Web server to interact with clients through the Internet. Such a middle tier allows us to publish data from a database onto the Internet. When a client sends a request to the Web server, the Web server will determine from which database it will get the requested data and retrieve the data for the client. The Web server can be configured to protect databases from Internet hackers. It also hosts various scripting languages such as VBScript and JavaScript, which are used to process requests from clients and dynamically create Web pages to respond to clients' requests.

Although the three-tier architecture is a great solution for implementing a network database, there are still some hurdles to clear. In the old way, data communication between a client and a server is a challenging task. Data sent by a client computer must be converted to the format that the server computer can understand. The data-conversion programs are often written by experienced programmers and are installed on the middle tier in a local area network or an organization's wide area network. As the Internet becomes a common infrastructure for database communication, the large number of different data formats makes it extremely difficult to handle the data-conversion tasks. One of the better solutions is to format all the data in XML. With the common representation in XML, data can be exchanged over heterogeneous computer systems and various programming languages. When sharing data in a multi-tier database system, XML is often used to represent the data and structure of database objects in a common format. In the next section, we take a closer look at the XML technology.

11.3 Introduction to Extensible Markup Language (XML)

The XML technique is a great contribution to database system development. XML allows information exchange between clients and database servers with heterogeneous application software, operating systems, and database management systems. The advantages of XML make it easier to do business over the Internet. For example, in our case study, `Hillcrest Computing`, assume that each sales center has a computer system different from that in the

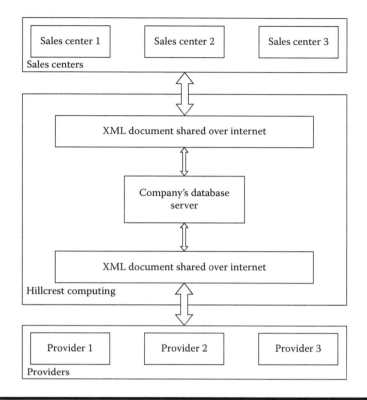

Figure 11.3 Doing business over Internet by using XML

company's headquarters. Also, the company requires that each sales center submit sales information in a specified format. Meanwhile, the company orders computer parts from various providers. The data formats and computer systems used by these providers may also vary. Therefore, to communicate with the sales centers and the providers, the company should require its sales centers to submit their sales information in an XML document and convert computer part order forms to XML files for part providers. The XML technology–involved business process is illustrated in Figure 11.3.

In later sections, we create a three-tier database system project. We use Windows forms, Web forms, or forms created in InfoPath as the front-end GUI interface, use Internet Information Services or XML Web services as the middle tier, and use the `Hillcrest Computing` database created on SQL Server as the back-end data source. Because the `Hillcrest Computing` database has been created in the previous chapters, we place our focus on the development of the client tier and the middle tier. Data files in Visual Studio .NET and InfoPath are formatted in XML, so we first introduce some basic concepts of XML.

By using a markup language such as **Hypertext Markup Language** (HTML), one can display information on a Web page. HTML uses a set of predefined tags to specify how information can be displayed on a Web page. However, for data communication over a client/server database system, HTML has its limitations. In the early 1990s, a more powerful markup language, **Extensible**

Markup Language (XML), was developed to handle data transactions over a client/server system. Like HTML, XML is a tag-based language. Unlike HTML, XML tags don't control how a Web browser displays text; they are used to define data types. XML contains a set of rules created by the World Wide Web Consortium (W3C). These rules are used to express data formats and structures. When compared with HTML, which is used to present data on a page, XML has the following advantages:

- XML allows developers to create tags to describe table structure. Better than HTML, XML does not depend on a fixed set of predefined tags.
- XML separates the document structure from the content. In this way, the same set of XML data can be used for different applications such as forms, reports, word documents, or spreadsheets.
- XML is a platform-independent language for defining and transforming data on the Web. From various data sources, data can be exported in the XML format and then the XML data can be imported to different applications for front-end users.
- XML can be used to represent some database objects such as views and can be used for document validation.

Usually, three files are involved in XML documents. Declarations of data types are stored in the **XML Schema Definition Language** file (.**xsd** file), the XML data defined by the data types declared in the .xsd file are stored in the **XML** data file (.**xml** file), and the style specifications of the XML data are stored in the **Extensible Stylesheet** file (.**xsl** file). The following sections give some brief descriptions of these files.

11.3.1   XML Data File (.xml File)

An XML data file contains elements, tags, attributes, and content. The example below shows the XML data file representing the data returned from the view PART_COST_VIEW, which returns two columns, SystemId and System_Cost.

```
<?xml version="1.0" encoding="UTF-8" ?>
- <dataroot xmlns:od="urn:schemas-microsoft-com:officedata">
  - <PART_COST_VIEW>
    - <SystemId>
      - <![CDATA[
        D0001
          ]]>
      </SystemId>
      <System_Cost>882</System_Cost>
    </PART_COST_VIEW>

  - <PART_COST_VIEW>
    - <SystemId>
      - <![CDATA[
        D0002
```

```
        ]]>
       </SystemId>
      <System_Cost>844</System_Cost>
     </PART_COST_VIEW>
        ...
 </dataroot>
```

In the above file, an element is defined by a pair of identically named tags. A typical XML element consists of a start tag denoted by angle brackets **<tag name>**, the element data, and an end tag denoted by a slash in angle brackets **</ tag name>**. The general format of an element tag and its attribute is

```
<tag_name attribute="value">element data </tag_name>
```

where **attribute** is a value that adds additional formatting information to the tag or content that follows the element. In the above example, the root element dataroot has one child element PART_COST_VIEW, and each PART_COST_VIEW element contains two child elements, SystemId and System_Cost. The meanings of commonly used syntax in an .xml file are listed in Table 11.1.

Table 11.1 Syntax in .xml File

Syntax	Meaning
<?xml version="1.0" ?>	XML declaration statement
<!--Insert system Id -->	Comment statement
<dataroot>	Document element
<PART_COST_VIEW>	Data element
version="1.0"	Attributes
<![CDATA[D0002]]>	DATA section where no markup in the content
D0002	Data value

In an .xml file, you can define your own XML tags to uniquely identify your data elements. You can also add attributes to the tags to include additional information about your data. User-defined tags are declared in an XML Schema Definition Language (.xsd) file. The following section shows you how to declare user-defined tags.

11.3.2 XML Schema Definition Language File (.xsd File)

The XML schema is used to define the data type and structure used in an XML data file. There are some advantages of using XML schema files.

1. One of the advantages of XML is that the definition of structure is separated from data. In this way, when data are transmitted from one application to another, the two applications need only convert the data by interpreting

the definition in the XML schema file. That is, if the sales centers transmit their spreadsheet data to the company's database at a remote location, there is no need to develop a special set of rules to perform the transformation from spreadsheet data to database data; all they need to do is interpret the data through the XML schema.

2. When we transmit XML data over the Internet, for example, by sending the XML data from the middle tier to a client, the client side verifies whether the document sent from the middle tier is an .xml file and checks the definition of the data types. After the verification is complete, the client side starts to process the XML data. The verification procedures on the client side need a set of standards so that the client can compare the structure of the incoming XML data with the standards. An .xsd file can be used to specify the standards.

3. The XML schema can be used to define standards for an entire industry. Once the standards are published, they can be used to interchange data within the industry. Each user in the same industry can use the predefined data types and structures to create his or her own XML data files without recreating the standards. Currently, industries such as real estate, insurance, banking, and accounting have their own XML standards.

4. By defining data types that correspond to the columns in a table or a view, the XML schema can be used to represent a database table or view. Usually, we use SQL statements to create a view. By using the XML schema, we have a better way to create a more sophisticated view with multiple data types.

The following is an example of an .xsd file related to the XML data file created in the previous section.

```
<?xml version="1.0" encoding="UTF-8" ?>
- <root xmlns:xsd="http://www.w3.org/2000/10/XMLSchema"
  xmlns:od="urn:schemas-microsoft-com:officedata">

- <xsd:schema>

  - <xsd:element name="dataroot">
    - <xsd:complexType>
      - <xsd:choice maxOccurs="unbounded">
        <xsd:element ref="PART_COST_VIEW" />
        </xsd:choice>
      </xsd:complexType>
  </xsd:element>

  - <xsd:element name="PART_COST_VIEW">
    - <xsd:annotation>
      <xsd:appinfo />
    </xsd:annotation>

    - <xsd:complexType>
      - <xsd:sequence>
        - <xsd:element name="SystemId" od:jetType="text"
          od:nonNullable="yes">
          - <xsd:simpleType>
            - <xsd:restriction base="xsd:string">
```

```
                     <xsd:maxLength value="10" />
                 </xsd:restriction>
              </xsd:simpleType>
          </xsd:element>
        <xsd:element name="System_Cost" minOccurs="0"
          od:jetType="currency" type="xsd:double" />
      </xsd:sequence>
      </xsd:complexType>

   </xsd:element>

 </xsd:schema>
```

To make sure that user-defined tags can be used by broad Web browsers or applications, the above .xsd file is used to define the meanings of the tags. On Line 2 and Line 3, two namespaces, **XML Schema Definition** (**xsd**) and **Office Data** (**od**), are defined. An XML namespace contains tags that can be used to uniquely identify an element or attribute. In an XML schema file, **xsd** and **od** are the two namespaces supported by Access in its XML documents. The .xml files in Access use the attributes from these two namespaces. The **xsd** namespace contains schema document–specific tags and the **od** namespace contains Microsoft Office–related tags such as **Table**, **Primary Key**, and **Not Null**. For example, in the above code, **od** is used as a prefix of **jetType** (as in **od:jetType=text**). With this prefix, an application in Microsoft Office will consider **text** as an Office-specific attribute. A namespace is identified by **Uniform Resource Identifier** (**URI**). The **xsd** is often uniquely identified by **Uniform Resource Locator** (**URL**) and **od** is often uniquely identified by **Uniform Resource Number** (**URN**). There is no requirement to use URL or URN as URI; the real requirement is that URI must be worldwide unique.

A namespace plays an important role in keeping the uniqueness of defined data types. For illustration purposes, if we define a set of data types to represent the table SALES_CENTER with columns such as CID, Name, and Phone and another set of data types to represent the table PART with columns such as PID and Name, we will have the duplicated **Name** data type. To avoid confusion, we can define two different namespaces for the two representations. One namespace is defined for SALES_CENTER with the elements CenterId, Name, and Phone. The other namespace is defined for PART with the elements PartId and Name. For example, to declare and use the data types to represent the above tables, we may use the following code in an .xml file that combines the data type declarations and the XML data:

```
<?xml version="1.0"?>
<Shipping xmlns="http://localhost/myxml/Shipping"
   xmlns:center="http://localhost/myxml/Sales_Center"
   xmlns:pt="http://localhost/myxml/Part"
   <ShippingDate>10-1-2005</ShippingDate>
   <center:Sales_Center>
      <center:CID>3</center:CID>
      <center:Name>Austin</center:Name>
      <center:Phone>281-275-3350</center:Phone>
```

```
     </center:Sales_Center>
     <pt:Part>
        <pt:PID>CD001</pt:PID>
        <pt:Name>24X CD ROM</pt:Name>
     </pt:Part>
  </Shipping>
```

Table 11.2   Syntax in .xsd File

Syntax	Meaning
<xsd:schema>	Defines a schema element to hold the definitions of data types and other elements
<xsd:complexType>	Defines a data type that contains child elements
<xsd:sequence>	Defines subsequent elements that must appear in that order
<xsd:element>	Defines the data type or tag that will be used in an XML data file
<xsd:simpleType>	Defines a new data type that inherits from a built-in data type
<xsd:restriction>	Defines restrictions to a built-in data type when creating an inherited data type
<xsd:maxLength>	Defines the maximum length restriction for the built-in data type String
xmlns:prefix="*namespace*"	XML *namespace* (xmlns) used to define a short *prefix* for a long *namespace* name

The above code defines three namespaces, the default namespace identified by the URI "http://localhost/myxml/Shipping," the namespace **center** identified by the URI "http://localhost/myxml/Sales_Center," and the namespace pt identified by "http://localhost/myxml/Part." When we define the XML data, the prefix **center** is added to the Name element for SALES_CENTER, and the prefix **pt** is added to the Name element for PART. In this way, we can maintain the uniqueness of element names. If there is no prefix, an element is from the default namespace.

In addition to the definition of namespaces, the meanings of commonly used syntax in an .xsd file are listed in Table 11.2.

11.3.3   Extensible Stylesheet File (.xsl file)

Unlike HTML, an XML data file does not provide data style formatting information. To specify styles such as color and font, we need to have a document stylesheet file, an **.xsl** file, which provides a set of formatting information about our XML data. Currently, the W3 Consortium splits **xsl** into two parts, the document transformation part **XSLT** for formatting and transforming XML documents to HTML and the formatting object part **XSL-FO** for more sophisticated formatting. An example of **xsl** is given below:

```
<?xml version="1.0" ?>
- <xsl:stylesheet xmlns:xsl="http://www.w3.org/TR/WD-xsl"
    language="vbscript">
- <xsl:template match="/">

    - <HTML>
      - <HEAD>
      <META HTTP-EQUIV="Content-Type"
        CONTENT="text/html;charset=UTF-8" />
     <TITLE>Computer System Cost Form</TITLE>
     <STYLE TYPE="text/css">.Style0 { BORDER-STYLE: solid;
        COLOR: #000000; BACKGROUND-COLOR: #ffffff;
        BORDER-WIDTH: 1px;

      …
      }</STYLE>
     </HEAD>

    - <BODY link="#0000ff" vlink="#800080" style="BACKGROUND-
      IMAGE:url('Images\Computer%20System%20Cost%20Form.bmp');
      BACKGROUND-POSITION: center center; BACKGROUND-REPEAT:
      repeat">

    - <xsl:for-each select="/dataroot/PART_COST_VIEW">
     <xsl:eval>AppendNodeIndex(me)</xsl:eval>
       </xsl:for-each>
         - <xsl:for-each select="/dataroot/PART_COST_VIEW">
             <xsl:eval>CacheCurrentNode(me)</xsl:eval>
               - <xsl:if expr="OnFirstNode">
             <DIV style="BORDER-STYLE: none; WIDTH: 2.9791in;
             BACKGROUND-COLOR: #d4d0c8; VISIBILITY: visible;
             HEIGHT: 0in; POSITION: relative" />
               </xsl:if>
    - <DIV style="BORDER-STYLE: none; WIDTH: 2.9791in;
      BACKGROUND-COLOR: #d4d0c8; VISIBILITY: visible; HEIGHT:
      0.6145in; POSITION: relative">
      - <SPAN class="Style0" style="LEFT: 1.3333in; TOP:
          0.0833in; WIDTH: 1.6041in; HEIGHT: 0.1979in;
          OVERFLOW: hidden; POSITION: absolute">
        <xsl:eval no-
            entities="true">Format(GetValue("SystemId",
            200),"" ,"")</xsl:eval>
        </SPAN>

        …
        </DIV>

      …
      </xsl:for-each>

    </BODY>
  </HTML>

- <xsl:script>
  - <![CDATA[
    'variable declaration
    dim cNodes
    dim iCurrNode
```

```
    ...
function CacheCurrentNode(objNode)
    set objCurrNode = objNode
    CacheCurrentNode = ""
end function
                    ...
    ]]>
  </xsl:script>

  </xsl:template>
</xsl:stylesheet>
```

Table 11.3 Syntax in .xsl File

Syntax	Meaning
<xsl:stylesheet>	Defines a top-level stylesheet element used to hold other style elements.
<xsl:template match="/">	Defines an output with HTML tags and text. match="/" means the process starts at the beginning of the XML data file. The xsl works only on the context that has been matched.
<HTML>	Defines a document as an HTML document.
<HEAD>	Defines the document title.
<META>	Passes the document's hidden information to clients and servers. No closing tag is needed.
<STYLE>	Defines the style rules.
<BODY>	Defines the document body.
<xsl:for-each>	Creates a for-loop and applies the template repeatedly.
<xsl:eval>	Evaluates the expression in a scripting language.
<xsl:if>	Defines an if-condition block.
<DIV>	Defines an HTML block to format several paragraphs as a unit.
<SPAN>	Defines an inline text container.
<xsl:script>	Defines a script block.

More syntax is used in .xsl files. The meanings of commonly used syntax in an .xsl file are listed in Table 11.3.

Once data in a database table, form, or report are exported to an XML file, they can be displayed on a Web page or shared by many other database applications. In the next few sections, you will first learn how to export and import XML data and then how to display data stored in an XML file. After that, you will learn how to develop an XML Web service to allow other people to share data over the Internet.

11.3.4 Export/Import XML Data

One of the important capabilities of XML is that it can be used as a method of exchanging data between applications. You can export data from a table, form, or report to an .xml file and then import the data stored in the .xml file to other applications. In the following example, we use Microsoft Access 2002 or later to export data from the form **Computer System Cost Form** to an .xml file. **Computer System Cost Form** is based on the view PART_COST_VIEW and is used to display the cost of each type of computer system. The data in this form are from the database Hillcrest Computing created on SQL Server. To export the data from the **Computer System Cost Form**, follow the steps below. (Note that the steps using Access 2003 are similar to those of Access 2002.)

1. To start Access, click **Start**, **All Programs**, **Microsoft Office**, and **Microsoft Office Access 2003**. Open **Mytest**. Select **Forms** in the **Objects** pane, and then select **Computer System Cost Form**. Click the **File** menu and select **Export**.
2. In the **Save as type** combo box, select **XML**. Enter **System_Cost** as the file name, and then click **Export**.
3. Check the **Data (XML), Schema of the data (XSD), and Presentation of your data (XSL)** check boxes. In addition to exporting the XML data file, you can also export the schema file that contains information about the structure of the XML data and the document stylesheet file. To configure the export file, click the **More Options** button. There are three tabs. The **Data** tab provides the options for configuring the characteristics of your data such as the coding style and the location to save your data (see Figure 11.4).

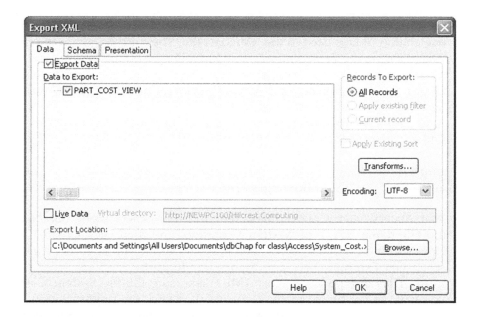

Figure 11.4   Export XML data dialog box

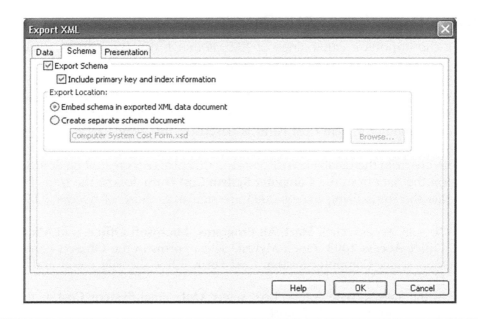

Figure 11.5   Export XML schema dialog box

The **Schema** tab provides information about the structure of your data. The schema information can be either exported to a separate file with the file extension .xsd or embedded directly into an XML data file. Here, we configure the schema information directly embedded into the XML data file (see Figure 11.5).

When other applications import the XML data, these applications will be able to validate the XML document with the schema information such as the document structure, the arrangement for data display, and the declaration of tags used in the XML data file. The third option in the Export XML dialog is the **Presentation** tab, which allows you to save the document stylesheet of the XML data in an .xsl file. The .xsl file can be used to format the presentation of your XML data on Web pages and in other database applications (see Figure 11.6).

4. After you have reviewed the types of XML files and their functions, click **OK**.

To import the data stored in the `System_Cost.xml` file to another database project, use the following steps.

1. Start **Access**, click **Create a new file**, and then select **Blank database**. In the **File name** box, type **System_Cost.mdb**, and then click **Create**.
2. Now you have a blank Access database. To import the .xml file, click **File**, select **Get External Data**, and then select **Import**.
3. In the **Files of type** box, select **XML** (make sure the file **System_Cost.xml** you want to import is highlighted), and then click the **Import** button. Click **OK** to complete the import. When selecting **Tables** in the **Objects** pane, you should have `Part_Cost_View` imported from the .xml file (see Figure 11.7).

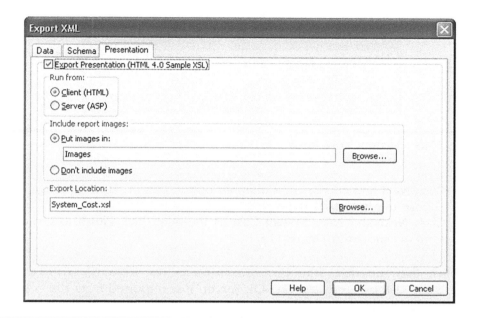

Figure 11.6 Export XML presentation dialog box

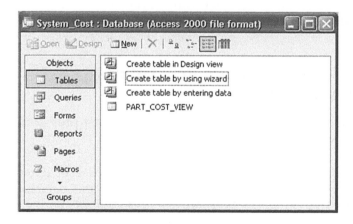

Figure 11.7 Import data from .xml file

After the data are imported into Access, we can use the data to reconstruct the form or simply use the stylesheet to display the XML data. Based on the imported data, you can create a form similar to the one in the Mytest project. To do this:

1. Click **Forms** in the **Objects** pane, and then double-click **Create form by using wizard** to open **Form Wizard**.
2. Select **Part_Cost_View** in the **Tables/Queries** combo box. Move all the fields to **Selected Fields**.

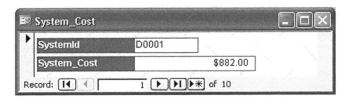

Figure 11.8   System cost form

3. Click **Next** and choose the **Columnar** option button. Click **Next** again and choose the **Industrial** style.
4. Click **Next** and enter **System Cost** as the title. Click **Finish** to create the form, as shown in Figure 11.8.

Notice that the data source of this form is not from the Hillcrest Computing database created on SQL Server; it is imported from the .xml file System_Cost.xml.

In this section, we have discussed the XML technology and its applications in a database. You have learned the definitions of the XML elements and types of files related to the XML technology. An example has been used to demonstrate how to export and import an XML file for exchanging data. For more examples on how to exchange data with the XML technology over the Internet, please read the next section.

11.4 Developing Database Applications with Visual Studio .NET

In this section, we create a three-tier database system project. We accomplish this task in three steps.

1. Create data sources such as a relational database or other types of data files. In previous chapters, we have created the database Hillcrest Computing on SQL Server. We use this database as the back-end data source.
2. Create forms and reports for front-end users. For the project in this section, we create a Windows form and a Web form with Visual Studio .NET and some other forms with InfoPath.
3. For the middle tier, a Web Server or XML Web services are developed to implement the application logic and process data transactions. Then deploy the services to the applications on the client side.

Because the database Hillcrest Computing has already been created in the previous chapters, we place our focus on the development of the client tier and the middle tier.

Visual Studio .NET is an application development tool that can be used to create Windows forms, Web forms, and reports. It can also be used to create a Web service application to serve as a middle-tier component. Visual Studio .NET provides the following features.

- It allows multiple programming languages to share the same development environment.
- It can be used to create different types of applications, such as Windows forms and Web forms in the same development environment.
- It includes several programming languages for Windows application development.
- It includes ASP.NET for Web-based application development.
- It provides ADO.NET for database accessing.
- It supports the XML standards and XML development tools.
- It has a component-based development environment. Several modules can be grouped into a project, and several projects can be grouped into a solution.

Complete coverage of Visual Studio .NET could fill several books. We are not able to cover everything about it in this book. In the following sections, we explore the topics closely related to network databases such as ADO.NET, ASP.NET, Windows forms, Web forms, and XML Web services. We first develop two applications using Visual Studio .NET: one is a Windows-based form, and the other is a Web-based form. Later, we develop an XML Web service project. A Windows application provides rich functionalities for data accessing and provides the XML parsing components for reading and writing XML data. A Web application is an ASP.NET-based technology used to build an interactive dynamic Web form.

11.4.1 Developing Windows Application

A *Windows application* is designed to run forms and reports in the Microsoft Windows environment. To take advantage of ADO.NET and ASP.NET, in this section, instead of creating forms and reports with Microsoft Access, we create them with VB.NET. The process in developing a Windows application is summarized below.

- Identify input and output variables, and then design a GUI interface for entering input values and displaying output values.
- Specify the database-accessing scheme by configuring ADO.NET.
- Identify activities involved in data manipulation, and then write code to implement these activities.

The following steps show you how to create a Windows application.

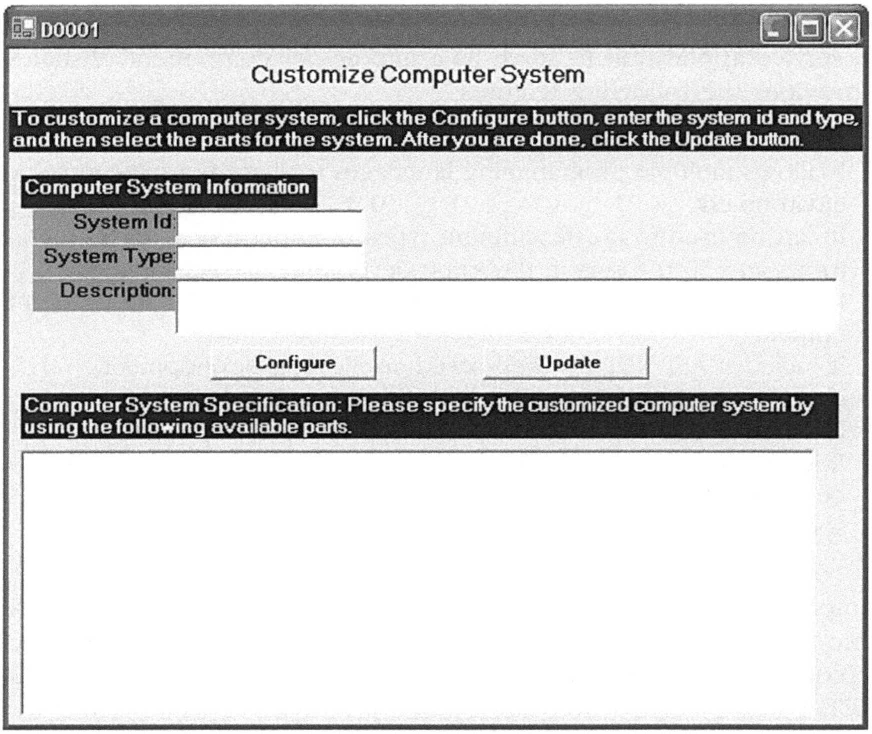

Figure 11.9   GUI design for Customize Computer System Form

GUI Design for Windows Application

As a Windows application, a Windows form created with Visual Studio .NET can be used as a front-end GUI within a three-tier structure. A Windows application can also provide rich data-processing functionalities for an application server on the middle tier.

To illustrate the development of a Windows application, we consider an example that creates a form used to customize computer systems based on customer requests. The form will display a list of available computer parts for the assembly manager and assembly workers to choose. After entering the information of a system id and computer type, the user can add computer parts to the system by clicking the parts' names listed in a list box. The input for the form will be system id, computer type, and computer system description. The output of the form will be part ids and part names. Based on the input and output, we can design the form shown in Figure 11.9.

The **Description** text box can also be used for the output to display the selected parts. The other text boxes are used for input. The list box at the bottom of the form is used to display the available parts for the system assembly. The configurations of these controls are listed in Table 11.4.

**Table 11.4   Control Specifications for Customize Computer System
Windows Form**

Control Name	Property	Meaning
lblTitle	Text Font size Font bold	Customize Computer System 12 True
lblSystemInfo	Text Font size Font bold BackColor ForeColor	Computer System Information 10 True HotTrack HighLightText
lblId	Text Font size Font bold BackColor	System Id: 10 True InactiveCaption
lblType	Text Font size Font bold BackColor	System Type: 10 True InactiveCaption
lblDesc	Text Font size Font bold BackColor	Description: 10 True InactiveCaption
lblSpecification	Text Font size Font bold BackColor ForeColor	Computer system specification: Please specify the customized computer system by using the following available parts. 10 True HotTrack HighLightText
lblInstruction	Text Font size Font bold BackColor ForeColor	To customize a computer system, click the Configure button, enter the system id and type, and then select the parts for the system. After you are done, click the Update button. 10 True HotTrack HighLightText
txtId		
txtType		
txtDesc	Multiline	True
btnConfigure	Text	Configure
btnUpdate	Text	Update
lstPart		

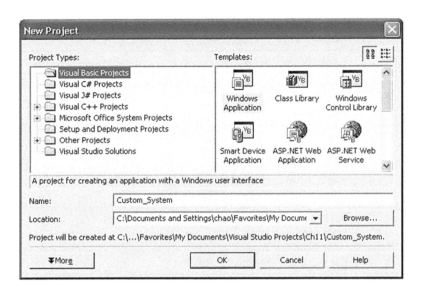

Figure 11.10   Specify new VB.NET project

After we have specified the properties of the controls, we are ready to create the GUI in VB.NET. Follow the steps below to start Visual Studio .NET, which provides a developing environment for you to edit and run VB.NET applications.

- *Launching Visual Studio .NET:* If you have installed Visual Studio .NET 2003, you can launch it with the following instruction.
  - Click **Start** and select **All Programs**. Then choose **Microsoft Visual Studio .NET 2003** and click the menu item **Microsoft Visual Studio .NET 2003** to open it.
  - Click **My Profile** on **Start Page** and select the **Visual Studio Developer** profile.
  - Click the **Projects** tab and then click the **New Project** button. Make sure that the **Visual Basic Projects** folder is highlighted. Select the **Windows Application** template, and specify the name of the application as **Custom_System** and the location path as shown in Figure 11.10. Then click **OK**.
- *Adding controls on blank form:* To add controls, move the cursor to the **Toolbox** icon ✿. When **Toolbox** is open, select the label control **A** and drag it to the form. Resize the label control and move it to the top of the form. While the label control is selected, specify the properties in the **Properties** window located at the lower-right corner of the screen. According to Table 11.4, you need to specify the properties such as **Name**, **Text**, **Font Size**, and **Font Bold**. Similarly, you can add other controls and configure them according to Table 11.4, as shown in Figure 11.11.

After the GUI is created, the next step is to specify a data-accessing scheme.

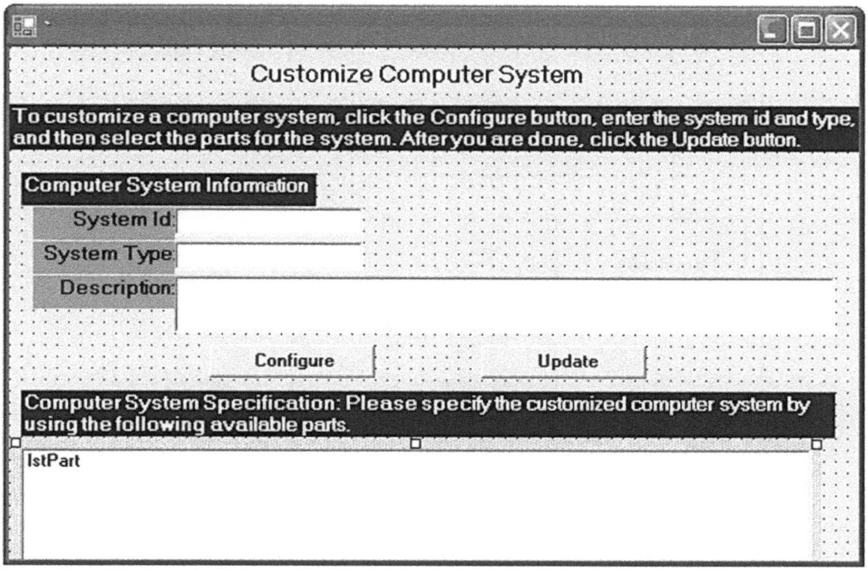

Figure 11.11 Controls on GUI

Accessing Data with ADO.NET

Compared with the traditional ADO, *ADO.NET* has the following important improvements.

- It provides a disconnected data structure. Unlike ODBC and ADO, which establish a connection to a database and keep it open while the application is running, ADO.NET first connects to a database, makes a dataset which is a copy of records, and then closes the connection. When changes are made to the dataset and an update to the database is requested, ADO.NET reconnects to the database. In this way, more users can access the same database simultaneously. By using the disconnected dataset, the traffic on the network can be reduced.
- It is integrated with the XML technology. By using XML, data communication over the Internet becomes easier. More and more database applications use XML to share data. Data in datasets created by ADO.NET are stored in the XML format. A dataset can be structured by an XML schema file and can be filled with data from an XML data file.
- The dataset created by ADO.NET has all the structures and functionalities of a regular database. A dataset can contain multiple tables that are related by foreign keys to keep the referential integrity. Tables in a dataset can be constructed from multiple databases managed by different DBMS systems. Using a dataset is equivalent to using a database created in memory on the client computer. This has made the data-accessing process much more flexible.

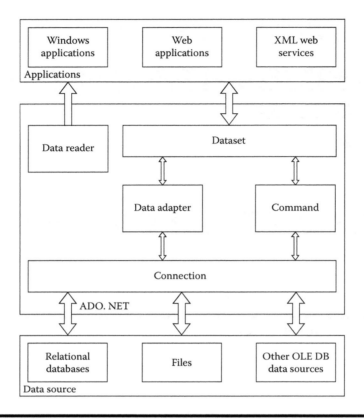

Figure 11.12   ADO.NET architecture

ADO.NET contains components that are used to handle tasks such as connecting to a data source, managing data, and generating datasets. The architecture of ADO.NET is given in Figure 11.12.

The functionalities of the objects in ADO.NET are summarized below.

- *Connection:* It is used to connect to data sources. If the data source is SQL Server, use the object SqlConnection. Otherwise, use the OleDbConnection object.
- *Data adapter:* It is used to manage communication between database applications and data sources. Use the object SqlDataAdapter for SQL Server and the object OleDbDataAdapter for other types of data sources.
- *Command:* It is used to create commands to perform some user-defined activities. There are two types of command objects. Use SqlCommand for SQL Server and OleDbCommand for other types of data sources.
- *Data reader:* It is used to retrieve read-only data from data sources.

Next, you will learn how to generate a dataset by using ADO.NET. You can use the graphical tool Server Explorer to create a dataset. In general, the dataset generation process requires three steps:

- Create a connection to your data source.
- Create a data adapter to manage data communication.
- Generate and fill a dataset for your applications.

In our example, we create a connection object connecting to our database Hillcrest Computing and then create three data adapters to manage the data in the tables COMPUTER_SYSTEM, SYSTEM_PART, and PART, respectively. The dataset is filled with the data from these three tables. The relationships among the three tables are also enforced in the dataset. The advantages of ADO.NET allow the salespeople to load the disconnected dataset onto their notebook computers and take the notebook computers with them to visit their customers. After coming back from the trips, they can update the changes made in the dataset to the database.

To connect to the Hillcrest Computing database, we create a **connection** object as shown below.

1. If Visual Studio .NET is still open, in the design window, move the cursor to the **Server Explorer** icon 🖳 located in the upper-left corner.
2. Right-click the **Data Connections** node and select **Add Connection** to open the **Data Link Properties** window.
3. Click the **Provider** tab and make sure that **Microsoft OLE DB Provider for SQL Server** is selected.
4. Click the **Connection** tab. Select your server, the database to be connected, and the database authentication method. For example, a possible configuration may look like the one in Figure 11.13, where the NEWPC8 server is connected, the Windows NT Integrated security is used, and the database Hillcrest Computing is selected.
   Note: The server name on your computer will be different. It is possible that your server name is the host computer name where you have installed your SQL Server.
5. Click the **Test Connection** button. If the database is connected, click **OK** to complete the configuration.
6. Drag the newly created connection to the form and you will see an icon labeled as **SqlConnection1**. Right-click **SqlConnection1** and select **Properties**. In the Properties window, change the **Name** property to **cnSystem**.

After the connection to the database is established, we create **data adapters**, which use the newly created connection for data manipulation. First, we create a data adapter to manage the data in the table COMPUTER_SYSTEM.

1. In the design window, move the cursor to the **Toolbox** icon on the left-hand side of the screen. When **Toolbox** is expanded, click the **Data** tab.
2. Drag **SqlDataAdapter** to the form to open **Data Adapter Configuration Wizard**.
3. Click **Next** to select the connection object. Choose the connection you have just created in the previous step, and then click **Next** to move to the **Choose a Query Type** page.

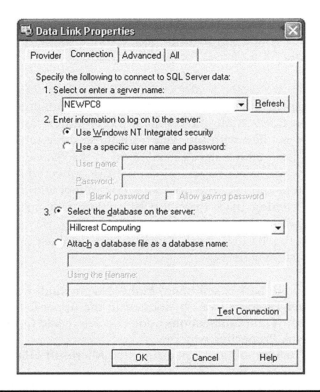

Figure 11.13   Configure connection

4. Check the **Use SQL statements** option and click **Next**. Enter the SQL statement shown in Figure 11.14.
5. Click **Next** to view the configuration result. If there is no error, click **Finish**.
6. In the design window, right-click the newly created data adapter **SqlDataAdapter1**, choose **Properties**, and change its **Name** property to **daSystem**.
7. To check if the newly created data adapter is working properly, right-click **daSystem** and select **Preview Data**. Once the Preview Data window is open, click the **Fill Dataset** button. You should see the data grid control filled with data.

Similarly, we can create the data adapters **daPart** and **daSystemPart** using the following SQL statements, respectively:

```
SELECT * FROM PART
SELECT * FROM SYSTEM_PART
```

We can generate a **dataset** for our database application by using a data adapter.

■ In the design window, right-click the data adapter **daSystem** and select **Generate Dataset**. Check all three tables COMPUTER_SYSTEM, PART, and SYSTEM_PART, and click **OK**.

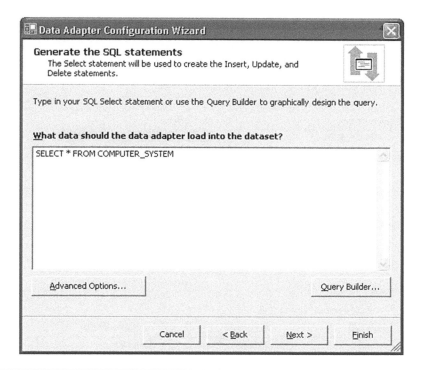

Figure 11.14   Data adapter configuration

- Right-click the newly generated dataset and rename it **CsDataSet1** for both the **Name** property and the **DataSetName** property in the **Properties** window.

In the above steps, three tables are placed in the dataset. Next, we create **relationships** among the tables in the dataset. There is a many-to-many relationship between the tables COMPUTER_SYSTEM and PART. To represent the relationship, an intersection table SYSTEM_PART is added. We use a one-to-many relationship to connect the tables COMPUTER_SYSTEM and SYSTEM_PART and another one-to-many relationship to connect the tables PART and SYSTEM_PART.

1. In the design window, right-click the dataset CsDataSet1 and select **View Schema**. You should see three table boxes.
2. Right-click the **COMPUTER_SYSTEM** box, select **Add**, and then select **New Relation** in the pop-up menu.
3. In the **Edit Relation** dialog box, specify **COMPUTER_SYSTEM** as the parent element and **SYSTEM_PART** as the child element. Select the column **SystemId** for both **Key Fields** and **Foreign Key Fields**, as shown in Figure 11.15.
4. Click **OK** to complete the configuration.
5. Similarly, create another one-to-many relationship to connect the tables **PART** and **SYSTEM_PART**. Make the table **PART** the parent element and the table **SYSTEM_PART** the child element. Use the **PartId** column for **Key Fields** and **Foreign Key Fields**.
6. After we are done, we should have a diagram like the one in Figure 11.16.

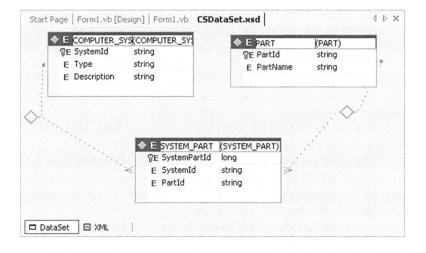

Figure 11.15   Configure one-to-many relationship

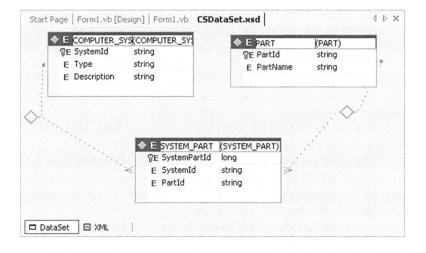

Figure 11.16   Relationship diagram

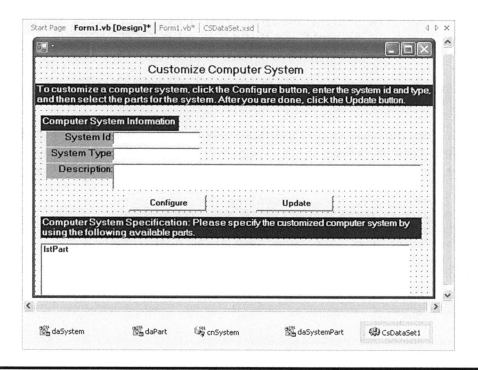

Figure 11.17   Design window for Customize Computer System application

Now we have completed the configuration for ADO.NET. The design window should look like the one in Figure 11.17.

The dataset is now ready to be filled with data. We are going to do this by using the **Fill** method that is defined in the data adapter objects.

Writing Code to Perform Activities for Windows Application

In the form **Customize Computer System**, two buttons are used to perform the following activities:

- When the form is loaded, the first task is to fill the dataset with data selected from the tables **COMPUTER_SYSTEM, PART**, and **SYSTEM_PART**.
- When the **Configure** button is clicked, a list of available computer parts will be displayed in the list box where a user can select parts to be added to the customized computer system.
- After entering information about the system id and computer type, the user can add part names to the Description text box. This can be done by clicking the part name in the list box. As soon as a part name is clicked, it will be automatically added to the Description text box.
- Once all the parts have been added to the **Description** text box, the user can click the **Update** button to insert the new computer system to the table **COMPUTER_SYSTEM** in the dataset **CsDataSet1**. Because the dataset is a fully functional database, after the new row is inserted into the table

COMPUTER_SYSTEM, the table **SYSTEM_PART** will also be updated by inserting the **SystemId** and **PartId** data related to the newly customized system.

■ After the dataset is updated, the user will be prompted to decide if the database in SQL Server should also be updated. If the **Yes** button is clicked, the corresponding tables in the data source will be updated.

We write the code to perform these activities. First, we write the **code** for the **Form_Load procedure**. In the design window, double-click an empty spot on the form to open the code window. Enter the code as shown below:

```
Friend Shared alAddSystemId As New ArrayList()
Friend Shared alAddPartId As New ArrayList()

Private Sub Form1_Load(ByVal sender As System.Object, ByVal e As
    System.EventArgs) Handles MyBase.Load

    If Me.cnSystem.State <> ConnectionState.Open Then
      Me.cnSystem.Open()
    End If

    Me.daPart.Fill(CsDataSet1.PART)
    Me.daSystem.Fill(CsDataSet1.COMPUTER_SYSTEM)
    Me.daSystemPart.Fill(CsDataSet1.SYSTEM_PART)
End Sub
```

The code first verifies if the connection to the database has been established. If not, it will open the connection. The keyword **Me** stands for the current form. Three data adapters, **daPart**, **daSystem**, and **daSystemPart**, are used to fill the three tables in the dataset **CsDataSet1**.

Now we write the **code** for the **Configure** button. The activities invoked by the **Configure** button will retrieve data from the `PartId` and `PartName` columns in the table `PART` generated in the dataset and then add the data to the list box. To make it easier for the user to read, we display the two columns side by side in the list box. To write the code for these activities, double-click the **Configure** button in the design window and enter the following code into the **Click Event** procedure:

```
Private Sub btnConfigure_Click(ByVal sender As System.Object, ByVal
    e As System.EventArgs) Handles btnConfigure.Click

  Dim strCol(2) As String
  Dim intColCounter As Integer

  'Clear the text boxes
  txtId.Clear()
  txtType.Clear()
  txtDesc.Clear()

  'Create a data table and rows
  Dim PartTable As DataTable
  PartTable = CsDataSet1.PART
```

```
    Dim PartRow As DataRow

    'Insert column title to the list box
    lstPart.Items.Add("PartId" & vbTab & vbTab & "PartName")

    'Insert PartId and PartName to the list box
    For Each PartRow In PartTable.Rows
        Dim PartCol As DataColumn
        intColCounter = 0
        For Each PartCol In PartTable.Columns
           strCol(intColCounter) = PartRow(PartCol)
           intColCounter = intColCounter + 1
        Next PartCol
        lstPart.Items.Add(strCol(0) & vbTab & strCol(1))
    Next PartRow
End Sub
```

The code first clears up the text boxes and then instantiates a **DataTable** object to hold the **PART** table. It also declares the **DataRow** object **PartRow** and the **DataColumn** object **PartCol** for retrieving individual elements from the **DataTable** object. The code adds a title line to the list box and then uses a double for-loop to assign each element in a row of the table **PART** to the array **strCol**. The **strCol** array is then used in the **Add** method to add a new row including **PartId** and **PartName** to the list box.

Next we write the **code** for the **SelectedIndexChanged** event. When you click a new row in the list box, the SelectedIndexChange event will be fired. By using this event, we can add selected items to the Description text box. Double-click the list box **lstPart** and enter the following code:

```
Private Sub lstPart_SelectedIndexChanged(ByVal sender As
    System.Object, ByVal e As System.EventArgs) Handles
    lstPart.SelectedIndexChanged

    Dim strSubstring As String
    Dim strPartName As String
    Dim strPartId As String

    Dim SystemTable As DataTable
    SystemTable = CsDataSet1.COMPUTER_SYSTEM

'Find the row specified by txtId.
    Dim SystemRow As DataRow = SystemTable.Rows.Find(txtId.Text)

'Verify if a system id and type have been entered.
    If (Microsoft.VisualBasic.Len(txtId.Text) = 0 Or
    Microsoft.VisualBasic.Len(txtType.Text) = 0) Then
        MsgBox("Please enter the new system id and type",
    MsgBoxStyle.Critical, "Missing Information")
    ElseIf (Not SystemRow Is Nothing) Then
'Inform the user that the system id already exists
        MsgBox("The system already exists. Please enter a new system
    Id", MsgBoxStyle.Critical, "Missing Information")
    Else
```

```
'Select the parts to be added to the description of a computer system
          strSubstring =
   Microsoft.VisualBasic.RTrim(lstPart.SelectedItem())
       strPartName = Microsoft.VisualBasic.Mid(strSubstring, 12)
       strPartId = Microsoft.VisualBasic.Left(strSubstring, 7)
       strPartId = Microsoft.VisualBasic.RTrim(strPartId)

'Add a system id and part id to the ArrayList object
       alAddSystemId.Add(txtId.Text)
       alAddPartId.Add(strPartId)

       If (Microsoft.VisualBasic.Len(txtDesc.Text) = 0) Then
         txtDesc.Text = txtDesc.Text + strPartName
       Else
         txtDesc.Text = txtDesc.Text + ", " + strPartName
       End If
   End If

End Sub
```

The code first defines a **Datatable** object as **SystemTable** to hold the data in the table **COMPUTER_SYSTEM**. The **Find** method is used to search for the row based on the content in the text box **txtId**. If the text box is empty, prompt the user to enter a system id. If the system id entered in the text box already exists in the dataset, inform the user so that he or she can re-enter a different system id. The **Left**, **Mid**, and **RTrim** methods in **Microsoft.VisualBasic** are used to extract the part id and part name from the row returned by the **SelectedItem** method. Add the system id and the corresponding part id to the global **ArrayList**, which will be used to update the dataset later. One of the advantages of the **ArrayList** object is that it allows the automatic increasing of the array dimension. This is a desired property for our program because the dimension of the array that is the total number of parts is dynamically determined by the user. The last **If ... Else...End If** structure is used to add the part name to the **Description** text box. If the **Description** text box is empty, it adds the part name directly. If the **Description** text box is not empty, it enters a comma and then appends the part name in the text box.

Now we write the **code** for the **Update** button. When the **Update** button is clicked, a new row including system id, system type, and system description is inserted into the table COMPUTER_SYSTEM in the dataset. Meanwhile, the related system id and part id are inserted into the table SYSTEM_PART in the dataset. Then a message is displayed to the user asking if he or she wants to update the tables in the database. When the **Yes** button is clicked, the corresponding tables in the database will be updated based on the changes to the dataset. Double-click the button **Update** and enter the following code to the **Click Event** procedure:

```
Private Sub btnUpdate_Click(ByVal sender As System.Object, ByVal
   e As System.EventArgs) Handles btnUpdate.Click

   Dim intCounter As Integer
   Dim AddSystemPart As DataRow
```

```
Dim AddSystem As DataRow

'Insert a new system in the table COMPUTER_SYSTEM
AddSystem = CsDataSet1.Tables("COMPUTER_SYSTEM").NewRow
AddSystem("SystemId") = txtId.Text
AddSystem("Type") = txtType.Text
AddSystem("Description") = txtDesc.Text
CsDataSet1.Tables("COMPUTER_SYSTEM").Rows.Add(AddSystem)

'Insert the corresponding parts in the table SYSTEM_PART
For intCounter = 0 To alAddSystemId.Count - 1
    AddSystemPart = CsDataSet1.Tables("SYSTEM_PART").NewRow
    AddSystemPart("SystemId") = alAddSystemId(intCounter)
    AddSystemPart("PartId") = alAddPartId(intCounter)
    CsDataSet1.Tables("SYSTEM_PART").Rows.Add(AddSystemPart)
Next
Dim intResponse As Integer
intResponse = MsgBox("Would you like to update the database?",
MsgBoxStyle.YesNo, "Database Update")
If (intResponse = 6) Then

    'Update the table COMPUTER_SYSTEM in the database
    Dim dsChanges As DataSet =
Me.CsDataSet1.GetChanges(DataRowState.Added)
    Dim dtInsertSystem As DataTable =
Me.CsDataSet1.Tables("COMPUTER_SYSTEM").GetChanges(DataRowState
.Added)
    If Not dtInsertSystem Is Nothing Then
      Me.daSystem.Update(dsChanges.Tables("COMPUTER_SYSTEM"))
    End If

    'Update the table SYSTEM_PART in the database
    Dim dtInsertSystemPart As DataTable =
Me.CsDataSet1.Tables("SYSTEM_PART").GetChanges(DataRowState.Add
ed)
    If Not dtInsertSystemPart Is Nothing Then
      Me.daSystemPart.Update(dsChanges.Tables("SYSTEM_PART"))
    End If
End If

End Sub
```

At the beginning of the code, a new row **AddSystem** is created. The content in the text boxes **txtId**, **txtType**, and **txtDesc** is added to the row object **AddSystem**. Then **AddSystem** is added to the table **COMPUTE_SYSTEM** in the dataset. Similarly, the system id and part id stored in the global **ArrayList** are inserted into the table **SYSTEM_PART**. After the data are inserted into the tables in the dataset, a message box is used to ask the user if he or she wants to update the database. When the **Yes** button is clicked, the number 6 (as defined in VB.NET) is returned. Then the code declares a **DataSet** object **dsChanges**, which will be used to hold the changes made to the dataset. If there is a change, the data adapter **daSystem** is used to update the table **COMPUTER_SYSTEM** in the database. Similarly, the data adapter **daSystemPart** is used to update the table **SYSTEM_PART** in the database.

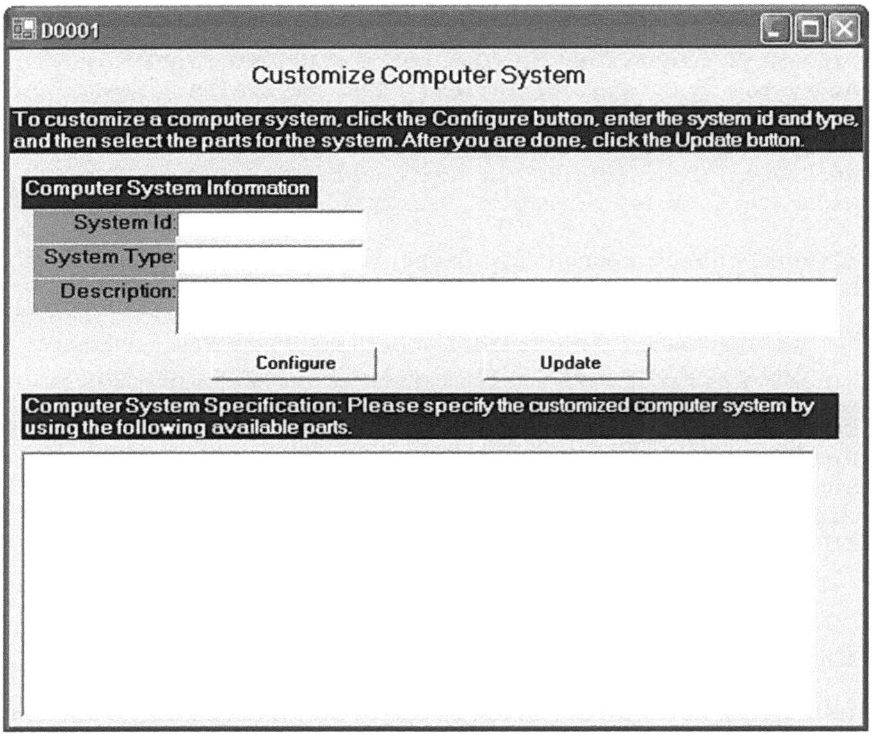

Figure 11.18　Customize Computer System form

Testing Windows Application Project

After the code is entered, save the code and click the **Start** button ▶ on the toolbar. If everything works correctly, we should get the screen shown in Figure 11.18. Click the **Configure** button. Enter **D0008** for System Id and **Desktop** for System Type. In the list box, click the part names needed for the customized computer system as shown in Figure 11.19. After the parts are added to the customized computer, click the **Update** button. When the Message window appears, click **Yes** to update the database. You may verify the update in Enterprise Manager.

　　In the above section, you have learned how to create a Windows application as the front-end GUI. ADO.NET is used to generate the dataset, which is a fully functional database in memory. We have written the code to carry out the application activities. In the next section, we study another important type of database application, the Web database application.

11.4.2　Developing Web Application

A *Web application* is designed to run forms and reports on a Web page that communicates with a Web server for data manipulation. With the fast development of electronic commerce, Web-based data access has become an

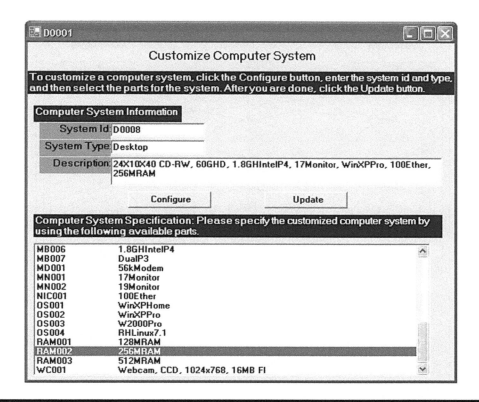

Figure 11.19 Add parts to customized computer

important database application. The Internet technology has changed the way data are accessed and used. Internet-based applications enable database users to perform tasks such as online shopping, banking, stock trading, hotel reservations, and teaching. A network database faces the following challenges when performing Web application tasks:

- It must provide support to many different types of database applications and services through the Internet.
- It must support database applications written in different programming languages.
- It must make DBMS systems from different vendors work together.
- It must be backward-compatible to previous versions of DBMS systems.
- It must be able to handle a large workload volume.
- It must handle a large number of users logging on to the database at the same time.

A Web application is ideal for the situation in which a database application is developed in an environment where there are heterogeneous operating systems such as Windows, UNIX, and Macintosh. It works on an organization's network or in an environment where some of the computers are not part of the organization's network; for example, some of the employees may want to access data from their home computers.

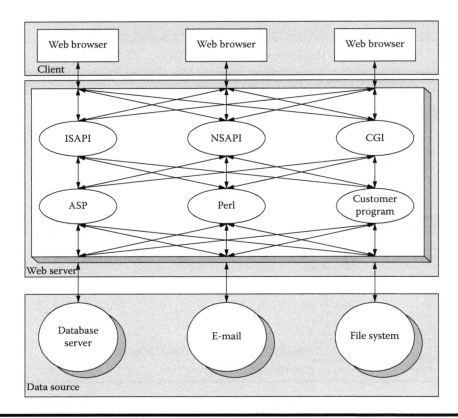

Figure 11.20   Three-tier architecture for Web-based network database

The three-tier client/server architecture is one of the solutions that meet the requirements of network-based databases, especially Web-based databases. A Web browser works as the front end with Web pages for displaying and entering data. Most of the data-processing tools will be placed on the middle tier where the Web server is installed. The back-end database provides data storage and functionalities to handle database security and to manage a large amount of data. The three-tier architecture of a Web-based network database is illustrated in Figure 11.20.

When a browser communicates with a Web server, the parties involved in the communication must agree on a set of rules to exchange messages. The set of rules used for Internet communication is called *HyperText Transfer Protocol* (HTTP). In the next few paragraphs, we take a closer look at Web browsers and Web servers.

A *Web browser* works as the front end. It contains Web pages to display and enter data. A Web browser is installed on a client computer and is used to present Web pages. When Web pages are retrieved from a Web server, the Web browser interprets markup languages such as HTML and XML, whose code is used to specify the appearance and behavior of a Web page. The other function of a Web browser is to run the client extensions such as Plug-ins and ActiveX.

A *Web server* is considered the middle tier in the three-tier client/server architecture. It can carry out the following tasks:

- Interpret requests from Web browsers.
- Return responses to the browsers.
- Execute programming code.
- Interact with data providers.

The commonly used Web servers are *Apache Web Server* for the UNIX operating system and *Internet Information Services* (IIS) for the Windows operating system. In the examples given in later sections, we use IIS as our Web server.

In IIS, there is an interface called *Internet Server Application Program Interface* (ISAPI). ISAPI is a DLL program that is used to enhance the compatibility of a Web server; that is, it allows *Active Server Pages* (ASP) and many other custom programs to process HTML messages. Based on HTML messages, an ASP page uses the information retrieved from the database to build Web pages dynamically and then passes the Web pages to the client through the Web server IIS. If you have the Windows 2000 Professional operating system or later installed on your computer, IIS and ISAPI are built into the operating system.

NSAPI, which is part of the Netscape Web server, performs similar tasks as ISAPI. NSAPI supports JSP, which is a Java-based program and has functionalities similar to ASP. NSAPI and *Common Gateway Interface* (CGI) are used with UNIX-based Web servers. When CGI is used, it requires a Web application to establish a communication session that takes more resources. The programming language Perl is often used with CGI to create Web pages.

Now that we have briefly reviewed some basic Web application concepts, we build a Web application similar to the Windows application Customize Computer System developed in the previous section. The key step to establishing a Web database application is developing ASP programs, which are used to create Web pages. ASP.NET is one of the tools that can help us accomplish the task. In a similar environment, Visual Studio .NET not only allows us to develop Windows applications but also to develop Web applications. With ASP.NET, we can create dynamic Web pages by following a procedure that is similar to the procedure used in developing the Windows application. That is, all the knowledge and skills used in developing the Windows application in the previous section can be reused in developing the Web application. Compared with the traditional ASP technique, it takes much less time to build a new Web application if we have already developed a similar Windows application. Before we can play around with ASP.NET, we need to make sure that the middle tier, Internet Information Services (IIS), is running properly.

Before you start the Web application–developing process shown below, verify that Internet Information Services (IIS) 5.0 or later is running on your computer. As mentioned earlier, IIS will serve as the middle tier for our database application. If you have Windows 2000 Professional, Windows XP Professional, or Windows 2000 Server or later running on your computer, the IIS server should already be included. In later versions of Windows, for security reasons, IIS may not be automatically installed on your computer. If it is not, go to **Control Panel**, click **Add or Remove Programs**, **Add/Remove Windows Components**, and check the box **Internet Information Services (IIS)**. For our Web application development, we assume that you have Windows 2000 Professional or Windows XP Professional installed on your PC with the IIS server running.

Similar to the Windows form developed previously in the design window, ASP.NET uses a **design page** to hold the controls for a Web form. ASP.NET automatically generates the HTML code to display controls on a Web browser. Behind the design page, the VB.NET code is used to perform the activities for the controls. Using the following steps, you will create the **Customize Computer System** application as a Web application. Similar to Windows applications, there are three steps in developing Web applications.

- Identify input and output variables, and then design a GUI for entering input values and displaying output values.
- Specify database accessing by configuring ADO.NET.
- Identify activities involved in data manipulation, and then write code to implement these activities.

In the following paragraphs, we go over the details of each step through the same example used in developing the Windows application.

GUI Design for Web Application

The following instruction shows how to start ASP.NET and how to place controls on the design page.

1. Open **Microsoft Visual Studio .NET**. On **Start Page**, click the **New Project** button. In the **New Project** dialog, select the **ASP.NET Web Application** template. Then, in the **Location** text box, enter the path and file name, for example, `http://localhost/Custom_System_Asp`, as shown in Figure 11.21. After you have specified the path and filename, click **OK** to start the project. If you like, you may name the file here slightly differently from the one in the Windows application.
2. Double-click the file **WebForm1.aspx** in the **Solution Explorer** window on the right-hand side of the design window. On the Web form design page, move the cursor to **Toolbox** on the left-hand side of your screen and click the **Web Forms** tab. You should see a list of available controls. The controls used in this application and their properties are listed in Table 11.5.
3. Drag the controls needed for this application to the design page and configure the properties according to the above table. Your design page should look like the one in Figure 11.22.

Because the connection has been established in the previous section, next we focus on developing data adapters for the Web application.

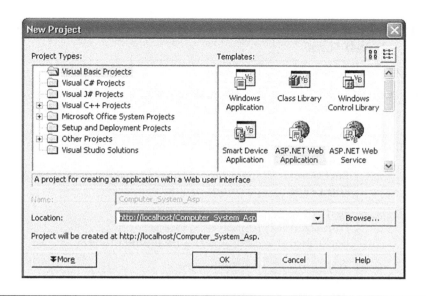

Figure 11.21   Create ASP.NET Web application

Creating Data Adapters and Generating Dataset

Our data adapters select all columns from each table involved in this application, so we can use another way to create the data adapters.

1. If **Visual Studio .NET** is still open, in the design window, move the cursor to the **Server Explorer** icon located in the upper-left corner and expand the **Tables** node in the data connection to the database **Hillcrest Computing**. Drag the table **COMPUTER_SYSTEM** to the design page. The new connection object **SqlConnection1** and the data adapter object **SqlDataAdapter1** should appear at bottom of your screen, as shown in Figure 11.23.
2. Right-click **SqlConnection1** and select **Properties**. Change the **Name** property to **cnSystem**. In the same way, rename the data adapter **daSystem**.
3. Similarly, drag the tables **PART** and **SYSTEM_PART** to the design page. Rename the data adapters **daPart** and **daSystemPart**, respectively.
4. Right-click **daSystem** and select **Generate DataSet**. In the text box of the **New** option, enter **CsDataSet1** as the new dataset name. Check all three tables **COMPUTER_SYSTEM**, **PART**, and **SYSTEM_PART**. Click **OK** to generate the new dataset.
5. Right-click **CsDataSet11** and select **Properties**. Change the **Name** property to **CsDataSet1**.
6. Right-click **CsDataSet1** and select **View Schema**. You should see that the three tables are in the dataset. To create the relationship between the tables **COMPUTER_SYSTEM** and **SYSTEM_PART**, right-click the **COMPUTER_SYSTEM** box, select **Add**, and then select **New Relation**. In the **Edit Relation** dialog, select the table **COMPUTER_SYSTEM** as the parent element and the table **SYSTEM_PART** as the child element. Use **SystemId**

Table 11.5   Control Specifications for Customize Computer System Web Form

Control ID	Property	Meaning
lblTitle	Text Font size Font bold	Customize computer system Medium True
lblSystemInfo	Text Font size BackColor ForeColor	Computer system information Small Navy White
lblId	Text Font size BackColor	System id: Small #COCOFF (the lightest blue)
lblType	Text Font size BackColor	System type: Small #COCOFF
lblDesc	Text Font size BackColor	Description: Small #COCOFF
lblSpecification	Text Font size BackColor ForeColor	Computer system specification: Please specify the customized computer system by using the following parts. Small Navy White
lblInstruction	Text Font size Font bold BackColor ForeColor	To customize a computer system, click the Configure button, enter the system id and type, and then select the parts for the system. When you are done, click the Update button. Small True Navy White
txtId		
txtType		
txtDesc	TextMode	MultiLine
btnConfigure	Text	Configure
btnUpdate	Text	Update
lstPart	AutoPostBack	True

in both **Key Fields** and **Foreign Key Fields**. Click **OK**. Similarly, create the relationship for the tables **PART** and **SYSTEM_PART**. Use **PART** as the parent element and **SYSTEM_PART** as the child element. Use **PartId** for both **Key Fields** and **Foreign Key Fields**.

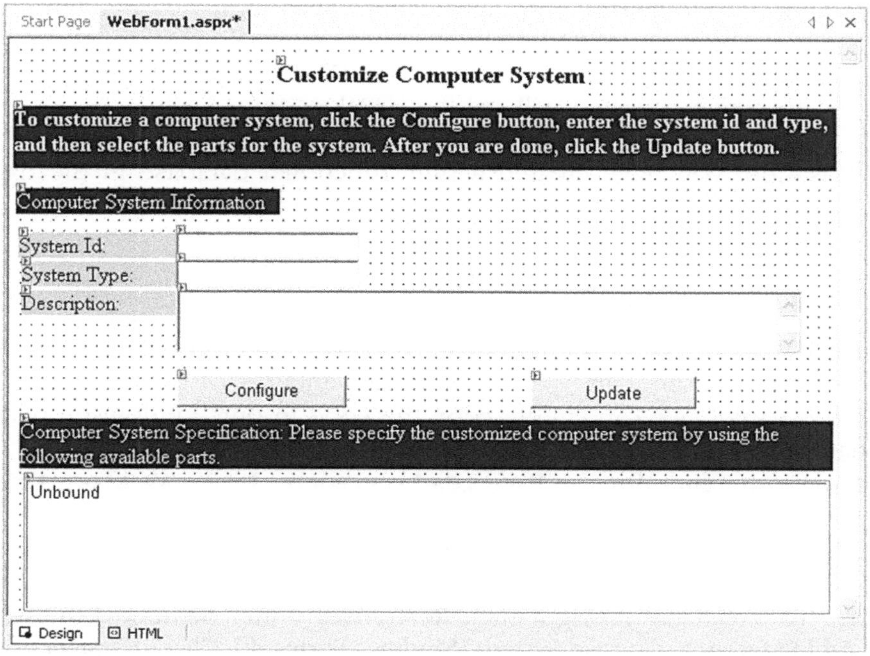

Figure 11.22   Controls on design page for Web application

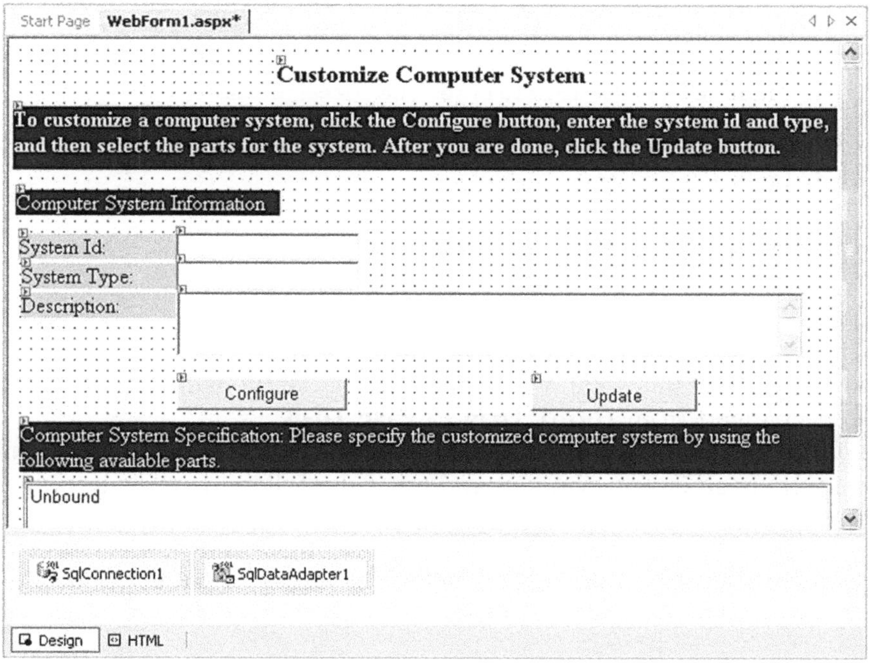

Figure 11.23   Create new connection and data adapter objects

7. Go back to **WeForm1.aspx**. To make the Web form viewable through the Internet browser, ASP.NET automatically generates corresponding HTML code. To view the HTML code, click the HTML tab in the lower-left corner of the screen and you will see the HTML code.

At this step, you have created a fully functional database in the dataset. Next, we add some code to perform activities for the Web application.

Writing Code to Perform Activities for Web Application

The code used in the Web application is almost identical to the one for the Windows application. This is one of the advantages of Visual Studio .NET mentioned earlier. We can simply copy the code in our Windows application and make some minor changes for the Web application.

We write the **code** for the **Page_Load procedure**. In the **WebForm1** design page, double-click an empty spot on the page and the code window will open. Copy and paste the code from the corresponding **Form1_Load** procedure in the Windows application.

Note: To avoid errors, right-click **References** under **Solution Explorer** and select **Add Reference**. Choose **System.Windows.Forms.dll**. Click the **Select** button and then **OK**.

```
Friend Shared alAddSystemId As New ArrayList()
Friend Shared alAddPartId As New ArrayList()

Private Sub Page_Load(ByVal sender As System.Object, ByVal e As
    System.EventArgs) Handles MyBase.Load

    'Put user code to initialize the page here
    If Me.CnSystem.State <> ConnectionState.Open Then
        Me.CnSystem.Open()
    End If

    Me.daPart.Fill(CsDataSet1.PART)
    Me.daSystem.Fill(CsDataSet1.COMPUTER_SYSTEM)
    Me.daSystemPart.Fill(CsDataSet1.SYSTEM_PART)
End Sub
```

You can see that this code is the same except that the name of the procedure has been changed from **Form1_Load** to **Page_Load**.

To write the **code** for the **Configure button**, double-click the **Configure** button in the page design window and enter the following code into the **Click Event** procedure for the Configure button:

```
Private Sub btnConfigure_Click(ByVal sender As System.Object, ByVal
    e As System.EventArgs) Handles btnConfigure.Click

    Dim strCol(2) As String
    Dim intColCounter As Integer

    'Create a data table and rows
```

```
    Dim PartTable As DataTable
    PartTable = CsDataSet1.PART
    Dim PartRow As DataRow

    'Insert column title to the list box
    lstPart.Items.Add("PartId" & vbTab & vbTab & "PartName")

    'Insert PartId and PartName to the list box
    For Each PartRow In PartTable.Rows
        Dim PartCol As DataColumn
        intColCounter = 0
        For Each PartCol In PartTable.Columns
           strCol(intColCounter) = PartRow(PartCol)
           intColCounter = intColCounter + 1
        Next PartCol
        lstPart.Items.Add(strCol(0) & vbTab & strCol(1))
    Next PartRow

End Sub
```

The above code is almost the same as the one in the Windows application except that we have removed three lines that clear the text boxes **txtId**, **txtType**, and **txtDesc**.

To write the **code** for the **SelectedIndexChanged event,** double-click the list box **lstPart** and enter the following code:

```
Private Sub lstPart_SelectedIndexChanged(ByVal sender As
    System.Object, ByVal e As System.EventArgs) Handles
    lstPart.SelectedIndexChanged

    Dim strSubstring As String
    Dim strPartName As String
    Dim strPartId As String

    Dim SystemTable As DataTable
    SystemTable = CsDataSet1.COMPUTER_SYSTEM

'Find the row specified by strSystemId.
    Dim SystemRow As DataRow = SystemTable.Rows.Find(txtId.Text)

'Verify if system id and type have been entered.
    If (Microsoft.VisualBasic.Len(txtId.Text) = 0 Or
    Microsoft.VisualBasic.Len(txtType.Text) = 0) Then
        Windows.Forms.MessageBox.Show("Please enter the new system
    id and type", "Missing Information",
    Windows.Forms.MessageBoxButtons.OK,
    Windows.Forms.MessageBoxIcon.Error,
    Windows.Forms.MessageBoxDefaultButton.Button1,
    Windows.Forms.MessageBoxOptions.ServiceNotification)
    ElseIf (Not SystemRow Is Nothing) Then

'Inform user that the system id already exists
        Windows.Forms.MessageBox.Show("The system already exists.
    Please enter a new system Id", "Missing Information",
    Windows.Forms.MessageBoxButtons.OK,
```

```
        Windows.Forms.MessageBoxIcon.Error,
        Windows.Forms.MessageBoxDefaultButton.Button1,
        Windows.Forms.MessageBoxOptions.ServiceNotification)
      Else
   'Select the parts to add to the description of a computer system
        strSubstring =
      Microsoft.VisualBasic.RTrim(lstPart.SelectedItem.Text)
        strPartName = Microsoft.VisualBasic.Mid(strSubstring, 12)
        strPartId = Microsoft.VisualBasic.Left(strSubstring, 7)
        strPartId = Microsoft.VisualBasic.RTrim(strPartId)

   'Add System id and Part id to the ArrayList objects
        alAddSystemId.Add(txtId.Text)
        alAddPartId.Add(strPartId)

        If (Microsoft.VisualBasic.Len(txtDesc.Text) = 0) Then
          txtDesc.Text = txtDesc.Text + strPartName
        Else
          txtDesc.Text = txtDesc.Text + ", " + strPartName
        End If
     End If
End Sub
```

You can copy the code from the Windows application, and there is no change to the code in this procedure. As we have seen here, ASP.NET has significantly reduced developing time compared with the traditional ASP technology.

To write the **code** for the **Update button,** double-click the **Update** button and enter the following code for the **Click Event** procedure:

```
Private Sub btnUpdate_Click(ByVal sender As System.Object, ByVal
    e As System.EventArgs) Handles btnUpdate.Click

    Dim intCounter As Integer
    Dim AddSystemPart As DataRow
    Dim AddSystem As DataRow

    'Insert a new system in the table COMPUTER_SYSTEM
    AddSystem = CsDataSet1.Tables("COMPUTER_SYSTEM").NewRow
    AddSystem("SystemId") = txtId.Text
    AddSystem("Type") = txtType.Text
    AddSystem("Description") = txtDesc.Text
    CsDataSet1.Tables("COMPUTER_SYSTEM").Rows.Add(AddSystem)

    'Insert the corresponding parts in the table SYSTEM_PART
    For intCounter = 0 To alAddSystemId.Count - 1
        AddSystemPart = CsDataSet1.Tables("SYSTEM_PART").NewRow
        AddSystemPart("SystemId") = alAddSystemId(intCounter)
        AddSystemPart("PartId") = alAddPartId(intCounter)
        CsDataSet1.Tables("SYSTEM_PART").Rows.Add(AddSystemPart)
    Next

    Dim intResponse As Integer
```

```
intResponse = Windows.Forms.MessageBox.Show("Would you like to
update the database?", "Database Update",
Windows.Forms.MessageBoxButtons.YesNo,
Windows.Forms.MessageBoxIcon.Question,
Windows.Forms.MessageBoxDefaultButton.Button1,
Windows.Forms.MessageBoxOptions.ServiceNotification)
If (intResponse = 6) Then

    'Update the table COMPUTER_SYSTEM in the database
    Dim dsChanges As DataSet =
Me.CsDataSet1.GetChanges(DataRowState.Added)
    Dim dtInsertSystem As DataTable =
Me.CsDataSet1.Tables("COMPUTER_SYSTEM").GetChanges(DataRowState
.Added)
    If Not dtInsertSystem Is Nothing Then
      Me.daSystem.Update(dsChanges.Tables("COMPUTER_SYSTEM"))
    End If

    'Update the table SYSTEM_PART in the database
    Dim dtInsertSystemPart As DataTable =
Me.CsDataSet1.Tables("SYSTEM_PART").GetChanges(DataRowState.Add
ed)
    If Not dtInsertSystemPart Is Nothing Then
      Me.daSystemPart.Update(dsChanges.Tables("SYSTEM_PART"))
    End If
  End If
End Sub
```

Again, there is no change in the code for the **btnUpdate_Click** event procedure.

Testing Web Application Project

Before testing, go to **Control Panel**, open **Administrative Tools**, and then open **Internet Information Services**. Expand the local computer node (each local computer name is different), and expand **Default Web Site** under the **Web Sites** folder. Right-click **Custom_System_Asp** and select **Properties**. Click the **Directory Security** tab. Click the **Edit** button and uncheck **Anonymous access**. Click **OK** to complete the configuration and close **Control Panel**. Go back to **WebForm1** of your Web application in Visual Studio .NET. Double-click **Web.config** under Solution Explorer. After the line **<authentication mode="Windows" />**, add the following line:

```
<identity impersonate="true" />
```

Then save the code. To test, click the **Start** button ▶ on the toolbar. If everything works correctly, click the **Configure** button.

Note: You need adequate privilege to access Default Web Site. If you are prevented from accessing Default Web Site, you may first log on as Administrator and allow the users who need Default Web Site to have full control of the Inetpub folder in the C drive.

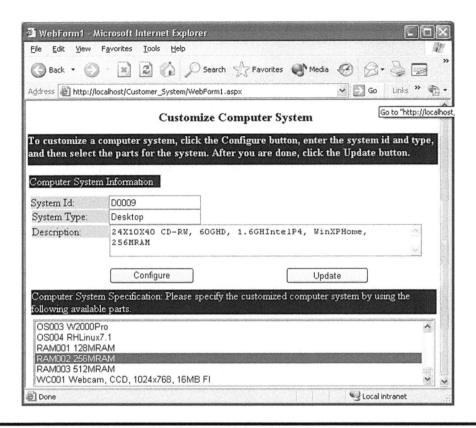

Figure 11.24   Web-based Customize Computer System form

Enter **D0009** for System Id and **Desktop** for Type. In the list box, click the parts needed for the customized computer system, as shown in Figure 11.24. After the parts are added to the customized system, click the **Update** button. When the message window appears, click **Yes** to update the database. You may verify the update in Enterprise Manager.

In this section, you have learned how to use the ASP.NET technology in developing Web-based database applications. Web-based forms allow front-end users to access a database remotely through the Internet; this has significantly extended the scope of a network database. ASP.NET enables us to create a Web-based form by using the same visual environment used in developing a Windows form. We have used the ASP.NET platform to create a Web form for Internet browsers and at the same time created the Visual Basic code to be executed on the Web server.

11.5   XML Web Services and InfoPath

One of the important database tasks is to exchange data between clients and a database server over the Internet. To access data stored on a database server, we can use data-accessing methods such as ODBC, OLE DB, and ADO, discussed in previous chapters. For a more flexible solution, XML is the language of choice for transforming various types of data. To transform data among different types of data sources and database applications over the Internet, we may create an XML Web service to supply the data and XML-compatible functions and stored procedures to implement business logic. The client can perform database operations by calling the server-side templates, user-defined functions, stored procedures, and other database objects provided by the XML Web service. The client's requests will be sent to a server that is running the Web service. The Web service executes the requested operations and returns responses to the clients. This leads to other advantages of a Web service; it allows front-end users to run highly interactive browser-based applications on the Internet while keeping these users from directly accessing the back-end database. This means the system has better security and performance because the Web service takes some business logic computation load from the database. Nowadays, due to these very neat features, Web services are quite popular.

The development of a Web service project includes two tasks: creating an XML Web service and accessing the XML Web service. Our first step is to create a Web service with Visual Studio .NET and then to develop a front-end project with InfoPath to access the Web service.

11.5.1   Creating Web Services with Visual Studio .NET

Visual Studio .NET provides convenient tools for developing Web services on a Web server. We build a Web service project using the ASP.NET Web Service template included in Visual Studio .NET. In the Web service project, we make the tables COMPUTER_SYSTEM, SYSTEM_PART, and PART from the `Hill-crest Computing` database available to front-end users. We also create some functions to help the front-end users query information about computer systems and parts used for a selected computer system. Follow the steps below to get started.

1. Open **Visual Studio .NET**. On the **Start** page, click the **New Project** button. Select **ASP.NET Web Service** in the **Templates** pane and select **Visual Basic Projects** in the **Project Types** pane. In the **Location** combo box, enter **SystemPartWS** as the Web service name shown in Figure 11.25. Then click **OK**.

2. Double-click the file **Service1.asmx** in the **Solution Explorer** pane to open the design page (if it is not already open). Press **F7** to view the code for the project. Enter the following code to import the namespaces:

```
Imports System.Web.Services
Imports System.Data.SqlClient 'required for data source
    connection
Imports System.Web      ' required for Server & Request classes
Imports System.IO       ' required for File I/O operations
Imports System.Xml      ' required for XmlDocument operations
```

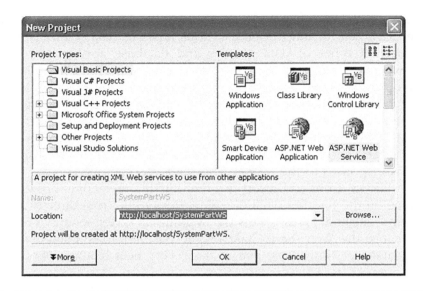

Figure 11.25   Create new Web service project

3. To connect to the database `Hillcrest Computing`, add the following database connection string between **Web Services Designer Generated Code** and **End Class**.

```
Dim CnSystem As New SqlConnection("Persist Security Info=
    False;Integrated
    Security=SSPI;server=NEWPC100;database=Hillcrest Computing")
```

In the above code, **server** is assigned the name of the PC and **database** is assigned the database **Hillcrest Computing**. When entering code, you may want to type all the code in a single line.

4. Enter the following code below the previous code to create a function that returns all system ids. Later, these system ids will be assigned to a combo box for selection.

```
<WebMethod()> _
Public Function GetSystemId() As Xml.XmlDataDocument

    Return GetXMLInfo("SystemId", "COMPUTER_SYSTEM", "")

End Function
```

The function has no input parameter and returns an **Xml.XmlDataDocument** object. In the **Return** statement, the function calls another function by passing the values **SystemId** for the column list and **COMPUTER_SYSTEM** for the table name in a query. The code for the function **GetXMLInfo** is given as the following:

```
<WebMethod()> _
```

```
Private Function GetXMLInfo(ByVal ColumnList As String, ByVal
    TableList As String, ByVal WhereCondition As String) As
    Xml.XmlDataDocument

    'Create a data adapter to query the database
    Dim daSystem As New SqlDataAdapter("SELECT " + ColumnList +
    " FROM " + TableList + " " + WhereCondition, CnSystem)
    'Create a dataset and fill it with the query result
    Dim ds As New Xml.XmlDataDocument()
    daSystem.Fill(ds.DataSet)
    Return ds

End Function
```

In the above code, a data adapter **daSystem** is created to query the database and a dataset **ds** is created to hold data returned by the query.

5. Create a function to return information about parts used in a specified computer system:

```
<WebMethod()> _
Public Function GetParts(ByVal SystemId As String) As
    Xml.XmlDataDocument
    Dim strColumn As String
    Dim strTable As String
    Dim strWhere As String

    strColumn = "P.PartId, PartName"
    strTable = "SYSTEM_PART S, PART P"
    strWhere = "WHERE S.SystemId = '" + SystemId + "' AND S.PartId
    = P.PartId"
    Return GetXMLInfo(strColumn, strTable, strWhere)

End Function
```

This function will return the part ids and part names of the parts used in the computer system specified by the parameter **SystemId**.

6. Create a function that will return the information about a specified computer system:

```
<WebMethod()> _
Public Function GetSystemInfo(ByVal SystemId As String) As
    Xml.XmlDataDocument
    Dim strColumn As String
    Dim strTable As String
    Dim strWhere As String

strColumn = "Type, Description"
    strTable = "COMPUTER_SYSTEM C"
    strWhere = "WHERE C.SystemId = '" + SystemId + "'"
    Return GetXMLInfo(strColumn, strTable, strWhere)

End Function
```

This function will return the type and description of a specified computer system.

7. The next function will insert a new row into the table **COMPUTER_SYSTEM** and then insert part ids corresponding to the parts used in a specified computer system into the **SYSTEM_PART** table. Because the data entered into an InfoPath form are used to construct the new row, this program includes the code to connect the InfoPath page.

```
<WebMethod()> _
Public Function SubmitInfoPathDocument(ByVal objXmlDoc As
   XmlDocument)

   Dim dsSystem As New DataSet()
'Update the table COMPUTER_SYSTEM
'Create a new data adapter daSystem and fill the dataset dsSystem
   Dim daSystem As New SqlDataAdapter("SELECT * FROM
   COMPUTER_SYSTEM", CnSystem)
   daSystem.Fill(dsSystem)
'Create a new datarow
   Dim dcSystem As New SqlCommandBuilder(daSystem)
   Dim newRow As DataRow = dsSystem.Tables(0).newRow
'Assign the submitted XML document objDocument to SystemDoc
   Dim SystemDoc As New XmlDocument()
   SystemDoc = objXmlDoc
'Save the submitted XML document to a file in the virtual
   directory
   Dim strFileName As String
   strFileName = Server.MapPath(".") + "\" + "SubmittedDoc.xml"
   If File.Exists(strFileName) Then
       File.Delete(strFileName)
   End If
   SystemDoc.Save(strFileName)

'The last part of the name space is the time when you established
   'the submission connection.
'You can find the time in the file SubmittedDoc.xml
   Dim Namemgr As New XmlNamespaceManager(SystemDoc.NameTable)
   Namemgr.AddNamespace("my", _
            "http://schemas.microsoft.com/office/infopath/2003/
   myXSD/2003-12-29T17:25:38")

'Add a new row
   newRow("SystemId") = SystemDoc.SelectSingleNode("//
   my:txtSystemId", Namemgr).InnerText
   newRow("Type") = SystemDoc.SelectSingleNode("//my:txtType",
   Namemgr).InnerText
   newRow("Description") = SystemDoc.SelectSingleNode("//
   my:txtDesc", Namemgr).InnerText
   dsSystem.Tables(0).Rows.Add(newRow)
'Update the dataset dsSystem
   daSystem.Update(dsSystem)

'Update the table SYSTEM_PART
'Create a new data adapter daSystemPart and fill the dataset
   dsSystem
```

```
    Dim daSystemPart As New SqlDataAdapter("SELECT * FROM
    SYSTEM_PART", CnSystem)
    daSystemPart.Fill(dsSystem)

    Dim dcSystemPart As New SqlCommandBuilder(daSystemPart)
'Assign the submitted XML document objDocument to SystemPartDoc
    Dim SystemPartDoc As New XmlDocument()
    SystemPartDoc = objXmlDoc

'Select all nodes that match the name PartId and store these
    nodes in PartIdList
    Dim PartIdList As XmlNodeList
 PartIdList = SystemPartDoc.SelectNodes("//my:PartId", Namemgr)
'Use a For loop to insert the new rows to the table SYSTEM_PART
    Dim intCounter As Integer
    For intCounter = 0 To PartIdList.Count - 1
        If PartIdList.Item(intCounter).InnerText <> "" Then
'Redeclare the new datarow newSystemPartRow
        Dim newSystemPartRow As DataRow =
    dsSystem.Tables(0).newRow
'Redefine a new row
        newSystemPartRow("SystemId") =
    SystemDoc.SelectSingleNode("//my:txtSystemId",
    Namemgr).InnerText
        newSystemPartRow("PartId") =
    PartIdList.Item(intCounter).InnerText
'Insert the new row to the dataset
        dsSystem.Tables(0).Rows.Add(newSystemPartRow)
      End If
    Next
    daSystemPart.Update(dsSystem)

End Function
```

At first, the function creates a dataset **dsSystem** and a data adapter **daSystem** that is used to query the table **COMPUTER_SYSTEM** and to fill the dataset **dsSystem** with query results. Then the function declares a command object **dcSystem** to manage an XML document, a data row object **newRow** that holds the information of a newly added computer system in the data entry form on the client side, and an XML Document object **SystemDoc** that is used to hold the XML document passed by the function parameter **objXmlDoc**. The information contained in the XML document **SystemDoc** is saved in a file in the virtual directory that is created at the time you create the Web service. Later, the file can be shared by other projects. For the XML document, we create an object **nameMgr** to manage namespaces. First, the namespace for the InfoPath form on the client side is added to the **nameMgr** object. The method **AddNamespace** uses the alias **my** to represent the following namespace:

```
http://schemas.microsoft.com/office/infopath/2003/myXSD/2003-12-
   29T17:25:38
```

Then the statement

```
newRow("SystemId") = SystemDoc.SelectSingleNode("//
  my:txtSystemId", Namemgr).InnerText
```

will select the text entered in the text box **txtSystemId** placed on the InfoPath form and assign the text to the **SystemId** column in the **newRow** object. Similarly, the columns **Type** and **Description** in the **newRow** object are assigned the text entered in the text boxes **txtType** and **txtDesc** on the InfoPath form. Finally, the new row is added to the dataset **dsSystem** and the dataset is updated by the data adapter **daSystem**.

Similarly, a **SystemId** value for the newly added row and the corresponding rows of **PartId** are inserted into the table **SYSTEM_PART**. As mentioned before, an XML file contains a set of data elements. Each element in an XML file is also called a node. Because each specified computer system uses many parts, we define an **XmlNodeList** object, **PartIdList**, to store a list of parts used for a computer system. A **For** loop is used to insert multiple rows into the table **SYSTEM_PART**. Finally, **daSystemPart** is used to update the dataset **dsSystem**.

Note: If you have not done so, you need to do two things before you can run the Web service project.

1. Configure Internet Information Services as shown in the subsection Testing Web Application Project, contained in Section 11.4.2, Developing Web Application.
2. If you are using Microsoft Visual Studio .NET 2002, before executing your Web service, make sure that Microsoft .NET Framework 1.1 is installed on your computer. The older version of Visual Studio .NET has only .NET Framework 1.0 installed, which may cause errors when executing ASP.NET projects. You can download and install .NET Framework 1.1 from the following Web site:

```
http://msdn.microsoft.com/netframework/downloads/default.aspx
```

After you have completed these configurations, click the **Start** button ▶ on the toolbar. If there is no mistake, you will be prompted to test a function on the Web service. Click **GetParts** and specify the input parameter as **D0001**, and you should have the screen in Figure 11.26. Click the **Invoke** button, and you should get the information of the part ids and part names in XML format, as shown in Figure 11.27.

In this section, we have created a Web service project. The data stored on the Web service can be shared by various client applications. InfoPath is one of the client application development tools included in Microsoft Office 2003. In the following section, you are going to learn how to use InfoPath to create client applications and use them to interact with the Web service developed in this section.

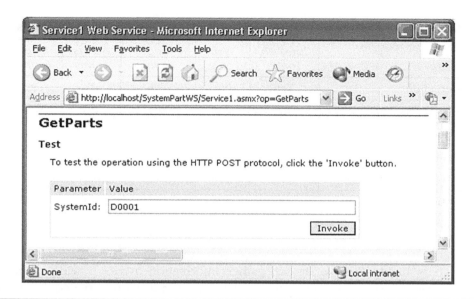

Figure 11.26 **Test Web service function GetParts**

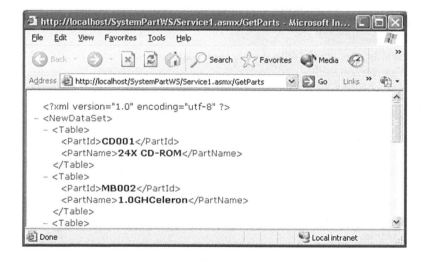

Figure 11.27 **XML document returned by GetParts function**

11.5.2 Creating InfoPath Forms

To meet the growing demand for business information processing, Microsoft Office 2003 has included InfoPath, which provides the tools that enable client application developers to create dynamic forms that can gather and share information across the Internet and an organization's intranet. Compared with the applications developed by the previous version of Office, InfoPath provides the following advantages:

Table 11.6 Features of Different Application Development Methods

Features	InfoPath Forms	Web Forms	Windows Forms	Access Forms	Excel Forms
Rich client	Yes	No	Yes	Yes	Yes
Structured data	Yes	No	Yes	Yes	Yes
Rapid development	Yes	No	No	Yes	Yes
Data validation	Yes	No	No	Yes	Yes
Internet accessing	Yes	Yes	No	No	No
Embedded reporting	No	No	No	Yes	No
Data analysis	No	No	No	No	Yes

- It is highly flexible. It can gather information across a wide range of business processes in a timely fashion. Applications created by using InfoPath can be seamlessly integrated into other Office 2003 programs.
- InfoPath fully supports XML and Web services. Therefore, it can communicate with existing enterprise systems, including non-Microsoft databases and middle-tier systems.
- Unlike other Web forms, forms generated by InfoPath have rich text editing, spell check, and AutoCorrect.
- InfoPath can work with groups of data and optional fields to customize forms dynamically.
- It has the ability to work offline to reduce network traffic and the load on a Web server.
- It provides functionalities to validate business logic on the client side online and offline.
- By creating trusted templates, InfoPath has strict security measures to control the access to a client machine through a form.
- With built-in support for form libraries, forms generated by InfoPath can be published in a form library. The forms published in the form library are available to support team-based data collection and collaboration of operation.

At this point you have learned several ways of creating client applications. In the previous chapter, you learned to create forms and reports in Access. In this chapter, you have created Windows forms with VB.NET and Web forms with ASP.NET. In fact, forms and reports can also be created with Microsoft Word and Excel. Table 11.6 illustrates the features of different application development methods.

Creating Form Based on Existing Data Source

As a quick start, we create a form to display the data in the PART table in the database Hillcrest Computing.

1. Start InfoPath by clicking **Start**, **All Programs**, **Microsoft Office**, and **Microsoft Office InfoPath 2003**.
2. Click **Design a Form** in the task pane. Then click **New from Data Source**.
3. Check the **Database** option and click **Next**.
4. Click the **Select Database** button. In the **Select Data Source** dialog box, click the **New Source** button to open **Data Connection Wizard**. Make sure that **Microsoft SQL Server** is selected and then click **Next**.
5. Enter your computer name as the server name and check the **Use Windows Authentication** option if the server and InfoPath are installed on the same computer. Click **Next** to select the database.
6. Select the database **Hillcrest Computing** and uncheck **Connect to a specific table**. Click **Next** and then click **Finish**.
7. Click the **Open** button. Select the table **PART** and click **OK**.
8. Click **Next** and check the option **Design query view first**. Click **Finish** to complete the configuration.
9. Change the form title to **Part Information Form** and enter the sentence "**This form contains information about part ids and part names**" as the introduction.
10. Because we want to display the data in the **PartId** and **PartName** columns in the list boxes, we should replace the default table control with a two-column table control. To do so, delete the default table control first, and then click **Layout** in the task pane. Drag the **Two-Column Table** control from the task pane to the design form.
11. Click **Controls** in the task pane and drag **List Box** to the first column of the Two-Column Table control. When prompted to select the list box binding, expand the **queryFields** node and select the **PartId** field. Click **OK**. Similarly, drag another list box to the second column of the table control and bind the list box to **PartName**. The resulting form is shown in Figure 11.28.
    Note: When selecting the database Hillcrest Computing in Data Connection Wizard, sometimes the tables are not displayed. To solve the problem, open **Enterprise Manager** and expand the **Hillcrest Computing** node. Right-click the **Users** node and select **New Database User**. Select **<new>** in the **Login name** combo box to open the **SQL Server Login Properties - New Login** dialog box. Use your Windows account to create a new database user account and set the database Hillcrest Computing as the default database. Then try to connect to the data source again.
12. Now configure the list box properties to display the part ids and part names in these two list boxes. Right-click the **Part Id** list box and select **List Box Properties**. Check the option **Look up in a database, Web service, or file** and then click **Secondary Data Source**. Click the **Add** button and check the **Database** option. Click **Next** to select the data source. Select the newly added data source **Hillcrest Computing** and click **Open**. Select the table **PART** and click **OK**. Click **Next** and then **Finish**. Close the **Secondary Data Sources** dialog box. Click the **Select XPath** icon ⬚ by the **Entries** text box. Expand the **dataFields** tree, select **PartId**, and then click **OK**. You should have the configuration as shown in Figure 11.29.

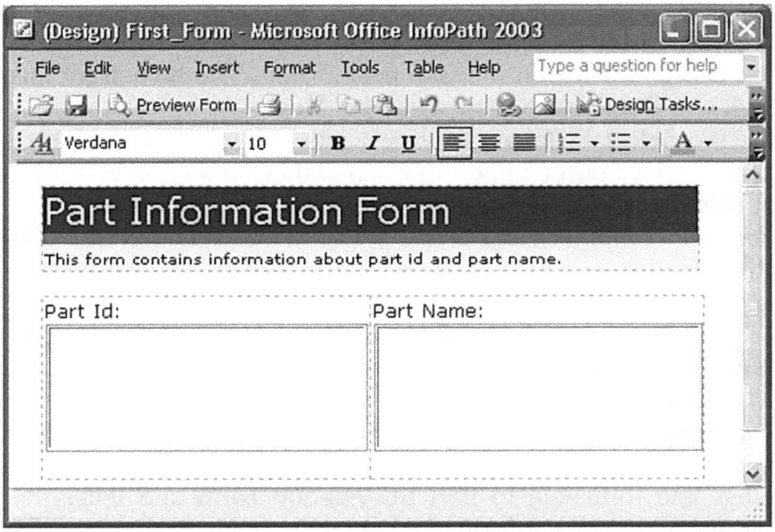

Figure 11.28   Design of simple form

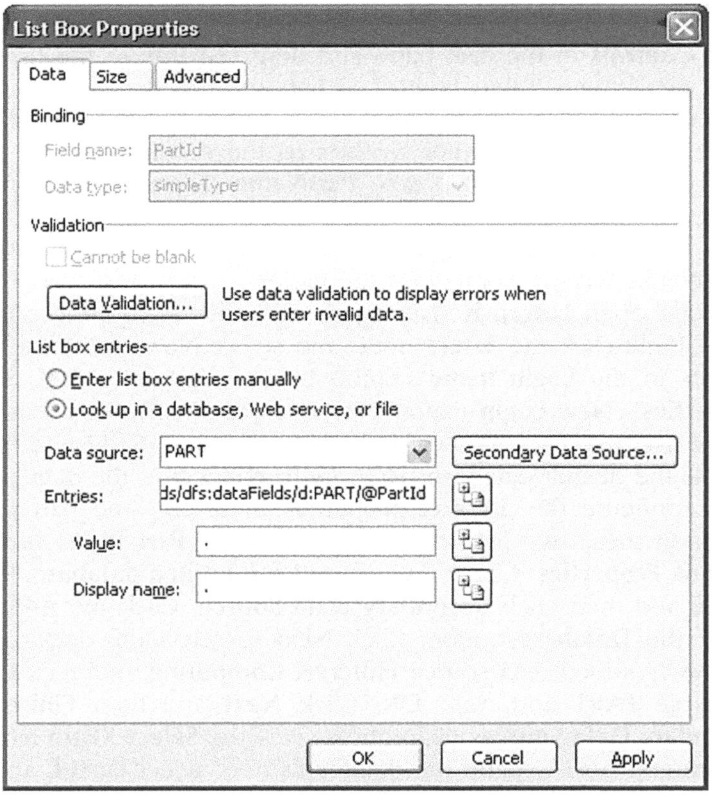

Figure 11.29   Configure data source binding for list box

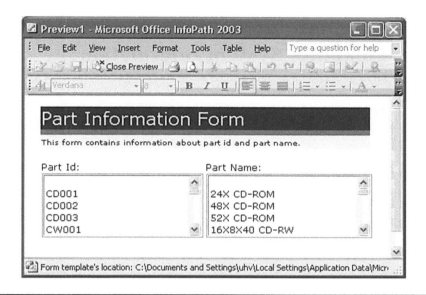

Figure 11.30 Preview of Part Information Form

13. Click **OK** to accept the configuration. Similarly, you can bind the **PartName** list box to the data source **PartName** in the table **PART**.
14. Click **Preview Form**. You should have the form as shown in Figure 11.30.

For a simple form like the one above, there is no programming involved in the form development. However, for forms that support interactions between clients and servers, some programming is necessary. InfoPath supports two scripting languages, JScript and VBScript. In the following, we develop two InfoPath forms that use the Web service as their data source. The first form displays all the parts used in a specific computer system and the second one allows the front-end user to submit information about a new computer system to the Web service.

Creating Form Receiving Data from XML Web Service Data Source

This form will use the functions GetSystemId, GetSystemInfo, and GetParts built on the Web service as its data source. It will use one drop-down list box to allow the front-end user to select a computer system through its id. After the computer system is selected, the information about its type and description will be displayed in two text boxes. All the parts used in the system will be listed in two list boxes. The following steps show you how to create this form.

1. Start **InfoPath** and click **Design a Form** in the task pane. Click **New Blank Form** in the task pane. To use VBScript for the coding, click **Tools** on the menu bar, **Form Options**, and then the **Advanced** tab. Select **VBScript** in the **Form script language** combo box. Click **OK** and save the form as **System InfoPath**.

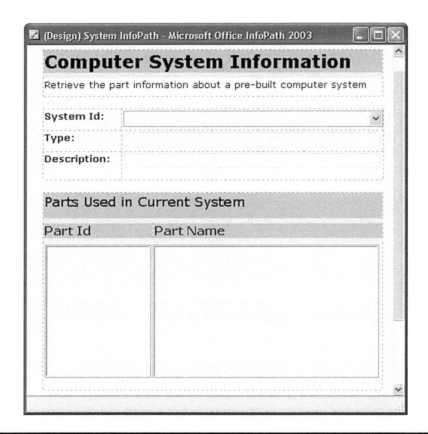

Figure 11.31   Design of system InfoPath form

Table 11.7   Property Specifications for Controls in System InfoPath Form

Control Name	Properties	Connection
lstSystemId	Data source entries	GetSystemId function on Web service /dfs:myFields/.../Table/SystemId
txtType		
txtDesc		
lstPartId	Data source entries	GetParts function on Web service /dfs:myFields/.../Table/PartId
lstPartName	Data source entries	GetParts function on Web service /dfs:myFields/.../Table/PartName

2. Add a **Table with Title** layout and a **Custom Table** layout where you can create a drop-down list box, text boxes, and labels to display the system information. Add another **Table with Title** layout that contains two list boxes and labels. Modify the form based on Figure 11.31.
3. Configure the controls with the specifications shown in Table 11.7.

4. To connect to the Web service data source, right-click the drop-down list box and select **Drop-Down List Box Properties**. Check the option **Look up in a database, Web service, or file**. Click the button **Secondary Data Source** and then click the **Add** button. Check the **Web service** option and click **Next**. Enter the Web service as http://localhost/SystemPartWS/Service1.asmx and click **Next**. Select **GetSystemId** and click **Next** three times. Click **Finish**. Similarly, add **GetParts** and **GetSystemInfo** to **Secondary Data Source**. This time when prompted, click the button **Set Sample Value** and enter the system id **D0001**; then click **OK**. Before you leave **Drop-Down List Box Properties**, choose **GetSystemId** in the **Data Source** combo box. Click the **Select XPath** icon ⬚ by the **Entries** text box. Expand the **dataFields** tree, select **SystemId**, and then click **OK**.

5. To bind **GetParts** to the two list boxes **Part Id** and **Part Name**, first right-click the list box **Part Id** and select **List Box Properties**. After you check the option **Look up in a database, Web service, or file**, select **GetParts** in the **Data Source** combo box. Click the **Select XPath** icon ⬚, expand the **dataFields** tree, and select the **PartId**. Click **OK** a couple of times to complete the binding. Similarly, you can bind the **PartName** field to the list box **Part Name**.

6. We need some code to add the information about the system's type and description after a computer system is selected from the drop-down list box to the text box. The following code will perform such activities. First, we create a function for the event **OnAfterChange** generated by the drop-down list box **lstSystemId**. To enter the code for the **OnAfterChange** event, right-click the drop-down list box **lstSystemId** and select **Drop-Down List Box Properties**. Click the **Data Validation** button, and select **OnAfterChange** in the **Events** combo box. Click the **Edit** button to open the editor and enter the code as shown below:

```
Sub msoxd_my_lstSystemId_OnAfterChange(eventObj)

' Write code here to restore the global state.

If eventObj.IsUndoRedo Then
' An undo or redo operation has occurred and the DOM is read
  'only.
  Exit Sub
End If

' A field change has occurred and the DOM is writable. Write
  'code here to respond to the changes.

UpdateSystemInfo
XDocument.View.ForceUpdate
UpdateTextBox

End Sub
```

Note: Later, to modify the code, you can open the editor by clicking **Tools** on the menu bar, **Script**, and then **Microsoft Script Editor**.

7. After the change is made to the drop-down list box, the code will call two subprocedures, `UpdateSystemInfo` and `UpdateTextBox`. `Update-SystemInfo` is used to update the namespace according to the selected system id so that the content in the other two list boxes can be updated automatically. The code is shown below:

```
Sub UpdateSystemInfo
   Dim IdValue
   set IdValue = XDocument.DOM.selectSingleNode( "/my:myFields/
   my:lstSystemId" )

'Get a reference to the SDS bound to the Web service.
   Dim objPart
   set objPart = XDocument.DataObjects.Item("GetParts")

'Set the SelectionNamespaces so that you can find the correct
   'field.
'Note: If the Web service was created with Visual Studio .NET
   '2003, the xmlns:s0 namespace is:
'http://tempuri.org/PopulateCities/Service1
   objPart.DOM.setProperty"SelectionNamespaces", _
    "xmlns:dfs=""http://schemas.microsoft.com/office/infopath/
   2003/dataFormSolution"" " &_
      "xmlns:s0=""http://tempuri.org/"""

   Dim prmtPart
   set prmtPart = objPart.DOM.selectSingleNode( _

   "/dfs:myFields/dfs:queryFields/s0:GetParts/s0:SystemId" )

   prmtPart.text = IdValue.text
   If prmtPart.text = "" Then prmtPart.text = "D0001"
   objPart.Query

End Sub
```

Several XML-related objects and related methods are used in the code. The following are their meanings:
 - *XDocument:* An XML document object for a Microsoft Office InfoPath 2003 form.
 - *DOM:* A property of an XDocument object. It returns the reference to a Document Object Model that describes the structure of the XDocument.
 - *selectSingleNode:* A method to search the specified node in an XDocument. It returns the first matching node.
 - *DataObjects:* It is a collection of DataObjects for each Secondary Data Source in a Microsoft Office InfoPath 2003 form.
 - *Item:* A property that returns the reference to a specified DataObject.
 - *SelectionNamespaces:* Specifies namespaces in XPath expressions.
8. After the part information in the list boxes is updated, call the subprocedure `UpdateTestBox` to update the text boxes **txtType** and **txtDesc**:

```
Sub UpdateTextBox
  Dim IdValue
  set IdValue = XDocument.DOM.selectSingleNode( "/my:myFields/
  my:lstSystemId" )

'The following code sets the textboxes
  Dim objSystem
  set objSystem = XDocument.DataObjects.Item("GetSystemInfo")

  objSystem.DOM.setProperty"SelectionNamespaces", _
  "xmlns:dfs=""http://schemas.microsoft.com/office/infopath/
  2003/dataFormSolution"" " &_
      "xmlns:s0=""http://tempuri.org/"""
  Dim prmtSystem
  set prmtSystem = objSystem.DOM.selectSingleNode( _

  "/dfs:myFields/dfs:queryFields/s0:GetSystemInfo/s0:SystemId"
  )

  prmtSystem.text = IdValue.text
  If prmtSystem.text = "" Then prmtSystem.text = "D0001"
  objSystem.Query

  Dim objType
  Set objType = objSystem.DOM.selectSingleNode("/dfs:myFields/
  dfs:dataFields/s0:GetSystemInfoResponse/
  s0:GetSystemInfoResult/NewDataSet/Table/Type")
  XDocument.DOM.selectSingleNode("//my:txtType").text =
  objType.Text
  Dim objDesc
  Set objDesc = objSystem.DOM.selectSingleNode("/dfs:myFields/
  dfs:dataFields/s0:GetSystemInfoResponse/
  s0:GetSystemInfoResult/NewDataSet/Table/Description")
  XDocument.DOM.selectSingleNode("//my:txtDesc").text =
  objDesc.Text

End Sub
```

Note: In the above codes, there are many long lines. Due to the size limitation, we have to present them in two or three lines. When typing the codes in Microsoft Script Editor, make sure to type all of them in single lines.

9. After you have entered the code, go back to the design page. Click the **Preview Form** button on the toolbar. After the preview window opens, select the system id **D0002** in the **System Id** combo box; you should have the system information displayed as in Figure 11.32. As you can see, the information of type and description is shown in the text boxes and the information about parts used in this computer system is in the list boxes.

Different from projects developed before, instead of directly pulling from the database, the data are from the XML Web service. Next, we create an InfoPath form that allows the user to submit data to the XML Web service.

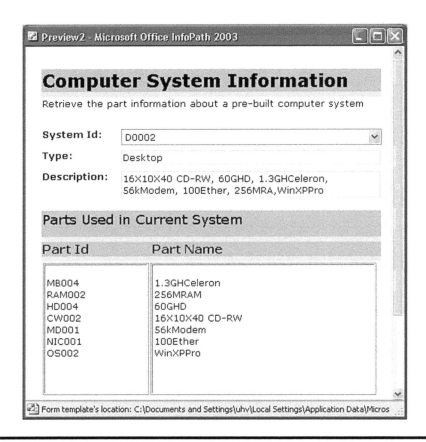

Figure 11.32   Display information for specified computer system

Creating Form to Submit Data to XML Web Service Data Source

In our case study, each sales center wants to submit the configuration of a customized computer system to the company's headquarters through the Internet. Suppose that the company's Web service accepts submitted information of customized computer systems. Now we need to create a form, Customized System Submission Form, for each sales center to enter data. To create this form, follow the steps below.

1. Start **InfoPath** and click **Design a Form** in the task pane. Click **New Blank Form**. Choose VBScript by clicking **Tools** on the menu bar, **Form Options**, and then the **Advanced** tab. Select **VBScript** in the **Form script language** combo box. Click **OK** and save the form as **SystemInfoSubmit**.
2. In the **Layout** list, drag the **Table with Title** control to the design page. Then add three text box controls in the table control. Modify the titles and labels as shown in Figure 11.33. In the **Controls** list, add a **Section** control below the table control. Then add nine **Optional Section** controls inside the **Section** control. Within each **Optional Section** control, add two text boxes with the labels as shown in Figure 11.33.

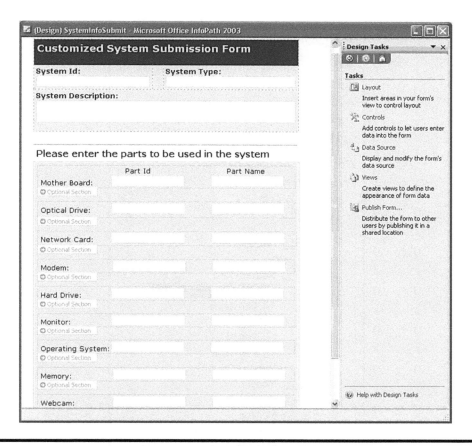

Figure 11.33   Design of SystemInfoSubmit form

3. In the **Data Source** list, right-click **myFields** and select **Add**. Enter **System** in the **Name** text box and select **Group** in the **Type** combo box. Click **OK**. You should see that a new group is added to the data source. Right-click the group **System** and select **Add**. Enter **txtSystemId** as the name. Click **OK**. You should see that a new field **txtSystemId** is added to the group. Similarly, add two more fields, **txtType** and **txtDesc**, to the group **System**. To add the group **Parts**, right-click **myfields** and select **Add**. Enter **Parts** as the name and select **Group** in the **Type** combo box. Click **OK** and you should see that the group **Parts** is added. In the same way, add the subgroups **MotherBoard**, **OpticalDrive**, **NetworkCard**, **Modem**, **Hard-Drive**, **Monitor**, **OperatingSystem**, **Memory**, and **Webcam** under the group **Parts**. To add fields for each subgroup, for example, the subgroup **MotherBoard**, right-click on it and select **Add**. Add two fields **PartId** and **PartName**. Because each subgroup has the same fields, an easy way to add the fields is to right-click the field **PartId** and select **Reference**. Click the subgroup **OpticalDrive** and click **OK**. The subgroup OpticalDrive gets the field PartId. Similarly, you can add the **PartName** to the subgroup **OpticalDrive**. Repeat the above process to add the fields **PartId** and **PartName** to all the remaining subgroups, as shown in Figure 11.34.

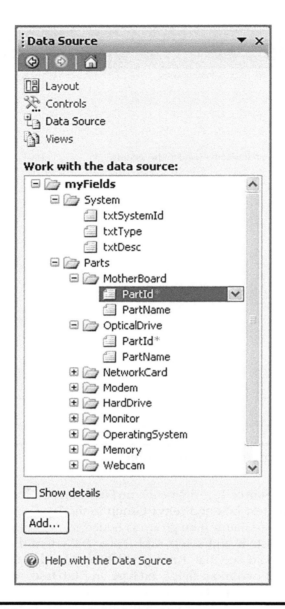

Figure 11.34   Add groups and fields in data source

4. To add the data source to the controls, right-click the text box for **System Id** and select **Change Binding.** Select **txtSystemId** from the tree and click **OK**. Similarly bind the fields **txtType**, **txtDesc**, **PartId**, and **PartName** to the other text box controls.
5. To add the VBScript code, click the **Tools** menu and then click **Submitting Forms**. Check the **Enable submit** option and select **Submit using custom script** in the **Submit** combo box. Click **OK**. Once the script editor is open, enter the following code:

```
Sub XDocument_OnSubmitRequest(eventObj)
```

```
'Get reference to the SubmitInfoPathDocument secondary data
  'source.
  Dim objSendXMLDoc
 Set objSendXMLDoc = XDocument.GetDOM("SubmitInfoPathDocument")
  objSendXMLDoc.setProperty"SelectionNamespaces",
  "xmlns:s1=""http://uhv.microsoft.com/schema"" " &
  "xmlns:s0=""http://tempuri.org/"" " &
  "xmlns:dfs=""http://schemas.microsoft.com/office/infopath/
  2003/dataFormSolution"" "

'Remove existing data from the SubmitInfoPathDocument secondary
  'data source. Here, objXmlDoc is the parameter passed into
  'SubmitInfoPathDocument
  Dim objData
  Set objData = objSendXMLDoc.selectSingleNode(          "/
  dfs:myFields/dfs:queryFields/s0:SubmitInfoPathDocument/
  s0:objXmlDoc")
  Dim objCurrentData
  Set objCurrentData = objData.selectNodes("@* | node()")
  objCurrentData.removeAll()

'Copy the XDocument.
  Dim objCopiedDoc
  Set objCopiedDoc =
  XDocument.DOM.documentElement.cloneNode(true )
  objData.appendChild( objCopiedDoc )

'Call the "Query" method of the secondary data source to send
  'the data.
  XDocument.DataObjects("SubmitInfoPathDocument").Query()

'Report the Submit results.
  eventObj.ReturnStatus = true

End Sub
```

In addition to the XML objects mentioned before, the following are the meanings of some new objects, properties, and methods used in this subprocedure:

– *GetDOM:* A method that returns the reference to the DOM of a specified DataObject defined in an XDocument object
– *documentElement:* A property used to hold the root element of a document
– *cloneNode:* A method used to copy a node
– *Query:* A method used to retrieve data from a specified data source and store them in an Xdocument's DOM

The next step will show you how InfoPath can seamlessly integrate with other programs.

6. To help the front-end user to configure a customized computer system, we can create an ASP.NET Web page that contains information about all the available parts. Then we add the Web page to the InfoPath form. We first create a Web page. To do so, start **Visual Studio .NET**. On the **Start** page, click the **New Project** button. Select the **ASP.NET Application**

template and enter the project name http://localhost/PartInfo in the **Location** combo box. Click **OK**. Double-click **WebForm1.aspx** to open the design page. In **Server Explorer**, drag the data connection to the design page. Right-click the data connection **sqlConnection1** and select **Properties**. Change the **Name** property to **cnPart**. Drag a **Label** control from **Toolbox** to the design page, and then change the **Text** property to **Part Information**. For the **Font** property, make **Bold** as **True** and **Size** as **Medium**. Go back to the design page. Drag a **Datagrid** control to the design page, name its **ID** as **grdPart**, and press **F7** to open the code window. Enter the following code:

```
Private Sub Page_Load(ByVal sender As System.Object, ByVal e
    As System.EventArgs) Handles MyBase.Load

'Declare a dataset
    Dim dsPart As DataSet
    Dim daPart As SqlClient.SqlDataAdapter

'Create a data adapter
 daPart = New SqlClient.SqlDataAdapter("SELECT PartId, PartName
    FROM PART ", cnPart)
'Fill the dataset with the data adapter
    dsPart = New DataSet()
    daPart.Fill(dsPart, "PART")
'Bind the Datagrid to the table PART in the dataset
    grdPart.DataSource = dsPart.Tables("PART").DefaultView
    grdPart.DataBind()

End Sub
```

7. Click the **Start** button on the toolbar. If everything works correctly, the Web page is ready to be added to the InfoPath form.

8. To add the Web page to the submission form, go back to the form's design page in **InfoPath**. Click **Tools**, **Form Options**, and the **Advanced** tab. Check **Enable custom task pane**. In the **Task pane name** text box, enter **Part Information**. In the **Task pane location** text box, enter the location of the Web page http://localhost/PartInfo/WebForm1.aspx, and click **OK**.

9. Suppose that the company requires that a system id must be present when submitting a new system configuration. We can add the data validation function to the **System Id** text box. To do so, right-click the text box **System Id** and select **Text Box Properties.** Click the check box **Cannot be blank** and then click **OK**. This will guarantee that each new system configuration contains a system id.

10. To test the form, click **Preview Form**. In the form preview, enter the information of a new system, as shown in Figure 11.35. The Web page is added in the task pane. The front-end user can configure a new customized system based on the available parts.

11. After you have entered the specifications for the new computer system, click **File** and **Submit**. If everything goes well, you should get the message **Submission is done successfully**.

12. To verify that the new customized system information is indeed submitted to the Web service, you can open the form System InfoPath created

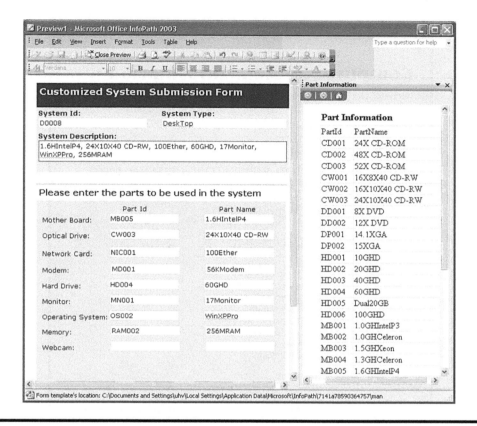

Figure 11.35 Configure customized system for submission

previously to display the information about a system, for example, D0008. To do so, click **File** and then click **System InfoPath** in the recently opened file list. Click **Preview Form** on the toolbar. In the form preview, select the system id **D0008** in the **System Id** combo box. You should get the configuration information about this system as shown in Figure 11.36.

In this section, we have discussed the XML Web service technology and the InfoPath technology. You have learned how to create a Web service in Visual Studio .NET. You have created several functions on the Web service to allow front-end users to retrieve and submit data. You have also learned how to create forms to interact with data sources such as databases and Web services. Several examples based on the database `Hillcrest Computing` have been used to demonstrate the usage of XML Web services and InfoPath for exchanging data between clients and a database server over the Internet.

11.6 Summary

In this chapter, you have learned various ways to develop network-based database applications. First, the client/server computing architecture was introduced. Both two-tier and three-tier architectures were discussed. Based on

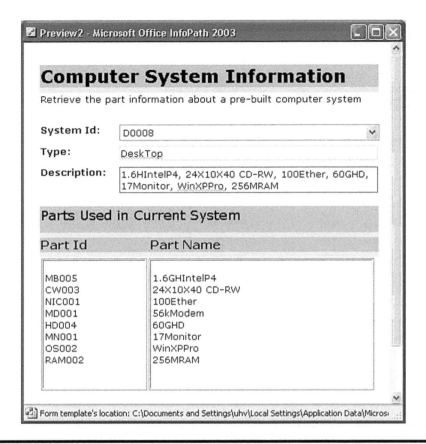

Figure 11.36 Display of submitted customized system information

the three-tier architecture, we developed four important network-based database applications: a Windows application, a Web application, an XML Web service created with Visual Studio .NET, and InfoPath forms.

Visual Studio .NET provides us with some convenient tools such as ADO.NET, ASP.NET, and VB.NET for developing network-based database applications. We have used Visual Studio .NET to create various network-based database applications in the same visual environment. Visual Studio .NET allows us to use the same knowledge and skills to develop Windows applications, Web applications, and Web services.

The XML technology has been used to exchange data among different database applications. We have implemented one of the important XML usages, which exchanges data between the database server and the client over the Internet, by setting up the XML Web service. Using the data provided by the XML Web service, we created some InfoPath forms to display XML data provided by the Web service and to submit data to the Web service.

Network-based database applications allow front-end users to access a database remotely through the local area network or the Internet. This has significantly extended the scope of a database. With these network database technologies, a business can expand itself through E-commerce to reach a wide range of customers.

As more and more users open their accounts on our database and more and more data are stored there, the next question is how we can efficiently manage the users and the data on our database. We answer this question in the next chapter.

Review Questions

1. What tasks can be done by network databases?
2. What are the advantages of a client/server solution to business processes?
3. What does the word "tier" mean?
4. What are the roles of the client and server in the two-tier architecture?
5. What are the advantages and disadvantages of the two-tier architecture?
6. What is the middle tier in the three-tier architecture used for?
7. How does the middle tier work in the three-tier architecture?
8. What are the advantages of the three-tier architecture?
9. How do you handle a large number of clients?
10. What are the advantages of XML when compared with HTML?
11. What are the advantages of using XML schema files?
12. What are the namespaces supported by Access 2002?
13. Explain the role of a namespace.
14. What is the purpose of an extensible stylesheet file?
15. Export the table PART as an XML file. Name the file as Part.xml. Then import the file Part.xml into a blank Microsoft Access database.
16. What are the features of Microsoft Visual Studio .NET that can be used in database applications?
17. Compared with the traditional ADO technology, what are the improvements of ADO.NET?
18. Summarize the functionalities of the ADO.NET objects `Connection`, `Data Adapter`, and `Data Command`.
19. What are the challenges in developing Web-based databases?
20. What are the tasks that can be carried out by a Web server?
21. What is the role of HTTP when a Web browser communicates with a Web server?
22. What are the advantages of the ASP.NET technology?

Case Study Projects

In the following case study projects, create some Web-based database applications with Microsoft Visual Studio .NET or InfoPath.

1. Computer Service

To assist front-end users in displaying the information stored in the `Computer_Service` database through the Internet, create the following database applications with either ASP.NET or InfoPath:

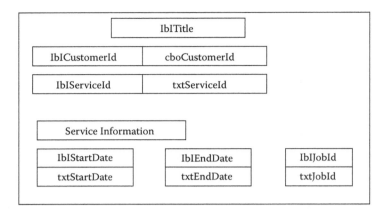

Figure 11.37   Form design sketch for service information

- Design a form according to the sketch in Figure 11.37. The GUI will be used by front-end users to display service information such as the service and service description after a customer is selected in the combo box.
- Develop a Web service by using Visual Studio .NET to make the tables CUSTOMERS and SERVICES available so that the information can be displayed on the form.
- Connect the form to the Web service. Also, add code to perform the following activities:
  - When the form is loaded, fill the combo box with customer ids.
  - When a row is selected in the combo box, display the service id and the information of the service.
- Test and show your final result in the Web browser.

2. University Registration

Create the following Web-based database applications to help students retrieve information about courses, class schedule, and classrooms from the Registration database over the Internet.

- Follow the sketch in Figure 11.38 to create a form that can be used to display course information. Once a course is selected, schedule and classroom information will be displayed.
- Develop a Web service by using Visual Studio .NET to make the tables COURSES, CLASSES, SEMESTERS, and CLASSROOMS available for the form application.
- After connecting the form to the Web service, add code to perform the following activities:
  - When the form is loaded, fill the combo box with course descriptions.
  - When a course description is selected in the combo box, display the class schedule and classroom information for the course.
- Test and display your final result in a Web browser.

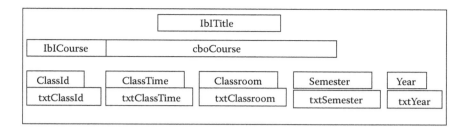

Figure 11.38　Form design sketch for course information

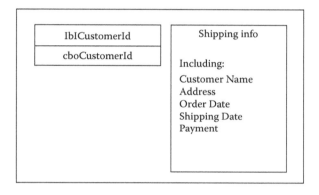

Figure 11.39　Form design sketch for shipment information

3. Mail Order

To allow the front-end user to use the database `Mail_Order` through the Internet, create the following Web-based database applications:

- According to the sketch in Figure 11.39, create a form to allow store managers to verify shipping information. Once a customer id is selected from the combo box, the shipping information will be displayed on the form.
- Develop a Web service by using Visual Studio .NET to make the tables `CUSTOMERS`, `ORDERS`, and `SHIPMENT` available for the form application.
- After connecting the form to the Web service, add code to perform the following activities:
  - When the form is loaded, fill the combo box with customer ids.
  - When a customer id is selected in the combo box, display the related shipping information.
- Test and display your final result in a Web browser.

Chapter 12

Database Administration

Objectives

- Manage user accounts and database security.
- Back up and restore databases.
- Perform database replication.
- Optimize database performance.
- Develop a database maintenance plan.

12.1 Introduction

A network database allows a large number of users to use the same database. Any database failure will have a great impact on many users as well as the entire organization or enterprise. This brings up some questions such as how to maintain user accounts, database security, and reliability. Therefore, we need to address issues such as managing user accounts and security, database backup and restoration, and database performance tuning. These tasks are normally handled by database administrators (DBAs). The following are common responsibilities of DBAs:

- *Implementing and maintaining databases:* DBAs participate in the database design process. They install and upgrade DBMS systems, perform proper data-transfer processes, schedule database turn-on and turn-off, maintain databases to allow users to access them at any time, and keep database-related documentation in a safe place.
- *Managing user accounts and database security:* DBAs create user accounts on a database and enforce security such as setting up different levels of log-ins, authentications, and permissions for users.

- *Performing database backup and restoration:* DBAs develop plans to recover a database as quickly as possible after a database failure. They set up a proper database backup plan to prevent the loss of data and perform scheduled backups and database recovery.
- *Monitoring and tuning database performance:* DBAs configure and tune database parameters to ensure that a database is running with optimal performance. They detect problems that cause a slowdown in performance.
- *Setting up replication services:* DBAs design a proper replication topology for reliability and performance in a distributed computing environment.
- *Providing data analysis services:* DBAs maintain the data warehouse or data mart for enterprises and provide services for data analysis and decision making.
- *Working with database application developers:* DBAs help developers implement application-related constraints on database objects and upload server-side stored procedures, triggers, and ASP programs.

A qualified DBA should be knowledgeable in many database fields such as having a good understanding of database design, DBMS systems, database applications, and an organization's network architecture. He or she should also have interpersonal skills. In this chapter and the next chapter, we study related topics to accomplish some of the above-mentioned tasks.

12.2 Managing Database User Accounts and Security

When a database is used in a network environment, it requires a variable security model so that users can perform database operations on various levels. Security requirements for data stored in a network database and for operations performed on database objects are different depending on the types of users. A DBMS system, such as SQL Server, often provides a security model to meet security requirements. The components of the SQL Server security model are described in Figure 12.1.

In the next few sections, we take a closer look at the SQL Server security model.

12.2.1 Server Authentication

SQL Server log-in is an authentication process, which is the first stage of security measures. The authentication process boils down to two parts: the Windows authentication mode and SQL Server authentication mode.

Windows Authentication Mode

By using this authentication mode, you can bypass the SQL Server log-in process by letting the SQL Server share the Windows log-in process. Once a Windows user logs on to the computer with the correct username and password, he or she automatically logs on to the SQL Server database. The benefits of Windows authentication are:

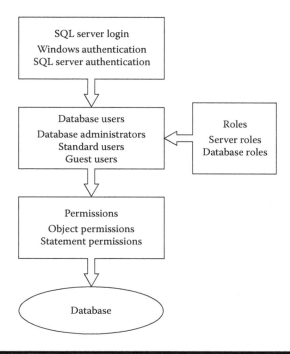

Figure 12.1   SQL Server security model

- It takes advantage of the Windows user security mechanism such as network encryption for log-in information and automatically logs out repeatedly failed log-in attempts.
- For each Windows user, there is no need to create and update another account for a SQL Server database. This can reduce the workload of a system administrator who manages a large number of users.

The default log-in mode for SQL Server is set as SQL Server Login. However, you can easily change the authentication mode to Windows authentication by following the steps below.

1. Start **Enterprise Manager** by clicking **Start**, **All Programs**, **Microsoft SQL Server**, and **Enterprise Manager**.
2. Expand your server's **Security** node under the **SQL Server Group** node, and right-click the **Logins** node. Select **New Login** to open the **New Login** dialog box (see Figure 12.2).
3. Check the **Windows Authentication** option to specify the log-in mode.

You may also be prompted to specify the Windows authentication mode in some other configuration processes, such as the process to link a client application to a database as covered in Chapter 9.

Mixed Authentication Mode

When using the mixed authentication mode, both the Windows authentication mode and SQL Server authentication mode are used. For users who have no

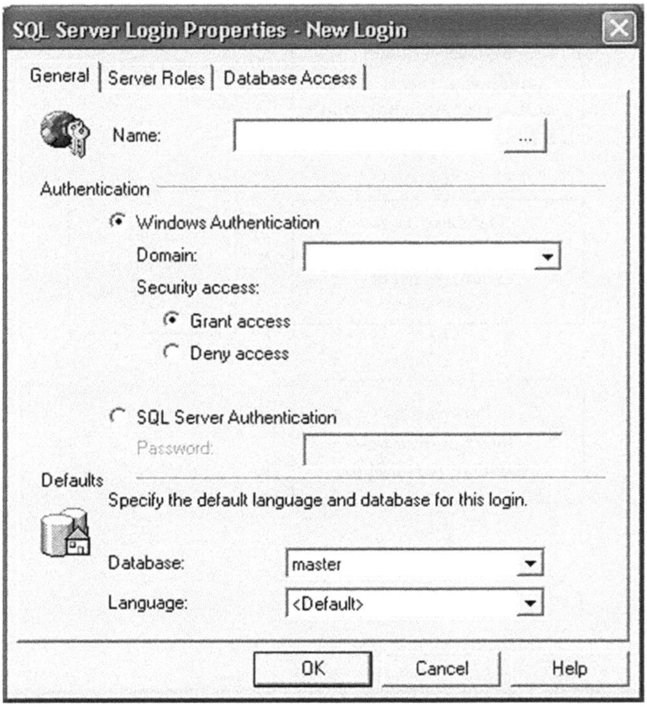

Figure 12.2   New log-in dialog

Windows accounts, the SQL Server authentication will allow them to use the SQL Server database. Often in an enterprise network environment, many computers use Linux or UNIX operating systems. In such a case, the SQL Server authentication mode is the choice. To configure security with the SQL Server authentication mode, select the SQL Server Authentication option in Figure 12.2 and enter the password for the SQL Server.

12.2.2   Server Authorization

After front-end users successfully log on to a database with the correct username and password, they will try to access some database objects and perform some database-related activities. These users are prevented from executing database administration commands or accessing the database objects without proper permissions. This leads to the authorization stage, which sets up security measures to specify permissions given to different types of users. We first create users and then add different roles to these users based on their job duties. Through the roles, we can specify database-accessing permissions for the users.

Database Users

There are three types of users: database administrators, standard users, and guest users. Each type has different security requirements.

1. *Database administrators:* DBAs are expected to do many database management jobs such as starting and shutting down database servers, installing and upgrading database server components, managing user accounts, tuning database server processes, creating and updating database objects, replicating databases, and backing up and restoring databases. For a small company, there may be one DBA who does everything. For a large company, there is a group of DBAs who share the above responsibilities.

2. *Standard users:* These users may be allowed to query only or to query and modify tables created in the database, depending on the permissions assigned to them.

3. *Guest users:* There may be public users who need to access a server's default database such as Northwind or pubs in SQL Server through the Internet connection for learning purposes. In such a case, guest users are created. With the correct username and password, a guest user can log on to SQL Server and access the Northwind and pubs databases, but he or she will not be allowed to access any other database objects.

Permissions

Basically, a permission gives you the ability to do certain things and controls the access to database objects. There are two kinds of permissions that are supported by SQL Server: the statement permission and the object permission. The *statement permission* allows a database user to use database manipulation statements such as CREATE, ALTER, DELETE, and BACKUP to create, change, drop, and back up database objects in a database. The *object permission* is used to allow a database user to read, write, update, or execute the content in database objects such as tables, views, or stored procedures.

Roles

A role allows a database administrator to apply a set of permissions to a group of database users who have similar tasks. When you change permissions to group users who are assigned the same role, the permissions are changed at the role level instead of at the user level. A database user can be assigned to different roles. For example, an accounting manager can be assigned to an accountant role and a manager role. SQL Server 2000 supports two types of fixed roles, *server roles* and *database roles*. We start with these two types of roles.

1. *Fixed server roles:* When a server role is assigned to a user, the user will be able to perform the defined database administration tasks. Table 12.1 lists the administration tasks permitted by the server roles included in SQL Server.

2. *Fixed database roles:* Once a database is created, the built-in database roles shown in Table 12.2 will be available to database users.

3. *User-defined database roles:* In addition to the fixed roles, SQL Server supports database roles defined by users to represent a job done by a group of database users. For example, in an accounting department, user-defined roles can be the accountant role and the account manager role.

Table 12.1   Permissions Assigned by Server Roles

Server Role	Permission
sysadmin	Permits any activity on SQL Server
serveradmin	Permits the configuration of database settings and the shutting down of SQL Server
setupadmin	Permits the setting up and managing of stored procedures and database replication
securityadmin	Permits the management of database security–related activities such as user log-ins and error logs
proceadmin	Permits the management of SQL Server processes
dbcreator	Permits a user to create and modify databases
diskadmin	Permits the management of disk files
bulkadmin	Permits a user to perform mass data import

Table 12.2   Permissions Assigned by Fixed Database Roles

Database Role	Permission
db_owner	Permits any activity within a database such as maintaining and configuring the database and assigning permissions to other users.
db_accessadmin	Permits the management of access requests from Windows users and SQL Server users.
db_datareader	Gives permission to query data in all user-defined tables by using the SELECT statement.
db_datawriter	Gives permission to insert, update, and delete data in all user-defined tables. Data query is not permitted by this role.
db_ddladmin	Gives permission to create, modify, and drop all database objects.
db_securityadmin	Can assign permissions of statements and objects to database users and roles within a database.
db_backupoperator	Gives permission to back up a database.
db_denydatareader	Does not give permission to query any data in all the user-defined tables within a database.
db_denydatawriter	Does not give permission to insert, update, and delete any data in all the user-defined tables within a database.
public	A default role assigned to every user who is permitted to access a database.

4. *User-defined application roles:* Sometimes, an individual application may need a special database access requirement. Application roles are defined to accommodate such a requirement. For example, a user has a standard fixed database role as db_datareader, with which the user is able to query the database from any application that connects to the database. Suppose that the user needs to insert new rows to the database using SQL Query Analyzer. To accommodate this special access requirement, we need to define an application role that permits the insert operation. When the user is using Query Analyzer, the application role is activated to allow the insert operation on the database tables there. When the user is using other applications such as Microsoft Access, he or she will be limited to the db_datareader role. This will prevent unauthorized users from modifying data directly in tables, which can be a big headache for database administrators.

12.2.3   Creating Roles and Users, and Auditing Log-Ins

After a quick overview of users and roles, we work on some hands-on practice. To illustrate the implementation of database authorization and authentication, we create some users for the database Hillcrest Computing with different types of roles. Users such as assembly worker, assembly manager, and IT manager (who will serve as the database administrator) will access tables such as PART, PART_DETAIL, ASSEMBLY_WORKER, ASSEMBLY_PROCESS, and COMPUTER_SYSTEM in the database. These users have the following database accessing requirements:

- Assembly workers need to enter assembly progress information in the table ASSEMBLY_PROCESS and update the tables PART and PART_DETAIL when parts have been used to assemble a computer system.
- Like the assembly workers, the assembly manager needs to update the tables ASSEMBLY_PROCESS, PART, and PART_DETAIL. In addition, the assembly manager needs to update the tables ASSEMBLY_WORKER, COMPUTER_SYSTEM, and SYSTEM_PART so that the assembly manager can assign jobs to the assembly workers and update the configurations of computer systems.
- The IT manager serves as a database administrator who can perform any activity on the database.

As a simplified example, we create three roles: Assembly Worker, Assembly Manager, and IT Manager. Table 12.3 summarizes the accessing requirements for the roles.

Next, we create three users: Smith as IT Manager, Jones as Assembly Manager, and Brown as Assembly Worker. Based on the above accessing requirements, three user-defined roles are created and assigned to the related database users.

Table 12.3   Accessing Requirements of Different Roles

Tables	Assembly Worker	Assembly Manager	IT Manager
ASSEMBLY_ WORKER		Query, Insert, Update, Delete	Query, Insert, Update, Delete, Grant rights, Create, Alter, Drop
ASSEMBLY_ PROCESS	Insert	Query, Insert, Update, Delete	Query, Insert, Update, Delete, Grant rights, Create, Alter, Drop
COMPUTER_ SYSTEM		Query, Insert, Update, Delete	Query, Insert, Update, Delete, Grant rights, Create, Alter, Drop
PART	Query, Update	Query, Update	Query, Insert, Update, Delete, Grant rights, Create, Alter, Drop
PART_ DETAIL	Query, Update	Query, Update	Query, Insert, Update, Delete, Grant rights, Create, Alter, Drop
SYSTEM_ PART		Query, Update	Query, Insert, Update, Delete, Grant rights, Create, Alter, Drop

Creating Roles

Expand the **Hillcrest Computing** node under **Databases** in SQL Server Enterprise Manager. Right-click **Roles** and select **New Database Role** on the pop-up menu. Enter the name **Assembly Manager** as shown in Figure 12.3. Then click **OK**. Similarly, create the role **Assembly Worker**.

After the roles are created, we can add permissions to the roles. Right-click the role **Assembly Manager**, and select **Properties** on the pop-up menu. Click the **Permissions** button. Check the permitted activities according to Table 12.3 and Figure 12.4. For the IT Manager, we assign the built-in role `sysadmin` when we create the user who will be the database administrator.

Creating Users

If SQL Server Authentication is used for the three users, configure the new log-ins as shown below.

1. Start **Enterprise Manager**. Expand the **Security** node. Right-click on the **Logins** node.
2. Select **New Login** from the pop-up menu. Enter **Smith** in the **Name** text box, check the **SQL Server Authentication** option, and select **Hillcrest Computing** from the combo box, as shown in Figure 12.5.
3. Enter **itadmin** as the password.
4. Click the **Server Roles** tab. Select the **System Administrators** option. Click the **Database Access** tab and check the database **Hillcrest Computing**.
5. Click **OK** to complete the configuration. Confirm the new password.

Similarly, create the user **Jones** with the password **asmanager** and the database access role **Assembly Manager**, and create the user **Brown** as **asworker**

Figure 12.3   Create new role

and the database access role **Assembly Worker**. The configuration of **Database Access** is illustrated in Figure 12.6.

Note: If you are working on a database that is copied from somewhere else, you may get an error message that says the user already exists. In this case, do the following to solve the problem:

1. Start **Enterprise Manager** and expand your SQL Server.
2. Expand the database, **Hillcrest Computing,** for example.
3. Select **Users**, and then delete the user who has the same username as the one you are trying to create.
4. Click **OK**. Create the new user again with the steps shown above.

To test the database access permissions we have just given, do the following:

1. Because we are using the SQL Server authentication for the users we have created, the first step is to make sure that SQL Server allows both the SQL Server authentication and the Windows authentication. To verify this, start **Enterprise Manager**. Right-click on the name of your SQL Server under the **SQL Server Group** node. Select **Properties**, and then click the **Security** tab. Check the **SQL Server and Windows** authentication option (see Figure 12.7). Click **OK** and restart **Enterprise Manager**.
2. After the SQL Server and Windows authentication is selected, start **SQL Query Analyzer**.

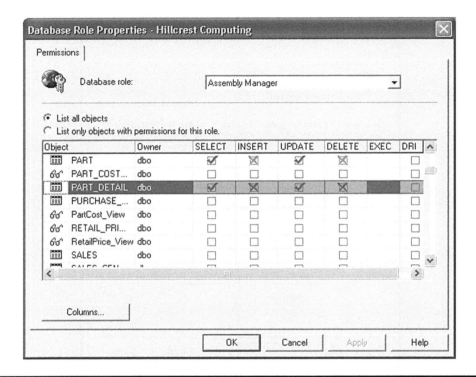

Figure 12.4   Assign permissions to new role

3. In the **Connect to SQL Server** dialog, check the **SQL Server authentication** option, and enter the user name **Jones** and password **asmanager** as shown in Figure 12.8. Click **OK** to enter Query Analyzer.
4. Jones is allowed to query the table ASSEMBLY_WORKER. To verify this, enter the SQL statement in Query Analyzer and execute the statement as shown in Figure 12.9.
5. Jones is not allowed to insert a row into the table PART. To verify this, enter the SQL statement and execute the statement as shown in Figure 12.10. As you can see, the INSERT activity is denied.

In the case in which one database object depends on other database objects, such as a view that may depend on several tables, we need to deal with the hierarchy of an *ownership chain*. If all of the objects, such as views and related tables, are owned by the same user, the owner of the view can grant permission to other users to access the view without their asking for permission from the table owner. On the other hand, if the view and the related tables are not owned by the same user, to grant the view access to other users, the view owner needs permission from the table owner.

Auditing Log-Ins

We take a look at another security measure, auditing, which is part of a DBA's job. For security reasons, it may be necessary to audit users who attempt to

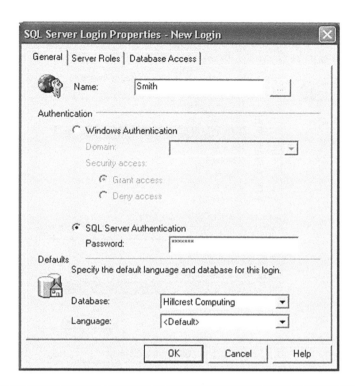

Figure 12.5   Create new user with SQL Server authentication

log in to a database. When something goes wrong, you may find clues by checking who has logged on or tried to log on recently. To audit the attempted log-ins by the users and track down possible security risks, you can configure SQL Server to audit user log-ins. The following steps show you how to configure security auditing.

1. Start **Enterprise Manager** in SQL Server. Expand the **SQL Server Group** node.
2. Right-click the name of your SQL Server and select **Properties**.
3. Click the **Security** tab. Check the **All** radio button under **Audit level** (see Figure 12.11).
4. Click **OK** and restart **Enterprise Manager**.

The following shows one way to trace auditing information.

1. Log on to **Query Analyzer** as **Jones** with the password **asmanager**.
2. Start **Enterprise Manager**, and expand your SQL Server node and then the **Management** node.
3. Expand the **SQL Server Logs** node, and click the **Current** log.
4. Move to the bottom of the log. You should see the log-in information as shown in Figure 12.12.

Figure 12.6   Configuration of Database Access

Another way to trace database activities is to use **SQL Server Profiler**. The following steps illustrate how to use the Profiler.

1. Click **Start**, **All Programs**, **Microsoft SQL Server**, and **Profiler**.
2. Click the **New Trace** icon on the toolbar. Select the **Windows authentication** option.
3. Under the **General** tab, enter **Audit Trace** as the trace name. Check the **Save to file** check box. Figure 12.13 shows the configuration of the General tab.
4. Click the **Events** tab. Double-click **Security Audit** to add it to the **Selected event classes** list box, as shown in Figure 12.14.
5. Click the **Data Columns** tab. Click the **Up** button to move the **LoginName** and **TextData** columns up. You may also add some other columns such as **Permissions** to the **Selected data** list box, as shown in Figure 12.15.
6. Click **Run** to start the trace.
7. Run the following two SQL statements in Query Analyzer:

```
SELECT * FROM ASSEMBLY_WORKER

INSERT INTO PART
VALUES('HD006', '100GHD')
```

8. In the Profiler trace window, you will have the trace results shown in Figure 12.16. The trace results show that the user Jones has attempted to run two SQL statements. One is to query the ASSEMBLY_WORKER table and the other is to insert a new row to the PART table.

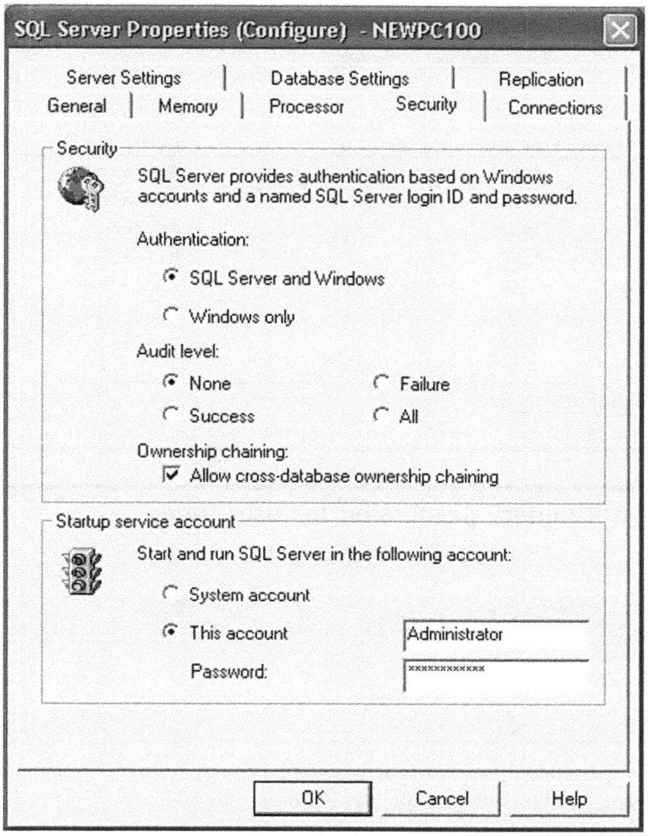

Figure 12.7   Select SQL Server and Windows authentication

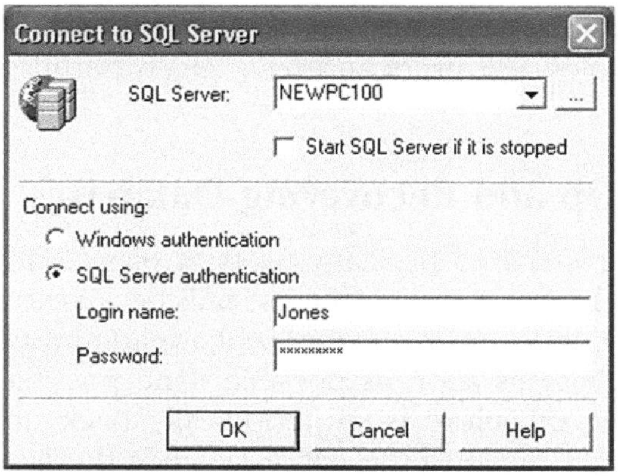

Figure 12.8   Log in with SQL Server authentication

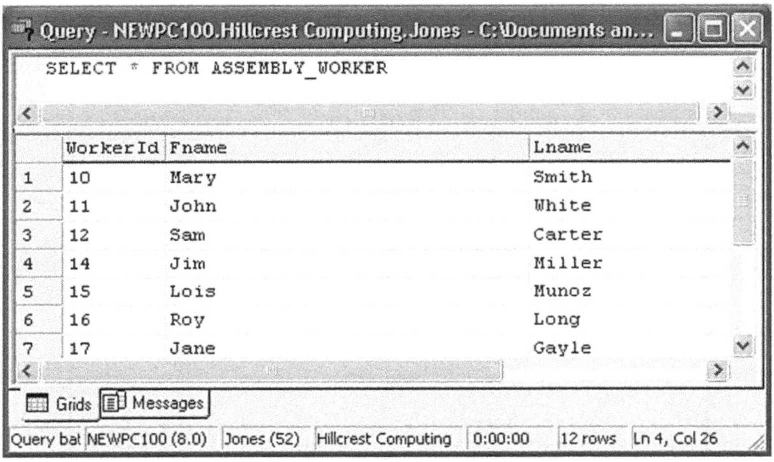

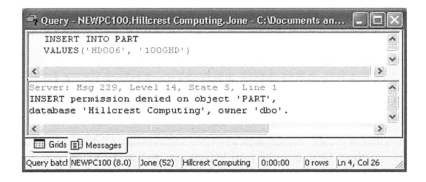

Figure 12.9   Verify query permission for user Jones

Figure 12.10   Verify insert permission for user Jones

In this section, we have discussed the issues concerning database authentication and authorization. Security requirements on data stored in a network database and operations performed on database objects are investigated. We have also created roles and users and have given permissions to the users.

12.3 Backing Up and Recovering Databases

A network database is shared by many users. It plays a key role for the daily operation of an enterprise. When a database fails because of hardware damage, software failure, or human error, it is the database administrator's responsibility to recover the database as soon as possible. One possible way to recover a database at the time of failure is to periodically back up the database and record all the changes made to the database since the last backup. Then the database can be restored by applying all the changes since the backup.

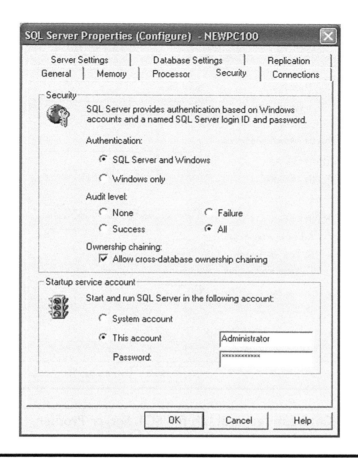

Figure 12.11   Configure audit level

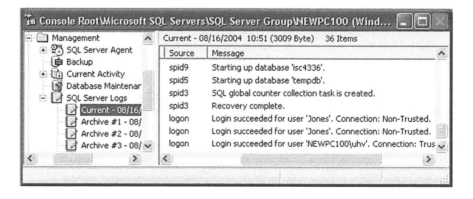

Figure 12.12   Trace auditing information

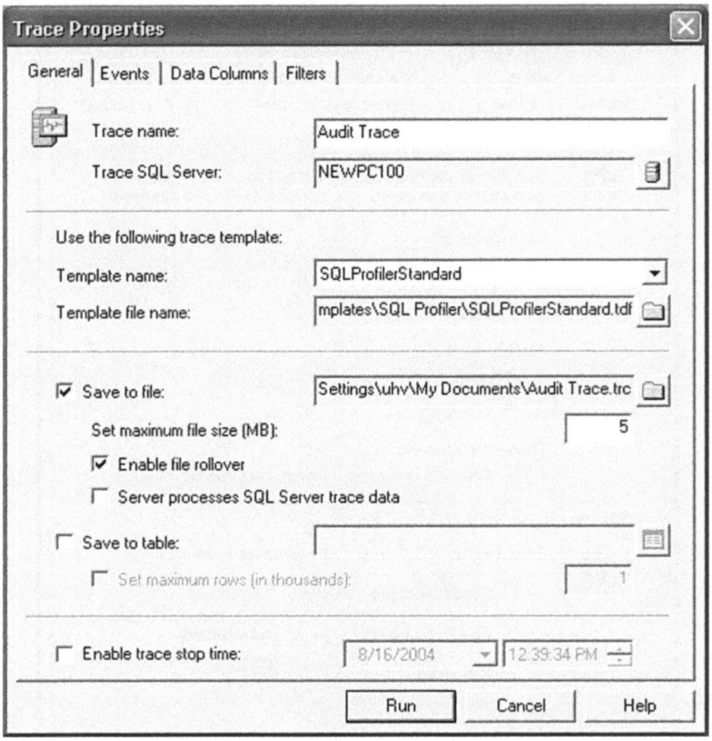

Figure 12.13   Configure general tab for SQL Server Profiler

12.3.1   *About Database Backups*

There are several ways to back up a database. Sometimes, you may need to make a complete copy of a database; other times, you may just want to record transactions to log files. The following are some types of backups.

- *Full backup:* This method creates a complete copy of a database. The full backup method will back up all the data in a database, including user-defined database objects, system-related database objects, and the data related to these objects. A full backup can be carried out while a database is running. Because a full backup copies all the data in a database, it slows down database performance considerably if a database contains a large amount of data. Normally, you should arrange a full backup during the off-peak time. For a large database, a full backup will also consume a large amount of storage space.
- *Differential backup:* This backup method records the data that have been changed since the last backup. In the case that only a small portion of the data is changed after a full backup, a differential backup enables you to back up only the changed data. The differential backup needs smaller storage space and executes faster. However, it takes more time to restore a database if you use differential backups because, during a database restoration process, database administrators will first restore the most recent full backup and then

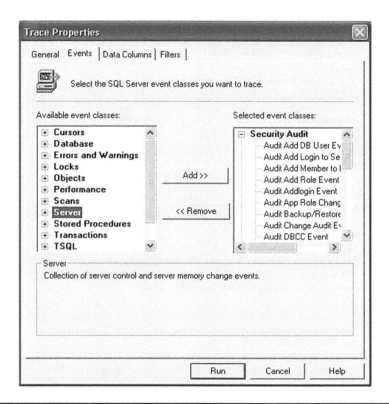

Figure 12.14   Configure event tab in SQL Server Profiler

restore the differential backups. Normally, database administrators schedule several differential backups between two full backups.

■ *Transaction log backup:* This backup method makes a copy of the transaction log since the last full, differential, or transaction log backup. A transaction log backup uses even less time and resources than a differential backup. This advantage will enable you to schedule more frequent backups between two differential backups, so that data loss can be reduced to a minimum. During the recovery process, apply all the transaction log backups since the last differential or full backup. If the last transaction log backup is missing in the recovery process, the transaction will be rolled back.

■ *File backup:* This method backs up specific database files that contain database data. This backup method enables you to back up a large database when you have limited time. However, the restoration of a database from data files is more difficult than with other backup methods. The restoration process can be performed by using the backup files and the transaction log backups since the last backup.

Backing up the database is an important part of a DBA's job. Sometimes, it is impossible to regenerate the lost data. When all else fails, database backup is the last resort to keep the company running. Next, we discuss how to recover a database from the backups.

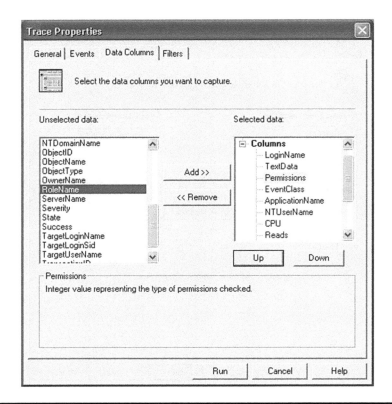

Figure 12.15   Configure data columns tab in SQL Server Profiler

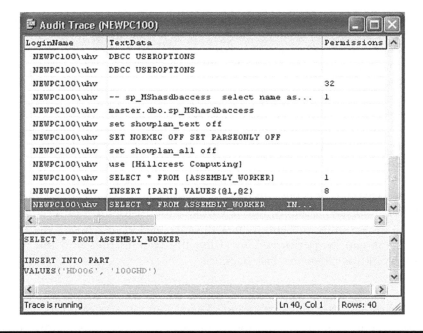

Figure 12.16   Trace results for activities done by user Jones

12.3.2 About Database Recovery

When a database crashes, you need to put the database backups back to SQL Server. This process is called database recovery. If a selected recovery process is properly configured, it will automatically recover the database when SQL Server restarts from a database crash. To restore a database, three activities will be performed during the recovery.

- Starting from the checkpoint, an analysis procedure is carried out to collect information about the uncommitted transactions. A checkpoint is a point at which all modifications to data and transaction log pages are written to disk. Many DBMS products provide checkpoint functionalities to assist database recovery. A transaction log contains the database records before they have been changed (**before image**), the records after they have been changed (**after image**), and the transaction activities performed on these data. By reading the transaction log, the analysis procedure can determine which transactions need to be recovered and which do not.
- If transactions made changes to data records and the changes were committed but the changed data were not written to disk, the recovery process will redo the transactions (**roll forward**) and write the changed data to disk. In a redo process, transactions are rolled forward by applying the **after image**. The redo process will make sure that every change made by the transactions has been restored in the database.
- If transactions made changes to data records but were not committed, the recovery process will undo the transactions (**roll back**). In an undo process, the partially processed transactions are rolled back by applying the **before image**.

Three recovery models are provided by SQL Server. These models are used to help database administrators to make decisions on balancing data loss, database performance, and disk space usage. A summary of the three models is given in Table 12.4.

To illustrate the use of database backup and recovery methods, let us consider the example of a backup and recovery process applied to the database Hillcrest Computing. Suppose that Hillcrest Computing is a mission-critical database; that is, we want to keep data loss to a minimum and reduce slowdown on the database performance by performing backup operations. Let us compare two backup schemes. The first one is to conduct a full backup on each Sunday and one transaction log backup on each weekday and Saturday. The second scheme is to conduct a full backup on each Sunday, a differential backup on each Wednesday and Friday, and a transaction log backup on each Monday, Tuesday, Thursday, and Saturday. These two schemes are listed in Table 12.5.

Both schemes will meet the requirements of keeping data loss to a minimum. The first scheme requires relatively smaller storage space and has less impact on database performance. During the recovery process, the first step is to restore the full backup, then apply Monday's transaction log backup,

Table 12.4   Recovery Models

Recovery Models	Data Loss	Database Performance	Disk Storage Usage
Simple	Changes since the last full or differential backup are lost.	Supports high-performance bulk data-loading operations such as SELECT INTO and BCP.	No backup for transaction logs, so it requires minimal disk storage usage.
Full	No data loss since the last transaction log backup if no failure occurs to the log file.	Supports high-performance bulk data-loading operations such as SELECT INTO and BCP. Has the ability to recover up to the point of failure. Needs additional time to back up every single user's operations.	Uses full, differential, and transaction log backups. The resulting backup can be quite large. Ideally, transaction logs should be stored on a different physical disk.
Bulk-logged	No data loss if no failure occurs to the log file and no database crash during a bulk operation.	Supports high-performance bulk data-loading operations such as SELECT INTO and BCP. These operations are only minimally logged; i.e., the operations are logged at bulk level instead of at single-entry level.	Uses full, differential, and transaction log backups. The resulting backup is much smaller.

Table 12.5   Backup Schemes

Sunday	Monday	Tuesday	Wednesday	Thursday	Friday	Saturday
Full backup	Transaction log backup	Transaction log backup	Transaction log backup	Transaction log backup	Transaction log backup	Transaction log backup
Full backup	Transaction log backup	Transaction log backup	Differential backup	Transaction log backup	Differential backup	Transaction log backup

then Tuesday's, and so on until the changes on Saturday have been recovered. This scheme needs more recovery time and causes more system downtime. The second scheme takes more time to perform the two differential backups and needs relatively greater storage space. During the recovery process, the full backup is restored first, then the most recent differential backup, and then the transaction log backup after the last differential backup. In the case of transaction log backup, if the database failure occurred on Saturday, you need to apply only Saturday's transaction log backup. This scheme requires relatively shorter system downtime and has less impact on users. We use the second scheme in our example.

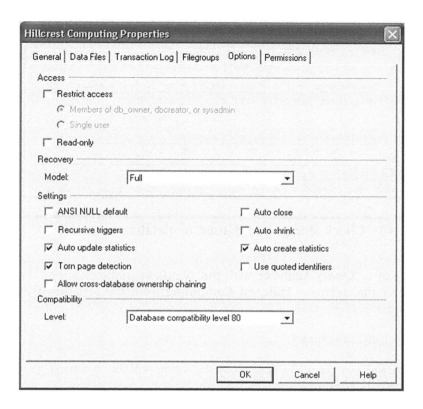

Figure 12.17   Configure recovery model

12.3.3   *Configuring Recovery Model*

Suppose that we need to minimize data loss or transaction loss between two backups. For the database `Hillcrest Computing`, we do not use many bulk loading operations such as `BCP` or `SELECT INTO` operations, so the requirement for the logging of operations is minimal. Based on the above needs, we choose the full recovery model for our database `Hillcrest Computing`.

- Start **Enterprise Manager**. Expand your SQL Server node.
- Right-click on the database **Hillcrest Computing**, and select **Properties**.
- Click the **Options** tab. From the recovery model combo box, select **Full** as shown in Figure 12.17. Click **OK** to complete the configuration.

12.3.4   *Creating Backup Device*

Before you back up a database, the first thing you need to do is to verify how large your database is by using the built-in stored procedure `sp_spaceused`. To do so, use the following steps:

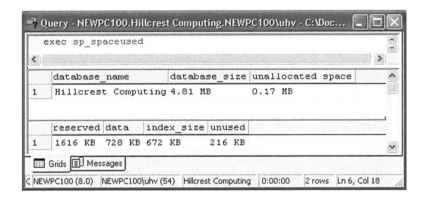

Figure 12.18 Check storage space used by database

1. Log in to **Query Analyzer** with the Windows authentication.
2. Select the database **Hillcrest Computing** from the pull-down menu, and enter the command

   ```
   exec sp_spaceused
   ```

3. Run the command. The execution result will be returned as shown in Figure 12.18.

After you find out the size of the database, the next step is to prepare a backup device to store the backup data. A backup device can be tapes or data files on a disk device. The following steps will show you how to create a backup device.

1. Start **Enterprise Manager**. Expand the **Management** node under your SQL Server.
2. Right-click the **Backup** icon and select **New Backup Device** to open the **New Device** dialog.
3. Enter **Hillcrest_Backup** as the backup device name and click **OK** to create a file on the hard disk as the backup device (see Figure 12.19).

After the backup device is created, the next step is to copy the database to the backup device.

12.3.5 Backing Up Database

By using Enterprise Manager, we will be able to perform a complete backup, differential backup, transaction log backup, and file/filegroup backup. The steps to perform a backup are given below.

1. Start **Enterprise Manager** and expand the SQL Server node. Click the **Tools** menu and select **Backup Database**.

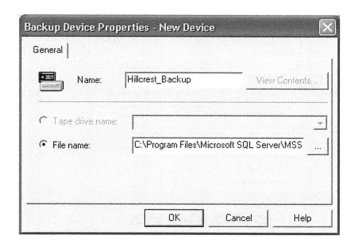

Figure 12.19 **Create database backup device**

2. Under the **General** tab, select the database **Hillcrest Computing** in the database combo box. Enter **Hillcrest Computing backup** as the database backup name. Based on Table 12.5, we need the full/complete, differential, and transaction log backups for our database. First, click the **Database-complete** radio button. To select the backup device, click the **Add** button. Click the **Backup device** radio button and select the **Hillcrest_Backup** device. To save disk storage space, choose the **Overwrite existing media** radio button. Click the **Schedule** check box and accept the default where the backup occurs on every Sunday at 12:00:00 AM, as shown in Figure 12.20. Click **OK** to accept the configuration.

3. Similarly, you can configure the **Database-differential** backup by checking the **Database-differential** radio button and naming the backup **Hillcrest Computing Differential backup**. Select the radio button **Append to media** to append the differential backup to the existing complete backup. Schedule the database-differential backup according to Table 12.5. Click the **Change** button for the **Recurring** schedule. The differential backup time is every Wednesday and Friday at 12:00:00 AM, as shown in Figure 12.21.

4. Use similar steps for the **Transaction log** backup. This time, name the backup **Hillcrest Computing Transaction Log backup** and set the recurring schedule as shown in Figure 12.22. Note that, for demonstration purposes, the transaction log is placed on the same device holding the database. In practice, the database should be placed on a different device from the transaction log and the backup database. In such a way, if the device holding the database crashes, the transaction log and the database backup files can be used to restore the database up to the point of failure. To verify that all three backups are created, you may navigate to the SQL Server **Agent** node under the **Management** node and then click **Jobs**, as shown in Figure 12.23. If the SQL Server Agent is not on, right-click on the SQL Server Agent and select **Start** to start SQL Server Agent.

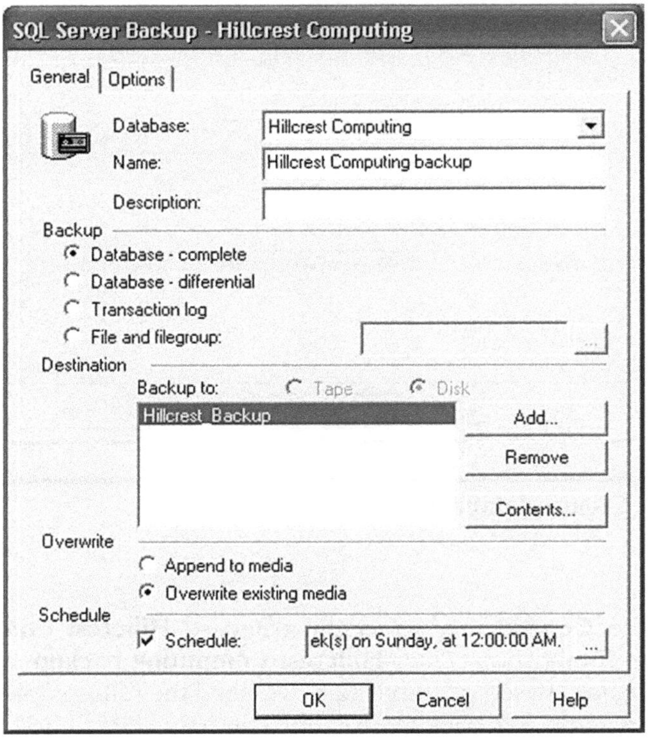

Figure 12.20   Configure database-complete backup

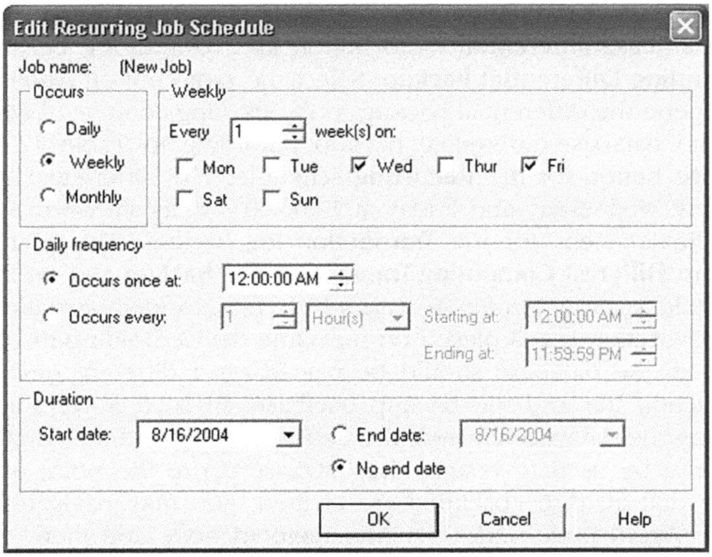

Figure 12.21   Configure database-differential backup recurring schedule

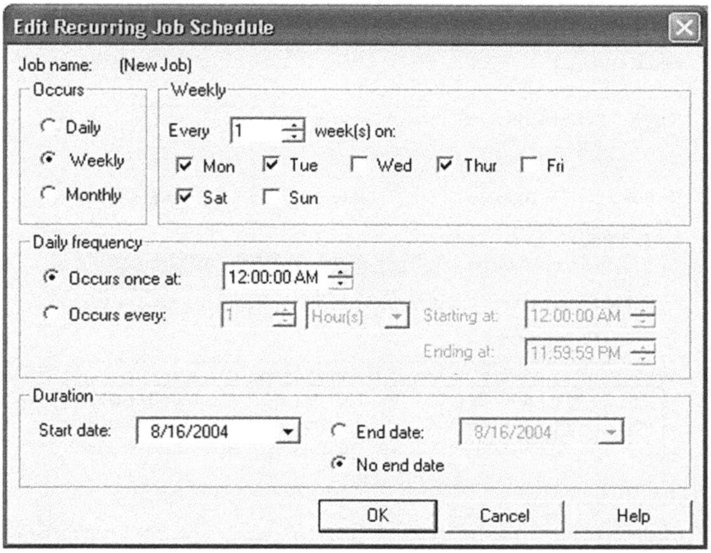

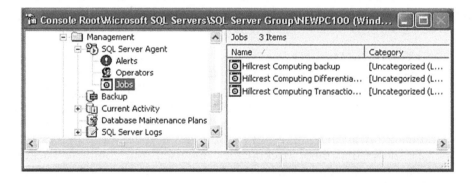

Figure 12.22   Configure transaction log backup recurring schedule

Figure 12.23   Three types of backups created

Note: To start SQL Server Agent, you need the system administrator privilege.

12.3.6   Restoring Database

Once a database failure occurs, a database administrator will solve the problem that causes the database to fail and use the database backups to restore the database up to a certain point, depending on the recovery model. For the full recovery model used in this example, the complete, differential, and transaction log backups can be used to restore the database up to the point of failure. As an example, suppose the database failed on Saturday. In this case, we can restore the database by using the complete backup on Sunday, the differential backup on Friday, and the transaction log on Saturday.

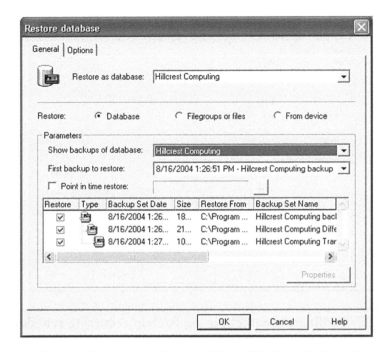

Figure 12.24 Restore database by using database backups

1. Start **Enterprise Manager** and expand the SQL Server node. Click **Tools** on the menu bar and select **Restore Database**.
2. Select the database to be recovered, such as **Hillcrest Computing**, in the **Restore as database** combo box. In the **First backup to restore** combo box, select the complete backup made on Sunday. Then SQL Server will automatically arrange the list of backup files in the backup process. Figure 12.24 shows that three backup files are used: the complete backup on Sunday, the differential backup on Friday, and the transaction log backup on Saturday.

The check box **Point in time restore** allows you to restore the database to a specified time. Under the option tab, you can also customize the restoration procedure such as forcing the database to be restored to another database or controlling the state after the restoration process is completed. Click **OK** to start the restoration process.

Note: For the above restoring practice, the backup jobs may not be available due the fact that these backup jobs are scheduled to start at midnight. If you cannot wait until midnight, go to **SQL Server Agent** under the **Management** node and click **Jobs**. Then right-click a backup you created and select **Start Job** to begin the backup right away.

In this section, you have learned how to develop and implement a backup plan. We have discussed the full/complete backup, differential backup, and transaction log backup. You have also learned how to implement and use a recovery model. There are three types of recovery models: simple recovery, full recovery, and bulk-logged recovery. The advantages and disadvantages of these recovery models are summarized in Table 12.4. For a large-scale database processing system, you may also consider running multiple copies of a database simultaneously to protect your data from database failure. This involves database replication, which is discussed in the next section.

12.4 Database Replication

Often, multiple applications use the same database. To improve the performance of an application, you may want to let the application work with a copy of the database. In some cases, for reliability purposes, you may want to create copies of the original database on standby servers. In a network database environment, a database may be run on multiple sites. To make data accessing easier, a copy of the database is placed at each site. To quickly create copies of a database, most DBMS systems support replication tools for duplicating the original database. A replication process can be applied in the following business circumstances:

- An airline ticket-ordering company runs a central database at its headquarters. Each ticket-purchasing outlet gets ticket information from the central database and stores the information on the local computer.
- A sales company employs a large number of sales representatives who store sales information on their notebook computers' local databases. The sales representatives need to communicate regularly with the central database to synchronize their local databases.
- A large online franchise computer store ships computers from several of its distribution centers. Each distribution center has its own local database. Daily database updating on the central server is required.

A replication process may be accomplished by three tasks: *publishing*, *subscribing*, and *distributing*. We take a closer look at these three tasks.

- *Publishing:* The task to detect the changes made to the database and make the modified data available to other servers is done by the **Publisher** server.
- *Subscribing:* The task to subscribe the data published by the Publisher server is done by the **Subscriber** server. The Subscriber server can also make changes to the Publisher server. Therefore, there are two types of subscriptions, *pull* and *push*. Subscribers use the pull subscription to initialize the replication. The push subscription will propagate all the changes to subscribers.
- *Distributing:* The task to store the published data and forward the data to **Subscriber** servers is done by the **Distributor** server.

Based on the requirements for a replication job, replication processes can be classified into three major types: snapshot replication, transactional replication, and merge replication. Table 12.6 summarizes the characteristics of these replication types.

Table 12.6 Replication Types

Type	How It Works	Usage
Snapshot replication	A replication is created by taking a snapshot of the database. The snapshot will then be published for subscription.	Good for the following cases: Small replication size. A replication contains few changes. Static replication is adequate for subscribers. Noncurrent replication is sufficient for subscribers. Subscribers can use offline replications.
Transactional replication	A snapshot is used as the initial replication. Then changes to the database are published to subscribers.	Good for the following cases: A replication contains frequent changes. Subscribers require an up-to-date replication. Subscribers need online replications.
Merge replication	Each subscriber is allowed to modify its own local database and then replicate the changes back to the publisher. When a conflict happens, a priority-based rule is used to resolve the conflict.	Good for the following cases: Multiple subscribers need to make changes to the same publisher. Multiple subscribers are working online or offline independently. The changes made by multiple subscribers need to be synchronized by a publisher.

Now that we have briefly discussed the concepts and characteristics of replications, we create some replications for our database with SQL Server. Common tasks in developing replications involve creating distribution databases, publishing replications, specifying subscribers, and removing replications. SQL Server provides several wizards to assist the configuration of replications. The configuration wizards and their functions are listed in Table 12.7.

In our example, suppose that each sales center uses a database that is updated by using the publication from the central database `Hillcrest Computing`. We are going to replicate `Hillcrest Computing` for the database at each sales center. It is ideal if the database at each sales center is updated as soon as the following information is available: an assembly process is completed, a new type of computer system is available, or a price change is announced. Based on these requirements, we implement a transactional replication.

12.4.1 Creating Distribution Database

The first step in developing a replication is to create a distribution database. This task can be done in SQL Server by using Enterprise Manager. The steps for creating a distribution database are listed below.

Table 12.7 Replication Wizards

Wizard	Usage
Configure publishing and distribution wizard	Specifies a computer as the distribution server and creates a distribution database on this server. Adds replication publishers to the distribution database.
Create publication wizard	Specifies publication options such as replication type, subscriber type, and data filtering for performance.
Push subscription wizard	Creates subscribers that receive subscriptions from the publisher automatically.
Pull subscription wizard	Creates subscribers that send requests to the publisher for subscriptions automatically.
Disable publishing and distribution wizard	Removes replication schedules, replication publications, distribution databases, and distribution services.

1. Start **Enterprise Manager**. Expand your SQL Server node.
2. To start the wizard, right-click the **Replication** node and select **Configure Publishing**, **Subscribers**, and **Distribution**.
3. Click **Next** to continue. By using the default setting in the **Select Distributor** dialog box, you make your current SQL Server the distributor. Otherwise, you may check the **Use the following server** option to choose a different server as the distributor. In our example, we choose the default and click **Next** to continue.
4. Accept the default for the **Snapshot** folder. Click **Next** to continue. When a message shows up, click **Yes**. Then move to the **Customize the Configuration** dialog box. Accept the default **No**, **use the following default settings**, as shown in Figure 12.25.
5. Click **Next**, **Finish, OK,** and **Close** to complete the configuration.

Now that the distribution database has been specified, we configure the replication publisher.

12.4.2 Configuring Replication Publisher

To specify the replication type, subscriber type, and data filtering for performance, follow the steps below.

1. From **Enterprise Manager**, expand the **Replication** node. Right-click **Publications** and select **New Publication** to open **Create Publication Wizard**.
2. Click **Next** to continue. Select the **Hillcrest Computing** database and click **Next**. Check the **Transactional publication** radio button.
3. Click **Next** to continue. Make sure that the check box **Servers running SQL Server 2000** is checked.
4. Click **Next** to go to the **Specify Articles** dialog box. To provide up-to-date information about the assembly processes and computer systems, specify the tables **ASSEMBLY_PROCESS** and **COMPUTER_SYSTEM** for publishing.

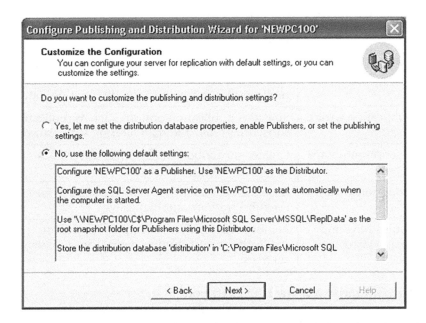

Figure 12.25   Use configure publishing and distribution wizard

5. Click **Next** and accept the default publication name and description. Click **Next** again to go to the **Customize the Properties of the Publication** dialog box.
6. Click **Next** to accept the default. Click **Finish** to complete the configuration. After closing the message page, you should be able to see the new publication **Hillcrest Computing** in the **Publications** folder.

Next, we specify a subscriber.

12.4.3   Configuring Replication Subscriber

You can either specify a remote SQL Server or a local SQL Server as a subscriber. In our example, to illustrate the use of replication, we create another instance on the local computer to represent the subscriber.

1. If you have not done so, install another SQL Server instance called **HOUSTON** by using the SQL Server CD before you do the following. Then restart the computer.
2. In **Enterprise Manager**, right-click on the **SQL Server Group** node and select **New SQL Server Registration** to start **Register SQL Server Wizard**.
3. Click **Next** and select the SQL Server instance **HOUSTON**. Click the **Add** button and then click **Next**.
4. Accept the default in the **Select an Authentication Mode** dialog box and click **Next**.

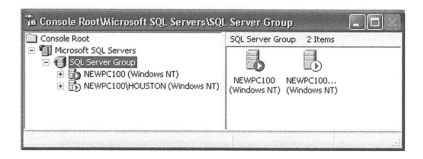

Figure 12.26   Create another SQL Server instance

5. Accept the default in the **Select SQL Server Group** dialog box. Click **Next** and then **Finish** to complete the configuration. You will see the result similar to the one shown in Figure 12.26.

In our example, we want the modification to the tables ASSEMBLY_PROCESS and COMPUTER_SYSTEM to be forwarded to the subscriber automatically. The push subscription will be able to do this. To configure the push subscription, follow the steps below.

1. Expand your SQL Server node and then the **Replication** node. Right-click the publication **Hillcrest Computing** we created earlier. Select **Push New Subscription** from the pop-up menu to open **Push Subscription Wizard**.
2. Click **Next** to go to the **Choose Subscribers** dialog box. Select the subscriber. In our example, the subscriber is **NEWPC100\HOUSTON**. Your subscriber may have a different name. It depends on the host name of your computer.
3. Click **Next** to continue. In the **Choose Destination Database** dialog box, you will select the database that uses the replication data. You may select an existing database or create a new database. In our example, the SQL Server instance is newly created, so there is no user-defined subscription database created yet. The next task is to create one. Click the **Browse or Create** button. Click the **Create New** button. Name the new database **Hillcrest Computing** and click **OK**. Click **OK** again to go back to the **Choose Destination Database** dialog box.
4. Click **Next** and accept the default setting for the dialog box **Set Distribution Agent Schedule**.
5. Click **Next** to go to the **Initialize Subscription** dialog box. Click the check box of **Start the Snapshot Agent to begin the initialization process immediately**.
6. Click **Next** to continue and accept the default setting in the dialog box **Start Required Services**.
7. Click **Next** and then **Finish** to complete the configuration.

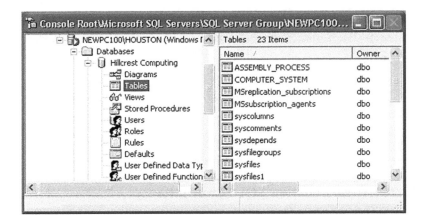

Figure 12.27   Subscription tables created on subscriber

To verify that the SQL Server instance HOUSTON has the subscription, expand **HOUSTON**, **Databases**, **Hillcrest Computing**, and **Tables**. You should see the two tables, **ASSEMBLY_PROCESS** and **COMPUTER_SYSTEM**, as shown in Figure 12.27.

In this section, we have discussed three types of replications: snapshot replication, transactional replication, and merge replication. You have learned how to perform some tasks in a replication process. As an example, we implemented the transactional replication on SQL Server. In the next section, we study another important database administration task, performance tuning.

12.5 Optimizing Database Performance

In a network database environment, multiple users share the same database. In such an environment, all sorts of performance and data transaction problems can happen. When a database is running, one of the DBA's tasks is to identify performance bottleneck and solve the problem by database tuning to make the database operate more efficiently and effectively. Database tuning may involve the following tasks:

- Identify the problem by listening to database users on performance and checking the performance with tools such as Enterprise Manager, SQL Query Analyzer, and Profiler.
- Alter options, add indexes, and modify database structures to improve performance.
- Report the changes made in a database-tuning process.

In the following, we first introduce the concept of transaction and discuss the transaction locks. Then we show how to use the performance-tuning tools to identify transaction deadlocks and solve performance problems.

12.5.1   *Transactions and Locks*

One of the tasks of performance tuning is to monitor SQL Server transactions and locking activities. For example, you can find out how many users are currently connected to the database, how their activities affect database performance, and if any database is currently locked.

To solve the performance-tuning problems, you need to first understand the concept of transaction. A SQL Server *transaction* consists of a sequence of related operations to complete one logical unit of work. A transaction can be started in one of three modes: *autocommit mode, implicit mode,* and *explicit mode.* By *autocommit,* we mean that each SQL statement operation is automatically committed when the operation is completed.

When a transaction process starts automatically and continues until the transaction is stopped by running the keyword COMMIT or ROLLBACK, it is in the *implicit* mode. For example, when you execute certain SQL statements, such as ALTER, CREATE, or OPEN, the implicit transaction process will occur.

For an *explicit* transaction, you need to explicitly start a transaction process with the keyword BEGIN TRANSACTION and explicitly end the process by using the keyword COMMIT or ROLLBACK. For example, the following sequence of SQL statements defines an explicit transaction:

```
BEGIN TRANSACTION

UPDATE STUDENT
SET FirstName = 'Liz'
WHERE SID = 10258

UPDATE STUDENT
SET FirstName = 'Bruce'
WHERE SID = 11505

COMMIT
```

For a committed transaction, changes to the records are written to the database. Otherwise, you can roll back an uncommitted transaction by using the keyword ROLLBACK.

A valid transaction should meet requirements such as *atomic, consistent, isolated,* and *durable.* By atomic, we mean that a transaction performs either all of its operations or none of them. By consistent, we mean that concurrent transactions should be executed in a serial order. There are two levels of transaction consistency: *statement level consistency* and *transaction level consistency.* As an example, we consider the above transaction. In that transaction, there are two UPDATE operations. For the statement level consistency, during each UPDATE process, the attempt to modify FirstName and SID in STUDENT from another transaction is disallowed. However, the modification is allowed during the interval between two UPDATE statements. For the transaction level consistency, modification from another transaction is disallowed for the entire transaction. By isolated, we mean that a transaction will not be

Table 12.8   Reading Problems during Concurrent Transactions

Problems	Meaning
Dirty read	Read records changed by an uncommitted transaction. When an uncommitted transaction is rolled back, the data retrieved during the read process is not in the database.
Nonrepeatable read	Inconsistent data are retrieved when rereading the same records within a transaction. The records have been changed by another committed transaction.
Phantom read	Inconsistent data are retrieved when rereading the records within a transaction. A new record has been inserted by another committed transaction.

Table 12.9   Isolation Levels

Isolation Level	Meaning
Read uncommitted	At this level, no physically corrupted data will be read. Reading of uncommitted data is allowed.
Read committed	At this level, no dirty read. Only committed data can be read.
Repeatable read	At this level, no dirty read and no nonrepeatable read, so that the same content can be read repeatedly within a transaction.
Serializable	At this level, no dirty read, no nonrepeatable read, and no phantom read. Concurrent transactions are completely isolated from one another.

affected by the values modified by other transactions. By durable, we mean that all the committed operations in a transaction are permanent. Any transaction that meets the above four requirements is called an *ACID* transaction.

When running concurrent transactions, the reading of records in a transaction has the problems shown in Table 12.8.

Depending on which reading problems are unacceptable, the 1992 ANCI SQL standard defines four levels of isolation: *read uncommitted*, *read committed*, *repeatable read*, and *serializable*. The default isolation level for SQL Server is read committed. The definitions for these isolation levels are listed in Table 12.9.

To avoid the inconsistency problem, a database object or transaction should be locked when you want to make changes during concurrent processing. The isolation level affects the *locking mode*. As the isolation level goes up, the lock becomes more restrictive. SQL Server provides six locking modes: *shared*, *update*, *exclusive*, *intent*, *schema*, and *bulk update*. The functions of these locking modes are listed in Table 12.10.

Locks are automatically managed by SQL Server. Usually, there is no need for a DBA to set and release locks on transactions or database objects. However, when multiple transactions try to modify the same resource, it is possible that *deadlock* and resource *blocking* problems may occur. The example in Table 12.11 shows how a deadlock takes place.

Table 12.10 Locking Modes

Locking Mode	Meaning
Shared	Allows concurrent transactions to read the same resource at the same time, but no modification.
Exclusive	Disallows other transactions to read or modify the resource.
Update	During an updating process, the update lock is converted to an exclusive lock if changes are made to the resource; otherwise, it is a shared lock.
Intent	Specifies that a transaction intends to place a lock on the resource, so that no other transactions can place locks on the same resource.
Schema	Prevents changes to schema-related transactions such as adding additional columns to a table when performing DDL operations or compiling queries.
Bulk Update	Prevents changes made by other transactions to a bulk update transaction.

Table 12.11 Occurrence of Deadlock

User	Activities	Processing Sequence
User A	Lock PartId in the table `PART` Update `PartId` Update `ItemId` in the table `PART_DETAIL`	Lock PartId for User A Lock ItemId for User B Update PartId for User A Update ItemId for User B User A waits for User B to release the lock on ItemId
User B	Lock ItemId in the table `PART_DETAIL` Update `ItemId` Update `PartId` in the table `PART`	User B waits for User A to release the lock on PartId Deadlock occurs

A blocking problem can be caused by a transaction that locks a resource for a long period of time. Other transactions must wait for the current transaction to release its lock. You may prevent a deadlock by allowing only one lock at a time or allowing locks from each application to be placed in the same sequential order.

In the following, we do some hands-on practice of performance tuning. We first introduce some tools used to monitor performance. Then we show how to use the information gained by using these tools to solve performance problems.

12.5.2 Tools Used in Performance Tuning

The following tools are useful in identifying performance problems. Look at what you can do with these tools.

- *SQL Server Enterprise Manager:* You can use this tool to identify locked database objects and types of locks enforced on them. You can also use it to get database processing information such as current users and queries performed by these users.
- *SQL Server Profiler:* By using Profiler, you can track detailed lock information, trace activities against a database, identify the bottleneck caused by queries and stored procedures, and examine log information about system performance.
- *Query Analyzer:* You can use Query Analyzer to examine an execution plan and make necessary changes to the plan to improve performance.
- *System procedures:* Some tasks accomplished by Enterprise Manager and Profiler can also be done by system procedures. The commonly used system procedures in performance monitoring are sp_lock, sp_who, sp_blockcnt, sp_trace_create, sp_trace_setevent, sp_trace_setfilter, and so on.

Using Enterprise Manager

One of the functions Enterprise Manager can perform is to monitor SQL Server transactions and locking activities. For example, you can find out how many users are currently connected to the database, how their activities affect the database performance, and if any database is currently locked.

Enterprise Manager can be used to monitor transaction processes and locking problems. Tasks that can be accomplished by Enterprise Manager are:

- Monitoring current transaction processes that are operating on the database
- Monitoring current users connected to the database and activities performed by them
- Monitoring locks held on transactions and database objects

To illustrate the use of Enterprise Manager in solving problems in transaction processes and locking, consider the example based on the database Student_Club created in Chapter 5. (Inasmuch as the database Hillcrest Computing has been replicated earlier in this chapter, it is not appropriate to use it to demonstrate the effect of blocking.)

1. Start **Enterprise Manager** and select your first SQL Server. In our example, it is **NEWPC100**.
2. To monitor processes against the database Student_Club, click **Tools** and then **SQL Query Analyzer**. Select the database **Student_Club** from the combo box on the toolbar.
3. Go back to **Enterprise Manager**. Under the node **Current Activity** in the **Management** folder, click the **Process Info** node. You will see many processes running against the database **Master** because it is the default database. You should also see that the process and the user connecting to the database **Student_Club** are listed in the result pane. (You may need to refresh **Current Activity** to see the most recent connection to a database.)

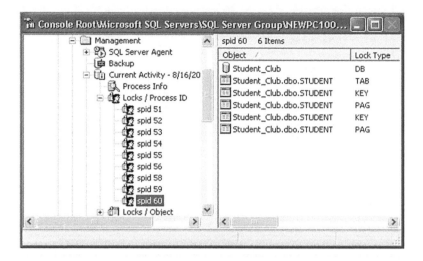

Figure 12.28   Locked processes

4. To demonstrate a blocking problem, we execute the following query in Query Analyzer:

```
BEGIN TRANSACTION

UPDATE STUDENT
SET FirstName = 'Liz'
WHERE SID = 10258
```

5. Go back to **Enterprise Manager**; right-click **Current Activity** under the **Management** node; select **Refresh**. Expand the node **Locks/Process ID** and click on the last process id. In the result pane, you should see that the lock is placed on the table STUDENT (see Figure 12.28).

6. To show that the lock is blocking other transactions from accessing the same resource, we execute another SQL statement. In Query Analyzer, open a new query window by clicking the **New Query** icon on the toolbar and enter the following SQL statement:

```
SELECT *
FROM STUDENT
```

7. This time, there are no records returned. Go back to **Enterprise Manager** and refresh **Current Activity**. Expand the **Locks/Process ID** node; you will see the blocking and blocked processes shown in Figure 12.29.

8. To solve the blocking problem, right-click the blocking process id, in our example, **spid 60 (Blocking)**, in the tree pane and select **Properties**. Click the **Kill Process** button to end the blocking process. Now go back to **Query Analyzer**, and you should see the records returned by the **SELECT** statement.

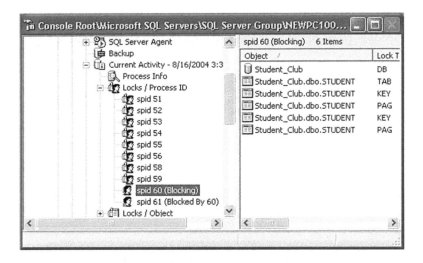

Figure 12.29   Blocking and blocked processes

Enterprise Manager is a convenient tool for diagnosing and solving blocking problems. Other tools such as SQL Profiler and Query Analyzer are also used in diagnosing and solving database performance problems.

Using Profiler

One of the Profiler's functions is to trace events that have occurred in SQL Server. Events are actions performed during an operation. There are more than 100 predefined SQL Server events. Profiler also allows 10 user-defined events. You can create an event trace and use the trace to keep track of details of how a SQL statement is executed, how a table is accessed, and how a lock is enforced. A trace can also be used to replay the activities against a database object for testing. By tracing the events, you can do the following:

- Find out what causes a query to run slowly by tracing the query step by step.
- Trace server events to find out the cause of a deadlock.
- Trace the activities in a process to find out which activity takes an unusually long CPU time.

In this section, you will learn how to use Profiler to trace SQL Server events and how to use tracked information to solve a performance problem. As an example, let us use Profiler to find which SELECT statement is taking more execution time when retrieving data from the database Hillcrest Computing. To open SQL Profiler and carry out performance-tuning tasks, follow the steps below.

1. Open **Profiler** by clicking **Start**, **All Programs**, **Microsoft SQL Server**, and **Profiler**.

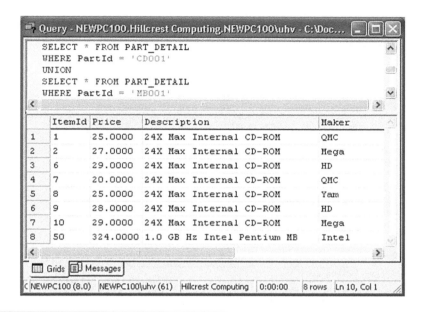

Figure 12.30 Query with UNION **operator**

2. Once Profiler is open, we need to define a trace template or use a predefined trace template. Several useful predefined trace templates are available; for example, *SQLProfilerTSQL_Duration* can be used to determine which SQL statement takes a longer execution time. To start the trace by using the SQLServerProfilerTSQL_Duration trace template, click **File**, **New**, **Trace**, and log in to the local SQL Server instance.

3. In the **Trace Properties** window, under the **General** tab, enter **Hillcrest Trace** as the trace name and select the predefined trace template **SQLProfilerTSQL_Duration**.

4. Under the **Events** tab, remove the event classes **Security Audit**, **Sessions**, and **Stored procedures** from the **Selected** event classes pane.

5. After you have configured the trace template, click **Run** to start the trace.

6. Next, we execute two SQL statements and analyze the information obtained by the trace template. We use the **UNION** operator to combine the output from two **SELECT** statements. The first statement selects detailed information about the part CD001, and the second selection is about the motherboard MB001. The query and the execution output are listed in Figure 12.30. To execute the SQL statement, we need to select the database **Hillcrest Computing** on the toolbar.

7. As a comparison, we use **UNION ALL** for the same query to see the difference in execution duration. Because the UNION ALL operator does not remove duplicates (if any) when returning query results, it should execute queries faster. The execution result is given in Figure 12.31.

8. We go back to **Profiler**; it has captured the execution duration for the two queries (see Figure 12.32).

The trace results show that the duration for the query with UNION ALL is 10 and the duration for the query with UNION is 20. This means UNION ALL has better performance.

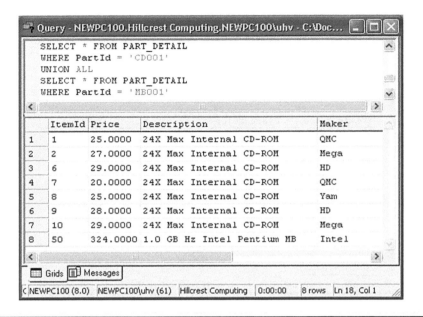

Figure 12.31   Query with `UNION ALL` **operator**

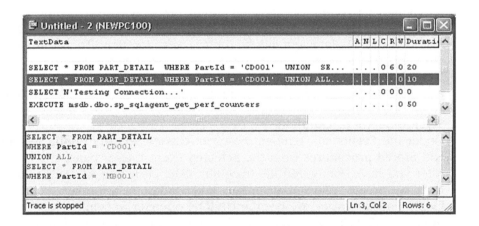

Figure 12.32   Trace results on execution duration for two queries

Using Query Analyzer

In this section, you will learn how to use Query Analyzer to analyze query execution. With Query Analyzer, you can view a query execution plan that is performed by the built-in query optimizer. The query optimizer compares the cost of each possible execution plan and uses the best one to execute the query. The built-in optimizer makes decisions based on the statistics about table columns. You can manually modify an execution plan generated by the built-in query optimizer. To demonstrate the use of execution plans, let us consider two queries. The first query is used to select data from multiple

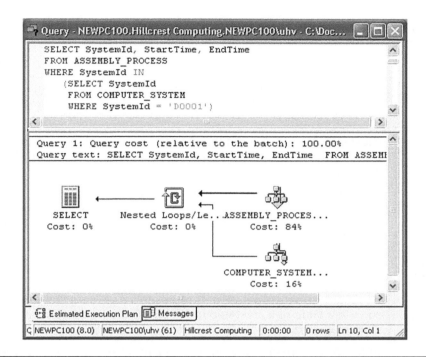

Figure 12.33   Execution plan for query with subquery

tables with a *subquery* structure. The second one selects the same information using a join structure.

- Start **Query Analyzer** and log in as a database administrator. Select the database **Hillcrest Computing** from the database selection combo box on the toolbar.
- Type the SQL statement as shown in Figure 12.33. Highlight the SQL statement and click the **Execution Plan** icon ▦▦ on the toolbar. The execution plan is displayed graphically (see Figure 12.33).

An execution plan displays resource costs for operations performed on database objects such as tables and indexes. There are two types of indexes: clustered index and nonclustered index. In a clustered index, the leaf nodes on the index tree contain actual data rows in a column (or columns). In a nonclustered index, the leaf nodes on the index tree contain references to the data rows in a column, instead of data rows themselves. The commonly used icons in an execution plan are listed in Table 12.12.

An execution plan finishes at the activity represented by the icon in the upper-left corner. Therefore, we read the execution plan from the upper-right corner to the leftmost icon. In Figure 12.33, for example, the index scan process on the table ASSEMBLY_PROCESS takes 84 percent of the cost. To see more details of how the resources are used, move the mouse cursor over the operation icons, for instance, the **Nested Loops** icon in the execution plan. A pop-up information window will appear, as shown in Figure 12.34. Table

Table 12.12   Commonly Used Icons in Execution Plan

Execution Plan Icon	Meaning
	Clustered or nonclustered Index Scan operation. The scan operator scans a given index. The use of keywords such as IN or LIKE will cause the scan operation.
	Clustered or nonclustered Index Seek operation. The index uses the SEEK operator to search for qualified rows. The use of keywords such as = will cause the seek operation.
	Nested Loops operation. It performs inner loop and left outer loop operations. The Nested Loops operator searches for rows in the inner table corresponding to each row of the outer table by using an index.
	SELECT statement. It represents the SELECT statement and its result set.
	Bookmark Lookup operation. It represents a process that searches rows in a table or a clustered index by using a bookmark (row ID or clustering key).
	Index Delete operation. It represents a process that deletes rows in a clustered or nonclustered index based on given criteria.
	Index Insert operation. It represents the process that inserts rows into a clustered or nonclustered index.
	Index Update operation. It represents the process that updates rows in a clustered or nonclustered index based on given criteria.
	Table Delete operation. It represents the process that deletes rows in a table based on given criteria.
	Table Insert operation. It represents the process that inserts rows into a table.
	Table Scan operation. It represents the process that scans a given table.
	Table Update operation. It represents the process that updates rows in a table based on given criteria.
	Sort operation. It represents a sorting process.
	Filter operator. It specifies a filter condition that is applied to SQL statements.

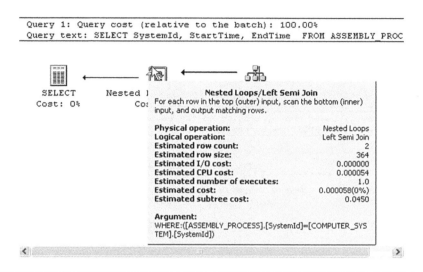

Query 1: Query cost (relative to the batch): 100.00%
Query text: SELECT SystemId, StartTime, EndTime FROM ASSEMBLY_PROC

SELECT   Nested]   **Nested Loops/Left Semi Join**
Cost: 0%   Co: For each row in the top (outer) input, scan the bottom (inner)
                      input, and output matching rows.

Physical operation:	Nested Loops
Logical operation:	Left Semi Join
Estimated row count:	2
Estimated row size:	364
Estimated I/O cost:	0.000000
Estimated CPU cost:	0.000054
Estimated number of executes:	1.0
Estimated cost:	0.000058(0%)
Estimated subtree cost:	0.0450

Argument:
WHERE:([ASSEMBLY_PROCESS].[SystemId]=[COMPUTER_SYS
TEM].[SystemId])

Figure 12.34   Detailed information of operations in execution plan

Table 12.13   Meanings of Information List in Detailed Information Window

Information	Meaning
Physical operation/ logical operation	Operations performed by SQL statements. The commonly used operations are listed in Table 12.12.
Estimated row count	The estimated number of rows processed by an individual operation.
Estimated row size	The estimated size of the result set retrieved by an operation. The size is measured in bytes.
Estimated I/O cost	The estimated I/O resources consumed by an operation.
Estimated CPU cost	The estimated CPU resources consumed by an operation.
Estimated number of executes	The estimated number of times that an operation will be executed during the execution of a query.
Estimated cost	The estimated resource cost of an operation. The cost is measured by the percentage of the total cost.
Estimated subtree cost	The estimated resource cost of the current and related preceding operations.
Argument	Parameters used by a SQL statement.

12.13 gives definitions of the list of information in the pop-up window. In our example, the detailed information window shows that the cost of the subtree, including the operations of clustered index scan, clustered index seek, and nested loops, is about 0.0450.

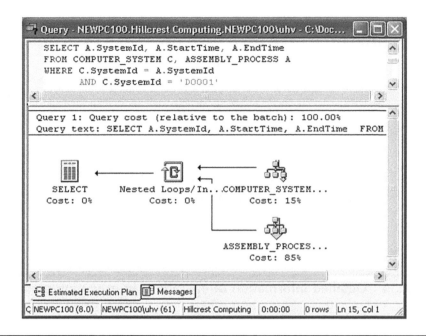

Figure 12.35   Execution plan for query with inner join

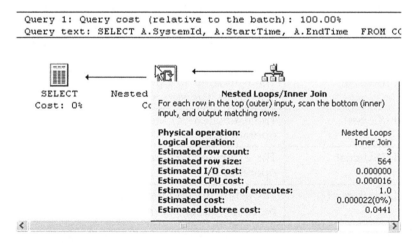

Figure 12.36   Detailed information window for query with inner join

As a comparison, we execute another query that will select the same set of data but use the inner join structure instead of the subquery structure. Enter the SQL statement and display the execution plan as shown in Figure 12.35.

To compare the costs of the queries with two different structures, open the detailed information pop-up window as shown in Figure 12.36. For the query with the inner join structure, the subtree cost is 0.0441, which is slightly less than that of the query with the subquery structure.

The performance can be further improved by correctly using a *hint* which forces the query optimizer to perform some manually specified operations. The commonly used hints are:

- *Join hint:* Used to make the query optimizer perform specified join operations such as loop, hash, and merge.
- *Query hint:* Used to force the query optimizer to perform operations such as GROUP BY and ORDER BY.
- *Union hint:* Used to force the query optimizer to perform operations such as concatenation, merge, and hash.
- *Table hint:* Used to force the query optimizer to perform operations such as retrieving the first *n* rows and using predefined indexes.

As an example, let us create an index, SystemId, on the table ASSEMBLY_PROCESS and then make a query to use the index SystemId. Enter the following SQL statements in Query Analyzer. (Be sure to run the CREATE INDEX statement first, and then run the rest of the code.)

```
CREATE INDEX [SystemId]
ON [dbo].[ASSEMBLY_PROCESS] ([SystemId])
ON [PRIMARY]

SELECT A.SystemId, A.StartTime, A.EndTime
FROM COMPUTER_SYSTEM C, ASSEMBLY_PROCESS A
WITH (INDEX(SystemId))
WHERE C.SystemId = A.SystemId
  AND C.SystemId = 'D0001'
```

The hint is represented by the statement WITH (INDEX(SystemId)). The execution plan of the query with the hint gives the detailed information shown in Figure 12.37.

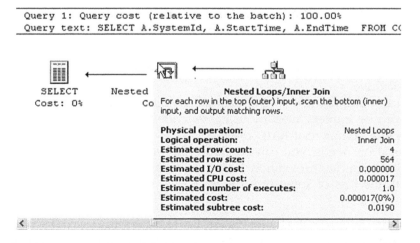

Figure 12.37 Detailed information window for query with hint

From the detailed information, the estimated subtree cost is 0.019, which shows that the performance has been improved significantly. However, we need to be careful when using hints. When using a hint, you overwrite the query optimizer. There are risks that some hints might make performance worse.

12.5.3 Impact of Database Structure on Performance

The structure of a database has a great impact on performance. The performance of a well-designed structure is improved significantly. One of the bottlenecks on databases is disk I/O. There could be thousands of users reading and writing to the same database concurrently. In such a case, *filegroup* is one of the structures that can be used to manage database files. When a DBA wants to store different tables on different disk drives, he or she needs to use a filegroup. The following are structure-related issues and tasks that should be considered for intensive database I/O operations.

- Once a database object is created, you can control where to place it. Place a heavily used table into a filegroup across a number of disk drives. In this way, the table is shredded to several disk drives, and this allows parallel I/O processing for the same table.
- When you place related tables in different filegroups, operations on these tables can be performed concurrently to improve performance.
- Placing nonclustered index files and table data in different filegroups allows users to run the index and process the data at the same time.
- Place data files, system files, and transaction log files on separate disk drives. In this way, files can be accessed concurrently and the time spent on disk I/O will be shorter.

When developing a large and highly reliable database, consider using the *Redundant Array of Inexpensive Disks* (RAID) structure to accomplish the above-mentioned tasks. The advantages of the RAID structure are as follows:

- It can make multiple disk drives work together and act like a single logical disk drive.
- It can automatically spread data across multiple disk drives.
- It can be implemented by using software with existing disk drives or by using a commercial RAID drive.
- Based on needs, you can configure different RAID levels.
- It has great fault tolerance. It can be configured to provide services, even with the loss of some disk drives.

The commonly used RAID levels are RAID 0 (striping), RAID 1 (mirroring), RAID 5 (striping with parity), and RAID 10 (striping and mirroring). We show how these levels function and how much fault these levels can tolerate.

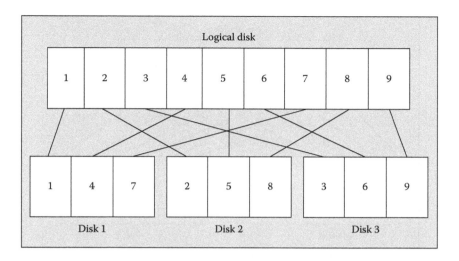

Figure 12.38   RAID 0 structure

RAID 0

This structure improves performance by using *disk striping*. The process of disk striping divides a set of data into blocks called *stripes*. The stripes are then distributed to multiple disk drives, as shown in Figure 12.38. The multiple disk drives work together as if we were using a single logical disk drive.

Although it improves performance, the RAID 0 structure has no data redundancy. This means it does not have hardware fault tolerance. If any disk fails, the entire logical disk fails with it. Therefore, RAID 0 is not appropriate for a mission-critical database.

RAID 1

This structure provides hardware fault tolerance by duplicating a set of data to multiple disks. In this way, if one disk drive fails, its duplicate (*mirror*) will continue to function so that no data are lost. The RAID 1 structure is shown in Figure 12.39.

Although it provides fault tolerance, the RAID 1 structure degrades performance and raises the cost of running the database. Every operation must be performed twice and the cost on the disk drives is doubled.

RAID 5

This structure provides good reading performance and tolerance by using *parity* information (see Figure 12.40). If a disk drive fails, parity can be used to re-create the lost data and store them on any other disk drive.

RAID 5 provides fault tolerance without costing twice as much disk space. It uses only a fraction of a disk drive to store parity information. Its reading

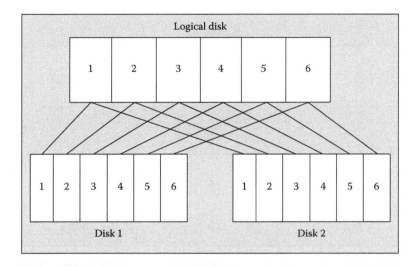

Figure 12.39   RAID 1 structure

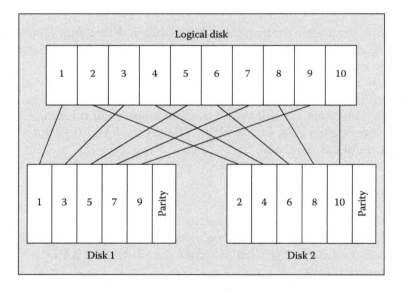

Figure 12.40   RAID 5 structure

performance is good by using disk striping. However, when data are written to a disk drive, the first step of RAID 5 is to get the information from both the destination disk stripe and parity block, recalculate the parity value, and then write the data to the destination disk stripe and at the same time modify the parity block. Therefore, its written performance is degraded.

To see how to achieve the fault tolerance goal by using parity information, we look at an example. Consider the RAID 5 structure with two disk drives, as shown in Figure 12.40. At each moment, data are represented by binary bits; that is, a data value is either 1 or 0. Parity can be either odd or even.

Table 12.14 Odd Parity in RAID 5 Structure

Disk 1-Bit Value	Disk 2-Bit Value	Parity Bit Value	Sum of Bits
0	0	1	1
0	1	0	1
1	0	0	1
1	1	1	3

Being an odd parity, the parity bit is created to make the sum of the bit from Disk 1, the bit from Disk 2, and the parity bit an odd number. Similarly, the sum for the even parity should be an even number. Suppose that we are going to use the odd parity. Table 12.14 lists the possible bit values from both disk drives and the corresponding values for the parity bit.

If one of the disks fails, say Disk 1, the bit values in Disk 1 can be re-created by using the bit values in Disk 2 and the values of the parity bit. You can re-create the bit values for Disk 1 to make each sum of bits equal to an odd number.

RAID 5 is a good structure for a mission-critical database that has fewer than ten concurrent writing operations. It provides a cost-efficient solution for small businesses.

RAID 10

This structure is a combination of RAID 0 and RAID 1. It provides both disk striping and data mirroring. The original data set is striped to multiple disk drives. Each stripe is mirrored to other disk drives. It has the performance advantage of RAID 0 and fault tolerance advantage of RAID 1. The structure of RAID 10 is demonstrated in Figure 12.41.

As in RAID 1, the writing in RAID 10 takes more time, but it is still faster than that of RAID 5. Its reading speed is faster, too. The RAID 10 structure is good for a mission-critical database that requires better performance and has less concern about the cost of disk drives.

In this section, you have learned how to use three tools — Enterprise Manager, SQL Profiler, and Query Analyzer — to diagnose and solve performance and locking problems. We have discussed the concepts of transactions and locking. Some details about locking modes and isolation levels are also discussed in this section. Examples are used to demonstrate how to use these tools in diagnosing and solving blocking and performance problems. The last part of this section discusses design issues on database structures to avoid the bottleneck problem caused by intensive I/O operations.

12.6 Database Maintenance Plan

For routine database management tasks, you can create a maintenance plan in SQL Server to perform these tasks automatically. By using **Database Maintenance**

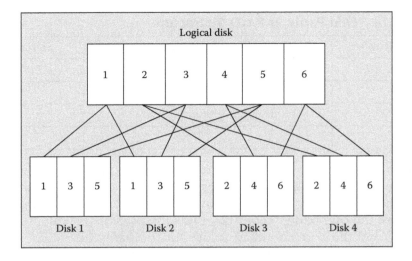

Figure 12.41 RAID 10 structure

Plan Wizard, you will be able to do database backups, performance optimization, and transaction consistency checking. To create a maintenance plan by using Database Maintenance Plan Wizard, follow the steps below.

1. Start **Enterprise Manager** and expand your SQL Server node. Under the **Management** node, right-click **Database Maintenance Plans** and select **New Maintenance Plan** to start **Database Maintenance Plan Wizard**.
2. Click **Next** to go to the **Select Databases** dialog box; select the database **Hillcrest Computing** under **These databases**.
3. Click **Next** to go to the **Update Data Optimization Information** dialog box. The following optimization options are available:
   - *Reorganize data and index pages:* This option allows you to rebuild all the indexes on all the tables in a selected database. For the tables being updated frequently, free space of index and data pages will be used to store newly added rows quickly. When the page is full, page split will occur. Half of the data on the original page will be moved to a new page. Page split slows down operation performance caused by delay and overhead. To avoid page split, you can rebuild the index to re-establish free space for later use. This option allows you to specify the percentage of free space allocated for each index page. If the percentage is too low, page split will occur frequently. If it is too high, free space will not be used efficiently and data reading will be slow.
   - *Update statistics used by query optimizer:* This option allows you to resample data to calculate the statistics used in the query optimizer. As an index and a data page are modified, the statistics used in the query optimizer should be updated accordingly. If the index is completely rebuilt as specified in the previous option, you don't need to specify this statistics updating option.
   - *Remove unused space from database files:* This option allows you to shrink the database files by removing unused space. Removing unused space makes a database run more efficiently and improves performance.

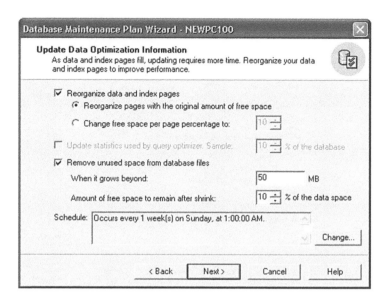

Figure 12.42 Configure optimization options

4. Check the **Reorganize data and index pages** option and the **Remove unused space from database files** option. Select the **Reorganize pages with the original amount of free space** radio button (see Figure 12.42).

5. Click **Next** to go to the **Database Integrity Check** dialog box. When the **Check database integrity** option is selected, it allows you to examine the integrity of indexes and tables. Click the radio button **Include indexes** and click the check box **Attempt to repair any minor problems**. Also, click the check box **Perform these checks before doing backups** (see Figure 12.43). Keep in mind that if integrity is violated, the database backup will be discarded.

6. Click **Next** to go to the **Specify the Database Backup Plan** dialog box. Here you can create an automated backup plan as you did in the database backup section. Because we already developed a database backup plan in the previous section, we uncheck the check box **Backup the database as part of the maintenance plan**. Click **Next** twice and make sure to uncheck the check box for the **transaction log backup plan**.

7. Click **Next** to go to the next dialog box, **Reports to Generate**. You can create a report about execution results for the maintenance plan. Check the option **Write report to a text file in directory** and enter the folder in which you want to keep the report. Also, click the check box **Delete text report files older than**.

8. Click **Next** to show the **Maintenance Plan History** dialog box. You can specify if you want to write the maintenance history to a database table. In our example, we uncheck this option.

9. Click **Next** to display the last wizard screen. Name the plan **Hillcrest Computing Maintenance Plan**, and then click **Finish**. You will see the maintenance plan you have just created in the folder **Database Maintenance Plans**.

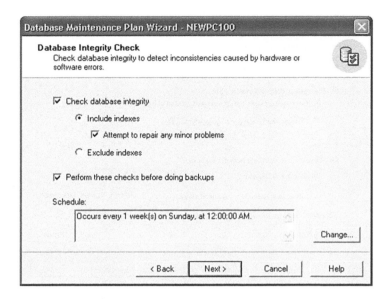

Figure 12.43   Configure integrity check

In this section, you have learned how to create a maintenance plan to automate daily maintenance jobs. As an example, a maintenance plan for the database `Hillcrest Computing` was developed.

12.7 Summary

In this chapter, various database administration tasks have been discussed. The first thing you learned was managing user accounts and database security. You then learned how to back up a database with three types of backups: full backup, differential backup, and transaction log backup. Next, these backups were used in a database recovery process. You also learned how to duplicate data by using database replication. Copies were created by replication and were used to improve performance of database applications and reliability. Three replication types have been discussed and compared in this chapter. You have learned, in detail, various methods of performance tuning. You have learned how to use tools such as Enterprise Manager, Profiler, and Query Analyzer to diagnose and solve performance and locking problems. In theory, we introduced the concepts of page splitting, transactions, and locking modes. We also discussed database structure design issues such as filegroups and RAID structures for avoiding bottleneck problems caused by intensive I/O operations. To assist daily database maintenance tasks, we have created a maintenance plan to automate the job. To demonstrate how to handle administrative tasks, database management examples based on the database `Hillcrest Computing` and `Student_Club` have been developed to help you gain some hands-on experience. At this point, you have gone through the topics of database design, SQL language, database accessing, database applications, network databases, and database administration. One important topic in the database processing system is still missing, that is, data analysis. We cover this topic in the next two chapters.

Review Questions

1. What are the common tasks for a database administrator?
2. What are the benefits of Windows authentication?
3. Describe the mixed authentication mode.
4. What is the difference between authorization and authentication?
5. List the tasks that can be done by a standard user and by a guest user.
6. State the meanings of statement permission and object permission.
7. How can roles be used to reduce the work of a database administrator?
8. Explain how the ownership chain works.
9. Describe the full backup, the differential backup, and the transaction log backup.
10. Explain the meanings of before image and after image.
11. Explain the differences between roll forward and roll back.
12. Describe the simple recovery model, the full recovery model, and the bulk-logged recovery model.
13. Explain how and in what situations a snapshot replication, transactional replication, and merge replication can be used.
14. What are the tasks involved in a database-tuning process?
15. Describe the tools used in a database-tuning process.
16. What are the implicit transaction and explicit transaction?
17. What is an ACID transaction?
18. Describe the problems in running concurrent transactions.
19. Describe the isolation levels.
20. Describe the locking modes.
21. Give an example in which a deadlock can occur.
22. What is displayed by using an execution plan?
23. Describe the hints used to improve performance.
24. How do you manage database structures to solve disk I/O problems?
25. What are the advantages of the RAID structure?
26. State the advantages and disadvantages of the RAID 0, RAID 1, RAID 5, and RAID 10 structures.

Case Study Projects

For the following case studies, you will be asked to work on some hands-on database management projects.

1. Computer Service

For the `Computer_Service` database, perform the following database management activities.

- Create the role Cashier that is allowed to read, delete, and update CUS-TOMERS and read the tables SYSTEMS, PARTS, and SERVICES. Create a user named Carter with "cashier" as the password. Assign Carter the cashier role.
- Back up your database with a full backup every Sunday.
- Suppose that a database failure occurs; use the most recent Sunday's backup to restore the database.

2. University Registration

Perform the following database management tasks for the Registration database.

- Create three roles: one for students, one for faculty, and one for database administrators. Make sure that students can read only the tables COURSES and CLASSES and faculty can read the tables COURSES, CLASSES, and STUDENTS.
- Create a user named Smith with "faculty" as the password. Assign Smith the faculty role.
- Suppose that you need to minimize data loss or transaction loss between two backups. Back up your database with a full backup on Sundays, a differential backup on Tuesdays and Fridays, and a transaction log backup on Mondays, Wednesdays, Thursdays, and Saturdays.

3. Mail Order

For the database Mail_Order, carry out the following database maintenance tasks.

- Create two roles, one for customers and one for sales representatives. Make sure that the customer role can read only the table PRODUCTS. Create three customers in SQL Server log-in mode — Bailey, Bach, and Harris — with the passwords as customer1, customer2, and customer3, respectively.
- Use Profiler to trace log-on information of the three customers you have just created.
- For comparison, execute two queries. One query displays the columns in the tables CUSTOMERS, ORDERS, and SHIPMENT with the subquery structure, and the other query selects the same set of data but uses the inner join structure. Use an execution plan to show which structure has better performance.

Chapter 13

Data Analysis Services

Objectives

- Learn the concepts of data warehouses and data marts.
- Use Data Transformation Services (DTS) for data transformation.
- Use On-Line Analytical Processing (OLAP) in data analysis.

13.1 Introduction

After implementing databases and applications in a network environment and setting up user accounts for a company, you have accomplished the tasks such as collecting and storing data in an organized way and supporting database applications. The next task is to use the data in the company's databases to provide information for helping the company to make the right decision about its business. The *On-Line Analytical Processing* (OLAP) system is one of the data analysis applications to support decision making. OLAP is used to present data in a way that provides the following benefits:

- OLAP can quickly respond to iterative analytical queries.
- OLAP allows you to make a decision with queries based on the "what if" question.
- Through a multidimensional view, OLAP can present data in various detailed levels.
- The data provided by OLAP can be shared by a large number of users.
- OLAP provides numerical and statistical analysis tools to assist decision making.

OLAP has been used in different businesses such as sales, marketing, finance, and manufacturing. We show what OLAP can do:

- Developing business process models such as marketing models for trend analysis
- Forecasting the sales and production in multiple regions
- Analyzing data about the cost, revenue, and profitability of a new product
- Generating reports that contain analytical information for decision making
- Identifying problems in a business process such as problems in resource allocation or product inventory

There have been many successful applications of OLAP in business. For example, to ensure high performance, OLAP has been used to analyze site traffic and patterns in sales data for many Internet computer product stores. Large retailers have hundreds of stores across the country. Allocating resources and keeping a proper product inventory level at each store is one of the key factors for a retailer to run a successful business. In fact, based on the finding from the OLAP analysis, Office Depot's profits were increased after eliminating unnecessary inventory. CompUSA, a large computer product retailer, applies OLAP to identify trends in the sales of video games and music CDs and then uses the findings from OLAP to adjust the inventory level at its stores.

As you can see, OLAP is often used to deal with a large amount of data from a variety of sources. When dealing with a lot of data from different sources, OLAP prefers to work with a *data warehouse*, which is a centralized data storage facility that contains and processes various types of raw data. One of the reasons to use a data warehouse instead of the original database is that it is difficult to design a database that has good performance for both daily data transactions and decision making. Often, the requirements from these two systems conflict with each other. For example, the *decision support system* (DSS) can improve performance by searching a denormalized table that contains all the information needed to make a decision. On the other hand, a denormalized table is not good for data transactions. It can lose data integrity and generate a large amount of redundancy. Some companies configure the database for transactional operations during the day and change the configuration to support decision making at night. It is awkward to switch the database configuration back and forth, and it does not work for companies with a large number of data transactions 24 hours a day. In addition to performance, many companies want to store not only relational database data but also other types of data such as spreadsheet data, data from e-mail, and data from other operating systems.

A data warehouse includes not only data but also data processing utilities and data analysis tools such as OLAP. It is designed for planning, analysis, and decision-making support. The performance of OLAP is greatly improved by extracting and organizing data in a data warehouse. Through the data warehouse, OLAP is able to work on various types of data and a wide array of applications. The benefits of data warehouses are as follows:

- Offering one-step shopping to allow OLAP to select all the requested data across an entire organization
- Improving OLAP's performance for decision-making activities

- Providing OLAP with clean data by automatically performing prescheduled load, filter, and format convert operations on various types of data

Even though OLAP prefers to work with a data warehouse, data warehouses are not just for OLAP. They are good for E-commerce and support many other decision-making tools. In the next two sections, we first introduce the concepts and design issues about data warehouses and then develop OLAP for data analysis.

13.2 Data Warehouse

Developing a data warehouse is a difficult process. A data warehouse must make data from various sources and locations work together. You may want it to do the following:

- Vary the structure of a query or a report. For example, you may want to present the same set of data in different ways and at different levels depending on the results from the ad hoc queries you have performed.
- Allow a user to specify the range of data needed for his or her investigation. For example, based on the return from a previous query, you may want to go to a more detailed level with a different set of data for the next query.
- Permit users to make use of metadata to convert data from one type to another type acceptable by other applications consistently in the time domain, for example, if you have two sets of data, one from a spreadsheet that is updated daily and the other from a relational database that is updated weekly. Tools should be provided to conduct consistent conversion from one time domain to another time domain.
- Provide integrated analysis tools with graphical output to present data in various formats. For example, data from Excel is represented by the spreadsheet format and data from Access is represented by the table format. Tools to convert the data to a consistent appearance should be supplied by a well-developed data warehouse.

For some of these requirements, the solutions are not trivial. The design and implementation of a data warehouse require advanced and complex technology. The construction of a complete data warehouse needs a team of experienced IT professionals. You may need to organize a team of in-house programmers or pay a consulting company to implement the required features. It is also expensive to operate and support the software. To ease the difficulty in developing a data warehouse, a scaled-down version of a data warehouse, a *data mart,* is often used to solve the problems in a limited way.

The emphasis of a data mart is to meet specific demands such as handling a specified data type, or a particular database function, or data management tasks in a departmental level. By restricting the data mart to handle a specific type of data, the metadata will be much simpler and easier to maintain. By restricting it to handle a particular business function, the data mart only supports users with common tasks. That is, the tools used by these users are similar. By restricting the data mart to the departmental level, the amount of data is limited and it is easier to manage the data. For some companies, data marts are used as the components of a data warehouse to run the data warehouse operations at the detail level.

The cost and the time spent in developing a warehouse make it impossible to cover everything in one chapter. In this chapter, we focus mainly on the introduction to the data warehouse and discuss the data warehouse developing tools that are available in SQL Server. For readers who want to know more about this subject, many books specializing in data warehouses are available.

13.2.1   *Data Warehouse Components*

As stated earlier, the functions of a data warehouse are to collect raw data from various sources, store and manage the data, convert the data to useful information, and deliver the information to various end users' applications. A basic data warehouse may include the components shown in Figure 13.1,

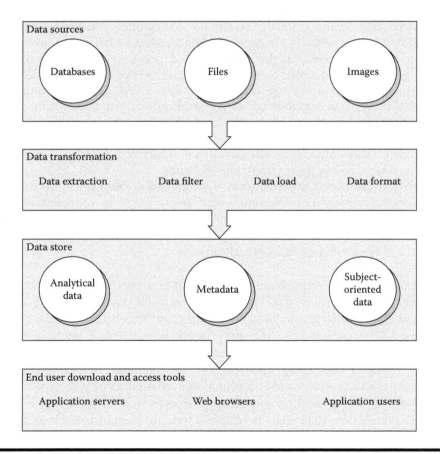

Figure 13.1   Data warehouse components

where the *data sources* of a data warehouse are the operational data that can consist of several databases, data files, images, and other types of data.

The *data transformation* component moves the operational data into the data store. This component will handle tasks such as extracting data, filtering data, and consolidating the data into a format required by the data store.

The *data store* is another database that is designed to improve performance for a decision-support system. The data store is equipped with data management tools used to maintain the data store in a clean, accurate, and consistent condition. The data store keeps an organization's historical data, analytical data generated by OLAP, metadata for data structure, and subject-oriented data such as data in the subjects of accounting, advertising, and sales. A data warehouse may include several data marts for processing the subject-oriented data.

Tools for efficient data accessing are available for front-end users to download the data stored in data warehouses. The data-accessing tools are available from commercial products or programmed by experienced programmers for some special purposes.

13.2.2   Data Warehouse Developing Tools

Based on the high demand for assistance in data warehouse development, many DBMS vendors, such as Oracle, Microsoft, and IBM, have started to offer data warehouse development tools in their database products. The tools provided to develop data warehouses by SQL Server are as follows.

- *Databases:* A data warehouse may contain multiple databases. Some of them may be used as data sources to keep the operational data. The others may be used to store decision-support-related data. SQL Server provides some tools for data warehouse design, construction, and maintenance. Many tools used for database design and manipulation can also be used for data warehouse development.
- *Data Transformation Services (DTS):* During the process that moves data from many sources to a data store, the data are converted to the format that is appropriate for data warehouse operations. SQL Server provides a data transformation tool, Data Transformation Services, which can be used to accomplish such tasks. DTS has two important functionalities needed in developing a data warehouse. It can access data from a wide variety of sources and transform these data into a format that is consistent with the data warehouse specifications.
- *Analysis services:* SQL Server provides analysis tools for decision making. The massive data in a data warehouse can be organized by the OLAP technology provided by SQL Server. OLAP allows the client applications to create reports presenting the data through a multidimensional view. It also supports the more advanced data analysis tools such as data-mining technology, which is used to discover and analyze the information from the data stored in a data warehouse.

Table 13.1   Differences in Designing OLTP System and Data Warehouse

OLTP System	Data Warehouse
For supporting a large number of users and transactions	For supporting decision making and ease of data retrieving
Needs rapid data transactions and very few analysis and reporting activities	Needs to rapidly deliver data for analysis and reporting
Requires transaction/rollback logging to keep track of changes made to a database	No need for transaction/rollback because only a few modifications occur to the historical data stored in a data warehouse
Database backup and restore are necessary to prevent data loss	Requirements for database backup and restore are minimal
Prefers more normalized small tables	Prefers fewer denormalized large tables
Uses entity-relationship data modeling in database design	Uses dimensional modeling in data warehouse design
For tables with frequent data modification, indexes may degrade performance	Needs a large number of indexes to improve performance

- *Metadata services:* SQL Server stores metadata in a centralized repository in the system database **msdb**. The metadata service tools supported by SQL Server provide a browser for viewing the metadata. SQL Server also supports the tools for developing metadata applications.
- *Database replication:* When distributing data from a database to a data store or moving data from a central data warehouse to a local data mart, replication tools can be used to coordinate the updates of distributed data.

13.2.3   Data Warehouse Design

At this point, the goals of database design are to increase data integrity, avoid anomalies, and be able to handle many users and transactions. An operational database that meets these goals is often referred to as the *OnLine Transactional Processing* (OLTP) system.

Design Goals

The goals of data warehouse design are very different from those of the OLTP system. To understand the issues in designing a data warehouse, we compare the design of data warehouses and the design of OLTP systems. The differences are listed in Table 13.1.

About Dimensional Modeling

As shown in Table 13.1, the main purpose of a data warehouse is to provide quick response to queries. This has suggested that the data model used for

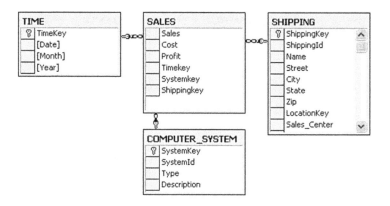

Figure 13.2   Star schema

data warehouse design should be based on the query structures used in data analysis or reporting. The data representing the business fact should be placed in a *fact table*. The data representing a set of attributes that are used to describe the fact should be placed in several *dimension tables*. This kind of modeling is called *dimensional modeling*. For example, for a query selecting the sales of computer systems in Houston during the first two months of 2002, the fact can be identified as the sales and the attributes of the fact are computer systems, shipping, and time. You can create a schema with four tables, one fact table SALES and three dimension tables COMPUTER_SYSTEM, SHIPPING, and TIME. Each dimension table has its own primary key and is connected to the centralized fact table through a foreign key. The schema is illustrated in Figure 13.2. The schema produced by dimensional modeling is called a *star schema* and has been effectively used in data warehouse design.

An alternative to the star schema is the *snowflake schema*. In a snowflake schema, some of the dimension tables can be further decomposed, as we did in E-R modeling. Multiple subdimension tables are connected to a primary dimension table and the primary dimension table is connected to the fact table. In the example shown in Figure 13.3, the SHIPPING dimension table is further divided into three tables. The table SHIPPING is the primary dimension table and the tables LOCATION and CENTER are the subdimension tables.

Compared with the star schema, the snowflake schema uses more inner joins to the primary dimension table in order to load the dimension information. The snowflake schema structure is more complicated and is harder to maintain. Using a snowflake schema will cost the performance slightly because of the additional joins. The benefit of the snowflake schema is that it will save some space in a data warehouse. You may consider the snowflake design for a data warehouse with limited storage space. Otherwise, star schemas are preferable because they include fewer joins when retrieving information from data warehouses and are easier to manage.

Fact Table

In a star or snowflake schema, the centralized fact table usually contains large numbers of rows that hold years of the organization's historical data. For a

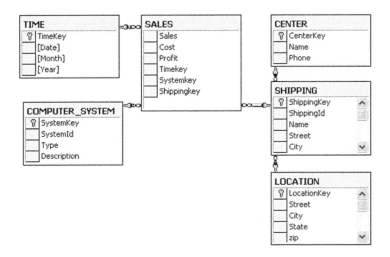

Figure 13.3   Snowflake schema

large organization, the fact table could contain millions of records. The content in a fact table includes foreign keys used to connect to the dimension tables and the columns with numerical fact data. The numerical columns are used to store data from various measurements, such as data about sales of computer systems in the first two months of year 2002. The numerical columns allow summation operations and data analyses over a time period, which is a required characteristic of many data analysis tools. To speed up operations of the data stored in a fact table, indexes are created for the fact table. Every fact table should have an index for the primary key, which is often a combination of the foreign keys from the dimension tables. Based on the structure of the queries and reports, additional indexes should be added to those columns that are frequently queried. A fact table should not contain columns with descriptive data. That kind of data does not allow summary operations on them, which is an undesired characteristic for data analysis.

Dimension Table

A dimension table contains data that describe the attributes of the facts in a fact table. Often, these data are descriptive and nonnumerical. For example, the dimension table TIME is used to specify the time line for the fact table SALES to summarize the cost and profit.

To maintain data integrity, a dimension table must contain a primary key, which is used to connect to the fact table. The keys from more than one data source may conflict with each other. The keys from data sources may be removed or reused and the data in a data warehouse remain the same. Therefore, instead of using the keys from data sources, surrogate keys should be used for all dimension tables to make sure the primary keys are reliable. Also, each dimension table should be indexed on its primary key. Often, the columns in a dimension table represent the detail level for an attribute. For

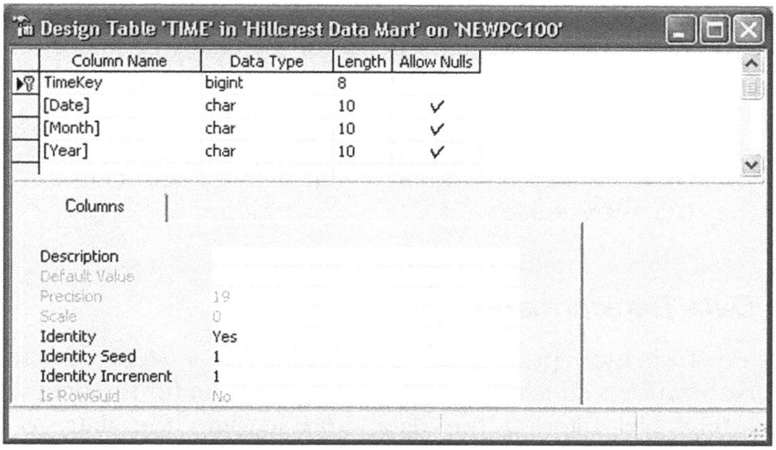

Figure 13.4 Create dimension table `TIME`

example, in the dimension table `TIME`, the detail levels are the columns `Year`, `Month`, and `Date`. Columns representing the detail levels in the hierarchical structure should also be indexed to improve query performance.

For more complicated data warehouse structures, there are multiple fact tables. In such cases, the multiple fact tables may share some of the dimension tables to keep consistency. For example, multiple fact tables can share the `TIME` dimension table for the consistent time period.

As you have seen, the creation of fact tables and dimension tables is straightforward. To create a database to store data for a data warehouse, use a data diagram in SQL Server to connect these tables according to the primary–foreign key constraint. As an example, we create a database using the star schema as shown in Figure 13.2.

1. Open **SQL Server Enterprise Manager** by clicking **Start**, **All Programs**, **Microsoft SQL Server**, and **Enterprise Manager**.
2. Expand the SQL Server. Right-click on the **Databases** node and select **New Database**. Name the new database **Hillcrest Data Mart** and then click **OK**.
3. To create the dimension table **TIME**, expand the **Hillcrest Data Mart** node under the **Databases** node. Right-click on **Tables** and select **New Table**. Enter **Column Name**, **Data Type**, and **Length** as shown in Figure 13.4. Set the column **TimeKey** as the primary key column. To make the primary key column an `auto-incrementID` column, select **bigint** as the data type and select **Yes** for the **Identity** property.
4. Similarly, you can create the tables **COMPUTER_SYSTEM** and **SHIPPING** for the database **Hillcrest Data Mart** according to the design in Figure 13.2. Make sure that the primary key column is an `auto-incrementID` column for each of the tables and the data types match those in the data source. Last, create the fact table **SALES**.
5. Right-click on the **Diagrams** node under **Hillcrest Data Mart** and select **New Database Diagram** to open **Create Database Diagram Wizard**. Click **Next** and add tables **COMPUTER_SYSTEM**, **SHIPPING**, **SALES**, and **TIME**.

Click **Next** and then **Finish**. Rearrange the icons according to Figure 13.2, and you have created the star schema for the data warehouse (or you may call it a data mart because the demonstration example is too small to be a data warehouse).

After the database is created, the next step is to transfer data from the data source to the data warehouse.

13.2.4   Data Transformation

The data transformation process includes three major steps: extracting data from the organization's data sources, preparing the data for the data warehouse by reformatting and filtering the data, and loading the data to the data warehouse.

Data Extraction

The commonly used the data extraction tools available in SQL Server are the following:

- TRANSACT-SQL statements for extracting data from relational databases
- BULK INSERT statement for extracting a large number of data from data files
- The bcp utility for extracting data from data files, tables, or views
- Distributed queries for extracting data from multiple heterogeneous data sources and storing them on one or multiple computers
- Data Transformation Services for extracting, transforming, and consolidating data from a wide range of data sources into one or multiple destinations

Before extracting data from data sources, we should implement the error-checking procedures in the data source to make sure that the data are valid for daily business operations. Invalid data will affect an organization's business as well as the data warehouse built with them.

Data Cleaning

During a data transformation process, we may need to clean data in situations such as the following:

- Eliminating inconsistency in format. Data from different data sources may have inconsistent formats. For example, date and time may be coded differently from different sources. Some data sources may use the format mm/dd/yyyy and others may use dd/mm/yy. Similarly, data sources may code telephone numbers, zip code, numerical numbers, and the length of character strings in different formats. We must reformat the data into a common format. A data warehouse cannot permit data with different formats to be inserted into the same column.

- Eliminating inconsistency in data expression. Data recorded from different data sources may be expressed differently. For example, the expression for the state of Texas in an address may be coded as TX in one data source and as Texas in another data source. For date, we may need to break the original expression mm/dd/yyyy into three new columns — date, month, and year — to fit the requirement of the time dimension table. As another example, we may need to convert the value Success to 1 and Failure to 0 for statistical analysis. Keep in mind that inconsistency in data expression causes difficulty in data analysis.
- Eliminating inconsistency in queries. Often, data are retrieved by using inner joins between the fact and dimension tables. The inner join will select only the row that matches the records in both the fact table and dimension table. If a numerical value in the fact table does not have the corresponding description in the dimension table, the inner join query will not select the record. This may cause some possible inconsistency when different queries are used, for example, if a particular record has no related description in the TIME dimension table. An inner join query searching the fact table and the TIME dimension table will ignore this particular record. However, other inner join queries that are not involved in searching the TIME dimension will return this particular record. The calculations in the data analysis will give different results when using different queries. To solve the problem, for each record in a fact table, we must include the corresponding description in the dimension table.
- Calculating numerical values by summarizing data from multiple data source columns.
- Merging data from multiple columns into a single column, such as merging street, city, and state into a single address column in the dimension table.
- Adding surrogate keys for the newly cleaned records.

Tools commonly used in a data cleaning process are as follows:

- SQL procedures and trigger
- Data Transformation Services (DTS) packages
- Other scripts such as ActiveX scripts

After the data have been cleaned, they are ready to be loaded into a data warehouse.

Data Loading

Data loading is the process to populate tables created for the star schema. When a large number of data are loaded into a data warehouse, the operation can slow down the database performance significantly. In such a case, we should perform the data-loading process during the time of relatively low system use. The tools used for data loading are the following:

- The bcp utility
- SQL statement
- Data Transformation Services

Data Transformation Services (DTS)

The data transformation tool, Data Transformation Services, provided by SQL Server is commonly used to assist the data transformation process. DTS can accomplish the following tasks:

■ Transfer data from heterogeneous data sources to a data warehouse. When moving data with DTS, you can handle the transformation for the following types of data sources and destinations:
  – *OLE DB data sources:* Including data stored in Oracle, SQL Server, MS Office, and others.
  – *ODBC data sources:* Including relational databases created with DBMSs sold by most of today's database vendors.
  – *Text files:* Including files with ASCII code.
■ Integrate data with the transformation controls that decide how and when to carry out actions such as connection, validation, and transformation. The package that integrates both data and control activities is the DTS package, which contains three types of objects.
  – *DTS connection:* This kind of object is used to connect to data sources. The information contained in the object specifies the data provider, log-in information, and network information of remote data sources.
  – *DTS task:* This type of object contains information about control activities such as reformatting data to make them data warehouse ready, executing SQL statements based on the dynamic parameter values, executing the code in scripting languages, performing bulk insert, and sending e-mail.
  – *DTS step:* This type of object can be used to set up data transformation workflow. It is used to coordinate the workflow by determining the order of execution based on the outcome of other tasks.
■ Graphically design and implement a complicated data transformation plan that involves exporting various types of data from multiple data sources and importing these data to multiple destinations. The graphical tool allows the sharing of metadata information.

DTS is a convenient graphical data transformation utility for the above tasks. It provides the services for extracting, validating, formatting, and loading data. The tools provided by DTS are as follows:

■ *Import/Export Wizard:* It is used to select various data sources for exporting. It can be used to reformat data and import them to different destinations. To ease the daily maintenance workload, we can schedule an automatic data transformation process with the Import/Export wizard.
■ *DTS Designer:* It is used to design and implement complicated data transformation plans. A transformation plan involves exporting multiple data sources with many different data types and importing these data to multiple destinations. A graphical tool is used to illustrate the data sources, workflows, and destinations.
■ *DTS COM object:* This COM object is used to integrate the DTS functionalities to other programming languages.

These three tools can be used to construct DTS packages. For a relatively simple constructing task, use the Import/Export wizard. For more complicated DTS constructing tasks, the DTS designer is the choice. To extend DTS functionalities to scripts in other programming languages, consider using the DTS COM object.

To illustrate the use of DTS, consider the example that transforms the data from our OLTP database Hillcrest Computing to the SALES schema created for the data mart. The first step is to create a DTS package in SQL Server Enterprise Manager.

1. Expand our SQL Server in Enterprise Manager. Right-click **Data Transformation Services**, and select **New Package** to open the **New Package** window.
2. On the left-hand side of the **New Package** window, there are connection objects and task objects. In this step, we create a source connection. Because our OLTP database is built on SQL Server, we first drag a **SQL Server connection** object to the New Package pane. The **Connection Properties** dialog box opens for us to enter information. Name the new connection **Computer_System.** Select the database **Hillcrest Computing** and keep the default for other options as shown in Figure 13.5. Click **OK** to complete the configuration for the source connection.

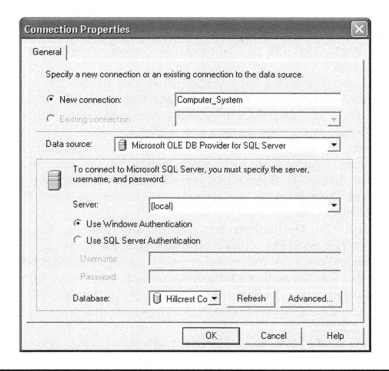

Figure 13.5   Configure connection object

Figure 13.6   Configure transform data task properties

3. For the destination connection, we drag another **SQL Server connection** object into the **New Package** pane. This time, choose the database **Hillcrest Data Mart**. Click **OK** to complete the configuration for the destination connection.

4. In this step, we add a transformation between the source and destination connections. Click the **Transform Data Task** icon 🦋, click the source connection, and then click the destination connection. You should see a transformation line between source and destination.

5. Now we can specify how to move the data from the data source to the data mart. Double-click the transformation line to open the properties window. Under the **Source** tab, enter **Transform Computer System Info to Hillcrest Data Mart** as the description. Select the table **COMPUTER_ SYSTEM** (see Figure 13.6).

6. Click on the **Destination** tab; choose the existing destination table **COMPUTER_SYSTEM**. Click the **Transformations** tab and select **DTS Transformation_1** as the transformation name. Click the **Edit** button to open the **Transformation Options** dialog box. Make sure all the columns are selected. Click the **Test** button to test the transformation. Click **OK** to complete the transformation editing. The configuration result is shown in Figure 13.7.

7. The data can be saved to SQL Server, a structured storage file, or a Microsoft Visual Basic file. Click **Package** and **Save As**. Name the new package **Computer_System Package** and choose the default for the other items. Click **OK** to save the package. To execute the transformation, right-click

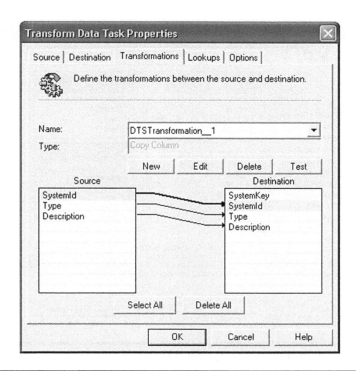

Figure 13.7 Configure transformation properties

the newly configured transformation line and select **Execute Step** to transform the data.

To illustrate the use of a SQL statement and ActiveX Script for transferring data from data sources to a data warehouse, consider the next example that will transfer the data from the tables SHIPPING and SALES_CENTER in the database Hillcrest Computing to the table SHIPPING in the data mart.

1. Drag a new **connection** object to the **DTS Package** window.
2. In the **Connection Properties** dialog box, change the new connection name to **Shipping**, select **Hillcrest Computing** as the database, and click **OK**.
3. Create a **transformation line** connecting the new connection object and the destination connection object created for the data mart. Double-click the **transformation line** to open the **Transform Data Task Properties** dialog box. Click the **SQL query** option box and the **Build Query** button. Click the **Add table** button on the toolbar, and then add the tables **SHIPPING, SHIPPING_ORDER, PURCHASE_ORDER**, and **SALES_CENTER**. From the selected tables, check the columns **ShippingId, Lname, Fname, Street, City, State, Zip, Name**, and **Phone**. The SQL statement is automatically generated, as shown in Figure 13.8.
4. Click **OK** to go back to the **Data Transformation Task Properties** dialog box. Click the **Destination** tab and select **SHIPPING** as the destination table. Click the **Transformations** tab to configure the data transformation properties. You will edit the new transformation by matching **Fname** and

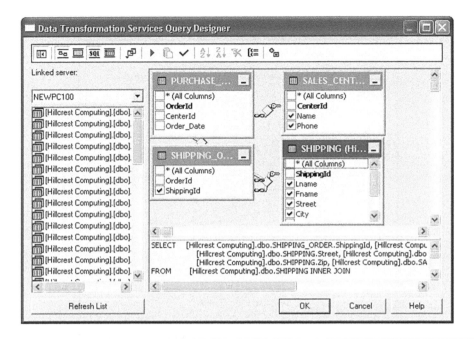

Figure 13.8   SQL statement in Query Designer

Lname in the source to **Name** in the destination. To integrate two columns in the source into a single column in the destination, highlight both **Lname** and **Fname** in the source and click the **New** button. Select **ActiveX Script** and click **OK**. Click the **Destination Columns** tab and move the column **Name** from the **Available columns** pane to the **Selected columns** pane. Go back to the **General** tab, click the **Properties** button, and enter the following code:

```
Function Main()
   DTSDestination("Name") = RTrim(DTSSource("Fname")) & _
      " " & DTSSource("Lname")
   Main = DTSTransformStat_OK
End Function
```

5. Click **OK** a couple of times. The resulting configuration is shown in Figure 13.9.
6. Click **OK** to complete the configuration. Right-click the newly configured **transformation line** and select **Execute Step** to transform the data.

Note: If the connection lines do not exactly match those in Figure 13.9, you need to delete the wrong connection lines and add new ones manually by clicking the **New** button and specifying the columns under the **Source Columns** and **Destination Columns** tabs.

To populate the TIME table, consider the next example, which inserts the data about date, month, and year into the columns Date, Month, and Year in the table TIME. Because there is no table containing the time data in the data

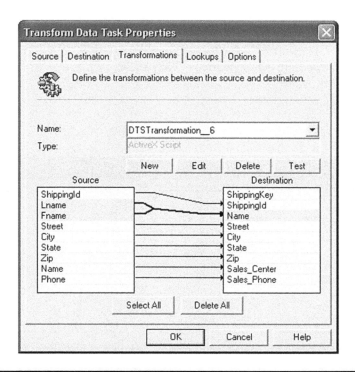

Figure 13.9   Configure transformation properties

source, we can simply generate the time data by a stored procedure without using DTS. In the destination database Hillcrest Data Mart, create the stored procedure with the following steps.

1. Open **Query Analyzer**. Select the database **Hillcrest Data Mart** from the combo box.
2. Enter the following code in Query Analyzer:

```
CREATE PROCEDURE Time_Proc AS
-- Declare the counter variables
DECLARE @M INT, @D INT, @I INT
-- Initialize the variable.
SET @M = 1
-- Test if the loop for Month is finished.
WHILE (@M < 13)
BEGIN
   -- Set the number of dates in a month
   IF (@M = 2) SET @D = 28
   ELSE IF (@M = 4 OR @M = 6 OR @M = 9 OR @M = 11) SET @D = 30
   ELSE SET @D = 31
   -- Insert the time data
   SET @I = 1
   WHILE (@I <= @D)
   BEGIN
       -- Insert a row into the table TIME
       INSERT INTO [TIME] ([Date], [Month], [Year])
         VALUES (@I, @M, 2002)
```

```
            -- Increment the counter variable
            SET @I = @I + 1
       END
       -- Increment the counter variable
       SET @M = @M + 1
  END
  RETURN
```

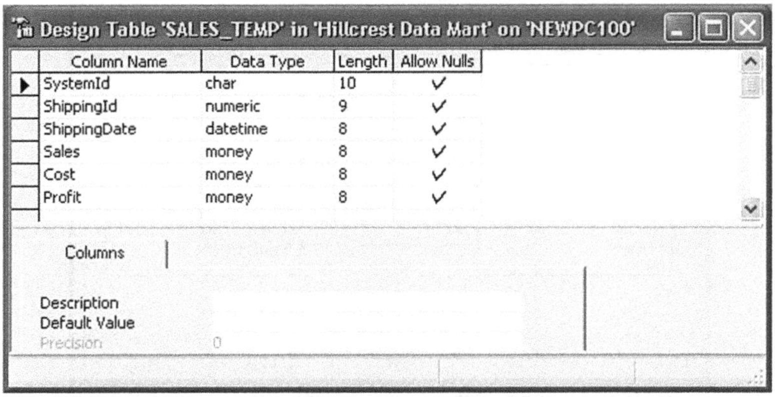

Figure 13.10   Create temporary table

3. In the above code, the outer `WHILE` loop is used to specify each of the twelve months. The `IF...ELSE` structure is used to define the number of dates in each month. The inner `WHILE` loop is used to insert the values of date, month, and year into the table `TIME`.
4. After you have successfully created the stored procedure, execute it by running the command **EXEC Time_Proc** in Query Analyzer.

The next example illustrates how to transform the data summarized by using a stored procedure and mathematical formulas.

1. First, we create a temporary table **SALES_TEMP** in **Hillcrest Data Mart**, as shown in Figure 13.10. The temporary table is used to store the source data such as **SystemId**, **ShippingId**, **ShippingDate**, **Sales**, **Cost**, and **Profit**. Later, these data will be placed in the fact table **SALES**.
2. Then we create a stored procedure `Sales_Proc`, which is used to generate the information about the cost and retail price of each computer system. Open **Query Analyzer**, select the database **Hillcrest Computing**, and enter the SQL statement shown in Figure 13.11.
3. Add two new connection objects to **DTS Package**. For the first new connection object, in the **Connection Properties** window, select the database **Hillcrest Computing** and click **OK** as the data source. For the second new connection object, select the database **Hillcrest Data Mart** as the intermediate destination.

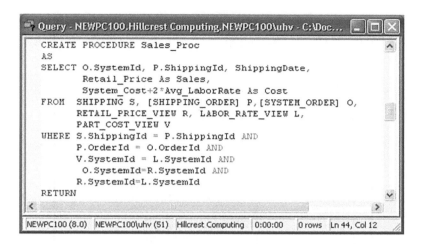

Figure 13.11   Create stored procedure Sales_Proc

4. Create a **transformation line** to connect the new data source to the intermediate destination. Double-click the **transformation line** to open the **Transform Data Task Properties** dialog box. Under the **Source** tab, click the **SQL query** option button. Enter the command **Exec Sales_Proc** to run the stored procedure Sales_Proc. Click the **Destination** tab and select the table **SALES_TEMP**. Click the **Transformations** tab. You will see that the columns **Sales** and **Cost** in the **Source** pane are automatically connected to **Sales** and **Cost** in the **Destination** pane. To transform the data to the column Profit by using the sales and cost information, highlight both **Sales** and **Cost** in the **Source** pane. Click the **New** button. Select **ActiveX Script** as the type of transformation. Click the **Destination Columns** tab and move the column **Profit** from the **Available columns** pane to the **Selected columns** pane. Go back to the **General** tab, click the **Properties** button, and enter the following code:

```
Function Main()
   DTSDestination("Profit") = DTSSource("Sales")-
   DTSSource("Cost")
   Main=DTSTransformStat_OK
End Function
```

5. Test the connection. If it is successful, click **Done** and then click **OK** twice to complete the configuration. Figure 13.12 shows the configuration result.
6. Click **OK** to complete the transformation line configuration. Right-click the newly configured transformation line and select **Execute Step** to transform the data.

   Now, we are ready to populate the fact table SALES.
7. Create a **transformation line** from the intermediate destination to the data mart. Double-click the **transformation line** to open the **Transform Data Task Properties** dialog box. Click the **SQL query** option button, and enter the following SQL statement:

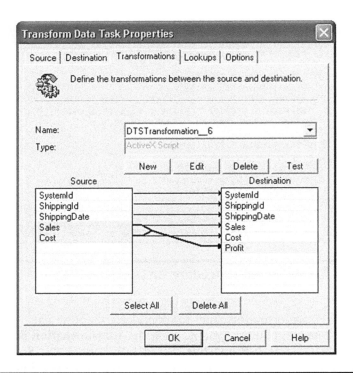

Figure 13.12   Configure transform data task properties using ActiveX script

```
SELECT  T.TimeKey,  P.ShippingKey,  C.SystemKey,
        S.Sales,  S.Cost,  S.Profit
FROM    COMPUTER_SYSTEM C,  SALES_TEMP S,
        SHIPPING P,  TIME T
WHERE   C.SystemId = S.SystemId AND
        S.ShippingId = P.ShippingId AND
        DatePart(dd,  S.ShippingDate) = T.[Date]  AND
        DatePart(mm,  S.ShippingDate) = T.[Month]  AND
        DatePart(yy,  S.ShippingDate) = T.[Year]
```

8. Under the **Destination** tab, select the table **SALES**. Click the **Transformations** tab and you will see the configurations as shown in Figure 13.13.
9. Click **OK** and execute the transformation by right-clicking the **transformation line** and selecting **Execute Step** to transform the data to the fact table **SALES**. After all these steps, the final transformation diagram is shown in Figure 13.14.

The above steps show you how to transform data from data sources to a simple star schema. In real business situations, the data warehouse will be much more complicated than the one in this demonstration.

After historical data are selected and organized in a data warehouse, it is time for front-end users to perform data analysis tasks for business decision making. Many application tools are available to assist front-end users in accessing data stored in a data warehouse. The commonly used data warehouse accessing tools are:

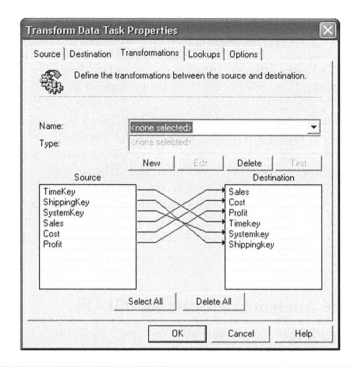

Figure 13.13   Transformation from intermediate destination to fact table

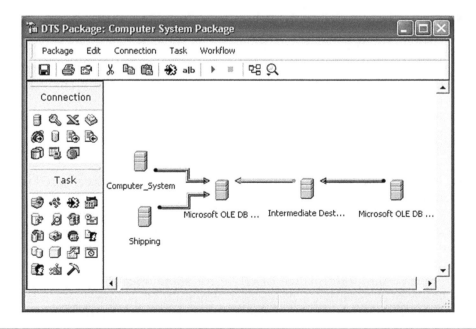

Figure 13.14   Transformation diagram

- *Microsoft Office:* Accessing a data warehouse through Access and Excel
- *SQL queries:* Directly accessing a data warehouse through queries
- *OnLine Analytical Processing (OLAP) Analysis Manager:* Accessing multi-dimensional data through cubes
- Other applications developed with programming languages

The OLAP technology enables data warehouses to be used effectively for online analysis by providing rapid responses to iterative complex analytical queries. Multidimensional data models and data aggregation techniques make it possible for OLAP to organize and summarize large amounts of data with its online analytical and graphical tools. In the next section, you will learn how to use OLAP to represent multidimensional data in cubes. To do so, a large number of data are needed. Therefore, instead of reinventing the wheel, we use the well-designed built-in data mart `FoodMart 2000` for the demonstration.

13.3 OnLine Analytical Processing (OLAP)

To help front-end users to access and navigate multidimensional data and perform sophisticated data analysis, a tool that can better interact with the multidimensional data is needed. In 1993, Dr. E.F. Codd, the inventor of the relational database, named the tool OnLine Analytical Processing (OLAP). With the OLAP technology, the real-time data analysis can be done in a fast and flexible way. SQL Server provides OLAP with the following features that will benefit users.

- It provides the GUI tools such as wizards, editors, and data manager to assist users. For example, users can use the cube wizard to create multidimensional data models.
- It not only allows users to dynamically reformat a star structure to perform the ad hoc data analysis but also improves performance by reducing the network traffic.
- It can be integrated with database administration tools and it is ready for a wide array of database applications.
- It includes the analytical query language for exploring complex business data relationships.
- It can precalculate the values derived from the original data to reduce the response time to ad hoc queries.

The *Analysis Services* package included in SQL Server supports several tools to assist data analysis. OLAP is included in the package. Figure 13.15 shows the structure of the data analysis services.

To improve the performance of OLAP for some special purposes, several OLAP alternatives have been developed. When OLAP is stored in a relational database structured by using indexes and managed with database administration tools, it is called *Relational OLAP* (ROLAP). When OLAP is stored in specified multidimensional data storage such as a star structure, it is called

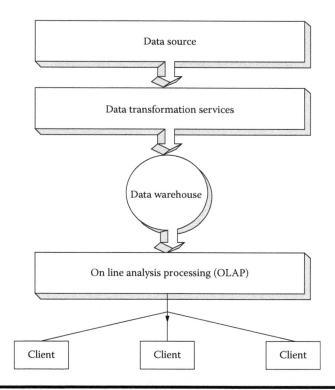

Figure 13.15   Structure of data analysis services

Multidimensional OLAP (MOLAP). The combination of ROLAP and MOLAP, which is the star structure developed and managed by a relational DBMS, is called *Hybrid OLAP* (HOLAP).

Usually, MOLAP outperforms ROLAP. Although ROLAP is slower in performance, it requires less storage. Also, ROLAP is created in an existing relational database; this means that it has a lower cost for investment and maintenance. HOLAP has the advantages of both MOLAP and ROLAP. It runs faster than ROLAP and costs less than MOLAP. In SQL Server, the OLAP included in the Analysis Services package is the HOLAP type.

13.3.1   OLAP Terminology

Before we investigate the architecture of the OLAP technology, we learn some basic concepts and terminologies.

Cube

In OLAP, multidimensional data are viewed by an object called *cube*. A cube is a set of data organized and summarized into a multidimensional structure represented by the star schema or snowflake schema. With the cube structure, the data can be presented at different levels of detail. For example, the time dimension data can be presented at three levels: year, month, and date.

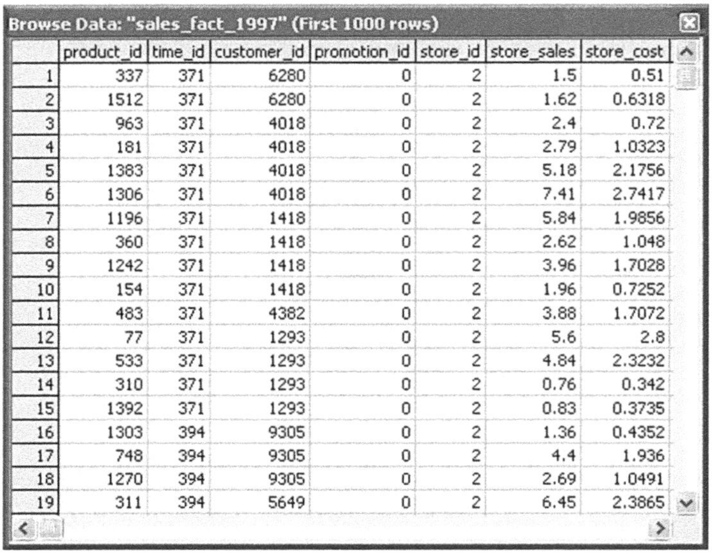

Browse Data: "sales_fact_1997" (First 1000 rows)

	product_id	time_id	customer_id	promotion_id	store_id	store_sales	store_cost
1	337	371	6280	0	2	1.5	0.51
2	1512	371	6280	0	2	1.62	0.6318
3	963	371	4018	0	2	2.4	0.72
4	181	371	4018	0	2	2.79	1.0323
5	1383	371	4018	0	2	5.18	2.1756
6	1306	371	4018	0	2	7.41	2.7417
7	1196	371	1418	0	2	5.84	1.9856
8	360	371	1418	0	2	2.62	1.048
9	1242	371	1418	0	2	3.96	1.7028
10	154	371	1418	0	2	1.96	0.7252
11	483	371	4382	0	2	3.88	1.7072
12	77	371	1293	0	2	5.6	2.8
13	533	371	1293	0	2	4.84	2.3232
14	310	371	1293	0	2	0.76	0.342
15	1392	371	1293	0	2	0.83	0.3735
16	1303	394	9305	0	2	1.36	0.4352
17	748	394	9305	0	2	4.4	1.936
18	1270	394	9305	0	2	2.69	1.0491
19	311	394	5649	0	2	6.45	2.3865

Figure 13.16 Data in regular relational database table

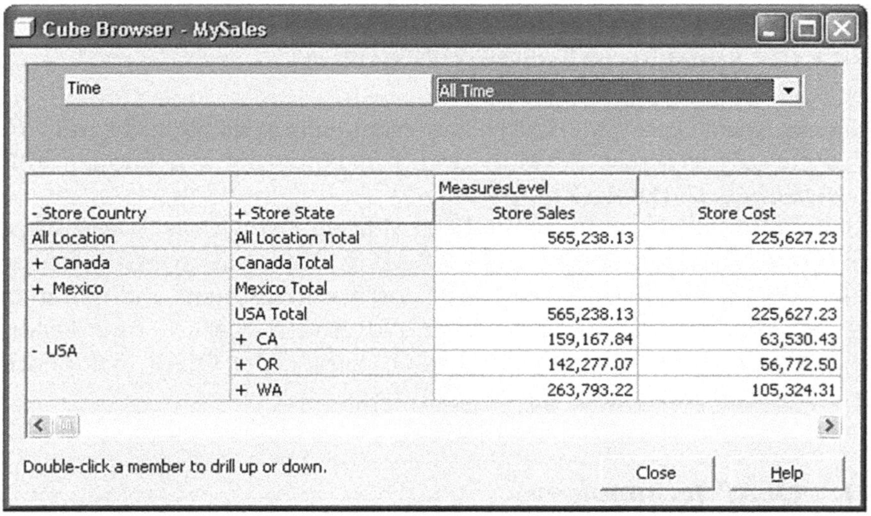

		MeasuresLevel	
- Store Country	+ Store State	Store Sales	Store Cost
All Location	All Location Total	565,238.13	225,627.23
+ Canada	Canada Total		
+ Mexico	Mexico Total		
- USA	USA Total	565,238.13	225,627.23
	+ CA	159,167.84	63,530.43
	+ OR	142,277.07	56,772.50
	+ WA	263,793.22	105,324.31

Figure 13.17 Data in an OLAP cube

Similarly, you may present the location data at the levels of city, state, and country. To see how a cube can make the user's job easier, we compare a regular database table with a cube created in SQL Server. First, we look at the relational database `tablesales_fact_1997` built in SQL Server Analysis Manager. As you can see in Figure 13.16, the data presented do not tell us what information we are supposed to pinpoint. As a comparison, we present the same set of data in an OLAP cube as shown in Figure 13.17.

On the left-hand side of the cube browser is the Location dimension. You can select the location levels Country, State, and City by double-clicking the plus sign. At the top of the cube browser is the Time dimension. You can select levels such as year, month, and date through the combo box. Once a value is specified in the Time dimension, a set of data values corresponding to the Location and Time specifications will be displayed in the table. This set of data is the *slice* of the cube. It is very clear this time that the data displayed in the cube represent the sales and cost values corresponding to the specified category levels. The data are separated and displayed according to categories.

The terms used in a cube are as follows:

- *Measures:* The source data values displayed in a cube. For example, the Store Sales and Store Cost values for CA, 159,167.84 and 63,530.43, are measures.
- *Dimensions:* For the cube displayed in Figure 13.17, dimensions provide the column headings, row headings, and subheadings. For example, you can select 1997 from the time dimension and USA from the location dimension; the sales and cost data will be returned in a tabular format. Location and time also supply a variety of subheadings that are part of a dimension.
- *Slices:* A cube with more than two dimensions is called a hypercube. To display the hypercube data on a two-dimensional computer screen, you can allow only two of the dimensions to be dynamically changeable and the values in the other dimensions must be constant. Each of the two-dimensional displays is called a slice.
- *Aggregations:* As seen in Figure 13.17, the data source provides only the data in Store Sales and Store Cost. To get information about the profit for each store at a specified time period, the values usually are computed in advance to improve performance. These precomputed values are called aggregations.

13.3.2 OLAP Architecture

On SQL Server, the OLAP architecture includes two major components: the server component and client component. The server component can do the following things:

- Allow the database administrator to design, create, and process cubes over various data warehouses.
- Access and store cube data in multidimensional structures or relational databases and populate cubes with original data from data sources.
- Store metadata in a private repository and export them to the Microsoft repository.
- Store data for data-mining models or convert the data to the XML format.

The OLAP client component is operated on a middle-tier computer or a Web server. The OLAP server provides the cube data to clients through the

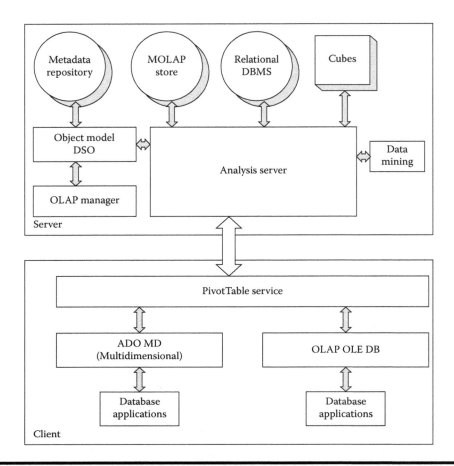

Figure 13.18   OLAP architecture

PivotTable service on the client side. The PivotTable service provides OLAP OLE DB, an extension of OLE DB, for accessing the data managed by the OLAP server. The goal of the client component is to pass the OLAP data to users in a simple and efficient way. The client side operations follow.

- Interact with the OLAP server to allow client applications to access the OLAP data.
- Present results returned from queries.
- Manage multiple users who are accessing the OLAP server.
- Download data from data sources and store the data in local cubes for offline data analysis.

The OLAP architecture is demonstrated in Figure 13.18.

In the server component, *Decision Support Object* (DSO) provides the programming environment for us to develop control programs for customizing the analysis server. By using DSO, we can create programs to control the cubes in the analysis server and manage the cube metadata in the repository. *OLAP Manager* is a built-in GUI administrative tool based on the objects included in DSO. OLAP Manager provides a GUI that allows users to design and develop cubes, access data in the relational DBMS for ROLAP and the multidimensional star schema for MOLAP, and populate OLAP data stores.

In the client component, the PivotTable service interacts with the analysis server and communicates with the client applications through OLAP OLE DB. The PivotTable service is the client to the analysis server, but it is also a server for the client applications such as Excel, Access, and Web-based applications. The PivotTable service is qualified as the middle tier. The client applications can also access the OLAP data through *ADO Multidimensional Extension* (ADO MD). You can develop your own data applications that include the PivotTable service to access the OLAP service on the analysis server. You can also access the analysis server through Microsoft Excel or Access because the PivotTable service is built inside these applications. From the client application, a request is passed to the PivotTable service, which carries the request to the analysis server. By using the aggregates saved in the cube, the analysis server builds a record set that meets the client request and returns the result to the PivotTable service, which then forwards the record set to the client application.

Data analysis can be performed either online or offline through the Pivot-Table service. You will like the offline operations for good reasons. When conducting a data analysis offline, a copy of the OLAP data store or a replication of the data source is saved on the client computer. By using the OLAP data stored on the client computer, you are able to create cubes through the PivotTable service. The offline cubes allow data analysis to be done locally to reduce network traffic and gain better performance. When multiple analytical users are accessing the same cube, the PivotTable service creates multiple processes for these users with its caching ability.

13.3.3   Analysis Manager

Analysis Manager provides a user interface in which users can access analysis servers and their metadata repositories. Analysis Manager can do the following:

- Configure analysis servers.
- Build, update, and process cubes.
- Create security roles.
- Build and process data-mining models.
- Specify storage options and optimize query performance.
- Link to third-party client applications.
- Restore and copy data.

Next, we do some hands-on practice to accomplish some of the above tasks with Analysis Manager.

The first thing you need to do is to check if **Analysis Services** is installed on your computer by clicking **Start**, **All Programs**, **Microsoft SQL Server**. If Analysis Services is installed, you will see the **Analysis Manager** item displayed on the menu, as shown in Figure 13.19. If not, you need to insert the SQL

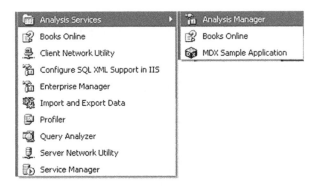

Figure 13.19   Analysis manager displayed on menu

Server 2000 CD in the CD-ROM drive and install the **Analysis Services** component.

Setting OLAP Data Source

Open **Analysis Manager**. In the Analysis Manager tree pane, expand the **Analysis Servers** node. To create a database with a star schema, right-click your analysis server node and select **New Database**. Name the database **MySales**. Type the description **OLAP Database for Sales Department**. Click **OK** to complete. Expand the **MySales** node.

Now we have the database. We need to connect the database to a data source. We use the data stored in the prebuilt database FoodMart 2000. To do so, right-click the **Data Sources** node and select **New Data Source**. Make sure that **Microsoft OLE DB Provider for ODBC Drivers** is selected under the **Provider** tab. Click **Next** to specify the connection properties. For the **Use data source name** option, select the data source **FoodMart 2000**. For the **Enter the initial catalog to use** option, select the path **C:\Program Files\Microsoft Analysis Services\Samples\foodmart 2000**, as shown in Figure 13.20. Click the **Test Connection** button. If the test is successful, click **OK**.

Defining Shared Dimensions

As mentioned before, a star schema database includes fact tables and dimension tables. We define dimensions first. To create dimensions that can be shared by multiple cubes, right-click the **Shared Dimension** node in the Analysis Manager tree pane and select **New Dimension** and then **Wizard** to open **Dimension Wizard**. Click **Next** and check the option **Star Schema: A single dimension table**. Click **Next** to select the dimension table. Select the **store** table for the location dimension. Click **Next** to specify the dimension type. Because we are going to use columns to define the dimensions, check the option **Standard dimension**. Click **Next** to select the levels for the location dimension. The columns should be entered from the most summarized level to the least

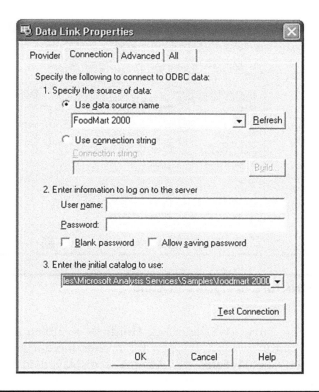

Figure 13.20   Configure data source

summarized level. Move the columns **store_country**, **store_state**, and **store_city** from the **Available columns** pane on the left to the **Dimension levels** pane on the right. Click **Next** a couple of times and accept the default. Name the dimension **Location** and click **Finish** to complete the configuration for the location dimension. Similarly, you can create another dimension, **Time**, by using the table **time_by_day**. For dimension levels, choose the three columns **the_year**, **the_month**, and **the_date**.

Creating Cube

As mentioned before, a cube is used to represent the star structure. To create a simple cube based on the data source FoodMart 2000 provided by SQL Server 2000, follow the steps below.

1.   The first step is to create a cube using **Cube Wizard**. In the Analysis Manager tree pane, right-click the **Cubes** node, select **New Cube,** and then select **Wizard** to open **Cube Wizard**.
2.   Click **Next** and select the table **sales_fact_1997** as the fact table. Click **Next** and select the columns **store_sales**, **store_cost**, and **unit_sales** as the measures of the cube. Click **Next** to enter the dimensions for the cube. Select the dimensions we have just defined, **Time** and **Location**. Click **Next**

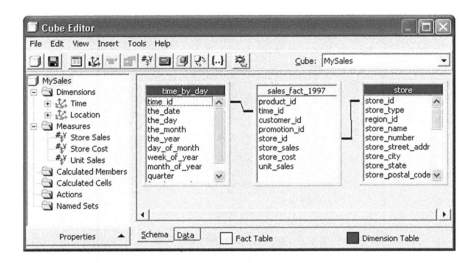

Figure 13.21   Structure of `MySales` **cube**

and name the cube **MySales**. Click **Finish** to complete the configuration. The **Cube Editor** window is open for further modification, as shown in Figure 13.21. The **MySales** star schema is displayed in **Cube Editor**. On the left-hand side of **Cube Editor**, there are dimension columns and fact table columns used in the cube.

3. Accept the default result. Click the **File** menu and click **Exit**. Click **Yes** to save the configuration. You will be prompted to define the storage option. Click **Yes** to start **Storage Design Wizard**. Click **Next** and select the **HOLAP** option.

4. Click **Next** to move to the **Set aggregation options** dialog box. To improve performance, OLAP will calculate the aggregation values based on the columns selected in the fact table and the existing dimensions. In our example, the values of profit based on the sales and cost in the fact table will be calculated. Suppose that we would like to gain performance up to 80 percent; select the **Performance gain reaches** option and enter **80%**. Click **Start**. As shown in Figure 13.22, four aggregations are calculated.

5. Click **Next** and **Finish**. If the process window indicates that the OLAP process is successful, close the process window. To view the data in the cube, right-click the **MySales** cube node and select **Browse Data**. You should get the result shown in Figure 13.17.

Note: If an error message such as "Unable to browse the cube …" appears, you need to download the latest service packs for SQL Server and Analysis Services from the Microsoft download Web site. For example, download the files **sql2ksp3.exe** and **sql2kasp3.exe** from the Web site http://www.microsoft. com/sql/downloads/2000/sp3.asp. (Detailed instructions of how to download the packs can be found in Chapter 14, *Preparing Data-Mining Tools in Analysis Services* section.) After you have installed the service packs, the problem should be solved.

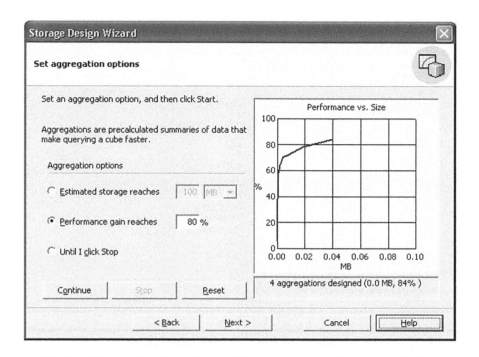

Figure 13.22   Set aggregation options

Data Analysis with Cube

A cube is a convenient tool to discover information about the data in a fact table. For example, from the **MySales** cube we have just created, we would like to know what impact the promotion has on the sales. The first thing we need to do is to add a new dimension to the cube. To do so, right-click the cube **MySales** and select **Edit**. Right-click on the **Dimensions** node and select **New Dimension** to open **Dimension Wizard**. Click **Next** and leave the default setting on how to create the dimension. Click **Next** and select the dimension table **promotion**. Click **Next** and keep the default **Standard dimension**. Click **Next** and select the columns **promotion name** and **cost**. Click **Next** three times to go to the last dialog box. Name the dimension **Promotion** and click **Finish**. Again, click the **File** menu and click **Exit**. Click **Yes** to save the configuration. You will be prompted to define the storage option. Click **Yes** to start **Storage Design Wizard**. Click **Next** and select the **HOLAP** option. Click **Next** to move to the **Set aggregation options** dialog box. Select the **Performance gain reaches** option and enter **80%**. Click **Start**, **Next**, and **Finish**. To see how the sales react to the **Best Savings** promotion from the cities in California, right-click the **MySales** cube and select **Browse Data**, choose **Best Savings** from the **All Promotion** combo box, and expand the **CA** member in the **Location** dimension. You will have the data displayed in the cube shown in Figure 13.23.

If you want to compare the sales response to different types of promotion from the cities San Francisco and San Diego in California, it is more convenient to make the Promotion dimension as the row heading and the Location

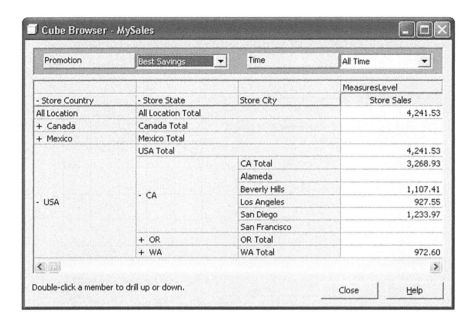

Figure 13.23   Sales response to best savings promotion

dimension as the column heading. To do so, click the **Promotion** dimension, hold the mouse, drag the Promotion dimension to the left side of the **Store Country** column, and then release the mouse. In the next step, click the **Location** dimension, hold the mouse, and drag the Location dimension to the column **Store Sales**. Expand the **California** node; you should have the result shown in Figure 13.24.

In the MySales cube, the measures are Store Sales, Store Cost, and Unit Sales. If we want to know the profit for the sales, we can add a new profit measure in the cube. To do so, consider the following steps. Right-click on the cube **MySales** and select **Edit** to open **Cube Editor**. Click the **Insert** menu and **Calculated Member** to open **Calculated Member Builder**. Enter the member name **Profit**. Expand the **Measures** node in the **Data** pane. Double-click the measure **Store Sales** to add it to the **Value expression** box. Click the arithmetic operator, and then click the measure **Store Cost**. You should have the configuration window as shown in Figure 13.25. Click **OK** to exit **Calculated Member Builder**.

To save the changes, click the **File** menu and then select **Save**. Rename the new calculated member **Store Profit**. Click **File** and **Exit** to quit **Cube Editor**. To see the new calculated member, right-click the cube **MySales** and select **Browse Data**. You will have the result shown in Figure 13.26.

Similarly, you can create calculated members for dimensions.

Creating Security Role

To allow users to access cube data and metadata through client computers, we need to create security roles and assign roles to the users.

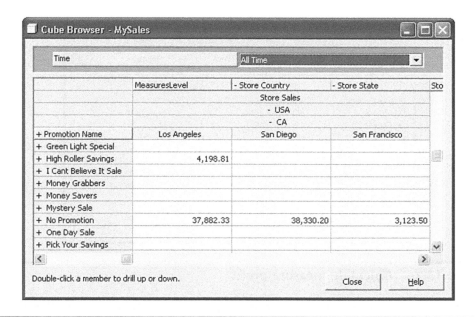

Figure 13.24   Sales response to different types of promotion

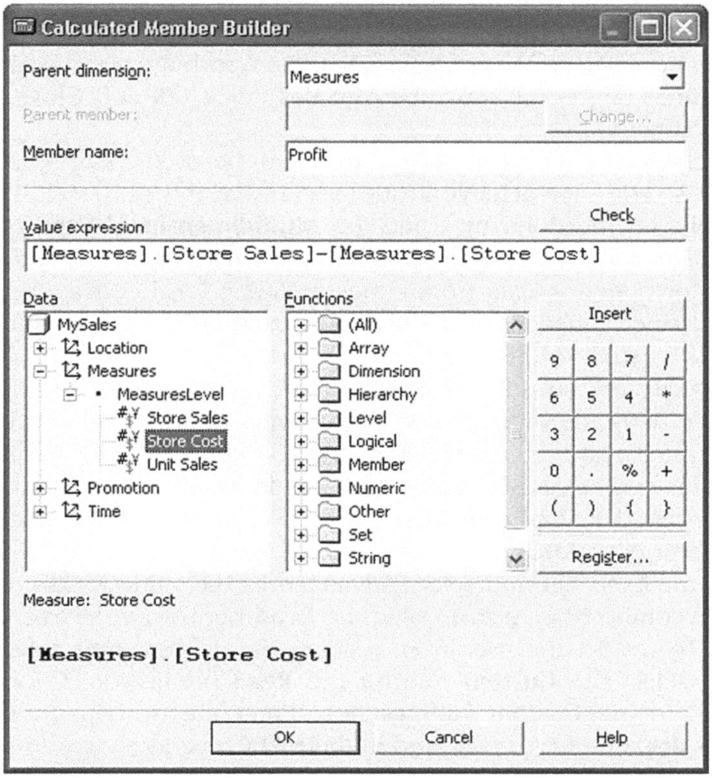

Figure 13.25   Configure calculated member

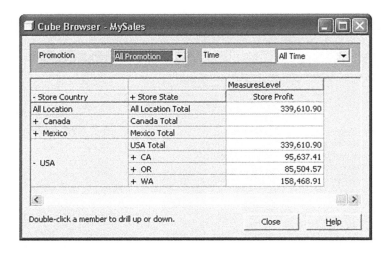

Figure 13.26   Calculate measure profit

- First, we create a database role. Right-click the database **MySales** in the Analysis Manager tree pane and select **Manage Roles** to open the **Database Role Manager** dialog box. Click the **New** button to open the **Create a Database Role** dialog box. Name the role **Analytical Database Role** and enter **Database role for analytical users** as the description. Under the **Membership** tab, click the **Add** button to open the **Add Users and Groups** dialog box. Select **Power Users**. Click the **Add** button and click **OK**. Under the **Cubes** tab, check the cube **MySales**. Click **OK** and **Close** to complete the configuration.

- By default, if a user can access the cube, he or she can read the data in all cells. You may achieve a finer security at the cell level. The cell-level security can be done by using the **Multidimensional Expressions (MDX)** language. MDX is used to manipulate multidimensional information. It is used for querying data from cubes, building local cubes, and developing user-defined functions. The commonly used MDX keywords for specifying cells are listed in Table 13.2.

- To specify the security of cells, you may either allow the access to the cells or deny the access. Suppose we want to add a cell-level security for the cube MySales; we need to create a cube role. Right-click the cube **MySales** and select **Manage Roles**. To add a new role, click the **Duplicate** button. In the **Duplicate Role** dialog box, name the role **Analytical Cell Role** and click **OK**. As the new role is highlighted, click the **Edit** button. Click the **Cells** tab and select **Advanced** as the value for the **Cell security policy** combo box. At this point, the **Read** permission has an **Unrestricted** rule. To restrict the user from reading the column **unit_sales** in the fact table, select the **Custom** rule for the **Read** permission. Click the **ellipsis** button in the **Custom Settings** box. Enter the description **Cannot read unit_sales**. Enter the command in the **MDX** box, as shown in Figure 13.27.

- The command specifies that when the reading process goes through the measures in the fact table, the reading of Unit Sales is denied. Click **Check** to verify if the MDX command is valid. If there is no error, click **OK** to

Table 13.2   MDX Keywords for Specifying Cell Security

MDX Keywords	Usage
Measures	Used to specify data in a column of a fact table
«Dimension».Name	Used to specify the name of a measure, a dimension, a member, or a level
«Dimension».CurrentMember	Used to specify the current member in a measure, a dimension, or a level
Ancestor(«Member», «Level»)	Used to specify the parent of a member from the dimension level
=	Used to identify the cells that can be accessed
<>	Used to identify the cells that cannot be accessed

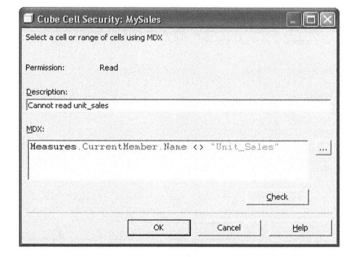

Figure 13.27   Specify cell security with MDX command

accept the security setting. Click **OK** again to close the cube role editing dialog box. To verify the cell security, click the **Test Role** button in the **Cube Role Manager** dialog box. As shown in Figure 13.28, the **Unit Sales** column is blocked for reading.

- For the next example, we deny the reading of the cells that belong to the members in Canada as well as the cells in Unit Sales. Again, click the **Edit** button. Click the **Cells** tab and select the **Custom** rule for the **Read** permission. Click the **ellipsis** button in the **Custom Settings** box, and enter the **MDX** command as shown in Figure 13.29.
- You can verify the result by clicking the **Test Role** button in the **Cube Role Manager** dialog box. Now you have the result shown in Figure 13.30.

In the above, we have demonstrated the use of Analysis Manager through a few examples. Many tasks can be accomplished by Analysis Manager.

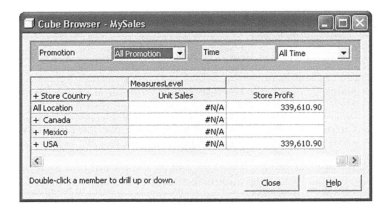

Figure 13.28   Unit sales column is blocked for reading

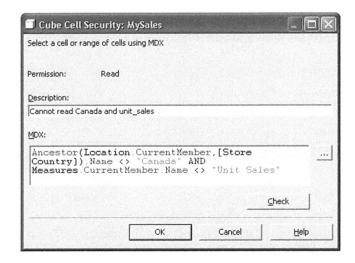

Figure 13.29   MDX command to block reading of Canada and unit sales

Detailed description of Analysis Manager is beyond the scope of this book. Interested users can read OLAP-related books for more information.

13.3.4   PivotTable Service

The PivotTable service is the middle tier between the analysis server and client applications. Through the PivotTable service, client applications can send requests to the analysis server and get responses back from it. Served as the middle tier, the PivotTable service supports a subset of SQL commands and the Data Definition Language that allows us to create and populate local cubes from relational data sources. It also supports the MDX language to retrieve and store multidimensional data for offline analysis. The following are some tasks that can be accomplished by the PivotTable service:

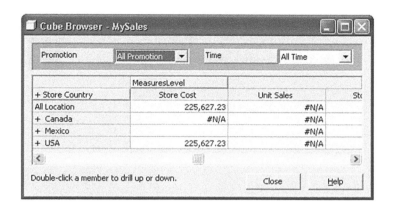

Figure 13.30   Block reading of Canada and unit sales

- Creating and populating cubes on local computers
- Retrieving and viewing data from local cubes
- Creating calculated members for local cubes
- Allowing client applications such as Excel and Access to use data stored on the analysis server in many different ways
- Allowing Internet applications to access the analysis server through the ASP page

In the following sections, we demonstrate how to accomplish some of these tasks through client applications.

Building and Manipulating PivotTable in Excel

In Excel, you can build a PivotTable through the graphical user interface or by using *Visual Basic for Applications* (VBA).

- *Creating PivotTable connected to server-based cube:* First, let us establish a connection to a remote server-based cube that can be used to download data and store the data in the local computer for offline data analysis.
    - Start Excel by clicking **Start**, **All Programs**, **Microsoft Office**, and **Microsoft Office Excel 2003**. Click the **Data** menu, select **Import External Data**, and then select **Import Data**. Click the **New Source** button to open **Data Connection Wizard**, as shown in Figure 13.31.
    - Select **Microsoft SQL Server OLAP Services** as the type of data source. Click **Next** to specify the database server name. Enter your database server name and click **Next** to go to the **Select Database and Table** dialog box. Select the **MySales** database and the **MySales** cube (see Figure 13.32).
    - Click **Next**, and enter the description and the search keyword. Click **Finish**.
    - Click **Open** to start **PivotTable and PivotChart Wizard**. Click **Finish** to create an empty PivotTable.

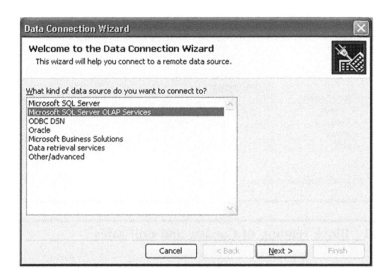

Figure 13.31   Connect to OLAP services

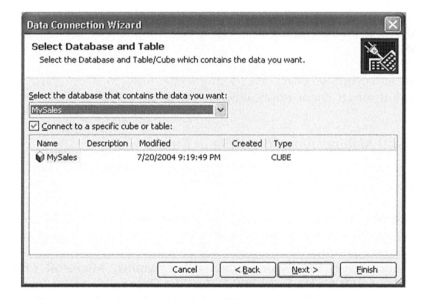

Figure 13.32   Specify database and cube to be connected

- *Building PivotTable report:* A PivotTable has four areas; three of them — the page area, the column area, and the row area — are called *axes* and are used to keep the names of the dimension members. The fourth one is the data area used to keep the values of the measures (see Figure 13.33).
  - In the PivotTable Field List dialog box, there are dimensions and measures from the server-based cube (see Figure 13.34).

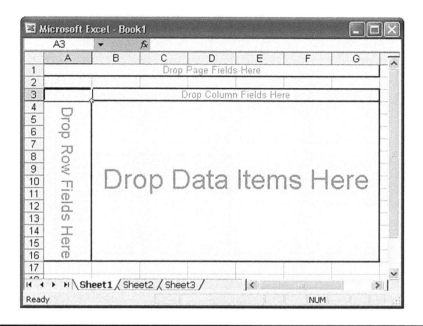

Figure 13.33   Format of PivotTable

Figure 13.34   PivotTable field list

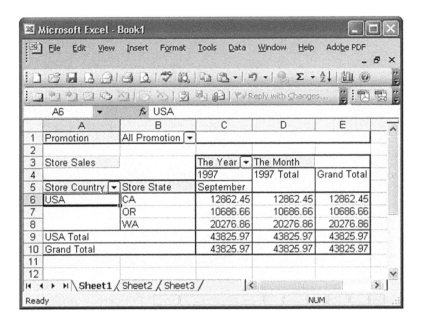

Figure 13.35   Store sales PivotTable

- Drag the **Location** dimension to the row area marked by **Drop Row Fields Here**. Drag the **Time** dimension to the column area marked by **Drop Column Fields Here**. Drag the **Promotion** dimension to the page area marked by **Drop Page Fields Here**. The page area is used to specify the slice in a dimension. Drag the measure **Store Sales** to the data area marked by **Drop Data Items Here**.
- To view the detail levels of the data, double-click **USA** under the level **Store Country**. From the combo box for the **Time** dimension, select **September**. You will have the result shown in Figure 13.35.

■ *Building PivotChart report:* Based on the PivotTable, you can create a PivotChart report to present the data.
- Click the **Chart Wizard** icon 📊 on the PivotTable toolbar. The PivotChart corresponding to the PivotTable is shown in Figure 13.36.
- You can view the information in the chart just as you do in the PivotTable. To view the information about store sales in the USA cities, click the **Store Country** button and select the all the cities under the states **CA**, **OR**, and **WA**. Click **OK** to accept the configuration. The bar chart created for store sales of these cities is displayed in Figure 13.37.

■ *Building local cube from PivotTable report:* To perform offline data analysis, we need to create a local cube. We can create it through PivotTable or query statements. Here, we create the local cube by using the Store Sales PivotTable.
- Go back to the spreadsheet by clicking the **Sheet1** tab. In the toolbar, select **Offline OLAP** from the **PivotTable** drop-down list. When the **Offline OLAP Settings** dialog box opens, click the button **Create offline data file** to open the **Create Cube File** wizard. Click **Next** to go to the dimension configuration dialog box. Accept the default setting and click

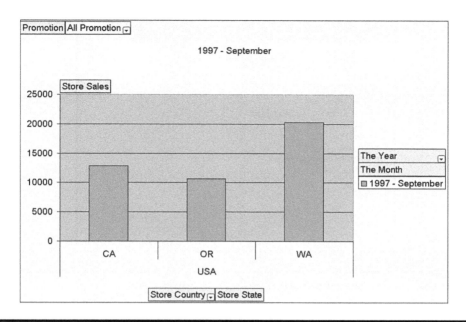

Figure 13.36   PivotChart corresponding to store sales PivotTable

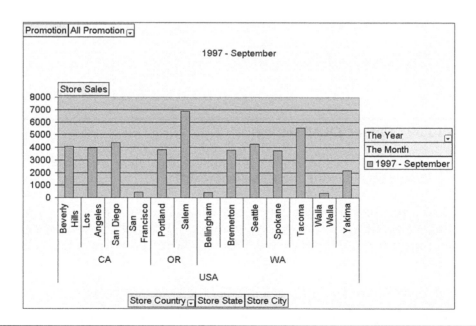

Figure 13.37   Bar chart for store sales information in USA cities

Next. Expand the **Measures** node and check all the measure members as shown in Figure 13.38.

- Click **Next**, specify the folder in which we want to save the local cube file, and click **Finish**. Now the data source is switched to the offline cube, as shown in Figure 13.39.

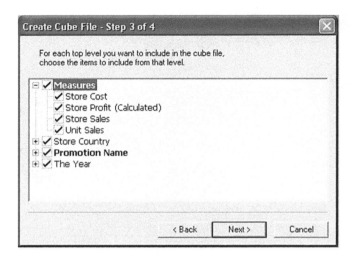

Figure 13.38   Include measure members in local cube

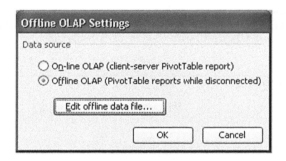

Figure 13.39   Offline OLAP settings

  – Click **OK** to complete the configuration. Save the spreadsheet in a file. You may name the file **CubeReport.xls**.

By now, you have learned how to create and manipulate a PivotTable in Excel. You can also create and manipulate a PivotTable through a data-accessing page for Web applications. You will learn how to do that next.

Building and Manipulating PivotTable List for Web Application

An easy way to publish PivotTable on a Web page is to build a PivotTable list. A PivotTable list is similar to a PivotTable report in many ways. The difference is that the PivotTable list is more flexible for working with OLAP cubes.

  ■ *Creating PivotTable list:*
    – If the file **CubeReport.xls** is not open, start **Excel** and open it. Click the **File** menu and select **Save as Web Page**. Click the **Publish** button in the **Save As** dialog box. Select **PivotTable** in the **Item to publish** box. Click

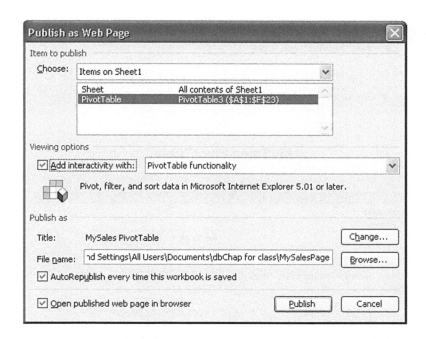

Figure 13.40   Configure PivotTable to be published as Web page

the **Change** button and enter the title **MySales PivotTable**. Change the file name to **MySalesPage**. Check the **Add interactivity with**, **AutoRepublish every time this workbook is saved**, and **Open published web page in browser** check boxes, as shown in Figure 13.40.
- Click the **Publish** button. (If security blocks the publication, click the **shield** icon and select **Allow Blocked Content**.) You will see the Web page in the browser. Double-click the plus sign by **USA**; you should have the Web page as shown in Figure 13.41.
- Save the page as **MySalesPage.htm**.
- *Manipulating Web-based PivotTable:* The advantage of a PivotTable list is that you have more power to manipulate the data on the Web page. Copy the file **MySalesPage.htm** to the folder **Inetpub\wwwroot**. Start the Web browser and enter the address http://localhost/MySalesPage.htm to open the PivotTable.
  - To add a new measure to the PivotTable, click the **Field List** icon to open the **PivotTable Field List** dialog box. Double-click **Store Cost** to add the measure.
  - To remove an existing dimension level from the current display, double-click the **USA** node and drag the level, for example, **Store City**, out of the current display. You will see that the level **Store City** is removed.
  - To look at the data corresponding to the different types of promotion, switch the dimensions **Location** and **Promotion**. If you need to sort the promotion types in descending order, right-click the **Promotion** column and select **Sort Descending**. To show only the top ten promotion types, right-click the **Promotion** column and select **Show Only the Top**, and then select **10**. You will see that only the top ten types of promotion are displayed.

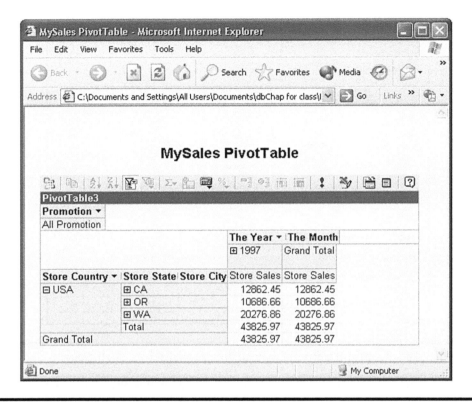

Figure 13.41   Publish PivotTable as Web page

- To add a calculated measure, click the **calculator icon** 🔢 on the PivotTable toolbar and select **Created and Calculated Total**. Enter **New Profit** as **Calculation Name** and the formula for profit, as shown in Figure 13.42.
- Click the **Change** button. Remove the measure **Store Cost**; you will have the PivotTable shown in Figure 13.43 on the Web page.

In this section, you have learned the terminology and structure of an OLAP process. Analysis Manager supported by SQL Server is a convenient tool for creating and manipulating the cubes. Several examples have been used to demonstrate how to use Analysis Manager to develop cubes for data analysis. On the client side, the PivotTable reports have been created to access the cubes. Through PivotTable, you can create a local cube for offline analysis. We have also demonstrated how to create and manipulate a PivotTable list for the Internet application through a Web page.

13.4 Summary

In this chapter, we have discussed the topics of data analysis services. To provide data sources for data analysis, we have introduced the concepts and architecture of a data warehouse. The requirements and usage of the data

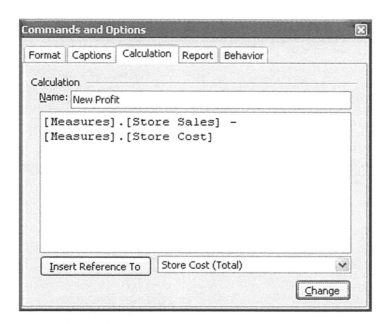

Figure 13.42   Create calculated measure through PivotTable list

warehouse have also been studied in this chapter. Different from the OLTP structure used for handling database transactions, the star structure or snow-flake structure is used for the data warehouse.

To efficiently transfer data from various sources to a data warehouse, we used the tool Data Transformation Services (DTS) to transform data into a simple star schema. DTS provides services for extracting, validating, formatting, and loading data before the data are transferred into a data warehouse. Many front-end application tools are available to help users access data stored in a data warehouse. One of the most powerful data warehouse accessing tools is the OLAP technology. OLAP allows front-end users to quickly and efficiently navigate and analyze data in a data warehouse. The OLAP technology makes the real-time data analysis easier and more flexible. The concepts and structure of the OLAP technology have been studied in this chapter.

You have learned how to use the tool Analysis Manager to create cubes for data analysis. To help the client application access the cubes built on the analysis server, the PivotTable technique has been investigated in this chapter. PivotTable reports can be created to access cubes from database applications such as Excel. For offline data analysis, local cubes can be created through PivotTable. To access a cube on an analysis server through a Web page, we can develop a PivotTable list. Various examples were used to demonstrate how to use Analysis Manager and how to create and manipulate a PivotTable. If a user knows what information he or she is looking for, OLAP can be used to interactively query the information. However, if users are not sure exactly what information they are looking for or they want to identify the patterns of customer behavior, they need a different data analysis tool called data mining, which is covered in the next chapter.

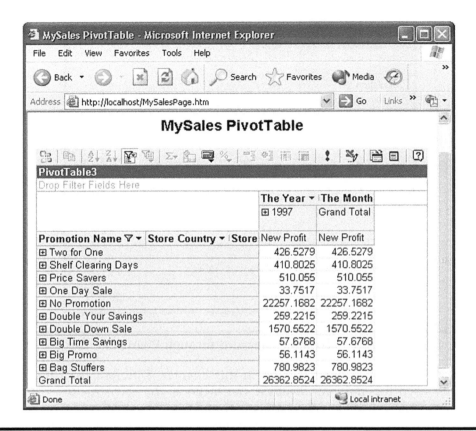

Figure 13.43   PivotTable with calculated measure

Review Questions

1. What are the applications of OLAP?
2. State the benefits of a data warehouse.
3. What are the requirements for a data warehouse?
4. Briefly describe the components included in a data warehouse.
5. What are the data warehouse development tools available in SQL Server?
6. What is the difference between designing OLTP and designing a data warehouse?
7. Use an example to describe the functions of the star schema and snowflake schema.
8. Describe the fact table and dimension table.
9. List the major steps in a data transformation process.
10. Summarize the tasks that can be accomplished by DTS.
11. For analytical users, what are the benefits of the OLAP technology?
12. Define the terms ROLAP, MOLAP, and HOLAP.
13. Define the terms cube, measure, dimension, slice, and aggregation.
14. Summarize the operations of the server component and the client component in the OLAP architecture.
15. What are the tasks that can be accomplished by Analysis Manager?
16. What are the tasks that can be accomplished by the PivotTable service?

Case Study Projects

You will create some OLAP-related projects. You can use the database you created, the database `Hillcrest Computing`, or the built-in data mart FoodMart 2000.

1. Create a star schema with tables in the database of your choice.
2. By using DTS, transform data from the tables in the database to the star schema you created in the previous step.
3. Implement a cube to display the data in the fact table.

Chapter 14

Data Mining

Objectives

- Learn the concepts and architecture of data mining.
- Identify the tasks in a data-mining process.
- Select proper data-mining modeling techniques.
- Implement data-mining models on SQL Server.

14.1 Introduction

In the previous chapter, we studied OLAP as one of the data analysis tools. OLAP is used to present multidimensional data to users in a fast and easy way. It supports decision making by providing numerical and statistical analysis tools. If you know what to look for, you can use OLAP interactively to query the information. However, for some data analysis tasks such as those listed below, OLAP may not be the best choice.

- Users are not sure exactly what information they want. In such a case, they may end up examining each slice of the cube until they find the useful information. Even though a cube has just a few dimensions, it requires a great deal of work to examine every slice that presents the data specified by a pair of dimension members.
- Many business decisions are based on the trends and patterns in the business process. It may not be clear to users what these trends and patterns are. Without knowing the trends or patterns, the users will not be able to tell OLAP what to do.
- Business processes are changing dynamically. This means that the structure of dimensions and measures will be changed accordingly. Once OLAP is created, it is difficult for it to change its structure dynamically.

It would be helpful if there were a data analysis tool that could accomplish the following tasks:

- It could conduct data analysis even when analytical users had only some vague idea about what information they wanted.
- Data analysis could be done with data stored in a data warehouse or an operational database.
- It could deal with dynamically changing business processes by providing self-learning abilities.
- The result of the data analysis would provide the trends and patterns for the business process.

The technology that can accomplish the above tasks is the *data-mining* technology. Through data mining, we can identify the trends and patterns of the business process. It can provide us with some potentially useful information even when we have not thought about it. Nowadays, data mining has become a popular tool in information management. The types of tasks appropriate for data mining are the following:

- *Uncovering abnormal patterns:* Data mining is an effective tool to detect fraud in credit card transactions, fraudulent telephone usage, and so on. Data-mining technology has been widely used in banking and investment and by telephone companies for fraud detection.
- *Risk management:* Data mining can be used to detect risk factors for insurance companies and healthcare organizations. For example, you can use data mining to identify the pattern of high-risk populations for a certain disease or identify certain types of cars that may cause higher insurance rates.
- *Pattern classification:* Through the data-mining process, a set of data can be divided into several subsets based on existing patterns captured about the data. Based on these patterns, we can make decisions on strategy. For example, banks can make decisions on which services should be available for customers based on their spending patterns.
- *Trend analysis:* Business process data often reflect the trend of customer behavior. Marketing strategy should change dynamically to fit the trend. For example, marketing and sales departments may use data mining to analyze the trend for the need of technology so that they can modify their advertising accordingly.
- *Predicting future behavior:* The result of data mining can be used to predict future tendencies in customer behavior. For example, a computer manufacturer can use a trend model to predict the demand for some products in next six months.
- *Discovering relationships:* Business relationships and dependencies are embedded in data collected during the business process. For example, based on their demographic backgrounds, some customers may require a different combination of services from an investment company. Data mining is a good tool for identifying relationships between customers and services.

To support data analysis with data mining, SQL Server has included a data-mining package since its 2000 version. In the early days, data mining was usually performed by large enterprises or academic institutions because it required high-level computer equipment and sophisticated programming skills. Including the data-mining package in SQL Server makes the data-mining job easier. Even small companies are able to conduct their own data analysis with data mining. The SQL Server data-mining package has the following high points:

- It has greatly reduced the cost of data mining.
- Data mining can be done directly on data stored in a database created on SQL Server. It eliminates intermediate transactions.
- Wizards are available to assist the development of data-mining models.
- Users can share source data and data-mining results through the utility OLE DB for Data Mining.
- To help with data preparation, tools are included for data cleaning and filtering.
- To help with data presentation, tools are included for presenting data-mining results.
- It includes some commonly used data-mining algorithms. It also provides interfaces that can be used to work with external data-mining algorithms.

In the next section, we introduce the data-mining process, in which you will learn the concepts and infrastructure of data mining. After that, you will learn some basic data-mining algorithms and how to perform data analysis with data mining on SQL Server.

14.2 Data-Mining Process

In a data-mining process, we first collect a set of business process data from databases, text files, or OLAP cubes. We use these data to train a data-mining model to identify the historical patterns of the business process. Then we use the patterns or trends learned from the training process to make decisions or predict the future behavior of the process. In this section, we introduce some basic concepts of the data-mining process. We also investigate the requirements for the data-mining process and how to develop a data-mining model to meet the requirements. Several data-mining analysis methods are investigated in this section. You will learn where and how to use these methods.

14.2.1 Data-Mining Process Standards

Data mining is a data analysis process that identifies trends and patterns. It uses a computer learning algorithm to extract and analyze data stored in a database. Data-mining development is a complex process. It requires a great deal of experience and understanding of both business practice and computer technology. For a computer learning process to return valid results, careful planning is necessary. To help data-mining developers do the job right, two major data-mining development standards were developed in the late 1990s. They are the *Cross-Industry Standard Process for Data Mining* (CRISP-DM) standard and the *Sample, Explore, Modify, Model, Assess* (SEMMA) standard. The statistics software company SPSS and companies including Daimler-Chrysler and NCR jointly developed CRISP-DM. The other statistics software company SAS created the SEMMA standard. There is no licensing fee for using the CRISP-DM standard. On the other hand, SEMMA is a proprietary standard and is supported by SAS's data-mining package Enterprise Miner. There are some other data-mining standards that are similar to CRISP-DM. The CRISP-DM standard consists of six phases, and some overlap may occur between the phases. Some phases are modified based on the outcomes of the other phases. Figure 14.1 shows the general steps in a data-mining process proposed by the CRISP-DM standard.

Understanding Business

In this phase, we perform the following tasks in order to understand the underlying business process:

- *Identifying business requirements:* We need to conduct a needs analysis to find out the requirements of a business process. We can do this by interviewing the key personnel, inspecting the business process, and evaluating the production outcomes.
- *Identifying business objectives:* We should find out what needs to be achieved. Based on our findings, we will specify the success criteria for our data-mining project. In a data-mining development process, we may need to modify the data-mining objectives based on the feedback from users. We may also need to conduct a cost-benefit analysis of the data-mining project to see if the project is worth the effort.
- *Identifying constraints:* We may want to identify the constraints that need to be resolved for our data-mining project.
- *Making data-mining plan:* We first convert the business objectives to data-mining objectives, draft a data-mining project timeline, and then identify the resources, inputs, outputs, and dependencies of the data-mining project.

As an example, consider the situation in which a food franchise wants to know how to use promotions effectively to increase sales. From interviews and discussions, the company comes up with the following business objectives:

- First, the company will be able to know how its customers from different demographic backgrounds react to different types of promotions.
- Second, the company will be able to know how to use the promotions effectively to increase sales.

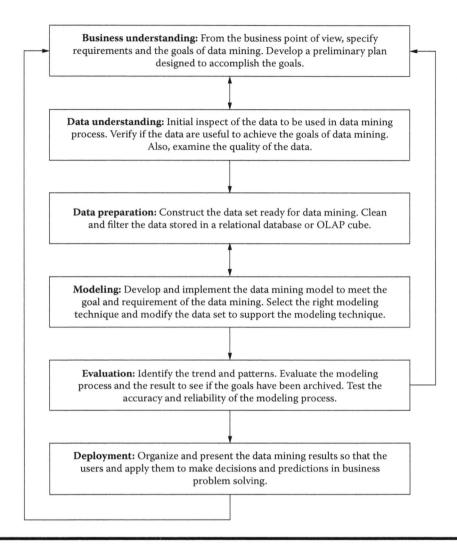

Figure 14.1   CRISP-DM data-mining process

- Third, the company will have a promotion management plan that includes a guideline about when and where to use the promotions. The guideline should also include the funding levels of these promotions.

The difficulties of accomplishing these objectives are that the data are collected from multiple regions and that customers have various backgrounds. It is not clear what characteristics should be used to classify the customers. The funding should depend on how the consumers react to the promotions and the media used to promote the products. A mathematical model may help with making this type of decision. However, sophisticated mathematics skills are needed to build the model. To overcome the difficulties, you may consider using the data-mining tools included in SQL Server. If you have already installed SQL Server, it has no additional cost. Also, it includes a number of data-mining algorithms and wizards to help you get a quick start on model building. It can also help you to deliver the results to decision makers. To be more precise, the business objectives mentioned above can be interpreted in terms of data mining as the following:

- To find out how customers react to the promotions, we need to create a data-mining model trained by the customer demographic data with the customers' responses to the promotions. This model will be used to classify the customers based on their common characteristics.
- To discover the relationship between sales and promotions, train a data-mining model with sales data that respond to the promotions. The model will be used to discover the patterns of the sales responses to the promotions.
- Based on the findings from data mining, a funding allocation map will be created. Based on the trend discovered from data mining, proper scheduling will be developed for promotion management.

To accomplish the above tasks, we need to work through the understanding data phase, as shown in the following.

Understanding Data

After the data-mining plan is drafted, our next move is to collect data. The tasks in the initial data collection process are as follows:

- *Identifying data sources:* To support a data-mining process, we need to identify the data sources that provide the data to be used to achieve the data-mining objectives.
- *Data transformation plan:* Because data will be collected from different data sources managed by different operating systems, we need to come up with a data transformation plan to move the data to our data-mining project.
- *Examining data:* We need to understand the data by examining the structure and size of the data. We may want to inspect the associated metadata to gain deeper understanding of the data structure. We should also inspect the data to see if any subset of the data may show some interesting characteristics.
- *Checking data quality:* Getting quality data is essential for achieving the data-mining objectives. Typical data problems are inconsistent data storage, inconsistent data formats, inconsistent data values, and missing data values. Some data sources may contain data with better quality than others. Data used in a data-mining process can be collected from OLAP cubes, data warehouses, relational databases, or flat text files. Data collected from data warehouses or OLAP cubes have better quality because most of the data-cleaning tasks are already done. By comparing data qualities, we can make a decision on which data source should be included in our data-mining project.

For the example mentioned in the understanding business phase, data can be collected from tables in the database `FoodMart 2000` or related OLAP cubes. Because `FoodMart 2000` is a built-in database, the data have been cleaned. Thus, all the data in `FoodMart 2000` are available for our data-mining process. We include the data in the data-mining related columns. For a real-life business process, understanding data is much more complicated than shown in the examples of this chapter. Data come from various sources with various formats. Data mining is a mixture of art and science. No one can tell you exactly how to choose the attributes to be included in your data-mining model. There are no fast rules you can follow when deciding which attribute will be helpful for the final model. For this reason, it is important to understand how the data behave before beginning to mine them. To achieve this level of understanding, you need to know how the data are distributed and how the attributes relate to each other. This is the process of exploring data, which can be done with both visual and numerical techniques.

- If you want to get a quick look at a large number of attributes and get a general sense of how they interact, use visual techniques. To visualize numeric data, you can use both histograms and scatter plots.
- On the other hand, if you want a more concrete and accurate understanding of how data interact, use numeric techniques. As the term "numeric" implies, you use numeric techniques only with numeric columns in a table. When exploring the numeric columns, you can build a correlation matrix that shows the relationships among numeric columns.

Later, during the data-mining process, you will learn both visual and numeric techniques.

Data Preparation

After a data-mining problem is defined, the next step is to get data ready for the data-mining project. The tasks in this phase are as follows:

- *Filtering data:* Based on the data-mining objectives, data will be filtered to get a subset of the data that is relevant to the data-mining problem.
- *Cleaning data:* For data collected from relational databases and flat files, additional effort is needed to convert data structures in order to eliminate inconsistencies. For the missing data, we need to specify a default value to replace the missing values. We also need to reformat the data value appearance, data value scale, and data value range in a consistent way.
- *Reconstructing data:* Sometimes, data also need to be reorganized in a tabular format. Some multiple attributes may need to be merged into a single attribute. Some numerical calculations also need to be done to summarize the values from multiple data sources. Occasionally, we may have to generate new attributes or new records to meet the data-mining requirements.

■ *Integrating data:* To perform data mining more efficiently, we may need to move data from various sources into a single table such as a fact table in OLAP. We should specify data transformation tools for data integration tasks such as data transformation, data reconstruction, and data cleaning.

To move data into the data-mining project, we can use the techniques such as OLE DB for Data Mining or Data Transformation Services (DTS). With OLE DB for Data Mining, we can develop a data-mining model from various client applications against a data source. It serves as a bridge to connect data-mining techniques and data sources. With the DTS technique, we can plan when and how to move data from a data source to the data-mining project while performing necessary data-cleaning tasks. For data cleaning, data reconstruction, and data integration, please refer to the previous chapter where DTS was introduced.

For our data-mining project, the tables such as `customer`, `promotion`, `product`, `product_class`, `store`, and `sales_fact_1997` are used. After the tables are selected, we need to specify the columns and rows to be used for model training. The set of columns used to define the information used by the data-mining process is called the *case*. Because we are interested in the customers' demographic data, we use the columns `customer_region_id`, `birthdate`, `marital_status`, `yearly_income`, `gender`, `num_children_at_home`, `education`, `occupation`, `house_owner`, and `num_cars_owned` from the customer table. From the `promotion` table, we choose the columns related to promotion types and promotion cost such as `promotion_name`, `media_type`, and `cost`. We also need to include the information about the stores such as `store_type` and `region_id`. For the sales data, we should include the columns `store_sales`, `store_cost`, and `unit_sales`. The decision tree algorithm in SQL Server provides **Dependency Network Browser** to unseal the relationship among attributes that can be used to help us decide which columns should be included in our data-mining model.

Mining

Once the data are filtered and cleaned, the actual data-mining operation will be carried out in this phase. First, we need to choose a modeling technique for our data mining according to the data-mining objectives. Then we select modeling parameters. The following tasks may be performed for this phase:

■ *Select modeling techniques:* The data-mining objectives have a major impact on the selection of modeling techniques. Some modeling techniques serve the purpose of finding trends, patterns, or relationships. Others may serve the purpose of predicting future behavior. For example, the neural network technique is good at identifying patterns but is inadequate for predicting behavior change with time. Some data-mining objectives can be achieved by multiple modeling techniques.

■ *Develop data-mining model:* After the modeling technique is specified, the next task is to select a data-mining software package that can get the job done. Then compute the modeling algorithms to prove or disprove the hypotheses. Once the data-mining model is initially created, use a set of testing data to verify that the model works properly. The model should have a number of adjustable parameters. Tune the parameters to make them work properly.

For large companies, data-mining development is often done by a group of experienced technology professionals or by a consulting company. The data-mining process is designed to deal with huge numbers of various data types and may take a long time to be completed. For medium-sized and small companies, the selection of data-mining tools focuses more on the cost, time, and complexity. To select suitable techniques for developing data-mining models, let us review some general requirements for a data-mining development tool.

- It should reduce the complexity of data mining so that analytical users and database administrators can get a quick start on developing data-mining models.
- The cost for developing a data-mining model should be affordable.
- It should be able to handle large amounts of data.
- It should provide tools to seamlessly input data into a data-mining model and seamlessly output results to a report.

The *Analysis Services* tool included in SQL Server is one of the tools that will meet those requirements by providing the following functionalities:

- The Analysis Services tool can handle a variety of data sources through the OLE DB for Data Mining technique. With OLE DB for Data Mining, users can create and train data-mining models in various applications.
- Results of data mining can be viewed by *Data-Mining Model Browser*, a graphical tool included in the Analysis Services package. By integrating a database with data-mining tools, the data transformation and data-cleaning tools included in the DBMS will provide seamless data input.
- The Analysis Services tool provides a number of data-mining algorithms, such as decision trees and clustering in its data-mining model development tools. It also supports third-party data-mining tools. Data-mining model development can be done by using wizards that specify the data-mining techniques, case tables, case key columns, input columns, and predictable columns.
- In Analysis Services, the data-mining technique is directly embedded into a database. That is, the data-mining model is implemented by a relational table. In this specially defined table, columns are used to store information about patterns and relationships that the data-mining process reveals. This enables the tasks of data-mining development to be done in the same way that we manipulate tables in a database. For example, DTS and OLE DB for Data Mining provide the JOIN operation similarly to the SQL syntax used in queries. The JOIN operation can be used to join existing data models against new data sources. DTS and OLE DB for Data Mining will also allow us to modify a data-mining model just like modifying a table.

- The Analysis Services tool supports *Predictive Model Markup Language* (PMML), which is an XML-based language. PMML provides a quick and easy way for integrating data-mining tools and capabilities into database applications. After parsing by an XML parser in a database application, PMML provides the application with information such as the types of data input to and output from data-mining models, technical details about the models, and interpretation of the data-mining results. It provides users with an open interface for integrating data-mining tools with a broad range of applications.
- The data-mining techniques in SQL Server can be integrated with Analysis Manager, *Decision Support Object* (DSO), and the PivotTable service. Those who are already familiar with these OLAP development tools can use these tools for data-mining modeling in a fast and easy way.

Once the modeling technique is chosen, the next step is to develop the data-mining model. Data-mining models can be developed based on a set of columns in relational database tables or OLAP data stores. For illustration purposes, we use both types of data-mining models. We use a relational database-based data-mining model to discover the relationship between customers and promotions and use an OLAP data store-based data-mining model to discover the relationship between the promotions and sales.

Evaluation

In this phase, we need to verify if the data-mining model can achieve the objectives specified in the understanding business phase. Modify the data-mining model based on the feedback from experienced users and testing results. Consider performing the following tasks to evaluate the model:

- *Verify data-mining results:* Verify if the data-mining results have achieved the business objectives. If it is short in achieving them, find out what factors are causing the deficiency. Review the output to see if any unexpected results are returned by the data-mining model.
- *Test accuracy and consistency:* Compare the results from the testing data set with the results from the operational data set. Determine how well the data model can reflect the reality. We should test the model repeatedly to verify consistency.
- *Modify data-mining model:* Based on the feedback, modify the data-mining model accordingly. We may also want to review the overall data-mining process to see if we have missed any important factor or task that should be included in the model.

To test the data-mining model, divide the entire data records into two parts. Use the first half of the records to train the data-mining model and use the second half to test the model. You will learn how to do this later in this chapter.

Deployment

To apply the data-mining results to business processes, the information gained from data mining should be delivered to business users. We should reorganize the data-mining results so that the users can easily understand them. A graphic description of the data-mining results will help. The steps involved in this phase are given below.

- *Plan deployment:* Determine how the results should be delivered to the decision maker. You need to specify if the results are delivered as a written document or a computer program that can be executed by the business application software automatically.
- *Plan maintenance:* You also need to make a maintenance plan. The plan should include a schedule for delivering the data-mining results. As more and more results are returned, you should have a plan of how to manage these results. You need to come up with some ideas on how to coordinate the multiple results so that the results can be delivered quickly.
- *Document reports:* The final step in a data-mining process is to write a report to summarize the data-mining results. The report should include conclusions and recommendations for future activities and should show the impact of the data-mining results on decision making.

In SQL Server, creating a data-mining report can be made easy by using DTS, which has greatly reduced the complexity of the reporting task by integrating data-mining results with reports developed on the client applications.

In this section, we have discussed the data-mining process. Among the data-mining process standards, the CRISP-DM standard has been given a closer look. CRISP-DM consists of six phases, from understanding business to deployment. There is a close-loop connection to these six phases. A data-mining process is not a linear process. It involves repeating and cycling through the development of a data-mining project. The data-mining process involves collaborative effort from decision makers, business managers, and IT personnel. It also involves various technologies. A wide range of knowledge and technical skills is essential for the success of data mining. In the next section, you will learn how to use SQL Server to get some of the tasks done.

14.3 Data-Mining Algorithms

To uncover patterns and trends, the task of data mining is to identify data with similar characteristics. A data case is a data record in a table. An ideal data-mining tool should be able to create a prediction model to forecast the outcome of a given data case. The data-mining tool should be able to identify common characteristics shared by a cluster of data cases. It should also be able handle both qualitative and quantitative data cases.

Based on whether the outcome will be classified, two algorithms — classification and clustering — are used to carry out the data-mining tasks.

- For a data classification task, an algorithm is used to classify the values in a predictable attribute (also called target attribute, dependent variable, or outcome attribute) based on a set of input attributes. The values in a predictable attribute can be either discrete or continuous. The result of the classification is used to predict future business behavior. For example, a *decision tree algorithm* included in SQL Server can be used to identify customers who are likely to use promotions to purchase certain products. In SQL Server, the decision tree algorithm is used for classification.

■ For a data clustering task, an algorithm is used to group data from a set of input variables into neighborhoods (clusters) that exhibit some similar characteristics while no outcome is involved. Sometimes, the characteristics may not initially be obvious to the analytical user. For example, we can group customers based on demographic information such as annual income, education, and occupation. The *clustering algorithm* is included in SQL Server.

We first create a classification model that can be used as a prediction model. Then we will use a cluster model to identify data with similar characteristics.

14.3.1   Decision Tree Algorithm

A commonly used classification algorithm is the decision tree algorithm. The algorithm builds a decision tree that predicts the outcome value for a given input value. The decision tree algorithm has a structure in which *terminal nodes* (called *leaves*) in the tree represent decision outcomes and *nonterminal nodes* represent particular testing values to further classify data. For example, consider the set of customer information data in Figure 14.2.

	Member_Card	Promotion_Result	Income	Occupation	Marital_Status	Education
1	Normal	0	$10K - $30K	Manual	M	Partial High School
2	Normal	0	$10K - $30K	Manual	S	Partial High School
3	Silver	0	$10K - $30K	Skilled Manual	S	High School Degree
4	Normal	0	$10K - $30K	Skilled Manual	S	Partial High School
5	Normal	0	$30K - $70K	Manual	S	High School Degree
6	Normal	0	$70K - $110K	Skilled Manual	M	Bachelors Degree
7	Golden	0	$110K - $150K	Professional	M	Bachelors Degree
8	Normal	1	$30K - $70K	Manual	S	High School Degree
9	Normal	1	$30K - $70K	Manual	M	High School Degree
10	Silver	0	$30K - $70K	Professional	S	Graduate Degree
11	Silver	1	$110K - $150K	Management	M	Graduate Degree
12	Golden	1	$110K - $150K	Professional	M	Bachelors Degree
13	Silver	1	$70K - $110K	Professional	S	Graduate Degree
14	Silver	1	$30K - $70K	Manual	S	Partial College
15	Silver	1	$70K - $110K	Professional	M	Bachelors Degree
16	Silver	1	$30K - $70K	Skilled Manual	M	Partial College
17	Silver	1	$70K - $110K	Professional	S	Graduate Degree
18	Normal	1	$10K - $30K	Skilled Manual	M	High School Degree

Browse Data: "Promotion_Customer" (First 1000 rows)

Figure 14.2   Customer information table

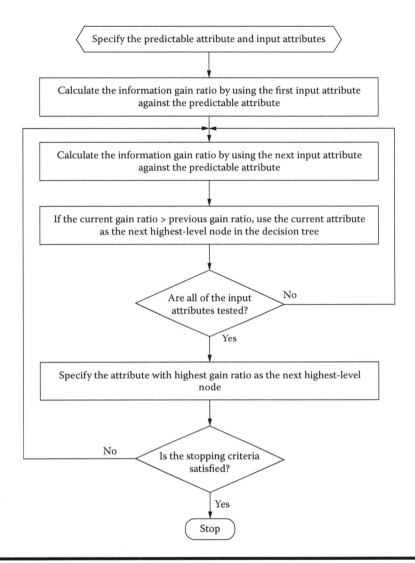

Figure 14.3   Decision tree algorithm flowchart

The data set contains information such as Member_Card, Income, Marital_Status, and Education. Suppose that we want to find out how a customer chooses his or her membership card based on the demographic information. The column Member_Card is chosen as the *predictable attribute* and the columns Income, Marital_Status, and Education are chosen as the *input attributes*. We can create a data-mining model with a basic decision tree algorithm by following the steps shown in the flowchart in Figure 14.3.

Constructing Top-Level Node

After the predictable attribute and input attributes are selected, the next step is to calculate the *information gain ratio* by using one of the input attributes

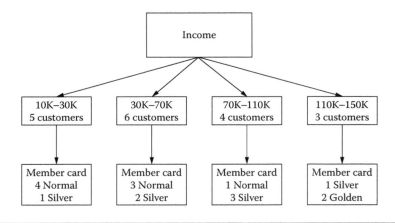

Figure 14.4   Member card count in each Income category

Table 14.1   Predicted Value Assigned to Each Income Category

Income Category	Predicted Value: Member Card
10K–30K	Normal
30k–70K	Normal
70K–110K	Silver
110K–150K	Golden

against the predictable attribute. For example, we first select the input attribute Income to calculate the gain ratio. In the column Income, there are four categories and each category corresponds to the predicted values, types of member cards, in the predictable attribute Member_Card, as shown in Figure 14.4.

Based on the count of member cards by type for each income category, we assign a predicted value to each category; that is, we assign to the 10K–30K income category the predicted value Normal based on the fact that four out of the five customers are using the Normal member cards. If there is a tie in one of the categories, for example, three customers are using the Normal cards and three are using the Silver cards, we count the total number of customers (including other categories) who are using the Normal cards and the total number of the customers who are using the Silver cards. If the total number of the Normal cards is greater than that of the Silver cards, we assign Normal to this category. Based on these rules, the predicted value for each income category is given in Table 14.1.

If the predicted value Normal is assigned to the 10K–30K category, one of the customers who is using the Silver card is incorrectly predicted. Thus, for

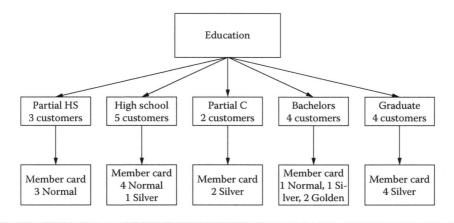

Figure 14.5   Member card count in each Education category

Table 14.2   Predicted Value Assigned to Each Education Category

Education Category	Predicted Value: Member Card
Partial high school	Normal
High school	Normal
Partial college	Silver
Bachelors	Golden
Graduate	Silver

this category, we correctly predict only 80 percent of the customers. For all of the four categories, we correctly predict 13/18 customers. Therefore, the gain ratio is 13/18.

Next, let us pick another input attribute, Education, and count the member cards by types in each category (see Figure 14.5). The predicted values for the categories in the Education attribute are given in Table 14.2. The gain ratio for the correctly predicted customers is 15/18.

For the input attribute Marital_Status, the count of member cards by types in each category is listed in Figure 14.6. After we assign the predicted value to each category for this input attribute, we have the result shown in Table 14.3. Based on the predicted values, the prediction has missed five customers for the Married category and missed four for the Single category. The gain ratio for Marital_Status is 9/18.

According to the comparison of the gain ratios from the three input attributes, the gain ratio from Education has the highest score. Therefore, the decision tree algorithm uses the input attribute Education as the top-level node in the data model.

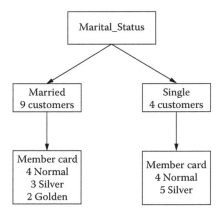

Figure 14.6 Member card count in each Marital_Status category

Table 14.3 Predicted Value Assigned to Each Marital_Status Category

Marital_Status Category	Predicted Value: Member Card
Married	Normal
Single	Silver

Constructing Second-Level Node

After the top-level node is selected, we continue to specify the next-level node. Notice that only two categories, High School and Bachelors, from the Education node have the next level because the other three categories have 100 percent correctly predicted values. A new input variable will be selected to form the second-level node. If the input attribute used to form the top-level node is a category attribute, it cannot be used to form the second-level node. However, if it is a continuous attribute, it can be used again to further split the current node to form the second-level node. In our example, the Education attribute is a category attribute. It will not be used to form a new node. The new node can only be constructed from the input attributes Income and Marital_Status.

For the High School category in the Education attribute, the member card count for the Income attribute is listed in Figure 14.7.

There is a tie for the category 10K–30K. Because the total count of Normal is 4 and the total count of Silver is 1, we assign Normal to the 10K–30K category. The predicted value for the category 30K–70K is Normal. In this case, the 30K–70K category is a perfect predictor. The 10K–30K category is mixed. The gain ratio for the attribute Income is 4/5.

The member card count for the Marital_Status attribute of the High School category is shown in Figure 14.8. The predicted value for the Married

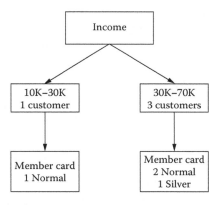

Figure 14.7   Member card count in income attribute for High School category

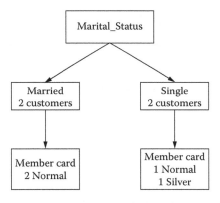

Figure 14.8   Member card count in Marital_Status attribute for High School category

category is Normal and that for the Single category is also Normal. Because the gain ratio for `Marital_Status` is not greater than that for `Income`, we keep `Income` as the second-level node for the High School category in `Education`.

With the same method, the second-level node for the `Education` category Bachelors is constructed by `Income`, which is split into two categories 110K–150K and not 110K–150K. For the `Income` not = 30K–70K category for High School, there is one case that is incorrectly identified. We may further split this node by using the input attribute `Marital_Status`, as shown in Figure 14.9.

Figure 14.9 shows the predictive structure of the data, which indicates that `Education` is the strongest predictor for member card types. In Figure 14.5, for the Graduate category, there are four customers and all of them have Silver cards. Thus, the predicted value for Graduate is set to Silver. If all the data cases in a node have the same category, there is no further splitting of

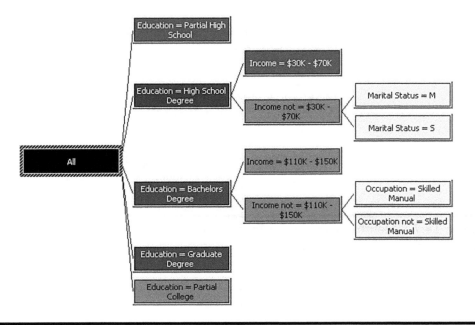

Figure 14.9   Decision tree data-mining model

the node. For the categories High School and Bachelors, some mixed classification occurs. The second-strongest predictor Income is used to further classify the data cases.

The process of identifying patterns and characteristics from a given set of data is called model training. The trained model is then used to predict the outcomes of new data cases. For example, for a new customer who has a high school education with income in the 30K–70K category and married, you can predict that the customer will have a Normal type of member card with the trained model.

Although we have correctly classified every case in the training data set, the data-mining results may not have a strong predictive value. The model in Figure 14.9 is often called an *over-fitted model*. That is, it is too specific. In real-life situations, due to randomness, it is almost impossible to classify a given set of data cases exactly according to the trained model. This can cause a large number of cases in a data set to be incorrectly classified. In practice, a less specific model should be used so that more cases can be correctly classified. In our example, this means we may just accept the model without the Marital_Status level or even without the Income level. To prevent the over-fitting problem, the decision tree algorithm included in SQL Server provides two parameters, MINIMUM_LEAF_CASES and COMPLEXITY_PENALTY. By increasing the values of these two parameters, you can reduce the number of nodes in the data-mining model. The decision tree algorithm built into SQL Server is similar to the decision tree algorithm in the above discussion, except that it uses a Bayesian score as the default splitting criterion. For more information about the Bayesian approach, please search the Web site http://research.microsoft.com.

Notice that an input attribute with more categories usually has less incorrectly predicted values. For example, for the `Education` attribute, the customers in the category Partial College are predicted 100 percent correct. However, this might be misleading. As the number of categories gets larger, the number of cases in each category gets smaller. A more sophisticated way to calculate the gain ratio is to divide the score of correctly predicted values by the number of categories in an input variable. For example, if the gain ratio for the input attribute `Income` is calculated by dividing the score 13/18 by 4, which is 0.1806, and the gain ratio for input attribute `Education` is 0.1667, the input attribute `Income` should be used as the top-level node in the decision tree.

14.3.2   Clustering Algorithm

Unlike the decision tree algorithm, the clustering algorithm does not classify data cases based on an outcome variable. The clustering algorithm partitions a set of data cases into clusters with similar characteristics. These clusters may also be called *segments*. For example, the clustering algorithm can be used to partition customers into several clusters based on their demographic backgrounds and purchasing behavior. If you want to see how data cases are divided based on their similarities, choose the clustering technique. From partitioned clusters, you can gain some insight on common characteristics of each cluster. The common characteristics can be used as clues for planning the business process. Based on the common characteristic, you can rearrange your products or services toward each cluster of your customers. There are various methods of cluster analysis, such as the *K-mean cluster analysis* and the *nearest-neighbor cluster analysis*. The basic idea of cluster analysis is shown in the flowchart in Figure 14.10.

The above algorithm groups data with similarities into neighborhoods. To demonstrate the application of the clustering algorithm, consider the set of income data in thousands of dollars:

```
D = {30, 50, 190, 60, 230, 130, 90, 20, 80, 120}
```

Suppose that we partition this set of data into two clusters, that is, C = 2. The next step is to randomly select two incomes from the data set. For example, the first picked income is 80 and the second one is 60. In the next step, we calculate the difference $|x - 60|$ and the difference $|x - 80|$ for each data case in the data set D. Based on the these differences, we group the data set into two clusters, as shown in Table 14.4. The two clusters' results in the first iteration are:

```
C₁ = {20, 30, 50, 60}    C₂ = {80, 90, 120, 130, 190, 230}
```

After recalculating the mean M_1 for Cluster 1 and the mean M_2 for Cluster 2, we have

```
M₁ = (20 + 30 +50 + 60)/4 = 40
M₂ = (80 + 90 + 120 + 130 + 190 + 230)/6 = 140
```

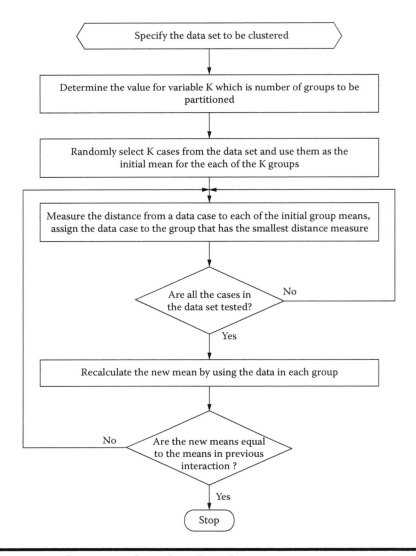

Figure 14.10   Clustering algorithm flowchart

In the second iteration, we recalculate the distances and regroup the data as shown in Table 14.5. The two clusters' results in the second iteration are:

```
C₁ = {20, 30, 50, 60, 80}    C₂ = {90, 120, 130, 190, 230}
```

After recalculating the new means M_1 for Cluster 1 and M_2 for Cluster 2, we have

```
M₁ = (20 + 30 + 50 + 60 + 80)/5 = 48
M₂ = (90 + 120 + 130 + 190 + 230)/5 = 152
```

In the third iteration, we recalculate the distances and regroup the data as shown in Table 14.6. The two clusters' results in the third iteration are:

Table 14.4   Group Data into Two Clusters in First Iteration

Data Case	Distance $|x - 60|$ and $|x - 80|$		Cluster 1 Includes 60 Cluster 2 Includes 80
30	$|30 - 60| = 30$	$|30 - 80| = 50$	30 goes to cluster 1
50	$|50 - 60| = 10$	$|50 - 80| = 30$	50 goes to cluster 1
190	$|190 - 60| = 130$	$|190 - 80| = 110$	190 goes to cluster 2
230	$|230 - 60| = 170$	$|230 - 80| = 150$	230 goes to cluster 2
130	$|130 - 60| = 70$	$|130 - 80| = 50$	130 goes to cluster 2
90	$|90 - 60| = 30$	$|90 - 80| = 10$	90 goes to cluster 2
20	$|20 - 60| = 40$	$|20 - 80| = 60$	20 goes to cluster 1
120	$|120 - 60| = 60$	$|120 - 80| = 40$	120 goes to cluster 2

Table 14.5   Group Data into Two Clusters in Second Iteration

Data Case	Distance $|x - 40|$ and $|x - 140|$		Cluster 1 with Mean=40 Cluster 2 with Mean=140
30	$|30 - 40| = 10$	$|30 - 140| = 110$	30 goes to cluster 1
50	$|50 - 40| = 10$	$|50 - 140| = 90$	50 goes to cluster 1
190	$|190 - 40| = 150$	$|190 - 140| = 50$	190 goes to cluster 2
60	$|60 - 40| = 20$	$|60 - 140| = 80$	60 goes to cluster 1
230	$|230 - 40| = 190$	$|230 - 140| = 90$	230 goes to cluster 2
130	$|130 - 40| = 90$	$|130 - 140| = 10$	130 goes to cluster 2
90	$|90 - 40| = 50$	$|90 - 140| = 50$	90 goes to cluster 2
20	$|20 - 40| = 20$	$|20 - 140| = 120$	20 goes to cluster 1
80	$|80 - 40| = 40$	$|80 - 140| = 60$	80 goes to cluster 1
120	$|120 - 40| = 80$	$|120 - 140| = 20$	120 goes to cluster 2

```
C₁ = {20, 30, 50, 60, 80, 90}    C₂ = {120, 130, 190, 230}
```

After recalculating the new means M_1 for Cluster 1 and M_2 for Cluster 2, we have

```
M₁ = (20 + 30 + 50 + 60 + 80 + 90)/6 = 55
M₂ = (120 + 130 + 190 + 230)/4 = 167.5
```

In the fourth iteration, we recalculate the distances and regroup the data as shown in Table 14.7. The two clusters' results in the fourth iteration are:

```
C₁ = {20, 30, 50, 60, 80, 90}    C₂ = {120, 130, 190, 230}
```

Table 14.6   Group Data into Two Clusters in Third Iteration

Data Case	Distance $\|x - 48\|$ and $\|x - 152\|$		Cluster 1 with Mean=48 Cluster 2 with Mean=152
30	$\|30 - 48\| = 18$	$\|30 - 152\| = 122$	30 goes to cluster 1
50	$\|50 - 48\| = 2$	$\|50 - 152\| = 102$	50 goes to cluster 1
190	$\|190 - 48\| = 142$	$\|190 - 152\| = 38$	190 goes to cluster 2
60	$\|60 - 48\| = 12$	$\|60 - 152\| = 92$	60 goes to cluster 1
230	$\|230 - 48\| = 182$	$\|230 - 152\| = 78$	230 goes to cluster 2
130	$\|130 - 48\| = 82$	$\|130 - 152\| = 22$	130 goes to cluster 2
90	$\|90 - 48\| = 42$	$\|90 - 152\| = 62$	90 goes to cluster 1
20	$\|20 - 48\| = 28$	$\|20 - 152\| = 132$	20 goes to cluster 1
80	$\|80 - 48\| = 32$	$\|80 - 152\| = 72$	80 goes to cluster 1
120	$\|120 - 48\| = 72$	$\|120 - 152\| = 32$	120 goes to cluster 2

Table 14.7   Group Data into Two Clusters in Fourth Iteration

Data Case	Distance $\|x - 55\|$ and $\|x - 167.5\|$		Cluster 1 with Mean=55 Cluster 2 with Mean=167.5
30	$\|30 - 55\| = 25$	$\|30 - 167.5\| = 137.5$	30 goes to cluster 1
50	$\|50 - 55\| = 5$	$\|50 - 167.5\| = 117.5$	50 goes to cluster 1
190	$\|190 - 55\| = 135$	$\|190 - 167.5\| = 22.5$	190 goes to cluster 2
60	$\|60 - 55\| = 5$	$\|60 - 167.5\| = 107.5$	60 goes to cluster 1
230	$\|230 - 55\| = 175$	$\|230 - 167.5\| = 62.5$	230 goes to cluster 2
130	$\|130 - 55\| = 75$	$\|130 - 167.5\| = 37.5$	130 goes to cluster 2
90	$\|90 - 55\| = 35$	$\|90 - 167.5\| = 77.5$	90 goes to cluster 1
20	$\|20 - 55\| = 35$	$\|20 - 167.5\| = 147.5$	20 goes to cluster 1
80	$\|80 - 55\| = 25$	$\|80 - 167.5\| = 87.5$	80 goes to cluster 1
120	$\|120 - 55\| = 65$	$\|120 - 167.5\| = 47.5$	120 goes to cluster 2

Because this time the clusters contain the same data cases as in the previous iteration, the new mean for each of the clusters will remain the same. The iteration can stop here. As shown above, all the incomes less than 100K are grouped into Cluster 1 and all the incomes greater than 100K are grouped into Cluster 2.

The clustering algorithm used in SQL Server is based on the *Expectation Maximization* (EM) algorithm, which is similar to the above clustering algorithm. Instead of partitioning data into C distinct clusters, the EM algorithm uses C probability distributions to represent C clusters. Each individual data case is assigned by a probability specified by a set of parameters. These parameters are recalculated in each of the iterations until they converge to the desired values. For more information about the Expectation and Maximization method, please search the Web site http://research.microsoft.com.

14.4 Developing Data-Mining Models in SQL Server

SQL Server 2000 has included data-mining tools in its *Analysis Services package*. By integrating the tools with a database, the data management utilities can be shared by data-mining processes. The database utility Data Transformation Services can be used for data preparation tasks such as data cleaning and data transformation. It can also be used to deploy data-mining results in front-end database applications. This makes the utilization of data-mining results in database applications seamless. SQL Server also provides data-accessing tools such as OLE DB for Data Mining to allow data-mining models to be broadly accessible. By using OLE DB for Data Mining, both OLAP and relational data can be used as data sources in a data-mining process. OLE DB for Data Mining is also an interface that allows various third-party vendors' data-mining software to access SQL Server databases.

In SQL Server, data mining and OLAP share the same graphic user interface, Analysis Manager. Additional data-mining wizards are built into Analysis Manager. These wizards facilitate analytical users in their interaction with data-mining models. Through Analysis Manager, you can also edit and execute both OLAP and data-mining queries. The wizards provided by SQL Server can run the decision tree and clustering algorithms.

SQL Server treats a data-mining model as a special relational table. Unlike a relational table that stores data, a data-mining model table stores the resulting patterns and relationships revealed by a data-mining process. Information contained in the columns of the data-mining model table can be used for prediction. In the rest of this section, we demonstrate how to create data-mining models in SQL Server and how to use the results from a data-mining process in database applications. Our examples are based on the built-in database `FoodMart 2000`.

14.4.1 Preparing Data-Mining Tools in Analysis Services

To make the data-mining wizard work properly, you need to download and install the SQL Server 2000 database component Service Pack 3 and the SQL Server 2000 analysis service component Service Pack 3 if you have not done so. The following are the steps for installation.

1. Open the Web page **http://www.microsoft.com/sql/downloads/2000/sp3.asp**. From the language select combo box, select **English** and click **Go**.
2. Double-click the database component service pack file **sql2ksp3.exe**. Click **Open** to start the downloading process. Follow the instruction and specify the destination folder as **sql2ksp3**.

3. Double-click the analysis service component service pack file **sql2kasp3. exe**. Click **Open** to start the downloading process. Follow the instruction and specify the destination folder as **sql2kasp3**.

4. To install the database component service pack, double-click the **Setup.exe** file in the folder **sql2ksp3** and follow the installation instruction.

5. To install the analysis service component service pack, double-click the **Setup.exe** file in the folder **sql2kasp3/msolap/install/** and follow the installation instruction. You may need to restart your computer to implement the changes.

14.4.2 Using Data Transformation Services to Prepare Data for Data Mining

As mentioned earlier, DTS can be used to prepare data and to deploy data-mining results. In the following, you will learn how to use DTS to create the `sales_fact_1997_Mining` table that includes all the columns in the table `sales_fact_1997` plus the columns `promotion_result`, `product_result`, `sales_result`, and `store_result`. In these new columns, specified outcome values are assigned to each row. Later, these outcome data are used in data-mining model training.

1. In Microsoft Access, open the database **FoodMart 2000.mdb**. Select **Tables** in the **Objects** pane. Copy the table **sales_fact_1997** and paste it as **sales_fact_1997_Mining**. Make sure that the **Structure Only** paste option is chosen. Open the new table **sales_fact_1997_Mining** in the **Design** view and add four new number columns, **promotion_result**, **product_result**, **sales_result**, and **store_result**.

2. Open **Enterprise Manager** and expand your SQL Server node. Right-click on the **Data Transformation Services** node and select **New Package** to create a new DTS object. Drag a **Microsoft Access** object to the center of the dialog. When the **Connection Properties** dialog box opens, enter the following file name in the **File name** text box:

```
C:\Program Files\Microsoft Analysis Services\Samples\foodmart
    2000.mdb
```

3. Click **OK** to create the DTS object. Similarly, create another **Microsoft Access object**, one as the source and the other as the destination. Highlight the source object, click the **connection** icon 🔁, and then click the destination object to create a connection between the source and destination.

4. Double-click the **connection line**; under the **Source** tab (see Figure 14.11), select the **SQL query** option and enter the following code:

```
SELECT sales_fact_1997.product_id, sales_fact_1997.customer_id,
    sales_fact_1997.promotion_id, sales_fact_1997.store_id,
    sales_fact_1997.store_sales, sales_fact_1997.store_cost,
    sales_fact_1997.unit_sales, store.store_type,
    product_class.product_family, promotion.media_type,
    customer.total_children, customer.yearly_income,
```

```
      customer.marital_status, customer.birthdate,
      customer.education, customer.houseowner,
      customer.num_cars_owned, customer.occupation
FROM store INNER JOIN (promotion INNER JOIN (product_class
   INNER JOIN ((sales_fact_1997 INNER JOIN product ON
   sales_fact_1997.product_id = product.product_id) INNER JOIN
   customer ON sales_fact_1997.customer_id =
   customer.customer_id) ON product_class.product_class_id =
   product.product_class_id) ON promotion.promotion_id =
   sales_fact_1997.promotion_id) ON store.store_id =
   sales_fact_1997.store_id;
```

Figure 14.11   Specify data source for DTS object

5. Under the **Destination** tab, select the destination table **sales_fact_1997_Mining**.
6. Click the **Transformations** tab. Delete the link to the destination column **promotion_result**, if there is a link. Highlight **promotion_id** in the **Source** pane. Click the **New** button and select **ActiveX Script**. Click **OK**. Click the **Source Columns** tab; make sure that **promotion_id** is in the **Selected columns** pane. Click the **Destination Columns** tab; make sure that **promotion_result** is in the **Selected columns** pane. Click **OK**. Click the **Properties** button and enter the following code for the **promotion_result** column:

```
'   Visual Basic Transformation Script
'******************************************************************
```

```
'  Copy each source column to the destination column
Function Main()

If DTSSource("promotion_Id") = 0 Then
   DTSDestination("promotion_result") = 0
Else
   DTSDestination("promotion_result") = 1
End If

Main = DTSTransformStat_OK

End Function
```

7. Test the code by clicking the **Test** button. Similarly, for the column `sales_result`, enter the following ActiveX Script code.

```
'  Visual Basic Transformation Script
'*************************************************************

'  Copy each source column to the destination column
Function Main()

If DTSSource("store_sales") >=0 AND
   DTSSource("store_sales")<4.0
Then
   DTSDestination("sales_result") = 0
ElseIf DTSSource("store_sales") >=4 AND
   DTSSource("store_sales")<8
Then
   DTSDestination("sales_result") = 1
ElseIf DTSSource("store_sales") >=8 AND
   DTSSource("store_sales")<12
Then
   DTSDestination("sales_result") = 2
ElseIf DTSSource("store_sales")>=12 AND
   DTSSource("store_sales")<16
Then
   DTSDestination("sales_result") = 3
Else
   DTSDestination("sales_result") = 4
End If

Main = DTSTransformStat_OK

End Function
```

8. (If the source and destination columns do not match the specifications in the code, edit them under the **Source Columns** and **Destination Columns** tabs.) If everything works, enter the following ActiveX script to specify the column `store_result`:

```
'  Visual Basic Transformation Script
'*************************************************************
```

```
'   Copy each source column to the destination column
Function Main()

If DTSSource("store_type") = "HeadQuarters"  Then
    DTSDestination("store_result") = 0
ElseIf DTSSource("store_type") = "Supermarket" Then
    DTSDestination("Store_result") = 1
ElseIf DTSSource("store_type") = "Small Grocery" Then
    DTSDestination("Store_result") = 2
ElseIf DTSSource("store_type") = "Gourmet Supermarket" Then
    DTSDestination("Store_result") = 3
ElseIf DTSSource("store_type") = "Deluxe Supermarket" Then
    DTSDestination("Store_result") = 4
Else
    DTSDestination("Store_result") = 5
End If

Main = DTSTransformStat_OK

End Function
```

9. For the column `product_result`, enter the following ActiveX script:

```
'   Visual Basic Transformation Script
'**************************************************************

'   Copy each source column to the destination column

Function Main()

If DTSSource("product_family") = "Food"  Then
    DTSDestination("product_result") = 0
ElseIf DTSSource("product_family") = "Drink" Then
    DTSDestination("product_result") = 1
Else
    DTSDestination("product_result") = 2
End If

Main = DTSTransformStat_OK

End Function
```

10. You should have the final result as shown in Figure 14.12.
11. To execute the transformation, right-click the newly configured transformation line and select **Execute Step** to transform the data.

14.4.3 *Exploring Relationships between Predictable Columns and Input Columns*

In the example, we use the decision tree algorithm to analyze the relationships between the predictable columns such as `store_sales`, `store_cost`, `unit_sales`, `promotion_name`, and `media_type`, and the input variables

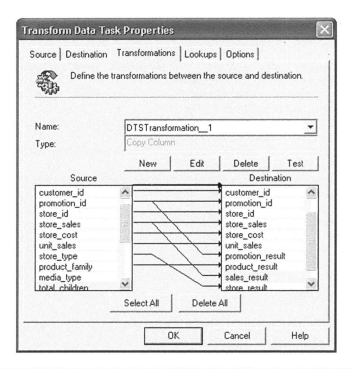

Figure 14.12   Specify transformations for DTS object

such as `customer_region_id`, `birthdate`, `marital_status`, `yearly_income`, `gender`, `total_children`, `education`, `member_card`, `occupation`, `houseowner`, `num_cars_owned`, `promotion_name`, and `media_type` from multiple tables to investigate how customers' purchasing behavior is related to their demographic backgrounds. First, because we are not sure what the relationships are among the columns in the tables `customer`, `promotion`, and `sales_fact_1997`, we include all the columns that can possibly be used to achieve the objectives of this data-mining project and let the decision tree identify the relationships.

1. To open Analysis Manager, click **Start**, **All Programs**, **Microsoft SQL Server**, **Analysis Services**, and **Analysis Manager**.
2. To start **Mining Model Wizard**, expand the **FoodMart 2000** node under the **Analysis Servers** node. Right-click **Mining Models** and select **New Mining Model**.
3. Click **Next** to go to the dialog box to specify the data source type. Check the **Relational data** option. Click **Next** to select the case tables. Check the option **Multiple tables contain the data**. Expand the **Default Schema** node under **FoodMart**. Move the tables **customer**, **promotion**, and **sales_fact_1997** in the **Available tables** pane to the **Selected tables** pane, as shown in Figure 14.13.
4. Click **Next** to select the data-mining technique. In the **Technique** combo box, select **Microsoft Decision Trees**.

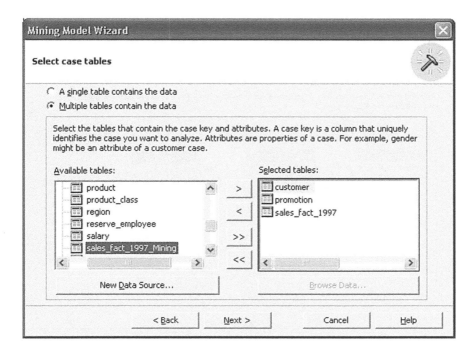

Figure 14.13   Select case tables for data mining

5. Click **Next**. You will see the **Create and edit joins** dialog box. By default, the tables should be automatically connected. If not, connect them using the key columns **customer_id** and **promotion_id** (see Figure 14.14).

6. Click **Next** to select the case key. Because we are going to use each customer as a case in this study, select the table **customer** in the **Case key table** combo box and select the **customer_id** column in the **Case key column** combo box (see Figure 14.15).

7. Click **Next** to select the input and predictable columns. Move the columns **store_sales**, **store_cost**, **unit_sales**, **promotion_name**, and **media_type** to the **Predictable columns** pane. Move the columns **customer_region_id**, **birthdate**, **marital_status**, **yearly_income, gender**, **total_children**, **education**, **member_card**, **occupation**, **houseowner**, **num_cars_owned**, **promotion_name**, and **media_type** to the **Input columns** pane, as shown in Figure 14.16. The columns **promotion_name** and **media_type** can be used as both predictable columns and input columns.

8. Click **Next** and name the model **Cust_Promotion_Sales**. Then click **Finish**.

9. Save the data model. Close the **Relational Mining Model Editor** window. Here we can reset the decision tree data-mining model parameters **MINIMUM_LEAF_CASES** and **COMPLEXITY_PENALTY**. Because the data set contains well-defined data, we can leave the default value unchanged. Right-click the newly created data-mining model **Cust_Promotion_Sales** and select **Browse Dependency Network**. The relationships between the columns are displayed in Figure 14.17.

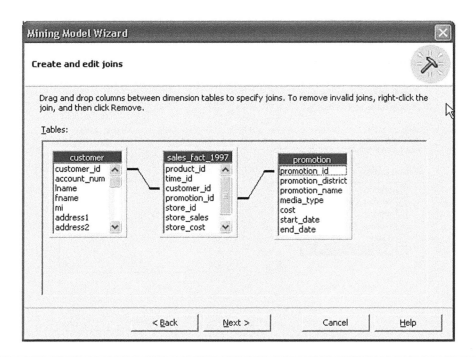

Figure 14.14   Relationships among tables

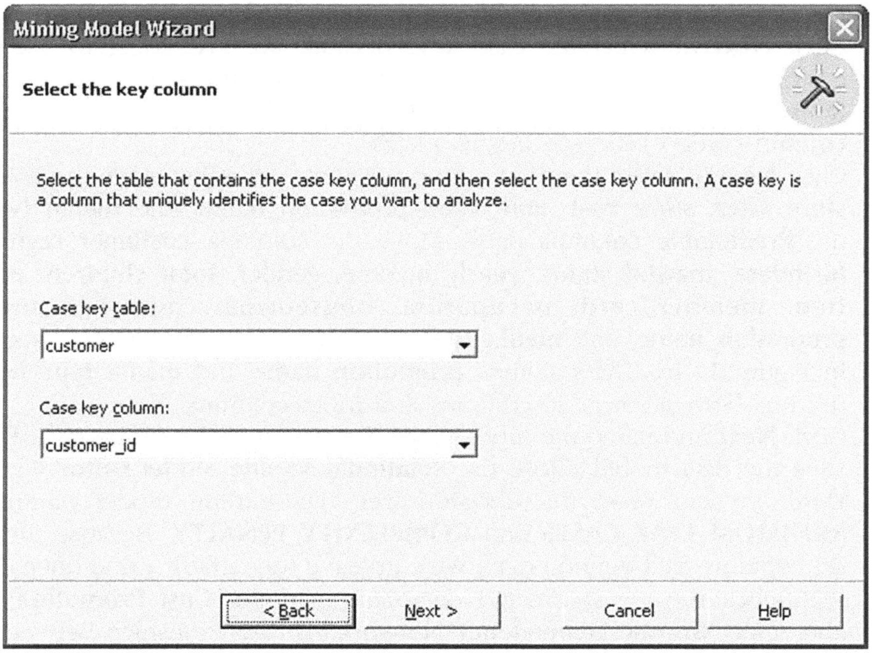

Figure 14.15   Select case key table and case key column

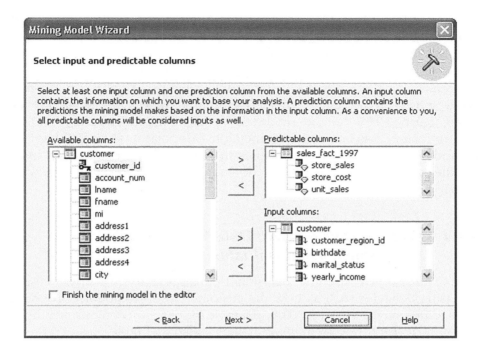

Figure 14.16   Specify predictable columns and input columns

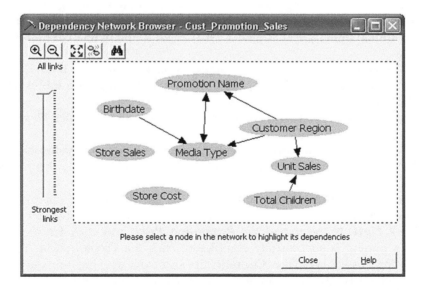

Figure 14.17   Dependencies between predictable columns and input columns

Now that we have found the relationships between some of the columns selected in the development of the data-mining model, let us examine the predictable columns such as unit sales, promotion_name, and media_type. From the dependency network, we can find out that there are no columns from the tables `customer` and `promotion` that are related to `store_sales` and `store_cost`. The column `customer_region_id` from the table `customer` predicts the columns `unit_sales` in the table `sales_fact_1997` and `media_type` and `promotion_name` in the table `promotion`. In the `promotion` table, the columns `promotion_name` and `media_type` predict each other. The column `unit_sales` in the table `sales_fact_1997` can be predicted by the columns `total_children` and `customer_region_id` from the table `customer`. The scroll bar on the left-hand side of the window measures the strength of a relationship. As you drag the pointer of the scroll bar down, the weaker relationships will be eliminated.

14.4.4   Creating Decision Tree Data-Mining Model Using Single Relational Table

As an example, we use the decision tree algorithm to analyze customer purchasing behavior such as how the customers use promotions on products with a different price range. This example is used to demonstrate how to develop a decision tree by mining a single relational table.

1. Open **Analysis Manager**. Expand the **FoodMart 2000** node under your analysis server.
2. Right-click the **Mining Models** node and select **New Mining Model** to open **Mining Model Wizard**. Click **Next** to select the source type. Check the **Relational data** option and click **Next** to go to the **Select case tables** dialog box.
3. Make sure that the option **A single table contains the data** is selected. Choose the table **sales_fact_1997_Mining** in the **Available tables** pane and click **Next** to select the data-mining technique.
4. Make sure that **Microsoft Decision Trees** is selected and click **Next** to select the case key column.
5. In the **Case key column** combo box, select the column **customer_id**. Click **Next** to move to the dialog box that allows you to specify the predictable and input columns.
6. Choose the **promotion_result** column as the predictable column and the **sales_result** column as the input column, as shown in Figure 14.18.
7. Click **Next**. Name the model **Promotion_Price** and click **Finish**. After the data mining is successfully completed, click the **Close** button. To see the mining result, click the **Content** tab and you will see the decision tree generated by Analysis Services, as shown in Figure 14.19.

Figure 14.19 shows that the **Relational Mining Model Editor** window contains three major areas: the **Content Detail** area in the center of the editor window, the **Content Navigator** area at the top-right corner, and the **Attributes** area at the middle-right side. Detailed information about the decision tree is displayed in the **Content Detail** area. Each node in the tree is marked by its name. The overall view of the decision tree is displayed in the **Content Navigator** area.

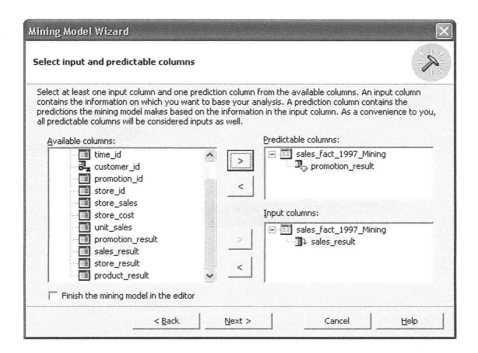

Figure 14.18   Select input and predictable columns

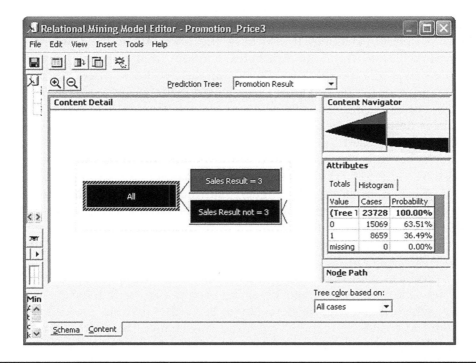

Figure 14.19   Decision tree created for Promotion_Price data-mining model

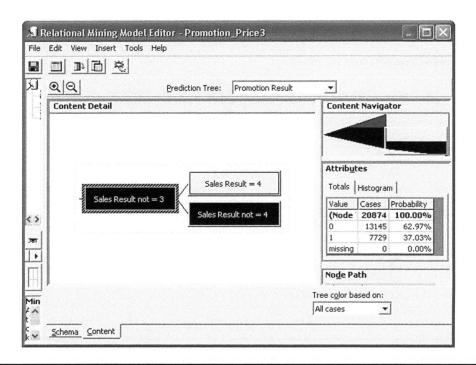

Figure 14.20   Second-level decision tree nodes

By clicking on a different part of the view in **Content Navigator**, you can see that part of the information is in **Content Detail**. Statistical information is summarized in the **Attributes** area. The statistical information will be used to help with decision making. If you click the node **All** in the **Content Detail** area, you will see, from the **Attributes** window, that 36.49 percent of the purchases used the promotions. Based on the products' price range of the data-mining result, the products are divided into two categories. The first category contains products with the price range from $12 to $16. Click the node **Sales Result = 3**. In the **Attributes** area, you will see that 32.59 percent of the purchases used the promotions; this is a little lower than the overall rate. Click the node **Sales Result not = 3**, which means not in the price range between $12 and $16. The percentage of purchases that used the promotions is 37.03 percent, which is a bit higher than the overall rate. The node **Sales Result not = 3** is further split into two categories. Double-click the node **Sales Result not = 3**, and you will see the content detail as shown in Figure 14.20.

Click the node **Sales Result = 4**. The statistical information in the **Attributes** area indicates that only 29.47 percent of the purchases used the promotions for the products with prices greater than $16. Click the node **Sales Result not = 4**. This time, the percentage of using promotions in purchasing is 37.17 percent, which is the highest percentage. From the analysis, we can see that the more expensive the product was, the less chance the promotions would be used. If a promotion is created to cover all products, the analysis indicates that fewer customers will use the promotion for products costing more than $16. If this is the case, fewer promotion resources should be allocated to the higher-priced products. Otherwise, the result may indicate that some of the promotions do not cover the higher-priced products. The company may need to change the coverage policies of some of the promotions.

14.4.5 Creating Cluster Data-Mining Models

Unlike the decision tree technique in which classification is performed on a predictable column based on a set of input columns, the cluster data-mining technique does not require the specification of predictable columns. By using the clustering algorithm, data contained in a set of input variables are classified based on their similarities.

Creating Cluster Data-Mining Model Using Single Relational Table

To demonstrate the use of the clustering algorithm in data mining, consider the following example in which we classify customers based on their purchasing behavior, which includes the types of stores from which the customers buy their products, the types of products the customers are likely to purchase, the amount of money the customers usually spend on these products, and if they use promotions. To do this, consider the following steps.

1. Start **Analysis Manager** and expand the database **FoodMart 2000** under your analysis server.
2. Right-click the **Mining Models** node and select **New Mining Model** to open **Mining Model Wizard**.
3. Click **Next** to select the source type. Because we are going to use the table **sales_fact_1997_Mining**, we choose the **Relational data** option.
4. Click **Next** to select the case table. For our example, select the table **sales_fact_1997_Mining**.
5. Click **Next** to select the data-mining technique. Because we are going to cluster the customers based on their purchasing behavior, we select the **Microsoft Clustering** technique.
6. Click **Next** to select the case key column. In our example, the customers will be grouped, so select **customer_id** in the **Case key column** combo box.
7. Click **Next** to specify the input columns. Select the columns **store_sales**, **promotion_result**, **store_result**, and **product_result**, as shown in Figure 14.21.
8. Click **Next**. Name the model **Customer_Cluster** and click **Finish**.
9. After the process is successfully completed, click **Close**. **Relational Mining Model Editor** will open automatically. Click the **Content** tab to show the clusters. By default, the Microsoft Clustering algorithm creates ten clusters. If you prefer five clusters, you can change the **Cluster Count** value from ten to five in the **Properties** pane located at the bottom-left part of **Relational Mining Model Editor**. Reprocess the model by clicking the **Process Mining Model** icon in the toolbar. You should have the result shown in Figure 14.22.
10. To examine the characteristics of the first cluster, click on the **Cluster 1** node. The characteristics of **Cluster 1** can be read from the **Node Path** pane.

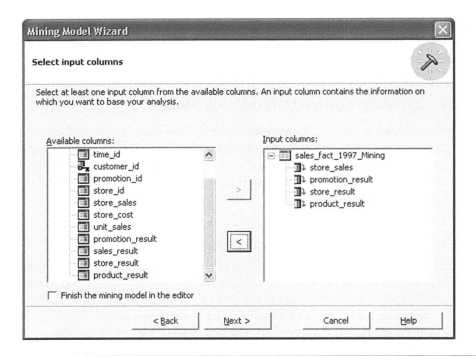

Figure 14.21　Select input columns for cluster analysis

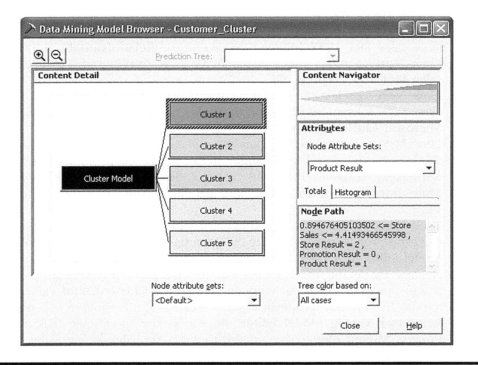

Figure 14.22　Clusters created in cluster data-mining model

You can see in Figure 14.22 that the following characteristics are specialized:

■ Cluster 1:
  – Store Sales (money spent): Ranging from $0.90 to $4.42
  – Store Result (type of stores) = 2 (Small Grocery)
  – Product Result (family of products) = 1 (Drink)
  – Promotion Result (if a promotion is used) = 0 (No)
From these characteristics, we have the description of Cluster1 customers. When purchasing drinks at a small grocery store with a small amount of expense, the customers tend not to use promotions. Similarly, the characteristics for the other clusters are as follows:

■ Cluster 2:
  – Store Sales (money spent): Ranging from $3.20 to $6.73
  – Store Result (type of stores) = 1 (Supermarket), 3 (Gourmet Supermarket), 5 (Mid-Sized Grocery)
  – Product Result (family of products) = 0 (Food)
  – Promotion Result (if a promotion is used) = 1 (Yes)

■ Cluster 3:
  – Store Sales (money spent): Ranging from $2.49 to $10.63
  – Store Result (type of stores) = 4 (Deluxe Supermarket)
  – Product Result (family of products) = 0 (Food) and 2 (Nonconsumable)
  – Promotion Result (if a promotion is used) = 0 (No)

■ Cluster 4:
  – Store Sales (money spent): More than $16.31
  – Store Result (type of stores) = 1 (Supermarket), 3 (Gourmet Supermarket), 5 (Mid-Sized Grocery)
  – Product Result (family of products) = 0 (Food) and 2 (Nonconsumable)
  – Promotion Result (if a promotion is used) = 0 (No)

■ Cluster 5:
  – Store Sales (money spent): Ranging from $5.62 to $9.89
  – Store Result (type of stores) = 1 (Supermarket), 3 (Gourmet Supermarket), 5 (Mid-Sized Grocery)
  – Product Result (family of products) = 1 (Drink) and 2 (Nonconsumable)
  – Promotion Result (if a promotion is used) = 1 (Yes)

From the above findings, we can see that customers tend to use promotions at supermarkets, gourmet supermarkets, and mid-sized grocery stores for food at a price range between $3.20 and $6.73 and for drinks and nonconsumable goods at a price range from $5.62 to $9.89. It is less likely that the customers will use promotions to purchase drinks at a small grocery store, food and nonconsumable goods at a deluxe supermarket, or products that cost more than $16.31. Based on these findings, decision makers may reallocate promotion resources to get better effects.

Creating Cluster Data-Mining Model Using Multiple Relational Tables

In the next example, we conduct a cluster analysis on multiple tables. This time, we classify the customers based on the types of promotion media and

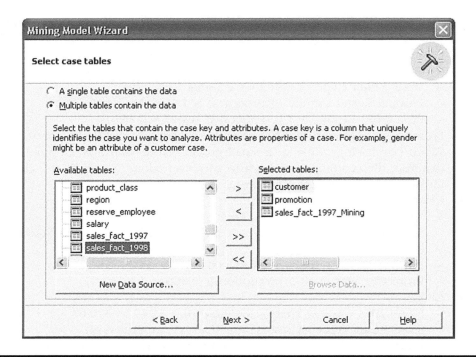

Figure 14.23   Select multiple tables for cluster analysis

the customers' demographic information such as yearly_income, occupation, and num_children_at_home. The steps to develop the data-
mining model are similar to the previous example, which uses a single
relational database table.

1. Start **Mining Model Wizard** as shown in the previous example. Select the
   Relational data source and click **Next** to go to the **Select case tables** dialog
   box.
2. Choose the option **Multiple tables contain the data**. Move the tables
   customer, **promotion**, and **sales_fact_1997_Mining** from the **Available
   tables** pane to the **Selected tables** pane, as shown in Figure 14.23.
3. Click **Next** to select **Microsoft Clustering** as the data-mining technique.
   Click **Next** and connect the tables, as shown in Figure 14.24.
4. Click **Next** to choose **customer_id** as the case key column.
5. Click **Next** to select input columns. In this example, we choose the columns
   yearly_income, **num_children_at_home**, **occupation**, **houseowner**, and
   media_type.
6. Click **Next** and enter **MultiTable_Cluster** as the model name. Click **Finish**
   to complete the configuration for the mining model.
7. Again, set the default number of clusters to five. Reprocess the model, and
   you will get the result shown in Figure 14.25.

The characteristics of Cluster 1 are given below.

- Cluster 1:
    - Yearly Income > $50K
    - Occupation = Professional, Management

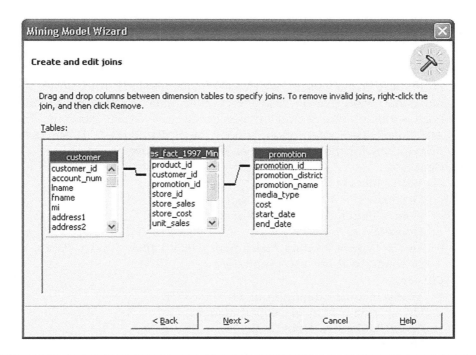

Figure 14.24   Create joins to relate multiple tables

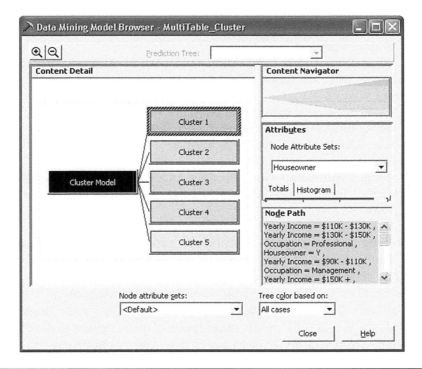

Figure 14.25   Clusters created from multiple tables

- Num Children At Home = 1, 2, 3, 4, or 5
- Houseowner = Yes
- Media Type = Street Handout, Product Attachment, In-Store Coupon, Sunday Paper, TV, or Radio

From these characteristics, we can see that a customer from Cluster 1 earns more than $50K, has at least one child at home, owns a house, and has used some of the promotion media such as Street Handout, Product Attachment, In-Store Coupon, Sunday Paper, Radio, and TV. Similarly, the descriptions for the other clusters are given below:

- Cluster 2:
  - Yearly Income > $50K
  - Occupation = Professional, Management
  - Num Children At Home = 0 or 2
  - Houseowner = No
  - Media Type = Product Attachment, Daily Paper, Sunday Paper, Radio, or simply will not use promotions
- Cluster 3:
  - Yearly Income ranging from $10K to $50K
  - Occupation = Manual, Skilled Manual
  - Num Children At Home = 0
  - Houseowner = No
  - Media Type = Product Attachment, In-Store Coupon, Daily Paper, Radio, or TV
- Cluster 4:
  - Yearly Income ranging from $10K to $50K
  - Occupation = Manual, Skilled Manual
  - Num Children At Home = 1, 2, 3, 4, or 5
  - Houseowner = Yes
  - Media Type = Bulk Mail, Product Attachment, In-Store Coupon, Sunday Paper, TV, Cash Register Handout, or Radio
- Cluster 5:
  - Yearly Income ranging from $10K to $50K
  - Occupation = Clerical, Manual, and Skilled Manual
  - Num Children At Home = 2, 4, or 5
  - Houseowner = No
  - Media Type = Bulk Mail, Product Attachment, Daily Paper, Radio, TV, Sunday Paper, Cash Register Handout, or simply will not use promotions.

Some of the customers who do not use promotions are in Cluster 2 and Cluster 5. Both clusters have the characteristic of not being a houseowner. Cluster 3 has similar characteristics to Cluster 2 and Cluster 5. The difference is that the number of children in the family is 0 for customers in Cluster 3. This may indicate that some of the customers from Cluster 3 are single. Further research may be needed to create some types of promotions that will encourage customers from Cluster 2 and Cluster 5 to use promotions.

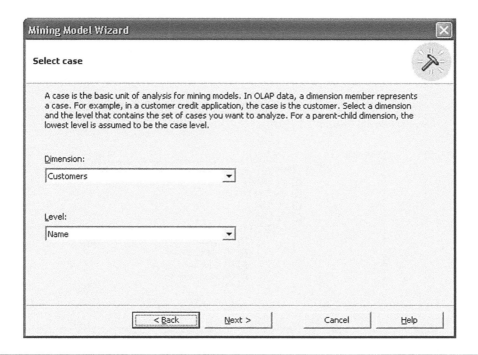

Figure 14.26 Specify dimension and level for OLAP-based clustering analysis

Creating Cluster Data-Mining Model Using OLAP

In the next example, we conduct a cluster analysis on a prebuilt OLAP object. This time, we use the OLAP cube `Sales` as the data source for the cluster data-mining model. We classify the customers based on their demographic information such as `Gender`, `Marital Status`, `Income`, `Education`, and `Member Card`. Based on the findings from this analysis, the stores can rearrange their services for different types of customers. The steps to develop the data-mining model are similar to the previous example.

1. To open Analysis Manager, click **Start**, **All Programs**, **Microsoft SQL Server**, **Analysis Services**, and **Analysis Manager**.
2. To start **Data Mining Wizard**, expand the Cubes node under the database **FoodMart 2000**. Right-click the cube **Sales** and select **New Mining Model**.
3. In the **Select data-mining technique** dialog box, select **Microsoft Clustering** from the **Technique** combo box.
4. Click **Next**. In the **Select case** dialog box, pick **Customers** from the **Dimension** combo box and **Name** from the **Level** combo box, as shown in Figure 14.26.
5. Click **Next**. Make sure all the columns under the **Member Properties** node of **Name** are checked, as shown in Figure 14.27. Because **Name** is the level, we use it in this model, so uncheck the levels **Country**, **State Province**, and **City**. Also, check **Store Sales** under **Measures**.

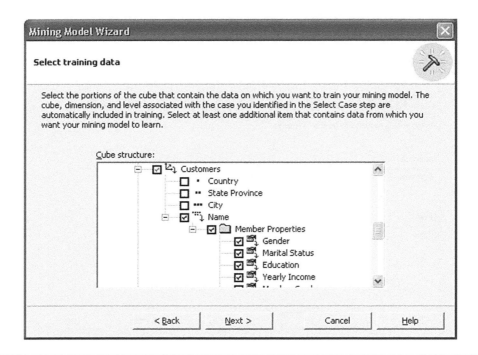

Figure 14.27 Select input columns as training data

6. Click **Next**. Enter **Customer_OLAP_Mining** as the model name and click **Finish**. After the data-mining model is successfully processed, click the **Close** button. Again, change the **Cluster Count** value to **5** and reprocess the data-mining model.

The following is the description of Cluster 1:

- Cluster 1:
  - Education = Bachelor's Degree and Graduate Degree
  - Yearly Income = $50K–$150K+
  - $0.57 <= Store Sales <= $123.77
  - Member Card = Bronze, Silver, Golden
  - Marital Status = Single
  - Gender = F

  From the above description, we can see that Cluster 1 customers are single females with higher education degrees and yearly income. They are also qualified for the Bronze, Silver, and Golden member cards. Their spending range is from $0.57 to $123.77, based on Store Sales. Based on the findings, the stores may arrange some products toward the purchasing characteristics of these single female customers, who are well educated with higher yearly income. The characteristics of the other clusters are shown below.
- Cluster 2:
  - Yearly Income = $10K–$30K
  - Member Card = Normal

- Education = Partial High School
- $0.57 <= Store Sales <= $256.29
- Gender = M
- Marital Status = Married
- Cluster 3:
  - $0.57 <= Store Sales <= $90.63
  - Education = High School Degree, Partial College
  - Yearly Income = $30K–$50K, $90K–$150K+
  - Member Card = Bronze, Silver, Golden
  - Marital Status = M
  - Gender = F
- Cluster 4:
  - Yearly Income = $30K–$50K
  - Education = High School Degree, Partial College
  - Member Card = Bronze
  - $0.57 <= Store Sales <= $208.71
  - Marital Status = S
  - Gender = M
- Cluster 5:
  - Store Sales > $578.34
  - Education = Bachelor's Degree, Graduate Degree
  - Yearly Income = $50K–$150K+
  - Member Card = Bronze, Silver, Golden
  - Marital Status = M
  - Gender = F

By comparing the customers in Cluster 3 and Cluster 5, we can see that they are married females with Bronze, Silver, and Golden member cards. However, the spending amount is quite different. The amount spent at a store for Cluster 3 customers is $0.57–$90.63. For Cluster 5 customers, the amount is more than $578.34. The main difference between these two clusters is the education level. The customers in Cluster 3 have completed high school or partial college, but the customers in Cluster 5 have bachelor's or graduate degrees. Also, the customers in Cluster 3 have incomes of either $30K–$50 or $90K–150K+, whereas those in Cluster 5 have incomes of $50K–150K+. The customers in Cluster 2 are married males with lower yearly income. They did not finish high school and carry Normal member cards. The customers in Cluster 4 have a similar spending level to those in Cluster 2. However, Cluster 4 customers are single males. They completed high school or have partial college education. They carry Bronze member cards. Based on these findings, stores can create some specific services for the customers in each cluster.

14.4.6   *Deploying Data-Mining Results with DTS*

In this section, you will learn how to apply the data-modeling technique to predict what type of member card a customer tends to have based on his or her demographic information such as income and marital status. The result of the data-mining process is then presented in a form such that a store

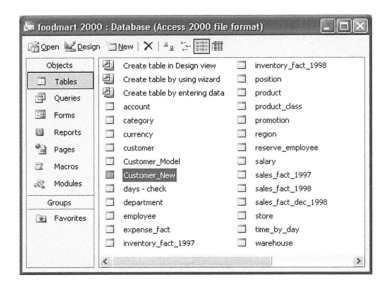

Figure 14.28   Create two new tables

manager can find a better way to increase the number of members for each type of card by providing appropriate services to potential customers.

In this example, we first divide the customer table into two tables. One of them is used for data-mining model training. In the training process, we learn the patterns based on customers' demographic information and the types of member cards they have. Then these patterns are used to predict which member card a potential customer will use. Information about potential customers is placed in the second table. To predict future behavior, you can use the PREDICTION JOIN statement included in the Data Transformation Services utility. PREDICTION JOIN relates the data-mining model to the table containing information about the customers. Because data mining is treated as a specific table, the JOIN statement connects the two tables, data-mining model and potential customer table, just as does a regular JOIN statement in a SQL query.

Creating Table for Data-Mining Model and Table for Prediction

The first step is to create two new tables that have the same structure as the table customer. In Microsoft Access, this can be easily done by copying the table **customer** in the database **FoodMart 2000** and pasting it as **Customer_Model** and **Customer_New**, as shown in Figure 14.28.

Delete the first half of the records from the table **Customer_New** and delete the second half of the records from the table **Customer_Model**, so that we can use the records in **Customer_Model** for training and use the records in **Customer_New** for testing. Although we should delete the column **member_card** in **Customer_New** because we are going to predict what member card each potential customer will use, we will keep this column to compare it with the predicted **member_card** column.

Training Data-Mining Model

The next step is to train a new data-mining model by using the table `Customer_Model`. The data-mining model developed here can be used to predict member cards stored in the `Customer_New` table.

1. Open **Analysis Manager**, and expand the **FoodMart 2000** database node under your analysis server.
2. Right-click the **Mining Models** node and select **New Mining Model** to open **Mining Model Wizard**. Click **Next** to select the source type. Check the **Relational data** option and click **Next** to go to the **Select case tables** dialog box.
3. Make sure that the option **A single table contains the data** is selected. Select the table **Customer_Model** in the **Available tables** pane and click **Next** to select the data-mining technique.
4. Make sure that **Microsoft Decision Trees** is selected and click **Next** to select the case key column.
5. In the **Case key column** combo box, choose the column **customer_id**. Click **Next** to move to the dialog that allows you to specify the predictable and input columns.
6. Choose the **member_card** column as the predictable column and the **yearly_income, marital_status, education,** and **num_cars_owned** columns as the input columns.
7. Click **Next**. Enter **Customer_MemberCard** as the model name and click **Finish**. To see the mining result, click the **Content** tab and you will see the decision tree generated by Analysis Services, as in Figure 14.29.

Predicting Member Cards with DTS

After the model is created, we predict the types of member cards held by the customers. The following steps show you how to use DTS to relate the data-mining model to the table `Customer_New` for prediction.

1. To start DTS, click **Start**, **All Programs**, **Microsoft SQL Server**, and **Enterprise Manager**.
2. Expand your **SQL Server** node. Right-click the **Data Transformation Services** node and select **New Package**.
3. Once the **DTS Package** editor opens, drag the **Data Mining Prediction Task** icon ⋟ from the task bar to the workplace.
4. In the **Data Mining Prediction Query Task** dialog box, enter **Member Card Prediction** as the name and add the description for the data-mining task. Also, enter your SQL Server name in the **Server** textbox and choose **FoodMart 2000** in the **Database** combo box. In the **Mining models** list box, select the model **Customer_MemberCard**, which will be used in the query task as shown in Figure 14.30.
5. To enter a query script, click the **Query** tab. First, we need to create a connection string. To do so, click the button ⋯ by the **Input data source** textbox.

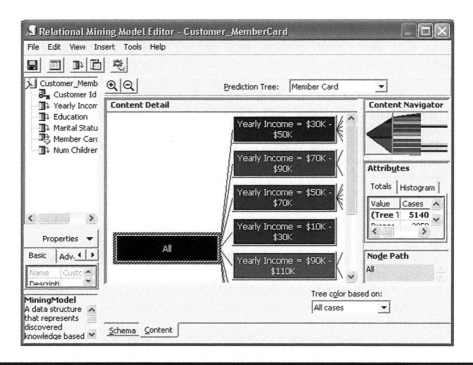

Figure 14.29　Create data-mining model Customer_MemberCard

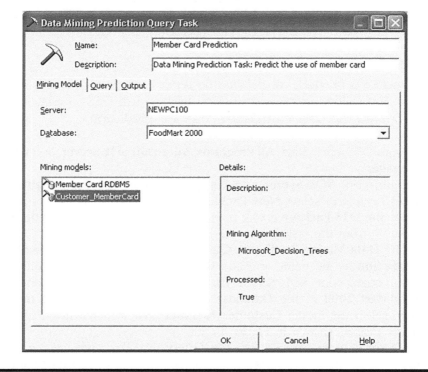

Figure 14.30　Select training model

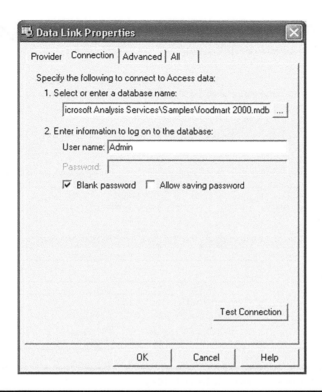

Figure 14.31   Configure data link properties

6. Make sure that **Microsoft Jet 4.0 OLE DB Provider** is selected. Click **Next** to configure the connection.

7. In the textbox **Select or enter a database name**, enter the file **C:\Program Files\Microsoft Analysis Services\Samples\foodmart 2000.mdb** for the data source, as shown in Figure 14.31.

8. Click the **Test Connection** button. If the test is successful, click **OK** to accept the configuration.

9. To enter the code in the **Prediction query** pane, click the **New Query** button. In the **Case Table** combo box, select the table **Customer_New**. For the input columns, select **Customer Id**, **Education**, **Marital Status**, **Num Children At Home,** and **Yearly Income**. Because we will predict the content of the **Member Card** column, uncheck it. Specify the predicted column as **Member Card** (see Figure 14.32).

10. Click **Finish** to generate the query. The prediction query has the format shown below:

```
SELECT [FLATTENED] <list of columns containing
   input data and predicted values>
FROM <name of the data-mining model>
PREDICTION JOIN <list of data source>
ON <join conditions>
[WHERE <select conditions>]
```

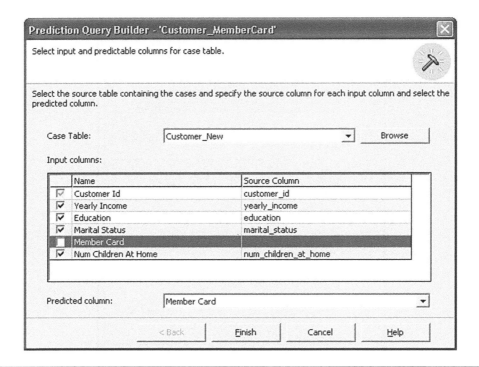

Figure 14.32   Generate prediction query

11. When working with multidimensional data, a flattened dataset has only two dimensions. If a flattened dataset is specified, additional dimensions are mapped onto the two existing dimensions. Figure 14.33 shows the prediction query generated by DTS.

12. In Figure 14.33, we can see that the input columns are **Customer Id**, **Education**, **Marital Status**, **Num Children At Home**, and **Yearly Income**, and the predicted column is **Member Card**. The data-mining model used is **Customer MemberCard**. The data source is a list of columns selected from the database **FoodMart 2000**. The alias for the data source is **T1**.

13. Next, we specify the output table. Click the **Output** tab. In the **Output data source** textbox, specify the connection where you want to place the output and, in the **Output table** textbox, specify the output table name. In our example, we accept the default for both, as shown in Figure 14.34.

14. Click **OK** to accept the specification and complete the package configuration. Save the result.

15. To execute the prediction query, right-click the icon of the newly created data-mining prediction task, and select **Execute**.

16. After you have successfully executed the prediction query, open the database **FoodMart 2000** in Access. Double-click the table **PredictionResults**, you should have the input and predicted values as listed in Figure 14.35.

17. The column **Customer_Member Card** contains predicted values. To verify the prediction results, run the following query in Access:

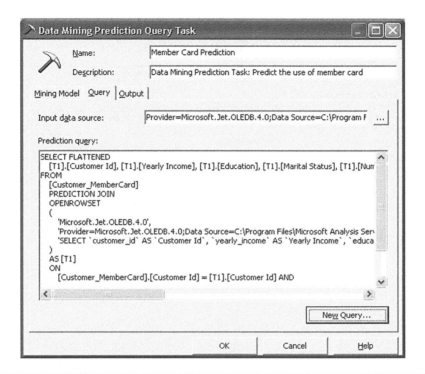

Figure 14.33 Prediction query

```
SELECT PredictionResults.[T1_Customer Id],
   PredictionResults.T1_Education,
   PredictionResults.[T1_Marital Status],
   PredictionResults.[T1_Num Children At Home],
   PredictionResults.[T1_Yearly Income],
   PredictionResults.[Customer_MemberCard_Member Card]
FROM PredictionResults
WHERE (((PredictionResults.[Customer_MemberCard_Member Card])
      ='Normal'));
```

18. The query selects customers who will possibly use the Normal type of member cards. The prediction results are shown in Figure 14.36.
19. From the above figure, we can see there are 1129 customers who will use the Normal member cards. We now compare this number with the number of customers who are using the Normal member cards in the original table by using the following query:

```
SELECT customer_id, education, marital_status,
   num_children_at_home, yearly_income, member_card
FROM customer_new
WHERE ((customer_new.member_card)='Normal');
```

20. The result of this query is shown in Figure 14.37.

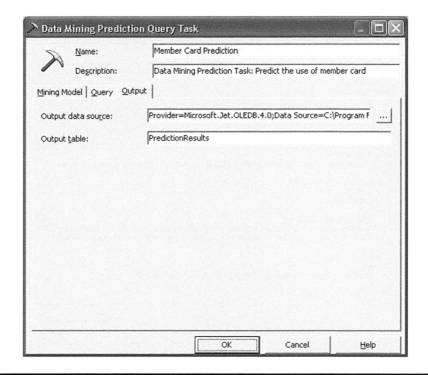

Figure 14.34   Specify output of prediction query

T1_Customer Id	T1_Yearly Incor	T1_Education	T1_Marital St	T1_Num Child	Customer_Mem
10262	$30K - $50K	High School De	M	5	Golden
10263	$30K - $50K	Partial College	S	0	Bronze
10264	$10K - $30K	Partial High Sch	S	0	Normal
10265	$110K - $130K	Partial High Sch	M	0	Bronze
10266	$130K - $150K	High School De	S	0	Bronze
10267	$10K - $30K	Partial High Sch	M	3	Normal
10268	$30K - $50K	High School De	S	0	Bronze
10269	$70K - $90K	Bachelors Degr	M	1	Bronze
10270	$30K - $50K	Partial College	S	0	Bronze
10271	$70K - $90K	Bachelors Degr	S	0	Bronze
10272	$110K - $130K	Partial High Sch	S	0	Bronze
10273	$70K - $90K	Bachelors Degr	S	0	Bronze
10274	$50K - $70K	Bachelors Degr	S	0	Bronze
10275	$30K - $50K	High School De	M	0	Bronze
10276	$30K - $50K	Partial College	M	0	Bronze
10277	$90K - $110K	Partial High Sch	M	3	Bronze
10278	$30K - $50K	Partial College	M	0	Bronze
10279	$130K - $150K	Partial High Sch	S	0	Bronze
10280	$150K +	High School De	M	2	Golden
10281	$50K - $70K	Bachelors Degr	S	0	Bronze

Record: 1 of 5141

Figure 14.35   Prediction results on member cards

Figure 14.36   Prediction results on normal member cards

Figure 14.37   Customers with normal member cards in original table

21. In Figure 14.37, there are 1219 customers who are using the Normal member cards. To find out the number of correctly identified cases, run the following SQL statement in Access:

```
SELECT C.customer_id, P.[Customer_MemberCard_Member Card]
FROM PredictionResults P INNER JOIN customer_new C ON
    C.customer_id = P.[T1_Customer ID]
WHERE (((P.[Customer_MemberCard_Member Card])='Normal') AND
    ((C.member_card)= P.[Customer_MemberCard_Member Card]));
```

22. The result of this query indicates that 1039 out of 1219 cases (85 percent) are correctly predicted by the data-mining model.

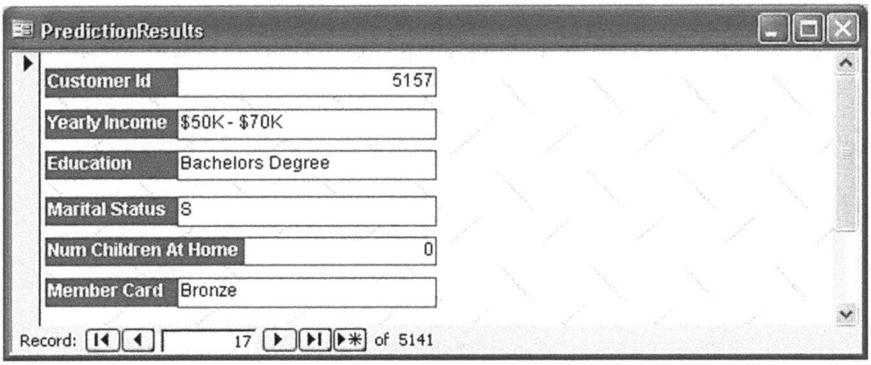

Figure 14.38   Form presentation of prediction results

Creating Form to Display Data-Mining Results

The final step of this example is to create a simple form to present the prediction results of this data-mining process. To present the data in the table `PredictionResults`, follow the steps below.

1. Start **Microsoft Access** and open the database **FoodMart 2000**. Click **Forms** in the **Objects** pane.
2. Double-click **Create form by using wizard**. In the **Tables/Queries** combo box, select the table **PredictionResults**. Move all the columns from the **Available Fields** pane to the **Selected Fields** pane.
3. Click **Next** to specify the layout format. Select the option **Columnar** for the layout.
4. Click **Next** to specify the form style. Select the option **Industrial**.
5. Click **Next** and then **Finish**.
6. In the Design View window, modify and rearrange the labels and text boxes. The final result should look like the one in Figure 14.38.

In this section, you have learned how to implement a data-mining process in SQL Server. Various tools have been used in the development of data-mining models. Analysis Manager is a convenient tool for creating and manipulating data-mining models. Examples have been given to demonstrate how to use Analysis Manager to create decision tree models and cluster models. DTS has also been used to connect data sources, prepare data for the data-mining modeling process, and display the data-mining results.

14.5 Summary

In this chapter, we have covered the topics in data mining. We first discussed the major steps in a data-mining process — understanding business, understanding data, data preparation, data mining, evaluation, and deployment — based on the Cross-Industry Standard Process for Data Mining (CRISP-DM) standard. We have studied the requirements and objectives for each of the above tasks. We have also discussed the tools available in SQL Server to handle these tasks. With the examples, we illustrated how to develop data-mining models with two data-mining algorithms, decision tree and clustering. The development and implementation of data-mining models in SQL Server were practiced in the last part of this chapter. To efficiently transfer data from various sources to a data-mining model, the SQL Server utility Data Transformation Services (DTS) can be used for data preparation. DTS provides services for extracting, validating, formatting, and loading data before the data are transferred into a data-mining model. By using the wizards provided by Analysis Manager, data-mining models based on the decision tree and clustering algorithms were created in the examples. We have developed data-mining models based on one or multiple tables from a relational database. Data-mining models based on OLAP cubes have also been developed. Finally, to assist decision makers in predicting future business behavior, DTS has been used in a prediction process based on the model created in a data-mining process. The prediction results were saved in a table, so that they could be easily used in a form or report to display the findings. These tools make it possible for a small business to conduct its own data-mining process.

Review Questions

1. What types of tasks are appropriate for data mining?
2. List the advantages of the data-mining package included in SQL Server.
3. Name two commonly used data-mining standards.
4. Briefly describe the major data-mining steps in the CRISP-DM standard.
5. What do you need to do to understand the business for data mining?
6. What tasks can be performed to understand data?
7. Describe the visual and numerical techniques used to explore data.
8. What are the tasks performed in data preparation?
9. What is Dependency Network Browser?
10. What are the tasks performed in the mining phase?
11. What are the tools provided by SQL Server to meet the data-mining requirements?
12. What is the advantage of treating the data-mining model as a table?
13. What are the tasks you will perform in the evaluation phase?
14. List the planning and documenting work you need to do when deploying the data-mining results.
15. Given a set of data D = {2, 15, 6, 8, 11, 5, 10, 7, 21, 17}, group the data into two clusters with the clustering algorithm introduced in this chapter.
16. Which algorithm is used in SQL Server for data classification tasks?
17. When do you use PREDICTION JOIN?

Case Study Projects

You will develop some data-mining related projects with the built-in database FoodMart 2000. To complete the projects, you need to create a new database FoodMart 2000 Mining in Analysis Manager, as described in this chapter.

1. With DTS, create a fact table, sales_fact_1998_mining, which includes the columns from the table sales_fact_1998. Recode the values in the columns, store_sales, store_cost, and promotion_id according the following rules:
   a. Divide the values in store_sales into six categories and code these categories with integers 1, 2, 3, 4, 5, and 6. Rename store_sales as sales_mining in the new fact table.
   b. Divide the values in store_cost into four categories and code these categories in the fact table with the integers 1 to 4. Rename store_cost as cost_mining.
   c. Divide the values in promotion_id into two categories and code these categories in the fact table with the integers 0 to 1. Rename promotion_id as promotion_mining.
2. Use the Dependency Network Browser to analyze the relationships between the predictable column promotion_name and the input variables such as marital_status, yearly_income, gender, education, customer_region_id, and store_sales from multiple tables to investigate how the types of promotions are related to the customers' demographic backgrounds and store sales.
3. Based on the findings in the previous step, analyze how the customers use promotions with the decision tree algorithm.
4. Conduct a cluster data-mining analysis on the columns sales_mining, cost_mining, promotion_name, and unit_sales in the table sales_fact_1998_Mining.

Appendix A

Sample Databases

To demonstrate the tasks addressed in developing database systems covered in this book, two databases, Student_Club and Hillcrest Computing, have been created and used in this book. In the following, some detailed information about these databases is given.

A.1 Student_Club **Database**

The database Student_Club is used in Chapters 3 and 5 through 8. Examples used to illustrate the topics in database design and SQL programming in these chapters are based on this database. The Student_Club database is used to store information about the student clubs at a university. It contains information about the clubs, students, mentors, and services. In SQL Server, the structure of the database can be represented by the diagram shown in Figure A.1.

Often you need to re-create the database. For example, after you completed the hands-on practice in a previous chapter, the structure of the database and data were changed. If you need the original database for the practice in the next chapter, you need to rebuild the database. To simplify the task, a script file is provided to include all the SQL statements to rebuild the database. The script file includes the following sections:

1. In the first section, the SQL statement is to drop the existing Student_Club database.
2. In the second section, a new version of the database Student_Club is created.
3. The third section of the script is used to create the tables included in the database Student_Club.
4. The last section of the script inserts the data into the tables.

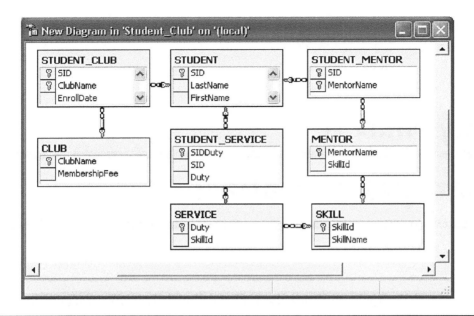

Figure A.1 Structure of Student_Club **database**

The following are the SQL statements included in the script file:

```
--Script to create the Student_Club database

---Drop the existing database
DROP DATABASE Student_Club
GO

---Create the database Student_Club
CREATE DATABASE Student_Club
GO

---Create tables
Use Student_Club
GO
CREATE TABLE CLUB
(
    ClubName CHAR(30) PRIMARY KEY,
    MembershipFee MONEY
)
GO
CREATE TABLE SKILL
(
    SkillId INT PRIMARY KEY,
    SkillName CHAR(30)
)
GO
CREATE TABLE STUDENT
(
    SID INT PRIMARY KEY,
    LastName CHAR(20),
    FirstName CHAR(20)
```

```
)
GO
CREATE TABLE MENTOR
(
    MentorName CHAR(30) PRIMARY KEY,
    SkillId INT,
    CONSTRAINT Mentor_SkillId_fk FOREIGN KEY (SkillId)
            REFERENCES SKILL (SkillId)
)
GO
CREATE TABLE SERVICE
(
    Duty CHAR(30) PRIMARY KEY,
    SkillId INT,
    CONSTRAINT Service_SkillId_fk FOREIGN KEY (SkillId)
            REFERENCES SKILL (SkillId)
)
GO
CREATE TABLE STUDENT_MENTOR
(
    SID INT,
    MentorName CHAR(30),
    CONSTRAINT Mentor_MentorName_fk FOREIGN KEY (MentorName)
REFERENCES MENTOR (MentorName),
    CONSTRAINT Mentor_SID_fk FOREIGN KEY (SID)
            REFERENCES STUDENT (SID),
    CONSTRAINT SID_MentorName_pk PRIMARY KEY (SID, MentorName)
)
GO
CREATE TABLE STUDENT_SERVICE
(
ClubName CHAR(30),
    SID INT,
    Duty CHAR(30),
    CONSTRAINT Club_ClubName_fk1 FOREIGN KEY (ClubName)
            REFERENCES CLUB (ClubName),
    CONSTRAINT Service_SID_fk FOREIGN KEY (SID)
            REFERENCES STUDENT (SID),
    CONSTRAINT Service_Duty_fk FOREIGN KEY (Duty)
            REFERENCES SERVICE (Duty),
    CONSTRAINT ClubName_SID_Duty_pk PRIMARY KEY (ClubName,
SID, Duty)
)
GO
CREATE TABLE STUDENT_CLUB
(
    SID INT,
    ClubName CHAR(30),
    EnrollDate DATETIME,
    CONSTRAINT Club_ClubName_fk FOREIGN KEY (ClubName)
                        REFERENCES CLUB (ClubName),
    CONSTRAINT Student_SID_fk FOREIGN KEY (SID)
                        REFERENCES STUDENT (SID),
    CONSTRAINT SID_ClubName_pk PRIMARY KEY (SID, ClubName)
)
```

```
GO

--- Insert records into STUDENT
INSERT INTO STUDENT (SID, LastName, FirstName)
VALUES(12784, 'Chen', 'Liz')

INSERT INTO STUDENT (SID, LastName, FirstName)
VALUES(13654, 'Dean', 'Jan')

INSERT INTO STUDENT (SID, LastName, FirstName)
VALUES(12153, 'Fry', 'Don')

INSERT INTO STUDENT (SID, LastName, FirstName)
VALUES(12105, 'Green', 'Linda')

INSERT INTO STUDENT (SID, LastName, FirstName)
VALUES(10258, 'Smith', 'Liz')

INSERT INTO STUDENT (SID, LastName, FirstName)
VALUES(14592, 'Smith', 'Mary')

INSERT INTO STUDENT (SID, LastName, FirstName)
VALUES(11690, 'Wyer', 'Joe')

INSERT INTO STUDENT (SID, LastName, FirstName)
VALUES(11505, 'Young', 'Bruce')


--- Insert records into SKILL
INSERT INTO SKILL (SkillId, SkillName)
VALUES(1, 'Accounting')

INSERT INTO SKILL (SkillId, SkillName)
VALUES(2, 'Leadership')

INSERT INTO SKILL (SkillId, SkillName)
VALUES(3, 'Typing')

INSERT INTO SKILL (SkillId, SkillName)
VALUES(4, 'Web-develop')


--- Insert records into SERVICE
INSERT INTO SERVICE (Duty, SkillId)
VALUES('Accountant', 1)

INSERT INTO SERVICE (Duty, SkillId)
VALUES('President', 2)

INSERT INTO SERVICE (Duty, SkillId)
VALUES('Recruiter', 4)

INSERT INTO SERVICE (Duty, SkillId)
VALUES('Secretary', 3)
```

```
INSERT INTO SERVICE (Duty, SkillId)
VALUES('WebMaster', 4)


--- Insert records into MENTOR
INSERT INTO MENTOR (MentorName, SkillId)
VALUES('Long', 2)

INSERT INTO MENTOR (MentorName, SkillId)
VALUES('Garza', 3)

INSERT INTO MENTOR (MentorName, SkillId)
VALUES('Jones', 2)

INSERT INTO MENTOR (MentorName, SkillId)
VALUES('Lee', 3)

INSERT INTO MENTOR (MentorName, SkillId)
VALUES('Moore', 2)

INSERT INTO MENTOR (MentorName, SkillId)
VALUES('Smith', 4)

INSERT INTO MENTOR (MentorName, SkillId)
VALUES('Wang', 4)


--- Insert records into CLUB
INSERT INTO CLUB (ClubName, MembershipFee)
VALUES('Book', 60)

INSERT INTO CLUB (ClubName, MembershipFee)
VALUES('Poetry', 50)

INSERT INTO CLUB (ClubName, MembershipFee)
VALUES('Soccer', 150)


--- Insert records into STUDENT_MENTOR
INSERT INTO STUDENT_MENTOR (SID, MentorName)
VALUES(10258, 'Jones')

INSERT INTO STUDENT_MENTOR (SID, MentorName)
VALUES(11505, 'Moore')

INSERT INTO STUDENT_MENTOR (SID, MentorName)
VALUES(11690, 'Lee')

INSERT INTO STUDENT_MENTOR (SID, MentorName)
VALUES(12105, 'Smith')

INSERT INTO STUDENT_MENTOR (SID, MentorName)
VALUES(12153, 'Long')

INSERT INTO STUDENT_MENTOR (SID, MentorName)
```

```
VALUES(12153, 'Wang')

INSERT INTO STUDENT_MENTOR (SID, MentorName)
VALUES(12784, 'Smith')

INSERT INTO STUDENT_MENTOR (SID, MentorName)
VALUES(13654, 'Garza')


--- Insert records into STUDENT_CLUB
INSERT INTO STUDENT_CLUB (SID, ClubName, EnrollDate)
VALUES(12153, 'Soccer', '9/12/2001')

INSERT INTO STUDENT_CLUB (SID, ClubName, EnrollDate)
VALUES(10258, 'Book', '10/2/2001')

INSERT INTO STUDENT_CLUB (SID, ClubName, EnrollDate)
VALUES(11505, 'Soccer', '11/12/2001')

INSERT INTO STUDENT_CLUB (SID, ClubName, EnrollDate)
VALUES(12105, 'Book', '11/16/2001')

INSERT INTO STUDENT_CLUB (SID, ClubName, EnrollDate)
VALUES(11690, 'Book', '2/11/2002')

INSERT INTO STUDENT_CLUB (SID, ClubName, EnrollDate)
VALUES(11690, 'Soccer', '2/11/2002')

INSERT INTO STUDENT_CLUB (SID, ClubName, EnrollDate)
VALUES(12784, 'Poetry', '3/29/2002')

INSERT INTO STUDENT_CLUB (SID, ClubName, EnrollDate)
VALUES(12153, 'Poetry', '4/14/2002')

INSERT INTO STUDENT_CLUB (SID, ClubName, EnrollDate)
VALUES(13654, 'Poetry', '7/31/2001')


--- Insert records into STUDENT_SERVICE
INSERT INTO STUDENT_SERVICE (ClubName, SID, Duty)
VALUES('Book', 10258, 'President')

INSERT INTO STUDENT_SERVICE (ClubName, SID, Duty)
VALUES('Book', 11690, 'Secretary')

INSERT INTO STUDENT_SERVICE (ClubName, SID, Duty)
VALUES('Book', 12105, 'Recruiter')

INSERT INTO STUDENT_SERVICE (ClubName, SID, Duty)
VALUES('Poetry', 12153, 'President')

INSERT INTO STUDENT_SERVICE (ClubName, SID, Duty)
VALUES('Poetry', 12784, 'Recruiter')

INSERT INTO STUDENT_SERVICE (ClubName, SID, Duty)
```

```
VALUES('Poetry', 13654, 'Secretary')

INSERT INTO STUDENT_SERVICE (ClubName, SID, Duty)
VALUES('Soccer', 11505, 'President')

INSERT INTO STUDENT_SERVICE (ClubName, SID, Duty)
VALUES('Soccer', 11690, 'Secretary')

INSERT INTO STUDENT_SERVICE (ClubName, SID, Duty)
VALUES('Soccer', 12153, 'WebMaster')
```

To run the script, start **Query Analyzer** and open the script file such as **StudentClub.sql** that will be available. Make sure that the database `Student_Club` is not selected in the combo box on the toolbar. If `Student_Club` is selected, you will not be able to drop the database. In such a case, select another database such as `Northwind` in the combo box. Click at the beginning of the first line and then click the **Execute Query** button on the toolbar or press **F5**. The tables in this database are populated with the data as shown from Figure A.2 to Figure A.9.

All the data stored in these tables are made up for illustration purposes. Feel free to modify the data to serve your own learning purpose.

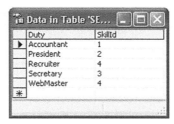

Figure A.2   CLUB **table**

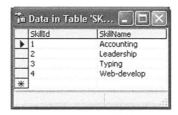

Figure A.3   SKILL **table**

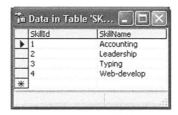

Figure A.4   SERVICE **table**

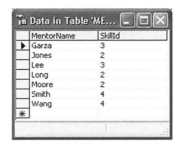

Figure A.5   MENTOR **table**

SID	LastName	FirstName
10258	Smith	Liz
11505	Young	Bruce
11690	Wyer	Joe
12105	Green	Linda
12153	Fry	Don
12784	Chen	Liz
13654	Dean	Jan
14592	Smith	Mary

Figure A.6   STUDENT **table**

SID	MentorName
10258	Jones
11505	Moore
11690	Lee
12105	Smith
12153	Long
12153	Wang
12784	Smith
13654	Garza

Figure A.7   STUDENT_MENTOR **table**

SID	ClubName	EnrollDate
10258	Book	10/2/2001
11505	Soccer	11/12/2001
11690	Book	2/11/2002
11690	Soccer	2/11/2002
12105	Book	11/16/2001
12153	Poetry	4/14/2002
12153	Soccer	9/12/2001
12784	Poetry	3/29/2002
13654	Poetry	7/31/2001

Figure A.8   STUDENT_CLUB **table**

Data in Table 'STUDENT_SERVICE...

ClubName	SID	Duty
Book	10258	President
Book	11690	Secretary
Book	12105	Recruiter
Poetry	12153	President
Poetry	12784	Recruiter
Poetry	13654	Secretary
Soccer	11505	President
Soccer	11690	Secretary
Soccer	12153	WebMaster

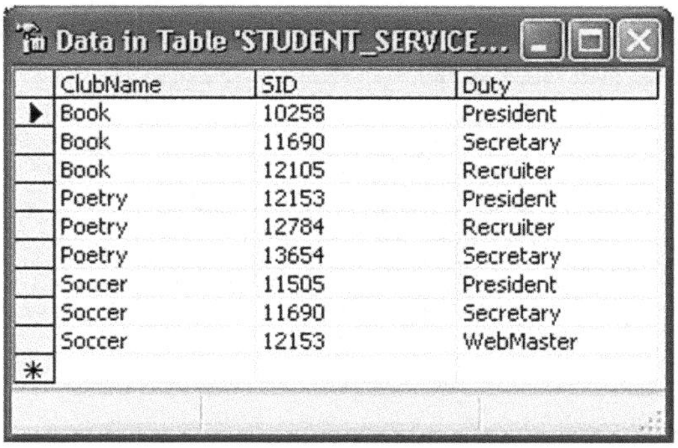

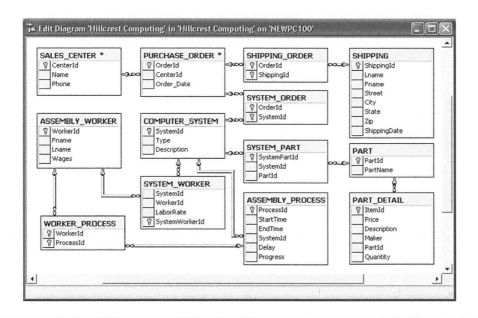

Figure A.9 STUDENT_SERVICE **table**

Figure A.10 Structure of Hillcrest Computing **database**

A.2 Hillcrest Computing **Database**

We have used the database Hillcrest Computing in Chapters 2 and 4 and Chapters 7 through 13. We use Hillcrest Computing to illustrate conceptual design, database creation, SQL procedures, database accessing, database application development, network-based database, database management, and data analysis. We use the database Hillcrest Computing to illustrate how to use a database to solve problems in a business process. The database is used to store the information about a computer company with multiple sales centers. It contains information about the sales centers, assembly processes, computer systems, parts, and purchase orders. The database Hillcrest Computing has a structure as shown in Figure A.10.

Data in Table 'COMPUTER_SYSTEM' in 'Hillcrest Computing' on '(LOCAL)'

SystemId	Type	Description
D0001	Desktop	1.0GHz Celeron, 128MB RAM, 40GB hd, 24X CD-ROM, 10/100 Ethernet, 17 Monitor, Win XP Home
D0002	Desktop	16X10X40 CD-RW, 60GHD, 1.3GHCeleron, 56kModem, 100Ether, 256MRAM, WinXPPro
D0003	Desktop	1.6GHz Intel P4, 256MB RAM, 40GB hd, 16X8X40 CD-RW, 56K, 10/100 Ethernet, Win XP Home
D0004	Desktop	1.6GHz Intel P4, 256MB RAM, 40GB hd, 52X CD-ROM, 10/100 Ethernet, 19" Monitor, Win 2000 Pro
D0005	Desktop	1.8GHz Intel P4, 256MB RAM, 40GB hd, 48X CD-ROM, 10/100 Ethernet, Win XP Pro
D0006	Desktop	1.5GHz Intel Xeon, 256MB RAM, 20GB hd, 48X CD-ROM, 10/100 Ethernet, Red Hat Linux 7.1
D0007	Desktop	1.0GHz Dual P3, 512 MB RAM, Dual 20 GB SCSI hd,10/100 Ethernet, Red Hat Linux 7.1
N0001	Notebook	1.0GHz Celeron, 128MB RAM, 10GB hd, 24X CD-ROM, 56K, 10/100 Ethernet, Win XP Pro, 14.1" XGA
N0002	Notebook	1.0GHz Intel P3, 256MB RAM, 20GB hd, 8X DVD, 56K, 10/100 Ethernet, Windows XP Pro, 15" XGA
N0003	Notebook	1.0GHz Intel P3, 512MB RAM, 60GB hd, 12X DVD, 56K, 10/100 Ethernet, Windows XP Pro, 15" XGA
N0004	Tablet	P4/1GHz 15"LCD GripPen 4DMouse 256GBHD

Figure A.11 `COMPUTER_SYSTEM` **table**

Data in Table 'ASSEMBLY_PROCESS' in 'Hillcrest Computing' on ...

ProcessId	StartTime	EndTime	SystemId	Delay	Progress
1001	2/2/2002	2/4/2002	D0001		
1002	3/14/2002	3/16/2002	D0001		
1003	3/14/2002	3/15/2002	D0002		
1004	4/4/2002	4/7/2002	N0001		
1005	4/10/2002	4/11/2002	N0003		
1006	3/24/2002	3/26/2002	D0001		
1007	4/14/2002	4/15/2002	D0003		
1008	5/17/2002	5/18/2002	N0002		
1009	5/7/2002	5/8/2002	D0002		
1012	6/3/2002	6/5/2002	D0001		
1013	6/13/2002	6/15/2002	N0001		
1014	6/23/2002	6/24/2002	D0003		
1015	7/1/2002	7/2/2002	N0003		

Figure A.12 `ASSEMBLY_PROCESS` **table**

A script is also provided to help you rebuild the database. Similar to the script for the database `Student_Club`, the script includes the SQL statements for the following tasks:

1. Drop the existing `Hillcrest Computing` database.
2. Create the new `Hillcrest Computing` database.
3. Create the tables included in the database `Hillcrest Computing`.
4. Insert data into the tables.

The script file is too large to be printed here. It is available in the supplementary materials. To run the script file, start **Query Analyzer** and open the file **HillcrestComputing.sql**. Click the beginning of the first line and click the **Execute Query** button or press **F5**. You will create the tables that are populated with data as shown from Figure A.11 to Figure A.23.

The data in the tables are fictional and are used to demonstrate database-processing system development. Before you can start the hands-on practice, run the two scripts to create the databases `Student_Club` and `Hillcrest Computing`. Except for some of the data analysis examples, most of the examples in this book are run against these two databases.

Data in Table 'ASSEMBLY_WORKER' in 'Hillcrest ...

WorkerId	Fname	Lname	Wages
10	Mary	Smith	64000
11	John	White	73000
12	Sam	Carter	36000
13	Jim	Miller	56000
14	Lois	Munoz	75000
15	Roy	Long	48000
16	Jane	Gayle	41000
17	Laura	Brown	62000
18	Gail	Rice	34000
19	Frank	Green	58000
20	Toni	Jones	52000
21	Bud	Wyer	45000

Figure A.13 `ASSEMBLY_WORKER` **table**

Data in Table 'PART' in 'Hillcrest Co...

PartId	PartName
CD001	24X CD-ROM
CD002	48X CD-ROM
CD003	52X CD-ROM
CW001	16X8X40 CD-RW
CW002	16X10X40 CD-RW
CW003	24X10X40 CD-RW
DD001	8X DVD
DD002	12X DVD
DP001	14.1XGA
DP002	15XGA
HD001	10GHD
HD002	20GHD
HD003	40GHD
HD004	60GHD
HD005	Dual20GB
HD006	100GHD
HD007	200GHD
MB001	1.0GHIntelP3
MB002	1.0GHCeleron
MB003	1.5GHXeon
MB004	1.3GHCeleron
MB005	1.6GHIntelP4
MB006	1.8GHIntelP4
MB007	DualP3
MD001	56kModem
MN001	17Monitor
MN002	19Monitor
NIC001	100Ether
OS001	WinXPHome
OS002	WinXPPro
OS003	W2000Pro
OS004	RHLinux7.1
RAM001	128MRAM
RAM002	256MRAM
RAM003	512MRAM
WC001	Webcam, CCD, 1024x768, 16MB Fl

Figure A.14 `PART` **table**

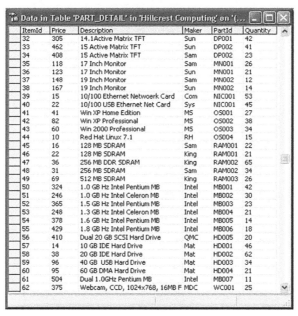

Figure A.15   PART_DETAIL **table: (a) Part I and (b) Part II**

Data in Table 'PURCHASE_ORDER' in...

OrderId	CenterId	Order_Date
1020	1	2/1/2002
1021	4	3/12/2002
1022	2	3/13/2002
1023	1	4/3/2002
1024	3	4/9/2002
1025	4	3/22/2002
1026	3	4/12/2002
1027	2	5/15/2002
1028	1	5/6/2002
1029	2	6/1/2002
1030	4	6/11/2002
1031	3	6/22/2002
1032	1	6/30/2002
1033	1	7/10/2002
1034	1	7/17/2002
1035	1	8/3/2002
1036	1	8/15/2002
1037	1	8/20/2002
1038	1	8/30/2002
1039	1	9/10/2002
1040	1	9/12/2002
1041	1	9/23/2002
1042	1	9/26/2002
1043	1	10/1/2002
1044	1	10/25/2002
1045	1	11/4/2002
1046	1	11/18/2002
1047	1	11/28/2002
1048	1	12/10/2002
1049	1	12/10/2002

Figure A.16 `PURCHASE_ORDER` **table**

Data in Table 'SALES_CENTER' in '...

CenterId	Name	Phone
1	Houston	7135672300
2	Dallas	2146791122
3	Austin	5124501529
4	Amarillo	8063753600

Figure A.17 `SALES_CENTER` **table**

Data in Table 'SHIPPING' in 'Hillcrest Computing' on 'NEWPC100'

ShippingId	Lname	Fname	Street	City	State	Zip	ShippingDate
1	Burge	John	214 Nelson	Dallas	TX	75201	2/7/2002
2	Wu	Keren	345 Bagby	Houston	TX	77002	3/17/2002
3	Parr	Dan	324 Miori	Victoria	TX	77903	3/20/2002
4	Garcia	Lisa	874 Wilson	Amorillo	TX	79105	3/22/2002
5	Holly	Susan	4848 Lakeside	Austin	TX	78767	4/9/2002
6	Dean	Al	1398 International Rd	Dallas	TX	75201	4/18/2002
7	Jouns	David	267 College	Houston	TX	77487	5/22/2002
8	Fry	Bud	2396 Anderson	Austin	TX	78767	5/12/2002
9	Young	Jane	1563 Madison	New York	NY	10159	6/2/2002
10	Smith	Robert	2995 Post	Huntsville	AL	35824	5/14/2002
11	Munoz	Roy	201 Bellaire	Denver	CO	80222	6/5/2002
12	Sitka	Paul	1240 Villa	Mountain View	CA	94041	6/15/2002
13	Sherman	Gary	145 Corporate	Cambridge	MA	02142	6/25/2002
14	Hursh	Larry	1248 Katy Frwy	Houston	TX	77429	7/14/2002
15	Reed	David	579 S. Mason	Houston	TX	77290	7/28/2002
16	Shum	John	389 Brooks	Houston	TX	76385	8/12/2002
17	Brand	Joe	2970 Hwy 6	Houston	TX	77638	12/20/2002
18	Revis	Eric	9108 Travis	Houston	TX	76325	8/30/2002
19	White	Lilla	1590 Memorial	Houston	TX	77389	9/1/2002
20	Dees	Frank	337 First St.	Houston	TX	78330	9/10/2002
21	Ramos	Aian	466 Sugar	Houston	TX	77449	9/17/2002
22	Garcia	Mike	1400 Richmond	Houston	TX	77562	9/18/2002
23	Kersh	Dana	8879 Telephone Rd.	Houston	TX	77541	9/29/2002
24	Rose	Jeff	735 Tomball	Houston	TX	77339	10/3/2002
25	Parker	Sam	6839 Antoine	Houston	TX	77456	10/7/2002
26	Wood	Helen	179 Greens	Houston	TX	77894	10/31/2002
27	Burton	Wanda	4221 Gulf Frwy	Houston	TX	77903	11/8/2002
28	Perry	Steve	827 Louetta	Houston	TX	76450	11/29/2002
29	Jackson	Jay	1849 Westheimer	Houston	TX	76889	12/3/2002
30	Vela	Toya	163 Fugua	Houston	TX	77398	12/15/2002

Figure A.18   `SHIPPING` **table**

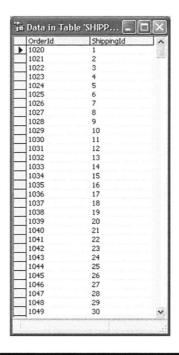

Data in Table 'SHIPP...

OrderId	ShippingId
1020	1
1021	2
1022	3
1023	4
1024	5
1025	6
1026	7
1027	8
1028	9
1029	10
1030	11
1031	12
1032	13
1033	14
1034	15
1035	16
1036	17
1037	18
1038	19
1039	20
1040	21
1041	22
1042	23
1043	24
1044	25
1045	26
1046	27
1047	28
1048	29
1049	30

Figure A.19   `SHIPPING_ORDER` **table**

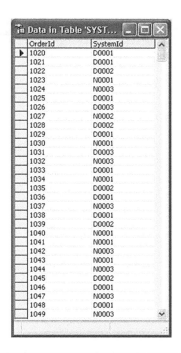

Figure A.20 SYSTEM_ORDER **table**

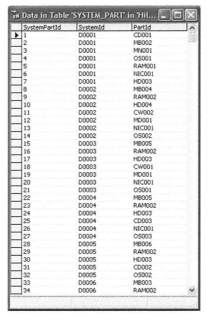

(a)

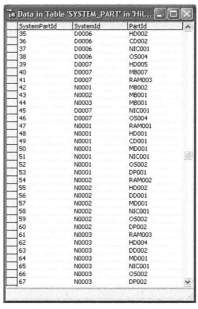

(b)

Figure A.21 `SYSTEM_PART` **table: (a) Part I and (b) Part II**

Data in Table 'SYSTEM_WORKER' in 'Hillcrest Comp...

SystemId	WorkerId	LaborRate	SystemWorkerId
D0001	10	224	1
D0002	12	270	2
D0002	11	219	3
N0003	14	224	4
D0003	15	188	5
D0003	16	264	6
N0001	17	246	7
N0001	18	217	8
D0001	19	255	9
N0002	20	232	10
N0003	21	234	11
N0002	22	270	12

Figure A.22 `SYSTEM_WORKER` **table**

Data in Table 'WOR...

WorkerId	ProcessId
10	1001
10	1002
10	1006
10	1012
11	1003
11	1009
12	1003
12	1009
14	1005
14	1015
15	1007
15	1014
16	1007
16	1014
17	1004
17	1013
18	1004
18	1013
19	1001
19	1002
19	1006
19	1012
20	1008
21	1005
21	1015
22	1008

Figure A.23 `WORKER_PROCESS` **table**

Appendix B

Installation of SQL Server

Several software packages have been used in the development of database-processing systems. SQL Server is installed for hosting databases. It is powerful enough to let us carry out the work for enterprise-level topics such as multi-tier architecture, database security, database management, Internet database, data mart, and data analysis. Microsoft Visio is installed for developing data models. For the software on the client side, we have installed Access 2003 and InfoPath 2003 for creating forms and reports. Microsoft Office–based database applications are popular in today's IT industry. To illustrate the development of network-based databases, we have installed Microsoft Visual Studio .NET for creating online forms and Web services. You need Windows 2000 Professional, Windows XP Professional, or Windows Server 2003 for hosting these software packages. The software used in this book is supported by the MSDN Academic Alliance (MSDNAA) program at http://www.msdnaa.net/. Under the agreement with MSDNAA, these software products can be used by the entire department. The MSDNAA program makes teaching and learning database systems easier and more affordable.

It is relatively easy to install and configure the software provided by MSDNAA for the class. It does not require a powerful computer to host SQL Server in the lab, office, or home. PCs with 400-MHz Intel P3 CPU, 256-MB RAM, and 10-GB hard drive should be good enough for all the hands-on exercises in this book.

SQL Server Installation

SQL Server has different editions: Enterprise Edition, Standard Edition, Developer Edition, Personal Edition, and Windows CE Edition. For the hands-on exercises, we can use the Standard Edition or Developer Edition. To run these editions, besides the operating system mentioned above, you also need to

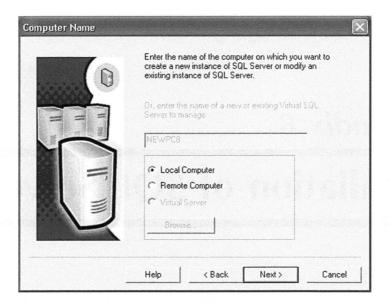

Figure B.1   Select the computer to install SQL Server

install Internet Explorer 5 or above and the latest service packs for SQL Server 2000. Follow the steps below to install SQL Server 2000 on your computer.

1. Log on to the computer as Administrator. Insert the SQL Server 2000 disk into the CD-ROM drive. If you want to create some users who will use Windows authentication to log on to SQL Server, you should create a Windows Administrator account for each of these users.

2. Navigate to the folder that contains the setup file **AUTORUN.EXE**. Double-click the **AUTORUN.EXE** icon to start the installation process.

3. Click **SQL Server 2000 Components**, and then **Install Database Server**. At the Welcome page, click **Next**.

4. On the Computer Name page, you are prompted to enter the name of the computer on which you want to install the SQL Server instance. You can install the SQL Server on the local computer, a remote computer on the network, or a virtual server in an existing cluster. Because you are going to install SQL Server on the local computer, select the **Local Computer** option, as shown in Figure B.1.

5. Click **Next** to go to the Installation Selection page. On this page, you have the choices to make a clear installation of a SQL Server instance, update the existing SQL Server, or perform some advanced installation tasks. To install SQL Server, select the option **Create a new instance of SQL Server, or install Client Tools**.

6. Click **Next** to enter user information. By default, you can use the same name and company information you have used for your Windows operating system.

7. Click **Next**, and then click **Yes** for the Software License Agreement.

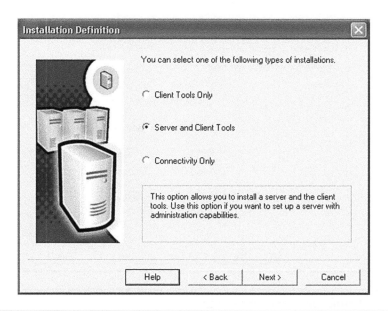

Figure B.2   Select installation type

8. Click **Next** to move to the Installation Definition page. On this page, you can select the option to install only the client management tools, or to install database server and client management tools, or to install only the connectivity components that include Microsoft Data Access Components (MDAC 2.6) and network libraries. In a client/server computing environment, there are one or more servers and many clients. For the hands-on practice in this book, you can use the same computer for both client and server, or you can create a network with one or two servers and at least one client. Assume that you are going to install the client and server on a single computer; select the option **Server and Client Tools**, as shown in Figure B.2.

9. If you install SQL Server for the teaching lab, you may want to divide the computers into several groups. Connect the computers in each group through a local area network. In each group, install the server on one of the computers and install the client tools on the other computers in the group. To install the client tools, you need to select the option **Client Tools Only**.

10. Click **Next** to go to the Instance Name page. If this is your first installation, make sure the **Default** check box is checked. Otherwise, you will be prompted to enter the instance name.

11. Click **Next** to bring up the Setup Type page. You can choose one of the options. The **Typical** option will allow you install all the SQL Server components with the default installation options. The **Minimum** option will install only the necessary components to run SQL Server. The **Custom** option will allow you select the components to be installed manually. The **Typical** option is good enough for the hands-on exercises in this book. Let us select **Typical**.

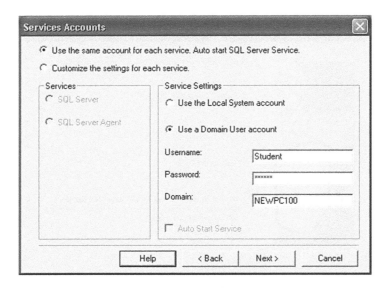

Figure B.3   Configure service account

12. Click **Next** to configure the service account. You can either use a single account for both SQL Server and SQL Server Agent Services or use separate accounts. Let us select the option **Use the same account for each service. Auto start SQL Server Service**. For the Service Settings section, you have two choices, **Use the Local System account** or **Use a Domain User account**, If you are going to install the client and server components on a single computer, choose the option **Use the Local System account**, which does not support the network access. On the other hand, if you are creating a client/server environment for your teaching lab, use the option **Use a Domain User account**. For this option, the computers in your lab should be the members of an existing Windows domain. Although we assume you are going to install both client and server on the same computer that is not a member of an existing domain, you may still need some network functionalities. We select the option **Use a Domain User account**, as shown in Figure B.3. Enter the username and password for the account you have created at the beginning of installation.

     If you install SQL Server for your teaching lab, make sure to choose the option **Use a Domain User account**. In this way, the server makes itself available to the client computers. For this option, make sure that you have set up a user account in the existing domain or have a Windows administrator account for the computer on which you are going to install the database server. If you install SQL server on your PC, you should check the option **Use the Local System account**.

13. Click **Next** to go to the Authentication Mode page. You have two options, **Windows Authentication Mode** and **Mixed Mode** (Windows Authentication and SQL Server Authentication). If you work on a single computer, select the Windows authentication mode. If you are setting up a client/server computing environment, you should select the mixed mode. Again, assume that you are working on a single computer, so select the **Windows Authentication Mode** option.

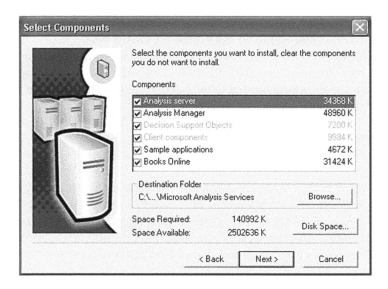

Figure B.4   Select Analysis Services components

14. Click **Next** twice to start the installation process. After the installation process is completed, click **Start**, **All Programs**, **Microsoft SQL Server**, and **Enterprise Manager** to start SQL Server.

Next, you can install the Analysis Services component. Suppose that the SQL Server CD disk is still in the CD-ROM drive. Follow the steps below to install the Analysis Services components.

1. Double-click **AUTORUN.EXE** to start the installation process again. Click **SQL Server Components**, and then click **Install Analysis Services**.
2. At the Welcome page, click **Next**. Click **Yes** for the Software License Agreement.
3. On the Select Components page, check all the available components as shown in Figure B.4.
4. Click **Next** to go to the Data Folder Location page. On this page, you can specify the folder in which to install the Analysis Services components. For this installation, we accept the default folder.
5. Click **Next** twice to start the installation process. After the installation is completed, click **Finish**.

For the teaching lab, you need to make sure that, from the client computers, you are able to connect to the server. Perform the following steps to verify if the connection to the server is established.

1. Log on to one of the client computers in your group. To open SQL Server Enterprise Manager, click **Start**, **All Programs**, **Microsoft SQL Server**, and **Enterprise Manager**.
2. Once Enterprise Manager is open, right-click **SQL Server Group** and select **New SQL Server Registration** to start **Register SQL Server Wizard**.

3. Click **Next** and select the server for your group. The server name for your group is the host name of your group's server computer.
4. Click **Next** and check the option **SQL Server login information**. Click **Next** and enter the log-in name and the password. The default log-in name is **sa** with an empty password. You have changed the password during the installation.
5. Click **Next** and make sure that the option **Add the SQL Server(s) to an existing SQL Server group** is checked. Click **Finish** to complete the configuration.

As mentioned in the text, for some of the hands-on practices, you should also install the latest service packs for SQL Server and Analysis Services. Please refer to the related chapters for more information. The installation for the other software such as Microsoft Visio, Microsoft Office, and Microsoft Visual Studio .NET is relatively easy. Read the Readme.txt files for more detailed information.

Appendix C

Suggested Resources

A database-processing system involves various technologies. There are a large number of books and Web sites for these technologies. The following is a short list of books and Web sites that have a lot of information that is related to this book. For those readers who are looking for more information about database-processing systems, this list of books and Web sites will provide in-depth information.

Web Sites

Check the following Web sites for recent development in database-processing system-related technologies.

- A comprehensive coverage of the technologies developed by Microsoft
  - http://msdn.microsoft.com/
- Sites dedicated to database design
  - http://databases.about.com/od/development/
  - http://database.ittoolbox.com/nav/t.asp?t=349&p=349&h1=349
  - http://www.utexas.edu/its/windows/database/datamodeling/
- Sites dedicated to database application development
  - http://www.devx.com/dbzone
  - http://www.devguru.com/home.asp
  - http://www.w3schools.com/ado/
- A site about developing enterprise-level databases, including decision-making-related topics
  - http://www.intelligententerprise.com/
- A site about the IDEF1X standard
  - http://www.idef.com/idef1x.html
  - http://www.idef.com/Downloads/pdf/Idef1x.pdf

- Sites of computing associations
  - http://www.w3.org/
  - http://www.acm.org/
  - http://www.xml.org
- A site about the MSDNAA program
  - http://www.msdnaa.net/

Books and Articles

Check the following books and articles for in-depth coverage of database-processing system theories and related technologies.

Professional Books

- Alex Berson and Stephen J. Smith. *Data Warehouse, Data Mining, and OLAP.* New York: McGraw-Hill, 1997.
- Rhonda Delmater and Monte Hancock. *Data Mining Explained: A Manager's Guide to Customer-Centric Business Intelligence.* Woburn, MA: Digital Press, 2001.
- Marci Frohock Garcia, Jamie Reding, Edward Whalen, and Steve Adrien Deluca. *SQL Server 2000 Administrator Companion.* Redmond,WA: Microsoft Press, 2000.
- Philip Koneman. *Programming with Visual Basic.NET for Business.* Upper Saddle River, NJ: Prentice-Hall, 2004.
- Ken Henderson. *The Guru's Guide to Transact-SQL.* Indianapolis, IN: Addison-Wesley, 2002.
- Microsoft Press. *Microsoft SQL Server 2000 Database Design and Implementation.* Redmond, WA: Microsoft Press, 2001.
- Graeme Malcolm. *Programming Microsoft SQL Server 2000 with XML.* Redmond: Microsoft Press, 2001.
- OLAP Train and Reed Jacobson. *Step by Step Microsoft SQL Server 2000 Analysis Services.* Redmond, WA: Microsoft Press, 2000.
- David Sceppa. *Microsoft ADO.NET (Core Reference).* Redmond, WA: Microsoft Press, 2002.
- Mark Spenik and Orryn Sledge. *Microsoft SQL Server 2000 DBA Survival Guide,* 2nd edition. Indianapolis, IN: Sams, 2003.
- William Stanek. *Microsoft SQL Server 2000 Administrator's Pocket Consultant.* Redmond, WA: Microsoft Press, 2000.
- Barry de Ville. *Microsoft Data Mining: Integrated Business Intelligence for E-Commerce and Knowledge Management.* Woburn, MA: Digital Press, 2001.
- Mark H. Walker and Nanette Eaton. *Microsoft Office Visio 2003 Inside Out.* Redmond, WA: Microsoft Press, 2003.
- Stephen Walther. *ASP.NET Unleashed,* 2nd edition. Indianapolis, IN: Sams, 2003.

Textbooks

- David Kroenke. *Database Processing,* 9th edition. Upper Saddle River, NJ: Prentice-Hall, 2004.
- Michael V. Mannino. *Database Design, Application Development, and Administration*, 2nd edition. New York: McGraw-Hill, 2003.
- Patrick O'Nell and Elizabeth O'Nell. *Database: Principles, Programming, and Performance*, 2nd edition. San Francisco: Morgan-Kaufmann, 2001.
- Gerald V. Post. *Database Management Systems: Designing and Building Business Applications*, 3rd edition. New York: McGraw-Hill College, 2005.
- Philip J. Pratt and Joseph J. Adamski. *Database System Management and Design*, 3rd edition. Cambridge: Course Technology, 1994.
- Peter Rob and Carlos Coronel. *Database Systems: Design, Implementation, and Management*, 5th Edition. Cambridge: Course Technology, 2002.
- Abraham Silberschatz, Henry F. Korth, and S. Sudarshan. *Database Systems Concepts with Oracle CD*, 4th edition. New York: McGraw-Hill, 2002.

Articles

- Peter Chen, Editor. "The Entity-Relationship Model: Toward a Unified Model of Data." *ACM Transactions on Database Systems* 1 (March 1976).
- R. Fagin. "A Normal Form for Relational Databases That Is Based on Domain and Keys." *ACM Transactions on Database Systems* 6 (September 1981).

Index